ABC's of the HUMAN MIND

A FAMILY ANSWER BOOK

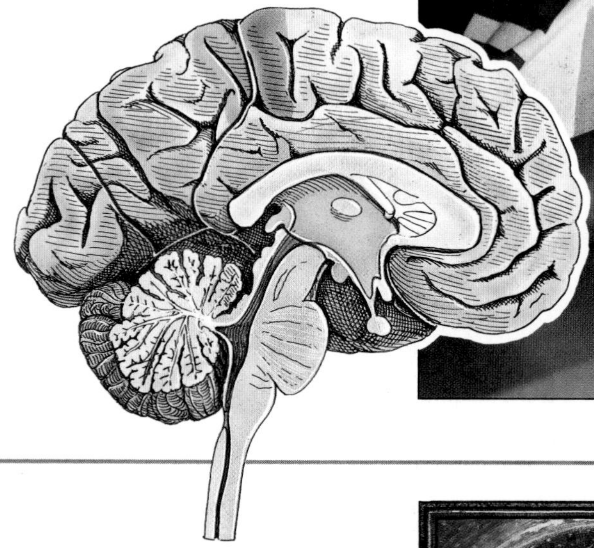

Clockwise from left: Brain basics, page 62. Learning, page 286. Creativity, page 183. Astrology, page 56. Previous page: Emotions, page 166.

ABC's of the HUMAN MIND

A FAMILY ANSWER BOOK

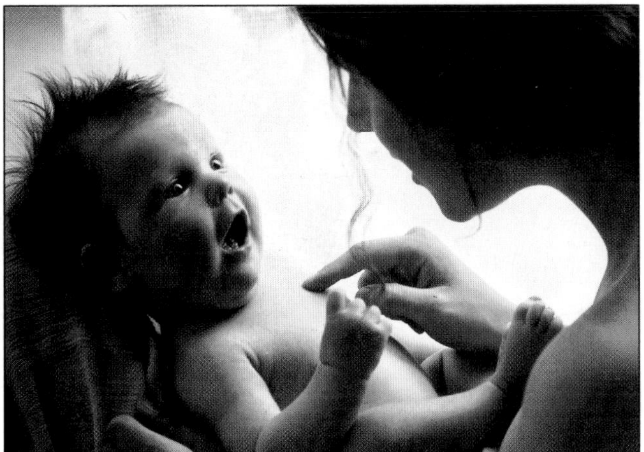

Top: Psychologists, page 149. Bottom: Family bonding, page 237.

Reader's Digest

THE READER'S DIGEST ASSOCIATION, INC.
PLEASANTVILLE, NEW YORK • MONTREAL

ABC's of the HUMAN MIND

EDITOR: Alma E. Guinness
ART EDITORS: Penny L. Howard, Henrietta Stern
CHIEF RESEARCH EDITOR: Eileen Einfrank
ASSOCIATE EDITORS: Don Earnest, Barbara C. Loos
ART ASSOCIATE: Nancy Mace
RESEARCH EDITOR: Christine Morgan
RESEARCH ASSOCIATE: Barbara Guarino
ASSISTANT EDITOR: David Diefendorf
LIBRARY RESEARCH: Nettie Seaberry
EDITORIAL ASSISTANT: Jean Ryan

CONTRIBUTORS

ASSOCIATE PROJECT EDITOR: Edmund H. Harvey, Jr.
CONTRIBUTING EDITOR/WRITER: Jozefa Stuart
WRITERS: Harriet Brown, Peter Burchard, David Caras, Rita Christopher, Thomas Christopher, Kate Ernst, Marjorie Flory, Charles Flowers, Sandy Fritz, James I. Killgore, Myron H. Marks, Margaret Moore, Wendy Murphy, Donald Pfarrer, Thomas L. Robinson, Nancy Wartik, Joseph F. Wilkinson
PRODUCTION COORDINATOR: Tracey Grant-Starker
PICTURE RESEARCHER: Mary Leverty
RESEARCHERS: Josephine Reidy, Joan Tedeschi, Kate J. Weiner
PROOFREADER: Karen Homan
INDEXER: Sydney Wolfe Cohen
EDITORIAL INTERN: Melanie Williams

CONSULTANTS

CHIEF CONSULTANT: Herbert H. Krauss, Ph.D., Professor of Psychology, Hunter College, CUNY
SPECIALIST CONSULTANTS: Martin Wilner, M.D., Instructor in Psychiatry, Cornell University Medical College
Murk-Hein Heinemann, M.D., Associate Professor of Ophthalmology, Cornell University Medical College
Helen E. Fisher, Ph.D., Department of Anthropology, American Museum of Natural History
Donald Mender, M.D., Founder of Neuropsychiatric Service, Payne Whitney Clinic
Patrick R. Bradley-Moore, M.D., M.R.C.P., D.M.R.D., Researcher in Nuclear Medicine, Medical Director, Bronx Medical Clinic

READER'S DIGEST GENERAL BOOKS

EDITOR IN CHIEF: John A. Pope, Jr.
MANAGING EDITOR: Jane Polley
ART DIRECTOR: David Trooper
GROUP EDITORS: Will Bradbury, Norman B. Mack, Susan J. Wernert, Evelyn Bauer (Art), Joel Musler (Art)
CHIEF OF RESEARCH: Monica Borrowman
COPY CHIEF: Edward W. Atkinson
PICTURE EDITOR: Robert J. Woodward
RIGHTS AND PERMISSIONS: Pat Colomban
HEAD LIBRARIAN: Jo Manning

Library of Congress Cataloging in Publication Data
ABC's of the human mind : a family answer book.
p. cm.
At head of title: Reader's digest.
ISBN 0-89577-345-7
1. Psychology—Miscellanea. I. Reader's digest.
BF145.A23 1990
150—dc20 89-36711
CIP

About This Book

From the first day the staff began work on ABC'S OF THE HUMAN MIND, we felt an ever growing sense of awe. One by one, our preconceptions fell away, to be replaced by a sense of the miracle that is the human mind. We came to understand that the brain is not one thing, or even the sum of its parts, but literally millions of things happening at once—and then a million more in the blink of an eye, and then a million more—all combining to make us who we are.

ABC'S OF THE HUMAN MIND explores fantastic new discoveries about the brain and the way it works. In a highly readable question-and-answer format—minus confusing jargon—readers of all ages will gain insight into their own minds. How do we learn? Why do we forget? What makes us tick? ABC'S OF THE HUMAN MIND is up-to-date and authoritative, based on consultations with distinguished experts in psychology, brain physiology, nuclear medicine, anthropology, and other specialties. However, although you will find many checklists and how-to features throughout, it must be emphasized that our purpose is only to inform and entertain. This book should not be used to diagnose a mental illness or prescribe treatment—that is the proper realm of professionals.

Our hope is that you will come to share the wonder and excitement we experienced in producing ABC'S OF THE HUMAN MIND.

Read about real situations*—as for example why some kids rebel in the teen years and others do not.* *(Turn to page 252.)*

In *Part I, The Mysterious Human Mind,* find out how psychology began as a science, what actually happens during psychotherapy. In *Part II, The Geography of the Brain,* read how the brain is formed, how scientists watch it work. In *Part III, Our Amazing Senses,* discover why we sometimes see things that aren't there, how deaf people cope in a hearing world, what causes persistent dizziness. In *Part IV, The World Within,* learn how and when the human personality is formed, how creativity can be cultivated, how depression can be conquered. In *Part V, The All-Important Family,* explore the ways family traditions are passed along, how families shape a child's mind, whether opposites really do attract, how important sex is in marriage. In *Part VI, The Outside World,* consider the psychological ups and downs of school, sports, work, and vacations; how we choose friends, why some people are good Samaritans and others are not.

For easy access, every question is listed in the table of contents. As you browse through this book, note the many entertaining illustrated features, such as *Classic Cases, Theorists and Theories, Perspectives* (insights by distinguished thinkers on subjects ranging from ethics to emotions), and *Did You Knows. . . ?* A comprehensive index will lead you quickly to any subject of interest. Like the human mind itself, this book is a rich broth of marvelous facts and revelations.

—The Editors

Contents

PART I

The Mysterious Human Mind

Freud's famous couch, page 41.

Vase-profile illusion, page 122.

Creativity, page 182.

PART V

The All-Important Family

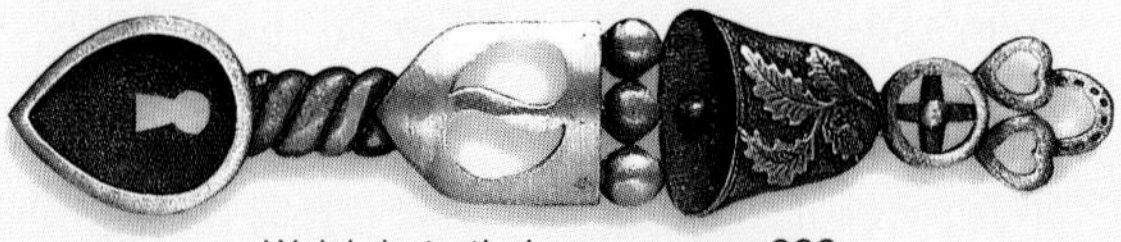

Welsh betrothal spoon, page 222.

Running, page 308.

PART I

The Mysterious Human Mind

The wonder grows with every new discovery about our marvelous, versatile minds. And today we stand on the threshold of even greater discoveries.

As far as anyone knows, human beings are the only creatures with a capacity for fantasy. In the mind's eye, we can, like artist René Magritte, conjure up castles in the air.

The Art and Science of Psychology

How did psychology begin?

"Psychology," a scholar observed, "has a long past, but only a short history." As a science, it can be said to have begun about 100 years ago, when Wilhelm Wundt opened a psychological laboratory in Germany. Yet an interest in mind and behavior is at least as old as human records.

Most of the great themes of modern psychology can be traced to ancient Greece. Almost three thousand years ago, the poet Homer marveled at the range of human personality and credited the gods: "To one man a god has given deeds of war, and to another the dance, to another the lyre and song, and in another wide-sounding Zeus puts a good mind."

Aristotle's concept of catharsis was partly a theory of psychotherapy. In watching tragic dramas, he said, people felt terror and pity, and this purged their minds of negative emotions. In the same vein the dramatist Aeschylus wrote, "Words are the physicians of a mind diseased." Over two millennia later, Sigmund Freud not only turned to Greek drama to illustrate his theories of the unconscious but also used "words"—the talk of a patient in psychoanalysis—as the basis of therapy for mental disorders.

Hippocrates, called the father of medicine, was very modern in his views that mental illness had natural causes and that the brain was the seat of emotion and thought. And many of today's findings about the brain and behavior simply amplify Aristotle's assertions that the human psyche (or mind) is a part of the body and that our capacity for reason and moral choice develops as the brain processes more and more data from the senses.

Is psychology really a science?

Scientists in other fields, such as physics and chemistry, often criticize psychology as "soft." Many jokes reflect doubts about its validity as a science. British psychologist Hans Eysenck cites the cartoon in which one laboratory rat says to another, "I sure got my human well conditioned—whenever I press this lever, he drops a food pellet into the chute."

Some doubts are reasonable. Is it really valid to apply the results of animal experiments to human behavior,

What People Want from Psychology

Most of us want to know how recent advances in psychology and brain physiology can help us and our families get more out of life. There are tantalizing indications that, with new information, we will be better able to manage our feelings, better able to use our minds. What many people want most is information on how to rear healthy, outgoing children. Our children need to be armored against dangers, confident in carrying on our cherished traditions.

Susan and her grandfather enjoy a family party together.

Museum-goers Jeffie, Joey, and their mother survey dinosaurs.

just because the animals' nervous systems are somewhat like our own? Can rats in a maze reveal anything significant about how humans think, or for that matter about rats?

Although most scientists do not deny that "talk therapy" on the Freudian model has helped many people, it bothers some scientists that nobody can say for sure how or why it works, after almost a century of use.

One philosopher, Patricia Churchland of the University of California at San Diego, has pointed out that the portion of the brain reachable by talk—our conscious, thinking, introspective self—is "only a little bubble on the froth," beneath which the huge preponderance of brain activity proceeds, in effect, on its own. Thus, suggests Harvard University psychologist Howard Gardner, the classic introspective dimension of psychology, dealing with such questions as character and motivation, is really closer to cultural studies and the issues addressed in great literature.

What lies ahead for psychology?

Three vast areas will probably dominate future study of the mind. First is the investigation of how we learn, or cognitive science. Second, there is the search for general principles of human behavior, which has much in common with sociology.

Most important, there is neuroscience, which focuses on the microscopic structures and fine processes of the brain. Since about 1960, neuroscience has been a whirlwind of discovery, employing extraordinarily powerful magnifiers, scanning devices, and computers. The picture that emerges is of a brain far more complex and far more capable than scientists imagined a generation ago. Nothing ever stands still in the brain. Ceaseless interaction is the rule, as billions of cells respond to one another in uncounted ways. So far, all that scientists have been able to detect is a pattern here, a process there, though that in itself is perhaps a kind of miracle. A clock is not expected to know how a clock works. Can a human mind understand the human mind?

PERSPECTIVES

On Mind and Spirit

Beyond such marvelous capabilities as reason and emotion, the human brain has a spiritual force that can only be described, never defined.

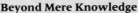

Beyond Mere Knowledge

"The most beautiful experience we can have is the mysterious. It is the fundamental emotion which stands at the cradle of true art and true science. Whoever does not know it and can no longer wonder, no longer marvel, is as good as dead. . . . A knowledge of the existence of something we cannot penetrate, our perceptions of the profoundest reason and the most radiant beauty, which only in their most primitive forms are accessible to our minds—it is this knowledge and this emotion that constitute true religiosity."

—Albert Einstein

◆

A Therapist's View

"There is vast mystery and beauty surrounding the human soul. It would be as presumptuous of me to attempt to overhaul that system as for an astronomer to remake the solar system. If I can help patients understand who God made them to be and then help them to *be* those men and women, it is enough."

—Alan Loy McGinnis
The Friendship Factor

◆

Our Own Doing

"The mind is its own place, and in itself
Can make a heaven of hell, a hell of heaven."

—John Milton
Paradise Lost

◆

Inspired Audacity

"In 1944, Raoul Wallenberg, a Christian and a member of the wealthy and powerful family often called the Rockefellers of Sweden, left the sanctuary of Stockholm to rescue Jews in Budapest. Wallenberg's plan was to provide temporary citizenship papers . . . . The *Schutzpasse* looked impressive and claimed the bearer was a ward of the king of Sweden.

"For the most part [the Nazi pogrom led by Adolf Eichmann] . . . was efficient and ruthless, often ignoring the Swedish flag, loading hundreds of Jewish men and women on cattle cars destined for Auschwitz and other death camps. When he knew of such a movement, Wallenberg would arrive at a railway station with long lists of holders of protective passes, demanding in an authoritative tone that they be turned over to him.

"Early in January 1945 . . . about 70,000 Jews had been moved to a sealed ghetto, and the Nazis planned to blow it up and machine-gun the survivors. When Wallenberg learned of the plot he warned the German commander that if the plan were carried out, he, Wallenberg, would personally see to it that the commander would hang as a war criminal. Obviously shaken, the commander halted the operation.

"It may also have been Wallenberg's downfall." *After the Soviet Union invaded Hungary, Wallenberg insisted on staying in the section of Budapest where the majority of the Jewish population lived. He continued to work for the safety of Hungarian Jews. Then, without warning, Wallenberg vanished. Six days after his disappearance, on January 16, 1945, a deputy Soviet minister sent word to the Swedish minister in Moscow that Wallenberg had been placed "under Soviet protection." Perhaps he was mistaken for a spy. The Soviets claimed that Wallenberg died of a heart attack in prison in 1947. But former Soviet prisoners reported seeing him alive many years after that date.*

"The mystery of Wallenberg's disappearance may never be solved. But one thing is clear. One man in six months saved between 20,000 and 25,000 Jews—more, if one includes his role in preventing the Budapest ghetto, with its 70,000, from being destroyed."

Says one whose family Wallenberg had saved from the death camps: "He was the Moses of the 20th century. The world in its history has known few Wallenbergs."

—Gerald Clark

Deciding What Is Normal

How do we know what's normal and what isn't?

Human beings are as immersed in their own cultures as fish are in the sea. Notions of normal or abnormal behavior must always take into account the social setting, or culture, in which someone's behavior occurs.

Culture is a blanket term for a society and its traditions, religion, government, and customs such as ceremonies, dress, songs, dances, and games. Each culture cherishes its ways, and throughout history, groups have sought to preserve their traditions by instilling beliefs and obedience in their members, starting from early childhood. Before written language, traditions were passed from one generation to the next by priests, storytellers, and bards.

What is normal or approved in one culture is generally widely endorsed within it, but similar deeds may be seen differently in a second culture. For example, most cultures think nothing of killing insect pests, but the Jain sect of India refuses to kill any creature, even a gnat or mosquito.

Reverence for a supreme being, sanctions against certain forms of killing, and incest taboos seem to exist in every culture. Other than these, there are few if any universal cultural laws.

If you said of someone's odd behavior, "That is not normal," your friends would likely agree. But your friends probably share your biases. The adjustable standards we have for others, related to age, sex, and social position, compound the difficulty of making absolute distinctions between normal and abnormal behavior.

Given these factors, it is clear why psychologists exercise great caution in evaluating human behavior. An inaccurate diagnosis could lead to both social stigma and improper treatment for the misdiagnosed person.

If you seek the foundations of Western civilization, *you will find them in the Bible. The Ten Commandments underlie all our laws and philosophy. In this medieval painting, Moses brings the tablets down from Mt. Sinai. From the 23rd Psalm to the Sermon on the Mount, the Bible is our spiritual source.*

Is religion fundamental to human nature?

Many scientists see religion as central to human existence. The Anglo-Polish anthropologist Bronislaw Malinowski wrote, "Religion gives man hope of immortality and the ritual means of achieving it; it reveals the existence of God or Providence and tells how communion can be established; it affirms the meaning of the world and the purpose of life; and, through its sacraments, it allows men to obtain a greater fullness of life. Religion gives man the mastery of his fate, even as science gives him the control of natural forces."

Religion offers answers to anxiety about the unknown, which seems to be a basic human trait. Philosopher André LaCocque remarks, "The human being is a creature that worries."

Certainly a sense of awe before the power and beauty of nature is central to religious faith. Spiritual revelations have provided both solace in times of uncertainty and inspiration for great art. Religious rituals also help to build cohesive societies by imbuing social and moral rules with sacred value.

Theorists and Theories: **Pioneers of Psychology**

Until the end of the 18th century, the study of human nature, which we call psychology, belonged to philosophy. Since then, psychology has been expanded and altered by the work of scientists such as those listed below.

Wilhelm Wundt, German, 1832–1920

One of the earliest scientists to try to establish objective criteria about human behavior, Wundt set up a lab where he collected data and analyzed his findings in the manner of a physical scientist. His approach is called *structuralist* because it sought the underlying structure of the mind through testing the subject's perception of externally presented stimuli. Wundt's work influenced the German psychiatrist Emil Kraepelin, originator of classification of mental diseases.

William James, American, 1842–1910

America's first prominent psychologist, James published *The Principles of Psychology* in 1890. He emphasized adaptation to the environment and became known as a *functionalist* for his premise that our behavior is not random but serves a purpose, or function.

Sigmund Freud, Austrian, 1856–1939

Freud's name overshadows all others in psychology. A true intellectual revolutionary, he postulated that we are all born with powerful, instinctual drives, which must be tamed if we are to become civilized. The conflict between gratification or repression of these drives leads to neuroses and psychoses. Freud introduced psychoanalysis as a treatment of these conflicts.

The son of a Protestant minister, Carl Jung always evinced a strong interest in religion and in mythology. When he became a psychoanalyst, he drew on these subjects in the development of his theories. Although Jung was not an orthodox Christian, he saw himself as belonging to the Christian tradition.

Alfred Binet, French, 1857–1910

By developing quantitative tests to measure intelligence in children and introducing the concept of mental age, Binet hugely expanded the practical application of psychology.

Carl Jung, Swiss, 1875–1961

A profound thinker and influential psychologist, Jung defined the ideally healthy human personality as one that has achieved a balance between the conscious and the unconscious, between interior and exterior life.

John B. Watson, American, 1878–1958

Founder of *behaviorism,* Watson believed that learning springs from conditioning and that conditioning is the most important force in shaping who we are. Environment, not heredity, counts.

Karl Lashley, American, 1890–1958

Through intensive neuropsychological lab work, Lashley concluded that the whole brain, not just specific areas of it, responded to new information. He named his thesis *equipotentiality.*

Is psychotherapy ever in conflict with religion?

Some people for whom religion is very important fear that if they undergo psychotherapy, their beliefs will be questioned. Most therapists try to avoid either attacking or justifying a patient's religious faith as such. But if a person's religious attitudes are linked with neurotic problems, the therapist may encourage him or her to examine the attitudes' psychological origins and implications. As a psychiatrist who has also studied religious ideas has remarked, many patients emerge from this process with a stronger, more solidly based faith.

Psychotherapists reinforce many attitudes shared by religious groups, such as the importance of love to human growth, the value of honesty and compassion, and the relevance to human life of hopes, images, and goals. Many priests, ministers, and rabbis have long had an understanding of human nature. Using the insights of psychology in their pastoral counseling is often just an extension of this time-honored pursuit.

Stories From the Unconscious

There are no dragons in the world *and never have been, yet judging by how frequently they appear in stories from every corner of the globe, humankind is enamored of these ferocious creatures. They appear to spring from deep within our unconscious.*

What is myth?

People often use the word *myth* to mean a false story or belief. Politicians speak about the myth of a nation's invincibility; scientists contrast primitive myths about sun and moon gods with the findings of modern astronomy. This echoes the attitude of the Greek philosophers Plato and Aristotle, who rated the mythic imagination inferior to logical thought.

Yet the Greek words *logos* (from which our *logic* comes) and *mythos* (our *myth*) have similar meanings. Both can be translated as "word," in the sense of information. *Logos* refers to a rational thought or calculation, while *mythos* has come to mean a fictitious narrative or legend involving supernatural beings.

Psychologists believe that such legends, or myths, play an important part in the thinking of many people, even those who claim to be guided by pure reason. "Mythology is not a lie, mythology is poetry, it is metaphorical," said Joseph Campbell. Another mythologist, Sam Keen, adds: "Myth is cultural DNA, the software, the unconscious information, the program that governs the way we see 'reality.' "

How can age-old myths shape our minds?

Psychologist Carl Gustav Jung asserted that we all carry in our unconscious minds the potential to have certain elemental ideas or "archetypes" and be transformed by them. This "collective unconscious" is expressed in myths that have been repeated in various forms throughout history. Basic themes do, in fact, recur in the mythology of many cultures. Just as traditional societies prescribed rituals to mark turning points in people's lives, they created myths to dramatize such events as coming of age, marrying, and meeting death.

The daring adventurer appears in the myths of many peoples, and his journey to distant, dangerous lands signifies the inner struggle that everyone must go through to become an adult. The mythical hero's goal is usually not just personal success but an achievement that will help society: he often defeats a monster that threatens his people. Or, like Prometheus who brought the gift of fire to mankind, he brings to them a new wisdom.

In Homer's *Odyssey*, the youthful Telemachus leaves his mother's home and sets out in search of his father, the legendary warrior Odysseus, who has been wandering about the Mediterranean since the end of the Trojan War. During his quest, the boy becomes a man, worthy of his father's respect.

Our culture both shapes and is shaped by myths. In dramatizing our deep preoccupations with self and family, nature and divinity, myths help frame what we think. A myth affects us not only by telling what heroes accomplish, but *how* they accomplish it. For example, how a mythical hero is said to feel about a slain enemy is a clue to the values of the society that finds the myth memorable.

Why did psychologists draw on ancient myths to explain the development of mental illness?

Some mythical heroes face profound, even insoluble problems. For the ancient Greeks, their tragic stories demonstrated human fallibility that caused their misfortunes to seem like fate. For Freud and his followers, they offered vivid illustrations of the unconscious conflicts that children must pass through to reach maturity.

Perhaps the most famous tragic hero is Oedipus, whose name is used in the term *Oedipus complex.* When Oedipus was born, an oracle predicted he would grow up to kill his father, the king of Thebes, and marry his own mother. To avoid this fate, the king ordered the infant put to death, but a servant secretly left him alive on a hillside; he was rescued and raised in a distant city. As a young man, Oedipus had an argument with a stranger on a highway and killed him. He then traveled to Thebes, where he was chosen to replace the city's dead king and marry the widowed queen. Later, he learned to his horror that the stranger he had killed was his father, and that his wife was his mother.

Freud saw this story as representing every small boy's unconscious sexual desire for his mother and rivalry with his father—a critical conflict that can lead to neurosis if it is not resolved. The female equivalent of the Oedipus complex was named for Electra, another mythical figure. Electra was the daughter of Agamemnon, king of Mycenae and leader of the Greek forces against Troy. While Agamemnon was at war, his wife, Clytemnestra, took a lover; the two conspired to murder him on his return and usurp his throne. To avenge her father's death, Electra plotted the murder of her mother and the evil lover.

How are myths and legends related to the societies that created them?

Some myths are based on historic events, which later generations imbue with special significance and which reflect the ideals of their own time. The myths in turn influence the culture in which they evolved.

The Trojan War was once thought to be purely imaginary. Now that the site of Troy has been discovered, we know that a battle really took place there, though it probably had less historic importance than Homer's epic suggests. The poem celebrates virtues admired in classical Greece, especially loyalty and courage in battle.

In modern times, movies have created some popular mythical heroes. The cowboy hero of the classic American Western, for example, personifies the courage and independent spirit prized in a young nation. As portrayed by John Wayne in such films as *Red River* and *Stagecoach,* he is a tamer of the wilderness and a strong, silent fighter against evil. In *Shane,* the Western hero is seen through the eyes of a little boy, emphasizing his status as a mythic role model for youth. Shane (Alan Ladd) was a former gunfighter trying to settle down as a hired hand on the homestead staked out by the boy's family. But when the family was threatened by a ruthless cattle baron, he used his gun again to save them, then rode off without waiting for thanks. A mysterious loner cut off from society, he nevertheless bravely defended civilized values.

A Deadly Test of Principle at *High Noon*

Just as Will Kane, the marshal of Hadleyville, turns in his badge and prepares to leave with his new wife for a quiet life elsewhere, word comes that a pardoned murderer, Frank Miller, will arrive on the noon train. Three confederates await Miller, and together they plan to kill Kane for his part in Miller's conviction. The new marshal hasn't arrived, so Kane turns to his former deputy and the people of the town for help. Everyone urges Kane to flee, taking the danger with him. His Quaker bride implores him to leave, threatens to leave him if he stays and fights. The drama, which spans only the hour and 20 minutes till the train comes, builds to unbearable suspense as Kane deals with the impossible odds. In the end, his wife puts his life ahead of her beliefs and backs him with a rifle. The killers die, and, exhausted and disillusioned, the couple rides off.

Deserted by all, his young bride Amy (Grace Kelly) and the townspeople alike, Will Kane (Gary Cooper) goes grimly forth to confront a killer.

Of Heroes and Quests

His wax wings failing him, Icarus hurtles to his death. *For a human to fly like a bird was a wildly extravagant notion in ancient times. But today, with hang gliding and skydiving, the myth has come true.*

Do myths become obsolete?

Writer Thomas Berry speaks of a mythical "story" that once expressed our basic assumptions about life. "The old story sustained us for a long time—it shaped our emotional attitudes, it provided us with life's purpose, it energized our actions, it consecrated suffering, it guided education. . . . Now the old story is not functioning. And we have not yet learned a new."

Myths tied closely to an extinct culture may well prove meaningless today when the survival of the planet is at stake. But for Joseph Campbell, the old myth of the hero's spiritual journey—the "vision quest"—retained mythic force, as in the movie *Star Wars,* whose hero, Luke Skywalker, carries ideals of honor into space.

Certain ancient myths also have special lessons for our technological age. The story of Icarus, who flew so high that the sun melted his man-made wax wings, plunging him into the sea, is often cited as a warning against too much faith in science. But, as Campbell saw it, the story is really about a flaw in the human character. Icarus became so ecstatic about flying that he lost control. His father, the prototypical inventor Daedalus, who had made wings for Icarus and himself, wisely took the middle way—flying between the sun and the waves—and reached his goal.

Do fairy tales have the same psychological value as myths?

"There are proper myths for proper times of life," Joseph Campbell said, and he called the fairy tale "a child's myth." The psychiatrist Bruno Bettelheim tells of a five-year-old boy whose mother was reading him "Jack, the Giant Killer." "There aren't any such things as giants, are there?" the boy suddenly asked. Before his mother could answer, he went on, "But there are such things as grown-ups, and they're like giants." When parents read such fairy tales, Bettelheim believes, they show that they understand the child's fears of being powerless in a world of adults, and recognize the child's need to grow toward independence.

What about women's myths?

Although male figures tend to dominate mythology, there are numerous female prototypes in myths, from the earth mother to the huntress, from warlike to peace-loving, wise to giddy, virtuous to amorous. As with male figures, the female prototypes that are most popular in a given culture reveal much about that culture and its values.

Many mythical heroines have traditionally feminine adventures. In the fairy tale "Beauty and the Beast," a young woman overcomes her repugnance for a "beastly" man—representing sexuality, according to Bruno Bettelheim—and transforms him through her love into a prince. The ending is doubly reassuring because she need not reject her parents to find fulfillment. In fact, she goes to the Beast's castle to save her father, and her love for her father prepares her to recognize a suitable romantic partner.

Are myths ever destructive?

Myths can have both positive and negative effects. A nationalistic myth may temporarily inspire some people, but be devastating to those they conquer, as the Nazi myth of a "master race" notoriously proved.

The King Who Lived in a World of Dreams

They called him Mad King Ludwig. And the Bavarian monarch's eccentric manners may well have bordered on insanity. But his support of Wagner's operas and his fanciful palaces proved him to be an art patron and master builder par excellence.

Ludwig, *here with family crest, wanted "to remain forever an enigma."*

When Ludwig II visited France in 1874, the newspaper *Figaro* observed, "One would think that the Bavarians had taken him from a fairy tale." In fact, the strange, reclusive monarch could well have been a storybook character, a romantic eccentric whose mind seemed filled only with dreams of mythical heroes, thoughts of other times, and elaborate building plans. Even his manner was peculiar. Tall and aloof, he walked with an odd high-stepping gait, head thrown back, making grand, sweeping gestures.

Ludwig was infatuated with the great German legends, especially Richard Wagner's operatic portrayals of them. When he was crowned in 1864, at age 18, he immediately sent for Wagner. Ludwig was soon the patron of the desperately debt-ridden composer and became passionately preoccupied with his work. Never modest, Wagner took the king's largess as his proper due and continued to amass debts.

Wagner's extravagant life-style and his exceptional influence on the young king became a topic of gossip—and a major concern to the king's ministers, who ultimately forced Ludwig to expel him. But even after leaving Munich, the composer received a stipend from his admiring patron for the rest of his life.

The Bavarian king also developed an insatiable passion for building. His first and best-known edifice is the multitowered fairy tale castle called Neuschwanstein. His next structure was even more imposing. The palace named Linderhof is a lavish baroque fantasy, surrounded by formal gardens, fountains, pavilions, statuary, and a grotto with waterfall and lake.

The king's building projects and support of Wagner were certainly extravagant. But what really set him apart was his eccentric personal behavior. The intensely shy monarch not only avoided court functions whenever possible, but he ordered private full-scale performances of plays, concerts, and operas. He usually ate alone, or barricaded himself behind flowers at state banquets.

Ludwig spent most of his time in his country retreats, alone with servants and aides. Sleeping by day, he would rise in the evening. One of his favorite pastimes was going for moonlit journeys to imaginary destinations in his gilded sleigh, his attendants in 17th-century attire. He became increasingly obsessed with his fantasies and withdrew more and more from affairs of state. Ministers were often kept waiting for hours while he staged elaborate picnics or costume parties with his servants and guardsmen.

Ludwig's downfall resulted from his last building project, Herrenchiemsee. In it, he undertook no less than to re-create the French royal palace at Versailles. But by now, the king was deeply in debt, and he threatened the stability of the state with his demands for money and schemes for raising it.

The king's ministers finally decided to depose him, using his odd behavior as an excuse. Prominent medical mental specialists were called in. They questioned Ludwig's servants and aides about his behavior and encountered reports of the king beating attendants, loudly partying with imaginary guests, bowing to a "holy" tree, and giving outrageous orders to imprison and flog his enemies. He also would prance around for hours or stare off vacantly into space. The doctors declared him incurably insane and sequestered him in a castle. Two days later, he went for an evening walk with the chief physician. Neither returned, and their bodies were found in a nearby lake. Inconclusive evidence suggests that a despondent Ludwig killed the doctor and then himself.

We will never know how Ludwig died—nor if he could be called insane. Millions who enjoy Wagner's operas and visit Ludwig's buildings would probably agree with his cousin Elisabeth, empress of Austria: "He was not insane; he was just an eccentric living in a world of dreams."

For his fantasy castle, *Neuschwanstein, the king selected a dramatic alpine site and hired a theater set designer to sketch the initial plans.*

Modern Views of Men and Women

Casablanca, a Love Story for Our Times

In a final, poignant scene at the airport, Rick (Humphrey Bogart) tells Ilsa (Ingrid Bergman) they must part forever. Her husband's fight against the Nazis and need for her take precedence over their hopes. Their pain is assuaged by the knowledge that they have been faithful to their moral convictions and to their pledge of love.

Rick and Ilsa meet and fall in love in Nazi-occupied Paris, from which they must flee. Just as Ilsa is about to join Rick at the railroad station, she learns that her husband, Victor, whom she believed to be dead, is, in fact, alive but injured. Bound to Victor by his desperate need and by her sense of honor, Ilsa fails to meet Rick. Ignorant of Ilsa's dilemma, an embittered Rick leaves alone, taking refuge in Casablanca. When, in turn, Ilsa and Victor go to Casablanca, they find Rick in his café. Ilsa appeals to Rick to help her get her husband away from Casablanca, where he is in imminent danger of arrest. Rick pours out his scorn, but then discovers what she has denied: she still loves him. He agrees to aid their escape.

The enduring appeal of *Casablanca* is in its portrayal of love in the crucible of life's ambiguities. Nothing could have prevented the lovers from seizing happiness. But what really counted was the knowledge that there had never been a betrayal, that their love and loyalty were indestructible.

How much have ideas of proper roles for men and women really changed from times past?

Not long ago, many girls and boys were brought up almost as if they were members of different species. Males were expected to grow up to be breadwinners, prosper in their work, and, if circumstances allowed, take part in community affairs. By contrast, females were expected to take subordinate roles. So much has changed in this century that today's young people are often astonished by some of the male-female stereotypes that were accepted in the past.

A woman in 17th-century Russia, Robert K. Massie writes in *Peter the Great: His Life and World,* "was regarded as a silly, helpless child, intellectually void, morally irresponsible and, given the slightest chance, enthusiastically promiscuous. In good families, children of opposite sexes were never allowed to play together. As they grew older, even the most innocent contact between youths and maidens was forbidden. Instead, to preserve their purity while teaching them prayer, obedience and a few useful skills such as embroidery, daughters were kept under lock and key. A song described them 'sitting behind 30 locked doors, so that the wind may not ruffle their hair, nor the sun burn their cheeks, nor the handsome young men entice them.' Thus they waited, ignorant and undefiled, until the day came to thrust them into the hands of a husband."

In 1807, Napoleon established a school for young women, with the following orders: "What we ask of education is not that girls should think, but that they should believe. The weakness of women's brains, the instability of their ideas, the place they will fill in society, their need for perpetual resignation—all this can only be met by religion. Girls must be taught writing, arithmetic, and elementary French, but care must be taken not to let them see any Latin. Competition should be banned: we don't want to rouse their passions, or to give play to the vanity which is one of the liveliest instincts of their sex."

Are friends of the same sex important to male and female psychological development?

Most but not all studies find that when there is a choice, boys tend to play with boys, girls with girls. A boy typically finds companionship in team sports and other competitive group activities. A girl more often associates with one best friend or a small circle of intimates.

In the teenage years, the need for friends escalates, as does the influence of other youngsters. Concern about clothing, hairstyles, and music seems to take center stage, but these are really a means of finding one's identity. Interest in the opposite sex increases, but for a sense of security, most youngsters depend on their own sex.

In adult life, women commonly have close women friends in whom they freely confide. Most men have close friends, too, but there is generally less discussion about personal matters. Owen Wister's 1902 novel, *The Virginian,* expressed a traditional male reticence about sharing feelings. The hero felt "guilty with emotion" when he met two close friends after a long separation; he knew, "as all men know . . . that many things should be done in this world in silence, and that talking about them is a mistake." Today, many men feel freer to express their emotions, but others still believe in the "strong, silent type" of masculinity described in *The Virginian.*

Aren't men and women similar in many ways?

Psychologist Carol Gilligan observes that though the psychological development of men and women may start from different points, the developmental paths often converge in adulthood. Men tend to aim first for individual achievement, "making it" in their chosen fields, but later come to value caring and mutual support.

Women traditionally define themselves first in terms of relationships with others: husband, family, and friends. Later a woman's need for self-determination asserts itself and she sets other goals.

As both men and women move away from rigid sexual stereotypes, convergence may begin earlier in life, bringing rewards for both sexes. Women nowadays are less dependent and contribute more to society. Mainly out of economic necessity, many Western women now work outside the home; studies indicate that both men and women approve of this trend. But, of course, most women still want marriage and motherhood.

Men and women also seem to agree on the qualities of the ideal man. According to a recent poll, he is family-oriented (though most men spend relatively little time with their families), intelligent, humorous, and loving; power and money are less important.

PERSPECTIVES

On Men and Women

Though permanently joined, the two sides of a coin never look out on the same world. It's a little like the predicament in which men and women find themselves.

A Separate Task

"Women do not really know as much about men as they think they do. They have developed, over the centuries, considerable expertise in the techniques of adapting to men, but that is not the same as truly understanding them. Women often labor under the delusion that life is really pretty easy for men, at least when compared to their own lot, and have no idea what a complicated struggle is really involved in the transition from male childhood to real manhood. They have no idea of the long and arduous road that must be traveled by the male child who *must* separate himself from the original, indispensable, nurturing mother and venture forth into a way of experiencing himself that is not her way and that he cannot learn from her either by example or by instruction. Considered in these terms, it is easy to see that a girl must learn to be like her mother, while a boy must learn to be different from her without this difference deteriorating into either antagonism or fear."

—**Robert A. Johnson**
He: Understanding Masculine Psychology

◆

A Puzzled Man

"What does woman want?"

—**Sigmund Freud**

◆

Fancy Footwork

"There's evidence that some women are now functioning very much like men, doing what men do, seeking the same kinds of short-term goals that men have been taught to seek. There is also evidence that discussions go differently when there are women involved, that there are changes of tone and attention. . . .

"We talk now about the conflict that women have between work and the home, and how terrible it is to be torn in two directions. But women have always been torn. We forget that when a woman who's been married for a period of time gives birth to a baby, she has to serve two masters. She has to respond to two different kinds of needs. . . .

"This is what it is to be a woman. And this is what it is to keep a household going, to have multiple skills, to deal with transitions, to deal with the health of the whole. There is a sense in which women have retained the capacity to be generalists, to live in an ecology in which there is more than one life, and you have to balance them off. . . .

"You know what people say about women—that they're easily distracted, and that success has to do with focusing on specific goals. But what if the health of the world depends on the same kind of capacity that allows you, while you're feeding one child, to see that the other child is reaching up and about to pull a cooking pot of hot liquid on his head? This capacity to see out of the corner of your eye, and care about the health, not just of one child, but of three or four and a husband and other members of the family—that is the beginning of the capacity to care about the health of a multitude of nations, or an environment of many species."

—**Mary Catherine Bateson**
Bill Moyers, A World of Ideas

◆

A Sweet Enhancement

"Young people are increasingly preoccupied with their capacity to love as well as be loved. . . . Sexual relations . . . come about less frequently from a desire on the part of the boys to present trophies to their own male vanity than to secure themselves against the anxiety that they may not be truly and deeply loved, or capable of love. Many men and women agree that when physical sex is part of a positive, caring relationship, it 'sustains, supports, and heals in the individual life journey.' "

—**David Riesman**

The Ways We Have Changed

The Beatles were wildly popular *in Great Britain, but when they arrived in the U.S. in 1964, they caused pandemonium, or "Beatlemania." They changed our tastes in music, clothing, hairstyles, and humor. Here (left to right) are Paul McCartney, Ringo Starr, George Harrison, and John Lennon.*

How has television changed the way we look at the world?

It is hard for almost everyone, but especially the young, to imagine a world without television. We take for granted that all the important news of the day, worldwide, will be there at the flip of a switch. In times past, only the literate knew what was going on in the world, and then only after long delay. But it is now possible for any of us, if we so choose, to attend a royal wedding in London, watch Olympic games broadcast from South Korea, witness the tragedy of a forest fire. Nothing has shortened the distance between the outside world and our private lives so much as television.

Television takes us to the habitats of rare and beautiful animals, and we feel kinship with them. Concern for the environment, whether acid rain or the destruction of tropical rain forests, is now general. We worry about the influence of technology not just on our cities but on ourselves. This is truly something new under the sun.

More people know more about the past than ever before. Whereas once scholars were the only ones to know ancient civilizations in depth, now countless TV viewers have seen excavations in the Holy Land and the architecture of ancient Greece. If popular knowledge is often superficial, it has nevertheless taken a great stride forward, providing a broad foundation for human understanding.

Our lives have changed in many significant ways, not the least of which is a much longer life span for many people. Extended life gives scope for changes in life-styles, something constantly discussed on TV. And television has made us very entertainment-minded. We casually adopt as our heroes and heroines a variety of celebrities, from talk-show hosts to country-western singers. We feel entitled to our own opinions to an extent that would make the Pilgrim settlers gasp. All these differences have changed the way we think about ourselves—and the psychology of our relationships with others.

Can the new ways of listening to music affect the brain?

Music, says Dr. Avram Goldstein, a pharmacologist at Stanford University, has the power to alter the brain's chemistry. Listening to highly dramatic music—especially the kind full of thrilling "peaks and valleys"—can cause the brain to trigger the release of endorphins, chemicals that evoke pleasurable feelings.

In the not so distant past, people heard music only when a family member played the piano or some other instrument or by attending live performances. Later, radio and the record player brought orchestras into the family living room. Now, however, music can be played 24 hours a day, entirely at the whim of a listener.

Nothing has changed the way we listen to music so much as the pocket-sized cassette recorder with headphones. It is now possible to hear music even while walking through rush-hour crowds. As we eat, study, or ride the bus, the music plays on; a listener can effectively hide behind a "wall of sound."

Listening to loud music for short amounts of time can produce an annoying ringing in one's ear. Scientists have established that music played at very high volume, even for short periods of time, can result in hearing loss.

But there is another side to this world saturated by music. Allan Bloom, philosopher and author of *The Closing of the American Mind,* expresses misgivings about the effect such intense preoccupation with music, particularly rock music, will have on the minds of young people over the long term. In this regard, Professor Bloom is in respected company. The Greek philosopher Plato was the first to sound the alarm about music in his *Republic.* He recognized that music could both please the soul and lead it astray. He warned, "A change to a new type of music is something to beware of as a hazard of all our fortunes. For the modes of music are never disturbed without unsettling of the most fundamental political and social conventions." Many people believe these ancient—and modern—warnings should be taken more seriously.

Does television have a special effect on children?

Sociologist Joshua Meyrowitz believes that television blurs the lines between childhood and adulthood. In the recent past, most children were shielded from adult displays of doubts, fears, sexual activities, and anxieties over parenting. Now, however, children who watch adult-level television programs get an inside, but often distorted, view of the world of adults. Meyrowitz thinks television can be damaging, especially when youngsters see adults being manipulative or deceitful.

Many critics go further and blame the increase in crime and murder on TV shows that portray violence as a solution to a crisis. Moreover, Dr. Benjamin Spock cautions that children who continually watch violent TV shows come to see violence as standard human behavior.

Unlike motion pictures, television shows are not rated. This makes it almost impossible to know in advance if a TV program is suitable for children. Concerned parents are advised to closely monitor the programs their children watch.

Discovering the True Nature of Childhood

As long as children were considered incomplete, diminutive adults, there was no reason to wonder how their minds were developing. In fact, a child's mind was likened to a blank page, or *tabula rasa,* on which adults were responsible for writing lessons.

It is a peculiarity of the human mind that we retain only fleeting recollections of infancy and early childhood. In the absence of information to the contrary, it was easy to sentimentalize about the joys of childhood and to trivialize a child's emotions.

Not until the 19th century did scientists find that the thinking processes of children are different from those of adults. We now know that the child's mind is an incredible learning machine, and that the foundations of personality and emotional development are laid down in the crucial period from birth to age 3. The child who is well cared for and encouraged in infancy, who is included in the family group as a matter of course, has an incalculable advantage over the child who is habitually ignored.

A "little adult" was once the ideal of what a child should be.

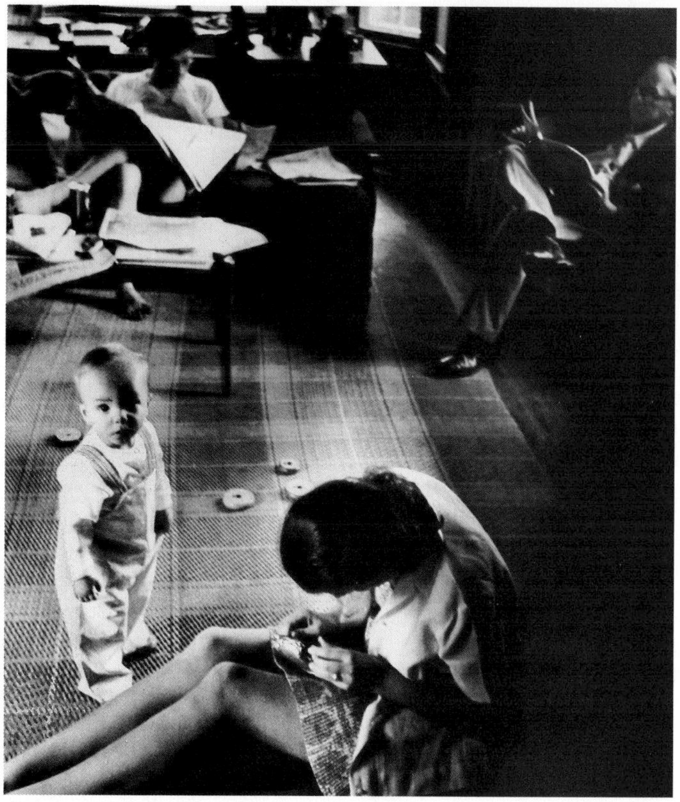

Though children today are the most studied in history, what this and every small child knows, and how he knows it, are locked in the brain's secret recesses, inaccessible even to loving parents.

The Human Face of War

Have people always fought one another?

The capacity for some aggression is probably inherent in human nature. Organized war has been called "a highly planned and cooperative form of theft," which arose after agricultural settlements appeared and others coveted their land and resources.

The causes of war are quite varied. Because people tend to develop loyalties to their own group, they often distrust outsiders and see others as inferior or hostile. In many early languages, the word for "people" was the same as the name of the tribe, and everyone else was "others" or "barbarians." Such attitudes can lead to an almost paranoid fear of foreign attack. For example, psychologist Sue Mansfield traces the outbreak of World War I to the belief of many leaders that their nations' power would be destroyed unless they took offensive action.

Most wars occur between close neighbors. Inevitably, neighboring peoples compete in some way. There may also be a tendency, as Freud suggested, to feel special scorn for people who seem familiar but have strange customs; perhaps one can "least well bear to see what is so much like oneself and yet so different."

***Francisco Goya's** searing portrait of war "The Executions of the Third of May, 1808" (above) was painted after Napoleon's invasion of the Iberian peninsula. The horrors of war are explicitly revealed. This vision supplanted the heroic images of combat commonly found in paintings, tapestries, and court chronicles. Increasingly, through such images as these, the world has become aware of the terrible suffering inflicted by war on innocent people, including young combatants who are not party to the quarrels of their leaders.*

The immediacy of photography has confirmed Goya's vision. A traumatized young American soldier in the Korean conflict (right) is comforted by a buddy.

Has war changed?

Some have argued that war has not changed since the dawn of history. Only the weapons have changed, with an exponential increase in the extent of killing and destruction that is possible. This seems to have made powerful nations less ready to go to war. The idea of war as an ennobling adventure, essentially a rite of passage for men, has also changed.

Television gave a vastly expanded audience front-row seats on news events in general and wars in particular, resulting in what has been called the first "living room war"—the Vietnam fighting of the 1960's and 1970's. TV reporting is thought to have stirred antiwar sentiments in America and hastened the pullout of U.S. troops from Vietnam.

Can war cause mental illness?

There is little doubt that the noise and terror of battle can drive people mad, or more precisely make them severely mentally disturbed. This can happen immediately, as a battle is raging; or the onset of mental disturbance can be delayed for days or even years. The condition has had various names. In World War I, it was shell shock. Later it was called combat, operational, or battle fatigue. Under the influence of psychiatry, *combat neurosis* became the preferred term. Today it is called post-traumatic stress disorder, or PTSD, and is recognized not just as a phenomenon of battle but as a mental disorder that can follow any disaster or traumatic event (such as rape or robbery) and affect surviving victims and bystanders alike.

Although records are unreliable, probably no war has brought as much concern and medical attention to the plight of PTSD sufferers as did the war in Vietnam. Depression and bereavement reactions (such as "survivor guilt") are common. Other symptoms are emotional indifference, reexperiencing the disaster in terrifying memories and dreams, and sleep, memory, and concentration difficulties. Alcohol and substance abuse occur frequently, probably as a misguided

In the Aftermath of War, the Emotions of Children

When we read heartbreaking stories of children injured and orphaned by war, we can't help wondering how they will ever recover—let alone grow up and feel safe in the world. We know from the many accounts of suffering that came out of World War II that few children ever forget the hellish experiences of war. Young survivors of the Holocaust who are adults today still have nightmares, still feel set apart by their suffering. Yet, there is a surprising spiritual resilience among young victims. In a *Time* magazine cover story on children of war, Roger Rosenblatt reports that in spite of being starved, brutalized, and deprived of parental love, few children carry hatred in their hearts. Kim Seng lost both parents in the war in Cambodia, but when he was asked about revenge, he said, "To me, revenge means that I must make the most of my life." Their experiences have made them wholehearted devotees of peace.

Home from a North Vietnamese prison camp, a U.S. Air Force pilot is greeted by his joyous family. Forgotten for the moment is the long agony of uncertainty about his fate.

At the Vietnam War Memorial in Washington, D.C., a little boy (left) kisses the name of his grandfather, who is missing in action. Another child is stunned by the chaos of civil war (above.)

form of self-medication. Other side effects include recklessness, marital problems, and withdrawal from friends and family. PTSD victims suffer from acute feelings of isolation and often show disregard for personal care.

Whether Vietnam veterans have been particularly hit by PTSD is a matter of some controversy; but one theory stresses the exceptional aspects of that war. In general, returning American soldiers were tainted, terribly unfairly, with the unpopularity of the war itself. The typical Vietnam combatant was also very young: whereas the average age of a World War II soldier who saw action was 26, in Vietnam it was 19. Furthermore, since he was rotated for duty on an individual timetable, the Vietnam soldier did not have the close attachment to a unit that was typical of previous wars.

As with any severe mental disorder, the treatment and outlook for PTSD is tremendously varied. Some sufferers recover almost on their own, often after a few sessions with a psychotherapist. Others are helped by antianxiety drugs and antidepressants. For a few, hospitalization is needed.

Alone in the Crowd

***Marilyn Monroe was adored by millions,** yet she often felt isolated. Ultimately she died a lonely death from an overdose of sleeping pills.*

Is alienation a common problem?

Probably everyone has felt a sense of isolation at some time in his or her life. A death in the family or of someone close, divorce, job loss, retirement, even leaving home for college can trigger intense feelings of loneliness. But alienation is deeper and more lasting than the loneliness that often follows misfortune or a major change in life-style. It is a sense of apartness or social isolation, a loss of values, a questioning of one's identity, a feeling of powerlessness.

For some people, such as elderly shut-ins and bedridden patients, chronic loneliness may result from the circumstances of their lives. Shy or introverted people are also prone to loneliness because they are not able to make friends easily. Numerous studies have shown that a lack of social support—the by-product of isolation—can pose serious health risks.

Are alienated people always loners?

Loneliness or alienation is not simply a matter of being alone or shy. Someone might be the life of the party—talkative, witty, and admired—and still harbor feelings of intense loneliness. Such feelings are hard to trace, but many experts believe early childhood experiences are the source.

Living in conformity with external values and expectations can also cause people to feel alienated—not from society but from themselves. A young stockbroker, for example, may feel deep inside that he would be more fulfilled by joining the Peace Corps. None of his coworkers or friends might expect such a feeling in him. They see only the successful businessman or the false self. The stockbroker lives a life surrounded by others, but alienated from his true self.

The 19th-century writer Henry David Thoreau captured this idea when he wrote that "the mass of men lead lives of quiet desperation. What is called resignation is confirmed desperation." Thoreau himself sought to escape this kind of desperation by living simply on the wooded banks of Walden Pond. Here he thought himself less alienated than any town dweller in his native Massachusetts.

Do certain economic or social conditions tend to produce alienated people?

Poverty, racism, cultural isolation— all breed alienation. Poor people experience rejection in the form of economic and educational barriers. In slums, shantytowns, and housing projects, a sense of helplessness and defeatism often takes hold. High rates of crime, family violence, and self-destructive behavior, such as alcoholism, drug abuse, and suicide, have been linked by some authorities to such circumstances.

One manifestation of alienation not easily ignored by society is homelessness. Alcoholism and mental illness characterize some of these people, but many are victims of extreme poverty and what writer Jonathan Kozol calls the "sledgehammer of dispossession." In some places, the homeless form a subculture of alienation in which normal values are transformed. Work may be replaced by welfare and begging; home becomes the steam grate or the welfare hotel.

Do people feel more alienated today than in the past?

Humankind has seen more technological advances in the last few hundred years than in the previous ten thousand. Just as many long-held ideals of science have been uprooted—so have many traditional values.

Today people are less likely to believe in God, or have any fixed set of morals. Questions of right or wrong, good or bad, no longer seem easily answerable. Doubt over how to live or what to believe has led to an increased sense of the meaninglessness of life, which is a form of alienation.

Technology has also brought about a radical shift in life-styles. Rural living with its emphasis on family and community has given way to a more urban, mobile society. Caught in this shifting, impersonal tide, people can lose a sense of belonging or belief in shared values.

In a trend that began with the Industrial Revolution, today's factory workers frequently lack a connection with the product they produce. That is, they are not likely to feel a sense of identification with or pride in their output. Many social theorists see this as a cause of alienation. Labor of all kinds, in factory or office, has become increasingly automated. Though computer technology can take much of the drudgery out of work, it can also leave workers even more divorced from traditional ideals of craftsmanship. As sociologist Kai Erikson writes of the computer's impact, "Experience becomes a matter of formula, intuition and judgment become matters of computation."

Can alienation be cured?

Much alienation stems from society's problems and not those of the individual. Still, hope does exist for alienated individuals. For example, loneliness among painfully introverted people can be eased through what psychologists call social skills training. Therapists can teach shy people, through role playing and other methods, how to make friends, initiate conversations, and be aware of messages passed on by their body language. Psychotherapy tackles alienation by unmasking the "false self." Once a person has a truer sense of his or her identity, the person is free to make more fulfilling choices.

What's the difference between alienation and solitude?

Whereas the alienated person may feel rejected or cast off, and is often stressed and resentful, the solitary person may well have sought time alone. The emphasis given by psychologists to the importance of *relationships* has tended to obscure the genuine benefits of solitude.

Certainly many creative people, ranging from the great physicist Isaac Newton to writer Rudyard Kipling, required solitude for work. Removing oneself from the clamor of social events is a relief. Solitude can be healing and consoling; it can allow time for prayer and for intellectual growth.

Those whose isolation is enforced, either because of circumstances such as loss of hearing (Ludwig van Beethoven and Francisco Goya, for example) or imprisonment of some kind, actually have a choice. They can respond by feeling alienated, or they can to some extent seek the consolations of solitude.

***"Christina's World,"** a painting by Andrew Wyeth, captures the feelings of a young woman whose life is circumscribed by paralysis and rural isolation. She gestures outward to a world beyond her reach.*

From Horror to Compassion

The final scene in "A Rake's Progress," *a series of paintings by 18th-century painter William Hogarth, shows the rake, insane after a life of sin, shackled in chains inside Bedlam—London's most notorious mental asylum.*

What were the early treatments for mental illness?

In the past, depending on the individual culture, severe mental illness that had no obvious cause was attributed to a variety of things: possession by demons, witchcraft, exposure to moon rays, an imbalance of bodily fluids, or humors, and a host of other such unverifiable agents.

The ancient Greeks treated depression as something the body could rid itself of—with the help of strong emetics and purges. In Europe in the Middle Ages, insanity was often seen as possession by the Devil or as the penalty for moral depravity, or possibly as punishment for parental sins. Some psychotic women were burned at the stake as witches.

In the 19th century, asylum keepers thought that a sudden shock could restore reason. Inmates were dropped without warning into tanks of icy water or strapped into chairs, which were then rotated rapidly to induce shock. Bloodletting was also a favored treatment.

Less sensational but cruelly efficient was the practice of abandoning adults and children whose intelligence or behavior did not measure up to the society's standards. Leaving a mentally impaired person in unfamiliar territory, far from home, was many times a sentence of death. There was little chance of being taken in by kindly strangers, although it occasionally happened. In rare cases the mentally disturbed were regarded as divinely blessed and treated well.

When did being crazy stop being a crime?

Although it survives in some parts of the world, the "insane asylum," where inmates are restrained and treated like dangerous animals, is no longer an acceptable institution in Western societies. The change has been brought about by a combination of expanding knowledge of the brain and behavior, effective medication, and humanitarian concerns for the rights and feelings of the mentally ill.

The idea of humane therapy is not new. Two centuries ago, care of mental patients took a dramatic turn for the better when Philippe Pinel became director of the Bicêtre asylum in Paris. Rejecting the notion that the mentally ill were possessed by demons, Pinel unchained the inmates and began a program of kindness.

Pinel's therapy included friendly discussions with the patients about their problems. His enlightened acts helped lay the foundations of modern psychiatry as a branch of medicine dealing with mental, emotional, and behavioral disorders.

Beginning in the 1860's the French neurologist and teacher Jean-Martin Charcot studied patients with such nervous-system disorders as epilepsy and multiple sclerosis. His observations greatly improved the diagnosis of these illnesses.

Later Charcot became interested in patients who displayed the symptoms of neurological damage but who had no organic disorders. While most of his colleagues dismissed this "hysterical paralysis" as malingering, Charcot believed that these patients were truly suffering. One of his students, Sigmund Freud, was intrigued by Charcot's use of hypnosis to treat such hysteria. The fact that Charcot took hysteria so seriously seems to have impressed Freud and may have been a factor in Freud's own search for explanations of neurotic behavior.

Who brought order to mental disorder?

In 1883, at the age of 27, the German psychiatrist Emil Kraepelin began publishing a classification of mental illnesses. He created categories based on the onset, symptoms, development, and outcome of an illness. Kraepelin kept expanding and revising his list for 40 years, and it became an indispensable guide to the diagnosis and treatment of mental illness through much of the first half of the 20th century.

Before Kraepelin's system, mental illnesses had few agreed-upon names. As a result, two psychiatrists discussing a patient might use different labels for the same problem; and if there was uncertainty about which patients had similar disorders (and therefore similar prognoses), each case in a sense presented a unique mystery. Neither patients nor doctors benefited from medical experience.

Theories and Theorists: **A Wide Array of Therapies**

Psychoanalysis

The aim of psychoanalytic therapy is to relieve a patient's anxieties by uncovering buried impulses and conflicts that were present in childhood but have since been repressed. During 50-minute sessions, four to five times a week, a patient talks about problems, hopes, fears, fantasies, dreams, relationships—anything at all. Psychoanalysts rarely talk or interpret a patient's problems during sessions. The goal is for patients to resolve their conflicts in their own way as they gain greater insight. Psychoanalysis is a lengthy process that may go on for years.

Brief Dynamic Psychotherapy

This therapy borrows from psychoanalytic theory, but focuses on specific emotional problems. To do this, a therapist strives to develop a therapeutic rapport quickly. Unlike psychoanalysis, brief dynamic psychotherapy aims to solve particular problems in a limited number of sessions.

Behavioral Therapy

Behavior therapists are concerned solely with behavior, which they believe is learned naturally in response to one's environment. Instead of analyzing the unconscious reasons that may motivate a person's behavior, a behavior therapist seeks only to help a client change or modify his or her problem behaviors.

Cognitive Therapy

The goal here is first to make clients aware of how their ideas and thoughts can distort their actions, attitudes, and emotions. Cognitive therapists then teach clients not to jump to the worst conclusions about themselves. Clients are encouraged to change their thinking patterns and take new, constructive actions to improve their lives.

Rogerian Therapy

Developed by Carl Rogers, this therapy is based on the belief that all human beings have the desire and capacity to achieve their full potential. Using therapeutic listening, a therapist restates what clients are saying and feeling. The goal is self-realization. A Rogerian therapist provides unconditional positive support, which is meant to help clients develop a positive sense of self-worth.

Gestalt Therapy

One's thoughts, feelings, and actions should be integrated to create a sense of wholeness. *Gestalt* in German means "form, shape, or structure." Based on work by Fritz Perls, this confrontational therapy encourages a client to achieve a sense of inner harmony by integrating all aspects of his or her inner self.

Group Therapy

People in group therapy talk about their personal problems and significant aspects of their lives and listen to the problems of other group members. Knowing that there are others with problems and hearing how they have coped are major benefits of group therapy, which also stresses building better interpersonal relationships. It has proved helpful to those who are in need of emotional support, but who resist the idea of individual therapy.

Hypnotherapy

Hypnosis may help control habits such as smoking and overeating. Its deep relaxation techniques are successful at helping relieve stress and anxiety. It is sometimes used as an adjunct to other therapies to help reduce a person's resistance to bringing repressed thoughts to the surface.

Play Therapy

Child therapists often use play therapy to help diagnose and treat children with psychological problems. Because young children have difficulty verbalizing their problems, it is easier for them to act out their concerns using dolls and other toys, which can symbolize troubling people or events in their lives. The goal of play therapy is to help children learn how to express and cope with their problems.

Probing for Understanding

Poisoning Was Behind the Madness of the "Mad Hatters"

For years it was so common for hatmakers to suffer from muscular tremors, mental confusion, and slurred speech that their condition gave rise to the expression "mad as a hatter." Scientists now know that the hatters' irreversible mental impairment was caused by the poisonous mercury-laden vapors they inhaled while making felt hats.

Other mental disturbances have been linked to toxic substances. The profound depressions of some famous artists in the past may have been due to the fact that their paints contained lead. Lead poisoning is especially harmful to young children. If they accidentally eat lead paint chips, children often develop severe learning disabilities. If detected early enough, lead poisoning can be treated with special drugs.

A bewildered Alice takes tea with the Mad Hatter and companions. A master of nonsensical chat, the Hatter asks Alice, "Why is a raven like a writing desk?"

How does psychotherapy affect a person's sense of self?

Most psychotherapists believe that they can only help a person who wants to be helped, and that when a person enters therapy, he or she takes on one of the toughest jobs imaginable. The task is to recognize and change habits that may serve some purpose but, on balance, are ultimately self-defeating. With the help of a caring therapist, a person sets out on a journey of self-exploration, pushing into areas where he or she has never been and, once glimpsed, may sometimes decide not to go.

The medium of most psychotherapy is talk, just as the medium of finance is money and the medium of boating is water. Really all the therapist knows is what the patient tells, although a well-trained therapist may see and hear nuances that add a dimension to what the patient is saying. Such insights are channeled back by the therapist into the growing self-awareness of the patient.

Can a hypnotist make you do something immoral?

When asked to do something considered wrong, a hypnotized subject generally rejects the command and comes out of the trance. However, up to a point, a hypnotist might be able to persuade a person that something had happened to justify an action that would otherwise be immoral.

One experimenter instructed a hypnotized person to offer poisoned tea to an expected guest, who (the experimenter said) was guilty of terrible crimes. The experimenter provided a bowl of sugar lumps, in which the lumps marked with an *X*, he claimed, were laced with a lethal dose of cyanide. The subject readily put the "poisoned" sugar into the guest's cup. When nothing happened, the experimenter explained that the dosage must have been too weak. He took out a box of pills labeled "potassium cyanide" and told the subject to put some into the tea. At this point, the man came out of the trance. He had evidently been willing to go along with what he thought was a form of role-playing, trusting that the experimenter would not tell him to do something wrong. But the clearly labeled poison broke the illusion.

Are some people more easily hypnotized than others?

Susceptibility to hypnotism seems to be related to an ability to concentrate all one's attention on something or to deeply immerse oneself in make-believe worlds beyond immediate experience. For example, some of us can almost *become* the characters in a book or movie. This link with fantasy casts doubt on the use of hypnosis to extract memories buried in the minds of witnesses to crimes. Events recalled by a hypnotized witness may turn out to be imaginary.

An electroencephalogram (EEG) shows the brain waves of a person in a hypnotic trance to be different from those of normal sleep, but they are nearly identical to the brain waves of ordinary wakefulness. Although the mind-controlling power of hypnosis has often been exaggerated by clever entertainers, there is no question that hypnosis makes people more responsive to certain kinds of suggestions. For example, if people with severe burns are hypnotized and told that their pain will be more tolerable, they may experience dramatic relief from the agonizing discomfort that accompanies healing. Scientists don't know why this happens, but one theory is that hypnosis enables the patient to block the perception of pain, though the pain is still there.

"Anna O" and the Birth of Psychoanalysis

She was the daughter of a wealthy, traditional Viennese family, brought up to marry and have a family. Instead, she became completely immobilized with an attack of hysteria. The therapy used to treat her led to the development of psychoanalysis.

IN 1895, TWO VIENNESE DOCTORS, Josef Breuer and Sigmund Freud, published a book, *Studies in Hysteria.* In it they described the therapy used by Breuer to help a woman suffering from hysteria. To respect her privacy, they called her "Anna O." Breuer and Freud coined the term *hysterical conversion* to describe the phenomenon whereby repressed emotions cause physical symptoms.

The case of "Anna O" helped shape Freud's epochal theories about the power of the unconscious. Furthermore, the technique that Breuer used in treating "Anna O" evolved into Freud's own method of psychoanalytic therapy.

When Breuer began treating "Anna O" in November 1880, he found a striking-looking, 21-year-old woman with an extraordinary number of dire symptoms. Both her legs were immobilized. She could barely move her head because of neck muscle paralysis. She was prone to hallucinations, had lost sensation in her right arm, and lay mute in bed, squinting defensively at the world. Breuer immediately diagnosed a case of hysteria.

As a young woman, *"Anna O" had mysterious illnesses.*

Hysteria had always been considered a woman's disease. Its name derives from the Greek word for the uterus. The Greek physician Hippocrates attributed the disease to a womb that had become unlodged and floated in the body. If a hysterical woman had throat trouble, it was believed that the womb had settled in her throat.

By the 1880's, hypnosis had become an accepted method of treating hysteria. The doctor would tell his hypnotized patient that the symptoms would be gone on awakening. While hypnotic suggestion often worked, the symptoms also had a way of returning. However, with "Anna O," Breuer went beyond mere hypnosis. He began to ask her about her life.

Gradually she revealed past experiences that had fascinating links with her present symptoms. For example, when questioned by Breuer about her inability to look directly at her surroundings, she remembered the night she had sat by her dying father's bed, sobbing. He awoke and asked her for the time. Her tears made it impossible for her to see the watch face without squinting. After she recounted this story, her squint disappeared.

In time, "Anna O" could slip easily into a hypnotic trance, and under questioning recalled more and more of her past. She herself called the process "the talking cure" or "chimney-sweeping." Breuer recorded that his treatment "took me completely by surprise and not until symptoms had been got rid of in this way in a whole series of instances did I develop a therapeutic technique out of it."

In later years, *"Anna O" became an effective social reformer.*

In the spring of 1882, Breuer decided that his patient no longer needed him, but "Anna O" may not have been quite so sure. She suddenly developed severe cramps. When Breuer was shown into her bedroom, he found her writhing in agony. A responsible physician and a respectable family man, Breuer was horrified to hear her say, "Dr. Breuer's baby is coming." Breuer calmed her with hypnosis and left. The next morning he sent another doctor and never treated her again.

"Anna O's" phantom pregnancy gave Freud another clue to how he could probe the unconscious in his therapy. It was clear that she had fantasized falling in love with Breuer and having his baby. Based on this and similar insights, Freud developed his theory of transference, which he described as the displacement of a patient's emotions from the parents to the analyst.

Not until 70 years after Josef Breuer treated "Anna O" was her identity revealed; her name was Bertha Pappenheim. When she died in 1936, she was a well-known, influential defender of women's and children's rights. To the very end of her life, she never mentioned her experiences with Breuer and gave no hint of her role in the birth of psychoanalysis.

Questions of Degree

The Trouble With Psychological Testing

In an effort to measure human behavior objectively, scientists frequently administer tests. In general, the results give an accurate indication of where a person stands in relation to others in, say, problem-solving ability. The three tests shown here are used to measure that very talent. To some degree, the more often a person takes them, the more skilled he or she becomes.

Students preparing for college entrance exams review the questions from past exams. In general, as they practice test-taking, their test scores improve. This is certainly a sensible way to pursue an objective: college entrance.

But when it comes to *psychological* testing, experience can skew the results. For example, in some psychological tests used in industry, a person may be asked about his or her father. Fathers are often considered as symbols of authority; love or hate of one's father may be interpreted as applying to the company. A person can sometimes outfox an examiner by knowing how answers are interpreted. Tests are here to stay, but they are far from perfect.

Answers to these tests are on page 320.

Assemble all six matches to form *four* triangles with each side one match length long.

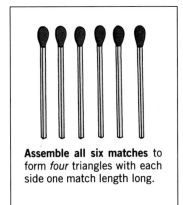

Trace these dots on paper. Without lifting up your pencil, connect all nine dots with four continuous straight lines.

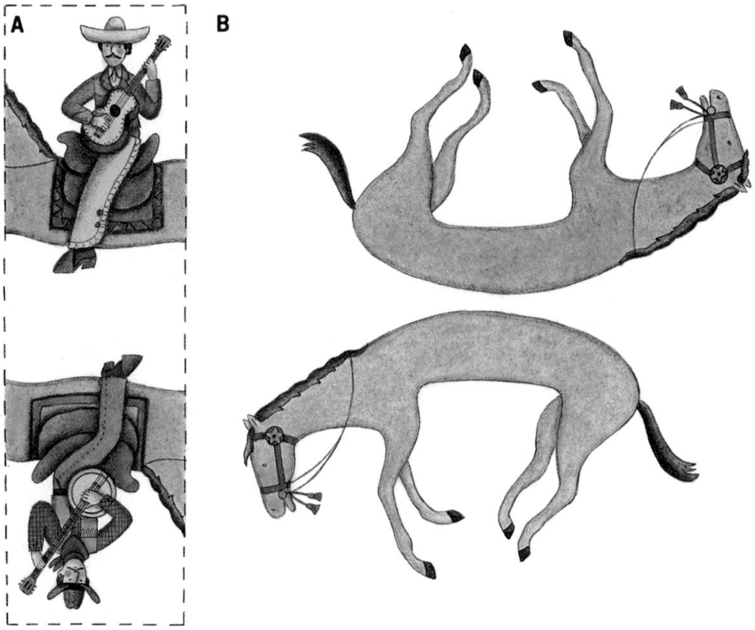

On a separate piece of paper, trace the two riders in panel A and then cut out the entire panel along the dotted line. (You can also make a photocopy.) Without cutting them apart, try to place the riders in panel A correctly atop the horses in panel B.

How do psychologists differ from psychiatrists and psychoanalysts?

Psychiatrists are physicians (M.D.'s) who have completed at least four years of postgraduate training. They are the only mental health specialists licensed to prescribe drugs and to give full physical examinations.

Psychologists work in some 40 different specialties. They may be experimenters studying rats in mazes or electrical impulses in nerve cells; animal-behavior specialists watching wild chimpanzees; or environmental psychologists observing people in crowded cities. Those who treat mental disorders are called clinical psychologists. They have Ph.D.'s or the equivalent and often have more training in psychological research and personality assessment than M.D.'s. Like psychiatrists, they have postgraduate experience and are trained to help patients with various therapies, some derived from the Freudian model.

Psychoanalysts may or may not be M.D.'s. They are generally graduates of training in Freudian, Jungian, or related analytical techniques.

What are the signs of mental illness?

Persistence is one of the main characteristics that distinguishes mental illness from life's normal allotment of unhappy feelings and missteps. Thus *if* they occur frequently and last for more than several days, the following feelings and ways of behaving warrant professional attention.

- Depressions that don't go away and whose intensity is dramatically out of proportion to any known causes.
- Suspicions (paranoia) that individuals and organizations are hatching harmful plots.
- Feelings of hopelessness or lack of control.
- Serious thoughts of suicide.
- Sleep problems, either insomnia or excessive sleeping.
- Withdrawal from society.
- Unreasonable fears or phobias.
- Episodes of sexual difficulties.
- Self-destructive behavior, such as

excessive gambling, drinking, drug use, overeating, and extreme dieting.

- Delusions and hallucinations.

What's the difference between neurosis and psychosis?

Using general terms to describe mental disorders is always a risky business. Each problem is unique, not exactly like any other. Furthermore, the meanings of general terms like *neurotic* and *psychotic* change over time and from country to country.

Broadly speaking, a psychosis is more serious than a neurosis. Psychotherapy—that is, one or the other of the "talking therapies"—is often helpful in treating neuroses, while psychoses (when confirmed by careful diagnosis) are usually best controlled with drugs, though talking is important for emotional support.

A key phrase in discussing neurosis is *maladaptive habit,* meaning a way a person has developed to deal with certain thoughts or events. This habitual response doesn't really work, although it may make the neurotic person feel temporarily better; it tends to create a bigger problem than dealing with the idea or situation directly. One example is the obsessive-compulsive neurosis. A psychotherapist would describe a person who repeatedly performs an action (compulsion), such as handwashing, as trying to expunge guilt for his or her irrational feelings (obsessions) of sinfulness.

A psychosis may involve behavior that seems little different from neurotic behavior; but a psychotic person's mind is in deeper disarray, in part due to a distorted sense of reality. Psychotic conditions include schizophrenia and manic depressions (also called affective psychoses).

Should people try to rid themselves of guilt?

Excessive guilt can be neurotic; psychologists say it arises when a person's natural aggression is turned against himself. But guilt feelings can also be useful. Communities generally try to promote the common good and prevent their members from harming one another. This works best when individuals internalize the group's values and avoid doing things they would be ashamed of, even when unobserved.

Amid a bevy of delighted bridal attendants, *a little boy smolders with resentment. What looks adorable to his elders clearly violates his sense of himself.*

Can people be their own psychotherapists?

The desire for self-improvement fuels whole industries. Books, magazines, videos, shops and parlors of every description offer to make you a better you, or at least feel better about the person you are.

What is often left unsaid is that the success of such programs depends in part on a person's commitment to change. No change for the better, even under the care of a highly competent psychotherapist, is possible unless you are determined to do whatever it takes to accomplish it. Change is always work. This is as true of achieving peace of mind as it is of breaking a habit, losing weight, or ridding yourself of old grudges.

Yet willpower, though always essential, may not be enough. Men and women who are miserable may spend months, even years, trying to solve personal problems or deal with fears or loss by relying only on their "inner resources." These people wouldn't think of taking out their own appendixes, but they think they are capable of dispelling sadness and confusion that may arise, at least in part, from long-ago childhood experiences.

Nor is great intelligence any guarantee that someone can solve problems that cause frustration and despair. Some of the smartest people, in fact, seem to have the hardest time changing habits that they *know* are essentially self-destructive. Just because someone knows all there is to know about agoraphobia (fear of leaving familiar surroundings) or impotence, for instance, doesn't mean he or she can cope with them successfully.

A real danger of trusting too much in do-it-yourself therapy is that it postpones getting the professional assistance that may be needed. The delay could make problems worse.

Classifying Mental Disorders

A Sampler of the Guidelines Used in Diagnosing Disorders of the Mind

The American Psychiatric Association (APA) divides mental illness into 16 different categories. Giving a name to any one condition, that is, diagnosing a person to have a certain mental disorder, is an extremely difficult job, sometimes as much art as science. For example, a diagnosis may call for a person to have at least three symptoms from a list of a possible 13, each symptom having been present for a certain amount of time and unrelated to any other illness the patient might have had.

Since the 1950's the APA has been publishing diagnostic guidelines in a volume entitled the Diagnostic and Statistical Manual of Mental Disorders. *The information given on these two pages is based on the revised third edition of that work, called* DSM-III-R *for short. This standard reference on diagnosis provides no information on treatment. (Suggestions about effective therapies are given in another APA publication.) It merely categorizes the disorders and briefly describes more than 200 different mental conditions. While* DSM-III-R *is used by psychologists and physicians in North America and increasingly around the world, another diagnostic reference, the* International Classification of Diseases (ICD), *is also widely consulted.*

In the United States, DSM-III-R *is followed by most health insurance companies when evaluating claims for coverage of mental illness. The APA cautions that its criteria for mental illness can be properly applied only by those with specialized clinical training and clinical skills. Here are the categories, with a sampling of the disorders they include, from* DSM-III-R*:*

- **Disorders First Evident in Childhood.** This category is made up of more than 42 different conditions and illnesses, all of which usually first appear in infancy, childhood, or adolescence. It includes *mental retardation,* for which two diagnostic signs are below-average intellectual functioning (IQ less than 70) and inability to meet standards of self-sufficiency that are normal for an age group. Retardation is further qualified by different levels of severity, from mild (55 IQ) to profound (below 20 IQ).

  Other conditions in this group are *attention-deficit hyperactivity,* which is characterized by at least six months of disruptive behavior before age 7 that impairs a child's ability to make friends and perform in school; and *Tourette's* (see page 42), which commonly appears before age 21.

- **Organic Mental Disorders.** This is the largest category, listing 69 different mental impairments that appear to result from organic (or physical) damage caused by drugs, diseases, or the degenerative effects of aging. Included here are several different mental disorders caused by *Alzheimer's* disease, and *alcohol amnestic disorder (amnesia),* in which both short-term and long-term memory may be impaired by prolonged heavy consumption of alcohol.

- **Psychoactive Substance Use Disorders.** All the 22 different conditions in this group involve abuse of or addiction to various psychoactive drugs. Among the symptoms listed for *alcohol dependence* are drinking in larger amounts or for a longer period of time than intended and an inability to stop drinking.

  Cocaine abuse is described as continued use of the drug for at least one month though the user knows that it is causing social, occupational, psychological, or physical problems. Substance abusers also frequently use a drug in dangerous situations, for instance, while driving a car.

  DSM-III-R suggests a distinction between dependence (mild, moderate, or severe) and abuse. Also remission may be partial (some dependence) or full (no dependence).

- **Factitious Disorders.** This category includes three disorders, all of which involve someone who craves a sick role and thus pretends to have a physical or psychological condition.

- **Schizophrenia.** All diagnosed schizophrenics share certain afflictions, such as hallucinations and incoherence lasting for a week or more (see page 44 for more on the general nature of this disease).

  The American Psychiatric Association recognizes five subtypes of schizophrenia, one of which is the *catatonic* type. Catatonic schizophrenics often do not speak and they may assume rigid postures for hours or days. This type of schizophrenia is marked by an emotional numbness or negativism that flattens motivation and can halt speech and limit movement.

  Paranoid schizophrenics are preoccupied with delusions and haunted by auditory hallucinations.

- **Delusional Disorders:** In this category are placed several types of delusions that persist for at least one month. For example, a *grandiose* delusion involves an inflated sense of self-worth, such as believing that one has far more knowledge or power than could possibly be the case. The *erotomanic* type describes someone who feels he or she is deeply desired or loved by somebody else, usually of higher status, who has no such feelings. The *jealous* type imagines that his or her sexual partner is being unfaithful.

- **Psychotic Disorders Not Elsewhere Classified.** This category covers psychosis—a form of mental derangement characterized by severely impaired ability to function effectively in the external world—that is not attributable to schizophrenia. Among the five disorders in this group is *brief reactive psychosis,* which refers to mental derangement lasting from a few hours up to a month, followed by a return to one's normal level of functioning. In the remarkable condition called *induced psychosis,* a close friend or relative is "infected" by a psychotic person's delusion.

- **Sleep Disorders.** Of 12 identified conditions affecting sleep patterns, one of the easiest to determine how to treat, once properly diagnosed, is *insomnia related to a known organic factor.* The insomnia can be cured by treating or eliminating the cause, which may be an illness or a medication.

  In this category are also various types of *hypersomnia*, or excessive daytime sleepiness and the inability to wake up quickly.

- **Mood Disorders.** This category covers nine extreme mood conditions, such as being chronically elated (manic) or morbidly depressed. Typical of the distinctions made among mood disorders is *major depression, single episode,* in which five of the following symptoms are constant for at least two weeks: depressed mood, loss of interest in daily activities, significant weight loss or gain, insomnia at night and sleepiness during the day, fatigue, feelings of worthlessness, and thoughts of death. *DSM-III-R* notes that this cluster of symptoms is not considered a normal reaction to the death of a loved one.

  At another extreme of mood is the *manic episode,* a distinct period of abnormally intense emotions with at least three of the following symptoms: inflated self-esteem, decreased need for sleep, pressure to keep talking, and excessive involvement in pleasurable activities, such as a buying spree. In a manic episode, a person is unable to work and socialize normally.

- **Anxiety Disorders.** The common thread in these conditions is a reaction that is disproportionate to any apparent objective cause, or stimulus. A person's fear, tension, or panic in the face of anticipated or imagined danger is so severe that it interferes with normal living.

  Of the nine phobias and disorders in this group, *panic disorder with agoraphobia* can be considered a prototype. This panic disorder causes a person to sweat, tremble, or feel faint or afraid of dying (to name just a few of the possible 13 symptoms) when attempting to leave familiar surroundings. Because of this anxiety a person may find leaving home extremely threatening.

  Some of the anxiety disorders, like *post-traumatic stress* (see page 30), can be traced to a specific time or event that terrified the person and continues to haunt him or her.

- **Somatoform Disorders.** *Soma* is the Greek word for "body." This category covers physical illnesses or complaints, such as pain or nausea, that have no identifiable physical cause. In all, seven somatoform disorders are recognized. Typical is *hypochondria,* the fear (lasting at least six months) of having a serious disease, despite medical assurance to the contrary. In *somatoform pain disorder,* a person feels pain for which doctors can find no appropriate physical cause.

- **Dissociative Disorders.** In the five conditions grouped under this label, an individual's personality is "split" or markedly altered. In the fascinating *multiple personality disorder,* a person has two or more distinct personalities that alternately take over and control the person's behavior. *Psychogenic fugue* is the sudden, unplanned, and unexpected travel away from home or place of work, accompanied by amnesia (inability to recall one's past) and the assumption of a new identity.

- **Sexual Disorders.** This category includes both sexually deviant disorders (of which nine are recognized, such as fetishism, exhibitionism, pedophilia, voyeurism, sadism, and masochism) and sexual dysfunctions, of which there are 11, including disorders involving arousal and desire.

- **Impulse Control Disorders Not Elsewhere Classified.** Sudden urges to act in a socially deviant or pathological way are called impulse control disorders. Three of the six listed in *DSM-III-R* are *kleptomania,* in which a person does not resist the impulse to steal objects that he or she does not need; *pathological gambling;* and *trichotillomania,* the inability to stop the impulse to pull out one's own hair.

- **Adjustment Disorders.** A person's reaction to everyday stress can sometimes go awry, resulting in maladaptive behavior. If such behavior interferes with one's work or family life and lasts as long as six months, it is considered an adjustment disorder. There are nine types of adjustment disorders, depending on a person's most dominant symptoms.

  For example, *adjustment disorder with withdrawal* describes a person who avoids the company of others but does not show signs of depression or anxiety. *Adjustment disorder with work inhibition* applies when a person feels unable to do a job or assignment despite having performed capably in the recent past.

- **Personality Disorders.** When the behavior and traits that make up an individual's personality become disordered, social and occupational functioning can be impaired. *DSM-III-R* calls these impairments personality disorders and lists 12 of them. *Antisocial personality disorder* is one of the possible diagnoses for an individual over the age of 18 who has a history of physical cruelty to people and animals, among other antisocial symptoms. A *histrionic personality* is marked by excessive attention-seeking beginning by early adulthood and displays such traits as constantly seeking praise, overconcern with physical attractiveness, and a need for immediate gratification of desires.

Freud's couch became a symbol for the release of repressed thoughts and the alleviation of mental torments. A relaxed patient, Freud thought, was more responsive to therapy.

The Ins and Outs of Therapy

Torturous Embarrassment of Tourette's Syndrome

The symptoms can be unsettling, to say the least: a person may suddenly start twitching uncontrollably and shouting obscenities. Called Tourette's syndrome after Dr. Gilles de la Tourette, who first described it in 1884, the strange disorder was thought to be a psychological problem, but psychotherapy proved useless in controlling the behavior of Touretters, as sufferers of the syndrome are called.

Doctors now believe that Tourette's syndrome is a neurological disorder that affects the chemical balance of neurotransmitters in the brain. However, little is known, and many Touretters are not properly diagnosed. For some reason it afflicts more males than females. Many researchers think the syndrome may be inherited. It generally begins in childhood with facial tics and can progress to spasms involving much of the body. As one Touretter described it, keeping his muscles from twitching was like "trying to stop a sneeze." Only during sleep are the symptoms absent.

In medieval times, some people who were burned at the stake as witches may have been Touretters. Today there is medication that, by altering the brain's chemistry, helps many Touretters control their spasms and their urges to yell and curse.

Uncontrollable outbursts of foul language in a Tourette's sufferer often cause passersby to stare and turn away in horror, as evoked here in Sue Coe's haunting illustration.

What is Freudian therapy?

Sigmund Freud believed that the mind is a battleground of conflicting impulses from three theoretical factions: the id, ego, and superego. The id is the mind's "animal," pleasure-seeking principle; the superego is our conscience; and the ego tries to mediate between the two and at the same time deal with external realities.

Most of the battle rages beneath the level of consciousness, and most of the conflicts have their roots in early childhood. Out of these theories emerged the prototype of psychotherapy, the first, the longest, and the most expensive form of talk therapy: Freudian psychoanalysis.

To get rid of unacceptable impulses (anger or lust, for example), the patient represses them, Freud believed. But they survive in the unconscious and produce anxiety, guilt, compulsive behavior, depression, or all of these. Psychoanalysis, Freud said, provided relief by uncovering these buried impulses. In bringing them out into the open and dealing with them, a more realistic balance was established among the id, ego, and superego. Anxieties became controllable.

To achieve all this was a lengthy, arduous, and sometimes tormenting job, Freud declared. After all, the patients had devoted a lifetime to burying unacceptable thoughts in their unconscious and could not be expected to dig them up easily.

What actually happens in psychoanalysis?

The setting for Freudian, or classical, psychoanalysis is designed to relax the patient. The decor is unobtrusive and lighting is subdued. There is indeed a couch on which the patient lies. The psychoanalyst sits out of the patient's line of sight.

The psychoanalyst urges the patient to free-associate, say whatever comes to mind. During a typical 50-minute session, the patient talks about hopes, fears, fantasies, dreams, experiences, relationships, anything at all. The psychoanalyst makes no attempt at conversation, although he or she may interject a brief comment or question now and then.

The psychoanalyst listens intently, alert for patterns. The ideas that the patient has been repressing may appear in symbolic form and the analyst must watch for hidden meanings.

Freud believed that as analysis progressed, something called transference took place. The patient begins to relate to the psychoanalyst, often as though to a parent, and feels a need to please or hurt the therapist. At this stage the patient reenacts with the analyst his or her childhood conflicts.

The ideal Freudian patient has been described as someone sick enough to need the analysis and well enough to tolerate it. It requires considerable resources of time and money. Done in the classic manner, analysis means four or five 50-minute sessions a week for as long as five years or more.

Did You Know . . . ?

- **Nothing is more convincing to a jury than an eyewitness** account, but according to psychologist Dr. Elizabeth Loftus it is far from foolproof. The stress of watching a crime often results in more memory mistakes, not fewer.
- **Men seem to be better than women** at detecting lies. Studies show that men are quick to spot the inappropriate smile or phony-sounding voice that often gives liars away. Women surpass men at reading nonverbal messages, but to be polite, they often ignore body language that appears inconsistent.
- **The seat of anxiety may lie in the temporal lobes** of the brain. A recent experiment using PET scans revealed an increased blood flow to the temporal lobes of volunteers who had been told to anticipate an unpleasant electrical shock.
- **Verbal slips of the tongue may not always represent** hidden thoughts or repressed wishes, as Sigmund Freud thought. New research shows that Freudian slips are often nothing more than speech errors due to memory lapses and inattention.
- **Psychotherapy is alien to most non-Western cultures.** As of 1988 there were only four psychiatrists in all of Tokyo.
- **In baseball, which eye a player favors** is just as important as which hand he or she prefers when batting. The best batters are cross-dominant. If they are lefties, they favor their right eye; if righties, they favor their left eye.
- **Compulsive ear-wiggling** fascinates scientists because unlike other uncontrollable nervous tics, such as eye-twitching, ear-wiggling involves involuntary muscles.
- **Shunning—the practice of treating people like pariahs** and excluding them from one's social group—is still practiced in many cultures today.
- **Drivers frequently step on the gas as they near home** because they are eager to get there and don't think of danger close to home.
- **Keeping secrets takes willpower.** Most secrets are eventually shared because the holder of the secret wants to demonstrate he or she knows something special.

Can you be trained to be mentally healthy?

Behavioral psychologist John B. Watson and his followers believed that neurotic disorders were caused by learned behavior and that this behavior could be unlearned.

For instance, a man pretends to be sick to get attention from his wife. The more he pretends, the more he is rewarded by attention. Carried to extremes, this behavior can disable the man and make life miserable for his wife. A behavioral therapist might treat the man by denying him attention at times of claimed illness and rewarding him with attention when he doesn't complain or act helpless.

How can you tell when therapy is working?

One way many people have used to gauge the effectiveness of therapy is to compare how they felt when they started with how they feel now. Those whom therapy has helped usually say they like themselves better and feel more relaxed and effective in dealing with others. Another approach is for the patient to ask the therapist for an evaluation at regular intervals.

The most noticeable improvements tend to occur early in treatment. Patients may feel elated with their progress after a few weeks. Then the pace may slow down as attention shifts to more deeply rooted problems.

Although psychotherapists offer hope, few promise a cure. No therapy can make the world a paradise. Sigmund Freud said that at best psychoanalysis could transform "hysterical misery into common unhappiness."

People who have been through it say that the two most difficult decisions of psychotherapy are when to start and when to stop. If a person set definite goals at the outset, such as feeling better about the loss of a loved one or being fired, then it's natural to consider stopping when those goals appear to have been met. Sometimes, a therapist will raise the question of whether or not to continue.

Some patients fear that all their gains will fall away without regular appointments. It is not uncommon for patients to grow attached to their therapists. A therapist, after all, is someone whom a patient can ask to listen to anything and everything.

Therapists, too, are human and don't want to lose a patient they have come to like. They may also feel that a patient wants to end treatment for the wrong reasons, such as an unwillingness to face certain deep-seated feelings. This resistance to further probing is a common occurrence in therapy and can take many forms, from making small talk to being late, missing appointments, or quitting abruptly.

Some therapists say that when a patient thinks that therapy is no longer needed but is hesitant about ending it, the best step may be a kind of trial separation. Therapy can always be resumed, even if not with the same therapist.

The Fearful World of Schizophrenia

What is schizophrenia?

Not one disease but a cluster of brain disorders, schizophrenia distorts the thoughts, emotions, and behavior of its victims. The term *schizophrenia* comes from two Greek words that mean "split" and "mind." When Swiss psychiatrist Eugen Bleuler introduced the term in 1911, he meant splitting or fragmenting of the thinking processes.

Schizophrenics should not be confused with victims of multiple, or split, personalities. The American Psychiatric Association also distinguishes schizophrenia from schizoid and schizotypal personality disorders. Though these conditions may involve traits and behavior (such as indifference to others, lack of interest in friends, excessive anxieties, and odd beliefs) that make relationships difficult, they are not marked by the delusions, hallucinations, and incoherence of the diagnosed schizophrenic. As evidence of its devastating effect on personality, schizophrenia used to be called *dementia praecox,* meaning "premature dementia."

Schizophrenics may have auditory hallucinations—hearing voices that urge them to perform acts that are often irrational. Schizophrenics may suffer delusions, such as believing that telephones are trying to rob their brains or that they are the rightful heirs to the throne of Great Britain. They may laugh at funerals and cry when others laugh. Some withdraw from the world, crouched in a corner, silent and unseeing.

Some schizophrenics have difficulty handling even the simplest of jobs, and they may be incapable of meaningful speech. They lose motivation and emotion and are unable to function in society at all. The only concentration they can apply is to whatever delusion obsesses them.

Schizophrenia can shatter not only the lives of its victims, but the lives of their immediate families. In the industrialized world, schizophrenia accounts for 50 percent of admissions to psychiatric hospitals.

Who gets schizophrenia?

Males and females are affected in equal numbers, generally in their teens or early adulthood. Most initial attacks occur between 17 and 25. Boys are likely to develop schizophrenia earlier, outnumbering girls four or five to one in the 17- to 18-year age range. About two in every hundred schizophrenics have their first attack before the age of 15. The onset of the disease rarely occurs after age 30.

Generally, among children with no schizophrenic relatives, the likelihood of developing the disease is one in 100. A child with one schizophrenic parent has a one-in-seven chance of becoming a schizophrenic. A child with two schizophrenic parents has about a 50 percent chance. If one identical twin becomes a schizophrenic, chances are almost even that the other will too. In nonidentical twins, the number drops to one in nine.

***The odds are 1 in 2 billion** that four identical quadruplets will develop schizophrenia, an illness that often runs in families. Nevertheless, by the age of 24, all four of the Genain sisters had been hospitalized with schizophrenia. Shown here at their 51st birthday party, the quads have been in and out of mental hospitals for years.*

What causes schizophrenia?

The theory that schizophrenia might have its origins in childhood experiences has been abandoned by most investigators, and parents of schizophrenic children need no longer add guilt to their hardships.

Although the cause of schizophrenia is unknown, there are several theories. Current research suggests that the illness is linked to biochemical imbalances in the brain. Many schizophrenics seem to have elevated levels of dopamine, one of the brain's chemical messengers; and antipsychotic drugs, which affect the action of dopamine, are used to help control schizophrenia. Among the possible causes being investigated are hereditary factors, viral infection, severe stress, early brain injury, and abnormalities in the immune system. Possibly the cause may turn out to be a combination of some or all of these.

What are the early signs of this severe illness?

The signs of schizophrenia may not be easy to recognize, especially those that are referred to as negative symptoms. These may include withdrawal, moodiness, problems at school or job, apathy, joylessness, and disregard for personal appearance. Initially, parents can miss the signs of schizophre-

Reexamining the Evidence of Schizophrenia in a Famous Case

For many years, the art of Louis Wain has been used to illustrate stages in the progress of schizophrenia. As madness overtook him, it was believed that he revealed his inner tumult in pictures.

Patricia Allderidge, archivist and curator in charge of these pictures at The Bethlem Royal Hospital and The Maudsley Hospital in Great Britian, has studied the evidence. She writes: "The theory that Wain's work became progressively more 'disintegrated' and 'hallucinatory' as his illness advanced is a complete myth. He continued to draw and paint in his old style throughout the 15 years after he was certified insane. The relatively few pictures which are supposed to represent his deterioration are, in fact, decorative patterns based on textile designs."

Louis Wain's reputation rested on his amusing representations of cats as people.

These pictures were considered to be evidence of mental deterioration. But there is no indication of the order in which they were painted, hence no evidence of a progression. The two pictures at right are actually Wain's renditions of textile patterns.

nia because these negative symptoms often seem to mimic irritating adolescent behavior.

The so-called positive symptoms are much easier for nonspecialists to spot: bizarre behavior, changes in sleep patterns, talk that makes no sense, imaginary health problems, internal voices and other hallucinations, paranoia, and delusions.

How is schizophrenia treated?

A wide range of antipsychotic drugs can reduce the symptoms of schizophrenia. When taken regularly, these drugs are effective in coping with delusions, hallucinations, bizarre behavior, and thinking disorders. They are less effective in dealing with apathy and ambivalence.

Like diabetes and hemophilia, schizophrenia is incurable, but with medication, controllable. Hospitalization is usually necessary for persons who are acutely ill with schizophrenia. Hospitalization permits examination and treatment of the patient. It also protects the patient and may give the patient's family a respite from coping with this difficult illness.

Doing the Right Thing

Instilling a Fear in a Baby in the Name of Science

Dr. Watson wears a bearded mask to test Albert's conditioned reaction to furry things. Watson's records show that he never tried to decondition his young subject.

Pioneer behaviorist John B. Watson believed that most fears are learned. To prove it, he deliberately set out in 1920 to condition an 11-month-old baby named Albert to fear white lab rats. Like most babies, little Albert was fearless and curious about the world. Watson, however, found that sudden loud noises caused Albert distress.

In a highly unethical experiment, Watson and a colleague used the sound of a hammer striking a steel bar to startle Albert whenever they presented him with a white lab rat. The moment Albert tried to touch the furry white animal, the bar was struck, scaring Albert. The more this grim experiment was repeated, the more afraid Albert became. Soon just the mere sight of a white rat caused him to cry. Worse, Albert's fear had generalized to other furry objects; seeing a fur coat, a dog, a rabbit, even a Santa Claus mask made Albert burst into tears.

Dr. Watson knew a month in advance that baby Albert would be leaving the hospital, but never attempted to remove his fear of furry objects. No one ever knew Albert's last name, nor if his fear persisted the rest of his life.

Is it ethical to use untested drugs or techniques on human beings?

However carefully a promising new treatment has been tested, the first person to receive it must in some sense be a "human guinea pig." The ethical dilemma is how to protect the individual from risk while pursuing potential benefits for a greater number. Some dedicated researchers have boldly performed the first human trials on themselves: Workers involved in Walter Reed's famous studies of yellow fever risked their lives by exposing themselves to the disease. And among those who experimented on themselves in the search for safe anesthesia was Sigmund Freud; he tried cocaine as a local anesthetic before its dangers were known.

Ideally, any human subject of an experiment should have enough scientific background to understand its implications. The dentist who received the first artificial heart probably met this standard, but the first patient to be given a transplanted baboon heart was the infant daughter of a couple with limited education; many wondered how well they understood the controversial procedure.

Children, the mentally retarded, and prisoners—once widely used in medical and psychological tests—are rarely in a position to give informed, truly voluntary consent to experimental procedures. And although terminally ill patients may agree to test new treatments out of a wish to help others, many experts urge that any therapy they receive should offer them personally some hope.

Ethical issues are also raised by random tests in which new drugs are compared with inactive placebos to determine if the drugs are safe and effective. If a drug works, shouldn't it be given to all patients? If it is useless, should anyone be exposed to its possible side effects? And what if desperate patients suffering from AIDS or other incurable diseases demand new, untried treatments? Bioethicists and physicians are searching for solutions to these painful dilemmas.

Is it ethical to mislead people about an experiment in which they are asked to take part?

Researchers studying human behavior sometimes mislead their subjects to test their reactions to unexpected events. A famous example was a series of experiments begun in 1965 by Stanley Milgram of the City University of New York.

Milgram told a group of paid volunteers that he was studying the effect of punishment on learning. Each volunteer in turn was introduced to a "learner"—actually a confederate of the researcher—who was to memorize and recite a list of paired words. Each time the "learner" made a mistake, the volunteer "teacher" was ordered to press a button that would give the pupil an electric shock. The shocks, mild at first, would increase with each error, up to an extremely painful, dangerous level of 450 volts.

No shocks were actually delivered, but the "learner" showed rising distress, finally screaming with pain and begging that the test be stopped. The experiment was carried out with 2,000 male subjects, from college students to adults of various ages and occupations. Although many protested about the pain they thought they were inflicting, 62 percent continued to push the button until the "shocks" reached maximum severity.

The results of this "Eichmann experiment" shocked both professionals and nonprofessionals. It implied how readily ordinary people follow immoral, Nazi-like orders if issued by a respected authority. The experimenter's actions also aroused shock; Milgram was severely criticized for deceiving his subjects and causing them mental anguish. He countered that the information gained outweighed the price of deception.

Professional guidelines have been revised to better safeguard subjects in psychological experiments.

Does fraud often go undetected in psychological research?

Even scrupulous scientists inevitably make errors, sometimes because of unconscious bias. Such errors are eventually caught and their study adds to an understanding of the psychological issues involved in research.

Bias apparently influenced the 19th-century researcher Richard L. Dugdale, who found a high rate of disease and depravity in a poor New York State family he called the Jukes. He blamed their ailments on inbreeding: cousins had married cousins for generations. Modern critics say he overemphasized the role of heredity and ignored environmental factors.

The Jukes later became linked in the public mind with the Kallikaks, a New Jersey family studied by H. H. Goddard, a researcher eager to rid the population of feeblemindedness and criminality. Goddard traced two branches of the family to a single ancestor who had fathered children by two women, one a virtuous wife and the other a promiscuous mistress. The "good" wife's descendants were said to be pillars of the community, but the other woman's progeny were morons, prostitutes, and thieves. His study, backed by a misinterpretation of early IQ tests, fueled the eugenics movement, which urged sterilizing or locking up mental defectives and restricting immigration from countries allegedly peopled by inferior stock.

Only recently has the Kallikak study been exposed as not merely biased but fraudulent. The researcher had falsified data and crudely doctored photographs to make the "bad" Kallikaks look idiotic and loutish. Ironically, Goddard decided late in life that mild feeblemindedness was probably not inherited after all, but he never corrected the records that had made the phrase "Jukes and Kallikaks" a dictionary entry, a synonym for hereditary imbecility.

PERSPECTIVES

On Ethics

In a single statement, the Bible sums up all anyone needs to know about ethical behavior. You must "do unto others as you would have others do unto you."

With the End in View

"If I'm willing to cheat, I could have a competitive advantage in playing golf. But it's not the same game. If we define the purpose of living only as the accomplishment of a particular task, accomplishing the task becomes the moral imperative—winning the election, getting the scoop, making a profit. But we know that nobody on a deathbed says, 'I wish I had spent more time at the office.' People's values begin to change when they reflect upon how futile most of the flurry of activity was. And the fact of the matter is that a good conscience is the best pillow. Living a good life is the most important thing for us." **—Michael Josephson**
Bill Moyers, A World of Ideas

◆

Beware Bad Leaders

"More hideous crimes have been committed in the name of obedience than in the name of rebellion."
—C. P. Snow

◆

Medical Ground Rules

"I swear by Apollo the healer, invoking all the gods and goddesses to be my witnesses, that I will fulfill this oath and this written covenant to the best of my ability and judgment.

"I will look upon him who shall have taught me this art even as one of my own parents. I will share my substance with him, and I will supply his necessities if he be in need. I will regard his offspring even as my own brethren, and I will teach them this art, if they would learn it, without fee or covenant. I will impart this art by precept, by lecture and by every mode of teaching, not only to my own sons but to the sons of him who has taught me and to disciples bound by covenant and oath, according to the law of medicine.

"The regimen I adopt shall be for the benefit of the patients according to my ability and judgment, and not for their hurt or for any wrong. I will give no deadly drug to any, though it be asked of me, nor will I counsel such, and especially I will not aid a woman to procure abortion. Whatsoever house I enter, there will I go for the benefit of the sick, refraining from all wrongdoing or corruption, and especially from any act of seduction, of male or female, of bond or free. Whatsoever things I see or hear concerning the life of men, in my attendance on the sick or even apart therefrom, which ought not to be noised abroad, I will keep silence thereon, counting such things to be as sacred secrets. Pure and holy will I keep my life and my art."
—The Hippocratic Oath

◆

The Honesty of Youth

"I love the fact that teenagers express all the emotions we adults have learned to suppress. When they are excited or depressed about something, they are not coy about their feelings. . . . I love their earnest passions, the urgency of their relationships, their capacity for outrage. Upon discovering an injustice, they demand in disbelief. 'Why isn't anyone doing anything about that?' Teenagers insist that we question our motives, our rules for them, our own behavior. They keep us honest." **—Letty Cottin Pogrebin**
New York Times

◆

The Ultimate Authority

"The one thing that doesn't abide by majority rule is a person's conscience." **—Harper Lee**
To Kill a Mockingbird

◆

Tried and True Advice

"This above all: to thine own self
be true,
And it must follow, as the night
the day,
Thou canst not then be false to
any man."
—William Shakespeare
Hamlet

The Puzzle of Criminal Behavior

***Over the years, the legend of Bonnie and Clyde** has turned this pair of outlaws into heroic Robin Hoods. Nothing could be further from the truth. They were petty thieves who robbed small banks and grocery stores and killed innocent people on whim. Incorrigible, amoral, and reckless, they were finally gunned down by the law in 1934.*

Are all criminals psychologically disturbed?

Each year American taxpayers defraud billions of dollars from the Internal Revenue Service by underreporting income and inflating deductions. Money stolen in this way probably far exceeds that taken in armed robberies. Yet no one would consider such white-collar offenses the work of insane criminal minds. The motives behind most crimes might even be thought of as "normal" in the sense that they are basic human urges: greed, lust, rage, a craving for excitement. Trouble arises when people allow these urges to stray beyond the bounds set by a society's laws.

Legal systems do recognize that not everyone can be held accountable for crossing these bounds. On March 30, 1981, John Hinckley leveled a gun at President Ronald Reagan and fired a bullet into his chest. Shots from Hinckley's gun also wounded three other men. Lawyers and psychiatrists at Hinckley's trial testified that he was suffering from "process schizophrenia" and was obsessed with the violent antihero of the film *Taxi Driver*. A federal jury later found Hinckley not guilty by "reason of insanity."

Schizophrenics display abnormal thought processes that can affect their emotional state and impulse control. Although schizophrenia and other serious mental illnesses are the causes of relatively few crimes, the ones they do commit are often dramatic. In 1985 a schizophrenic woman, Sylvia Seegrist, dressed in fatigues and carrying a semiautomatic rifle, opened fire on shoppers at a mall near Philadelphia, killing three people. It was later learned that she had a history of violent schizophrenia dating back to age 15. Doctors believe such brutality may be biological in origin.

What is a psychopath?

Insane criminal acts are relatively rare—at least in the eyes of the law. But many of the muggers, rapists, murderers, and chronic con artists arrested each year do fall into a disturbing psychological category. Nineteenth-century doctors called it "moral insanity." Today's texts prefer the terms *antisocial personality disorder* or *sociopath*. But the label that has stuck in the public's mind is psychopath.

Psychopaths can be charming, intelligent, and highly seductive. What characterizes them is a lack of any moral sense or true regard for others. Life for psychopaths is totally self-serving, and they will not hesitate to lie or cheat to gratify any desire.

"Normal" human emotions often seem absent in psychopaths; pain or sorrow in others leaves them untouched. They may commit the most callous of crimes with no hint of emotion or remorse. One teenager stabbed his 15-year-old former girlfriend repeatedly because she'd decided to stop dating him. Later that night he went to a party with another girl.

Antisocial behavior emerges early in adolescence. Young psychopaths are prone to impulsiveness, and often have histories of disruptive behavior, truancy, theft, fighting, and random acts of cruelty, such as torturing animals. By age 18 they may already have a long record of delinquency.

Are criminals born or made?

At the turn of the century an Italian criminologist, Cesare Lombroso, theorized that men could be "born criminal," with recognizable "degenerate" traits such as sloping foreheads and flat feet. That theory has long since fallen into disfavor. Most criminologists today see crime arising mainly from environmental conditions, such as urban pressures, poverty, and a poor home life. Statistics tend to bear this out. Urban areas have higher crime rates than rural areas. Crime is more common in slums than in suburbs. Violent criminals often come from violent homes.

What motivates a mob to act violently?

Mob violence is one example of what psychologists call mass hysteria. In a group, an individual may do, say, or feel things that he or she would find unacceptable in other circumstances. Researchers say that people caught up in mass hysteria are not usually acting out new emotions, but releasing existing feelings that are kept in check under normal conditions.

In general, two factors account for individuals being caught up in mass hysteria. First, the individual must be a member of a group that is in a "suggestible state." Second, the group must be exposed to a repeated "suggestion," usually a slogan or slogans. Alcohol, drugs, and rhythmical sounds like drumming help put a crowd into a suggestible state. A clever leader can sense when a group is ready for a message and time the repeated suggestions, which often play on the group's suppressed fears, to achieve maximum manipulation.

Mass hysteria in itself is not necessarily evil and occurs in many religious rites, political rallies, and sports and entertainment events. The surest defense against being caught up in mob violence is a strong sense of one's identity and values.

Why do people sometimes fail to help when they should?

There is little doubt that people exist who simply do not feel the emotions that are felt by normal people. Because of a brain defect or some other abnormality, they lack empathy. They cannot feel another human being's pain, either emotional or physical. Fortunately, they are a rarity.

More common are decent, normal people who, at one time or another, fail to help somebody who, in retrospect, obviously needed help. In the infamous Kitty Genovese case in New York City in 1964, 38 people had a chance to interrupt a murder in progress but did not. Why such things happen has perplexed philosophers for centuries, and today psychologists have joined the search for answers.

One general rule is that the better we know someone, or the more he or she is like us, the more likely we are to help the person. We seldom hesitate to help people we love. But we often think twice about helping strangers, especially if different from ourselves.

Oddly, a victim's chances of being promptly helped seem to decrease as the number of people observing the emergency increase. Bystanders tend to think that somebody else has already made a decision about what to do, and that further help is either on the way or unnecessary. This *diffusion of responsibility* seemed to be a factor in the Genovese case.

Finally, empathy has two sides. While feeling someone else's distress can lead to compassionate action, it can also make you want to run away or somehow shut out the pain you feel. Furthermore, if the person who needs help is offensive in some way—say, dirty, drunk, or bleeding—the idea of helping may fill you with revulsion. What may happen then, if you decide not to help, is that your mind will help you make a kind of cognitive escape from your guilt, better known as rationalization. You might convince yourself that the situation is not as serious as it appears or that the victim has only gotten what is coming to him, a response psychologists call "blaming the victim."

***The fear of being a victim** is captured by George Tooker's famous painting "The Subway." Crime insidiously feeds on people's fears, causing many to curtail their daily activities. Modern-day life demands being alert to danger, but when our attention turns into overwhelming dread, we become more victimized than ever, feeling that our freedom of movement is lost.*

The Manipulators

What's the difference between propaganda and brainwashing?

Slogans and exhortations, repeated over and over in an atmosphere of public crisis, are the essence of propaganda. People tend to accept the propaganda message, especially if they feel alienated and are cut off from reliable sources of information. Propaganda is very effective in wartime.

Brainwashing, on the other hand, is an extreme distortion of a person's mental processes. It works only under special circumstances, such as when individuals are isolated in prison or held by kidnapers. Experts who have studied victims of brainwashing believe that their captors appeal to a reservoir of general guilt that most people harbor. A captive deprived of sleep, food, and privacy, and dependent on his guards for his most elemental needs, is readily susceptible to persuasion. To further the process, manipulators use such techniques as exhausting interrogations at all hours of the day and night.

The effects of brainwashing are generally temporary, however, and some individuals resist it altogether. Few American prisoners in North Korea, for example, accepted the ideology their captors tried to impose. Even those who did accept it under stress discarded it after they returned home.

Can populations be controlled by mind-altering drugs?

In *Brave New World,* his nightmarish vision of a future totalitarian state, novelist Aldous Huxley depicted a society in which the whole population, beginning in childhood, was given a drug that kept them in a state of submission to authority by stimulating the pleasure centers of the brain.

Real people are not so easily controlled. It is conceivable that an evil dictator might insert drugs into a community's water system, but even if he did, experts point out that this would be a blunt instrument for manipulating a population. It is generally only in a closed environment like a prison or mental institution that people can be forced to take drugs.

When kidnap victim Patty Hearst *was brutalized by her captors, the Symbionese Liberation Army, she joined their cause. She helped them rob a bank, but later recovered her true identity.*

What is the Stockholm syndrome?

Several years ago a woman was taken hostage during a bank robbery in Stockholm, Sweden. In the course of her 131-hour captivity, she fell in love with one of the bank robbers. Although the woman's reaction was extreme, it has been observed in varying degrees in other hostage situations the world over. Thereafter, this response to captors has been dubbed the Stockholm syndrome.

Victims held captive by terrorists or other criminals know that at any moment during their ordeal they may be killed. Under the threat of death, their thoughts and feelings often take an irrational turn.

Hostages frequently develop a childlike trust in and dependence on those who terrorize them. By identifying with their captors, hostages assuage their feelings of isolation and helplessness. Studies show that the closer hostages feel to their captors, the less likely it is that they will be harmed. They come to view their captors as the "good guys." The people who try to liberate them without giving in to the captors' demands then become the enemy.

Once a hostage is released, it may take a few months for the acute effects of the syndrome to wear off. Psychologist Curt Toler notes: "Long-term follow-up studies show that this is a trauma that is there for life. It will poke its head up occasionally throughout a person's lifetime, when his or her resources are low."

The Cult Leader Who Became a Messenger of Death

Brainwashed into believing that Jim Jones was their "dad and savior," the followers of his Peoples Temple gave him all they possessed. For many the Temple provided their first sense of belonging. No one ever dreamed they would have to die for it.

A HANDSOME AND CHARISMATIC religious leader, Jim Jones preached a mixture of socialism, brotherly love, and racial equality. He offered free food and medical care to the poor and downtrodden of California. But more important, he gave a home to those who were lonely and ignored by society. They, in turn, gladly donated all their worldly possessions to help maintain his church, the Peoples Temple.

Like other cults, his movement had special appeal to people alienated from their families, friends, and traditional churches, who were searching for acceptance and spiritual comfort. For most Temple members, Jim Jones became a father figure, and they addressed him as "Dad." Anything he asked, they gladly would do.

Soon Jones's fanatical beliefs in religion and socialism turned into megalomania. He came to see himself as a reincarnation of Jesus, then as God himself. He demanded total loyalty. Anyone who asked to leave was threatened with death. He did not allow his authority to be questioned. Parents could not even protest when he ordered their children to be whipped.

In a move to consolidate his power, Jones took his followers to a remote outpost in Guyana, a socialist country in South America. In 1977, with official approval, he set up an independent colony that he advertised as a religious utopia. Letters back to relatives in the United States, however, revealed that Jonestown, as it was called, was more like a concentration camp than a haven for socialists.

In a form of brainwashing, members were awakened in the middle of the night to listen to hours of haranguing from Jones; anyone who failed to listen attentively was severely beaten. His physical and sexual abuse of children, which he had

***Jim Jones** began with good intentions but was overtaken by ambition and finally paranoia.*

managed to hide from child welfare agencies in California, escalated in Guyana. Children who didn't smile at the mention of his name had electric shocks applied to their arms and legs. Restless children were lowered into a well, which they were told was filled with snakes.

Adults fared just as badly. Those who dared disobey an order were imprisoned for days at a time in a wooden box in the steaming heat; a woman who became intimate with a male friend in defiance of Temple rules was forced to have intercourse with another man in public. To prove his authority further, Jones, himself a married man, demanded sexual favors of the married women in the commune.

The Jonestown settlement had meager food and medical supplies, but Jones had huge quantities of tranquilizers available. In a gruesome test of loyalty, Jones would give members a drink he said contained poison. If they believed in him, then they would drink from the cup together and be martyrs to the cause of socialism. They drank, and realized it was not poisoned.

The paranoia that brought Jones and his followers to Guyana soon reached new heights. He posted armed security guards around the compound to intimidate anyone who tried to leave. There were frequent rehearsals for mass suicide. Many people apparently remained devoutly loyal to their messiah even as he descended into madness. They believed Jones's tales that a worse fate awaited them if they dared to leave and return to the evil corruption of the United States. Like prisoners of war, the members of the Peoples Temple, mostly poor blacks, were soon broken in spirit by exhaustion, punishment, and lack of food. They had no choice but to depend entirely on Jones.

The end came when California congressman Leo Ryan, concerned by alarming reports from constituents with relatives at Jonestown, led a personal tour of inspection. At first he saw nothing but smiling, apparently happy people. But when a few dissidents asked to go home with the visitors, the mood grew tense. Before Ryan's plane could take off from the nearby airfield, it was ambushed by armed men. The congressman, two newsmen, and one departing Temple member were shot dead.

Back at Jonestown, Jones gathered his flock for a final sermon. He reported the deaths at the airfield, then vowed they would die rather than surrender to their enemies. Jones ordered them all to take a soft drink laced with cyanide. Those who hesitated were threatened with rifles.

Nearly everyone took the potion voluntarily. Survivors recalled that mothers squirted cyanide into their babies' mouths; family members held hands, calmly waiting for death. When Guyanese and U.S. officials later searched the site, they found more than 900 bodies. The 46-year-old Jones was discovered dead of a bullet wound, evidently a suicide.

Mind Over Matter

Can we use modern knowledge about the brain to improve our own well-being?

High on the list of self-help techniques endorsed by recent research on brain function is exercise. There is little doubt that exercise has a psychologically calming effect and benefits the heart, lungs, and muscles as well. "Runner's high" apparently occurs because strenuous activity stimulates the brain to increase its output of endorphins, opiate-like chemicals that produce a natural "high." The practice of meditation, in forms similar to those followed in Eastern religions, has also been widely accepted.

Less commonly, people are learning to hypnotize themselves as an aid to overcoming distressing phobias or habits, such as nail-biting and overeating. (Increasing recognition of hypnotism as valid therapy has at least partly dispelled the specter of the manipulating, malevolent hypnotist.)

Somewhat less experimental is biofeedback, in which people are taught through the use of electronic instruments to monitor certain bodily functions that are normally unconscious. Biofeedback techniques have been used to relieve tension headaches or migraine, for example.

The Fiery Feat of Walking, Unblistered, on Hot Coals

In a tribal ritual, brightly attired Fiji Islanders start to circle a pit filled with superheated stones. On other Pacific islands, people walk on molten volcanic lava.

A modern advocate treads on embers.

Walking barefoot across beds of glowing hot coals is an ancient practice, and variations of it are traditional in such diverse parts of the world as India, Greece, Japan, and Polynesia. In modern society, New Age gurus now promote it as an instant way to allay anxieties and bolster self-esteem.

Fire walkers say an elevated state of mind prevents them from feeling pain or getting burned. But scientists point out that even very hot coals are poor heat conductors and are unlikely to harm skin that touches them fleetingly, as a fire walker's feet do. When people walk on a more conductive surface, such as heated stone, water or perspiration on the feet may produce a protective buffer of steam. Even so, fire walking is not for amateurs; a miscalculation may cause serious injury.

What is meditation?

Long an integral part of many religions, meditation is a practice that is used to empty the mind of distracting thoughts. Hindu and Buddhist priests see it as the only way to achieve spiritual enlightenment. The poet William Blake's lines, "If the doors of perception were cleansed, every thing would appear to man, infinite," represent the goal of many meditators.

Beginners usually start by focusing on their breathing. The simplest way to do this is to sit in a darkened room, with the eyes closed, and for 20 minutes silently direct all attention to the act of breathing. To overcome the mind's natural tendency to wander, it may help to think the word *in* with each inhale, *out* with each exhale.

Is meditation therapeutic?

In the early 1970's Dr. Herbert Benson, a cardiologist at Harvard medical school, studied practitioners of transcendental meditation (also known as TM). In this form of meditation, people sit in a quiet room, with their eyes closed and silently repeat a mantra—a special word or sound used to facilitate meditation. Devotees meditate for a half hour, twice a day.

Dr. Benson observed that during meditation his research subjects' heart and respiratory rates were slower. For most of them, blood pressure was also lowered. Moreover, when they meditated, they were extremely relaxed, yet wide awake, a state Benson named the "relaxation response." Further studies showed that meditation could modify a person's reaction to stress.

Dr. Benson was so impressed with the physical benefits of meditation that he began prescribing a Westernized version of it to his patients with high blood pressure. Other doctors followed. Meditation may be an effective therapy for migraine headache and chronic pain.

Does the New Age movement relate to psychology?

The New Age movement has been described as a belief in a holistic approach to life, that is to say, a belief that all parts of living matter interact to create a whole.

New Age thinking is difficult to define because it encompasses everything from holistic medicine and vegetarianism to the healing power of rock quartz crystals. Some followers believe in reincarnation, some claim to have contacted extraterrestrial beings. Channelers, who are people possessed by spirits from another time or place, have attracted a wide following. Many New Agers are convinced that everyone has psychic powers and can communicate through telepathy, and there are numerous reports of out-of-body experiences. Some followers believe that each and every person is God, and that this divinity enables us to harmonize with the world around us.

Because they embrace so many diverse approaches and beliefs, the New Age followers do not lend themselves readily to a classical psychological profile. However, many experts agree that the movement is rooted, psychologically, in a deep uneasiness and sense of dissatisfaction with some of the values our society offers.

Can magic rituals cure mental or physical ailments?

Some rituals have been found to be curative in themselves. In addition, some primitive healers combine magical ceremonies with the use of drugs that have proven physiological effects.

A Tsimshian shaman of the Pacific Northwest *summoned healing spirits. Only he could see them; only he, with curing song, could urge them to aid the sick.*

Opium poppies, source of the powerful painkiller morphine, for example, have been used in many primitive rituals.

Other "magical" treatments may work by the placebo effect. This response may be the result of certain chemicals released by the brain in people who believe that a healer and his medicine will help them. It can lead not only to a sense of well-being but to measurable improvements in physical symptoms. The response is so common that medical scientists do not consider any drug effective unless its results have been compared to those of a placebo, or inert pill. *(Placebo* literally means "I shall please" in Latin.) About a third of all patients in any given study are found to be "placebo reactors."

Ritual cures or exorcisms for people whose mental illness is believed to be the result of possession by demons sometimes involve agitated dancing to the point of exhaustion. Therapists have suggested that these procedures may act much like electroshock therapy, which is used for the treatment of severe depression. But they caution that the benefits of exorcism are generally temporary; the condition will probably return unless the underlying cause is treated.

Can witch doctors really kill people by black magic?

Some deaths that credulous people attribute to black magic may really be due to natural causes, accidents, or even murder.

But scientists who have investigated otherwise unexplained deaths following voodoo rituals, for example, contend that the victims, deeply convinced of their enemies' magical powers, were actually frightened to death. The awful terror provoked by touching an object thought to be imbued with black magic could affect the brain centers that control breathing and heart contractions, perhaps triggering a fatal heart arrhythmia.

Roots of Superstition

Insatiable demons were everywhere in olden days, *lying in wait to snare the weak or imprudent. How else to understand dire misfortune—disease, madness, and evil? Small wonder superstitious practices arose to hold at bay such horrid monsters as these, in a detail of* The Temptation of St. Anthony *by the medieval artist Matthias Grünewald.*

What is superstition?

Few people in any era have been entirely free of superstitions, those illogical feelings that supernatural or magical forces influence the events in our lives. Especially among prescientific cultures, superstitions are a psychological defense in a world seemingly aswarm with menacing, unpredictable spirits that must be appeased in order to avoid disaster and to survive. Today, they have lost most of their desperate urgency and endure as easy, somewhat comforting learned responses to uncertainty. The word *superstition* comes from the Latin *superstites,* which means "those left standing after battle," in other words, survivors.

Many of today's common superstitions are descended from older superstitions whose origins are lost in the mists of time. For example, the belief that a broken mirror brings bad luck for seven years is believed to stem from the ancient notion that a man's reflection in water portrayed his soul, and that ripples in water destroyed it.

The horseshoe, which is roughly crescent in shape, seems to have derived its magical reputation from the Egyptian worship of the moon. Its iron makes it even more potent, because the first known specimens of iron fell from the sky as meteorites. It is mounted with ends facing up, so the luck doesn't fall out.

In pagan Britain, the hare (a relative of the rabbit) was an object of worship. With the advent of Christianity this practice was outlawed, but old habits die hard and many people still carry a rabbit's foot for luck.

What makes people superstitious?

Almost everybody gives the nod to superstition even if they laugh at themselves for doing so. Many inveterate scoffers, for example, have been caught knocking on wood—just to play it safe. (The sound of knocking on wood supposedly scares off evil spirits.) Another superstition that few have resisted is crossing the fingers, which goes back to the early days of

Christianity. Members of the church concealed their faith, fearing persecution. Crossed fingers were a secret greeting, a way of making the sign of the cross. When one spills salt, a pinch is tossed over the left shoulder as an offering to the spirits; many still do this without giving it a thought.

Many powerful people have had pet superstitions. Napoleon was terrified by black cats; Winston Churchill used to touch them for good luck. General Eisenhower carried a gold coin as a good luck charm. John D. Rockefeller clung to a lucky stone from an eagle's nest, and Alfred Gwynne Vanderbilt protected himself from evil spirits by sleeping only in beds whose legs stood in dishes of salt.

Why is 13 thought to be unlucky?

The number 13 has been a deeply ingrained symbol of bad luck in many countries and for many centuries. In ancient Babylon, 13 people were chosen to personify the gods in certain religious rites. One person, however, was always seated apart from the others and was put to death at the end of the ceremony. In the Bible, 13 were present at the Last Supper, and Christ foretold that one of them would soon betray him. Even today some people hesitate to sit down when there are 13 at a table.

Culture and language influence superstitions. In China and Japan, the number 13 has no particular significance, but 4 is unlucky, perhaps because the Chinese character, or ideograph, for *four* also signifies death.

Are superstitions ever based on fact?

Some superstitions have proved to be remarkably practical. There was once a superstition in England, that people infected by cowpox from cattle would be immune to smallpox. In the late 1700's, Edward Jenner took the superstition seriously and discovered that an inoculation of cowpox prevented smallpox. This led to the establishment of the principle of vaccination. The application of moldy bread to a wound was considered a superstition until Alexander Fleming's discovery of penicillin.

During World War I, a superstition arose that the third man to light his cigarette on one match would be killed. Few superstitions have ever had a sounder base, for in just the time it took for the third man to get his cigarette lit, the enemy was able to draw a bead on him with a rifle.

Do superstitions ever help?

Superstitions can be harmless or even helpful to people unable to make decisions or gripped by fear. Tossing a coin can resolve questions when there is no overriding practical reason to choose one answer over another.

The power of a positive attitude has been demonstrated as an aid in performance in everything from sports to taking exams. If wearing a lucky tie or ring makes you feel sure of success, then superstitions are indeed helpful. If you are convinced that you sleep better by consistently putting your right foot into pajama pants first, then you are using a superstition to make your life pleasanter.

For the most part, superstitions call for the suspension of logic and reason. One man who was afraid of flying happened to break a glass the day before boarding a plane. When the flight proved uneventful, he decided the broken glass had magically warded off danger. Although he knew it was irrational, he felt compelled to break a glass before his next flight, too.

A luxuriant black tomcat called Clawed Monet *is prized by his human family. A tiny tuft of white fur on his chest may exempt him from the drawbacks of black-cat superstitions. In any event, Clawed himself enjoys good fortune.*

Belief in Controlling Forces

The signs of the zodiac encircle the world, *which, in this medieval painting, is composed of four basic elements—earth, fire, water, and air.*

Do the stars and planets influence human life?

The ancient science, or pseudoscience, of astrology is the study of the position and movement of the sun, moon, stars, and planets as influences on one's personality and life. Astrology began in Babylon about 4,000 years ago, and its followers number in the tens of millions today. Worldwide, there may be many more astrologers than scientists.

Present-day champions of astrology try to link ancient conjectures with more recent scientific discoveries. They claim, for example, that the variations in earth's magnetic field caused by the changing patterns of the planets influence the neural circuits of the brain of human embryos. But physicists point out that a pregnant woman in a modern household is subject to far greater magnetic forces from a refrigerator and a television.

Some events in outer space do affect the earth. The gravitational pull of the moon influences the tides, and meteorites sometimes fall to earth, even though science was slow to accept their extraterrestrial origin. Since these seemingly fantastic occurrences have been proven true, believers in astrology (including some scientists) insist that it is unreasonable to reject the idea of celestial influence.

Most scientists, however, argue that even if the planets could influence earthlings, the ancient charts used by astrologers would be irrelevant. The positions of the planets as seen from the Earth on a given date have changed since those charts were drawn up, and three planets have been discovered, Uranus in 1781, Neptune in 1846, and Pluto in 1930.

How well do astrological signs predict personality?

A few researchers have conducted surveys to find out whether people's personality traits really corresponded with those traditionally assigned to individuals born under their astrological signs. One French statistician and psychologist, Michel Gauquelin, found a surprising correlation between the professions "eminent" people chose and the planet that was at a certain position in the sky when they were born. But others criticized his methods, and even Gauquelin did not claim that they "proved" the validity of traditional astrology; he found only certain planets pertinent. Other surveys have suggested no connection at all, except what might be expected under the laws of chance.

Why is astrology so popular?

Any technique that promises to foresee the future or identify a compatible friend or mate has always had a huge appeal to human nature. Publicity about astrological predictions that come true and prominent people who believe in astrology undoubtedly add to its allure.

Some people simply use astrological signs as a harmless game, checking their horoscopes in newspapers or consulting an astrologer as an exotic experience without attaching much importance to the result. Such people often laugh at their own brief lapses of critical thinking. Others may be reacting against the modern emphasis on science and scientific proof at the expense, they feel, of acknowledging unknown, irrational forces.

Are there benefits to astrology?

Astrology led mankind to study the stars and to keep detailed information on their movement for many centuries. Astrology, a superstition, laid the groundwork for the development of astronomy, a science.

In India and other Asian countries, astrology serves a useful social function today. It is the custom there for marriages to be arranged by parents. Sometimes the bride and groom don't meet until just before the wedding. Before the marriage takes place, an astrologer prepares horoscopes for the two young persons. If, when they finally meet, they can't stand each other, the excuse of incompatible horoscopes provides a graceful way to call off the marriage.

Is there a psychological risk to predictions?

Divining the future can take many forms, such as reading tea leaves, consulting a deck of tarot cards, or examining the palms of hands. Fortune-tellers consult these tangible items to answer questions their clients have about their futures. Psychics, on the other hand, rely only on their own special powers to tune into the future (and sometimes past) lives of those who consult them.

Psychologists note that most people who go to fortune-tellers or psychics are looking to be either amused or reassured. But such experiences can be seductive. For some, it is comforting to believe that there are people who have the power to see into the future.

When one is in a quandary, going to a so-called spiritual adviser can ease anxiety over making personal decisions. Regardless of the outcome, the responsibility of decision-making has effectively been transferred to the fortune-teller.

However, for people who are particularly vulnerable to suggestion and have come to believe implicitly in a fortune-teller's power, a negative prediction can be devastating. One highly educated young woman who counted on having children asked a tarot card reader how many she would have when she married. When the reader replied, "None," the young woman became hysterical. Even months later she could not shake her depression. She felt powerless to alter her "fate." Studies have demonstrated that the more personable and charismatic a fortune-teller is, the more credible he or she seems.

The Reappearance of the Human Spirit in Another Body

Reincarnation is an ancient belief that the soul survives and returns to earth in another form after the death of the body. Many Eastern religions regard reincarnation as a tenet of faith and some state the soul may be reborn as human, animal, or plant life. The Greek philosopher, Plato, held that the human spirit goes through nine cycles of rebirth either to a higher or lower level of existence. Those souls, he wrote, that achieved the ninth and highest cycle by inhabiting the body of an artist or philosopher—thus divorcing themselves from the material world—would be freed from returning to another cycle. The Egyptians believed that the spirit's cycle on this earth continued for 3,000 years. Today, in the West, there is a resurgence of interest in reincarnation, inspired in part by a widespread fascination with Eastern religions and philosophies.

The early expression of musical genius by Wolfgang Amadeus Mozart, who composed two sonatas at age seven, prompted some to attribute his powers to experiences gained in a previous life.

Henry Ford and Thomas Edison loved to go camping together, using the time to swap ideas. Both men, though critical of established religion, were nonetheless believers in reincarnation.

From ESP to UFO

Can extrasensory phenomena really be used to detect or influence distant events?

Some believers have suggested that such phenomena as mental telepathy and telekinesis (moving distant objects) might be explained by some form of radiation given off by the brains of people concentrating on a particular thought. But no proof has ever been found for this theory. Indeed, when people familiar with the tricks traditionally used by magicians have observed those who claim extraordinary psychic powers, they have exposed many as fakers. One such skeptic is professional magician James Randi, who has often uncovered deceptions that mystify less sophisticated observers.

A common technique is to create a distraction so that the audience fails to notice the sleight of hand involved in apparently pulling a rabbit out of a hat—or bending a spoon. With such help, a skilled magician's hand is indeed quicker than the eye. And "mindreaders" often do preliminary research on the lives of people they plan to interview, or have associates circulate among the crowd before a performance to eavesdrop on conversations, so that their guesses about the subjects' thoughts will not be shots in the dark.

Psychic performers also use "multiple outs"—ambiguous statements that can be interpreted in various ways. They fine-tune their remarks as the subjects volunteer further information (people often give away far more than they realize). If the psychics miss the mark, they are ready with alternative interpretations—some of which would seem extremely far-fetched to listeners who were not predisposed to believe or distracted by the tricksters' rapid-fire delivery.

The "one-ahead" ploy is another standby. A performer asks people to submit questions in sealed envelopes, which he will then "read" without opening them. Secretly, he has opened one envelope and memorized its contents before the session starts. Then he holds up a second envelope, pretends to read its contents, but actually recites the remembered message. When he opens the second envelope, supposedly to confirm that his reading was correct, he repeats the procedure, and continues to read one message ahead.

Why are so many people convinced that extrasensory perception is genuine?

The idea that some people have supernatural mental or spiritual abilities is naturally appealing. Among others, it has attracted detective-story writer Sir Arthur Conan Doyle and scientist Michael Faraday.

Perhaps the most exhaustive studies of ESP, or extrasensory perception, were carried out at Duke University. There, J. B. Rhine and his colleagues tried to eliminate cheating by setting up careful experiments such as one in which a deck of cards was shuffled, then subjects were asked to predict the order in which certain cards would be turned up. They found that many subjects were able to predict correctly more often than would be expected by chance. But independent investigators have been unable to duplicate Rhine's findings in other laboratories—an essential condition for proving the scientific validity of an experiment. Some speculate that Rhine's group, who hoped to prove that ESP was real, may have unconsciously influenced the subjects by giving them subtle visual cues.

Beyond the Boundaries of Science

There's no question about it, many of us are intrigued by the uncanny. This fascination with all kinds of psychic phenomena seems to be deep-rooted in human nature. Although scientists continually debunk paranormal claims, they endure.

Spiritualism. The oldest and best known of all such claims, spiritualism holds that people with special powers, known as mediums, can communicate with the spirits from another world. Mediums hold séances and, possessed by a spirit, bring back messages from the dead. Through mediums, the dead can respond to questions. Séances are often accompanied by such psychic phenomena as table rapping, furniture moving, and floating ectoplasm, indicating the presence of a spirit in the room.

Human aura. Believers in this theory say that everyone gives off a kind of radiation, an aura. There are people who claim that someone's aura is a visible emanation. The color of an aura varies and has meaning. Violet, for example, signifies a person of deep spirituality whereas yellow indicates the opposite.

Biorhythms. This concept is based on the belief that we are born with specific biorhythms, which influence our daily lives. Biorhythms run in cycles of 23 days for physical energy, 28 days for emotional well-being, and 33 days for intellectual skills. There are 'ups' and 'downs' within each cycle. If the deepest 'down' days of all 3 cycles should happen to coincide, it is best to spend the day in bed.

Is there any validity to psychics' claims that they can predict the future?

Since time immemorial, people have tried to predict coming events by various arcane techniques, from conjuring up spirits through mystical incantations to consulting the bones or entrails of sacrificial animals. Psychics still claim to be able to see into a spirit world where the future and the present are one.

Skeptics who have investigated some highly publicized predictions of psychics that came true point out that the many inaccurate predictions psychics make are rarely remembered. Among published but forgotten predictions for the years 1981 and 1982 were the following: "Startling new evidence of pyramids and massive statues on Mars will convince scientists that life flourished there millions of years ago. Cuban president Fidel

Castro is overthrown in a major uprising. An impeachment effort will be launched against one or more Supreme Court justices. A controversy will break out when it's discovered that a man-made explosive device sank the *Titanic.*"

How can we explain eyewitness accounts of UFO's and extraterrestrial beings?

When the first UFO reports appeared shortly after World War II, the U.S. air force started investigating them in case they represented hostile foreign activities. But the program was stopped when no evidence of either earthly or extraterrestrial enemies was found. Some people, unconvinced by the Air Force's denials, insist that it is suppressing facts. Several private groups still investigate UFO reports, but they have different criteria for evaluating the evidence, and sometimes debunk one another's findings. Some early believers in UFO's have become skeptics.

Although a few UFO stories remain unexplained, scientists insist that the burden of proof should be on those who claim to have seen the mysterious objects. They are especially skeptical of claims of "close encounters of the third kind"—actual contacts with extraterrestrial beings, or rides aboard their spaceships.

After all, why should an alien visitor appear to only one individual? Why have no clear photographs been taken or corroborating witnesses found? In contrast, writes one skeptic, when a real fireball (a meteorite) streaked through the earth's atmosphere over the Rocky Mountains one afternoon in 1972, it was seen by thousands of people and recorded in countless still photographs and at least two motion-picture sequences, even though it appeared unexpectedly over a sparsely populated area and was visible for only two minutes.

Alien visitors are often described as highly intelligent and friendly toward earthlings. Some investigators suspect that this reflects public fears about nuclear war and wishes for a refuge in outer space.

On the Lookout for Visitors from Outer Space

Many alleged UFO sightings have been explained as airplanes or satellites seen from an odd angle, or as natural phenomena. Light striking clouds can create visual effects that inexperienced observers could mistake for UFO's. Comets and meteor showers have also been misread. Ball lightning, pulsating electrical charges in the air, is rare enough to be totally unfamiliar, hence suspect. Even the aurora borealis seen for the first time might be misinterpreted.

Then too, science fiction is so much a part of our lives (think of *Star Wars* and *Star Trek*), it's hardly surprising that some people are ready to interpret any strange phenomena as invaders from space.

The man who faked this picture did so hoping to shore up his claim that he had encountered aliens.

Lens-shaped, or lenticular, clouds look remarkably like flying saucers. Seen in numbers, as here, over Santos, Brazil, they could be a UFO squadron.

PART II

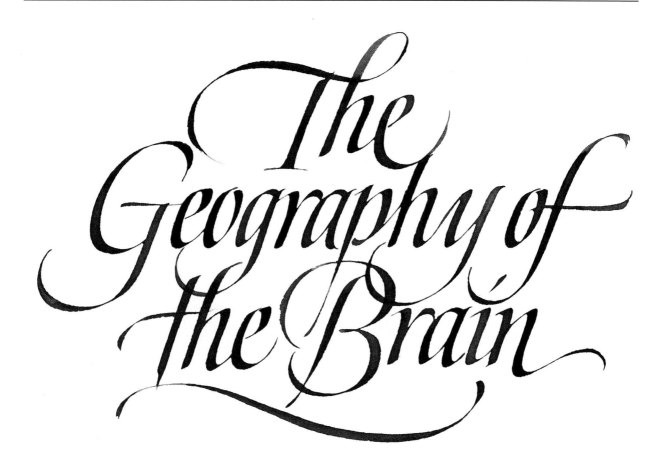

The Geography of the Brain

New scanners make it possible to explore the living brain—actually see it function—like watching news on TV. These magic probes have greatly extended our knowledge. The deeper we go into its intricate workings, the more marvelous does the brain appear. Each one of us carries a veritable universe within!

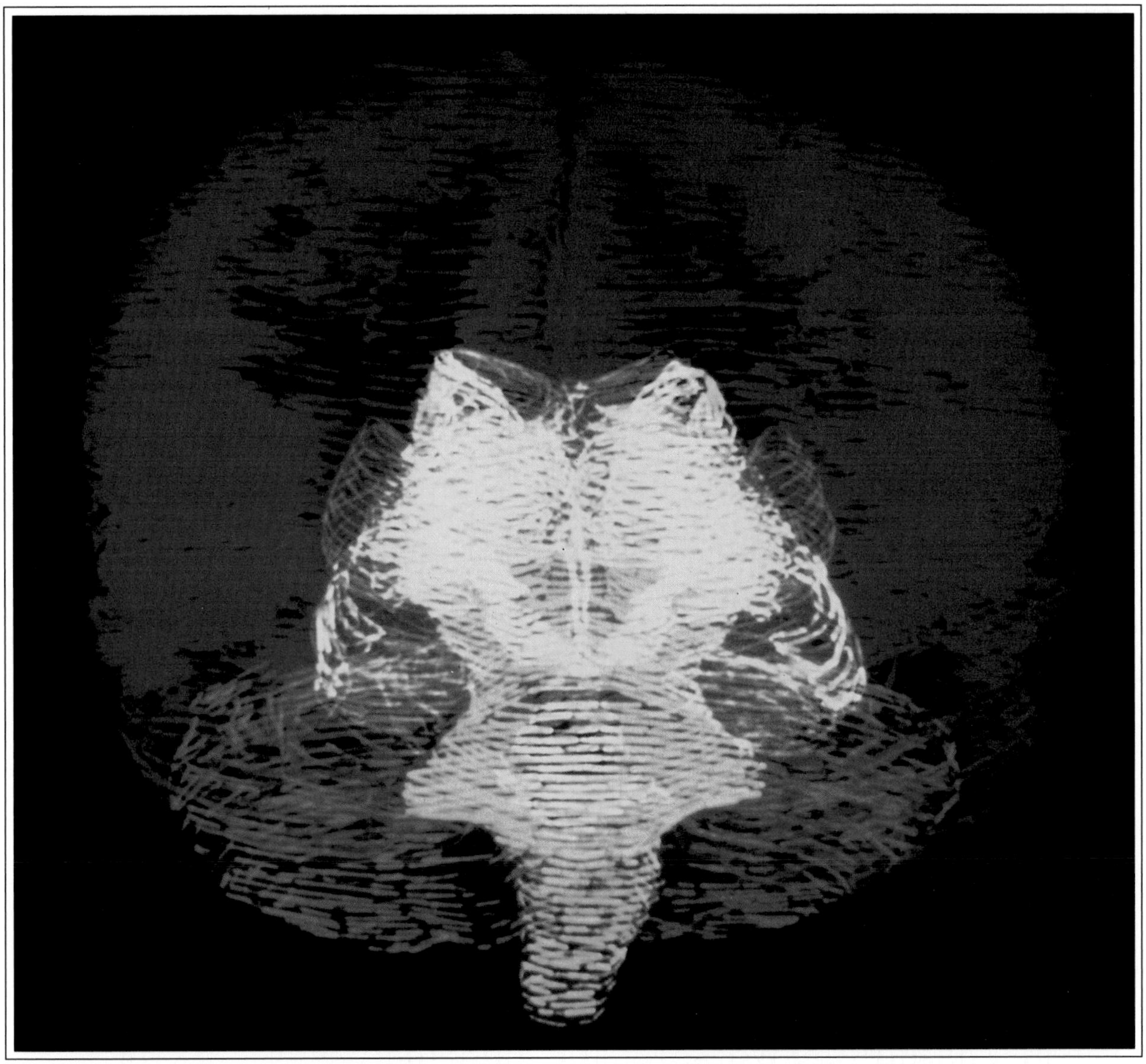

Astonishing, three-dimensional pictures of the brain, derived from CT scans, are artificially colored by computer to highlight the inner structure.

Our Great Advantage: The Cerebral Cortex

What is unique about the human brain?

In certain ways that involve their brains, some animals are clearly superior to human beings. Eels, salmon, caribou, and many kinds of birds perform astonishing feats of navigation in their long-distance migrations. Owners of dogs or cats know that these mammals have senses of smell and hearing that are better than our own. Behind each such superhuman talent is an area of the animal's brain, enlarged or tailored in some way that makes the special skill possible.

In turn, what distinguishes the human brain from other brains is the relative size of the cerebral cortex, the quarter-inch-thick covering of gray matter on the lobes and hemispheres of the cerebrum. Only in human beings is the cerebral cortex so large in relation to body size.

The human cerebral cortex is further distinguished by its great quantity of foldings and refoldings (convolutions, or gyri), valleys (fissures and sulci) and ridges, all of which increase the surface area of the cortex and allow a maximum amount of gray matter to be packed within the confines of the skull. The brains of lower mammals, with relatively smoother cortexes, have less surface area and less gray matter.

Most scientists agree that the unique abilities of the human brain are directly attributable to the cerebral cortex. The powers of speech and written language, for example, reside there and separate us from other animals. These powers go hand in hand with thinking—observing, analyzing, and integrating experiences to solve problems—planning ahead, and imagining what may happen in the future.

How the Brain Is Organized: A Matter of Perspective

The brain can be viewed from many vantage points—from beneath, above, either side, with magnification or not—and divided into many regions, which may overlap, depending on what interests an investigator.

These diagrams show the brain from the right side, with the front of the brain on your right. The two smaller brains give a developmental perspective, revealing the fetal formation of the telencephalon and the diencephalon, which will later include structures such as the cerebral cortex (in the telencephalon, part of the forebrain) and the hypothalamus (in the diencephalon at the top of the brain stem), as shown in the diagram below.

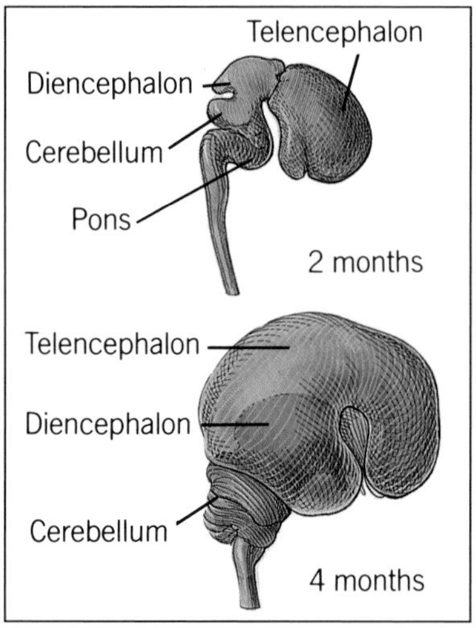

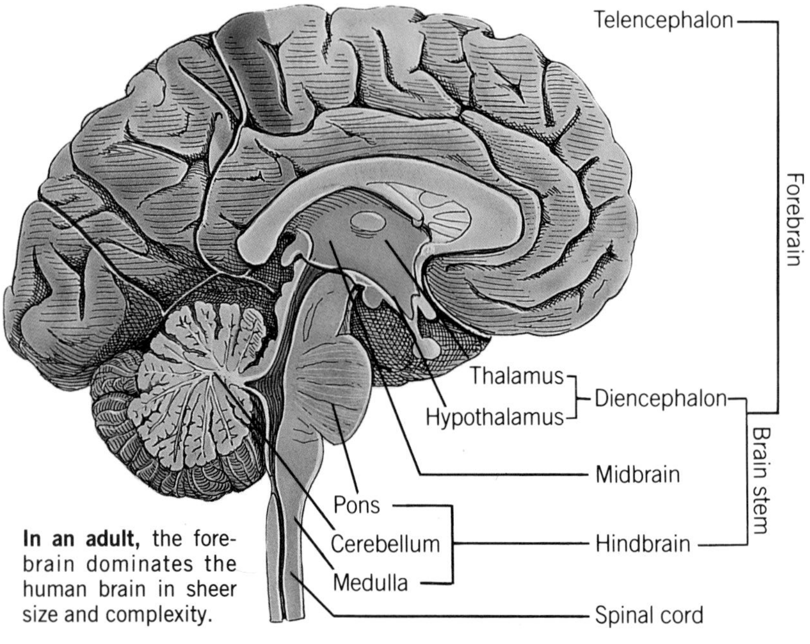

In an adult, the forebrain dominates the human brain in sheer size and complexity.

Why are some parts of the brain called reptilian and mammalian?

Neuroscientist Paul MacLean sees the human brain as really three brains. The first is made up largely of structures at the very top of the spinal cord, including portions of the brain stem. Because it resembles in some ways the total brain possessed by reptiles, this part of our brain is called reptilian in MacLean's terminology. Like the entire brain of a lizard or snake, it is mainly devoted to life support, such as the regulation of breathing, heartbeat, and muscle movements, and to basic drives such as eating, mating, and self-protection.

While retaining generally the brain abilities of reptiles, mammals add some dimensions to living. Their behavior, for example, involves complex emotional responses. They snarl, skulk, cringe, purr, growl, yelp in excitement or fear, nuzzle, teach their young, do tricks for rewards, wag their tails, show affection, and may even look ashamed or guilty when they have done something wrong.

Such behavior is linked with a section of the mammalian brain that is not nearly so well developed in reptiles: the limbic system. For this reason, MacLean sees the limbic system as the core of our "second brain." If it does not function properly, he found in experiments with hamsters, the young lose interest in play and mothers stop their maternal behavior. The loss of limbic functions makes mammals behave more like reptiles.

Our third brain, according to MacLean, is composed of the outer bulges of the cerebrum and the overlying cerebral cortex. It is the reasoning brain.

What is consciousness?

For thousands of years, consciousness and its significance have been the subject of endless arguments, and today psychologists and philosophers continue to disagree hotly on the matter. For some, consciousness means self-consciousness, that is, awareness of one's behavior, its causes and effects. In this sense, consciousness is something plants probably don't have, some animals may have, and most humans have in abundance.

Another way to define consciousness is by personal experience. We are unconscious, more or less, when we are asleep or knocked out by a drug or blow; we become conscious again when we wake up. In this sense, consciousness means much the same for us as it does for other animals. If unconsciousness is prolonged, as in a deep coma, special medical procedures must be used to prevent death.

Many of the arguments about the meaning of consciousness center on the question of whether or not human consciousness represents some kind of nonphysical attribute that transcends scientific understanding. Some of those who believe that "brain" and "mind" are essentially two different entities, one quantitative and the other qualitative, regard the brain, but not the mind, as accessible to ordinary scientific analysis. According to this view, at its highest levels, human consciousness is in fact unreachable; the mind is really the soul or spirit.

PERSPECTIVES

On Consciousness

We give the name consciousness to the essential identity that makes us what we are—which just goes to show that naming something doesn't explain it.

Hidden Sources

"Man's task is to become conscious of the contents that press upward from the unconscious . . . As far as we can discern, the sole purpose of human existence is to kindle a light in the darkness of mere being."

—Carl Jung
Memories, Dreams, Reflections

◆

Stream of Consciousness

"Consciousness, then, does not appear to itself chopped up in bits. Such words as 'chain' or 'train' do not describe it fitly. . . . It is nothing jointed; it flows. A 'river' or a 'stream' are the metaphors by which it is most naturally described. In talking of it hereafter, let us call it the stream of thought, of consciousness, or of subjective life."

—William James

◆

Now Hear This

"The conscious is the executive part of our total being. It is the conscious that makes decisions and translates them into action. Were we to become all unconscious, we should be indeed like the newborn infant, one with God but incapable of any action that might make the presence of God felt in the world."

—M. Scott Peck
The Road Less Traveled

◆

Putting Time Together

"Consciousness is a licensed rover, independent, free in time and free in space, a sort of psychological time machine dispersing itself in past, present and future simultaneously . . . . It goes back and forth, unifying our tomorrows with our todays and yesterdays . . . . Consciousness can traffic in things that are not, but perhaps could be. Its spontaneity is not even shackled by the laws of logic and deterministic cause and effect. It has the power to doubt and imagine, and in order to imagine it must be able to escape from the world. Its nature is to conjure up possibilities . . . . By unifying past and future, consciousness modifies the past by giving it a new context. The content of our lives up to the present moment is a fact, and must stand as it is. But we can interpret and reinterpret our past from the standpoint of what we are and of our future possibilities. As a result, the meaning of the past is always being altered, much as in a novel later chapters make the reader see earlier ones in a different light."

—Jeremy Campbell
Winston Churchill's Afternoon Nap

◆

Invisible but Real

"Few questions have endured longer or traversed a more perplexing history than this, the problem of consciousness and its place in nature.

"It is the difference that will not go away, the difference between what others see of us and our sense of our inner selves . . . . The difference between the you-and-me of the shared behavioral world and the unlocatable location of things thought about. Our reflections and dreams, and the imaginary conversations we have with others, in which never-to-be-known-by-anyone we excuse, defend, proclaim our hopes and regrets, our futures and our pasts, all this thick fabric of fancy is so absolutely different from handable, standable, kickable reality with its trees, grass, tables, oceans, hands, stars—even brains! How is this possible? How do these ephemeral existences of our lonely experience fit into the ordered array of nature that somehow surrounds and engulfs this core of knowing?"

—Julian Jaynes
The Origin of Consciousness in the Breakdown of the Bicameral Mind

◆

A Dissenting Note

"To be too conscious is an illness—a real thorough-going illness."

—Fyodor Dostoevsky

Crucial Events in Development

Dramatic Changes From Birth to Maturity

At birth, a baby's head is about a quarter of its total body length. In adulthood, the proportion of body to head is about seven and a half times the length of the head. Rates of growth of various parts of the body differ greatly, with brain development leading the way. The brain reaches between 75 and 80 percent of adult size within the first two years. By contrast, the extremities may not attain full length until the individual is in his or her late teens.

A newborn's head (left) can be cradled in a hand. A tremendous spurt of brain development, as in 15-month-old Anica (above), makes toddlers into tireless explorers.

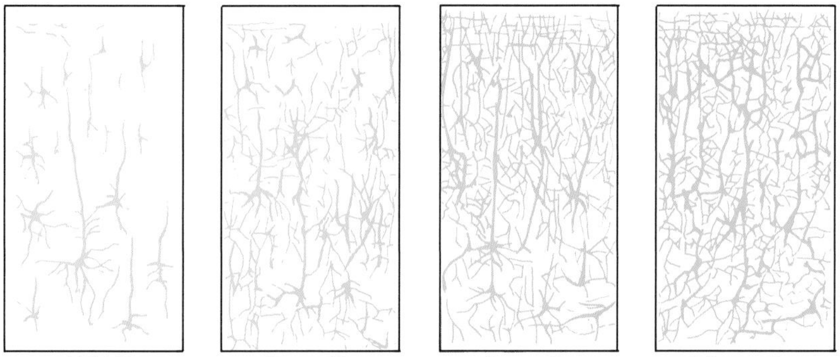

At birth | 3 months | 6 months | 15 months

Neurons are widely spaced at birth, but immediately, connections begin to form. These illustrations show the proliferation of the links, which organize experience.

How does development of the brain begin?

The brain, like every other part of our body, begins with a fertilized egg, a single cell. Although this cell is so tiny it can barely be seen by the unaided eye, it contains all the information needed to produce a human being.

Thirty hours after fertilization, the cell divides into two cells. Each of these two cells divides into two cells. The resulting four cells divide to create eight cells. Cells continue to multiply throughout gestation, constantly enlarging the fetus.

On the eighth day after fertilization, the cell mass implants itself on the wall of the uterus. Now cell differentiation starts. As it is formed, each cell is assigned to become a specific part of the body, such as skin, liver, or brain. Cells are assigned not just to an organ, but to a precise spot in the organ.

A fetus could be said to develop from the inside, or brain, out. First to take recognizable shape in the womb is an embryonic central nervous system—later to become the brain and spinal cord—and around this core the rest of the body forms.

When does the fetal brain begin to look like a brain?

Roundish and disk-like at first, the embryo becomes more oblong. It develops a layer called the ectoderm, which will become the central nervous system (brain and spinal cord). In a few days a groove forms lengthwise down the middle of the ectoderm. Then the edges of the groove fold over and fuse together to form a tube. To either side of this closure over the tube, the leftness and rightness of the brain and body develop. Defective closure can cause anencephaly (missing brain) and spina bifida.

After 30 days the embryo is about the size and shape of this capital C. At the top of the C are three small bumps, the beginnings of the forebrain, midbrain, and hindbrain. The rest of the C is the beginning of the spinal cord.

By the end of the fifth week of gestation the emerging shape of the brain and spinal cord (and to a lesser extent the rudiments of the peripheral nervous system) are evident in the embryo. Two weeks later the brain and spinal cord are readily recognizable. However, brain development in the gestation period can be adversely affected by the mother's poor health or nutrition.

When do we have the most brain cells?

We enter the world with the most neurons, or nerve cells, we are ever going to have, over 100 billion, and their number begins declining immediately. The rest of our body grows new cells to replace those that have worn out or died, but neurons are not replaced. These cells are believed to be formed only in the prenatal period. This sounds alarming until one considers the enormous numbers of cells involved—we are born with neurons to spare.

But neurons are not the only kinds of brain cells. Great numbers of other types are produced that support the neurons. A newborn's neurons start out, as a rule, largely isolated from one another. Through the experience of living and learning, new connections and patterns are forged among cells; thus the brain changes constantly. Obviously it also gets bigger. A newborn's brain is about a quarter the size and weight it will eventually be.

Why are babies commonly born headfirst?

Sometime after the sixth month the fetus usually turns within the uterus. Its head works its way down toward the pelvic gap and the headfirst birthing position. Gravity may be the chief reason for this shift, the head being by far the heaviest part of the body and accounting for a quarter of the baby's length. The head's great size is necessary to accommodate the baby's brain, which is nearer its adult size than other body parts.

At birth the baby's skull has developed into the perfect "opening wedge" for a birth that both mother and child can survive. The bony plates of the baby's skull are not yet as hard as they will later be. Nor do they quite yet meet at certain points where, as they grow larger, they will later fuse (forming the solid adult skull). These "soft spots" in the baby's skull are called fontanels. Thus the skull is soft and flexible enough to make it through the narrow birth canal, yet hard enough to keep the brain from injury in most cases.

An Expandable Skull Accommodates the Developing Brain, Then Hardens

Babies' heads are very large compared to the rest of their bodies, but still not roomy enough for the expansion of brain tissues that is to come. By leaving the baby's skull unknitted at birth, really unfinished in a sense, nature allows for a brain that will double in size during the baby's first six months, and double again before the skull bones fuse into a hard helmet.

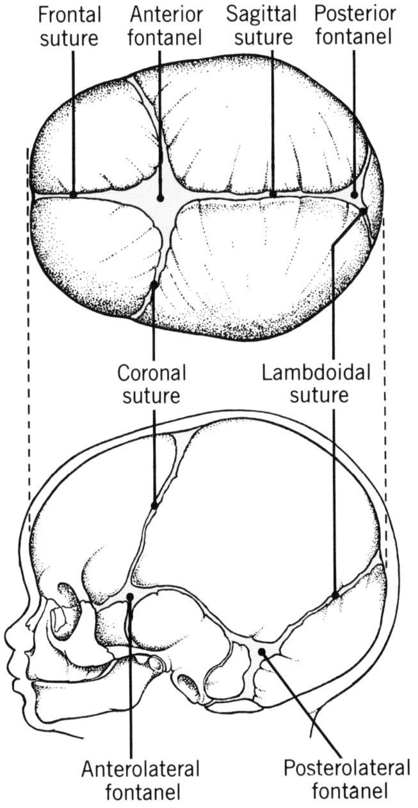

At birth, the bones of the skull, held in position by tough tissue at the suture lines, do not meet at gaps called fontanels, felt as the "soft spots" on a baby's head.

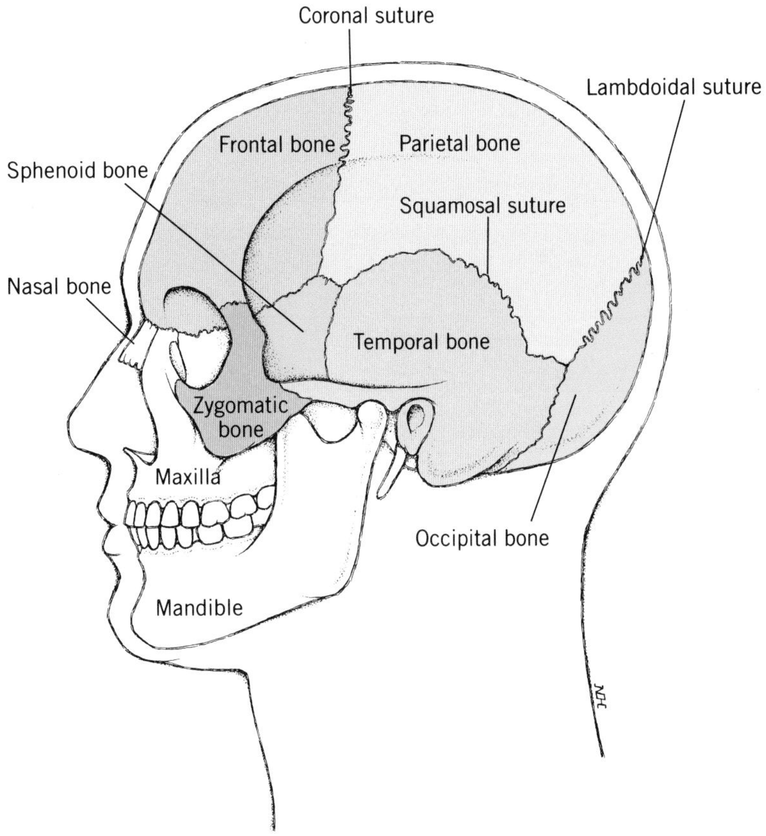

By the teenage years, all the skull bones have fused tightly, so that they feel like one solid bone. Sutures are still plainly visible on the skull of an adult skeleton.

Constantly Changing Networks

How Messages Travel From One Nerve Cell to Another

Nerve cells, or neurons, are the working units used by the nervous system to send, receive, and store the signals that add up to information. This ability separates living things from nonliving, and nowhere does it perform more marvelous feats than in the human brain. In trying to explain the wondrous work of neurons, scientists have compared them to switchboards or computers, but such comparisons can be misleading, for neurons employ a unique blend of electricity and chemistry.

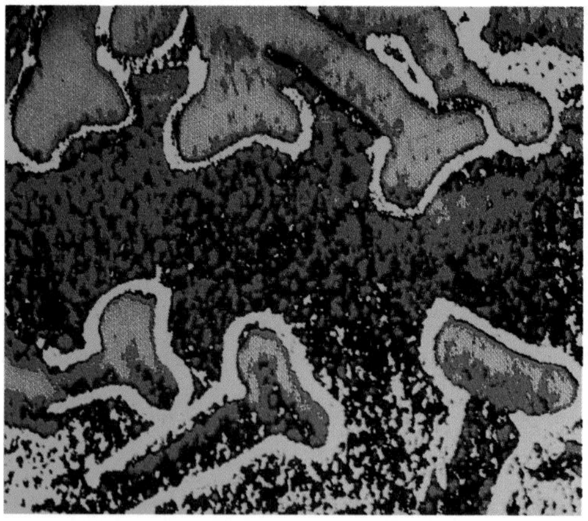

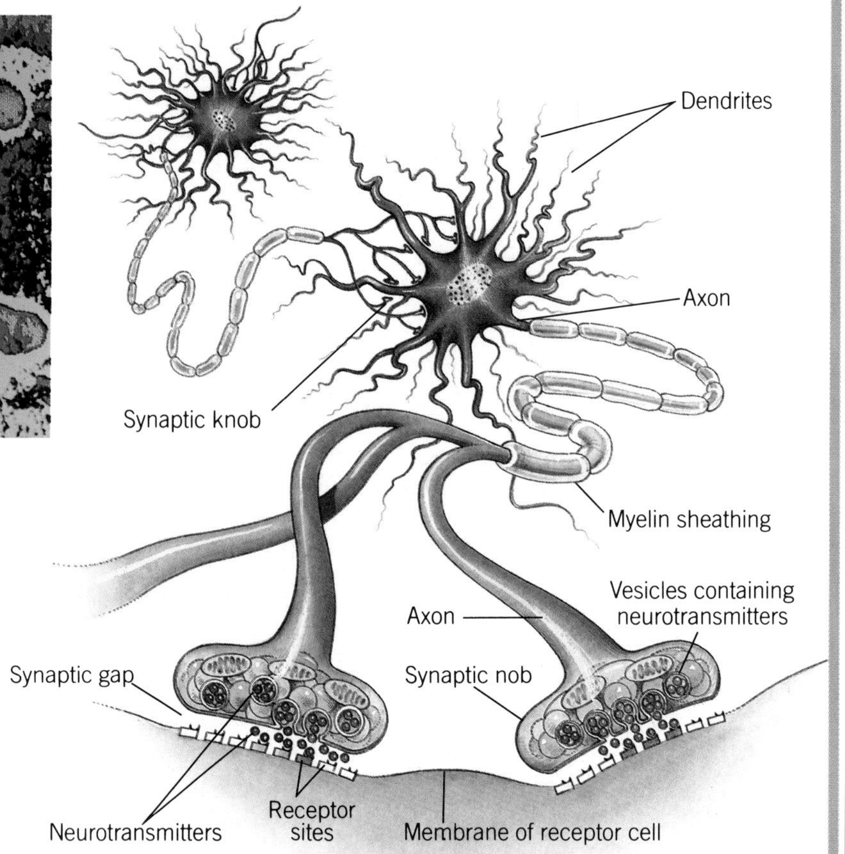

The synaptic knobs of actual neurons, ready to send signals, poke toward another brain cell in the photomicrograph above. The diagram at right, picturing two complete neurons (background and foreground), reveals how signals are transmitted.

An electrical impulse, traveling down an axon, causes the release of neurotransmitter molecules from the synaptic knob into the synapse (synaptic gap). The neurotransmitters then traverse the gap, causing an electric charge, or signal, to be passed on to the receptor cell.

What kinds of brain cells are there and what do they do?

In the brain (and throughout the nervous system), there are two main classes of cells: the neurons, or nerve cells, and all the rest, which for convenience are often described simply as non-neuronal cells. Roughly speaking, neurons are the brain's excitable cells, the ones that "fire" to send signals, while the rest are nonexcitable and support the neurons' work. Collectively, the bulk of support cells is called neuroglia (or glia), from Latin and Greek words for "nerve glue."

The neurons' main job is communication—sending and receiving information. Each neuron has hundreds to thousands of connections with other cells, and some neurons in the cerebrum may have a great many more links. The more than 100 billion neurons in the brain work together, in ever-changing relationships, to form an enlightened machine that makes us so successful on our planet.

In addition to neurons and glial cells, the brain has several other kinds of cells, such as those making up the blood vessels—capillaries, arteries, and veins—that serve brain tissue. Special cells line the canals and cavities that hold the brain's cerebrospinal fluid, which helps protect the brain by acting as a shock absorber.

Why do we need "nerve glue"?

Because the neurons are the key units in the brain's amazing ability to process information, they have received the lion's share of attention from scientists. However, neurons are outnumbered, five or ten to one, by the glial cells of the surrounding "nerve glue." During the development of the brain before birth, certain glial cells aid neurons in their migration to their ultimate places in the nervous system, acting almost as ladders or scaffolds for the neurons.

Furthermore, along with increases in the size and complexity of existing neurons, the formation of new glial cells adds significantly to the expansion of the brain after birth. By adulthood, up to half of the brain's volume consists of glial cells, wedged into the countless nooks and crannies among the far larger and dramatic-looking neurons.

Glial cells come in two major forms, the star-shaped astrocytes and the oligodendrocytes. Recent research suggests that these cells, long thought to be rather passive and inert, interact constantly with neurons and affect the electrochemical processes that underlie neural communication. In addition to a suspected role in how injured brain tissue tries to heal itself, the astrocytes also may play a part in forming the tight tangle of capillaries called the blood-brain barrier, which allows some substances into the brain and keeps others out. As for the oligodendrocytes, they form the myelin sheath that wraps around the main protruding tentacle, called an axon, of a neuron. The myelin covering seems to facilitate the transmission of signals by the neuron, although not all neurons have it.

What is gray matter?

The surface of the cerebrum, called the cerebral cortex, is covered with gray tissue containing billions of neurons. This is the "gray matter" that has come to be a colloquialism for intelligence, although a person with more gray matter is not necessarily smarter than someone with less.

Beneath the gray matter (and throughout the nervous system) is tissue called white matter. The whitish color comes from the myelin sheaths that are attached to the axons of neurons in these areas. In addition to gray and white matter, the brain has a great many other kinds of tissues, including the "red matter" of blood and blood vessels.

How do nerve cells communicate?

Everything we do and all we know depends on the transfer of signals from nerve cell to nerve cell. Underlying this extraordinary phenomenon is the unique structure of neurons and their ability to make certain chemical and electrical events happen.

A neuron has one big tentacle, its axon, and many smaller ones, its dendrites. The axon is responsible for sending signals, which are received by the dendrites of other neurons. For a signal to pass between an axon and a dendrite, these two structures must be very, very close—but not quite touching. The place where they almost touch is called a synapse, or synaptic gap, and it is no wider than a few billionths of an inch.

A message, traveling as an electrical impulse, moves down an axon toward the synapse. There it stimulates the production of molecules, called neurotransmitters, from the end of the axon into the synapse. A neurotransmitter diffuses across the narrow space between the two cells and affects the dendrite of the receiving neuron. This causes a change in the electric charge of the receiving neuron, with the resultant transmission of an electrical impulse that may excite or inhibit future impulse transmission.

The process of exciting neurons to transmit and receive messages is sometimes called "firing," suggesting sparks and explosions. That is a misleading image for very weak electrical events, involving tiny molecules, that occur silently in a chemical soup.

Can neurotransmitters fail?

An absence or an excess production of any of the dozen or so kinds of synaptic neurotransmitters can play a major role in brain disease and behavioral disorders. A decrease in acetylcholine, for example, has been noted in Alzheimer's disease, which causes deterioration of thought processes. Sufferers from Parkinson's disease have a very small amount of the transmitter dopamine in their brains. Elevated dopamine levels have been reported in schizophrenics.

Norepinephrine and serotonin are thought to be neurotransmitters associated with depression. Some antidepressants seem to work by triggering increased production of neurotransmitters, although knowledge of how to correct neurotransmitter imbalances remains sketchy.

The Cruel Effect of Alcohol on a Baby's Brain

In addition to the psychological damage (and often physical abuse) that alcoholic parents may inflict on their children, a woman who drinks heavily during pregnancy can injure the brain of her unborn child, a condition called fetal alcohol syndrome.

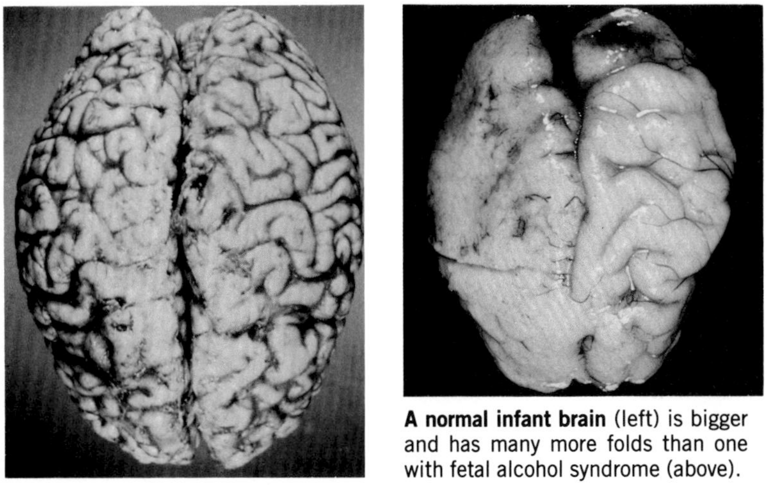

A normal infant brain (left) is bigger and has many more folds than one with fetal alcohol syndrome (above).

New Ways of Seeing the Brain

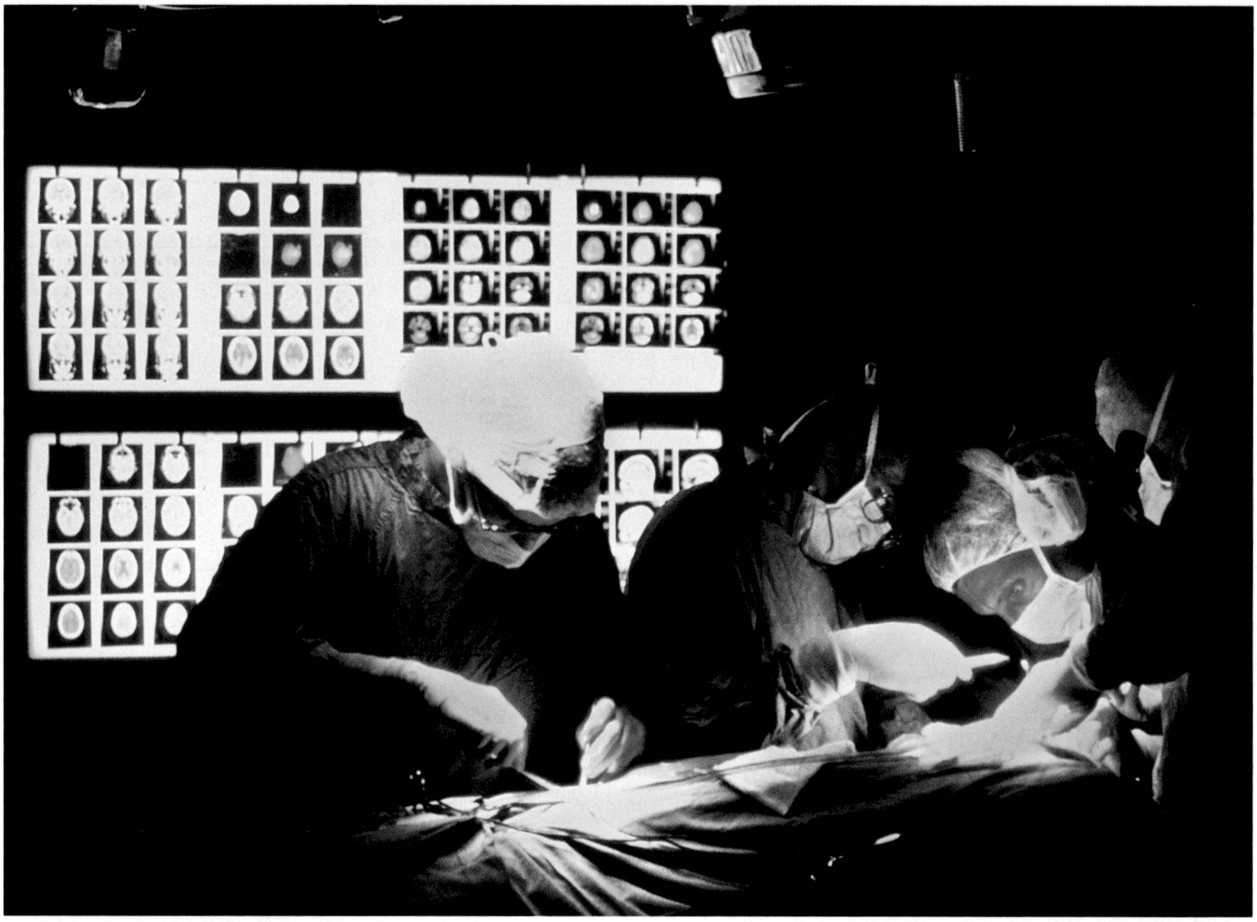

Installing a tube in the skull, *which will shunt excess fluid subcutaneously into the abdomen, surgeons are aided by brain scans. Note in the background an array of CT and PET scans of the kind commonly seen in today's operating rooms.*

How do scientists see the brain at work?

Until the early 1970's, scientists could get only crude pictures of the working brain. They had to use a good deal of guesswork and imagination to figure out exactly what they were seeing. The electroencephalogram (EEG) provided some information of the brain's activity. Examination of spinal fluid gave clues to infection or injury. A conventional X-ray showed mainly skull, because the brain has little density to block X-rays.

A new world of brain research opened up with the development of CT (or CAT, computerized axial tomography) scans and MRI (magnetic resonance imaging). The CT scan works by sending X-ray beams through a patient's head at 1-degree intervals over a 180-degree arc. A computer builds this information into an image on a screen that shows a cross section of the brain. More detailed images of the inner brain are possible with MRI, which operates similarly to CT (but without X-rays). By linking MRI with a computer, 3-D images of the brain are created.

While CT and MRI are valuable in studying brain structure and pinpointing the location of injury or abnormality, they are not much help in observing and measuring what happens *as the brain functions.* That is the great advantage of another brain-imaging technique called PET (positron emission tomography), which follows the movement through the brain of radioactive atoms introduced into the patient's blood. Fed into a computer, this information is built into colored cross-sectional images of the brain. These images, singly or in series, reveal brain metabolism, blood flow, and electrochemical processes.

What effect does aging have on the brain?

By the age of 20, our neurons are usually dying by the thousands, most probably never to be replaced. But since we are born with as many as 100 billion neurons, we could lose 5,000 of them a day and at age 90 still have 99,983,585,000 left. Partly as a result of the loss of nerve cells, our brains lose weight, about 1/30th of an ounce per year, beginning in our twenties.

The loss of neurons takes its toll, but not in any predictable way. Cognitive processes, the acts of knowing and perceiving things, slow down as we grow older, but to widely varying degrees. Some persons of 60 show declines in their mental abilities and some persons of 90 seem as sharp as they ever were.

About five percent of people over 65 suffer from some form of dementia a deterioration of mental processes. Alzheimer's disease is a leading cause. Other causes are small strokes and arteriosclerosis, or hardening of the arteries, which reduces the flow of blood to the brain.

Are the brains of men and women different?

The average man's brain weighs about 3 pounds, (1.35 kilograms); the average woman's, 2 pounds, 10 ounces (1.21 kg). Because men have bigger bodies on average, the relation of brain to body weight is about the same in both sexes. In any case, there is no evidence that a large brain means high intelligence. For example, the brain of the brilliant French author Anatole France was a mere 2 pounds, 4 ounces (1.02 kg).

Months before birth, a surge of the male hormone testosterone apparently affects the action of certain brain chemicals in the male fetus. Some researchers think this predisposes boys to react more strongly than girls to stress and perhaps causes the greater aggressiveness many boys begin to display at an early age. High testosterone levels in the male fetus may also be a factor in the greater frequency of left-handedness, dyslexia, and stuttering in boys. The same hormone has been linked to a slight male edge in mathematical and spatial skills, but this is speculative and controversial.

Some researchers think that certain kinds of verbal superiority shown by girls, on average, may be linked to the fact that sections of a woman's corpus callosum are usually somewhat thicker than a man's. The corpus callosum is the main bundle of nerve fibers that cross between the right and left halves of the brain.

If women do have extra connections between the two hemispheres, it may help them develop alternate pathways for specialized brain functions. If the left half of a woman's brain is damaged by a stroke, for example, she is more likely to overcome severe speech difficulties than a man with a similar injury, suggesting that her verbal ability is not as strictly localized in the left brain as the man's is.

Pattern Recognition: When Your Brain Fills in the Gaps

Our neurons store familiar images: places, family, friends, famous portraits. We need see only part of an image, or a faded outline, to call up the complete picture. An ingenious demonstration, using computer grids, puts this assertion to the test.

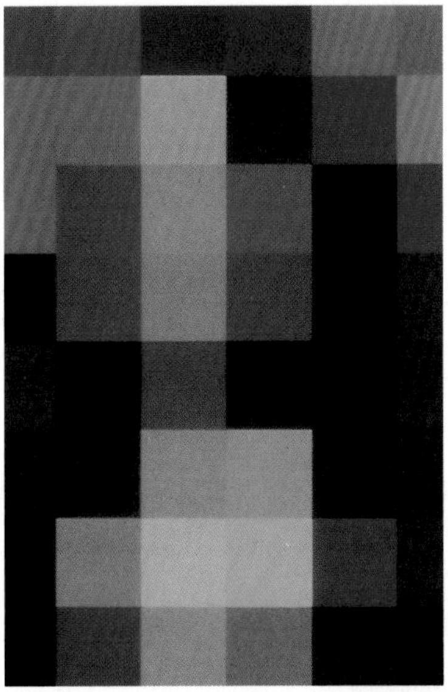

A picture is simplified in color blocks.

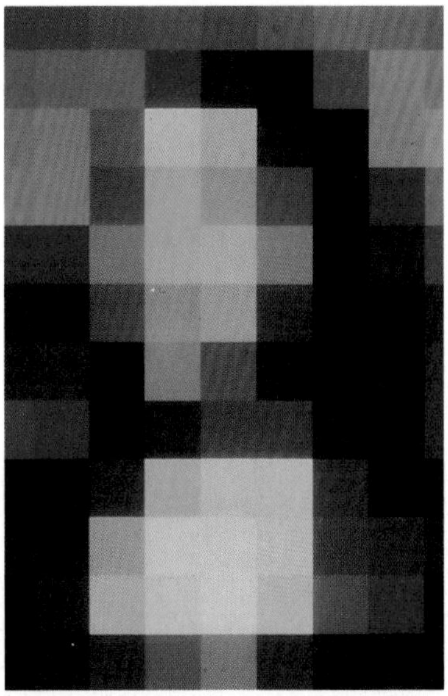

Smaller blocks of the face add detail.

Neurologists have discovered some of the secrets of human memory, how the myriad images that impinge on our consciousness are sorted and stored. How is it possible to call up a particular image, perhaps 50 years after first seeing it?

We now know that there are actual chemical changes in brain cells, neurons, that form a record of what we see, hear, taste, smell, and feel. The brain has such enormous numbers of neurons that there is no danger of ever using up the mind's storage capacity. (If a very old person of vigorous intellect wants to learn more, there is no impediment.) Scientists have found that a familiar context is helpful when you want to retrieve a particular piece of information.

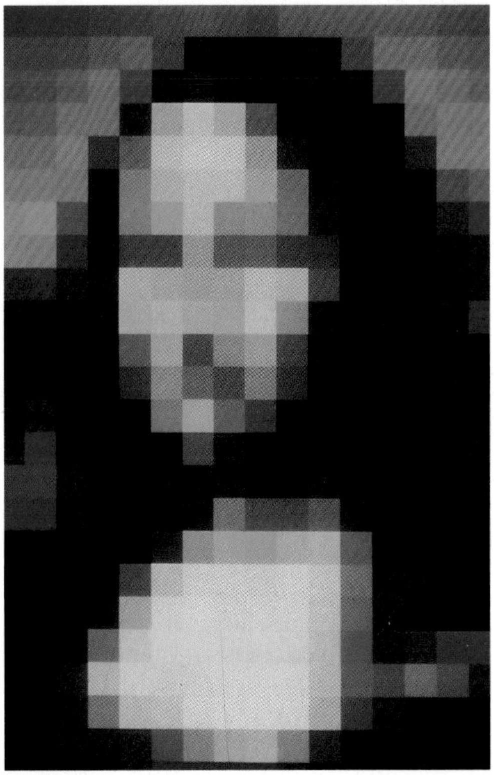

Who is this? Turn to page 320 for the answer.

Balance of Left and Right

A Great Bridge Between the Two Hemispheres

People are fascinated with the idea of our hemispheres being really two brains—the right one more "creative" in most people, the left one more "logical." But the hemispheres of a normal brain hardly exist in splendid isolation. Between them, in the words of neuroscientist Michael S. Gazzaniga, runs an "enormous interbrain connector," called the corpus callosum, which is packed with innumerable nerve fibers. In patients whose corpus callosum has been severed to control epileptic attacks, a lack of normal communication between hemispheres has been observed. For example, something sensed in one hemisphere, as well as certain thoughts and memories, may not register in the other.

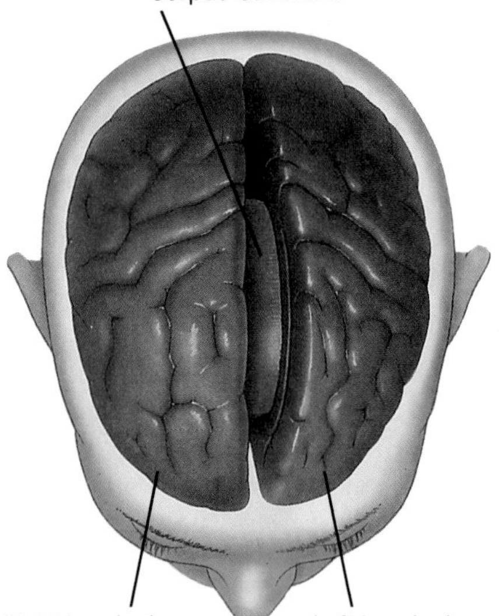

The corpus callosum is the main connecting link between the left and right hemispheres.

Why is the brain divided in two?

Our brain has two hemispheres, the right and the left. They share our thinking and the control of our body. The left half of the brain controls the right side of the body and the right half of the brain controls the left side.

One theory on why the brain is divided down the middle is that each half can provide a backup if one is damaged. This duality is common in other internal organs, such as the lungs and kidneys, and of course in eyes, ears, limbs, and so on.

When injury to the brain occurs at birth, a healthy hemisphere can often take over successfully the function of the damaged one. Infants who have had a hemisphere removed surgically have shown relatively normal physical and mental development. A stroke in a child of six or seven often does not severely impair language development, although in an adult it could mean permanent loss of speech. Thus adaptability diminishes as a child ages, as the brain hemispheres normally become more specialized.

Although our brains are divided in half, the two halves are not identical. For that matter most persons have faces that aren't quite symmetrical, and one foot that is usually a bit larger than the other. The asymmetries in the brain's halves are a clue to the different specialties of each hemisphere.

Is each hemisphere really an independent brain?

In the early 1940's, brain surgeons began to treat sufferers from life-threatening epilepsy by cutting the major nerve link, called the corpus callosum, between the two halves of the brain. In an epileptic attack, the brain's neurons sometimes discharge in an abnormal, erratic way, sending what have been described as electrical storms across the corpus callosum. The neurologists thought that cutting the corpus callosum might calm these storms, and up to a point they were correct. The operation reduced epileptic seizures and left the patients otherwise apparently unchanged.

Cutting of the corpus callosum became a frequent treatment for intractable epilepsy. Follow-up studies of the split-brain patients led to the popular belief that we have two brains in our heads. That is, each hemisphere is capable of working independently, and we can get by with one or the other.

However, later studies revealed that although separated hemispheres can function well, a split-brain patient may have measurable deficits in connecting images and language. Normally, the two hemispheres don't operate independently, but interact.

What makes you right-handed or left-handed?

Why some 90 percent of people possess a greater degree of strength and coordination in their right hands than in their left—and why the opposite is true for the other 10 percent—is something that remains unexplained.

There are many theories. The Greek philosopher Plato believed that humans were by nature ambidextrous, and the "folly of our nurses and mothers" imparted the "bad habit" of right-handedness. Today, theories on why individuals have a dominant right or left hand tend to place more emphasis on inheritance and less on learning. Even infants seem to demonstrate, by the direction in which they turn their heads and by their strength of grip, a preference for one side over the other.

If your parents are left-handed, the probability that you will be, too, is 23 times higher than if both parents are right-handed. British researcher Marian Annett thinks that most people are born with a gene inclining them to right-handedness. The 18 percent without this gene, she suggests, become lefties or righties depending on childhood influences.

Other theories propose that fetal or birth events may be a cause of left-handedness. Among twins—who are somewhat more prone than single babies to fetal injuries—the incidence of left-handedness is more than double the average. However, there is not conclusive evidence that left-handed people have experienced any form of brain damage.

What is it like being a leftie in a right-handed world?

Many left-handers today remember being told in school not to use their left hand for writing, and how difficult it was to oblige. Author and leftie Michael Barsley has written of his kind, "It is remarkable that so little has been written about this minority, and the prejudice against it."

The bias against left-handers is ancient and deep-rooted, although its origin is impossible to trace. Perhaps it stems from some instinctive human distrust of differentness. Or perhaps the explanation lies in ancient codes of hygiene that decreed the right hand should be kept clean for eating, leaving the left to do dirtier tasks. In Europe in the Middle Ages, left-handedness was associated with witches and devils. In areas of rural Japan, left-handed women had to hide their handicap in order to find a husband. Cultural anthropologists surmise that right-handedness has been the norm throughout history.

In our right-biased world, left-handers suffer many inconveniences: scissors, can openers, tools, sports equipment, office furniture, and knitting instructions are designed for use by right-handers. However, a few companies now offer products made specially for left-handers.

Can some people do things equally well with either hand?

Nineteenth-century British artist Sir Edwin Landseer entertained party guests by simultaneously drawing a horse with one hand and a stag with the other. This super-achiever among the ambidextrous (literally, "doubly right-handed") was, in fact, not outstandingly rare in being able to do skilled work with both hands. Tests used to determine handedness find many people who switch hands to do different tasks.

It is still unclear, however, whether there are degrees of handedness that fall on a continuum between two extremes, or whether there are just three distinct categories of handedness: left, right, and ambidextrous.

The Remarkable Resilience of a Child's Brain

For many people, epilepsy is a manageable affliction that does not interfere with normal life. But in rare instances, it is catastrophic. With the help of PET scans, it is now possible to discover with clinical precision where in the brain these storms occur.

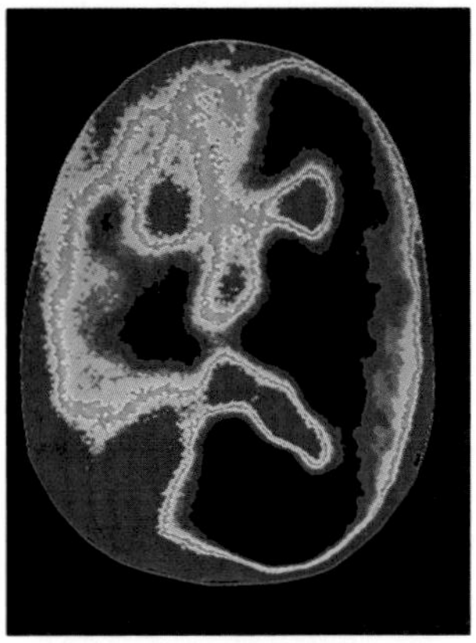

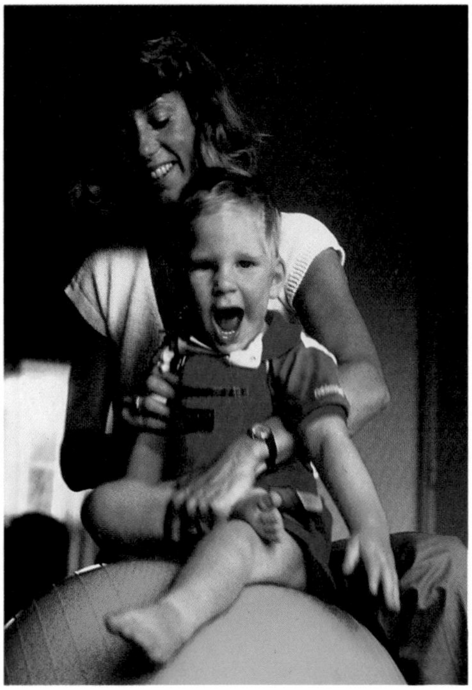

The large, empty space, a dark area in the pre-operative PET scan above, is the left hemisphere of Ryan's brain. Tissue was excised in order to stop epileptic seizures so devastating as to be life-threatening. Afterward, a therapist worked with Ryan to help with muscular coordination and weakness on the right side of his body.

Only eight hours after Ryan Petersen was born on September 23, 1984, he had his first epileptic attack. By the time he was three months old, his seizures were coming at the rate of five a day. Later, they increased to 15 to 20 a day, and the baby was not helped by medication. Children with such severe epilepsy seldom live beyond the age of 10.

While the Petersens were on a visit with Ryan to his grandparents' home in southern California, his epileptic seizures worsened. The attacks increased in duration and sometimes lasted for as long as 40 to 50 minutes. The family took Ryan to the University of California, Los Angeles, School of Medicine. Using PET scans, pediatric neurologists determined that the tissue of Ryan's left hemisphere was diseased. At the age of 15 months, Ryan underwent an operation that lasted more than seven hours. The surgeon removed large parts of his left hemisphere. Such an operation is undertaken only as a last resort on children who are otherwise unlikely to survive.

The drastic surgery brought Ryan's seizures under control. His subsequent progress can be credited to the nature of a child's brain, which can often reorganize itself and develop compensatory capacities. An adult brain, on the other hand, lacks such flexibility to a large degree.

There are fundamental differences between the brain of a child and that of an adult. For one thing, a child's brain from about age 3 to 11 has a much higher rate of metabolism, that is, it consumes and applies more energy, indicating a great amount of brain-building activity. Furthermore, during childhood, the brain has a surplus of both neurons and of the synapses across which neurons communicate. Apparently, in the event of tissue injury or loss, the child's brain makes good use of these surpluses.

His mind no longer dominated by seizures, Ryan learned to talk within four years. So great was his improvement that his mother told the UCLA doctors that it was almost as though Ryan had been born on the day of his surgery.

The Interacting Hemispheres

Stroke: A Case of Blood-Starved Brain Tissue

Most strokes occur when brain tissue loses its blood supply. The extent and location of mental or physical impairment depends on the brain tissue affected. One cause of a stroke can be an embolism, a blockage of a cerebral artery by an air bubble or some other material circulating in the bloodstream. Or a stroke can result from a thrombus, a blood clot formed in the artery itself. In either case, the blood supply to brain tissue is blocked. When tissue is deprived of the oxygen and the glucose (the body's fuel) carried by the blood, it is either damaged or does not survive.

Brain hemorrhages can also cause strokes. A blood vessel bursts, sometimes as a result of high blood pressure, and brain tissue is destroyed by the escaping blood as well as by the cutoff of its normal blood supply.

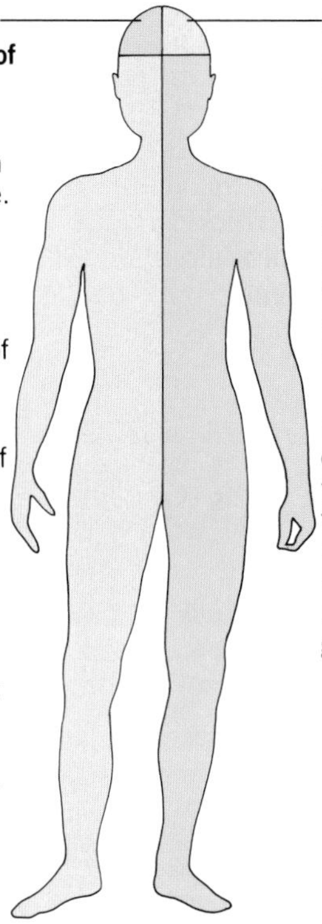

Paralysis on the left side. Can be partial or complete. Sometimes loss of sensation.
Distortion of visual perceptions, unable to estimate distances.
Impairment of memory. Forgetful of intention.

Paralysis on the right side. Can be partial or complete. Some loss of sensation.
Impairment of speech from minor to loss of memory. Unable to remember language.

What are the specialized abilities of the brain's two hemispheres?

The notion that we carry two independent brains in our head is somewhat misleading, but each hemisphere does seem, as a rule, to specialize in (though very rarely monopolize) certain functions. The left brain's specialties are spoken and written language, logic, number skills, and scientific concepts. Work that might involve primarily the left brain includes writing, bookkeeping, selling, and laboratory jobs.

The right brain excels in recognizing patterns and shapes and how they relate to one another. It is, for example, probably instrumental in remembering faces. It is the half of the brain that seems to contribute most to insight and imagination and that appreciates the arts and understands humor. The work of an architect would draw heavily on the right hemisphere, as would that of a musician or gardener.

Although it doesn't initiate speech, the right hemisphere apparently has a role in creating and perceiving the emotional nuances of speech. Take, for instance, the remark: "You're unbelievable!" It can be critical or admiring, depending on how it is said. One man with stroke damage in the right brain couldn't understand the intonation. Another man with right-brain damage, though he could say "you're unbelievable," might only say it in a monotone.

Is one hemisphere dominant?

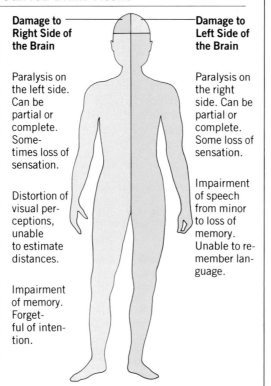

In 1861 Paul Broca, a French physician, observed that damage to the left side of the brain was associated with loss of speech. This discovery led, in time, to the conclusion that the left hemisphere controls speech.

Because damage to the right half of the brain seemed to produce no comparable deficit, the right hemisphere was thought to be less important for human success. The left half of the brain came to be called the dominant hemisphere and the right half was then termed the minor hemisphere.

Subsequent research has shown the role of the right hemisphere in perceiving spatial relationships and in many kinds of creativity. In fact, so much attention has been given so-called "right-brain thinking" in recent years that some people believe that the right hemisphere, not the left, is the dominant one. Probably the middle ground is closest to the truth: both hemispheres, working together, are important.

Does each lobe have a special function?

In the last 20 or 30 years, the idea that each lobe has specific tasks has undergone revision as neuroscientists probed deeper into the secrets of the brain. Although the lobes do specialize in certain functions, there is more and more evidence that many important responsibilities are shared by more than one lobe. Thus, it is wise to remember that certain functions are *primarily,* not exclusively, the business of one lobe or another.

The frontal lobes, just behind and above the eyes, include the motor cortex at the rear of each lobe, a control center for body movements. The left frontal lobe plays a key role in speech. The prefrontal (nearest the front) part of the lobes seems to have much to do with the interaction of thought, emotions, and behavior.

The temporal lobes, named for their location at the temples, are involved in hearing and memory. If one temporal lobe is damaged, hearing is not lost, since nerves from both ears go to each temporal lobe. Through links with the limbic system, the temporal lobes seem to affect how we experience fear, anger, lust, and jealousy.

The parietal (from Latin *paries,* "wall") lobes are named after the bones that form the back top half and sides of the skull. These lobes are just to the rear of the frontal lobes, and the frontmost portion of the parietal lobe is the somatosensory cortex. It is directly across a groove from the motor cortex, the rearmost portion of the frontal lobes. The somatosensory cortex is a receiving area for sensations.

The occipital lobes, beneath the occipital bone that forms most of the lower back and base of the skull, are the smallest lobes, but no less important than the others. Among other functions, they are centers for vision.

How do the lobes work together?

About 12 years after the Frenchman Paul Broca identified a piece of the left frontal lobe as a center for producing speech, a German neurologist, Karl Wernicke, discovered an area on the left temporal lobe, not far from Broca's area, that was a center for understanding speech. The interdependence of lobe functions is beautifully demonstrated by the shared work of Broca's and Wernicke's areas in enabling us to repeat aloud a word that we have just heard spoken.

From the ears the sensation of a heard word travels by neurons to the auditory (or hearing) cortex on the temporal lobe. The word is not understood until it passes through Wernicke's area, also on the temporal lobe, where it is processed so that we recognize it in auditory form. Then it goes to Broca's area, on the frontal lobe, which sends instructions to the motor cortex, at the rear of the frontal lobe, to drive the muscles of your lips, tongue, and larynx to utter the word.

How the Cortex Is Divided Into General Working Areas

Very early in the study of the brain—almost certainly by inspecting corpses—it was observed that the surface of the brain could be divided into sections along more or less conspicuous grooves. It was the dawn of neuroscience. For the first time, early scientists could begin to talk specifically about the anatomy of the brain.

The longitudinal fissure, a deep groove down the center of the brain front to back, divides the cerebral cortex into left and right hemispheres. Other grooves divide the surface of each hemisphere into four sections, or lobes. Named for the skull bones that enclose them, they are, starting from behind the forehead and moving to the rear of the cerebrum: the frontal lobe, the temporal lobe, the parietal lobe, and the occipital lobe. While each lobe seems to specialize in certain functions, there is much shared work among them, and one lobe may take over the functions of another one if it is damaged.

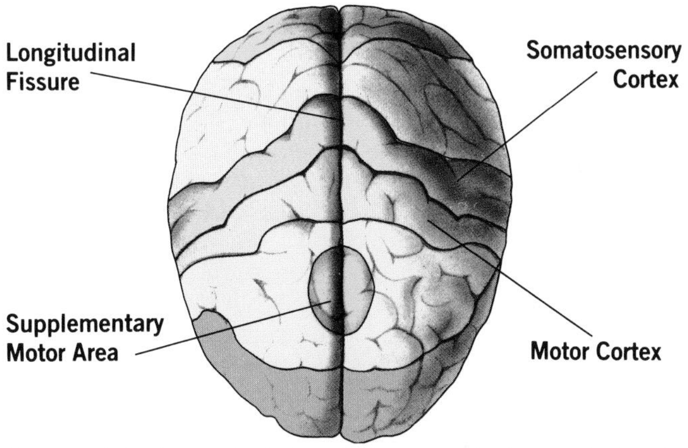

The top of the human brain is entirely covered by the cerebral cortex, which includes the lobes, motor cortex, and somatosensory cortex.

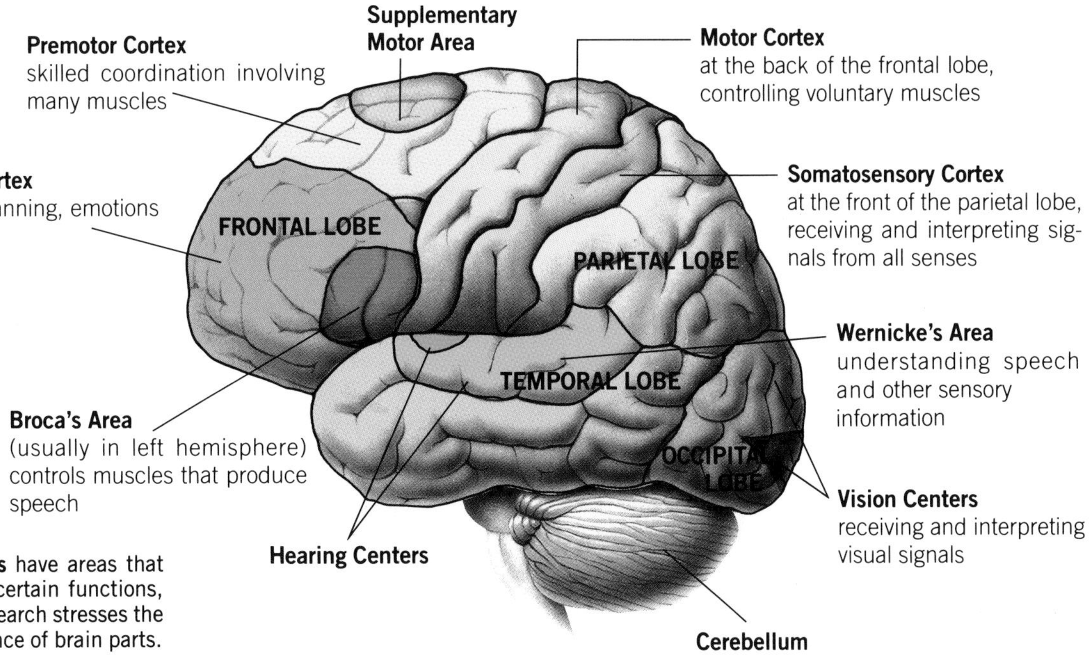

The four lobes have areas that specialize in certain functions, but recent research stresses the interdependence of brain parts.

Tracking Specific Functions

Where are the speech centers?

For 70 percent of left-handers, the left hemisphere controls speech, just as it does in all but a few right-handers. But for 15 percent of left-handed persons, the right half of the brain controls speech. For the remaining 15 percent, speech is controlled by both right and left hemispheres.

Interestingly, stuttering may be more common among left-handed males. One theory on a cause of stuttering is that in some left-handed persons, the two hemispheres of the brain compete for control of speech.

Autism may also be linked to variations from normal patterns of speech control by the hemispheres. It appears that a majority of autistic children are left-handed, and childhood autism is characterized by speech difficulties that vary from muteness, to delayed onset of speech, to strange speaking patterns. Yet autistic children often show considerable artistic or musical abilities.

What happens when the frontal lobes are injured?

In 1848 Phineas Gage was blasting rock in a Vermont gorge when he accidentally sparked an explosion that sent a 3½-foot iron rod ripping through his head. It apparently destroyed most of his left frontal lobe.

Miraculously, Gage not only survived but went on to make a full physical recovery. But his personality underwent a dramatic change. Before the accident, Gage was, in the words of his physician, "shrewd, smart, . . . very energetic and persistent in executing all his plans." Afterward, he was "fitful, irreverent . . . impatient of restraint or advice when it conflicts with his desires." He constantly changed his plans and had become "a child in his intellectual capacity." He was reduced to working as a stable hand and, for a while, as a sideshow freak for P. T. Barnum.

As with Gage, damage to the frontal lobes always produces a change in the way a person feels and expresses emotion. But the exact effect on the person's behavior varies from erratic activity to emotional flatness. The full consequence of damage to the frontal lobes, wrote the psychologist A. R. Luria, "still remains the most baffling section of psychoneurology."

In the 1940's and 1950's, surgery on the frontal lobes, an operation called prefrontal lobotomy, was done on many patients who were extremely agitated or violent. Although the procedure calmed the patients, it has been all but abandoned because it rendered the patients irreversibly and profoundly apathetic.

What is meant by the neglect syndrome?

Some people who have suffered a stroke or extensive damage to the right rear of the head may behave as if the left side of everything, including their own body, does not exist. This is called the neglect syndrome.

Males with neglect syndrome shave just the right sides of their faces, and women apply makeup only to the right side. Their neglect of the left leads them to eat food only on the right side of a plate and complete only the right side of drawings.

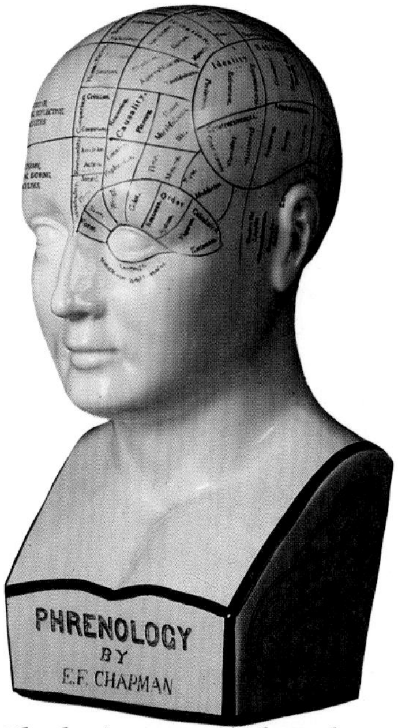

***The brain maps** of phrenologists were incorrect, but they were on the right track; many brain functions are localized.*

People with this kind of damage in the right hemisphere may deny that the left sides of their bodies exist. Oddly, patients with similar damage in the left hemisphere seldom show the neglect syndrome.

The reasons for the neglect syndrome are not yet clear. Many neglect patients are blind in their left visual fields. That is, they can't see anything to the left of the point on which they are focusing. It may be that the mechanisms that control selective attention are in the right hemisphere. Another possibility is that the left hemisphere cannot compensate when the right hemisphere's abilities to grasp spatial relationships are lost.

Why isn't the face familiar?

In the title essay of his book *The Man Who Mistook His Wife for a Hat,* the neurologist Oliver Sacks describes a man, called Dr. P., who suffers from prosopagnosia, the inability to recognize faces. The man's vision, intelligence, and memory were not affected, but he had lost the ability to associate names with faces, to link features with identity.

Dr. P.'s problem was traced to a tumor or degeneration that affected how his brain processed visual information. It is likely that the damage involved the occipital lobes of both hemispheres. Possibly these lobes do more than simply register stimuli. They could also play a part in matching incoming visual signals against images and patterns stored in memory.

What is the source of *déjà vu*?

Déjà vu, the feeling that something that you are seeing or experiencing for the first time is something you have seen or experienced before, may arise from electrochemical events in the temporal lobes. Not only does the sensation often follow injury to the temporal lobes, but also it is commonly experienced by people with temporal lobe epilepsy. Moreover, neuroscientists have produced sensations of *déjà vu* by giving minute electric shocks to those lobes.

The Man With a Shattered World

A bullet tore into a young officer's brain as he forded an icy river in March 1943. His mind in shreds, he fought to reclaim his life. Aided by a compassionate doctor, he won at last a kind of victory—and brought new hope for severely brain-damaged people.

MANY STUDIES of brain damage have helped researchers map the areas of the cerebral cortex that control perception, thought, and behavior. But none has been more inspiring and enlightening than the collaboration between A. R. Luria, a noted Soviet neuropsychologist, and his patient and friend, Zasetsky.

The two met during World War II, after a German bullet caught the 23-year-old Zasetsky in the head. A close friendship developed and lasted some 30 years. Out of it came a 3,000-page diary laboriously composed by Zasetsky, on which Luria based his classic study, *The Man With a Shattered World.*

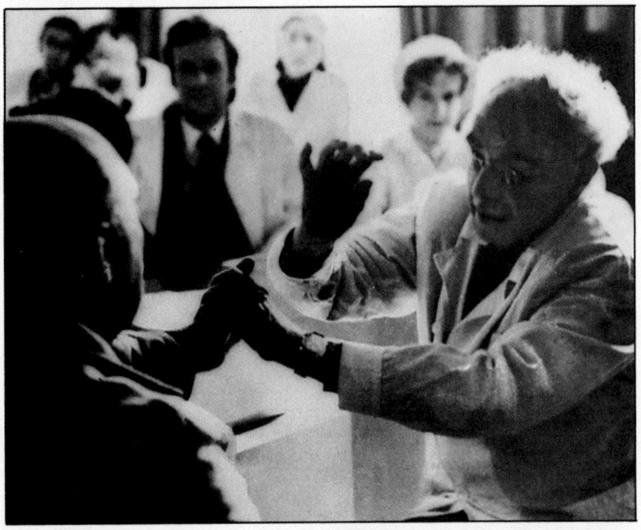

Examining a patient, *A. R. Luria radiates the warmth and intensity that gave courage to the terribly wounded Zasetsky.*

Except for a scar behind his left ear, Zasetsky looked little changed from the fourth-year engineering student who had gone off to war in 1941. Only if you asked him to do a simple task, or watched him struggle to answer a simple question, would you suspect the terrible effects of his brain damage.

■ The right half of the visual field of each eye was permanently gone. "I suddenly 'lose' the right side of my body because I'm always forgetting I can't see on my right side." Moreover, he saw objects in fragments—swimming and glimmering before his eyes. And when he tried to read, he could see, at best, three letters at a time.

■ In trying to read, Zasetsky faced an even greater obstacle. He had lost not only most of what he had learned through reading and study, but also his basic capacity to remember what words stand for. He could read only letter by letter. "Often after I've figured out the letters in a word, I forget the word itself and have to read every letter over again . . . . If I want to understand a word, I have to wait until the meaning comes to me."

■ Speaking was equally difficult. "My biggest problem was not being able to remember the right words." He had to search his mind until he hit upon the right one. Understanding speech was also an agonizing task. "Every word I hear seems vaguely familiar . . . except that it has lost its meaning."

■ Perhaps even more frustrating, Zasetsky lost his sense of space and direction. In the small town where he was raised, he quickly got lost when he ventured away from his home. He even had trouble relating his own body parts. "I always forget where my forearm is located. Is it near my neck or my hands?"

Zasetsky's disturbing partial loss of vision was probably caused by severed nerves. But Luria traced his other difficulties to the damage in his cerebral cortex. The bullet spared all the areas that receive stimuli from the senses and discern patterns in them. The area it hit—in the left hemisphere behind his ear—was instead one that carries out a more complex form of cognition. Combining information from other areas, it gives us the ability to grasp situations, associate words with ideas, understand grammatical constructions, and gauge spatial relations. Thus, Zasetsky could receive information from his senses, but as Luria noted, "he cannot immediately combine his impressions into a coherent whole; his world becomes fragmented."

One day Zasetsky made an astonishing discovery. He could write—in fact, he did it spontaneously, without thinking. How could he? For Zasetsky, an adult, writing had become an automatic skill, controlled by the cortex's motor region. "His injury had damaged his capacity to see and orient himself," Luria wrote, "but had not affected his kinetic-motor functions." Still, Zasetsky had to ransack his mind for the right words—an agonizingly slow, hit-or-miss search. Writing even a few words could exhaust him and he had to stop, his head aching and buzzing.

But Zasetsky continued his heroic struggle. In Luria's words, he "wrote with the precision of a man doing psychological research . . . . He painstakingly searched for the right expressions to describe his problems . . . . In doing so, he left a classic analysis of his disability . . . . In the long run, he won his fight."

The "Brain of the Brain"

The Power Behind the Endocrine System

The hypothalamus weighs a fraction of an ounce and is no bigger than the tip of your thumb, but it rules the entire endocrine system. When blood sugar levels drop, the hypothalamus triggers our desire to eat. Should the weather suddenly turn warm, the hypothalamus lowers our internal thermostat. Hormones activate nearly all of our biological functions. Of the more than 200 hormones in the body, 20 are produced in the brain.

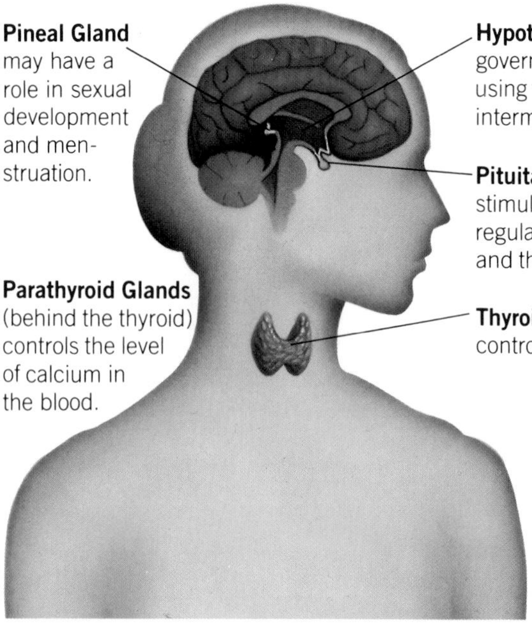

Other major endocrine glands (not shown) include the thymus, adrenals, pancreas, and ovaries or testes.

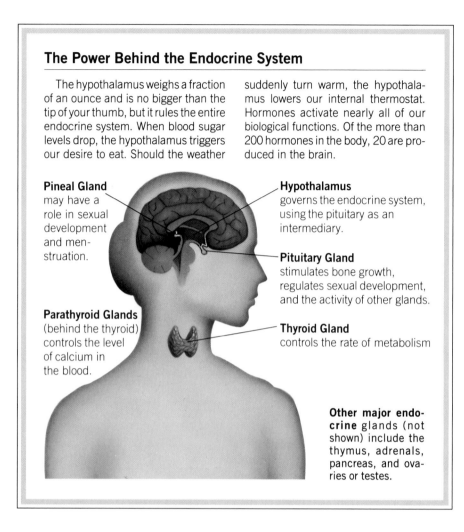

How does the brain manage the inner body?

Some of the most complicated body processes—breathing, digestion, circulation, growth, reproduction, and repair—are more or less involuntary. These functions are under the control of two different systems that work in concert: the nervous system and the endocrine system.

The nervous system (specifically the autonomic nervous system) sends short messages, as brief as a few thousandths of a second, by electrical impulses to produce rapid responses. These signals travel through nerve cells as rapidly as 650 feet (200 meters) per second.

The endocrine system sends most messages relatively slowly by means of hormones to produce more long-lasting effects. Hormonal messages travel through the bloodstream and may take several hours or days. Certain cells have receptors for one or more hormones. A receptor is like a lock and only the right hormones have the key to a particular kind of cell. When it links with a cell, the hormone then alters such cellular functions as protein production, storage or release of glucose (the carbohydrate fuel used for many body activities), and production of other hormones.

How does the endocrine system work?

The endocrine system is a collection of ductless glands throughout the body that secrete hormones directly into the bloodstream. The word hormone means to set in motion. These glands include the pituitary, thyroid, thymus, adrenals, pancreas, ovaries or testes, and many others. Their job is to control the internal environment, not only of each cell and organ, but of the entire body. Their main command center is the hypothalamus, which operates the system through the pituitary, a pea-sized gland that sits under it and, on its orders, directs the work of the other glands.

For instance, when the hypothalamus discovers the need to raise the level of thyroid hormone in the blood, it releases a hormone to the pituitary that orders the pituitary to send thyroid-stimulating hormone by way of the bloodstream to the thyroid gland. When the thyroid receives this chemical message it releases the thyroid hormone, thyroxine. The end result of all this is that metabolic processes are speeded up. A deficiency of thyroxine can cause fatigue.

Can you feel hormones being released?

You can't feel the release of a hormone any more than you can feel a message traveling in your nerve cells. But sometimes you can be very aware that a hormone has been released. When you blush, for example, you are feeling the effects of hormones. Or when you are in a dangerous situation, such as an imminent car crash, your hypothalamus signals a release of adrenaline into your system.

Adrenaline, the fastest hormonal message, acts immediately to prepare your body for fight or flight. Your heart beats more strongly, your breathing deepens, perspiration increases to cool your body, your pupils dilate to sharpen your vision, and your face turns pale as blood vessels at the surface of the skin contract, perhaps to reduce bleeding in the event of an injury.

What does the brain have to do with growth?

The process of transforming a helpless 7-pound infant into a fully developed man or woman is regulated by the hypothalamus, acting with the pituitary gland in an elegant duality. Each has its distinct role, and each depends on the other. Their movements are timed by a kind of biological music that only the hypothalamus can interpret, and then the hypothalamus translates the music into signals that can be understood by the pituitary.

Growth is the young body's response to the growth hormone (GH), a chemical synthesized in the pituitary gland. In one sense, the pituitary can be said to control the growth process because it emits the hormone. But, although the pituitary is often called the "master control gland of growth," it works directly under the influence of the hypothalamus.

GH is secreted during sleep and travels through the body via the bloodstream, but it activates growth only when it communicates with the so-called receptor molecules in the cells for which it is intended. In these cells it promotes protein synthesis, setting the growth process in motion.

What causes giantism and dwarfism?

Being very tall or short does not constitute either giantism or dwarfism. Men and women can range in height from 4 feet 7 inches (140 centimeters to 6 feet 7 inches (201 cm) and still be considered normal.

Giantism and dwarfism are specific growth disorders that can usually be traced to something that has gone awry in the pituitary, but sometimes dwarfism can be caused by malnutrition or by diseases of the kidney, heart, or liver. As a rule, too much GH (growth hormone) leads to giantism and too little to dwarfism, but the timing of the secretions is also important.

If the pituitary overproduces GH before the end of adolescence, the outcome is likely to be excessive growth. But if the oversecretion comes after adolescence, the hormone acts unevenly. Because growth in stature has essentially ceased, and because GH acts only on the parts of the skeleton still not completely hardened by mineralization, the excess hormone may cause large extremities or, in rare instances, a condition called acromegaly, marked by enlargement of the face, feet, and hands.

PERSPECTIVES

On Time and the Mind

The brain is a time machine, a metronome, orchestrating, second by second, the working of our bodies, all the while conducting us from birth to old age.

Uniquely Our Own

"I believe that only one person in a thousand knows the trick of really living in the present. Most of us spend 59 minutes an hour living in the past with regret for lost joys, or shame for things badly done (both utterly useless and weakening) or in a future which we either long for or dread. The only way to live is to accept each minute as an unrepeatable miracle, which is exactly what it is—a miracle and unrepeatable." **—Storm Jameson**

◆

Why Time Flies and Drags

"If scientists do manage to locate this 'clock' in our brains, they may find out what others have suspected all along, that the clock is responsible for our preoccupation with variable time. . . .

"In 1932 physiologist Hudson Hoagland began to ask why time tended to fly or drag when his wife was ill with the flu. She had been lying in bed with a temperature of 104 and had asked her husband to run to the drugstore to fetch some supplies. When he returned, she was angry. 'Although I was gone for only 20 minutes,' he wrote of the incident, 'she insisted that I must have been away much longer.' Hoagland was stunned, and fascinated. 'Since she is a patient lady, this immediately set me to thinking.'

"The reason for this is that heat speeds up chemical reactions. Indeed, the beating of the hearts of cockroaches and the frequency of chirping of crickets, which depend on chemical reactions, increases as a function of temperature.

"If time is determined by chemical velocities, then raising our body temperature should speed up the reactions. The increased reactions should make more chemical changes and hence make physiological time pass more quickly in a given interval of clock time than would normally be the case.

"Now, Hoagland believed, he had discovered the same phenomenon occurring somewhere in his wife's brain. . . .He asked her to count out loud to 60 'at a speed she believed to be one per second.' Days later, when she was well, Hoagland tested her again and was delighted at the results. He had discovered that his wife counted faster when she had a fever than when she did not."

—Kenneth Jon Rose
The Body in Time

◆

Life Cycles

"Yesterday, with the dry leaves shuffling in figure eights around my feet on the sidewalk, I thought about what it was like growing up, and the feeling came back to me, palpable as fever. . . . the ubiquitous feeling of waiting for real life to begin, knowing it was just the other side of the horizon, never really sure what it would be, what it was about. . . .

"Life was so close you could touch it by the time adolescence arrived. By then you knew that the only way to get any relief was to hitch your wagon to the milestones. Senior prom. Graduation day. Rehearsals for the main events, which would come later. . . .

"One moment we are waiting, waiting for real life to begin, racing toward milestones only to arrive and say, 'That's all?' And the next we look around and realize that that *is* all, that somehow without knowing it we have slipped sleepily into the next three decades of our existence. . . .

"One day we realize that we are not waiting but living. No more will we peg everything on the Christmas holidays, or a new job. It is only living with the slow beating of our own hearts that is real. This is your life. It is a strange sea change, pleasant if the horizon looks sunny, shot with long strands of pink and gold. Soothing even, after all the years of waiting."

—Anna Quindlen
The New York Times

Biological Cycles and Clocks

What are biological rhythms?

Every moment of our lives, we experience fluctuations in our temperature, blood pressure, brain waves, energy levels, attentiveness, appetite, hormone production, and much more. The beating of our hearts is one such rhythm; so is the menstrual cycle of women. The new science of chronobiology is concerned with identifying our cycles and internal clocks and seeing how they interact. Although the hypothalamus and the pituitary gland are undoubtedly influential in keeping us on our own schedules, no one yet knows how they do it. We are, of course, also influenced by the outside world. Sunrise is nature's prod to wakefulness, and the alarm clock is a man-made aid. But our biological rhythms—with or without external cues—have a persistence and strength that scientists are just beginning to appreciate.

When a biological cycle is completed in a period of 24 hours or so, it is called circadian, from the Latin for "about a day." The daily pattern of wakefulness and sleep is a circadian rhythm. Sleep is often accompanied by fairly regular temperature changes. No two people have identical rhythms, but a common pattern is for the body temperature to be at its lowest between 4:00 A.M. and 6:00 A.M. By 7:00 A.M., the temperature may be almost at 98.6°F (37°C); by midmorning, when temperature is at its highest, energy is highest too.

So-called "morning" people, who rise up raring to go, generally start their temperature rise not at 5:00 A.M., but at 3:00 A.M. Although their energy peak occurs earlier, so does the falling off of their energy at the other end of the day.

The temperature of "night" people may not rise till 9:00 A.M., which means feeling listless while others are in high gear. Their peak performance may not come until late afternoon or early evening.

What does it matter if people have different cycles?

One of the major stress points in human relations occurs when people have conflicting moods. Husbands and wives, particularly, find differences inescapable; he's up-and-at-'em at 6:00 A.M., she comes to life at night, or vice versa. Resentment builds as each person feels thwarted by the other's habits. In all probability, this frequently observed difference between "fowls" (morning people) and "owls" (night people) isn't anybody's fault; it's best to accept it.

What do round-the-clock sleeping and compulsive eating have in common?

The role of the hypothalamus in sleep was pointed up in the case of a man with a small inoperable tumor in this gland. The two hypothalmic nuclei associated with sleep and eating were destroyed, and he slumbered around the clock. When he was roused, he ate continuously. He died soon after the onset of this condition.

Disorders of the hypothalamus also influence appetite. One 20-year-old woman developed a voracious appetite. Unable to stay away from the refrigerator, her weight ballooned. She functioned fairly well for about a year, then became hostile and confused. Her emotional state could only be relieved by gorging. Her doctors discovered an inoperable tumor of the hypothalamus. When she died, she was taking in 10,000 calories a day.

Can being hit on the head kill interest in sex?

"In 1978, I was involved in a car accident. A few months later, I wasn't interested in sex any longer; I had lost all my chest hair."

Mitch Heller was normal in every way until that car accident in which he took a serious blow to the head. He was examined by brain researcher Dr. William Crowley at Massachusetts General Hospital.

"It appeared the defect was isolated to the reproductive hormone in the hypothalamus—that is, the gonadotrophin releasing hormone [GnRH]," Dr. Crowley said, "and that was extremely interesting because other hypothalamic functions were normal."

The particular neurons of the hypothalamus responsible for secreting the

Jet Lag: When Your Body Needs to Catch Up

When you travel by jet across several time zones, you may need a few days to adjust to the local time. Till then, you may experience fatigue, insomnia, and even nausea. Because jet lag is known to slow one's thinking, many business people try to arrive at least one day before important meetings. Experienced travelers find that jet lag is more severe when flying from west to east than from east to west. This is because it is harder to speed up your body's daily rhythms (to make up for time you "lose" when you travel from west to east) than it is to slow them down (to adjust to time you "gain" when going from east to west). No matter which direction you are traveling, there are steps you can take to help minimize the effect of jet lag:

- As soon as you start your trip, try to adjust to the waking and sleeping schedule of your destination. If you're flying west to east, avoid drinking caffeinated beverages and try to sleep on the plane. If you're traveling east to west, drink coffee or tea and exercise by walking up and down the aisles.
- Once you've landed, follow the mealtimes of your new location. Remember, what you eat can retard or accelerate your adjustment. Foods rich in protein, such as fish and chicken, will help keep you awake. To help you sleep, eat foods rich in carbohydrates, such as bread and pasta.
- Recent studies show that outdoor light can have a powerful effect on sleeping and waking schedules. By spending parts of the first two days of your trip in outdoor light, you can help speed your adjustment to the new time zone.

A Sojourn Underground Demonstrates How Inner Clocks Can Go Haywire

This underground wood and plastic compartment, where she developed her own timetable, was Stefania Follini's whole world for more than four months.

On May 23, 1989, Stefania Follini emerged into the midday sun near Carlsbad, New Mexico, after a long ordeal. As a volunteer for an Italian research team studying the effects of isolation on body rhythms, the 27-year-old decorator had spent 130 days alone in a cave 30 feet below ground, sealed off from natural light and with no clock to measure time. The temperature in her living area was set at a steady 69°F (21°C), and her only link to the outside world was a computer, on which she recorded her vital signs and the results of physical and mental tests.

With no external cues to define her days, her sleep-wake cycle changed: she would stay awake 20 to 25 hours, then sleep for about 10 hours. Her eating patterns changed, too; she took fewer meals.

Follini's four months in the cave seemed to her like only two. She also lost 17 pounds, stopped having menstrual periods, and was somewhat depressed. She took this occasion to learn English from instructional tapes. Books, playing cards, and two friendly mice helped her keep up her spirits.

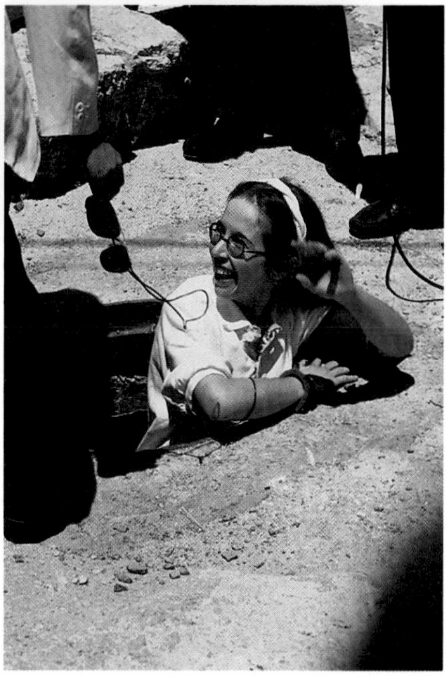

Sunglasses shield the volunteer's eyes as she comes out of her cave after the test.

crucial GnRH to the pituitary were traumatized by the head blow. So Dr. Crowley devised a pump through which the hormone could be administered subcutaneously through the abdomen. And to mimic the action of the hypothalamus, it had to be given at two-hour intervals. Soon his sex drive—and chest hair—returned, and he and his wife had a baby girl.

Is the hypothalamus the boss of the body?

Despite its vast responsibilities, the hypothalamus is just a part of the brain. Though the information that flows to the hypothalamus is voluminous, there is much it can't be aware of. Higher brain centers can and do override the hypothalamus.

The cerebral cortex, the part of the brain responsible for precise perception and conscious thought, compares information from both the internal and external environments. If, for instance, your home is on fire, the cortex will conclude that this is not the best time for lunch; sensory information on your low blood sugar and empty stomach will be put on hold.

The Body's Thermostat

A Reflex That Keeps Youngsters From Drowning

When 9-year-old Kendall Smith was pulled from a frozen pond after being submerged for more than 40 minutes, his body was cold and lifeless. But, amazingly, rescuers restored his heartbeat and breathing. Kendall is one of a number of young people who owe their lives not just to effective rescue work, but to a recently recognized human survival trait known as the mammalian diving reflex.

First noted in aquatic mammals, the reflex is found also in humans. Before the body submerges, the central nervous system halts breathing and slows blood flow to the body's surface. Most of the blood's oxygen goes to the heart and brain, allowing survival for a while without breathing. The reflex seems strongest in children, though it is not unknown in adults.

Five weeks after his icy plunge, an elated Kendall leaves the hospital, on his way to a full recovery.

What does the brain have to do with temperature?

In order for the 100 trillion or so cells in the human body to work efficiently, they need a constant environment. For most persons, this is a temperature of 98.6°F (37°C) or so. When the body temperature deviates even a little, the person is likely to feel ill.

A part of the brain, the hypothalamus, acts as the body's thermostat, maintaining this steady temperature no matter how hot or cold the weather. Though the extremities may be chilled, the body's core—and the brain—are protected.

Neurons in the hypothalamus constantly monitor blood flowing through it. When blood temperature rises, the hypothalamus promptly sends out messages through the autonomic nervous system, producing sweat and dilating the blood vessels in the skin.

Low body temperatures, picked up by sensors in the skin, signal the blood vessels in the skin to constrict. The muscles begin to produce heat-generating shivers. Your teeth start to chatter, and goose bumps appear as the fine hairs on the skin stand on end. In addition, the hypothalamus causes the release of the hormones epinephrine and norepinephrine into the blood. These hormones temporarily increase the body's metabolic rate and produce heat.

How does a fever affect the brain's control of temperature?

Fevers are a result of the body's reaction to bacterial toxins, foreign bodies, or by-products of damaged tissues. By means that are still uncertain, these substances, called pyrogens, have the ability to reset the hypothalamus's thermostat to a higher level. Once they reset it, the hypothalamus no longer orients its heating and cooling activities around the normal 98.6°F (37°C). Instead, it uses the new higher temperature established by the pyrogens as its standard.

When the thermostat is first reset to a new higher level, the hypothalamus reacts as if the body were too cold and goes into a heat-producing routine, complete with shivering and goose bumps, making the person feel cold. Thus, chills are the symptoms of a fever's onset, and throughout a period of fever a person may feel cold, even though the room is at a moderate or warm temperature. Similarly, when a fever is about to end, the body's thermostat returns to its normal setting and suddenly the hypothalamus senses the body is too hot. It causes sweating and the skin becomes flush with blood, producing the classic "crisis" that marks the end of a fever.

Body temperatures above 106°F (41.1°C) can be extremely dangerous. At that level, delicate enzymes are inactivated and cells throughout the body are destroyed. Damage to the liver, kidneys, and other organs can lead to death. Physicians can usually bring fevers down by combining medications and direct cooling methods such as alcohol sponge baths.

Does the brain help the body adjust to long-term exposure to a very cold climate?

If a person is exposed regularly to extremely cold weather for a period of several weeks or longer, the hypothalamus will act to speed up the body's basal metabolic rate. Working through the pituitary, it sends hormonal messages to the thyroid that cause that gland to grow in size and increase its production of thyroxine, the hormone that regulates the body's metabolic rate.

Tests on animals exposed to intense cold for long periods show that the thyroid can enlarge by one-third or more. Military personnel stationed in polar areas for months often develop a basal metabolic rate 10 percent above normal, and Eskimos generally have an even higher metabolic rate.

The Baffling Symptoms of King George III

Beginning at age 50, King George III suffered from episodes of mental instability. At the time, his strange physical and mental symptoms defied diagnosis, but now researchers believe that his insanity may have been due to a rare metabolic disorder.

As a young man, *King George III showed early signs of a disease that would later confound his doctors.*

THE POPULAR IMAGE of George III is of a mentally unstable monarch who responded unwisely to crises during his long reign, including the rebellion of his American colonies. King George may well have been politically inept. But many experts now believe that he became mentally impaired as a result of a metabolic disease that periodically affected his brain.

Unlike many of his predecessors, King George maintained an extremely healthy lifestyle. He ate sparingly, almost never indulged in alcohol, and took exercise regularly. He enjoyed hunting, one of the more demanding sports of his time. Today, a number of researchers feel that such healthy habits may have helped postpone the onset of the king's madness.

It wasn't until 1788 when the king turned 50 that he suffered his first severe episode of deranged thinking. The initial symptoms were physical. He developed severe gastric disturbances; then his legs and arms became painfully weak, his heart raced, and he sweat profusely. Finally his sensory perceptions were affected, and he became excitable, confused, and unable to sleep or stop talking. Within six months, however, he was well.

These symptoms are the mark of a rare metabolic disorder known as porphyria, which causes episodes of mental and physical disability. In this disease, the body fails to break down a blood pigment called porphyrin, which then builds up in the blood and begins to poison the nervous system and the brain, producing the same symptoms in the same sequence as the king's. But court physicians who examined the monarch recorded an even more persuasive clue of the disease: his urine had an unusual deep wine-red hue. Doctors today recognize this color as a telltale sign of excess porphyrin which, aside from causing a host of physical ailments, can also induce psychotic behavior.

Acute intermittent porphyria is an inherited disease. Medical histories of King George's blood relatives reveal that the disorder may have begun with Mary, Queen of Scots. She in turn passed it on to her son, James I of England, who described his urine as the color of his favorite port wine.

Of all the direct descendants of Mary, George III seems to have suffered the worst attacks of this disease. As King George's psychotic behavior increased, he became violent and attacked his doctors.

At last the king's advisers called in the reverend Dr. Francis Willis, one of England's leading authorities on mental illness. Dr. Willis was the first to discuss the king's mental ills publicly. He halted the bloodletting and blister packs that were being used to treat the king. Instead, when King George became agitated, Willis tried soothing conversation. When this did not work, then the "straight-waistcoat," or straitjacket, was applied. Within two months of Dr. Willis' arrival, George III was on the mend. His psychotic behavior lessened and he resumed his royal duties.

But in keeping with the episodic nature of porphyria, more bouts of mental instability occured. Finally in 1811, at the age of 72, King George suffered another attack of madness. Doctors at the time recorded that the king "appears to be living . . . in another world." George III was declared mentally unfit to rule, and his son, George IV, assumed the power of regent.

Some psychologists disagree with the porphyria theory. They say that King George more likely suffered from a manic-depressive disorder. Although the opportunity for a final scientific diagnosis is long lost, the riddle of of the king's condition had a far-reaching beneficial effect. It helped foster the first attempts to treat irrational behavior as a medical problem.

Late in life, *after 51 years as King, George III's increasing madness forced Parliament to order an end to his rule.*

Food for Thought

What does the brain use for food?

For its ceaseless work, the brain constantly needs energy from the foods we eat. The energy is most efficiently obtained from carbohydrates, such as bread, pasta, and rice. Metabolic processes break these foods down into glucose, blood sugar that circulates in the bloodstream and is the basic energy-yielding food for all the body's cells.

The brain is greedy in its demand for glucose-enriched blood. Although it accounts for about two percent of body weight, the brain uses nearly one-fifth of the body's total blood supply; and brain tissue requires 10 times as much blood to stay healthy as muscle tissue. One reason for this is that the brain cannot store glucose for later use as can muscles and other organs. Thus, the brain must be continuously fed. Glucose is critical to the brain's functioning. Without it, the brain would lack the energy to transmit messages between neurons.

Protein and fat are less readily converted to glucose. In times of need, the body's fat serves as a backup source of glucose. However, when fat is converted to glucose, toxic substances called ketones are given off. Circulating through the bloodstream, they cause irritability, apathy, and fatigue. Many crash diets lead to abnormal amounts of ketones in the blood.

Does the brain need a balanced diet?

The brain does not live by bread alone. In order to think, remember, or analyze, the brain needs more than glucose, it needs protein. This is because protein is required for the manufacture of certain key chemicals in the brain called neurotransmitters. In this sense, the folklore that fish is "brain food" turns out to have a scientific basis, for fish is a good source of protein, as are lean meats and most dairy products.

Of course, the protein we eat does not go directly into our brain. It is broken down by digestion into molecules of amino acids, which are the building blocks of neurotransmitters. Tryptophan, for example, is used to produce serotonin, a neurotransmitter that influences our mood and perception of pain. From the amino acid tyrosine comes dopamine, a neurotransmitter involved with experiencing pleasure and maintaining alertness.

Eating great amounts of protein will not make anyone smarter, nutritionists caution. However, the extra calories will certainly make you fatter. On the other hand, going without protein for too long a time will have a disastrous effect on your brain. Too much protein loss, and the brain begins to hallucinate. To avoid that, it must raid the protein in lean muscle tissue. This accounts for the weakened condition and gaunt, wasted appearance of people who have gone without food for long periods of time.

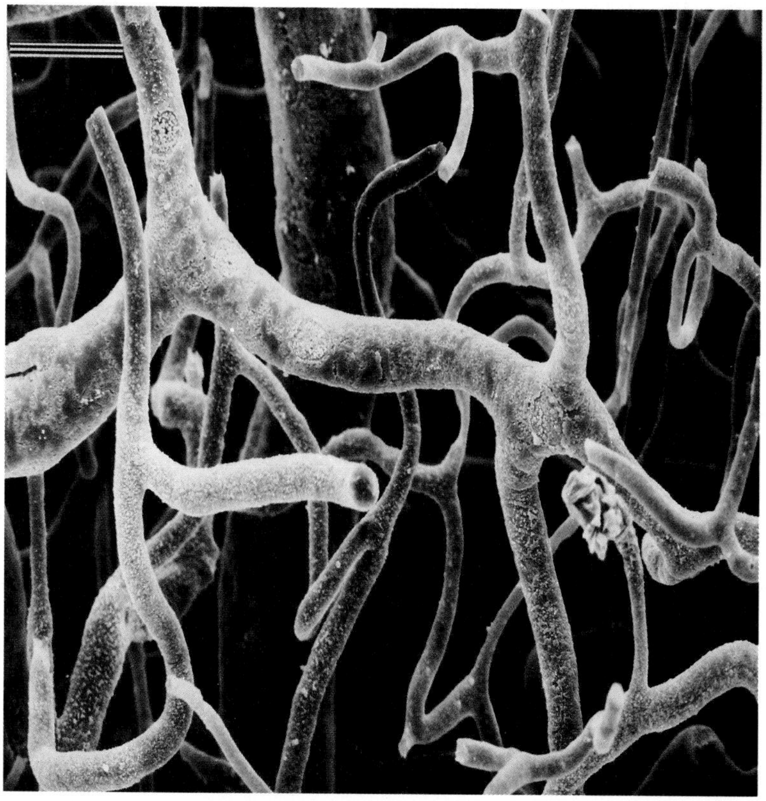

The microscopic capillaries shown here *are found only in the brain, where they help form a natural barrier to incoming substances. Called the blood-brain barrier, it screens out bacteria and many toxins.*

What is the blood-brain barrier?

In many ways, the brain is the most protected organ in the body. It even has a special arrangement with the bloodstream.

Before it can reach the brain, a substance in the bloodstream must pass through a dense thicket of cells and capillaries that scientists call the blood-brain barrier. These cells and capillaries mesh in such a way that only certain molecules can pass: small oxygen molecules, for example, gain easy access. They in turn help ferry glucose and amino acids across the barrier. Several mood-altering chemicals that are fat soluble, such as caffeine, alcohol, and morphine, are also allowed through the barrier.

The pituitary gland and certain areas of the hypothalamus are not protected by the blood-brain barrier. This lets these parts of the brain adjust and react to the levels of hormones in the blood. Thus, physiological changes that might adversely affect the brain's balance of such chemicals as blood sugar, sodium, and potassium can be swiftly corrected.

Is there an appetite control center in the brain?

The brain's hypothalamus seems to be mainly responsible for triggering the sensation of hunger. But the exact sequence of biological events has yet to be discovered.

Some scientists theorize that one of the main reasons we eat is to maintain a certain level of fat. They reason that because energy is stored as fat, the brain must have some way of monitoring how much reserve energy the body has in storage. The optimum level of fat—which varies from person to person—is set at a certain point. According to this theory, when fat levels fall below this set-point, the brain triggers the signal of hunger. We stop eating when certain hormones in the stomach signal that we have a sufficient amount.

By turning on the appetite, the brain protects our fat stores and so helps ensure our survival in times of privation. The set-point theory of hunger partly explains why losing weight and keeping it off is so difficult. When the body loses weight, the brain often signals the desire to overeat in order to replenish the body's original level of fat.

Does the brain control thirst?

The sensation of thirst is similar to the one for hunger. The hypothalamus tells us when to start and stop drinking liquids. Frequently the need for water is directly related to the intake of food, since metabolism of food proceeds best when the balance of water, salts, and other nutrients is within certain limits.

Would young children seek a proper diet without adult supervision?

A famous study conducted in the 1920's seemed to prove that when young children were presented with an assortment of nutritious foods, they ended up choosing a well-balanced diet. Apparently, no help from their parents was needed.

Smart Brains Like to Take It Easy

Someone who achieves high test scores does not necessarily use more "brain power" than someone who scores lower. This startling discovery was made by Dr. Richard Haier of the University of California when he tested volunteer subjects to see how much glucose their brains metabolized during an abstract reasoning test. (Glucose is the sugar from which both the body and brain get their energy.) Much to his surprise, he found that the brains of subjects with the highest scores consumed far less glucose than those who scored poorly. Moreover, the better test-takers concentrated their use of glucose to just a few areas in the brain. Those with lower scores ended up expending more glucose by searching just about everywhere in their brains for answers to the test questions. This waste of energy may be due to test anxiety, but one of Dr. Haier's theories is that brains with the most efficient neural circuitries use the least glucose.

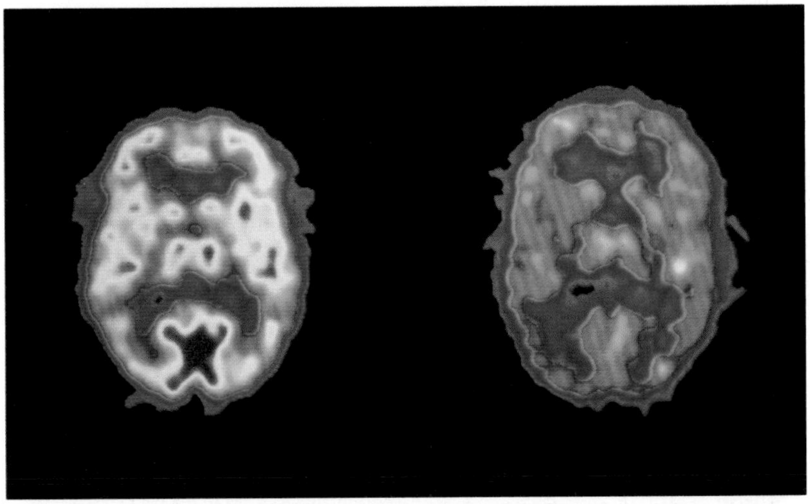

Using radioactive dye, these PET scans show how much glucose—the sugar our brains use to power our thinking—is being metabolized. The "smart" brain on the right uses less glucose (yellow) to find the correct answers to a test than the brain on the left.

This experiment fostered the belief, still held by many, that children know instinctively what is nutritionally best for them. This is not true.

More recent experiments show that children will almost always choose sweet-tasting over nonsweet-tasting food. Even newborns opt for sweet-tasting foods. Our brain seems to be programmed to prefer sugary foods. This may have helped us survive since foods that taste sweet usually provide the body with far more energy than foods that taste bitter.

Learning to select foods is part of any child's education. If your child is a fussy eater, or suffers from what is called neophobia—a fear of new foods—your example is probably the best way to overcome resistance.

Can a lack of vitamins drive you crazy?

Vitamins play a key role in brain metabolism. Studies show that even small vitamin deficiencies can derange the mind. Lack of the B vitamins, for example, is often associated with depression, intellectual impairment, and psychosis. One study found that over half of the people admitted to the psychiatric unit of a British general hospital were deficient in at least one of the eight B vitamins.

However, vitamins vary in retention rates. Thus nutritionists advise caution when taking vitamin supplements. Too much vitamin A, for instance, can severely injure the eyes, brain, and nervous system.

Our Emotional Switchboard

Is the heart the seat of emotions?

Poetry, song, and folklore have long portrayed the heart as the province of the emotions, while making rational thought the business of the brain. Actually such emotions as fear, love, hate, anger, elation, greed, lust, envy, and shame have not one cause or source but several, beginning with the internal or external event that provokes them. Although emotions often involve a quicker heartbeat and other "heartfelt" effects, the heart is just one part of a complex story.

Each conscious emotion is the result of a welter of signals traveling back and forth on nerve and brain pathways. If there is any one control center for all this activity, it is the limbic system, the collective name (from Latin *limbus*, meaning "border") for several interconnected structures that lie near the brain's core. Enveloping the top of the brain stem, they form a borderland between the "lower" or "animal" parts of the brain (mainly involved with instincts, drives, and automatic regulation of body processes) and the higher, uniquely human brain areas, associated with the cerebral cortex, which permit advanced reasoning and planning. In this strategic spot, a kind of crossroads where visceral feelings, cognition, and memory meet, the limbic system helps shape the basic motivations and emotions of our lives.

Does the limbic system control our behavior?

In defining what the limbic system does, a big problem is lack of scientific agreement about where this region of the brain starts and stops and exactly which structures it includes. Some scientists think the term *limbic system* should be discarded.

However, there is little question that structures such as the amygdala, hippocampus, and hypothalamus—all usually considered parts of the limbic system—have much to do with behavior. When functioning normally, the limbic area seems to act as a switchboard where emotional power is imparted to ideas, and reason tempers drives and emotions. In this complex interaction, the energizing force can be either an idea, a memory, a sensation, or any kind of stimulus, external or internal.

One way of looking at what happens is to imagine that the limbic system proposes and the cortex, the thinking part of the brain, disposes; but the cortex can also propose, or originate an emotion, in which case the emotion is routed back to the cortex for review and moderation by reason and experience, if necessary.

In providing a place where reason and emotion can mix, the limbic area seems to help keep our behavior within certain limits: neither too coldly rational nor too hotly emotional. What takes place in the limbic area may keep us from quitting a job after some slight criticism from a boss, for example; and conversely it may give us the courage of conviction when we must take a stand for what we believe.

How to Overcome Stage Fright

The thing many of us fear the most is speaking in public before a group. Just the idea of appearing before an audience can so overwhelm us that we react as if we were in physical danger. In times of danger, be it real or imagined, the brain releases adrenaline into the bloodstream. The result is stammering, trembling, heavy perspiration, and sometimes a loss of short-term memory. The effect of stage fright, as it is commonly called, can be devastating. Here are some tried and true tips to help you.

Know your material. Whether it is a speech, a comedy routine, or a musical performance, knowing and understanding your material thoroughly is essential to building confidence.

Assemble the ideas of your speech in your mind in their natural order, then jot them down on index cards. Never try to memorize a speech—always leave room for spontaneity.

Practice delivering your speech or part in a play out loud in front of a mirror. Remember, acting confident will make you feel more confident. Rehearsing in front of family or friends is helpful. So is videotaping your performance. Taping can help you spot such common errors as speaking too rapidly, or using too many or too few gestures.

Visualize your performance. Part of your practice time should be devoted to mentally going over each aspect of your performance, from start to finish. To boost your ability to memorize lines for a play, visualize your character in action.

Show your enthusiasm for your subject. In his book *Effective Speaking*, Dale Carnegie advises all speakers to "speak about something that you have earned the right to talk about through experience or study." Personal anecdotes are an effective way to enliven a talk.

Make friends with your audience. Pick out individual people in various parts of the crowd and talk directly to each one for a few minutes throughout your speech. Speak as naturally as possible: this helps put an audience at ease.

What if something goes wrong in the limbic system?

Some people whose amygdalae have been damaged at birth or in an accident have episodes of limbic rage, known medically as episodic dyscontrol syndrome. On slight provocation, its victims may strike out at anybody or anything, kick, throw furniture, and use obscene language, then fall asleep and remember nothing of the outburst on awakening. Treatable with antiseizure drugs, the condition strongly suggests that moderating extreme behavior is a key role of the limbic complex, whether acting on its own or as a relay station for instructions from the cortex.

A breakdown in limbic functions may also partly explain panic attacks. Usually for no apparent reason—although sometimes stress may be a factor—a person feels as if he or she must be having a heart attack or stroke. Often without warning and for about 20 terrifying minutes, a panic-attack victim experiences chest pain, heart palpitations, shortness of

The Limbic System: A Mini-Brain on the Borders of Reason

The structures of the limbic area have been called a mini-brain, automatically controlling our internal environment. In humans, the limbic region is dwarfed by the cerebrum (enclosed in a high forehead and spacious skull), the source of superior reasoning. The limbic system is relatively large in animals such as dogs and cats, whose cerebrums are small (and foreheads low). Such mammals' super smelling powers stem from giant olfactory connections in the limbic area.

Cerebrum—Compared to animal brains, the human brain is conspicuous for the great size of the cerebrum and its surface, the cerebral cortex. This "thinking brain" is often considered splendidly independent, but in fact parts of its frontal and temporal lobes constantly communicate and interact with limbic structures.

Thalamus—A key communications link between the senses and the cortex, the thalamus receives incoming signals, determines their source, and evaluates their importance before passing them on to the cerebral cortex.

Hypothalamus—Weighing about half an ounce and smaller around than a dime, the hypothalamus is considered by many scientists to be for its size the most versatile and powerful part of the brain. It has much to do with how we feel and express emotions, as well as with the regulation of autonomic body processes and the intensity of drives and appetites.

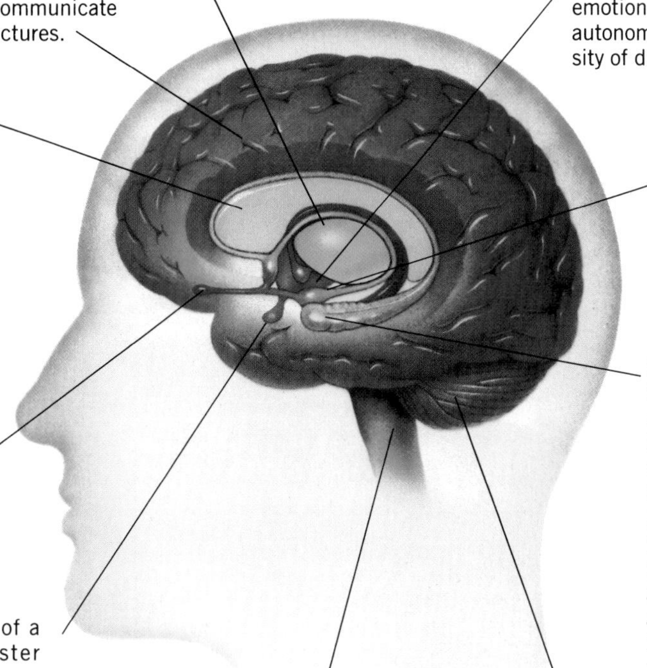

Corpus Callosum—Though not usually considered a limbic structure, this bridge of nerve tissue connecting the left and right hemispheres lies snugly adjacent to the limbic system and allows for the transfer of information across both hemispheres.

Amygdala—This almond-shaped bulge has been called an "aggression center," since its stimulation can cause hostile, angry emotions and its removal, in cases of severe epilepsy, has resulted in passive and childlike behavior.

Olfactory Lobe—Alone among senses, olfaction (smell) has a direct connection to the limbic system via the olfactory lobe.

Hippocampus—Taking its name from the Greek for "seahorse," whose shape it roughly resembles, this remarkable organ deals with a strange mix of signals about smells, short-term memories, and visceral goings-on. This may account for the power of smells to evoke strong memories and emotions. The hippocampus also seems to play a part in deciding if information received by the senses is worth remembering.

Pituitary—About the size of a pea, the so-called "master gland" technically belongs to the endocrine system and lies outside the limbic region, but the pituitary is linked through the hypothalamus to the brain and the rest of the nervous system, one indication among many of the interdependent functions of the endocrine and nervous systems.

Brain Stem—All the basic life processes—heartbeat, respiration, circulation, sleeping, and so on—are controlled by the brain stem and the structures connected with it, such as the medulla and pons. Signals from the limbic system affect the rate and duration of brainstem activities.

Cerebellum—Concerned with balance and the control of body movements, this primitive part of the brain links to the higher brain through the limbic region, which combines the cerebellum's unconscious directions with the cerebrum's conscious instructions on how and when to move body parts.

breath, a choking or smothering sensation, sweating, trembling, faintness, hot and cold flashes, and an over-all feeling of impending doom. Fear of suffering an attack away from the safety of home makes many victims afraid to go out, a condition known as agoraphobia. Often the conscious fear of having a panic attack produces a high level of anxiety that, in turn, triggers the frightening bodily reactions that seem beyond conscious control. Various forms of therapy can help people avoid recurring panic attacks.

The curious thing about the limbic system—and about the brain in general—is that stimulation of the same area can cause different behavioral effects. One person may feel elation, another anger, depending on when and exactly where brain tissue is stimulated. In the same person, a point that gives pleasure may be just a few cells away from a point that causes anxiety. Such findings challenge the idea of a single dominant "pleasure center" in the brain. More likely, there are many such centers, and they vary from person to person and from situation to situation.

Nerves: Extensions of the Brain

Systems Within Systems

Understanding the nervous system is like trying to comprehend an entire country. So much is going on, at so many places at once that we must look at the subject piece by piece. In the case of a country, we may consider it city by city, or in terms of highways and rivers. With the nervous system, scientists speak of its functions as if each were performed by an independent system, when in fact the systems are pieces of an interlocking, interdependent whole.

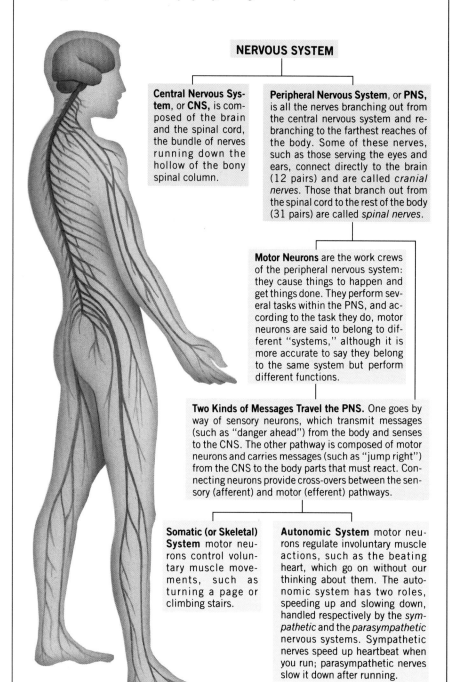

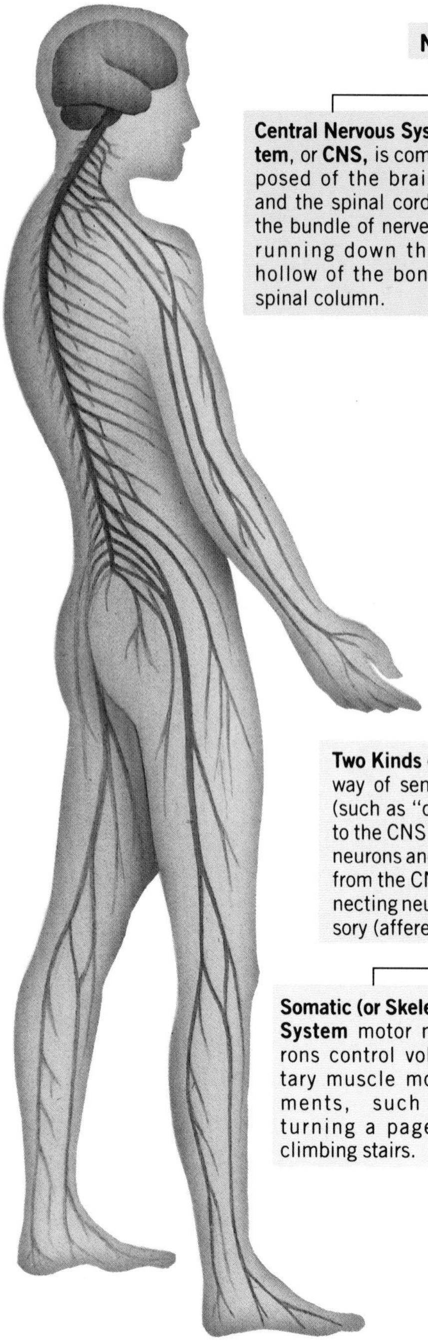

NERVOUS SYSTEM

Central Nervous System, or **CNS,** is composed of the brain and the spinal cord, the bundle of nerves running down the hollow of the bony spinal column.

Peripheral Nervous System, or **PNS,** is all the nerves branching out from the central nervous system and rebranching to the farthest reaches of the body. Some of these nerves, such as those serving the eyes and ears, connect directly to the brain (12 pairs) and are called *cranial nerves*. Those that branch out from the spinal cord to the rest of the body (31 pairs) are called *spinal nerves*.

Motor Neurons are the work crews of the peripheral nervous system: they cause things to happen and get things done. They perform several tasks within the PNS, and according to the task they do, motor neurons are said to belong to different "systems," although it is more accurate to say they belong to the same system but perform different functions.

Two Kinds of Messages Travel the PNS. One goes by way of sensory neurons, which transmit messages (such as "danger ahead") from the body and senses to the CNS. The other pathway is composed of motor neurons and carries messages (such as "jump right") from the CNS to the body parts that must react. Connecting neurons provide cross-overs between the sensory (afferent) and motor (efferent) pathways.

Somatic (or Skeletal) System motor neurons control voluntary muscle movements, such as turning a page or climbing stairs.

Autonomic System motor neurons regulate involuntary muscle actions, such as the beating heart, which go on without our thinking about them. The autonomic system has two roles, speeding up and slowing down, handled respectively by the *sympathetic* and the *parasympathetic* nervous systems. Sympathetic nerves speed up heartbeat when you run; parasympathetic nerves slow it down after running.

What does the nervous system do?

The nervous system, by which most scientists mean the brain, spinal cord, and all the body's nerves, allows us to register external and internal conditions and respond to them. With our brains, furthermore, we can actually shape the outside world to our liking, within limits. Our nervous system separates us from rocks, which have none, and from other forms of life, whose nervous systems are not crowned with brains like ours.

An engineer might call the nervous system the body's operations and communications network, whose main control center is the brain. It runs our lives. It carries out our conscious commands to our bodies, such as walking across a room.

Without any conscious help from us, the nervous system also plays a part in managing the many complex automatic functions of the body, such as heartbeat, breathing, circulation, digestion, regulation of internal temperature, and combating infection and disease. Our conscious selves must sleep but the unconscious, involuntary regulation of our body continues without rest, every minute of every day as long as we live. In some of these activities, the nervous system joins forces with the endocrine system, whose hormones and other chemical messengers also play a part in regulating the unconscious operation of the body.

Do we have more than one nervous system?

The term nervous system is used in a very confusing way. There is one over-all system, generally known as *the* nervous system. Though it is all one system, scientists have broken it down into many subsystems, or divisions, generally according to function, which scientists also tend to call systems (but which are really just parts of the whole).

The two great divisions of the nervous system are the central nervous system (CNS), which includes the brain and the spinal cord, and the peripheral nervous system (PNS), which connects the central nervous system to the rest of the body, head to toe. The PNS forms a vast network of nerve cells, or neurons, radiating out from the CNS to all parts of the body, skin, and extremities.

From an anatomical view, the peripheral nervous system PNS can be divided into two major divisions, the cranial nerves and the spinal nerves. These nerves come in pairs, usually one of the pair leading to the left side, the other to the right.

Does our nervous system need us?

Part of the job of the peripheral nervous system is making muscles move on orders from the brain, and this process is often described as the special work of the somatic (or skeletal) nervous system. It includes the actions we consciously decide to do, such as using a knife and fork to eat, playing tennis, or swatting mosquitoes.

But much important work is done by the peripheral nervous system with little or no awareness or direction on our part. These autonomic activities of the PNS modulate our internal behavior, and this in a sense allows our external behavior to proceeed normally. For instance, when we run, the autonomic division increases our heartbeat and breathing to get more oxygen-rich blood to our muscles. When we sit down to rest, autonomic nerves relay messages that adjust the heartbeat and breathing to the lower demand for oxygen.

***Some yoga practitioners can override** the autonomic nervous system during exercises. Once they stop exercising, the nervous system regains control.*

How do you pick up a pencil?

Nerves can carry information in only one direction at a time, which means that two pathways are almost always in use at any one time in the nervous system. The sensory nerves pick up information from sensors in the skin, eyes, tongue, nostrils, joints, and muscles and carry it to the central nervous system. For each sensory nerve pathway there is usually a motor nerve pathway along which directions from the brain and spinal cord move to rouse a muscle to action.

When the thinking part of the brain, in the cortex, decides to pick up a pencil, messages go out on the motor nerves that serve your hand. They tell the hand how to move toward the pencil. These directions are aided by information that has come to the brain by way of the optic nerve. As you pick up the pencil, sensory nerves in your fingertips report on your action and motor nerves send orders to your fingers about the amount of pressure to apply to the pencil.

Just standing still, something that most of us take for granted, involves a constant flow of reports from sensory nerves in the joints, muscles, skin, and organs of balance in the inner ear. These must then be acted upon with messages to the muscles involved. This activity sends millions of messages via billions of nerve cells.

Can the conscious brain override the commands of the autonomic nervous system?

Life without the autonomic nerve system would be one crisis after another. Imagine what a job it would be trying to control your liver, fine-tune the insulin secretions from your pancreas, and get just the right amount of blood with proper oxygen content into every corner of your body. You could never sleep!

However, under certain conditions individuals can override the autonomic nervous system. Some skilled yogis can change their heart rate, bring metabolism to a near halt, and lower body temperature. What's more, using biofeedback equipment that monitors body processes, many individuals have taught themselves how to lower their blood pressure.

Action, Reaction, Equilibrium

Can nerves calm us?

The autonomic nervous system, which manages our internal operations, is divided into two subsystems, which, in a sense, work against each other. They might well be labeled *war* and *peace*, or *speed* and *cruise*, or *spend* and *save*. They are, however, called the sympathetic and parasympathetic systems.

The sympathetic system takes over in emergencies and stress. It gets us ready for fight or flight. In times of great stress our pupils dilate to allow more light to enter our eyes, the heart beats faster, breathing deepens, digestion slows, blood pressure rises, blood moves to the limbs and brain, and blood sugar rises. This is the work of the sympathetic system, mobilizing us for maximum use of energy.

The parasympathetic system stores and conserves energy. Its role is to keep our internal organs and glands working at a normal rate. After a terrible fright, it is the parasympathetic system that urges rest and recuperation. It slows the heartbeat and breathing, narrows the pupils of the eyes, directs blood to internal organs, and lowers blood pressure.

Normally, the two systems complement each other. Under stress, the sympathetic system dominates. During times of relaxation, the parasympathetic system is dominant.

People can live without a completely intact sympathetic system. In some cases of extreme high blood pressure, sections of it have been surgically deadened. But survival outside a hospital would be extremely difficult without a functioning parasympathetic system.

Does the spinal cord think?

The spinal cord is basically a transmission cable of nerve fibers lying within the column formed by the vertebrae. But it does have some decision-making responsibilities.

The spinal cord is an important reflex center. When your hand touches a hot iron or the thorn on a rose bush, a sensory nerve sends a message to the spinal cord immediately. Just as fast, the spinal cord activates a motor nerve to make you pull your hand away. This is a reflex action that needs no consideration by the brain. It is accomplished before the brain—and you—feel the pain.

The brain can override the reflex action. You can, for instance, keep your hand on a hot iron and you can stop yourself from pulling your finger away when it is being pricked for a blood sample. But each override takes a conscious effort.

Invisible to the naked eye, *nerve receptors in the skin are seen here in a micrograph enhanced by computer imagery.*

What happens when the spinal cord is injured?

The nerves packed into the spinal column have been compared to telephone wires that provide communication between the brain and the various parts of the body. Slight damage to one of these nerves may amount to something like a temporary short circuit and may repair itself. Serious damage to nerves in the spinal column cannot be healed or as yet repaired medically. When a nerve—a wire, so to speak—is severely damaged, communication ends. When the brain cannot send a message to a muscle to act, that muscle is paralyzed. However, the paralysis may be temporary if the trauma is not severe. Sometimes, a concussion or a bruising blow to the spine may cause the loss of muscle control for a few days.

The spinal cord, well protected by the vertebrae, is not easily severed, but car accidents, diving accidents, and bullets, among other causes, can do it. The result is paralysis below the level of the injury. The higher up the spinal cord the injury occurs, the more of the body is paralyzed.

In addition to accidents and weapons, certain diseases and genetic disorders can hurt the spinal cord. The poliomyelitis virus, for example, can destroy motor nerves in the spine. How much paralysis polio causes depends on the extent of nerve damage.

What is the most sensitive part of the body?

There are millions of pain receptors distributed around the skin, muscle, bones, and internal organs. Some of these special nerve endings are more sensitive to pain than others.

The cornea of the eye, the thin transparent layer that covers the pupil, is the most sensitive part of the body. A nicked or torn cornea can be excruciatingly painful. We tend to develop protective calluses on the parts of the body we regularly put to rough use, such as the hands and feet. Thicker skin has fewer nerve endings and is less sensitive to pain.

The sensitivity of internal organs is somewhat curious. In the operating room they can be cut, crushed, or cauterized (burned) without causing a patient pain. But they are extremely sensitive to distension, spastic contraction, inflammation, obstructions, ruptures, and bleeding. Internal tumors tend to cause pain when they grow large enough to push organs out of shape.

The least sensitive organ of the body is the brain. Although the brain constantly processes pain signals, brain tissue itself has few pain receptors. However, the meninges, membranous sacs that enclose brain tissue, are highly sensitive to some kinds of stimulation, particularly pressure.

Stephen Hawking's Triumph of the Mind

Made a prisoner of his body by a devastating nerve disease, a young British physicist faced early death. But with courage, determination, and a high-tech talking wheelchair, he became one of science's most brilliant theorists—and popularizers.

A MIND IS TRULY A TERRIBLE thing to waste. Less than a generation ago the British physicist Stephen Hawking would have been such a mind, stunted and silent, locked inside the prison of a nerve-destroying disease called amyotrophic lateral sclerosis (ALS), better known as Lou Gehrig's disease. Today, though almost totally paralyzed and unable to speak or write, he functions brilliantly as a theoretical physicist and mathematician. He holds the prestigious Lucasian professorship at Cambridge University, once held by Isaac Newton. Far from wasted, his mind is exploring the universe's origins and developing a "unified" theory to explain all of reality. And he is communicating his ideas to people around the world.

Hawking's career is a story of intellectual achievement, but even more it is a drama of love and courage in the face of despair and death. In 1962, at age 20, Hawking had completed studies at Oxford as a brilliant but not very diligent student of physics. He had just moved to Cambridge to pursue a doctorate in theoretical physics and cosmology when he began to have difficulty walking. Doctors diagnosed ALS, which attacks the neurons in the brain and spinal cord that make the muscles work. The muscles—including those for swallowing, speaking, and breathing—weaken and waste away. ALS usually kills within two to five years. Despairing, Hawking at first gave up most of his work and turned inward.

But two wonderful things happened. Two years passed and the disease inexplicably stabilized. Equally important, he found, as he said, "something to live for" in his love for Jane Wilde, a fellow student. Suddenly, in spite of ALS, he longed to finish his studies and get a job so that they could marry.

He began work with a colleague on the concept of "singularities," also known as black holes. These are giant stars that have run out of fuel and collapsed. Gravity crushes each until it becomes infinitely dense and has no size at all. From such a singularity, Hawking argued, the universe was born in the "big bang." That idea, which he later amended, brought him fame.

Once begun, Hawking's career soared. He married Jane, and they have had three children. In 1974 he was inducted into Britain's highly esteemed Royal Society and in 1980 assumed his present professorship at Cambridge. He travels and teaches around the world and, when home, works nearly every day. In all, Hawking leads a vigorous life for a man so frail.

By 1985 Hawking's voice had weakened to a groaning mumble, intelligible only to a few. Then pneumonia forced him to have a tracheostomy, which made speaking impossible. Technology gave him back a voice, however, when his wheelchair was fitted with a computer and voice synthesizer. Now, operating a switch with a finger that he can barely move, he picks out words on his computer screen. At about 10 words per minute, he composes sentences, and the computer transforms them into speech. His only complaint now, he jokes, is that the computer program, produced in California, gives him an American accent.

Though plagued by disease, in many ways Hawking considers himself fortunate. He is supported by a loving family, by bright graduate students who aid his research, and by a faithful staff of nurses. He is blessed with a prodigious memory that allows him to develop complex mathematical equations in his head. And he works in one of the most exciting areas of modern science. "When one's expectations are reduced to zero," Hawking asserts, "one really appreciates everything that one does have."

Living with the prospect of imminent death, Hawking continues his quest for a unified theory that accounts for all of reality. "My goal is simple," he says. "It is complete understanding of the universe."

With loving family support, *physicist Hawking developed a thriving life of the mind despite failing control of his body.*

The Subjective Nature of Pain

What is pain?

Pain is a feeling of discomfort that can vary in intensity from mild to unbearable. Most pain works like an alarm. By alerting you to danger, it helps you avoid further harm. Without pain, for instance, you would have little warning that your appendix was infected and about to burst or that fingers holding a hot frying pan were getting burned.

The ability to feel pain is critical to our survival. Very rarely there are people born with an almost complete insensitivity to pain. These "pain-blind" individuals tend to die at a young age because they have no way of knowing when they are hurt.

How do we react to pain?

Nearly all of us have felt physical pain at some time in our lives. However, no one can ever really understand another's pain, because how we experience pain is entirely personal. Furthermore, our perception of pain is often influenced by our upbringing.

Pain experts have yet to determine if ignoring feelings of pain actually lessens its intensity. In part, we react to pain the way we saw our parents react when we were young. Children often have a harder time with pain than adults do, since their pain threshold is lower. Most of us lose sensitivity to pain as we get older.

Are there different kinds of pain?

Because pain is such a personal experience, doctors are hard-pressed to understand all the different kinds of pains we may feel. One important consideration is how long a pain lasts: this helps a doctor determine whether the discomfort is acute or chronic.

Acute pain is typically a sharp, piercing sensation. The word *acute* comes from the Latin *acus,* meaning "needle." Acute pain is the direct result of a painful stimulus such as an infection or a cut.

On the other hand, pain that is chronic (from the Greek word for time, *chronikos*) can continue even though whatever caused the pain is gone. A pain is considered chronic if it continues for more than six months, and is felt regularly throughout the day, day after day, either as a dull ache or sharp, recurring stabs.

How do we feel pain?

There are two main nerve pathways available for signals from pain receptors. One pathway sends signals quickly, the other more slowly. The express pain route is made up of large nerve fibers that allow pain messages to be transmitted at about 220 miles per hour—a speed that covers the distance from foot to head in less than one-hundredth of a second.

For safety's sake, sudden encounters require fast reactions. Thus, pain receptors send the painful news of a burned finger quickly to the spinal column and a reflex action is triggered, jerking the finger away.

After a few moments, the pain of the burn will be replaced by a dull throbbing sensation. The duller pain indicates that pain receptors are now sending messages along the body's slower pain pathway, which is made up of small nerve fibers.

Is there a pain center in the brain?

Whether the message of pain travels the fast or slow route, the destination is the same: the brain's thalamus. Pain impulses, once they have cleared the spinal column, head for the two oval-shaped lobes of the thalamus. They lie at the core of the brain, above the brain stem and beneath the cerebrum, in the area often called the limbic system. The thalamus registers signals from pain receptors and labels them painful.

The pain message is then routed to the cerebral cortex, near the front of the brain. The cortex is involved in identifying the intensity and specific location of the pain. Without the cortex, we would not understand that pain is usually the result of something dangerous or unpleasant that should be avoided now and in the future.

The Confusing Signals of Referred Pain

A person having a heart attack may feel pain down the left arm to the little finger. This is an example of referred pain, in which an internal organ's disorder is felt as pain in an unrelated surface part of the body. It results when nerve impulses from the two parts share the same neural pathway to the spinal cord. In this case, the brain receives pain messages from the more sensitive areas served by the pathway. Areas where referred pain is felt are shown below.

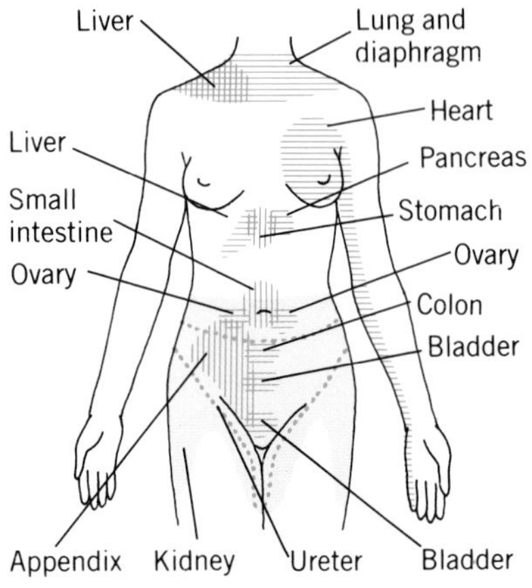

Front view

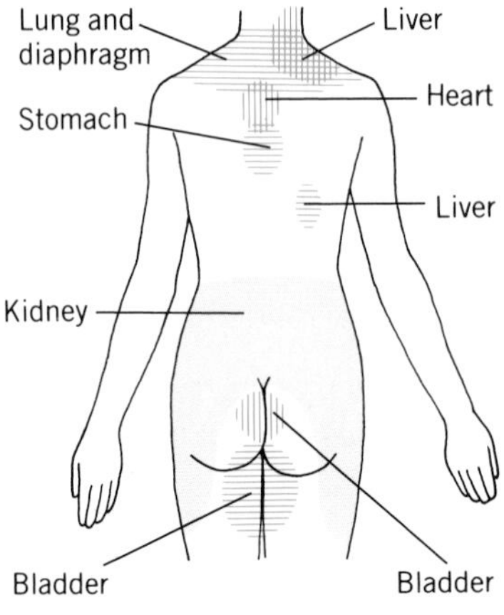

Back view

The Long Shadows Cast by Pain

***Theodore Roosevelt Sr.'s** early death devastated his family.*

THEODORE ROOSEVELT, the 26th president of the United States, was only three years old when he was first threatened by serious illness. Born in New York City in 1858 to loving and caring parents, the boy's growing years were a battleground with bronchial asthma, a disease that makes drawing a breath painful and difficult. Victims feel as if they were suffocating, even drowning. Attacks usually come at night. Young Roosevelt once noted in his diary that "I had a nightmare dreaming that the devil was carrying me away."

The asthma made the Roosevelts' family life a series of crises. When an attack came all plans had to be changed, often at the last minute. Nights were times of anguish when both parents sat with the boy, fed him coffee, walked him up and down, read to him, and even resorted to the extreme remedy of making him vomit by forcing him to smoke a cigar.

In 1876 young Theodore entered Harvard and the frequency of his asthma attacks lessened. In his sophomore year he learned that his father was suffering from painful intestinal attacks. At Christmas that year the pain seemed to have abated and young Theodore returned to college sure that his father was recovering. In fact, the elder Roosevelt was dying of a malignant tumor of the bowels.

In New York, the family tried by every means known at that time to control the elder Roosevelt's pain. His agony was so intense that nothing helped for long, though handkerchiefs, soaked in ether or chloroform, were applied to his face. On February 9, 1878, a telegram went off to Theodore urging him to come home. Arriving in New York, he heard that his father, aged 46, had died a few hours earlier.

The experience of pain is so personal that it cannot be shared. Yet those who have watched someone they love endure pain are forever changed. They can never forget the suffering. Biographers have surmised that the tragic life of Elliott, Theodore's younger brother, and his death at 34 from alcoholism can be linked to the time spent nursing his father. And Theodore himself may have been driven to live a life of daring and spectacular achievement by the memory of his father's early death. "I remember so well," he wrote, "how, years ago, when I was a very weak, asthmatic child, he used to walk up and down with me in his arms . . . and oh, how my heart pains me when I think I never was able to do anything for him during his last illness!"

***Young Theodore** never ceased to mourn his beloved father.*

Is psychosomatic pain real or imagined?

Physicians sometimes say that pain is imaginary, or "psychosomatic," when they cannot find an organic cause for a patient's discomfort, such as injury, nerve damage, or infection. For a few patients with a history of emotional problems, the diagnosis may be correct. However, for the vast majority, pain is rarely imaginary.

Diagnostic tools such as thermography, MRI, and CT (or CAT) scans now pinpoint causes of pain that were undetectable a few years ago. When the source of pain is finally located, the typical reaction of the sufferer is immense relief that the pain, after all, is not a cruel creation of the mind.

What is the gate-control theory of pain?

Pain researchers are still puzzled about one of the everyday methods we automatically use to ease acute pains: massaging a sore muscle, for example, rubbing a bruise, or pressing a scrape. What makes these dull sensations help? The scientists theorize that before pain messages reach the thalamus, they pass through a "gate" in the spinal column, which channels incoming messages of pain and outgoing messages of relief.

According to this gate-control theory of pain, the sensations of massaging a sore muscle or pressing on a scrape or bruise can temporarily close the gate, preventing pain signals from reaching the thalamus. Thus competing messages manage to trip the gate shut for a short time.

The Scourge of Chronic Pain

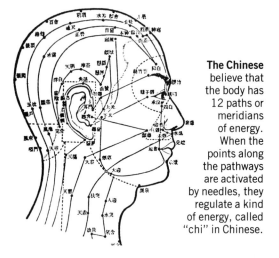

The Ancient Practice of Acupuncture

Acupuncture, which is the method of puncturing the skin with needles to treat disease and relieve pain, has been practiced in China for thousands of years. According to practitioners, acupuncture is particularly effective against chronic pain and certain infectious diseases such as bronchitis and tonsilitis. Westerners have long been unconvinced of its powers. But they took note, when in 1971, James Reston, a columnist for *The New York Times*, filed a dispatch from China describing how an acupuncturist treated him for pain after an emergency appendectomy. With just one treatment, Reston experienced relief. Research now reveals that acupuncture may relieve pain by stimulating the production of endorphins, the body's own painkillers.

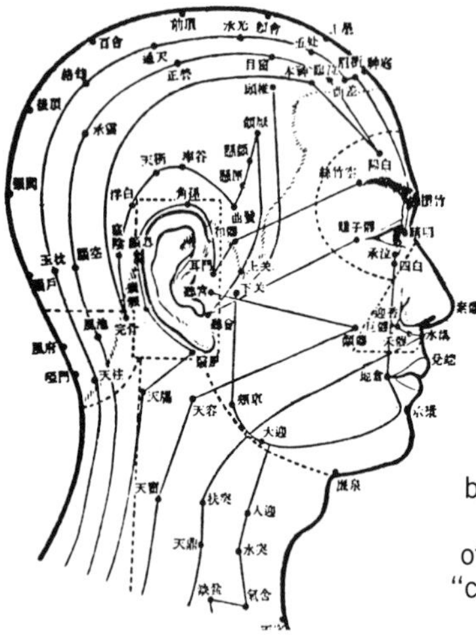

The Chinese believe that the body has 12 paths or meridians of energy. When the points along the pathways are activated by needles, they regulate a kind of energy, called "chi" in Chinese.

The placement of the stainless steel acupuncture needles, often far from the site of the pain or infection, are on meridian points.

What causes chronic pain?

Thanks to medical advances, people with such conditions as rheumatoid arthritis, ulcerative colitis, and heart disease can live longer than ever before. But often the price of living with these diseases is pain that will not go away.

Most chronic pain originates with an illness, a genetic defect, or an injury; but some pain continues for no apparent reason. For instance, there is a mysterious, searing pain that may begin months after a wound has healed. This type of chronic pain, sometimes called causalgia, baffles doctors because medical tests reveal no new tissue or nerve damage that might be causing it.

Ordinarily, once painful wounds heal, the brain sends out messages that cancel any lingering incoming signals of pain. But in the puzzling case of causalgia, the brain does not send out messages indicating that the injury has healed. Some psychologists theorize that a "gate" in the nervous system has somehow been left ajar, allowing pain to persist.

How do people cope with chronic pain?

Because pain is so subjective, many chronic sufferers may feel—often quite correctly—that no one really understands their misery. This tends to happen especially when a person has elected to use drugs or surgery to relieve pain, but the discomfort continues, unrelenting.

Severe continuous pain can be so totally absorbing that its victims feel isolated from others. People in pain often are depressed by their condition and guilty at the burden they think they are placing on their loved ones. In turn, family and friends who enjoy good health may feel helpless, frustrated, and even guilty to see loved ones in pain.

Enduring constant pain can overwhelm a person's desire and ability to lead a normal life. Someone in continuous pain affects the whole family, and upheavals in family routine can cause a great deal of anger. Writes Sefra Pitzele in her book *We Are Not*

Alone, Learning to Live with Chronic Illness: "It took many months for us to realize that his [her husband's] anger was not directed at me, but . . . at the changes that this illness has caused in our lives and in our lifestyle. While I regarded my illness as an up and down process that changed daily, he saw only the negative side that never seemed to improve."

Organizations such as the American Cancer Society and the National Chronic Pain Outreach Association have programs designed to provide emotional support for people who must deal with continual pain, either as victims or as caring companions.

How is pain suppressed?

Time and again in war, medics have been astonished when very seriously wounded soldiers refuse painkillers. The soldiers say they feel no pain; some have been known to remain oblivious to their injuries for as long as nine hours. This ability to suppress and postpone pain has survival value. It can grant relief from crippling pain until safety is reached. Survival comes first, then recuperation.

Postponing pain is partly a chemical process. Certain parts of the brain (most notably the hypothalamus and the pituitary gland) manufacture chemicals called endorphins. These natural chemicals act like the opiate morphine and deaden pain. Both opiates and endorphins may work by causing the brain to send messages that halt further incoming messages of pain. Theoretically, this causes a circuit overload at the "gate" through which pain signals travel. The circuit overload effectively blocks pain.

If the brain and nervous system can automatically block out pain in certain emergency conditions, the question arises why this ability does not swing into action in all cases of extreme pain. One theory sees pain as too useful to be deadened except when survival is at stake.

Recent findings suggest that chronic stress can lower the level of endorphins in the body. Some chronic-pain sufferers have been found to have an unusually low amount of endorphins.

What do analgesics do?

Analgesics, or painkillers, relieve pain without blocking all nerve impulses. They come in two types, non-narcotic and narcotic or opiate. In a sense, both types are poisons, and too much of either will harm or kill.

Some non-narcotics, such as aspirin and ibuprofen (all sold under various brand names), act locally, at the site of the pain. Aspirin and ibuprofen also reduce inflammation and fevers. Aspirin has been around since 1899. Scientists now know that aspirin works by blocking the production of chemicals called prostaglandins, which contribute to the swelling and pain in inflamed tissue.

Narcotics are related to opium and are potent painkillers. They seem to relieve pain by altering the brain's perception of it. Pain is felt, but is not appreciated as being painful. Morphine is one of the strongest painkillers used in medicine today.

How do anesthetics work?

Anesthetics are chemicals that make the entire body or specific areas of it insensible to pain. General anesthesia causes unconsciousness and must be administered by a specially trained anesthesiologist. Among the dangers is that too much anesthetic can stop vital automatic body processes, such as heartbeat and breathing.

For some operations, anesthesiologists use a neuromuscular blocking agent that is a refined version of curare, a poison used for hundreds of years by South American Indians.

Treatments to Help Manage Chronic Pain

Psychologists have learned that chronic pain cannot be understood as a simple transmission of messages along nerve fibers. Many other factors are involved, including the emotions. How we experience pain can change from day to day, even minute to minute, and the changes are often linked to our emotional state. The emotional dimension of pain suggests that it is possible to manage pain, at least to some extent, by managing the emotions. That is the premise of many so-called pain clinics. Such clinics may offer one or more of the following techniques for treating chronic pain.

- **Biofeedback**—Sufferers from tension headaches and lower back pain can learn to relax the muscular tension that causes or amplifies their pain. Sensors that monitor muscle tension are placed on patients. These sensors are then attached to a machine that produces frequent clicking sounds or light flashes when muscles are tensed. With practice, patients can lower the tension in their muscles by trying to lower the number of signals that the sensors emit.
- **Psychotherapy**—Many pain clinics offer individual and group therapy for chronic pain sufferers. Simply talking about chronic pain can sometimes make it less isolating, as can listening to others who know firsthand the emotional toll that pain can exact.
- **Hypnosis**—Not everyone can be hypnotized and not all of those who are hypnotizable will gain relief from pain, but when it works, hypnosis helps to block the perception of pain by directing one's attention away from it. Hypnosis is more effective in controlling pain caused by illness or injury than in easing emotionally induced pain. Some patients have learned to manage pain by hypnotizing themselves.
- **Surgery**—Surgically severing the nerves that transmit pain has helped some people, such as those with certain kinds of facial pain. But chronic pain is seldom easily vanquished and may reappear after the nerve surgery.
- **TENS**—One device called the TENS machine utilizes the gate-control theory to help ease pain. The TENS device works by stimulating nerves with tiny jolts of electricity. Electrodes are placed on the skin and hooked up to batteries. Electrical stimulation for up to thirty minutes will overload a patient's pain circuits and so close the gate to further pain. In some cases, relief from pain lasts for several months.

From Tension Headache to Migraine

How does tension cause headaches?

Most people think that the pain they feel from a headache comes from inside their head. However, the brain has so few pain receptors that a headache is almost always referred pain, which means the pain is actually coming from somewhere else. It is felt in the head because some nerve pathways are not designed to give exact pain locations.

A common source of the referred pain of a headache is the neck and shoulder muscles. When these muscles are tense or fatigued they trigger muscle contractions in the scalp muscles. The referred pain can feel like tight bands crushing the head.

Not surprisingly, tension headaches can also be traced to overwork or emotional turmoil. The stress from eyestrain or an angry outburst, for example, may cause the arteries that supply blood to the head to swell. This sets off pain-sensitive nerve endings in the afflicted vessels and is felt as a throbbing headache. The pain usually passes in a few hours. Relaxing tense neck and shoulder muscles helps to ease the pain of tension headaches.

What is intracranial pain?

The meninges, highly sensitive membranes that surround the brain and spinal cord, are sometimes the source of intracranial (within-the-skull) pain. This kind of headache occurs when the meninges become distended. One symptom of meningitis, a disease that causes inflammation of the meninges, is severe headaches.

Nerve fibers in the blood vessels within the brain are also sources of intracranial pain. When blood vessels dilate or constrict too rapidly they create head pain. High blood pressure can cause headaches because it constricts the brain's blood vessels.

Another example of intracranial pain is the hangover headache, caused by consuming alcohol faster than the body can absorb it. The reason for the morning-after headache is that alcohol dilates the blood vessels within the brain. The pain stops when the blood vessels return to normal.

Head pain that comes on like a "bolt out of the blue" may indicate a severe problem. One possibility is a leak from a blood vessel, which can cause fluid pressure to build up within the brain, push on the meninges, and cause blinding pain. Any rapid onslaught of acute head pain warrants immediate medical attention. CT (CAT) scans and spinal-fluid tests can help doctors pinpoint the problem.

What is a migraine headache?

Most victims of migraine are subjected to intermittent bouts of intense throbbing head pain, often accompanied by nausea, frightening visual hallucinations, and partial paralysis. These dreadful symptoms can last for hours or days. One migraine sufferer likened the pain of migraine to "an elephant using my temple as a trampoline." During a migraine attack, people may become highly sensitive to light and noise and frequently desire nothing more than to crawl into bed in a dark, quiet room.

There are two types of migraines. The common migraine comes on with little warning. The classic migraine, which afflicts one-fifth of migraine sufferers, is heralded by an "aura." The aura may involve such bizarre within-the-head effects as a display of light beams, sparkling stars, zigzag patterns in neon colors, exploding flash bulbs, and iridescent pinwheels.

What causes migraine attacks?

Researchers used to think that constriction of blood vessels within the brain triggered the severe throbbing pain of a migraine. But recent medical findings indicate that the constriction and dilation of blood vessels are not the cause of migraine, but rather one of its many wretched aftereffects.

What sets off migraine pain appears to be a problem with the brain's chemistry. Serotonin, one of the chemical neurotransmitters that is essential for normal brain activity, seems to be lacking in migraine suf-

Did You Know. . . ?

- **The list of migraine victims is long and illustrious,** with such disparate notables as Sigmund Freud, Thomas Jefferson, Charles Darwin, and George Bernard Shaw.
- **Too much alcohol often results in a headache,** which in America is called a hangover. In Germany the word for hangover is *katzenjammer* ("the wailing of cats"); in France it's *la gueule de bois* ("woody mouth"); in Norway it's *jeg har tømmermenn*, which loosely translated means construction workers in my head.
- **General Ulysses S. Grant,** the commander of the Union forces during the Civil War, suffered from headache pain. One of his worst headaches occurred after he had surrounded General Robert E. Lee and his Confederate army at Appomattox, Virginia. When Lee refused Grant's demand to surrender, Grant came down with a raging "sick headache." The next morning, however, when a note from General Lee announced his intention to surrender, Grant's headache disappeared.
- **Eyestrain commonly causes tension headaches.** Exercises for the eyes can help. Try moving your eyes in a clockwise circle several times, then counterclockwise. It also helps to give your eyes a rest every few hours by covering them lightly with the palms of your hands for a few minutes.
- **Listening to relaxing music** and imagining tranquil scenes is one of the best ways to ward off migraines. Some researchers think that music makes migraine sufferers feel better because it releases endorphins, the body's natural painkillers.
- **Some allergists claim that 70 percent of headaches** are due to food allergies. Milk, wheat, and eggs top the list. Though it is difficult to discover which food triggers your headache, allergists note that we often develop allergies to foods we crave.

ferers. Serotonin suppresses the perception of pain, apparently by blocking pain messages from reaching the thalamus. Thus, when serotonin is depleted, messages of acute head pain are no longer prevented from reaching the thalamus. This may explain why migraine pain can last for days.

Serotonin also plays an important role in the constriction of blood vessels within the brain. If the brain does not have enough serotonin, then excessive swelling or constriction of blood vessels may result.

Headache experts theorize that migraine sufferers have an abnormally low amount of serotonin. One support for this theory is the fact that ergotamine, a drug that eases migraine pain, helps boost the level of serotonin.

Some researchers speculate that a defect in the functioning of serotonin may be inherited. This would explain why migraines run in families.

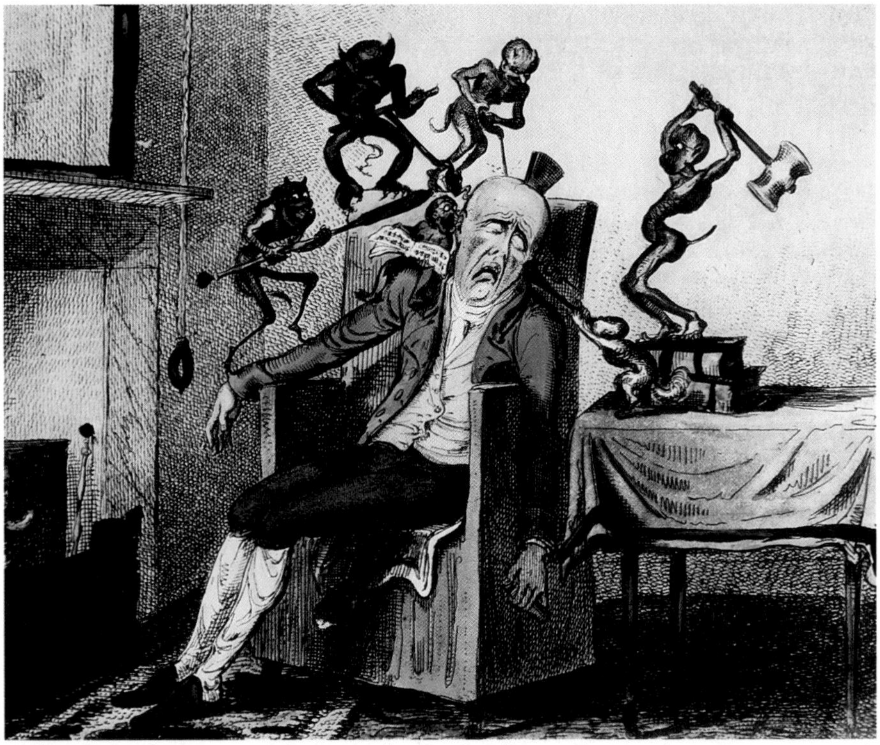

A thundering hangover conjures up *a horde of malicious demons doing their worst with hammer and tongs in this cartoon by the British artist, George Cruikshank.*

Who gets migraine headaches?

Women account for 60 to 80 percent of migraine victims. Migraine attacks usually begin in childhood or early adolescence. They rarely begin after age 40.

Men are more prone to cluster headaches, which are often treated like migraine and are even more painful. The pain always strikes the same side of the head, causing the eye on that side to tear. Cluster headaches can last from 20 minutes to two hours. They occur at least once a day for weeks or months, then stop for months or years before recurring.

For more than a century, it was accepted that migraine sufferers were perfectionists who were impatient for success. This led to the erroneous idea of a migraine personality. Research has since shown that migraine pain is a neurological disorder that can affect almost any personality type.

This Stone Age skull *(dating back some 10,000 years) shows it has been cut open or trephined. This may have been a religious rite to release evil spirits.*

What starts a migraine headache?

Just about anything appears to set off a migraine attack. Depending on the individual, any one of the following can trigger a migraine: smoking, alcohol, caffeine, aged cheese, Chinese food, chocolate, processed meats, onions, peanuts, cinnamon, sex, tension, relaxation, red wine, fatigue, napping, birth control pills, dieting, menstruation, bright lights, emotional pressures, and a change in barometric pressure.

To help pinpoint the cause of migraine, try keeping a diary of the substances or circumstances that seem to trigger attacks. Because of the wide variety of causes, doctors sometimes simply recommend avoiding excess and trying to live by the Greek ideal of "moderation in all things."

Are migraine headaches curable?

There is as yet no cure for people who suffer from chronic migraine headaches, but there are effective treatments to control the severity of the attacks. Since the 1930's, a major source of drugs to abort a migraine attack has been ergot, a fungus that grows on rye. Drugs based on ergot narrow the blood vessels and alter the level of serotonin in the brain.

British researchers have found that feverfew, an herb used since medieval times to treat fever, can reduce the frequency and severity of migraine headaches. Some migraine sufferers have reported being helped by biofeedback training, which is meant to teach a person to control the dilation of his or her own blood vessels.

Tracing the Patterns of Sleep

Does the brain sleep?

For William Shakespeare, sleep was "the death of each day's life," and another English literary giant, Samuel Johnson, saw it as "irresistible stupefaction." To the contrary, scientists have found that the brain buzzes with activity during sleep.

This modern view began to emerge in the 1920's and 1930's when the electroencephalograph, or EEG for short, was used to study the brain waves of sleeping people. These studies revealed that a sleeper's brain waves vary throughout the night.

Why do scientists call some sleep paradoxical?

In the early 1950's the pioneering sleep researcher Nathaniel Kleitman and his assistant, Eugene Aserinsky, made a discovery that shattered once and for all the idea of sleep as a time when the brain turns off. Monitoring an electrooculogram, or EOG, which can reveal eye movements even when the lids are closed, they found that at a certain point in sleep our eyes begin to dart back and forth.

Though we continue to sleep and our eyes remain shut, the eyeballs move as if watching a fast-paced three-ring circus. During these periods of frantic eye motion, moreover, an EEG registers intense brain activity. Yet another remarkable thing occurs at this time of sleep. Most of the body's muscular activity halts. This curious cessation shows up in an electromyogram, or EMG, a record of electrical impulses in the muscles.

All three of these changes happening simultaneously—a surge in brain activity, increased eye movements, and near paralysis of muscles—were so unexpected that scientists gave this period of sleep a special name, in fact two names. One is REM (from rapid-eye-movement) sleep. The other name is paradoxical sleep. The paradox is that we appear to be deep in sleep, but our brains are really working furiously.

People who are awakened during REM sleep invariably report vivid dreams. This is the time when most, though not all, dreaming occurs.

Are NREM and REM sleep really so different?

NREM sleep is characterized by fairly distinct and predictable brain-wave patterns, detectable by an EEG and broken into four stages by scientists. An NREM cycle is "quiet sleep," a time of measured breathing and little body movement, even though it is when

Brain Waves Reveal Stages of Sleep

Modern sleep research began with the use of the EEG, or electroencephalograph, a word meaning "electrical brain writing." Groups of nerve cells in the brain generate electrical impulses and, as these discharge, the EEG records them as lines on a sheet or roll of paper. The oscillating lines, or waves, indicate the activity in a sleeper's brain.

The meaning of a sleeper's brain waves

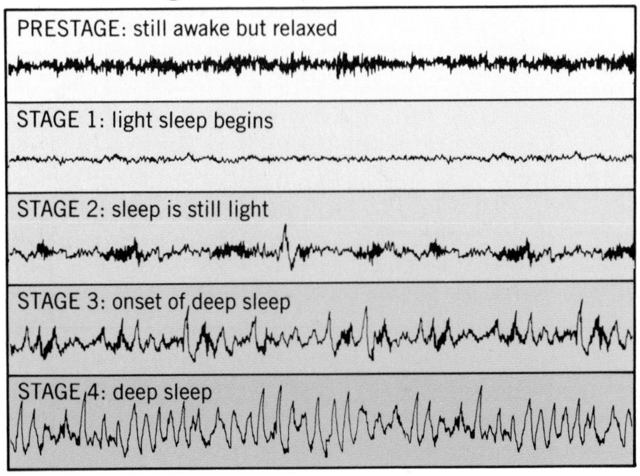

The stages of sleep recur in several cycles every night. Each stage has a distinctive brain-wave pattern, as on these simulated EEG printouts. The sequence and number of stages in a cycle vary.

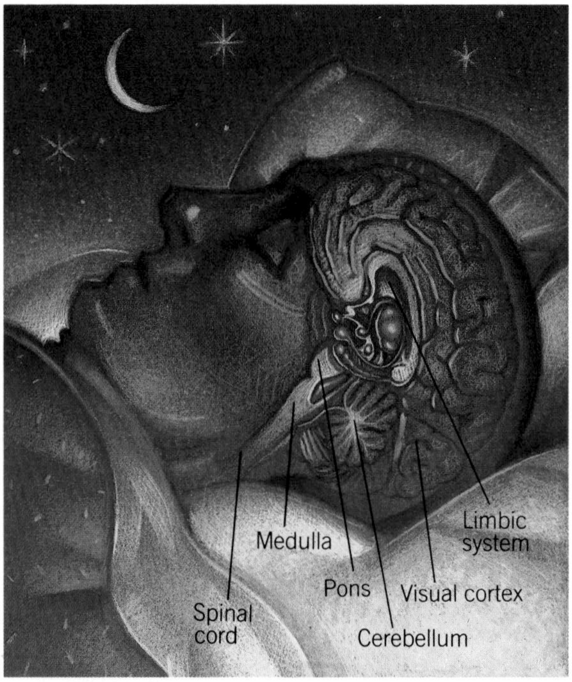

The mystery of what makes us sleep at certain times and then wake up seems to involve structures in the limbic area and brain stem, where chemicals are released in step with the rhythms of night and day and other grand cycles of nature.

sleepers snore. During NREM sleep our senses are at their least responsive.

Everything changes with the coming of REM (rapid eye movement) sleep. Snoring stops. Breathing varies from short sharp gasps to slow inhaling and exhaling. Blood flow to the brain increases and brain temperature rises. Facial and fingertip muscles may twitch.

Curiously, the arms, legs, and trunk, which are able to move during NREM, are usually paralyzed in REM sleep. How the brain produces this paralysis is still unclear, but being immobilized during REM sleep may save us from hurting ourselves or others.

Why do we need sleep?

For most of us the point of "a good night's sleep" is to wake up refreshed and ready to face the day. Common sense and experience tell us that we have to sleep to function well. Just why this should be so remains somewhat mysterious, though scientists are finding fascinating clues to sleep's restorative powers.

During the day, for instance, certain hormones are used up. While we sleep, new hormones are turned out by the endocrine system. Among these hormones is somatotropin, a growth substance released by the pituitary gland during NREM sleep. Researchers theorize that sleep may be a time when the growth of some kinds of cells speeds up and the body purges itself of the chemical by-products accumulated during waking hours.

In some ways, sleep seems to strengthen our capacity to remember. However, since the brain cannot absorb new information while we sleep, claims of "sleep-learning," while enticing, are nonsense.

How does the body go to sleep?

Falling asleep is a complicated and extremely active process. Moreover, it does not really take place gradually but rather suddenly, in the sense that one moment we are technically awake (however sleepy) and the next moment we are fast asleep.

Current research suggests that the brain stem controls when and how long we sleep, while structures in the brain's limbic system regulate the cycles and stages of sleep.

Certain chemicals in the body, among them peptides, have been found to be natural sleep-inducers. These compounds, which contain amino acids, also are known to bolster the immune system by increasing the production of antibodies. Thus modern research seems to confirm a bit of age-old medical wisdom: sleep can help fight illness and infection.

Charting the Ups and Downs of a Good Night's Sleep

Ignored for centuries as a subject of research, sleep has since the 1950's been a hotbed of scientific study. Tons of data about muscle activity, eye movements, and the brain's electrical activity during sleep have put to rest forever the notion of "unbroken" sleep. A typical eight hours of sleep is broken into four or five cycles every night. A cycle, in turn, is divided into the staged sleep (the fullest cycle being stages 1 to 4 and back to 1) revealed by an EEG. Also, sleep has periods of rapid eye movement (REM), in which dreaming occurs, and periods of little or no rapid eye movement (non-REM, or NREM), which occur during staged sleep.

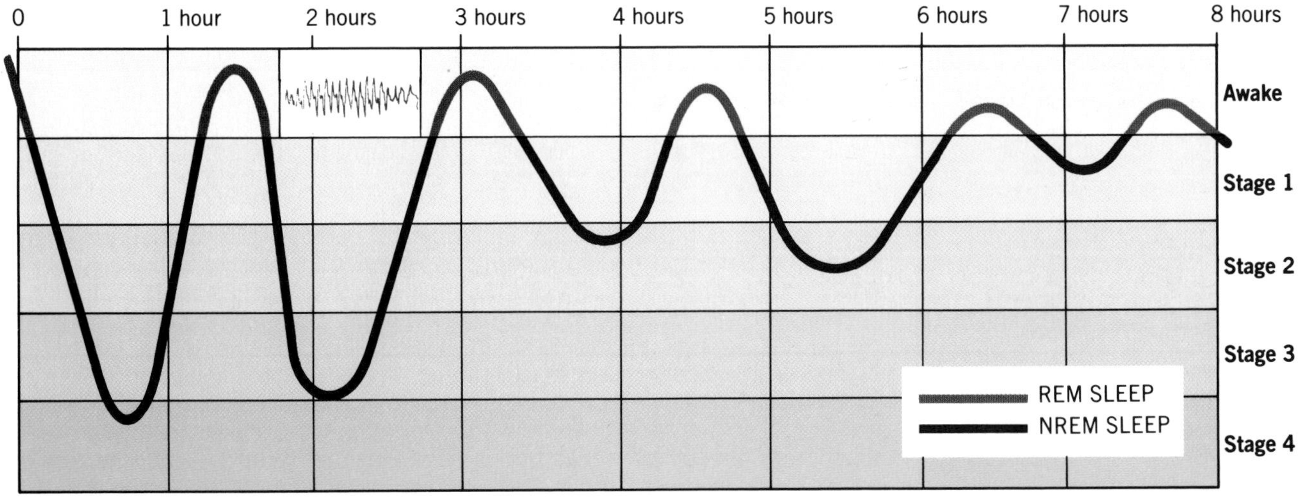

Each sleep cycle lasts up to 90 minutes or so and is mostly NREM sleep. During NREM sleep, the EEG has detected four stages of sleep, although all four usually occur only during the early hours of the night and stages 4, 3, and even 2 may be skipped toward morning. Each NREM cycle is followed by 5 to 35 minutes of REM, or dreaming, sleep.

When the Need for Sleep Changes

How much sleep do we need?

Most adults feel best getting somewhere around eight hours' sleep a night. But there are "natural short sleepers" who regularly sleep only a few hours a night and still maintain good health and vigor. In fact, if they happen to sleep longer one night, they may even feel tired and groggy the next day.

There's a limit, however. In Italy a man had a mysterious malady that was later discovered to be a deterioration of the thalamus in the limbic area of the brain. For months he could not sleep more than an hour a night. Then a lung infection attacked his exhausted body, and he died at the age of 53.

At the opposite extreme, there also seems to be a limit to how long a healthy person can sleep. Even people who have been up for days can seldom sleep more than 17 or 18 hours.

The body can "change its mind" about how much sleep it needs. One young scholar had always slept eight or so hours until one night he abruptly woke after four hours and could not doze off again. From then on, through a long and very active career as a university professor, he never slept more than four hours a night.

Is sleep our natural state?

Perhaps the most intriguing theory about why we sleep is that of sleep researcher Nathaniel Kleitman. He proposed that sleep is our natural condition and we must be stimulated into wakefulness by sensory experiences and by muscular activity. Without such stimulation, we stay asleep.

When Sleep and Dreams Are Lost Deliberately

Going without sleep is nothing new in human experience. In times of crisis—from warfare to cramming for exams—people are able to force themselves to stay awake. But it was not until well into the twentieth century that sleep and science came together. Since then, hundreds of sleep laboratories have sprung up around the world to study the nature and function of sleep and dreams.

Marathon dancing, with prize money going to those who danced the longest, was a Depression-era phenomenon—and an accidental exercise in sleep deprivation.

The discovery of rapid-eye-movement sleep, REM, in 1952 gave the first full-scale impetus to sleep research, some of which took place in the public eye. In 1959, in New York City, a disc jockey decided to stay up for eight days straight to publicize a charity. At the end of that time, he had become paranoid and subject to hallucinations, hearing voices and sounds that did not exist. From a scientific point of view, the experiment proved useless because the disc jockey, in his sleepless paranoia, refused to answer researchers' questions.

Dr. William C. Dement, a prominent sleep researcher, confirmed, from his own experiences, that sleep deprivation can lead to paranoia. He reported that after 48 hours without sleep "I sometimes became mildly suspicious that my roommates were hostile and plotting against me."

There are other consequences of lack of sleep. People often have difficulty focusing their eyes, and the desire for food increases. They may also be more sensitive to pain. In a study of soldiers involved in war games, the Israeli army reported that the men who had lost sleep did not lose their skill as marksmen but tended to ignore important basics, such as filling their water bottles (a *must* in desert warfare). Thus, though specific skills may not decline, lack of sleep apparently saps self-discipline, motivation, and will power.

Unexpectedly, the many experiments conducted in sleep deprivation prove that there are no serious long-term effects. One good night's sleep can make up for any number of hours lost in sleep-deprivation experiments.

Dream deprivation has also been investigated. In one experiment conducted by William Dement, a volunteer spent eight hours a night in a sleep lab. He was awakened immediately whenever he fell into dreaming sleep. Outside the lab, he was supervised to ensure his wakefulness. During the first night the volunteer had to be awakened five or six times to prevent dreaming. On each successive night he had to be awakened more often. Only with rough tactics—struggling with him, holding him up, and yelling in his ear— could he be awakened from his dream sleep. Dement realized that depriving the volunteer of dream time simply increased his need to dream and the rapidity with which he arrived at the dream state. It became clear to Dement that the need for dreaming is so great that, in order to stop a sleeper from dreaming, *all* sleep had to be prevented.

When we sleep or dream, we enter an altered state of consciousness, whose precise purpose in our lives is still not scientifically established. Human experience, however, tells us that when we are deprived of either, we no longer function at our best.

Does the need for sleep change with age?

Brand-new parents soon find out just how different the sleep patterns of infants are from those of adults. A newborn baby usually sleeps a total of 15 or 16 hours a day—twice as much as the parents—but its sleeping and eating are typically arranged on a four-hour cycle. That can make a nursing mother feel that she will never know a good night's sleep again. After about three months, however, the baby's sleep pattern begins to shift to the parents' schedule.

Nature allows for amazing variation. One baby girl suffering from colic slept only five and a half hours a day through her first months. The experience made her parents bleary-eyed but had no long-term effects on them or the girl.

As children mature, they need less sleep. By the teens, sleep time has usually stabilized and only very gradually declines during adulthood, with women as a rule sleeping slightly more than men. Compared to other age groups, people past middle age tend to have a greater variation in their sleeping patterns. For example, a substantial percentage of individuals in their seventies sleep only five or six hours, while other 70-year-olds average nine or ten hours a night.

Sleep Champions of the Animal Kingdom

Although almost all animals and even plants have regular cycles of activity and inactivity, only mammals and birds seem to have the kind of sleep we experience, with its several stages, including REM.

Based on studies of animals in captivity, the world's champion sleeper appears to be the two-toed sloth, logging a total of 20 hours every 24-hour day. That's truly slothful compared to the elephant, which may sleep as little as three hours a day. Why the difference? One reason may be that in its natural habitat the sloth slumbers in the treetops, relatively safe from danger, while the elephant must be always alert for big cats lurking in the grasslands. Matching the elephant in wakefulness is the giraffe, followed by such creatures as the horse, sheep, cow, and guinea pig.

Man and mole tie at eight hours of sleep. Opossums and armadillos fall just short of the sloth's 20 hours, while hamsters, rats, spiny anteaters, jaguars, and pigs snooze for about half of every 24-hour day.

In the comfort of our homes dogs and cats, as well as other kinds of pets and domesticated animals, sleep longer and sounder than they would if they had to exist in the wild. Their need for wakefulness—to hunt for food and to avoid being eaten—is reduced. A housebound cat or dog may sleep a total of 13 or 14 hours a day.

What happens when sleep and work are at odds?

Many kinds of workers, such as police officers and factory employees, are asked to accommodate their sleep schedules to changing work shifts. A week on the night shift, for example, might be followed by a couple of days off, then assignment to the swing shift, and after a while, on to the day shift. This constantly alters the time when alertness is required of a worker and can upset an individual's natural circadian rhythms, which are cycles of just under 25 hours, according to which a person may feel energetic at certain times of the day and lethargic at other times.

Shift workers often experience sleep disorders, as well as a tendency to develop ulcers or other digestive problems. Abnormal schedules and changing shifts may also have far wider implications. On the late night (or "graveyard") shift, many workers' circadian rhythms are telling them to sleep. The accidents at the Three Mile Island and Chernobyl nuclear plants and the massive disaster at a chemical plant in Bhopal, India, all occurred during graveyard shifts.

Certain drug or hormonal treatments may eventually prove effective in resetting circadian rhythms for shift workers. But for the present, researchers suggest two simple ways to minimize the disruptions and dangers of shift work. Shift changes should move forward from day to evening to night rather than the reverse. And workers should remain in a particular shift for at least three weeks.

Of Sleepwalking and Insomnia

***In the TV comedy,* The Honeymooners,** *Ralph Kramden (Jackie Gleason) boils with exasperation at the sleepwalking Ed Norton (Art Carney). Swooping around the Kramden apartment, Norton, with pooch, still calls for his long-lost dog, "Lulu, Lulu!"*

Why do people sleepwalk?

The old idea that sleepwalkers are acting out their dreams has been challenged by the finding that sleepwalking tends to occur early in the night and at stages 3 and 4 of NREM sleep—when little or no dreaming is thought to occur. However, despite a great deal of research and laboratory observation, the reasons for sleepwalking remain almost as mysterious today as they were in the past.

Sleepwalking is rare among adults, and rarer in women than it is in men. About 20 percent of children aged 5 to 7, especially when they are overtired, are likely to sleepwalk at some time. Most children outgrow sleepwalking, which may be associated with night terrors and bed-wetting. Dr. William C. Dement, founder of a sleep clinic at Stanford University, strongly believes that patience is the best policy for parents of sleepwalking children. "Most treatments are ineffective," says Dement, "and generally only make the child anxious."

Among adults sleepwalking has been found to occur as a side effect of certain drugs. Anyone taking medication who suddenly begins sleepwalking should check with the doctor. Because stress, too, can promote sleepwalking, a regular schedule and sufficient sleep are good preventive measures. Drugs that inhibit sleepwalking exist but are prescribed only in extreme cases.

Should you wake a sleepwalker?

Sleepwalkers who are shocked awake will likely be disoriented and confused. Try very gently to help them find their own way to a couch, the floor, or back to their beds. Sometimes a softly repeated suggestion will do the trick. When waking them is necessary, try repeating their names, very quietly, over and over again.

Sleepwalkers are rarely violent toward others. Their greatest threat is to themselves as they wander. There have been tragic instances of a sleepwalker falling headlong down stairs or mistaking a window for a door. Some chronic sleepwalkers have tied themselves to their beds. Others, before going to bed, have roped off dangerous areas.

Is it true that some sleepers must wake up to breathe?

Sleep apnea is a disorder in which a sleeping person repeatedly stops breathing and must at least partially wake up to breathe again. This may happen as many as 500 times a night, but the morning after, apnea sufferers seldom clearly remember their struggles with breathing.

Unsuspecting apnea victims often wonder why they are so terribly tired during the day. Worse, because the disorder is robbing their bodies and brains of oxygen, they have a greater risk of heart problems, high blood pressure, and behavioral and psychiatric disorders, including irritability, aggression, and depression.

In one type of sleep apnea, found most often in middle-aged men, the throat muscles relax too much and close off the air passage. After about a minute without air, the person comes partly out of sleep, usually with a terrific snort. Staying in a state of semiwakefulness just long enough to get oxygen, the person then falls back into sounder sleep, only to repeat the same process in a few minutes.

Another type of sleep apnea is more common among the elderly. The brain fails to tell the diaphragm muscles in the chest to expand and contract, and the person must periodically struggle to breathe, often with a violent heaving of the chest wall.

Certain medications and sometimes surgery are effective against apnea. There is also a nasal mask designed to help push air through the breathing passages during sleep.

Do some people fall asleep without warning?

Narcolepsy is sleepiness carried to an almost unbelievable extreme. A narcoleptic is someone who cannot help suddenly, uncontrollably falling asleep. It can happen in the middle of an important business conversation, working on an assembly line, driving a car, or even making love. A person with severe narcolepsy may experience dozens of sleep attacks a day, each lasting 15 or 20 minutes. In milder cases a person may have only a couple of episodes a month. Needless to say, narcolepsy can be life-threatening, not to mention socially and psychologically devastating.

To add to their troubles, narcoleptics may suffer cataplexy. Usually in a moment of strong emotion such as anger or laughter, a person loses muscle control and collapses in a heap while remaining fully conscious.

Considering all these symptoms, together with the fact that many narcoleptics experience paralysis and vivid hallucinations just before falling asleep, some researchers think that narcolepsy must involve the same brain processes that regulate REM sleep. They speculate that the brain's ability to paralyze the body during REM sleep, which prevents us from acting out our dreams, is out of control, producing paralysis and sleep any time, any place.

As many as 100,000 people in the United States have some form of narcolepsy. It runs in families, and researchers are zeroing in on the genes that may be responsible. No cure yet exists, but certain stimulants can limit narcolepsy attacks. Antidepressant drugs are used to control cataplexy.

Why do some people have trouble sleeping?

Nearly a third of American adults report some difficulty with sleep, and more than half of those consider their sleeping problems a major disruption in their lives. The complaints are usually of insomnia, the inability to sleep at night, and hypersomnia, excessive sleepiness during the day.

According to psychologists, most sleep problems have underlying causes that are either temporary or can be effectively treated. For example, family or job worries are a frequent cause of insomnia. When they clear up, so may the insomnia.

In recent studies, a number of sleep clinics investigated complaints of sleep loss. They found that 10 percent of the patients who reported severe insomnia actually slept a full eight hours a night. These "pseudo-insomniacs" apparently have a problem of perception that causes them genuinely to believe that they sleep as little as three or four hours a night. That belief is so firmly held that it affects their whole day, making them feel constantly tired.

Do sleeping pills help insomnia?

One trouble with sleeping pills and alcoholic "nightcaps" is that regular users can develop a tolerance for them and need ever greater doses to fall asleep. The risk of dependency and addiction is great.

Moreover, the sleep induced by pills and alcohol is rarely quality sleep. It tends to be shallow and fitful, with little REM or dreaming sleep. People who break a sleeping-pill dependency may have "REM rebound," which can temporarily cause severe nightmares and other disturbances. Former pill users say it is worth enduring to be free of dependency.

Not all medications for disturbed sleep are useless or, worse, harmful. If taken according to a physician's instructions and used for no more than a few weeks, some medications can help people get some badly needed sleep. However, many doctors would agree with one expert's wry comment that "the best treatment for insomnia is to grab patients by the feet and shake until all the medications fall out of their pockets."

One Strategy for Victims of Insomnia

This plan is based on one used by Richard M. Coleman, a former codirector of the Stanford University Sleep Disorders Clinic. Whereas Dr. Coleman may prescribe sedatives for short-term insomnia, the steps suggested here avoid their use.

Chronic insomniacs should aim for a specific number of hours of sleep, perhaps 4 to 5 hours, which approximates their current maximum sleep time. Once the insomniac sleeps about 90 percent of the allotted time—say 4½ out of 5 hours—then the sleep schedule can be increased by 30 to 60 minutes.

- Get into bed at 1:00 A.M. and get out of bed at 5:00 A.M., even if you are blissfully asleep. You are trying to establish a structured sleep schedule, so rigid timing is important. Set your alarm for the chosen wakeup hour.
- The bedroom must be completely dark while you sleep, but be sure to turn on the lights or raise the shades as soon as you get up.
- If awake and relaxed during sleep period, stay in bed.
- If you cannot help feeling anxious about being awake during a sleep period and efforts to relax do not work, get out of bed.
- When you are out of bed, do household chores (laundry, cleaning, paying bills, etc.). If you feel sleepy, get back into bed. No matter what time you return to bed, get up at 5 A.M.
- Avoid alcohol, caffeine, and cigarettes within 5 hours of your bedtime. If possible, stop smoking and drinking alcohol and cut back on caffeine drinks.
- Do not exercise within 2 hours of bedtime. Over all, exercise is not a key factor in improving sleep. Neither are meals. But it is best to avoid spicy foods near bedtime.
- If active thoughts persist near or during bedtime, keep a diary. Put aside 20 minutes after dinner and work on your worries. Write the problems down, along with short-term or long-term solutions.
- Avoid naps during the day.

If you stick to these rules, you should get good results within three to five weeks. Remember, following the sleep schedule is probably 75 percent of the battle. Keeping a sleep diary can contribute to the cure.

Those who are not helped by this treatment may suffer from a psychological or physiological problem and should consult a sleep specialist.

Fascinating Dream Worlds

What are dreams?

Each night, after the lights go out, the curtain goes up on a theater inside our heads. As actors or audience (or both), we replay fragments of the day's events as well as longer-ago experiences and emotions.

Dream scenarios range from the mundane to the marvelous to the macabre. No matter how extreme they are, our sleeping minds always accept these hallucinations as normal. They are "only dreams." When we dream, we inhabit a subjective, internal world, where reason and reality no longer dominate.

At least sometimes, dreams seem to help people cope with their daily lives. In one study, students were monitored by machines that indicated dreaming. The students were then presented with a problem just before falling asleep. Some of the students were allowed to dream uninterruptedly; the others were awakened when they dreamed. The experiment found that the students who had been allowed to dream had a clearer idea of how to solve the problems they had heard before going to sleep.

Why do I have trouble remembering my dreams?

Part of the reason dreams are hard to remember may be that many dreams are not that memorable. Much of the dreaming we do every night involves very mundane stuff.

It may also be that the brain is programmed to forget dreams. This intriguing theory starts with the fact that in some respects the brain is very much awake while we dream. For example, researchers have found that brain-wave patterns during REM sleep are almost identical to those of the waking state.

However, while some brain functions (such as vision and hearing) remain switched on during dreaming sleep, others (such as motor control) are switched off. If memory is also one of the brain functions that rests during dreaming, this could account for our difficulty remembering dreams.

The memory-shutdown theory might also explain the common misconception that most of us do not dream in color, when in fact people abruptly awakened by researchers from REM cycles often report dreaming in vivid colors. The memory of colors in dreams may be even quicker to fade than the memory of the dreams themselves.

Can you control your dreams?

The Senoi tribe of Malaysia believed that dreams reflected not only current feelings but also feelings that were about to develop. For this reason, the Senoi were most anxious to have their dreams suggest happy, positive experiences. To ensure this, a dream whose content was antagonistic to someone had to be followed by a dream that promised reconciliation. And children who had nightmares were encouraged to dream of the conflict again, either to conquer or to conciliate the threatening dream figure.

Some dream researchers have discovered that the power of suggestion can alter the content of dreams. Either autosuggestion (self-coaching) or suggestions from someone else may work. Such methods are said to have helped people suffering from recurrent and frightening nightmares, or even from occasional scary dreams.

The power to gain some control over one's dreams is an aspect of so-called lucid dreaming. An example of lucid dreaming is training oneself not to wake up at a terrifying moment in a nightmare but, instead, to remain asleep and face the dream monster the mind has created.

Sleep researcher Stephen LaBerge, who uses himself as a test subject in exploring the potential of lucid dreaming, has developed several techniques to help achieve a state of awareness while dreaming. In one technique, having awakened from a dream, a person focuses on the dream he or she has just had; as the person drifts back to sleep, he or she repeats over and over, "The next time I dream, I want to recognize that I'm dreaming." At the same time, the person tries to visualize himself or herself dreaming and *knowing* all the time that it is a dream.

In dreams we return to dwelling places of our past. *What the dream means depends on the dreamer—whether the house was where, in childhood, one was cherished, overwhelmed, or ignored. Or the house may be a home of one's adult years—or a place merely visited. It is often the abode of emotion: homesickness, nostalgia, fear, longing.*

Why keep a dream diary?

A dream journal helps you to remember your dreams and to explore the messages your unconscious mind is sending to your conscious mind. Keep a pad of paper and a pencil by your bed. Whenever you awaken (even in the middle of the night), take a moment to jot down quickly what you remember. With a little practice, you'll be able to scrawl quite legible notes in the dark.

In the morning, refer to your notes and write out your dreams. You'll be surprised how, with the aid of just a few key words, the dreams of the night before will come to mind.

Can dreams really produce great ideas and inspired solutions?

Elias Howe had worked for years on a machine to mechanize sewing, but couldn't get it right. Then one night he had a dream in which he was attacked by savages. They gave him an ultimatum: make a machine that sews or die! As the dream warriors raised their spears, Howe noticed holes through the tips of the weapons. That was the answer: a needle with a hole at the point instead of the shank!

Artists too have credited dreams with inspiring some of their best work. Samuel Taylor Coleridge claimed the entire poem "Kubla Khan" came to him in a dream. A dream supplied Robert Louis Stevenson with a plot twist for *The Strange Case of Dr. Jekyll and Mr. Hyde.*

But it is questionable whether dreams alone are ever the sole source of creative solutions or expressions, and it is hardly advisable to abandon all conscious efforts at problem solving in favor of letting dreams do it.

As the Nobel Prize winning biochemist, Albert Szent-Györgyi, said, "My work is not finished when I leave my workbench. I go on thinking about my problems. My brain must continue to think about them when I sleep because I wake up with answers to questions that have been puzzling me." Dream solutions are best arrived at after a liberal amount of good, old-fashioned, wide-awake work.

PERSPECTIVES

On Sleep and Dreams

Shakespeare's famous description of sleep holds true. Indeed, sleep "knits up the ravell'd sleave of care"—and it gives rise to mysterious dreams as well.

How Sweet Is Sleep

"Blessings light on him who first invented sleep!—it covers a man all over, body and mind, like a cloak; it is meat to the hungry, drink to the thirsty, heat to the cold, and cold to the hot; it is the coin that can purchase all things; the balance that makes the shepherd equal with the king, the fool with the wise man. . . ." **—Miguel de Cervantes**
Don Quixote

◆

Holing Up

"Psychologically, sleep can sometimes be a vehicle for retreating from reality. All of us have experienced the kinds of stresses in which the most comfortable thing to do upon awakening would be to duck under the covers and escape reality by sleeping some more. . . ." **—Dr. Julius Segal**

◆

Nightmare of Nightmares

"When you're lying awake with a
dismal headache, and respose is
taboo'd by anxiety,
I conceive you may use any language
you choose to indulge in, without
impropriety;
For your brain is on fire—the
bedclothes conspire of usual
slumber to plunder you:
First your counterpane goes, and
uncovers your toes, and your sheet
slips demurely from under you;
Then the blanketing tickles—you
feel like mixed pickles—so terribly
sharp is the pricking,
And you're hot, and you're cross,
and you tumble and toss till there's
nothing 'twixt you and the ticking.
Then the bedclothes all creep to the
ground in a heap, and you pick
'em all up in a tangle;
Next your pillow resigns and politely
declines to remain at its usual
angle!
Well, you get some repose in the
form of a doze, with hot eye-balls
and head ever aching,
But your slumbering teems with such
horrible dreams that you'd very
much better be waking. . . .

"You're a regular wreck, with a crick in your neck, and no wonder you snore, for your head's on the floor, and you've needles and pins from your soles to your shins, and your flesh is a-creep, for your left leg's asleep, and you've cramp in your toes, and a fly on your nose, and some fluff in your lung, and a feverish tongue, and a thirst that's intense, and a general sense that you haven't been sleeping in clover.

"But the darkness has passed, and it's daylight at last, and the night has been long—ditto ditto my song—and thank goodness they're both of them over!" **—Sir William S. Gilbert**
Iolanthe

◆

The Unconscious Mind at Work

"The German chemist Friedrich August Kekule von Stradonitz, who, had he lived another decade, might have been awarded a Nobel Prize for proposing the ring form of the benzene molecule, told how this radical idea came to him in a dream. In his fantasy, he imagined molecules were dancing about, some of them with the shape of snakes. One of these whirling snake molecules seized its own tail in its mouth. 'Like a flash of lightning,' Kekule's sleeping mind recognized that here lay the explanation for the puzzling properties of benzene! 'Learn to dream, gentlemen,' he wrote later. 'Then we shall, perhaps, find the truth. We must take care, however, not to publish our dreams before submitting them to proof by the awakened mind.' "
—Lorus and Margery Milne
The Senses of Animals and Men

◆

Time Out

"Dreaming permits each and every one of us to be quietly and safely insane every night of our lives."
—Charles Fisher, M.D.
The Senses of Animals and Men

Riddles from the Unconscious

When are we most likely to have nightmares?

A nightmare has been called a "dream anxiety attack." Most nightmares occur toward the middle or end of a night's sleep, rather than near the beginning, and we invariably remember some of them, although most of us would probably rather forget the feelings of terror, dread, oppression, and helplessness that characterize a nightmare. Few real-life events have the emotional intensity of a bad nightmare, from which we can awake panic-stricken, gasping for breath, hearts beating wildly.

Nightmares may be linked to stress. Traumatic experiences, such as an automobile accident or combat, often leave a legacy of emotional turmoil that erupts in nightmares. Physical illness can also bring on nightmares, though whether it is the illness or the accompanying emotional stress that is more at fault is not clear.

Drug and alcohol abuse can cause nightmares, and so, too, can prescribed medications. If you think a medicine is giving you bad dreams,

Theorists and Theories: **The Unsolved Mysteries of Dreaming.**

Fascination with the meaning of dreams reaches far back in history. To ancient peoples, dreams were messages from the gods to be interpreted by priests and oracles. Books on dream meanings have always been popular. A surviving papyrus from the 12th century B.C., the work of Egyptian priests, interprets 200 dream symbols. The Interpretation of Dreams, *from the second century A.D., was republished in England in 1644 and quickly became a best-seller, going into 24 editions.*

Aristotle, Greek, fourth century B.C.

Dreams echo our emotions distorted by sleep, hence dreams are fragmentary and confused.

René Descartes, French, 1596-1650

When we sleep our nerves, which connect the brain with the body, are at rest and slack, diminishing outside stimulation. But sometimes, during sleep, the nerves tighten, and then the sensations received by the brain produce dreams.

Sigmund Freud, Austrian, 1856-1939

In his pioneering work, *The Interpretation of Dreams,* published in 1899, Freud describes dreams as an expression of our unconscious desires and wishes that are suppressed during waking hours. These wishes usually take the form of repressed sexual drives, and much of the symbolism of dreams is connected to sexual desires. In our dreams, we ignore the acquired standards of thought and behavior imposed by society. Freud's theories, which saw dreams as wish fulfillment, left little room for an explanation of nightmares. At first, he proposed that nightmares are a form of wishing for punishment but, dissatisfied with this explanation, he later suggested that some nightmares may be part of a repetition compulsion—a need to repeat an experience. However, neither theory satisfied him, and Freud avoided the subject in his later writings.

Erich Fromm saw dream symbols as personal and often literal.

Alfred Adler, Austrian, 1870-1937

Dreams originate in the unresolved problems of daily life. They may deal with continuing problems or with those we expect to face. Danger, in a dream, may be symbolized by a fall or we may dream that we have lost our passport if we are worried about an impending trip.

Carl Jung, Swiss, 1875-1961

Dreams are a step in the development of a personality and as such are not just tools for treating neurotic people but can also help people seeking self-knowledge. We dream in term of opposities; if, for instance, we feel weak and timid, we dream of strength. Every dream must be interpreted differently for each individual because dreams reflect our personal relationship to universal experiences. Dreams can also be prophetic.

Erich Fromm, German-born American, 1900-80

In our dreams we express our inner feelings using knowledge we have gained from external experience. For instance, someone whom you believe to be a coward will turn into a chicken in your dreams. The symbolism of dreams follows an inner logic but not the logic of day-to-day reality.

Current Theories

Many researchers today tend to give physiological rather than psychological explanations of dreams. One theory states that dreams are triggered when random signals are spontaneously released by neurons in the lower brain (the pons), and these signals in turn activate other neurons involved with eye movements, balance, and voluntary movements. Dreams are the result of the cortex trying to make sense of the barrage of random signals. This theory has been named the activation-synthesis theory. It has been criticized for failing to account for the emotional content of dreams.

Another theory likens the brain to a computer that must file and sort incoming data. When we sleep, our brain sorts waking experiences, filing some and discarding others. Dreams are what we remember of this housecleaning process.

A somewhat similar theory states that while we sleep the brain discards useless information and also perhaps unacceptable fantasies, obsessions, and behavior. Dreams, in other words, are a process of forgetting and should not be examined. Psychologists refer to this and similar interpretations of dreams as "dumping" theories.

tell your doctor or pharmacist at once so that it can be adjusted or changed. In some cases, serious mental illness may be signaled by nightmares, especially if they are severe and recurring.

Scientists distinguish between nightmares and *night terrors*, the term for terrifying nocturnal experiences that mainly affect young children in deep sleep. The principal difference is that the sleeper seldom remembers a night terror. Sleepers in the throes of a night terror often awaken to the feeling of being suffocated or choked.

Can dreams foretell the future?

Most of us have heard a story of someone who had a prophetic dream. Grandma dreamed that lightning would strike the big oak tree, and it did. Joe down the street dreamed Old Paint would win the seventh race, and that's what the old horse did. On hearing such stories, skeptics often wonder how many such prophetic dreams turned out to be wrong.

Such skepticism has not always been shared by great thinkers, among them the hugely influential psychologist Carl Jung. He firmly believed that dreams sometimes foretold future events. In his memoirs, *Memories, Dreams, Reflections,* he relates how he dreamed that a cold Arctic wind was sweeping through the European countryside and freezing the land to ice. In his dream, the entire region was deserted by human beings and all vegetation had been killed by the frost. It was June of 1914, two months before the outbreak of World War I.

Sleep researcher Richard M. Coleman once predicted a sporting event in a dream, including the exact score and a scenario featuring the game-winning play by the player who made it. Coleman explains his prophetic dream by using the theory of probability. Figuring in the number of fans thinking about the upcoming game, the amount of dreaming time each fan would experience, the number of players on a team, and the combination of possible scores, it seemed probable that *somebody* would dream the correct outcome.

Other theorists might say that Coleman's sleeping brain had merely pulled together his knowledge of the sport and the players involved and handicapped the game (successfully) in his sleep. The same theorists might explain Jung's experience in a similar way: Jung had been reading the newspaper, knew how volatile the political situation was, and had a subsequent anxiety dream concerning a possible war.

The fact remains that dreams do sometimes foretell events that come to pass (just as they predict events that *never* come to pass). The reasons for this, as for so many questions about dreams, are likely to remain a mystery for some time to come.

This famous romantic painting, **Nightmare,** *by the British-Swiss artist, Henry Fuseli (1741-1825) portrays, literally, the terror evoked by a trampling steed. Fuseli himself once said, "One of the least explored regions of art is that of dreams."*

Do blind people see images in their dreams?

Though they do not use vision to relate to their dream world, people blind from birth report dreams in which other senses, such as touch, take the place of sight. One woman, for instance, heard the sound of a washing machine in her dreams. Those who were born with sight but later lost it report varying degrees of visual imagery in their dreams.

Researchers have recorded some eye movement during REM cycles in the congenitally blind. Moreover, eye movements have been observed in the blind who were born sighted.

The Brain-Computer Comparison

Is the comparison between the brain and computer valid?

There are similarities between the brain's neural network and a computer's intricate circuitry. Each one is a complex of well-coordinated interconnections that sends messages back and forth. Each one groups and regroups information, stores it, and uses it to solve problems. And either can be wrong if the information is wrong. "Garbage in, garbage out," is as true of the brain as it is of a computer.

Even though the computer is a marvelous invention, it is in no way as extraordinary as the human brain. The chief advantage of a computer is its phenomenal speed. It can retrieve a wealth of data or whiz through complex calculations in a matter of seconds or less. But in the end, a computer is simply a machine built by humans that reacts to the commands and data supplied by humans.

It is no longer quite accurate to say that machines cannot think, because some computers have been designed to apply reason in solving certain well-defined problems. However, no computer even comes close to matching the brain's simultaneous abilities to observe, imagine, initiate, anticipate, and be inspired. And, unlike any computer yet designed, the human brain is capable of constantly adapting to new experiences.

Impressed by the computer's prodigious speed and skill with numbers, we often underrate the brain's abilities. But commonly, if a person cannot find a screwdriver, he or she may decide to substitute a coin or even a fingernail, which a computer could not do without elaborate programming.

Computers are inferior to the brains of the simplest of creatures. When it comes to such things as seeing, moving, and responding to stimuli, no computer can rival a fly.

Is a computer better organized than a brain is?

The brain is not organized merely to solve a certain set of well-defined problems. Our vast reservoir of memory and our ability to call up ideas or feelings from the past and associate them with other ideas or feelings give the human brain creative powers that cannot be matched by a conventional computer's calculations and comparisons. Moreover, our minds supply meaning and context to new situations as they arise.

We have a unique ability to combine our thoughts with sensations and feelings. We can remember not only names, faces, facts, and figures, but can also recall a mother's soothing voice, the feel of terry cloth against sunburned skin, or the smell of a campfire. This ability to interweave information and sensation gives our thoughts their rich complexity.

High-Tech Friends and Foes in Modern Yarns

From lovable Robby the Robot in the 1950's classic *Forbidden Planet* to omnipresent HAL in *2001: A Space Odyssey* and the vicious hitman in *The Terminator*, our movies and other fictional media have been infiltrated by computers, both stationary and mobile. These stories demonstrate not only our awe at the capabilities of computers, but our ambivalence as well. We prize computers as intelligent companions and workmates but also fear they may become tyrannical masters and agents of wholesale destruction.

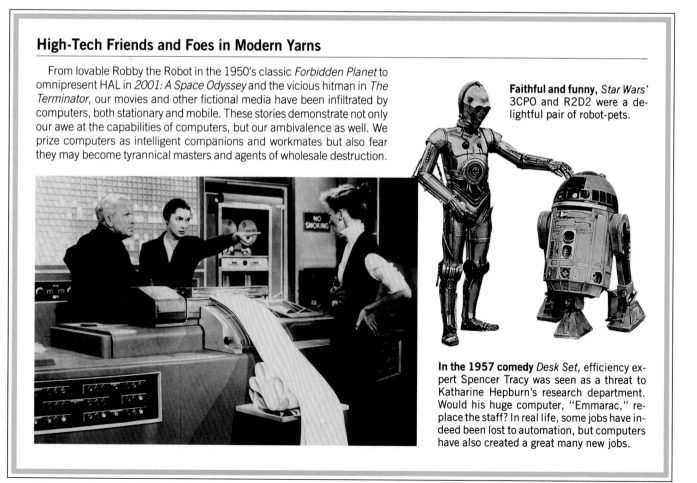

Faithful and funny, *Star Wars'* 3CPO and R2D2 were a delightful pair of robot-pets.

In the 1957 comedy *Desk Set*, efficiency expert Spencer Tracy was seen as a threat to Katharine Hepburn's research department. Would his huge computer, "Emmarac," replace the staff? In real life, some jobs have indeed been lost to automation, but computers have also created a great many new jobs.

How does computerized artificial intelligence compare with our brains?

After some 30 years of developing artificial intelligence, researchers have been able to imitate some of the brain's intellectual functions on computers, but others are still out of reach and are likely to remain so for the foreseeable future. For example, computers with artificial intelligence often perform well when used to make simulated models of new machines such as automobiles, and test the probable effect of various design changes on those models. But the computers offer less help when evaluating what kind of machine should be built in the first place. For this kind of design decision, the human brain is still indispensable.

When it comes to performing physical acts, the intelligent robots used in industry can move, detect motion, and perform repetitive tasks. But they cannot handle the unexpected, something that they have not been programmed to react to. Similarly, with language, computers can generate intelligible sounds and recognize speech patterns. But they cannot understand in the sense of being able to take into account the context of words.

Can a computer learn from experience as we do?

Nobel laureate Gerald Edelman developed a computer simulation of how we learn. In it, a small creature called Darwin III appeared on the screen, as in a video game. The creature did not follow a set pattern of action. Rather it had the ability to "see" and "feel" other creatures and it had a "brain" with thousands of connections and storage cells, which enabled it to receive, exchange, associate, and remember information. After thousands of trials, Darwin III "learned" to coordinate what it saw with what it felt. It was able to act on an acquired inclination: it responded to certain other computer "creatures" that it could both feel and see. In this very limited way, computers can learn from experience. But even the simplest animal can easily do far more.

Changing Models of the Brain Through the Ages

How the brain works has long been an intriguing puzzle, and in every age people tend to liken it to the most advanced technologies of their time. When aqueduct and sewer systems were great wonders in the second century A.D., for example, the Greek physician Galen viewed the brain primarily as a vehicle for carrying fluids that he called humors.

During the Industrial Revolution, a mechanical view of the brain and senses began to develop. Later, parallels were seen between the brain and electrical circuits. And in the early days of telephones, a switchboard run by a single operator seemed a perfect metaphor for the brain. It is only natural, then, that in our time the brain has been compared to a computer. But even the most advanced computer is a relatively primitive machine when set against the complex human brain.

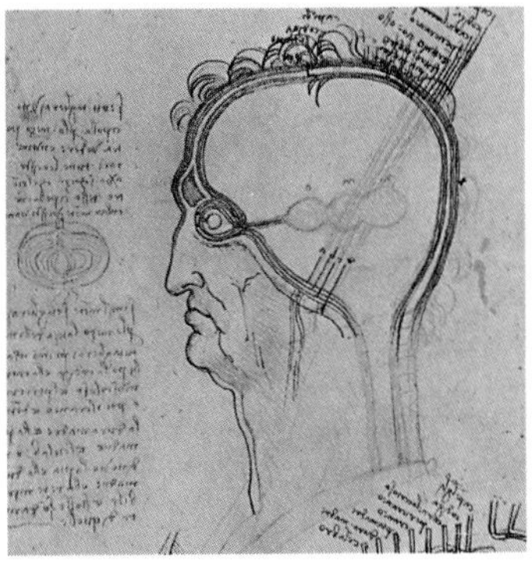

Leonardo da Vinci located the soul in the brain's "common sense cell."

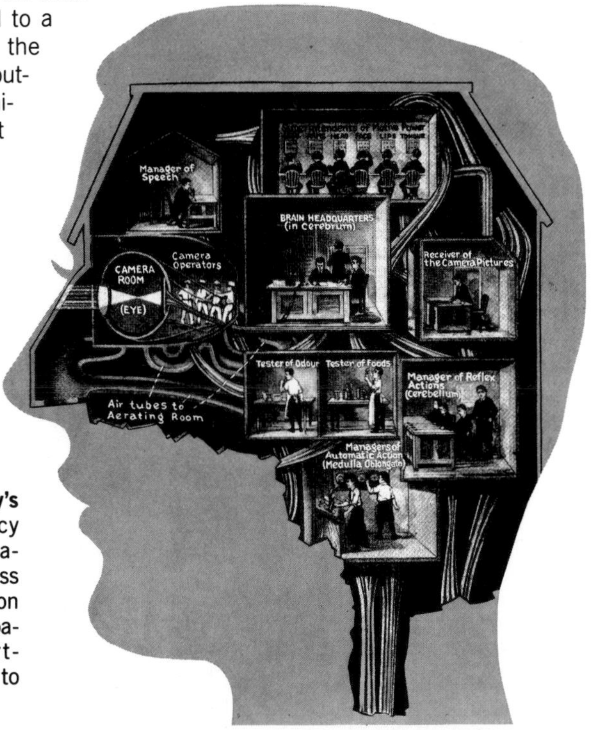

The early 20th century's faith in the efficiency and rational organization of modern business prompted this depiction of the brain. It is separated into compartments, each devoted to a special function.

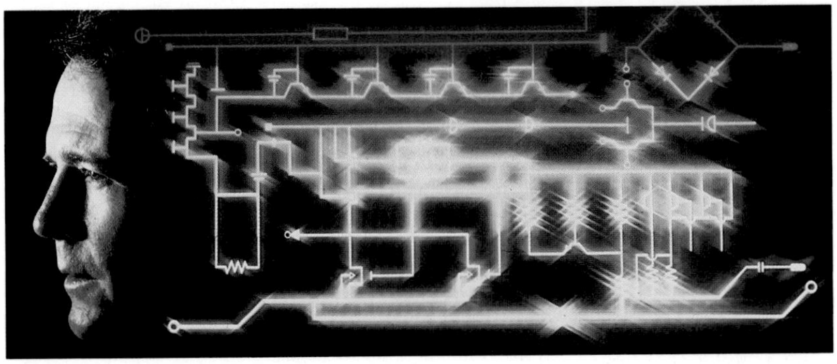

The complex circuitry of a computer chip is the common analogy for the brain today.

The Intrinsic Superiority of the Brain

Can computers help us to understand our brains?

More and more, neurologists who are engaged in brain research are working with computer scientists to explore the structure of the brain. One of the more interesting ways that they do this is by making computer models that try to mimic some of the brain's intricate connections. In effect, they create electronic networks of artificial neurons and synapses. These models have helped them develop a better understanding of how we learn and how information is processed in the human brain.

Because the brain is living tissue, however, it will always have many unique abilities that even the most complex computer simulation will be unable to duplicate. As Dr. Gerald Edelman, a leading brain researcher at New York City's Rockefeller University, notes, "No computer could begin to deal with the variation in the world, and no computer could work if it contained connections like the enormously variable nerve-cell connections that make up the brain."

Nevertheless, Edelman, who has created some exciting computer simulations of the brain, recognizes the key role of computers in brain research. "Suppose I understood everything about how the brain works," he says. "I couldn't possibly visualize the processes. Just to count the connections to the cortex at one per second would take 32 million years. For brain theory, you need computers. They're like pigment for a painter."

Why don't computers always win when playing chess?

A very fast supercomputer running a sophisticated chess program can vanquish all but the best chess players and may even beat some grand masters. In fact, a good chess program on an ordinary personal computer can be a real challenge to a skilled player.

Computer chess programs work mostly by calculating the relative advantages of potential positions for the chess pieces. And a supercomputer can calculate an enormous number of possibilities in a second. But as neurologist and author Richard M. Restak points out, "The capacity to compute hundreds of thousands of foolish or inappropriate moves is less important than selecting the one or two best."

***Computer chess expert Hans Berliner** developed a supercomputer program that has defeated many chess masters. But this program was routed by the program of a team of non-experts because their program was capable of learning from its mistakes.*

Will knowledge about how the brain works help scientists develop better computers?

If computers are ever to approach the brain's ability, they will have to process and compare information—along hundreds or even thousands of pathways at once—in much the same way as the brain's neural network does. Most computers can handle only a single stream of data, but some very advanced computers can process several parallel streams of information at the same time.

These so-called neural-network computers, researchers hope, may eventually be able to weigh the relative importance of the data in the different parallel streams. Such a computer's artificial neural network would then be able to give priority to some streams of data over others, depending on the over-all context of the situation. The great advantage of this is that it would permit the computers to recognize and put together patterns, such as shapes and sounds. Present-day computers often have to make thousands of computations to ascertain the identity of a form or a sound, something that a toddler can do in an instant without even stopping to think about it.

The development of these "neurocomputers" promises to produce enormous technological advances in such areas as speech recognition and artificial vision. Computers modeled on the brain would also be better able to "learn" than today's computers because they would have an ability to distinguish among patterns after being repeatedly presented with sets of them. With such capability, they could revolutionize the field of robotics, but they would still not be a serious challenge to the brain's abilities.

Why is the brain better able to fix itself than a computer?

Most computers today are not the easily damaged machines they once were. Some computers even have a limited capacity for self-repair, an ability instilled by human designers.

The brain is more resourceful in coping with damage. Composed of soft, fluidlike tissue, the brain is vulnerable to injury and disease. After a stroke, for example, the brain can often recognize the damage and in effect transfer some of the injured area's functions to healthy tissue. Over time, this may enable patients to regain speech, movement, and memory.

How do emotions fit into thinking?

Emotions are the wild card in human intelligence, and one of the major factors that distinguishes our thinking from even the most sophisticated machine intelligence. Emotions can result from thoughts as well as from sensory perceptions.

Emotions can also create thoughts, as when we hear a scary sound and imagine what caused it. By using emotion to interpret the clues in the environment, the brain puts the available information into a context, which then becomes a critically important part of a person's decision-making process.

It is only in science fiction that computers exhibit emotion. HAL, the sinister computer in the movie *2001*, who meddled in the affairs of the astronauts, was not just highly emotional but highly improbable as well.

PERSPECTIVES

On Brains and Computers

Who's in charge around here—the mind or the machine? When one feels threatened, it helps to remember that human beings don't need to be plugged in.

The New Energy

"Without the computer we would not have understood that information, like electricity, is a form of energy. Electricity is the cheapest, most plentiful, and most versatile energy for mechanical work. But information is energy for mind work. This is indeed the first era when energy for mind work has been available. Information through the ages has been all but completely lacking. At best it has been expensive, late, and quite unreliable. Most people in responsible positions today, whether in government, in hospitals, in research labs, or in business, spend most of their time scratching to get a little incorrect and unreliable information on what happened yesterday." **—Peter F. Drucker**
The Age of Discontinuity

◆

A Word of Caution

"The machine does not isolate man from the great problems of nature but plunges him more deeply into them."
—Antoine de Saint-Exupéry
Wind, Sand, and Stars

◆

Beyond Calculation

"Ever seen an abacus? You know, those centipedelike things with wooden beads in rows. They're sold mostly in knickknack import shops, for wall decoration. But, in fact, an abacus is an adding machine, calculator, and computer. On second thought, that's not quite true. The abacus is just a visual record of the computations going on in the mind of the person using it.

"Millions of people in Asia still use the abacus daily. And it has been in use there for a couple of thousand years or more. Not only is it an effective practical tool, but it is nice to look at. Nice to hold and touch. Wood and brass and ivory. And the older they get and the longer they are handled by a human being, the lovelier they get—smooth and dark and polished. They will last for a lifetime; they will never need updating; all the software needed to drive them is between your ears; and if they break they can be fixed by an eight-year-old with household tools.

"The presence of the abacus puts some kinds of progress in perspective. I remember a time when a Japanese-American computer conglomerate moved into the Chinese market in a big way. In order to demonstrate the value of its small pocket calculators, it arranged a contest. The great abacus-PC shootout. The guy who won—the one with the abacus, of course—was named Chan Kai Kit. Hong Kong Chinese—a senior clerk for a shipping company. It is true that the operator of the little computer did handle the pile of invoices forty-four seconds faster than Chan Kai Kit and his abacus. But the computer got the wrong answer. Seems the machine operator was in too big a hurry to prove how smart his machine was and fed it fuzzy facts. Much face was lost.

"Now don't get me wrong. Pocket calculators are here to stay, and they have their place. A Luddite I am not—machines are not evil in themselves. And a careful, thoughtful man like Chan Kai Kit might do even better with his own pocket calculator instead of his abacus—who knows? It's just that I'm a sentimentalist about the wonders of the human hand and mind. And when I find evidence that it can still hold its own in the face of the wizardry of the electronic circuitry of little chips, I am pleased. It is comforting to know that some very old and very simple ways of getting from one place to another still work." **—Robert Fulghum**
All I Really Need to Know I Learned in Kindergarten

◆

Like Magic

"The perfect computer has been developed. You just feed in your problems—and they never come out again." **—Al Goodman**

PART III

Our Amazing Senses

When do we feel most alive? Often it's on a vacation, when our senses are refreshed by change. We appreciate anew the play of shapes and colors, we savor the sea wind and enjoy the wet sand underfoot.

On a lovely, sunstruck summer day, two children shiver in delight as the icy water of a lawn sprinkler tickles their skin.

The Eye of the Beholder

Do people ever see things that aren't there?

The brain can lie about what comes to us through our senses. When we see or hear things that are not there, they are called hallucinations, and they can be caused by any number of things, including hypnosis. For example, in response to a command from a hypnotist, a person may see somebody who is not there.

Other causes of hallucinations are lack of sleep, stress, illness, drugs, and alcohol. An alcoholic suffering from delirium tremens may witness such alarming sights as purple spiders, flies crawling all over his body, or bizarre creatures like the famous "pink elephants." And someone under the influence of the hallucinogenic drug LSD may see lacelike patterns suspended before his eyes.

In a famous series of experiments in the 1950's, scientists induced hallucinations in participants by means of sensory deprivation. In the tests conducted by John C. Lilly, subjects were immersed naked in a dark, silent tank of water kept at body temperature. By thus removing most external stimuli, the researchers were testing the theory that if denied stimulation, the mind would fill in the blanks by creating its own stimulation.

After a short time the subjects of this experiment did indeed have vivid, mostly visual, hallucinations. What they saw was so remarkably graphic, in fact, that most were unable to tell when they were dreaming and when they were awake.

How Observant Are You?

Some people can glance at a scene and register everything. It's a skill you can teach yourself, just as good reporters and detectives do all the time. With practice, you will get better at noting details. To check the present state of your powers of observation, look at this painting for a minute or two, then turn to page 320 to see how much you noticed.

French painter Claude Monet sought to capture in this *Terrace at Sainte Adresse* (1856) the fleeting effects of light and color. It was not till five years later that an art critic gave a name to Monet's distinctive and influential style: impressionism.

What is the most unusual kind of hallucination?

Fatigue, among other things, can cause one of the rarest and most fascinating hallucinations known: that of the doppelgänger. A person who has this experience sees his mirror image, usually facing him from three or four feet away. It reproduces the viewer's facial expressions, posture, and movements as though reflected in a mirror. The image is said to be transparent, like a slide or movie projected on glass. In some cultures these hallucinations have been interpreted as visitations from the person's soul or as premonitions of death.

This hallucination, which usually occurs early in the morning or late at night and lasts only a matter of seconds, can appear to normal minds under stress or fatigue. However, it is more common among people with serious disorders such as epilepsy, brain lesions, migraine headaches, and states of delirium.

In particularly bizarre cases, the person may see the double standing in an adjacent room. Others have reported seeing this kind of apparition standing behind their own reflection in the mirror.

Does the average person ever "see things"?

Many of us have hallucinations every day, without remembering them. The reason they are hard to remember is that they occur in that twilight zone between waking and sleep, and only for a period of a few seconds as we are drifting off.

This phenomenon, called hypnagogic imagery, is extremely common and produces strikingly vivid hallucinations, both visual and auditory. Typical are the sounds of familiar voices, a telephone ringing, the laughter of children, or a dog's bark; sights include familiar faces, pets, beautiful landscapes, and water flowing in brooks or waterfalls. Those who are lucky enough to remember these hallucinations say that they are astonishingly real, with amazing detail, crisp clarity, and bright, lifelike colors.

PERSPECTIVES

On Our Senses

Sometimes, it takes the eyes and ears—the keen perceptions—of another person to open our minds to the richness of sensations around us.

The Skilled Observer

" 'I collect for my eye,' sculptress Louise Nevelson said. And she had an exceptional eye.

"She believed that any of us can live in great beauty anywhere, as long as we're alive to our environment. She lived near the Bowery in New York City. Even from there, she could 'see the world.'

"Sitting in her dining room and looking out at the huge building that stood across the street, she found varying patterns in the way the sun and the moon reflected on its windows. She could look at a chair and say, 'The chair isn't so hot, but look at its shadow.' "

—**Natalie S. Bober**
Breaking Tradition

◆

Everyday Miracles

"Consider the capabilities involved in strolling down the sidewalk. Leaving aside such things as balance and coordination, you still have to see where you are going, which means you somehow have to make sense out of the ever-changing swirl of motion and color and light and shadow.

"To accomplish this, you have at your command roughly 100 million receptor cells—the rods and cones—in the retina of each eye. The retina also contains four other layers of nerve cells; all together the system probably makes the equivalent of ten billion calculations a second before the image information even gets to the optic nerve. And once the visual data reaches the brain, the cerebral cortex has more than a dozen separate vision centers in which to process it. In fact, it has been estimated that vision in one form or another involves some 60 percent of the cortex.

"Of course, you remain blissfully unaware of all this. You simply glance across the street and say, 'Oh, there's Sally.' "

—**M. Mitchell Waldrop**
Science 85

Wonders to Wish for

"If, among the delights of the open world, I were to choose the sights, the sounds and the fragrances I most want to see and hear and smell on a final day on earth, I think I would choose these:

the clear, ethereal song of a white-throated sparrow singing at dawn;

the smell of pine trees in the room;

the lonely calling of Canada geese;

the sight of a dragonfly glinting in the sunshine;

the voice of a hermit thrush far in a darkening woods at evening;

and—most spirited and moving of sights—the white cathedral of a cumulus cloud floating serenely in the blue of the sky."

—**Edwin Way Teale**
Heirlooms

◆

The Body's Sense of Itself

"Climbing . . . is a paradoxically intellectual pastime, but with this difference: you have to think with your body. Every move has to be worked out in terms of effort, balance and consequences. It is like playing chess with your body. If I make a mistake, the consequences are immediate, obvious, embarrassing and possibly painful."

—**A. Alvarez**
The New York Times Magazine

◆

Links to Memory

"Smells are surer than sounds or sights to make your heart-strings crack."

—**Rudyard Kipling**
Lichtenberg

◆

Acquiring Taste

"Learning to taste is like learning to appreciate music. At first [the listener] can't distinguish one symphony from another, but gradually he can pick out the sound of the oboe, and the clarinet."

—**Louise Miller Mann**
The Christian Science Monitor

The Circuitry of Seeing

What makes seeing possible?

Pure and simple: we see with our brains. What we know as sight is actually the ultimate outcome of light's fantastic journey through the brain's visual system.

The processing of light begins in our eyes, which are an extension of the brain and the most exposed part of the central nervous system. In the eyes, light is filtered and focused before being translated into electrical impulses and sent on its way along the optic nerve to the brain.

The final destination of these impulses is the brain's vision center, the visual cortex located at the rear of the brain, where the impulses are interpreted as visual images.

How do we recognize what we are seeing?

We don't just see people and things, we recognize them for who and what they are. Most of us take this ability for granted, but it is a very complicated process—and one not yet fully understood by scientists.

One theory—called the feature-detection model of vision—suggests that individual cells along the visual pathway are pre-programmed to respond to certain shapes. Cells programmed to recognize different types of curved lines, for instance, might work together to recognize a face.

Feature detection led to speculation (most of it humorous) about the existence of a "grandmother cell," one single cell in your brain imprinted with the image of your grandmother. But the grandmother-cell model implied the brain would need to assign a different cell to everything seen in a lifetime, and this data-storage task would be too great even for the adept human brain. Critics of the feature-detection model have also pointed out that the process of assembling all those shapes into an image would be clumsy and take too long.

In recent years, the feature-detection model has been modified by the spatial-frequency theory, which sees images as compositions created by the brain out of variations of light and dark. In this model, the brain takes the differing wavelengths of light and dark reflected by an object and translates them into its own "computer code." The low-frequency wavelengths give the brain a kind of fuzzy outline of the image, while the high frequencies fill in the details.

Do you see the world as it really is?

Studies of the mechanics of the eye have revealed that the images reaching the retina are only two-dimensional, flat like a photograph. Yet the world is three-dimensional, and we perceive it that way. The image received by the eyes is also upside-down, yet our brains perceive the world as right side up.

We are able to make the necessary corrections, apparently, because the brain expects the physical world to have certain qualities, such as three-dimensionality. Furthermore, the certainty that up is up and down is down is part of the brain's innate equipment. From the beginning of our conscious lives, the brain looks for visual cues that conform to its inborn understanding of reality.

How can you find a white cow in a snowstorm?

The setup: To a potential buyer, an artist shows a canvas that is completely white.

Buyer's question: "What is it?"

Artist's answer: "A white cow in a snowstorm."

The joke is old, but here's why no buyer should be fooled:

Our visual system is expert at recognizing objects against all kinds of backgrounds. A real cow would stick out for a variety of reasons: The white of the cow would be different from the white of the snow. The cow's body would form a distinct outline against any non-snowy background. And if

A black-and-white muddle: *that is probably your first impression of this odd photo. But stored memories may help your mind organize the patches into a pattern. Check page 320 to see if you sorted out the spots correctly.*

Upside-Down, Crisscrossing Images in the Brain

We process information from our eyes about color, shapes, and depth in the back of our brain in an area known as the visual cortex. The way that light entering the eye is converted to signals that are then routed to this area of the brain is remarkable. In each eye, the lens focuses light on the retina, turning the image upside down in the process.

Receptors in the retina convert the image into nerve impulses, which travel along the optic nerve to the optic chiasm. As shown, at this point half of the nerves from each eye cross over to the other side of the brain and continue, on other pathways, to the visual cortex.

As a result of the crossover, whatever you see in the right half of your visual field (here, a boy) goes to the left hemisphere of the brain and whatever you see in the left half of your visual field (the dog) goes to the right hemisphere. But other connections in the brain allow each hemisphere to be aware of what the other is perceiving.

This locator shows what area of the brain is represented in the large cross section at right.

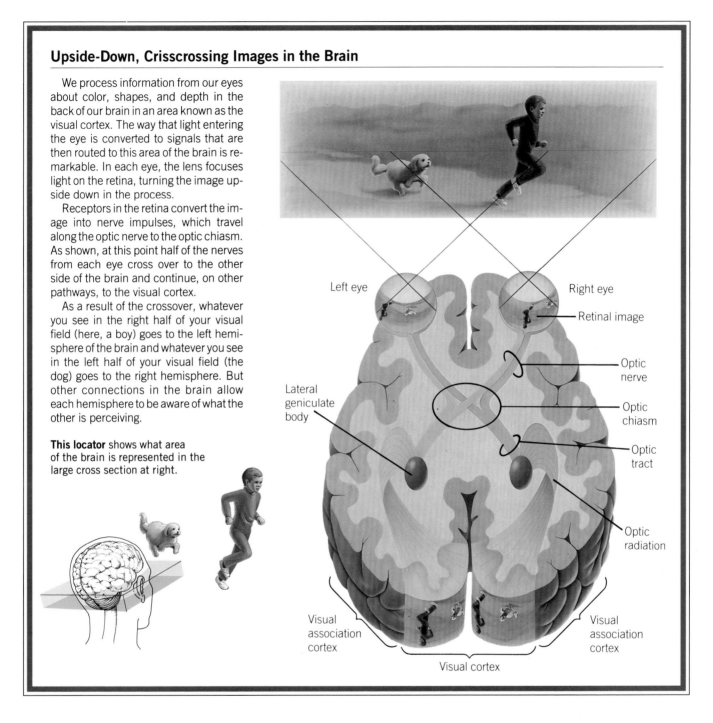

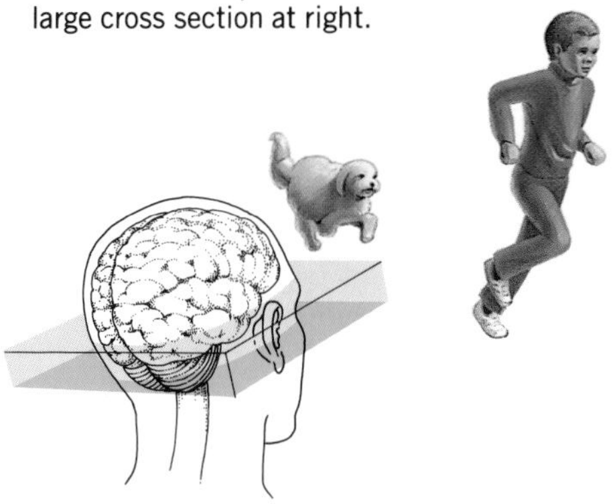

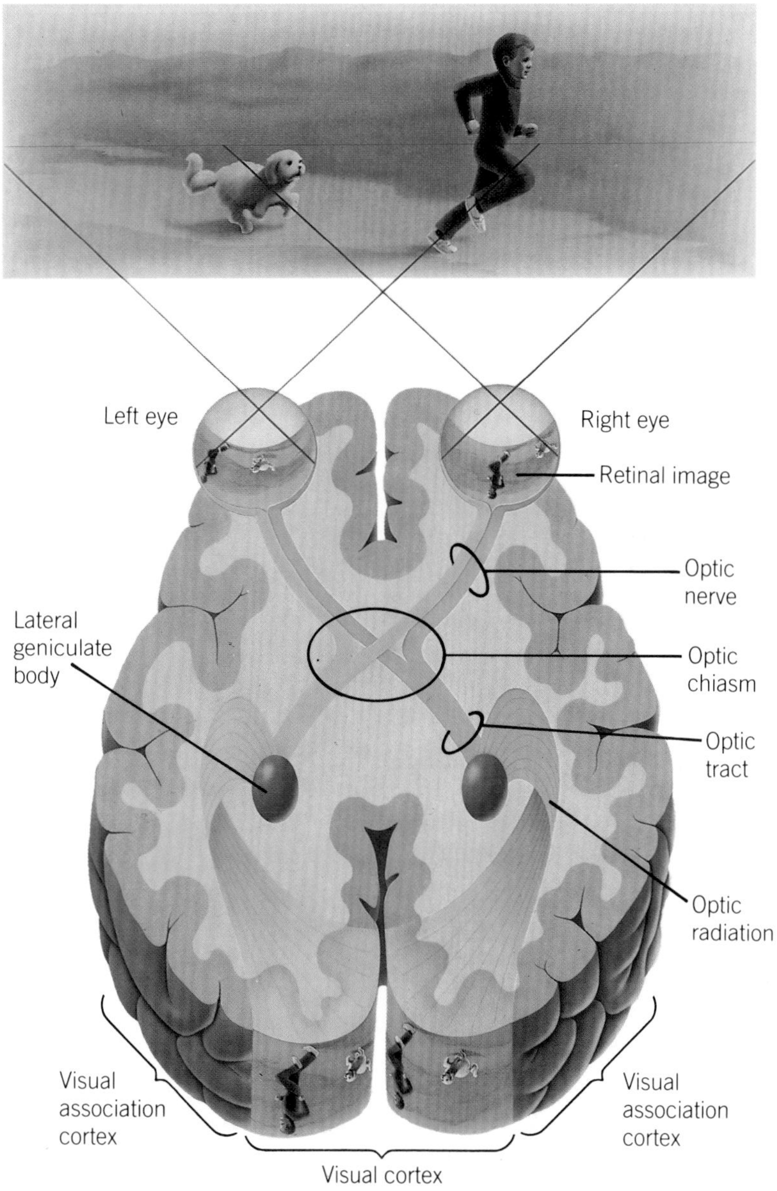

you argue that the cow is in front of a snow-covered hill, then there would either be two brown eyes staring at you or some variation of texture or brightness that, at least for the careful observer, would call attention to the cow's presence.

Every day our visual system distinguishes thousands of objects from very cluttered backgrounds. Whether we're searching for a phone booth in a crowded cityscape, the face of a friend in a crowd, or a mushroom on a forest floor, our visual system can find and focus on the desired object to the virtual exclusion of all others.

Such discrimination can fine-tune itself with amazing subtlety. For example, when you look at a face and see the baring of teeth, you not only can tell a smile from a sneer, but also a false smile from a genuine one.

The calculations made by your brain as it sorts through and processes all this information are so complicated that they would be impossible for all of the world's most powerful computers linked together to duplicate. Those calculations and the paths they follow in the brain are so complex, in fact, that very powerful computers are needed for scientists to begin even to theorize about them.

The Eye's Amazing Receptors

Converting Light to Nerve Signals in the Retina's Complex Pathways

The images we see are so clear that it is difficult to imagine the roundabout way in which an eye turns light into nerve impulses. After light enters the eye, the lens focuses it on the many-layered retina. Surprisingly the light-sensitive nerve receptors are not on the first layer of the retina that the incoming light hits. The light must first pass through several layers of the relatively transparent retina to reach the light-sensitive tips of the rod and cone cells. As shown, the tips are in a layer toward the back of the retina, near the optic nerve. So-called bipolar cells combine impulses from many receptors and send them on to ganglion cells, which in turn route them to the optic nerve and thence to the brain.

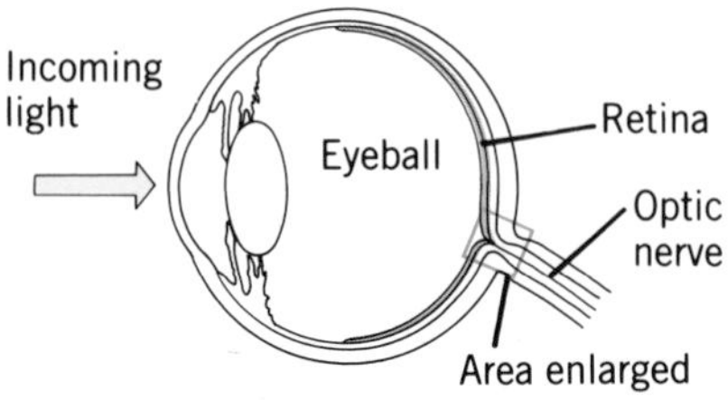

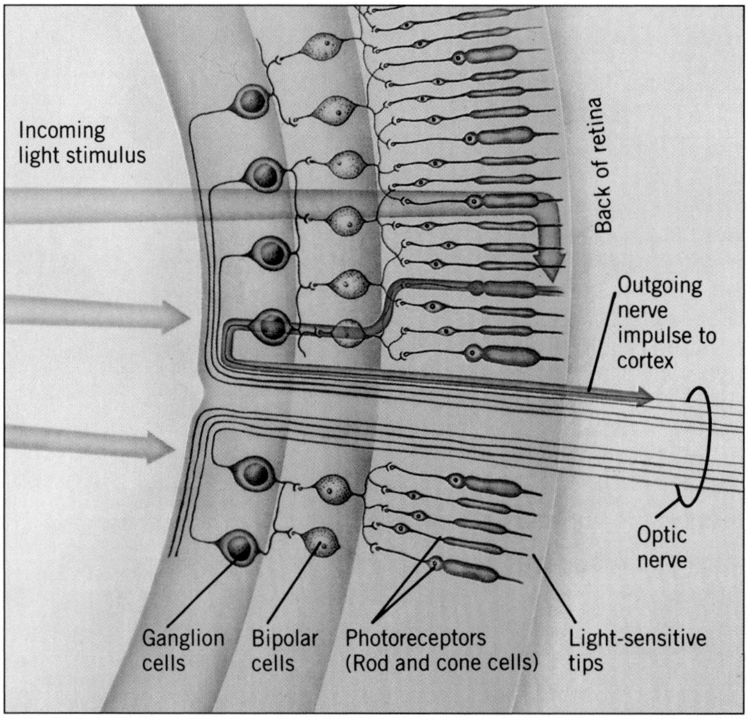

How much light do we need in order to see?

Human eyes react to even a small amount of light. Each eye contains over 100 million light-sensitive cells called rods, located in the retina at the rear of the eye, together with color-sensing cells called cones. The rods have no ability to see color but can react to the light produced by only one ten-billionth of a watt. That's the equivalent of a match struck on a clear, pitch-dark night 50 miles away! Of course, for someone to actually *see* that match, there would have to be impossibly ideal conditions: a total absence of other light sources and a perfectly clear atmosphere.

How do my eyes adjust to the darkness indoors?

When you are outside in bright sunlight, the eyes' rods and cones are chemically balanced to handle the large amount of light. Upon entering the darker indoors, however, you encounter a greatly lessened amount of light, and the rods and cones must adapt by means of a chemical reaction. Interestingly it is the cones (whose main function in brighter light is color vision) that adapt first, taking only 10 minutes to adjust. The super-sensitive rods, on the other hand, take as long as 30 or 40 minutes to reach their maximum effectiveness in dim light.

Why do you see an object at night more clearly if you don't look directly at it?

The two types of light receptors in the eye, rods and cones, perform different tasks and are concentrated in different areas of the eye. Rods, which are chiefly responsible for night vision, are concentrated more at the sides of the eye's back wall. Cones, which handle day and color vision, are packed into an area along the center of the eye's back wall called the fovea. Cones are not nearly as sensitive to light as rods, and there are no rods at all in the fovea! Therefore, objects at night are best seen at the sides, or "corners,"of your eyes, where the rods are.

Can carrots really improve your eyesight?

In World War II, when British RAF fighters were scoring spectacular night victories against German bombers, their success was attributed to improved eyesight from eating carrots. The carrot story was actually a ruse to keep the Germans from guessing the real secret of their success: radar. But research has shown that a diet rich in vitamin A foods, such as leafy green vegetables and, of course, carrots, can indeed help some people who suffer from night blindness.

People who are night-blind have

trouble adapting to diminished light. For them, the normal chemical reaction that allows the rods and cones to adjust to the amount of light is either absent or inhibited. In some cases the cause is a vitamin A deficiency. But, alas, eating carrots won't help everyone. Other causes include disease, heredity, and prolonged exposure to bright light.

And even when vitamin A might be the answer, it's possible to have too much of a good thing. Taken in great quantities (such as high-strength vitamin A pills), it can cause blurred vision, stomach and skin problems, headaches, and even brain damage. One sign that you're getting too much vitamin A is a yellowish tinge to your skin, due to the pigments found in carrots and other foods rich in vitamin A. As a rule of thumb, one large carrot every two days ought to be enough to counter any deficiency.

How do we see in color?

Color exists only in our head. Without our brain's ability to interpret the intricate and individual way light is reflected off every object in nature, the world would be entirely colorless. Objects themselves have no color, nor does the light reflected by them. What we see as color is actually the result of the way different wavelengths of light stimulate certain parts of our brain's visual system.

The light receptors called cones, located in the retina of the eye, are largely responsible for our color vision. Cones come in three types, each sensitive (by virtue of a chemical pigment they contain) to a certain range of light wavelengths. One type of cone recognizes certain wavelengths as aspects of the color blue, others see only red, and others only green. These three colors are in a way the eye's primary colors, and mixing them together in the eye's "palette" forms all the other colors.

From the cones, color signals pass farther into the system, where neurons along the visual path mix and match them until we can see the full spectrum of about 5 million colors that make up the world as we know it.

How to Fool Your Own Eyes

So keen and dependable is our vision most of the time that we tend to forget it has its quirks and limitations. And it can be gullible! In the three games here, you'll find your eyes seeing things that aren't there—and not seeing things that are there.

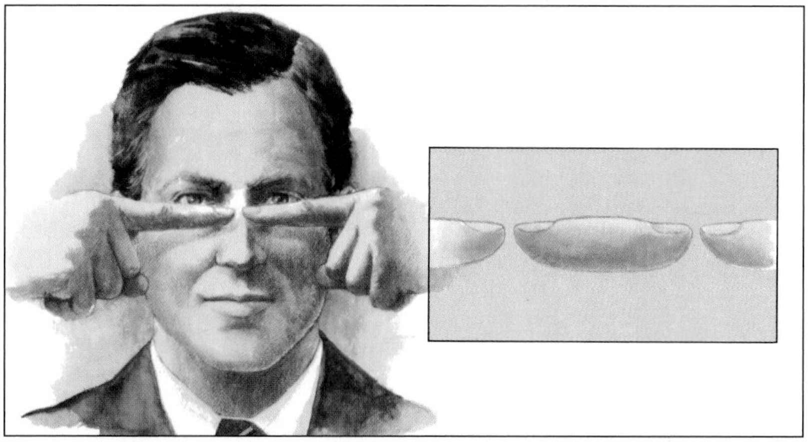

The floating sausage. To see a weird "fingertip frankfurter," hold your two index fingers about 5 to 10 inches in front of your eyes. Your fingers should be pointed at each other with the tips about half an inch apart. Now, without changing your line of vision, focus on a distant object and observe the odd result.

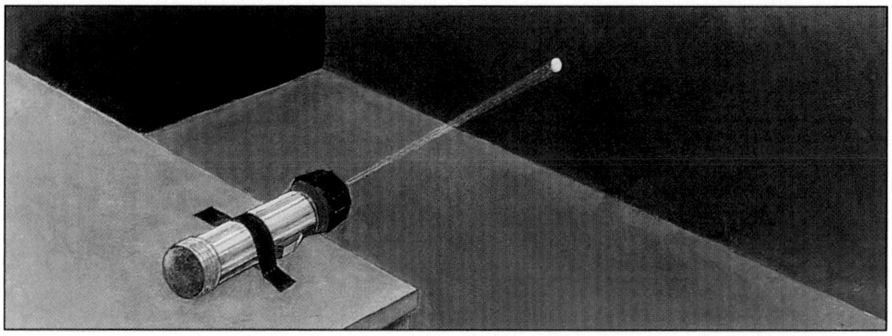

The moving spot. Cover the beam end of a flashlight with black tape so that only a pinpoint of light can escape. Shine the beam on the wall of a dark room and stare at the spot of light. Soon the spot will appear to move. However, it is your eyes that are moving, not the spot. The effect is called autokinetic movement.

Find your blind spot. The spot where the optic nerve enters your eye has no light receptors and is thus "blind." To find it, hold this book at arm's length, cover your left eye, and stare at the left button with your right eye. Move book toward you till the right button vanishes. To test your left eye, do the reverse.

The Many Dimensions of Color

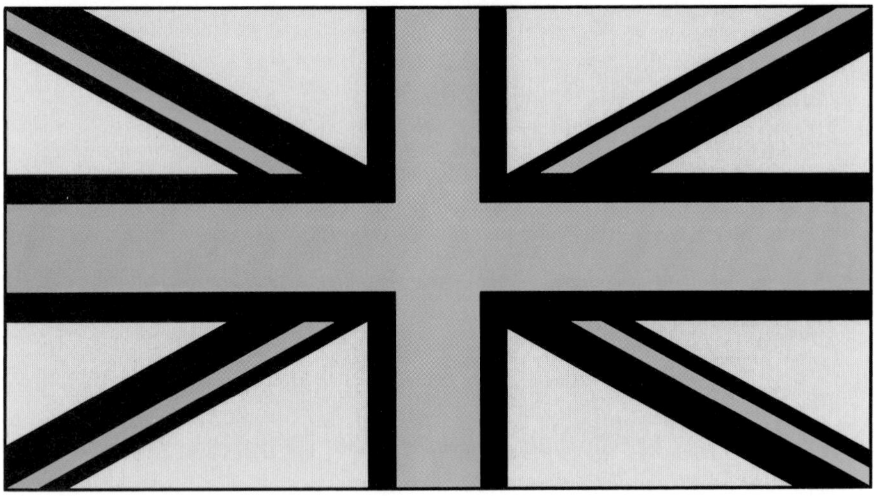

To correct the colors of these flags, stare at them for 20 seconds or more, then look at a white sheet of paper. You will see a negative afterimage that converts the wrong green, black, and yellow to the proper red, white, and blue.

Why can you sometimes see colors that aren't there?

If you stare at a green spot for a length of time, then look immediately at a piece of white paper, you will see a ghostly red spot. This phenomenon is called a negative afterimage. It is a result of the way your visual system mixes and matches colors. In this system every color has a contrasting color. The contrasting color of green, for example, is red. If those two kinds of light are put together, they'll cancel each other out and give you gray.

By staring at the green spot you excite the "green-seeing" neurons. When you turn to look at the white paper, however, *all* your neurons are excited because white (when combining lights) contains all colors. But your "green" neurons are tired from looking at the green spot and cannot cancel out the "red-seeing" neurons. Hence the red image.

Do we all see the same colors?

People with normal color vision seem to see the same colors. But how intense a certain color appears, or how subtle the difference between two shades of one color may be, probably varies from individual to individual. However, unless science devises a way for us to see through the eyes of another—a possibility that is now very much in the realm of science fiction—we will never know for sure.

Can color affect your moods?

It is almost impossible to deny that color can affect our moods. Yet science cannot explain why this is so, perhaps because reaction to color is extremely subjective, depending largely upon cultural and personal experience. A color that you find calming may cause your neighbor's blood pressure to rise.

One study pointed to the power of suggestion as a factor. People reacted negatively or positively to certain colors according to subtle hints previously given by interviewers.

Other studies, which tested children (in the hope of minimizing learned responses), showed that the majority chose colors such as yellow to depict happiness and brown to depict sadness. Still, this was no proof of a universal color symbolism, since even very young children have some cultural and personal experience that may influence their views.

Studies of infants, on the other hand, show that they seem to prefer toys of pure colors, such as red or blue, over pastels. In the workplace, companies are underwriting research designed to determine if the color of the wall paint makes a difference in workers' productivity.

How do advertisers use color to sell their products?

People want things to be the color they expect them to be, especially things they eat. Apples can be red, yellow, or green but not purple. In one test, psychologists altered appearance by shining specially filtered light on a table filled with delicious foods. Subjects found they had no appetite at all for gray meat, red milk, purple salad, and peas that looked like little black pellets. So people who process and package food pay special attention to the colors they use. In supermarkets, a vigorous competition is waged for shoppers' attention. Companies may spend millions to change the color of a cereal box, for example, in hopes of luring new buyers.

It isn't only the food industry that pays close attention to color. Automobile makers, clothing manufacturers, and the producers of thousands of everyday items spend enormous amounts of money on consumer testing and test marketing to determine exactly which colors will make their products acceptable to the public.

Product testers for at least one consumer advocate's group also make use of filtered lights but for the opposite reason. By performing their tests under neutral light they seek to remove color as a criterion for a consumer's decision to buy or not.

What is color blindness?

It is extremely rare that a person will have a total inability to see color. What is generally called color blindness might better be termed "color confusion." Most people with this disorder see colors, but tend to confuse some colors with others.

Color blindness, an inherited condition, is thought to be caused by either a lack of or a reduced number of cones of a given type. Which colors are affected and to what degree depend largely upon the type of cone involved. If all three types of cones are affected, the result is someone who sees the world like a black-and-white movie. But such a condition is rare.

Curiously, considering the universal traffic colors for stop and go, the most commonly confused colors are red and green!

Did You Know . . . ?

- **Your eyes may betray feelings** you would rather hide. The way our pupils open or close can give away our thoughts and emotions, in that the degree of pupil dilation can indicate the degree of interest in the person or thing being seen. For centuries, merchants trying to judge how high a price we'll pay, magicians guessing the card we've picked, and con men wanting to know if we've been duped have looked into our eyes for the answer.
- **A too-tight shirt collar** can affect your vision. Collars only half an inch too small can constrict the blood flow both to the retina, impairing vision, and to the brain, causing headache and slowing the reflexes. The solution? Loosen your collar.
- **Artists may actually see objects** in a different way, according to one theory of artistic talent. People who can draw exceptionally well may have an inborn ability to focus on the parts that make up the whole. When sketching a table, for instance, they see not only the table, but all of its individual parts and how the parts' lines, curves, and angles interrelate.
- **The color of your eyes may reveal** certain of your abilities. Researchers have noted an apparent link between eye color and sports ability. People with dark eyes do better in reactive sports like baseball, which require split-second hand-eye coordination. People with lighter eyes are better at sports like golf, which allow athletes to regulate their own timing. These findings suggest that eye pigmentation may play a role in determining how fast nerve impulses travel to the brain.

Is color blindness influenced by your gender?

Though women are not totally immune to color blindness, it is mostly men who are affected. The reason lies in the differing genetic makeup of men and women. The gene linked to color vision is carried on the X chromosome. Whereas men have only one X chromosome, women have two. For a woman to be born color-blind, *both* X chromosomes would have to carry the defect, which happens rarely. More commonly, a woman whose family has this trait inherits the defect in only one chromosome, and though she herself will see color normally, she may produce color-blind sons, or daughters who pass the trait on to their sons and the predisposition to their daughters. Race is also a factor in color blindness, with white men most likely to be affected.

Dr. Ishihara's Tests of Color Perception

Early in the 20th century, Shinobu Ishihara, a Japanese ophthalmologist, created color-blindness tests. Three are shown here. Left to right: a practice exercise used to familiarize people with the test; a pattern that detects red-green color blindness; and a design that reveals other kinds of color vision that vary from the norm.

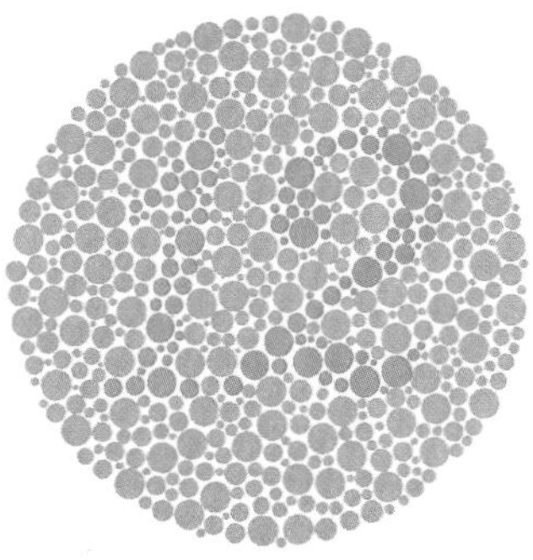

Whether your vision is normal or not, you will see the number 12.

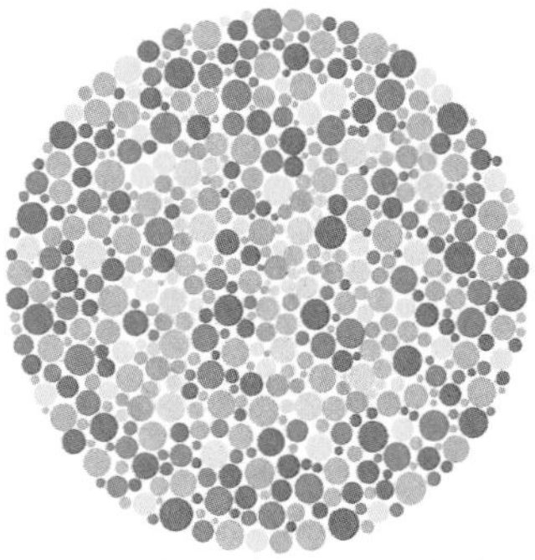

People with red-green confusion will not see the number 16.

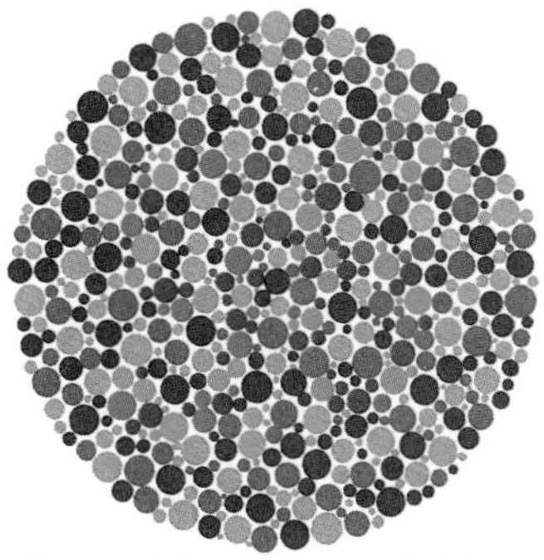

Those with other color deficiencies will see 9 or 6, not 96.

Binocular Vision: Seeing in Depth

Why are two eyes better than one?

Seeing an object isn't enough. It is also important to know where we are in relation to it. Our brain's ability to determine this is called depth perception. One of the most important visual cues in depth perception is binocular disparity, which refers to the two different (disparate) views of the world seen by our two eyes. Since eyes are spaced a distance apart in our heads, each eye is looking at things from a slightly different angle. The brain takes the information that is received from each eye and uses it to calculate our distance from the object. This process is called stereopsis.

So faithfully does the brain accept the images from both eyes, that even if the resulting single image defies all logic and experience, the brain will blend the two images together.

A simple experiment you can perform on yourself will show this is true. First, roll a piece of paper into a tube. Choose a small object across the room (a burning candle will give a dramatic effect) and look at it through the tube with your right eye, keeping both eyes open. Now, slowly start to pass your left hand in front of the paper tube. When your left hand reaches a certain point, you will observe that a hole appears in your hand and the candle is burning right in the middle of it!

A candle burning in a hole in your hand is not logical, or even believable, but you see it nonetheless.

What's the secret of 3-D pictures?

A popular diversion in 19th-century parlors was a device called the stereoscope, which gave the viewer the illusion of seeing a photograph in three dimensions. The device was invented in 1838 by British physicist Charles Wheatstone. To achieve the 3-D illusion, a scene was photographed twice, each time from a slightly different angle. (The two cameras, spaced slightly apart, imitated the spacing of our two eyes.) Then both photographs were mounted on the device, and mirrors were used to overlap their images.

Children today can buy stereo viewers based on Wheatstone's invention. The method of looking at one scene from two different angles also underlies 3-D movies.

Does everyone see in three dimensions?

Some people are stereo blind. They would find 3-D movies most disappointing. Their condition results from an inability to properly align their eyes, which makes it impossible for them to pick up the visual cues that binocular disparity normally provides. Even so, many people with this disability are able to see in three dimensions, rather than just two, because not all visual cues the brain uses for depth perception require two eyes.

Are we born with depth perception?

When you look along a railroad track, how do you know that the rails remain parallel? Were you born knowing or did you have to learn it? Could it be that the tracks really do converge, as it appears? Such questions have captivated philosophers and scientists for centuries; and three schools of thought have emerged.

One group says that when we see the rails converge, we know from our past experiences that they remain parallel. Thus our mind elects—correctly—to interpret the information from our eyes as distance.

Another group uses the term *gestalt* to explain how our eyes see, but our minds reject, the tracks converging. *Gestalt* is German for "pattern" or "form." According to this theory, when we look at a scene, our minds grasp its full significance intuitively. Thus it is pointless to try to analyze how the individual pieces create the total impression in our minds. They just do.

A third group says that the mind has plenty of other visual cues in the scene besides the railroad tracks that it can use to determine distance. One of

How the Mind Overrules the Eye in Judging Size

The tiny student (at right) is the same size as the one in back, who doesn't look small because we know he is farther away.

You recognize a friend coming toward you from a couple of blocks away. As he approaches, his image will fill more and more of the retina at the back of the eye, where receptors send visual signals to the brain. Yet your friend does not look as if he has shrunk when you first see him, nor has he grown into a towering giant by the time he reaches out his hand to greet you. Your mind keeps him the same size by a series of mental adjustments that impart *size constancy* to familiar figures moving toward you or away from you.

A camera does not make this automatic adjustment, and therefore a photograph, the rough equivalent of the retina, can plainly show that the image of a distant person is dramatically smaller than you think it is.

Perspective fascinated 20th-century Dutch artist Maurits Escher, whose woodcut of a vaulted staircase (above) creates distance and depth out of light and line. His lithograph House of Stairs *(right) features "curl-ups," imaginary beasts of his invention. He plays games with our perception: Which way is up?*

the most important of these is how outline and texture (of rocks in the track bed, for example) are clear up close, but blur as the distance from us increases. We thus associate sharpness of detail with nearness, and fuzziness with objects farther away.

Using mirrors and transparent glass plates to create the illusion of a dangerous drop, experimenters tried to find out if crawling babies had an innate ability to recognize heights (and depths). Since the infants hesitated at the edge of the laboratory-created "visual cliff," the researchers concluded that the babies already had some depth perception. But since even crawling infants have some experience of height and perspective to draw upon, the experiments are inconclusive as to whether or not the perception of height is inborn.

Can people with only one eye have depth perception?

Wiley Post, a famous aviator of the 1930's, was instantly recognizable in photographs by his white eye patch, which he wore to cover an unseeing eye. And most of us know people who can drive a car perfectly well with only one good eye, having done well enough on the required vision test to qualify for a driver's license.

Obviously, binocular disparity is only one of the methods the brain uses to determine depth. So-called monocular methods of depth perception require just one eye. When you gaze up a railroad track and see the rails seeming to come together in the distance, you are experiencing a monocular cue. When one object partially obscures another, you naturally assume the first object is closer than the second. Size is also an important cue. As a general rule, larger objects are thought to be closer and smaller objects farther away.

Patterns, Puzzles, and Deceptions

Is seeing always believing?

Have you ever misjudged a distance? Or seen the moon appear to race across the night sky? Or seen a green leaf (that was really a bug) fly away? In the world of vision, what you see is not always what you get. The same cues that permit visual perception can, if combined in a certain way, deceive us.

The world we know is made up of countless combinations of shapes, from the simple, straight lines of a desk ruler to the intricate patterns of a computer's integrated circuits. The shape of each object is made more complicated by variations of color and shadings of light and dark. Yet our brains sift through all this chaos and create order. That the eye is sometimes deceived by what it sees is perhaps not nearly so amazing as the fact that, most of the time, it sees exactly what is there.

What is an optical illusion?

In effect, everything you see is an optical illusion, for vision is nothing more than a reconstruction of reality inside your head. The brain, it seems, is programmed to expect certain things from reality. Everything it sees, it weighs against that knowledge of reality and draws its conclusions accordingly. New knowledge is added from infancy continually. Using both its innate and learned knowledge, our brain constantly analyzes the images it receives to achieve our moment-to-moment understanding of reality.

But what about those times when the brain draws the wrong conclusions? Has the brain made a mistake? Not necessarily. In most cases the brain has processed the information just as it was supposed to. It was the visual cues that were conflicting.

Many illusions depend on how you look at something. A famous illusion of this type is the girl–old woman drawing. Looked at in one way, it appears to be a picture of a pretty young girl. If we refocus our eyes, however, the features distort. The girl's chin now becomes an enormous nose and we see the image of a witch-like old crone. In the face-goblet illusion, the first thing many people see is a white goblet on a dark background. But then the black background becomes the silhouettes of two faces staring at each other on a white background.

In both these cases the artist has created pictures with conflicting sets of cues. Which image we see depends on what we're looking for.

***Classic double takes** occur as we reorganize visual patterns: a girl becomes a hag (above) and vase sides (left) reveal profiles of Elizabeth II and Prince Philip. The vase was made for the Queen's 1977 Silver Jubilee.*

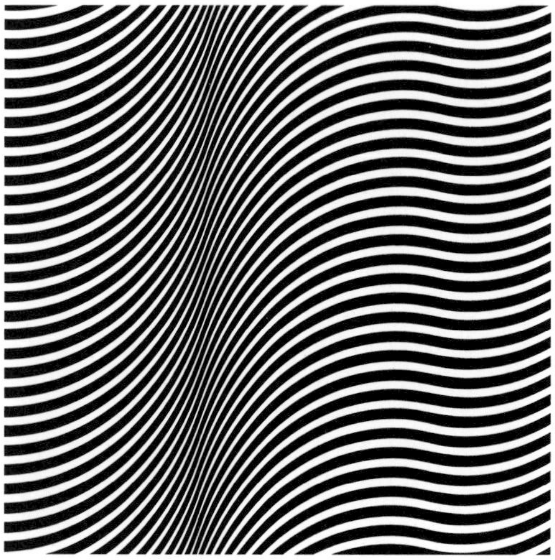

***Wavy lines wobble** as we stare at them: the brain cannot get a firm fix on the pattern.*

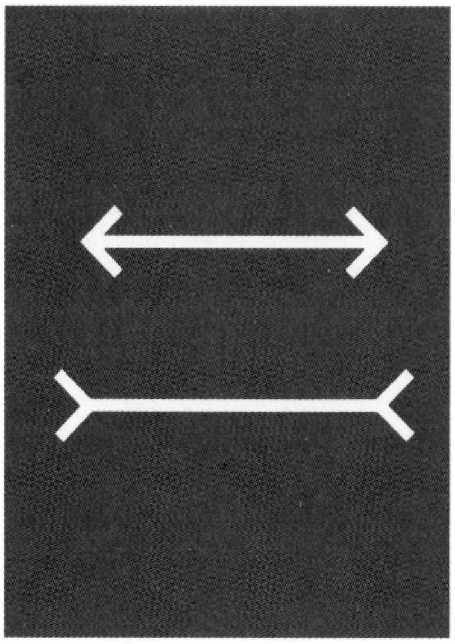

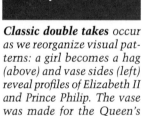

***In the Muller-Lyer illusion,** the horizontal lines are equally long.*

Are some shapes more likely than others to confuse our perceptions?

The brain seems to have difficulty obtaining and holding an accurate picture of certain geometric shapes. When we see a circle, we have a natural tendency to think it's smaller than it is. Even when looking at a shape seemingly as simple as a square, we are apt to say it is taller than it is broad. If the square is tilted or we look at it from an angle other than straight on, its shape becomes even more difficult to discern. In fact, we have learned to call squares standing on their corners diamonds!

We are inclined to think straight lines are longer than they really are, and wavy lines give most of us even more trouble. The movement you may see in pictures with wavy lines seems to be the result of the brain trying to make sense of the pattern made by these particular shapes.

When my train stops, why does the scenery outside seem to move in the opposite direction?

This is an example of the illusory aftereffects of motion, or the "waterfall illusion," as it was called in an 1834 description of this "peculiar optical phenomenon" by a British scientist. After shifting his gaze from a long contemplation of a waterfall, the scientist wrote, he was amazed to observe the surrounding riverbank slowly rising.

Researchers today believe that it is the same sort of reaction that gives us color afterimages. For every neuron in your brain programmed to perceive forward motion, there are opponent neurons programmed to perceive backward motion. Coming to a stop after a period of constant forward motion creates an imbalance in the stimulation of these neurons. As a result, your brain continues for a few moments to see the scenery moving, but in the opposite direction.

How does nature use optical illusions?

Many animals trick the eyes of their enemies, including human hunters, by simply disappearing into the background. Their natural coloration removes one of the most powerful cues for recognizing objects against a background: contrast. An example of contrast is a white ladder leaning upright against a red barn. It is easier to see, obviously, than a red ladder against the same barn.

But the eye also looks for continuity of patterns. Suppose the barn was painted in a criss-crossing pattern of red and white stripes. In that case, the eye would find it difficult to pick out the white ladder because contrast would be lost, obscured in what has become a continuity of pattern.

To Find Our Way, We Interpret Visual Clues

What we see is always compared in our minds with what we know. The following puzzle poses a problem that would be impossible to solve unless we know the meaning of the visual clues. But knowing leads us to a solution.

Visual clues in this maze reveal that each room has two sides that are mirrors and two open sides. Find the mirrored walls. Then, starting from the middle, walk through all eight rooms consecutively without going through a room twice. You may exit and re-enter the maze. (To avoid marking the book, put a clear plastic sheet over the puzzle.) The solution is on page 320.

In nature, an animal's continuity of pattern with its environment is called protective coloration, or simply animal camouflage. The coloring of many insects, for example, conceals them from predators. The same is true of the delicate white spots on a fawn and the patterns on a turtle's back. The dark backs of most fish make them hard to spot by birds of prey.

Predators too make use of camouflage. The golden coloring of an African lion blends into the sun-bleached grasses of its hunting ground.

Military planners utilize color and the eye's search for continuing patterns (called good continuation by scientists) to make tanks, gun emplacements, and sometimes whole armies "invisible" to enemy eyes.

Exploring Media Magic

How Lightning-Speed Fools Your Eye

It is a curious fact of movies and television that if you examine an individual frame, the picture is blurred. Yet the moving image can be razor sharp. The illusions of movement and sharpness are in the eye's reading of high-speed images.

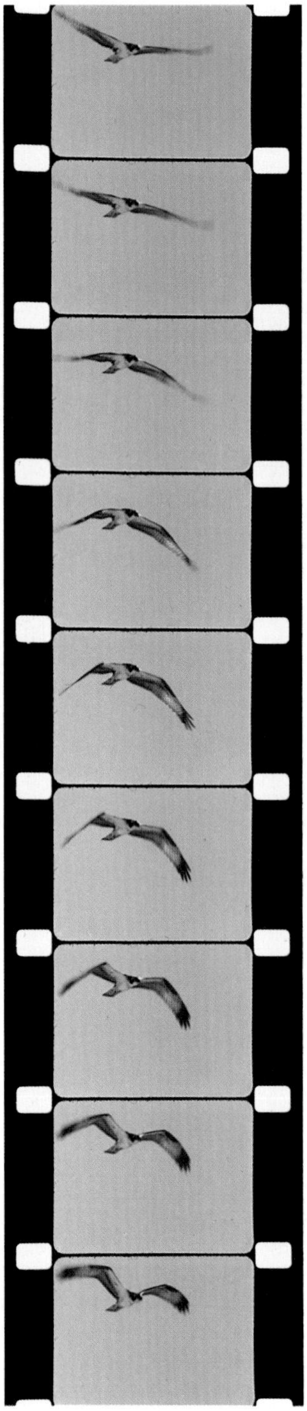

These nine frames of an osprey in flight reveal the graceful motion of the bird's beating wings. But in actual viewing time, amounting to less than a third of a second, one gets the impression of a swift gesture.

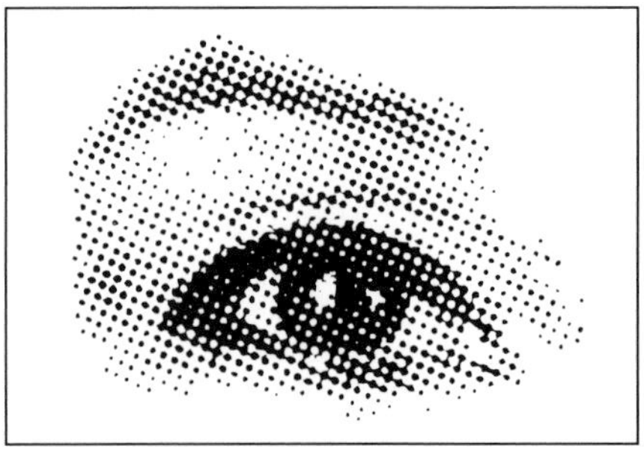

The dot patterns that create newspaper photos are called halftones. This one of an eye becomes sharper as you move away from it.

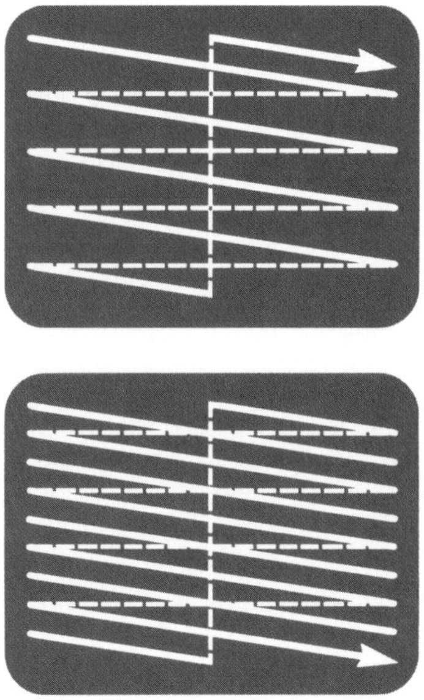

A TV's electronic beam "reads" left to right across the fluorescent dots of each frame. New high-resolution TV has fewer frames per second, but each has more dots, which gives a sharper picture.

How are newspaper photos optical illusions?

A picture on the front page of today's paper may look like a solid image; but if you peer at it with a magnifying glass, you will see that it is made up of tiny dots. When viewed normally, the dots blend together in our vision to appear solid.

Does TV affect our vision?

Parents often worry that too much television will ruin their children's eyes. Although watching TV for hours on end can be a waste of time and give both parents and kids a headache, it probably does not hurt the eyesight. However, one result could be to encourage passivity, both social and intellectual. TV requires very little interaction from a viewer, whether child or adult: all we have to do is sit there and watch. And compared to reading, which requires some imagination to transform words into mental pictures, TV's images are ready-made.

Is television an optical illusion?

Television tricks the brain into seeing whole pictures where there are only individual bits and pieces of visual stimuli. There are two kinds of deception (actually three if you are watching color television). Just as a magician uses hand movements that are "quicker than the eye," the secret of the TV illusion is *speed.*

When we see a picture, or frame, on our TV set, what is really happening is that thousands of fluorescent dots are lighting up with more or less brightness, one at a time, as an electronic beam sweeps over the screen from behind. This beam makes two split-second sweeps for each picture. So quickly is this done, in about one-thirtieth of a second, that we don't notice the dot-by-dot, line-by-line flashes of light. It looks like one complete picture.

Speed again explains why each individual frame seems to flow into the next to give the illusion of unbroken action. The frames change at the rate of 30 per second, which is more than fast enough to fool our brains into thinking we are seeing continuous movement. This is identical in principle to the illusion of action in movies.

In color TV, the screen has dots that glow in green, blue, and red. Guided by signals carrying color information about the original scene, the swiftly moving electron beam hits the dots in a way that re-creates the colors. All the colors of the rainbow can be produced before your eyes by hitting the red, green, and blue dots with different intensity and in varying patterns. The process is similar to that of an artist mixing primary colors to create a whole range of hues and tones.

How can movies make the impossible seem so real to us?

Films are illusions to begin with, simulating real life on a screen. Since the 1960's, the quest for special optical effects has carried the trickery to new heights. Old techniques have been combined with new ones that use the computer's talent for manipulating images with great speed and precision. The result was eye-dazzling space films like the *Star Wars* trilogy, action-adventure like *Raiders of the Lost Ark*, and fantasies blending cartoon characters and human actors.

The secret of almost all special effects is to insert, as seamlessly as possible, an image we know is real into a scene that we don't immediately recognize as fake. Or vice versa: to put a fake person or object in a real scene. Our minds are fooled because we cannot accept, at least until we have time to think about it, that the unreal can exist and act in a context of reality. So we take the whole scene as real.

Model-making is also a big part of special effects. A realistic model of a train, for example, can be put into a miniature landscape and made to chug realistically along—to its destination or disaster depending on the movie script. Or the model (photographically enlarged) can be inserted into a real environment, a trick accomplished by combining film of a moving model with film of an actual landscape, seascape, or spacescape.

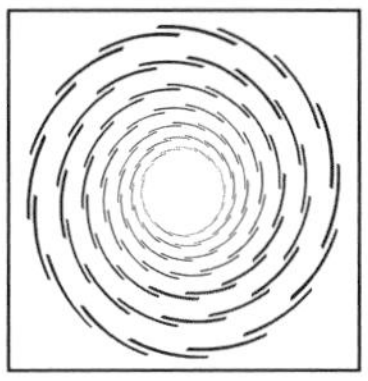

***Fraser's famous spiral** is an example of how a clever manipulation of visual cues can make the mind assume something that isn't so. The secret of Fraser's spiral is that it is not a spiral at all!*

***The illusion of a spiral** is created by arranging curved segments in a pattern of concentric circles, with one end of every segment angled slightly inward toward the center.*

What are some other favorite illusions of film makers?

One of the oldest tricks of the film trade utilizes the phenomenon of induced movement. In a scene calling for actors to talk in a moving vehicle, the director places them in front of scenery (or a film of scenery) that moves backward. To us, it looks as if the actors are moving forward.

Two other classic examples of movie illusions are found in the old black-and-white Sherlock Holmes and King Kong films. Holmes and evil Professor Moriarty grapple on a mountain ledge, a thousand-foot drop just inches away. Kong picks up Fay Wray and holds her in the palm of his hand. The precarious ledge would be merely a realistic sculpture built in the studio; the deadly drop, a perspective painting on glass filled with visual cues to deceive our brains into seeing depth.

To create the illusion of Ms. Wray sitting in Kong's hand, the director took shots of her perched in a huge mock-up of a gorilla's hand, then interspersed these with shots of a model gorilla amid scaled-down buildings and trees. To make Kong move, the film makers used stop-motion photography, a technique still much used today, which takes a great number of still photographs, then splices them together to simulate movement.

The World of the Blind

Can people have undamaged eyes yet still be blind?

Damage to certain areas of the brain can cause total blindness in people whose eyes otherwise function normally. In a way, people with this type of blindness can "see," yet have no vision. It is a phenomenon called blind sight or psychic blindness. Researchers have shown that such blind eyes follow and respond to light. Studies have also suggested that to some extent the behavior of these individuals is visually guided, though they perceive no images.

This phenomenon has led some scientists to speculate that there might actually be two separate yet parallel visual systems in the brain.

Located in the center of the brain are two clusters of nerve cell bodies. These clusters receive the same impulses (though along a separate pathway) that the eyes send to the rest of the visual system.

Many scientists believe this area handles reactive movement: something comes flying at your head and you move to avoid it. Only later do you see that it was a ball.

Proponents of the two visual systems theory carry this idea further, saying that the second pathway is responsible for all place recognition. That is, it tells us *where* objects are, while the main visual system is concerned with pattern recognition, or *what* objects are.

The Woman Who Saw With Her Hands

IN HER SECOND YEAR, Helen Keller was struck by an illness that left her permanently blind and deaf. For the next several years she was, in her words, "wild and unruly," expressing herself violently.

Then, when she was six years old, a teacher named Anne Sullivan entered her life. Using the sense of touch as the link between their two worlds, the new teacher tried again and again, by spelling words into her pupil's hand, to make Helen grasp the connection between words and the things they stand for. The breakthrough came with the word *water*. As water from a spout gushed over one hand, Anne Sullivan spelled "water" into the other. "I stood still, my whole attention fixed upon the motions of her fingers," Helen recalled. "Suddenly I felt . . . a thrill of returning thought; and somehow the mystery of language was revealed to me."

From that day on, Helen "saw" the world in a new way. Her sense of touch became a kind of vision: "Sometimes it seems as if the very substance of my flesh were so many eyes looking out. . . . It is not for me to say whether we see best with the hand or the eye. I only know that the world I see with my fingers is alive, ruddy, and satisfying."

She discovered ingenious ways to enjoy sights and sounds: "Occasionally, if I am very fortunate, I place my hand gently on a small tree and feel the happy quiver of a bird in full song." And with touch she could "detect laughter, sorrow, and many other obvious emotions. I know my friends from the feel of their faces."

***Helen Keller's face** still glowed with the joy of reading in 1948, at the age of 68.*

Helen Keller felt that the silence and darkness in which she lived had actually opened a door to a world of sensations that more "fortunate" people never perceive: "With my three trusty guides, touch, smell, and taste, I make many excursions into the borderland of experience which is in sight of the city of Light."

The Miracle Worker, *a 1962 film, recaptured the moment when Helen first connected touch to the word "water" and what it meant.*

Can stress hurt your vision?

Stress has been cited as a cause of detached retina. It may be that the surges in blood pressure associated with stress can undermine the retina's network of capillaries and tissue. This can cause part of the retina to tear free, affecting vision. Such a condition might result from an accumulation of stress over a long period—a hazard associated more with aggressive workaholics than with most people.

Does being blind affect one's personality?

People who are born blind, according to some researchers, tend to have more personality problems than those who lose their sight later in life. But blind people as a group have relatively few emotional disorders.

Studies have shown that the emotional difficulties of blind people are more often caused by other people's reactions to them than by the handicap itself. In one study, teenagers said they were most upset not by their blindness but by receiving pity from other people. Also, being restricted from going exploring by themselves or being overly protected often made them feel they were being treated like children. It was hard to be the only blind person in a group of sighted people and also to be excluded from games and social activities.

In most cases, blind people felt that whatever emotional problems they had were due to other people's exaggeration of their limitations, and their own frustration in dealing with this.

Are a blind person's other senses more acute than a sighted person's?

There is no physiological evidence to suggest that the senses of touch, taste, smell, or hearing are superior in the blind. It is true, however, that persons who lose one sense almost always become more adept at using the senses they have left, giving the impression that these remaining senses are inherently more acute.

What to Do When You Meet a Blind Person

Most people who meet a blind person would like to be of help, but don't know quite how to act. Here are a few suggestions that will make you and the blind person feel more at ease.

- On the street: If you think a blind person needs help, ask. If the answer is yes, offer your elbow rather than taking theirs. This allows them to follow your movements—stopping, turning, stepping up and down—more easily than if you are trying to "steer" them with your hand.
- Giving directions: Use the blind person as the reference point, not yourself. For example: "You are facing the coffee shop. To get to the park, turn right, cross the street, and continue for one block."
- Dining out: In a restaurant, guide the blind person by offering your elbow. Place their hand on the back of the chair so they can seat themselves. Offer to read the menu aloud.
- Traveling: A blind person likes to hear about sights—both indoor and outdoor ones—while in unfamiliar surroundings, so it is thoughtful to offer to describe them.
- Guide dogs: Do not pat a guide dog or try to get its attention. This can distract the dog and prevent it from doing its job.
- In general: Speak to a blind person in a normal tone of voice, and don't be afraid to use expressions like "See you later." If you enter a room where a blind person is alone, make your presence known with a greeting. In a group, address the person by name if you expect a reply. And always be sure to let a blind person know when you are leaving.

What is it like for a person born blind to gain vision later in life?

In the 1930's, a study was made of people who, born with cataracts that obscured their vision, gained their sight through surgery. At first somewhat flustered because of all the new visual stimuli, these patients were soon able to differentiate the fuzzy outlines of figures and to follow moving objects. Such abilities are, however, believed to be inborn.

They could not identify colors or tell the difference between shapes unless they first counted the number of corners, say, on a triangle or moved their fingers along the shape's edge. Faces and objects familiar to them by touch could not be identified by vision alone. When asked to compare two rods, they could not even say which was the longer one until they were permitted to touch them. After a period of training, these people learned to distinguish colors and shapes, but still were not always able to identify a triangle, say, when it was shown sideways or upside down.

The message, of course, is that any change in the status of our senses requires a period of learning and adjustment. Only through repeated trial and error can newly sighted persons learn to use their sense of vision.

Are there ever drawbacks to having one's sight restored?

In a famous case in England, S.B., a man blind since infancy, had his sight restored at the age of 52. At first all seemed normal. Soon, however, researchers began to notice problems of perception. Looking out a window 40 feet above the ground, for instance, S.B. felt sure the drop was no more than a few feet. The problems began to affect every aspect of his life.

As a blind man S.B. had been adept at navigating the city streets. Now those streets were a strange world he couldn't relate to. Eventually S.B. shut himself up in his room with the lights off, denying his sight, choosing to live his life as he had been accustomed—in the dark.

Making Sense of Sounds

How We Process Sounds in the Brain

We perceive sound in the left and right sides of the auditory cortex in the brain. Each side receives impulses from both ears. The language-processing centers of the left hemisphere (below) translate sound impulses into meaning.

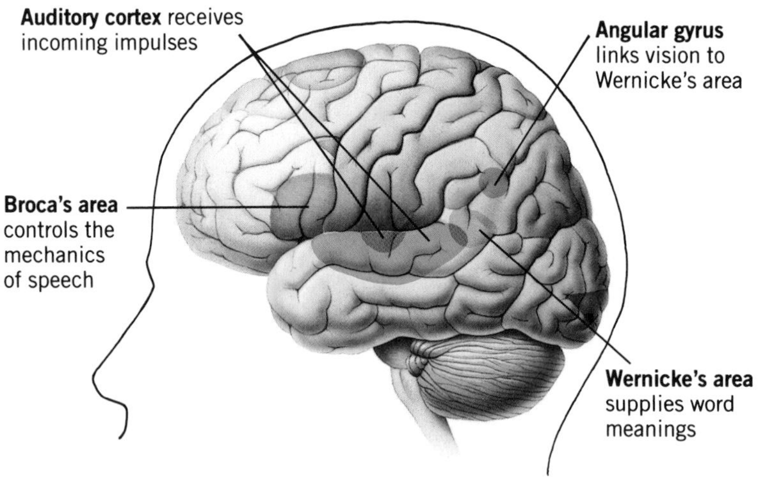

Auditory cortex receives incoming impulses
Angular gyrus links vision to Wernicke's area
Broca's area controls the mechanics of speech
Wernicke's area supplies word meanings

A signal reaching the left auditory cortex is just noise until it is interpreted by Wernicke's area. Thus people with damage to Wernicke's area hear words but do not understand them. They speak clearly but talk nonsense.

They can speak because control of the way we form words is located in Broca's area. Injury here leaves a person unable to enunciate correctly even though he knows what he wants to say and can comprehend others.

Another language area, the angular gyrus, links Wernicke's area with the visual area. It allows us to understand and articulate written words. If it is impaired, a person cannot read. If the auditory cortex itself is damaged, a person will not understand speech but can still read and speak.

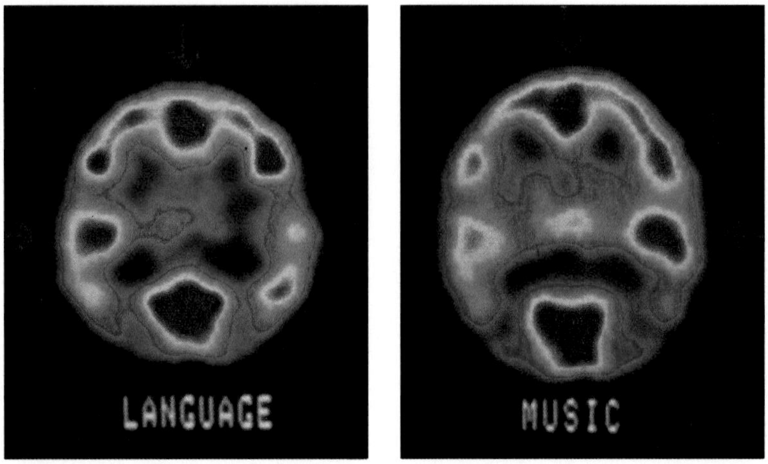

LANGUAGE
MUSIC

The dynamics of the brain receiving sound are revealed in these PET scans, which show areas of greatest activity in red. When a person listens to speech (left), the left auditory cortex is most active. Hearing music, another person has an active right auditory cortex. In both scans, activity in the front of the brain, at top, indicates stimuli being interpreted. Activity at the bottom of scans is related to vision.

How does the brain tell one sound from another?

The auditory, or hearing, centers of the brain are located in the temporal lobes, behind the temples. It is here that the brain "hears" sound, registering it as loud or soft, high or low. What the brain hears as loudness corresponds to the strength of the sound waves picked up by the ears. Pitch relates to the waves' frequency—the number of waves per second. Timbre is a blending of sound waves that each voice or instrument produces.

Our brain's hearing centers interpret the multitude of sound signals we receive, comparing them with one another and grouping them in orderly patterns. This process is all-important in deciphering speech.

But before they reach these higher brain centers, the sound signals from each ear are routed through the auditory nerve to the brain stem at the top of the spinal cord. There they pass through a series of relay stations; many signals then cross over to the opposite side of the brain before being collected in the thalamus, which routes them to the hearing centers. At many points along the way, nerve cells can "decide" whether or not to pass on a given signal. This tunes out much confusing noise.

When do we begin to hear?

Babies can actually hear in the womb. The sense of hearing is believed to develop in the 20th week of pregnancy, eight weeks earlier than vision. There is even evidence that babies may recognize their mothers' voices before birth. Studies of infants' sucking reflexes showed that newborns suck faster when they hear their mothers speak.

The hearing of newborn babies is somewhat less acute than that of children, but it becomes keener within a few days. It takes longer for their brains to develop the ability to interpret the sounds they hear. At first, they react to any loud noise by flinging their arms and legs about. This startle reflex is tamed as they learn to recognize common sounds. Soon they may smile when they hear a noise that signals their mothers' arrival. By about five months babies can make distinctions between spoken sounds, an ability that is important in understanding words.

Why is it pleasurable to listen to music?

In random noise, sounds of many different frequencies and in no particular order are mixed in such a way that we can make no sense of them. Music, however, presents our auditory system with sounds that have been arranged in orderly patterns. We respond to rhythms in the repetitious beat of drums, and pleasing harmonies in the varied pitch of stringed or wind instruments.

The frequencies of notes that sound pleasant when played together are related in specific mathematical ratios. For example, the frequency of middle C is exactly four-fifths that of the E above it; together they form a harmonious chord. Moreover, tests show that people tend to hear a succession of tones that are closely related in pitch as a connected series, even when other tones are interspersed with them. This is apparently how we pick out a melody played by one instrument in an orchestra.

As mothers know, babies respond well to orderly sound. Low notes and repetitious sounds are particularly soothing. In fact, recordings that repeat a tone every second are marketed as high-tech substitutes for mothers' lullabies. And when calming music is played for premature babies in some intensive-care nurseries, research shows that infants actually gain weight faster.

What's the difference between people who have absolute pitch and those who are tone-deaf?

A few people—probably less than one percent of us—have the ability to hear a single note and immediately recognize it as, for example, middle C. This mysterious faculty seems to be inborn or imprinted in childhood through early exposure to music. Even with intensive training, hardly anyone has been able to develop the same skill later in life.

It is far easier to learn to distinguish notes when we can compare them with one another. Almost everyone can tell that two notes are different in pitch as long as they are far enough apart. Some people who are tone-deaf may have trouble singing notes that are unlike those they use in speaking. Others may recognize that two notes are different but be unable to tell whether the second is higher or lower than the first. Both groups can usually improve greatly with practice. Heredity may play a part in this, but, as with absolute pitch, early experience with music is very important.

In any case, a musical ear and its opposite, tone deafness, seem to be functions not of the ear but of the brain. Late in his life, composer Maurice Ravel was in an automobile accident that severely injured the left hemisphere of his brain. The accident left him with an unusual form of aphasia (inability to use language): Ravel could no longer play the piano, sing in tune, or write down musical notes. Yet he could still enjoy listening to music and could even hear pieces in his head.

What is the cocktail-party effect?

What we hear depends in large measure on what we can screen out. We have the mysterious ability to tune in on one conversation amid the babble of a crowded room—a phenomenon called the cocktail-party effect. But even when we have filtered out most distractions, certain sounds we care about will jump out at us. We can't help noticing the sound of our own name, for example, however softly it is spoken. In the same way, a sleeping mother will be wakened by a cry from her baby, and a single wrong note by one player in a huge symphony orchestra will catch the ear of the conductor.

A country dweller who visits the city is often appalled by the relentless clamor of vehicles and people, which an urban cousin no longer hears; and a teenage student can concentrate while loud rock music is playing, to the amazement of his parents. Also, depending on their attitudes toward the source of the noise, people may hear noises as louder or softer. In one study, for example, people living near a military airport found the sound of jets taking off less noisy when they believed that the airport was vital to the national defense.

The ability of the ear to select *messages is demonstrated at any stock or commodity exchange, where traders yell buy and sell orders amid a bedlam of noise and commotion.*

Breaking Through the Silence

Does hearing get worse with age?

Unfortunately, the hearing level of adults declines year by year, and it is usually our ability to detect high-frequency sounds that we lose first. Many older people find speech hard to understand, chiefly because the consonants needed to decipher most words are pitched higher than vowels. Higher voices, such as those of children, are harder to follow than lower-pitched ones. In extreme cases, family communications can break down and the elderly can become isolated and lonely.

The reason for this decline in hearing was long thought to be the result of deterioration in the bones and membranes of the ear and in the nerves that carry sound to the brain. But now it is believed that at least part of the deterioration may be due to the noise of modern civilization. Studies have found that primitive Mabaan tribesmen in Africa, who are normally exposed to sounds no louder than that of rustling leaves, have far more acute hearing in their fifties than the average young American.

Is deafness often hereditary?

Hereditary deafness is relatively rare. However, hearing problems in newborn babies are sometimes caused by events in the womb or during childbirth. For example, rubella

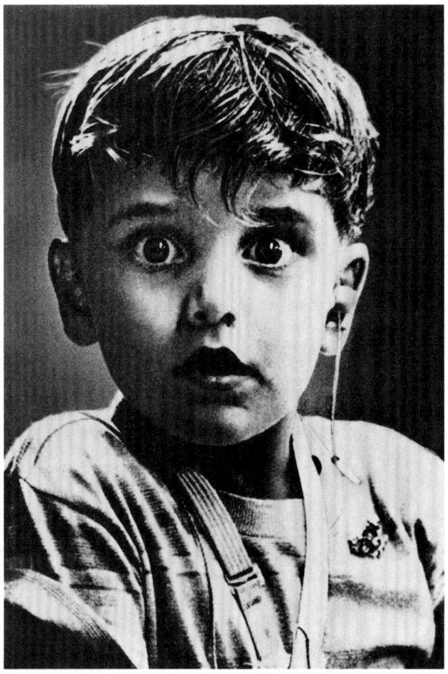

Born deaf, *this boy has just acquired a hearing aid. He is listening to a recording of his own voice for the first time.*

(German measles) during pregnancy may lead to hearing difficulty. Now that many young women are vaccinated against rubella, this problem is becoming less common. Lack of oxygen to the infant's brain or head injury during birth can also damage hearing.

Thanks to modern medicines, ear infections are less threatening to children than in the past. But such childhood diseases as mumps, measles, and meningitis can harm hearing. The hearing centers of the brain may be affected by a severe head injury, tumors, or strokes. Probably the most vulnerable link in our hearing system is the fragile hair cells of the inner ear. They are damaged much more often than the hearing centers, especially by antibiotics and certain other drugs and by noise. The noise of a single loud explosion can destroy hair cells. But authorities differ as to how much harm can be caused by less intense, continuous noise.

What is the difference between being hard of hearing and being profoundly deaf?

Some 21 million Americans are hard of hearing; their mild to moderate disability keeps them from hearing a ticking watch or following quiet conversation. Far fewer people—perhaps 2 million Americans—are profoundly deaf. They miss even loud crashes and cannot hear speech at all.

Many hearing problems are treatable. For example, various kinds of hearing aids or surgery to repair defects within the ear can help restore hearing. So far, the deafness that is caused by damage to the auditory nerve cannot be overcome.

Violinists who experience hearing loss use a simple test to determine their kind of deafness. They touch a vibrating violin to their teeth. If they hear its tone carried through the bones of the skull, their problem has a good chance of being curable; if not, the hearing nerve is dead.

How do deaf people cope in a hearing world?

Deaf people often feel cruelly cut off from the world because they cannot hear what people are saying. In the past, those who were totally deaf since infancy bore the added burden of being labeled "deaf and dumb." But deaf people can compensate superbly for their handicap, using sight and touch to substitute for sound.

In special schools or classes, deaf children learn to communicate by means of sign language or lipreading—more properly called speech-

How to Talk to Someone Who Is Hard of Hearing

If you have a friend or family member who is hard of hearing, you can work out effective ways of communicating. If talking to a hearing-impaired person is new to you, here are some tips on being a good communicator.

- Face the person you are speaking to; be sure you have his or her attention before you start talking.
- It's best not to eat, chew gum, or cover your mouth while talking: it distorts your speech.
- If you aren't being understood, don't repeat yourself. Try rephrasing what you've been saying.
- Speak clearly and at your normal voice level. Never shout.
- If you are in a noisy area, move to a quieter spot if you can.
- Try not to stand with bright light behind you; the glare makes it difficult to read your facial expressions and gestures as you talk.
- Naturalness can smooth over rough spots, so relax and be yourself.
- With practice, your communication with the hard of hearing will become easy and pleasant.

reading, since they watch the whole face for clues to meaning.

At Gallaudet University in Washington, D.C., the world's only liberal arts college for the deaf, many teachers are themselves deaf. As a result of a student protest—backed by deaf people everywhere—the college's current president is also deaf. The students felt that a hearing person, however highly qualified, could not fully understand or represent them.

A new appreciation of the needs of the deaf and the partially deaf has led to greater use of such devices as warning lights to replace hard-to-hear bells in the home, as well as sign-language interpretation and amplification equipment in theaters and on TV.

The telephone poses special difficulties, since hearing aids often pick up too much extra noise to work with telephones. Adaptive devices can partially alleviate this problem. Another option is TDD (Telecommunications Devices for the Deaf), which enables deaf people to send and receive typed messages with a keyboard and screen on both ends of the line. Ultimately, videophones could allow phone communication by sign, gesture, lip movements, and facial expression.

Will it ever be possible for the profoundly deaf to hear?

Alessandro Volta, the Italian physicist for whom the volt is named, tried a daring experiment in 1790: he wanted to find out what would happen if he directed a 50-volt electric current through his head using metal rods inserted into each of his ears. Immediately after closing the circuit, he sensed what felt like a blow on the head—followed by the sound of boiling liquid. Clearly, electricity could produce the sensation of hearing.

Two centuries later, Volta's discovery may help the deaf. Researchers are experimenting with "bionic ears"—properly called cochlear implants. These electronic devices translate sounds into electrical signals, transmit the signals through tiny wires snaked into the cochlea, and stimulate the hearing nerves of people whose hair cells cannot do their normal job.

One such experimental implant has been tested with several hundred patients. It allows the profoundly deaf to "hear" such sounds as doorbells and automobile horns, and helps them in lipreading. The hope is to develop implants that approach normal hearing, but the technical problems are enormous. It may never be possible to imitate the inner ear's complex workings closely enough to let the deaf understand speech without visual cues. And if the auditory nerve itself is dead, no electrical stimulation can help. Still, the brain is amazingly resourceful in deciphering partial hints and clues. Even a rough approximation of the normal hearing mechanism might be of great benefit.

Now, Following in the Footsteps of Seeing Eye Dogs, Come Hearing Ear Dogs!

The first Hearing Ear dogs were trained in Minnesota in 1975. Since then, other programs have systematically trained dogs to help the deaf. Many states now have laws that allow these dogs, like Seeing Eye dogs, to enter public places that are closed to ordinary pets.

The dogs are taught to lead their owners to the door when the bell rings and to alert them to such important sounds as a smoke alarm or a crying child. The animals can even learn to go "off duty" when there are people around who can hear. Then, when they are again left alone with their deaf owners, the dogs resume their role as flesh-and-blood hearing aids.

Training of a Hearing Ear dog can cost up to $2,500 per animal, but some agencies provide the dogs free. Enthusiastic clients appreciate not just their pets' help but their affection as well.

Hearing Ear dogs are trained to report a child's cry.

When a special phone rings, this dog lets her master know.

Our Delicate Balance

***Mohawk Indians are world famous** for their fearlessness on "high steel" jobs—bridges and skyscrapers. Their confidence stems from a rare, built-in sense of balance.*

How do the ears help us to keep our balance?

Our sense of balance largely depends on the vestibular system, which lies close to the cochlea in the inner ear and allows us to stand upright and walk in a straight line.

The vestibular system has two main parts: a group of three fluid-filled, semicircular canals, set at right angles to one another; and two vestibular sacs, also filled with fluid. Hair cells line the inside of the canals and sacs. As we move about, the fluid sloshes back and forth, pushing the hair cells to and fro. The movement of the hair cells triggers the release of nerve signals that inform the brain that the head is turning clockwise or counterclockwise or tilting forward, backward, or to the side. Some of the hair cells are highly sensitive to the pull of gravity. Their signals help tell the brain how far we are from an upright position. From the vestibular system, the signals pass along the vestibular nerve to the cerebellum, at the back of the head. It sorts out messages from the inner ear and coordinates them with information from other parts of the body to tell us from moment to moment where we are in space, and whether we are standing, sitting, lying down, running, walking, or standing on our heads.

What causes persistent dizziness?

Most of us have had brief dizzy spells. But some unfortunate people have two-hour attacks of dizziness that recur frequently and bring on nausea, sweating, vomiting, and such disorientation that they cannot stand.

Famous victims of this affliction in history include Julius Caesar, Martin Luther, and Jonathan Swift. But only in the 19th century was it named Ménière's disease, after Prosper Ménière, the French doctor who first described it scientifically.

The immediate cause of Ménière's disease is excess fluid in the semicircular canals, which leads to confused messages sent to the brain about balance; when the cochlea is also overloaded with fluid, hearing is affected, too. But the underlying causes of the disorder are not fully understood. In the past, when patients described the symptoms, some doctors routinely blamed emotional conflicts. Although stress does make symptoms worse, recent studies have found no basic emotional disorder in patients.

Among the known causes are food allergies, hormonal and circulatory disorders, and viral infections. Avoiding the troublesome food or treating the underlying ailment may solve the problem; drugs that dilate the blood vessels may help by relieving fluid pressure. If such measures fail, doctors may try a delicate operation to install a drain in the inner ear. This procedure allowed astronaut Alan Shepard, once grounded by Ménière's disease, to return to space.

Is the dizziness that troubles astronauts the same as seasickness?

The jury is still out on the exact cause of space sickness, which has afflicted almost half the astronauts on U.S. space flights. The motion sickness that people get on ships and in cars apparently results from a sensory mismatch between the messages the brain receives from the vestibular system of the inner ear and those from the eyes and other parts of the body. If your inner ear tells you your head is rocking back and forth, while the deck under your feet looks level, the result is confusion, dizziness, and often nausea, sweating, and vomiting. In space, an added complication is that there is no gravitational pull on the gravity sensors of the ear, which normally tell us which way is up. Astronauts who had rarely been seasick were miserable in orbit.

Yet the sickness felt by *Spacelab I* astronauts did show similarities with ordinary motion sickness. Head movements that jostled the inner ears were particularly upsetting, and rather than floating free, the men liked to cling to corners, where the sense of touch gave them reassuring cues as to their location—much as sailors overcome sensory confusion by fixing their eyes on the horizon.

Do muscles have a kind of memory?

Muscles can be said to have memory in several senses. Nerve endings in the muscles send faster, stronger signals when the position of your arm or leg changes, then the signals slow down when the limb stops moving or returns to its "remembered" place. Nerves also signal "felt effort" when the muscles are doing work; as they continue the same work and become fatigued, these signals become stronger because it takes more effort to make the muscles contract. This is why a suitcase feels heavier after you've carried it for a while.

Signals from the muscles and joints also play a part in forming the sense of self that we start developing as infants. As you touched the mattress and sides of your crib, and as you felt your muscles moving when your mother picked you up, you began to form an image of your body. As your body grew, this image was modified until it became the one you now carry in your brain.

Are some people naturally better coordinated than others?

Top athletes probably do have an unusually keen form of coordination, which gives them more physical grace and quickness than most people. And, with training, these natural abilities are enhanced. Other occupations that call for heightened kinds of proprioception include surgery, watchmaking, and playing the piano—which some blind pianists do very well. Aptitude tests can distinguish students likely to excel in these fields.

But almost everyone exhibits a high degree of coordination in familiar activities. If you regularly drive to work, chances are that you have no difficulty staying on the road while listening to a radio news program. And if you like to knit, you can undoubtedly carry on a conversation or watch television without dropping a stitch.

A torrent of signals from body to brain and back again *helps guide the legs, arms, torsos, heads, and even chins and fingers of acrobats performing a feat of balance. Their movements were captured by leaving a camera shutter open as bright lights flashed on and off.*

An Unknown Sense of Self

Do people really have a sixth sense?

Sight, hearing, smell, taste, and touch: these are the five senses that Aristotle named more than 2,000 years ago. But modern scientists recognize several others, including the perception of pain, heat, and cold, and a sense that few of us are aware we have—proprioception. The name, from the Latin *proprius* ("one's own") and *recipere* ("to receive"), was coined early in the 20th century by British Nobel Prize–winning physiologist Sir Charles Sherrington. He called proprioception "our secret sense, our sixth sense."

Also known as kinesthesis, this sense is vital to your awareness of your own body, reporting where you are in space and where your arms, legs, head, and other body parts are in relation to one another. Thanks to proprioception, you can touch your nose when blindfolded, and bring your fingers together behind your back with unerring precision.

Proprioception is basic to your sense of your physical self. Yet much of the time it is unconscious. Your brain is "on automatic pilot," constantly scanning signals from your body to check for errors in alignment and coordination. For example, even when you stand in one place you always sway slightly from side to side. When the movements are too wide, proprioceptive signals alert your brain, which tells your muscles to make adjustments.

Where is proprioception located in the body?

Special proprioceptors are located throughout your body. Working with them is the vestibular system of your inner ears, which detects the position of your head and is essential to maintaining balance.

Proprioceptors in the joints react specifically to changes in the angle between two bones; proprioceptors in tendons and muscles react when tendons are pulled or muscles contract or stretch. Together, these receptors can detect very slight changes in the angle between your forearm and upper arm, for example. When you bend your elbow, this angle may vary from 180 degrees (straight) to about 30 degrees; your proprioceptors can pick up changes as little as a third of a degree. Similarly, receptors in the skin and in deeper tissues report on interactions between your body and its surroundings, such as the pressure of the floor on your feet.

Your brain is able to monitor all these signals, along with those from your eyes and other sense organs, to control your balance and coordinate your movements. It makes sure that no one part of the body moves alone.

As a child learns to crawl, then walk, and finally run, *her sense of accomplishment can be almost unbearably exhilarating. Underlying these emotional highs is the steady maturing of another kind of sense of self: the nerve systems that impart body coordination.*

Does this sense of position change with age or illness?

Proprioception does seem to become less reliable with age. Sometimes a loss of this faculty affects only part of the body. One patient found that he could move one arm normally, but had to use extraordinary mental effort and concentration to move the other arm. Such people often have the strange sensation that parts of their body don't belong to them. You may have experienced something like this briefly when your hand or foot went to sleep.

Neurologist Oliver Sacks has described an unfortunate woman who had completely lost the sense of her body. "It's like the body's blind," she said. She was unable even to sit in a chair without conscious effort; as her facial muscles lost their tone, her face became flat and expressionless. This "disembodied lady" had a rare form of neuritis (nerve inflammation) that destroyed the proprioceptive nerves but left others intact.

Vision and other senses can compensate to some degree for proprioceptive loss. And different proprioceptors can apparently substitute for one another. For example, when an arthritic hip is replaced, the patient can walk smoothly even though the artificial hip joint contains none of the nerve endings that once played a part in proprioception. Other proprioceptive nerves, such as those in the muscles and tendons, are evidently able to fill in and do the job required.

Agnes de Mille's Personal Triumph

At the height of her career, choreographer Agnes de Mille suddenly became the victim of a debilitating stroke. Ironically the woman who for decades had taught others how to move now had to begin all over again to teach herself.

***Fame came** to Agnes de Mille with her 1942 ballet,* Rodeo.

KNOWN FOR HER ENERGY, will, and elegance, Agnes de Mille had long been one of America's premier choreographers. Beginning with her dances for *Oklahoma!* in 1943, she brought new life to the Broadway stage and gave new stature to dance in the American musical.

Then in May 1975, as she was completing last-minute work for a New York performance of her Heritage Dance Theater, something happened. Painlessly, a small blood vessel deep in her brain ruptured. Pressure from the hemorrhaging blood began to damage the surrounding tissue. Reaching out to sign the contract for a substitute dancer, Agnes de Mille found that her hand simply would not work. "I looked around in surprise," she recalled. "There was no pain. You expect, when your life alters, a thunderclap, or something drastic. Nothing. This is deadly. This is really deadly."

She soon realized that she was experiencing a dancer's worst fears. A stroke had emptied her right side of all feeling and control. That evening, doctors had warned her husband that she might not survive the night, and *The New York Times* was preparing her obituary.

A CAT scan revealed that a walnut-sized area deep in her brain had been affected by the stroke. The site was the thalamus, which receives, integrates, and sends on messages from the body's senses. From the thalamus, information is telegraphed to the cerebral hemispheres, where awareness and recognition occur.

To make matters worse, Agnes de Mille had long-standing high blood pressure, a condition that could prolong the hemorrhaging from the ruptured blood vessel. Death seemed imminent.

What was not calculated into the bleak prognosis, however, was her sheer will to survive. Though she was nearly 70 at the time of her stroke, she had maintained a lifelong discipline and seems never to have imagined that she might not overcome this obstacle as she had so many others. "The morning after I was officially pronounced dying I sat up and had breakfast with the remaining hand," she recalled. "The doctors were astonished."

More problems were to come: months of hospitalization, a heart attack, several small strokes, a pulmonary embolus, and continuing paralysis in her right side. She fought and exercised and cursed and struggled her way to a "reprieve"—as she titled her memoir of the experience—and to more work as a choreographer. The delayed performance of her Heritage Dance Theater was ultimately staged for television and a national audience. And in May of 1988, at the age of 82, she presented a critically acclaimed new ballet for the American Ballet Theatre.

Agnes de Mille's perseverance could not undo the physical damage of the stroke; she had to overcome the feeling that her left side was shackled to a "gigantically heavy . . . dike of unfeeling matter." She could not get her balance nor sense where her right arm and leg were. Her awareness of body position—kinesthesis or proprioception—so highly refined in a dancer, was gone. The information that the thalamus had processed from innumerable internal sensors telling the angle of every bone and the tenseness of every muscle had to be replaced with far less exact information from the eye. Her physician, Dr. Fred Plum, reported, "She relearned to walk and to use the hand and to function by looking at it . . . using her eyes, as it were, as feelers. Most patients with this kind of a deficit find it so hard to relearn that they give up. It's her determination, I think, which has gotten her as far as she has gotten."

And she succeeded; from a wheelchair she directed young dancers in a new production. As she stood onstage in 1988 acknowledging an ovation for her artistry, Agnes de Mille symbolized the indomitable human spirit.

***Triumphant** over her stroke, de Mille earned new accolades as a choreographer in the 1980's.*

Getting in Touch

Do people really need to be touched?

Infants and children have a special need for physical contact—to be held and touched. It is now believed that separating a baby from its mother at birth can interfere with the natural bonding between mother and child. Early contact stimulates the baby's development as well as the mother's maternal feelings.

In a famous experiment, young monkeys were raised in cages and denied physical contact with other animals. Each monkey could choose between two wire "surrogate mothers," one that gave milk but no tactile stimulation and another that had no milk but was covered in soft terry cloth, which the infants could cling to. They preferred the soft "mother" to the milk provider. Many monkeys deprived of touching actually died.

Pediatricians have noticed a similar tendency among human babies: at the turn of the century almost all infants placed in U.S. orphanages before they were a year old died, even though they were well fed and given good medical care after being admitted to the orphanage.

A Boston doctor, visiting a German orphanage, saw an elderly woman carrying a sick baby on her hip. When he asked the staff about her, he was told, "That is Old Anna. When we have done everything we can do medically for a baby, and it is still not doing well, we turn it over to Old Anna, and she is always successful." Just being picked up and carried apparently made all the difference. When such tender, loving care was tried at U.S. institutions, infant mortality declined.

More recently, researchers have found that premature babies in intensive-care nurseries gain weight faster if they are gently stroked by nurses for 15 minutes three times a day, or placed in tiny water beds, whose motion simulates the gentle, rocking embrace that full-term babies receive from their mothers. Touching apparently produces its physiological benefits in part by stimulating the secretion of certain brain chemicals necessary for growth and for the body's response to stress.

The Universal Language of Touching

Most babies begin sucking right after birth. Although the survival value of sucking is obvious, hunger is not the whole story. Between meals, babies suck industriously, clearly taking comfort from doing so. When babies put toys or other objects in their mouths, they may not be trying to taste or eat them but to *feel* them with their highly sensitive lips and tongues.

A cozy moment with grandpa is a head-to-head, hands-on experience.

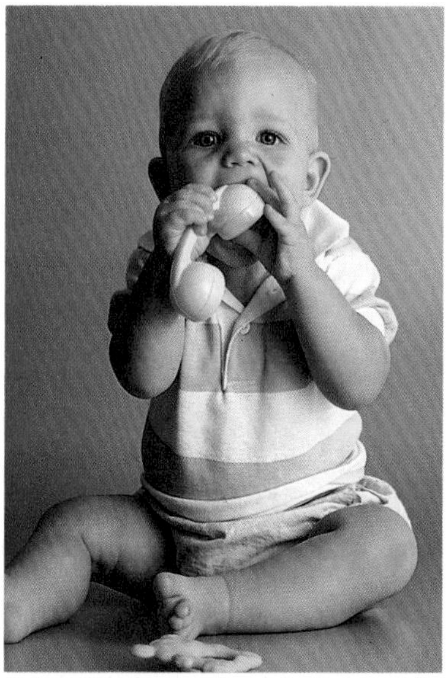

Exploration of the world, quite literally, includes getting the feel of things.

The fun of roughhousing often culminates in tickling and the helpless laughter of all.

Why is touch called "the mother of our senses"?

Touch is the earliest of the human senses to develop. It is already functioning during the seventh week of pregnancy, long before the ears or the eyes are fully formed. And it is literally the broadest of the senses, since the skin, where the touch receptors are found, covers the entire body.

At birth, babies use their sense of touch in their first efforts to understand their surroundings. Even after they have learned to recognize things by sight, they often try to confirm what they see through touch—by patting their mothers' faces or reaching out to the sides of their cribs.

Adults also seem to regard touch as fundamental. How often do you find yourself not believing what you see until you have actually felt it? A sign saying "Wet Paint," for example, often serves less as a warning than as an invitation to touch the paint and find out how wet it really is.

Is there a sense of pressure?

What we call our sense of touch actually consists of at least four different kinds of sensory receptors. Specialized pressure receptors react to light touch, deep pressure, or vibration; they can detect a touch as delicate as a butterfly's wing, even when it is so fleeting that it lasts only one-tenth of a second. Like most sense receptors, they "adapt" by sending slower, less intense signals as the same stimulus continues. This is one of the reasons why you stop noticing the pressure of your watch on your wrist or the feel of your clothing on your body.

"Royal Touch" of 11th-century *English king Edward the Confessor (shown in a 13th-century illustration) was thought to cure scrofula, TB of the lymph glands. In 1775, at his coronation, Louis XVI touched 2,400 ailing subjects.*

What sensations other than pressure does touch convey?

Receptors to both cold and warmth do not respond directly to cold or warmth but to relative changes in skin temperature. For example, a cool room feels warm to someone coming in from the cold. Our bodies respond to changes in temperature by rerouting the flow of blood. Cold receptors are the least densely packed of the touch receptors; if a cold knife touches certain parts of your body, for example, you may only feel the pressure of its weight, not its temperature.

Pain receptors are of two kinds: some send a quick, jabbing sensation to your brain and others send a slow, aching or burning sensation. Unlike other sensory signals, they remain strong even when they are stimulated for a long time. Unpleasant as this may be, it has the advantage of assuring that you will not ignore their warning of tissue damage. Because painkillers can block this important message from reaching your brain, it is best to use them sparingly and only under the supervision of a doctor.

Sensations of itching and tickling were once thought to be produced by mild stimulation of pain receptors. Now they are believed to be produced by other specialized receptors that trigger their own characteristic reflexes. While you automatically withdraw your hand from a painfully hot stove, for example, you have a different reflex to an itch: you scratch. If the reflexes are distinct, scientists reason, the receptors must also be different.

Why do people react so differently to being tickled?

Tickling apparently has an emotional as well as a physiological effect. It triggers laughter only in social situations, not when you are alone and tickle yourself. Children respond with special intensity to being tickled, but people from all cultures apparently enjoy the sensation as long as it is provoked by someone they like and is not continued too long.

People differ as to where they are most ticklish. The armpits, the sides of the body, the soles of the feet, and the abdomen are the most common areas. Ribs and the backs of knees may also be sensitive to tickling. As people age, their response to tickling lessens.

Can touch heal?

Belief in the healing power of touch goes back to ancient times. Up to the 18th century in England, some people were sure the monarch's "Royal Touch" could cure scrofula, a form of tuberculosis. Faith healing, which customarily involves touching, is based on trust and belief and is accepted by some religions, although its benefits are controversial. Apparent cures may be the result of the placebo effect: some patients feel better when given a pill containing no medicine, because they *believe* it will help.

Touching does appear to have specific value in relieving pain—as any child knows who has rubbed a bruise after a fall. Scientists think that the nerve signals triggered by gentle rubbing of pressure receptors may interfere with those from pain receptors, thus lessening the impact of pain signals on the brain's cerebral cortex.

Massage also seems to have real physical and psychological benefits; it not only relaxes the muscles but induces a sense of well-being reminiscent of the security babies feel when they are held in their parents' arms.

Signals Real and Imagined

In the Brain, Clues to the Sense of Touch

The area where we perceive touch stretches across the brain like a headband. The somatosensory cortex (bright blue, right) also responds to heat, cold, pain, and body position. An adjacent ribbon of tissue, the motor cortex (light blue), controls voluntary movements, from a wink to a leap.

The more sensitive a body part is, the more space the somatosensory cortex devotes to it. The cutaway view below shows the areas assigned to the various body parts.

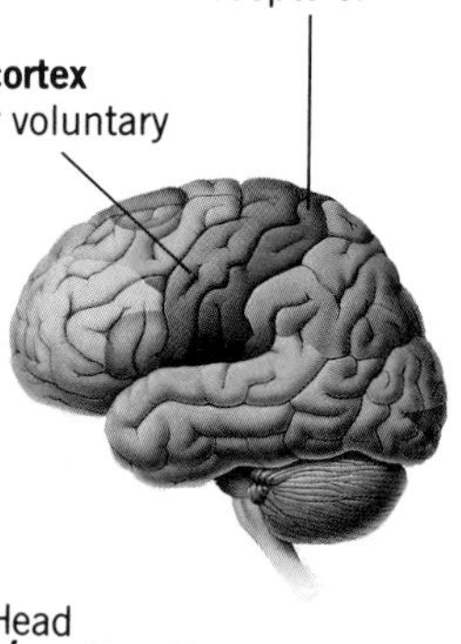

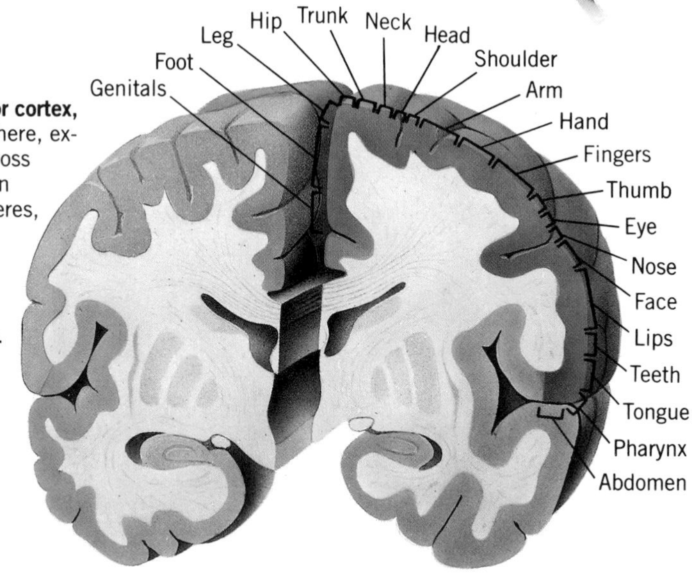

Touch's Exaggerated Sense of Proportion

If our bodies' parts were proportional to the space that the somatosensory cortex devotes to them, we would have a tiny torso and matchstick arms and legs. But our heads would be huge and our hands the size of tennis rackets, as the diagram at right shows.

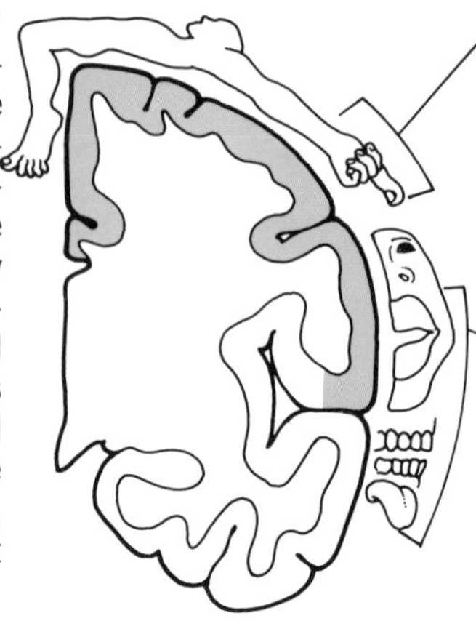

The hands and fingers receive a large amount of brain space, providing precise feedback when we manipulate objects.

The teeth, lips, and tongue owe their great sensitivity to the huge amount of brain tissue devoted to them—more than the entire torso.

Are some parts of the body more sensitive to touch than others?

Touch receptors are widely distributed throughout the skin. They even cluster around the bases of hair follicles; this allows you to feel the wind blowing through your hair.

But receptors are most densely packed in the tongue, lips, and fingers, as well as in the nipples and external genital organs, whose stimulation leads to sexual pleasure. The areas of the brain that register signals from these parts of the body are disproportionately large. For example, the importance of the human hand in manipulating objects and in communicating with other people is reflected in the relatively huge size of that part of the cortex devoted to processing messages to and from the hand.

You can demonstrate on your own body the various densities of touch receptors by a simple test of two-point pressure thresholds. If you touch two toothpicks simultaneously to your lip, you will feel pressure from two different points when the toothpicks are only about one twenty-fifth of an inch apart; on your back, where receptors are more widely spaced, you will feel as though the pressure of the two toothpicks is coming from only one point until the toothpicks are about two inches apart.

Why do amputees feel sensation in missing limbs?

The strange phenomenon of "phantom limb" is apparently related to an image of the body that persists after the limb or the use of it has been lost. In many cases, the image of the functioning limb has been stored in the brain since early childhood. Almost every amputee has "felt" pressure in a missing arm or leg when it is actually the stump that is being touched. Many amputees feel a persistent mild tingling in the lost limb; others may feel severe pain. Usually the problem disappears over time as the patient corrects his or her body image, but sometimes it becomes so annoying that psychotherapy is needed.

One woman felt that the fingers of

her missing hand were digging into its palm. Finally she came to believe that she could open her clenched fist and the pain disappeared.

If a person is born with a missing limb or loses a limb early in childhood, there is usually no phantom-limb effect, presumably because the image of the whole body has not yet been imprinted on the brain.

Can you improve your sense of touch?

In certain fields that call for a refined sense of touch, workers have been able to increase their sensitivity. Engravers at the U.S. Bureau of Printing and Engraving, for example, can detect a layer of ink only one molecule thick by feeling the plates.

Why do some people like to be touched more than others?

Childhood experiences evidently influence attitudes toward touching. Women generally appreciate it more than men, perhaps because little girls are held, kissed, and cuddled more.

Other differences are cultural. Southern Europeans and Latin Americans tend to be more comfortable with touching than the English, for example. One study of people sitting at coffee shops in Puerto Rico, Paris, and London found that Puerto Ricans touched each other 180 times an hour, Parisians 110 times an hour, and Londoners not at all. Generally speaking, although this varies with ethnic backgrounds, Americans are only slightly more physically demonstrative than the English.

Social context also affects the amount of physical contact people find acceptable. In the camaraderie of a sports contest, even men who are usually uneasy about touching will often hug and punch one another exuberantly. In the workplace, a boss may grasp a subordinate's arm or pat him on the back, but the subordinate rarely responds with similar gestures.

Within these contexts, normal individuals differ widely in their responses to touch. Generally, people with outgoing personalities tend to be most comfortable with touching. And people who were severely deprived of affectionate touching in childhood may develop extreme reactions—either phobias in which they avoid touching altogether, or cravings for constant cuddling and holding by others.

The Remarkable Power of Pets as Therapists

Some of our oldest legends tell how animals have saved human lives, or shown almost incredible devotion and loyalty. Today new chapters are being written to those stories as scientists document case after case of pets actually hastening people's recovery from illness—both physical and mental—and prolonging the lives of old people by strengthening their desire to live. In one study, 50 out of 53 of the heart-attack patients who owned a pet survived their first year, compared to 28 out of 39 non-pet owners.

Why pets, such as the cat above or the dog at left, work so well in making old people happier and healthier is still not fully understood. But commonsense says that sheer animal warmth must be a factor.

Are there rules for touching?

A light, friendly touch can often influence people's attitudes. When a touch signals appreciation, comfort, or reassurance, people react positively; it may even make strangers more cooperative. In one study, clerks at a library were asked to touch some patrons casually as they returned their identification cards. Those patrons who were touched, though unaware of the touch, were later found to have more positive attitudes toward the library than readers who had not been touched. In another study, when people using a telephone booth were asked to look for coins that "may have" been left there (the coins were left deliberately), they were more likely to return the coins if the questioners touched them lightly before asking.

Yet some sorts of touching are felt as intrusive. One group of researchers identified 17 kinds of touching that occur in everyday life; and most people considered seven of these negative, from over-aggressive "playful" taps to forceful touching accompanied by critical remarks. Even a friendly handshake can seem unpleasant if it is weak and flabby, crushingly strong, or held too long.

What the Nose Knows

Odors Stir Sensation, Emotions, and Memories

The power of smells to evoke strong feelings can be partly explained by the fact that odor signals travel by unique pathways to special destinations in the brain. Located in the top of each nostril, two small patches of olfactory cells dispatch odor signals directly to the olfactory bulbs, which are extensions of the brain's limbic system. In the diagram below, the limbic system (in blue) is shown in cross section with the cerebrum covering it and an olfactory bulb reaching toward the nose.

Since the limbic system processes emotions and gut reactions, a scent can cause a quick, involuntary response, such as recoiling from a bad smell or salivating at a good one.

The limbic system also plays a role in storing and recalling memories, which is probably why a whiff of an odor related to your past can bring a rush of long-forgotten memories. Smell is also involved in arousing sexual urges, since they are associated with the brain's limbic system as well.

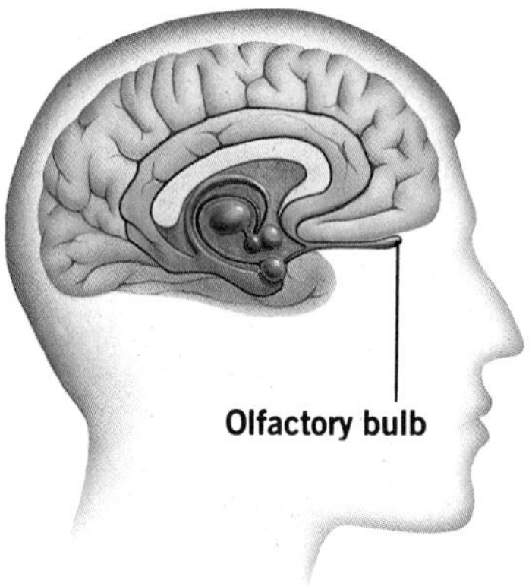

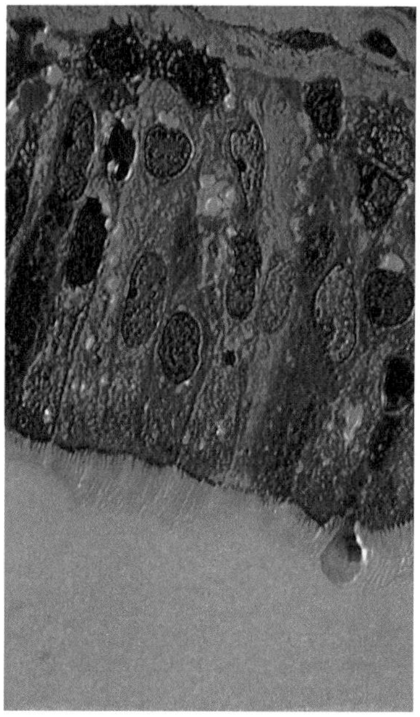

When airborne odor molecules dissolve in the nose, they interact with cilia, the threadlike filaments on the end of the olfactory cells shown in the micrograph at right. Impulses go directly to the olfactory bulb and the limbic system, seat of the emotions and memory.

How does the brain perceive odors?

Deep inside the nasal passages is a mat of mucus and raw nerves called the olfactory epithelium. It is only about half the size of a postage stamp, but it is packed with millions of receptor cells. Air inhaled through the nose brings with it various kinds of molecules. Some are water soluble and, after being captured by special molecules in the nose, are transported to the receptor cells in the mucus mat. From there, signals identifying the odor are sent along nerves to the brain, where the final perception is made. Some objects, such as glass and metal, don't give off water-soluble molecules, so have no smell. (Any smell such objects have comes from impurities on their surfaces.)

From the nerves in the nasal passages, the sensation of smell travels directly to the brain's olfactory bulbs, two lima bean–sized organs behind the bridge of the nose. From these organs, smell signals move to parts of the brain where memories are stored, as well as to areas responsible for stimulating the production of hormones that control appetite, body temperature, and sexual urges. Finally, following some as yet unknown pathways, smell sensations reach locations in the brain where they are consciously identified.

Do we actually need a sense of smell?

How smell affects our brains and behavior is not well understood; but its association with hormone production and sexual urges, for example, leads some scientists to believe that smell plays a greater part in our lives than we now recognize.

There is no question that smell adds to our enjoyment of food and drink, since it accounts for four-fifths of the flavor we experience. Smell also alerts us to the danger of an unseen fire or a gas leak; it attracts us to a fragrant flower or expands our appreciation of a day by the sea.

How keen is the nose?

It takes only 1/25,000,000,000 of a milligram of methyl mercapton in a milliliter of air for most people to smell it. This chemical, whose odor is essentially that of decaying flesh, is mixed with odorless natural gas to warn of gas leaks. And the smell of a single drop of highly concentrated perfume in a three-room house, or the equivalent of one part in 500,000,000, is detectable by most people. The lowest concentration of a substance that can be detected by human smell is called that substance's detection threshold.

Although the sense of smell can be triggered by just a few molecules, concentrations only 10 to 50 times above that detection threshold often reach maximum intensity for us. That is, we won't sense that a smell is stronger, no matter how much greater the concentration gets. The relatively small range between detection and maximum intensities of smell means that our noses are much better at detecting the presence or absence of odors than at differentiating their intensities. Many animals have a sense of smell that is far superior to ours.

Can our sense of smell be heightened or dulled?

Your age, your health, the weather, the altitude, and the humidity are just a few of the factors that influence the perception of smell. The simplest way to heighten the sense of smell is to inhale through your nose and thus draw more air over the receptor cells in the epithelium. On the other hand, clogged nasal passages dull smell because they block the passage of air to the receptors.

Colds are the most frequent cause of a temporary loss of smell. Since smell is 80 percent of a food's flavor, it is not surprising that many cold-sufferers complain of bland food while they are sick.

Victims of serious head injuries occasionally lose the sense of smell. The aftermath of a viral infection or exposure to toxic materials can also leave victims in a permanently odorless world. Some 2 million Americans suffer from anosmia—the inability to smell. About 25 percent of the people who lose their sense of smell also lose interest in sex. Apparently, odor plays an important role in sexual arousal, at least with some people.

How many odors can we identify?

Many attempts have been made to classify odors, but no one system is universally accepted. On the basis of psychological tests, it is believed that human beings can detect between 4,000 and 10,000 odors. Each of them is composed of various concentrations of seven primary odors: etheral (dry-cleaning fluid); camphoraceous (mothballs); musky (root oil); floral (rose), pepperminty; pungent (vinegar); putrid (rotten eggs).

Each primary odor may have a corresponding type of receptor cell in the nose. Depending on the type of receptor activated by an odor, and how strongly, a different series of electrical signals is sent to the brain. There, the signals are identified as a unique odor.

Do women have a better sense of smell than men?

Women are more sensitive than men to a number of smells. The female hormone estrogen may account for this sensory difference. As estrogen levels rise and fall during a woman's monthly cycle, her sensitivity to odors rises and falls.

Women are most sensitive to smell during ovulation, when estrogen levels are highest, and less sensitive during menstruation, when estrogen is lower. The estrogen levels of pregnant women drop drastically. It is estimated that a woman is 2,000 times more sensitive to smell before her pregnancy than during it.

The "pickles-and-ice cream" syndrome, in which pregnant women eat unusual combinations of food, is thought to be due at least partly to a dulled sense of smell during pregnancy. Hence pregnant women can tolerate unusual foods and even crave tastes that they found unappetizing before becoming pregnant.

These Women's Job Is to Smell Body Odor So You Won't Have To

The final hurdle for many new deodorants and mouthwashes is a battery of noses at Hill Top Research in Cincinnati, Ohio. There, odor experts sniff the natural smells of volunteers before the new product is applied. A second whiff determines whether or not the product has been successful in disguising the odor.

A Hill Top researcher says that housewives are the best smell experts. This could be true for two reasons. First, females have a superior ability to detect odor. Second, their many years as housewives and mothers have given them experience with a great variety of smells.

Is smell as important as advertising sometimes makes it out to be? Try this quick and simple smell test. Cut a one-half-inch cube from both an apple and an onion. Hold your nose. Eat the apple cube and then the onion cube. As long as no smell reaches your nose, the cubes will taste the same—do-it-yourself evidence of the importance of smell.

The *appeal* of a smell is heavily influenced by learning and memory. The aroma of smoke at a barbecue is pleasant. In a crowded theater it's alarming. And since there is no standard, universal vocabulary for describing different odors, we often cannot name familiar smells. Our olfactory vagueness helps explain why we are so susceptible to suggestions about how to describe an odor and whether it is pleasing or offensive.

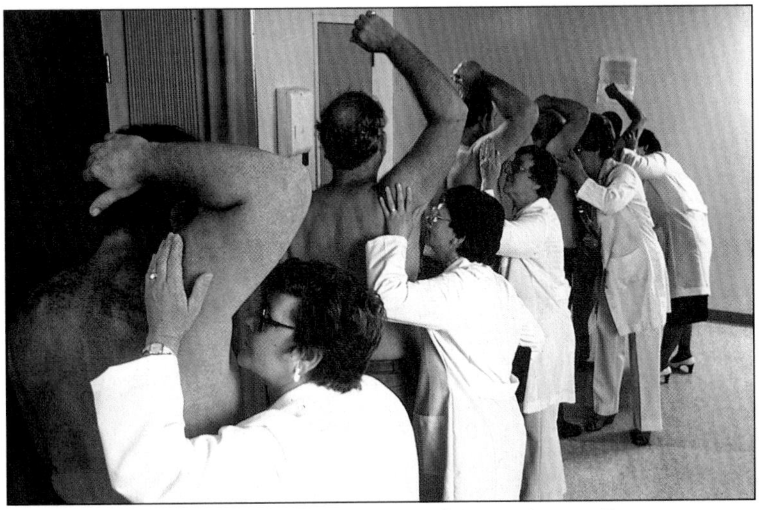

The proof is in the smelling—odor experts work to sweeten our lives.

A Whiff of Experience

Memories of home *are aroused by kitchen smells. Yet no one aroma has universal evocative power. An American might recoil from the odors of cinnamon, curry, garlic, ginger, mustard, and licorice-scented lovage seeds emanating from this kitchen in rural Nepal.*

Can we become adapted to a smell?

Many odors that at first seem noxious become less noticeable with time, especially if you are exposed to them frequently.

In the first second after a smell is encountered, electrical activity between the brain and the smell receptors rises sharply. After a minute or so, activity drops by about half and then levels off; the smell gradually fades from perception. The puzzling thing is that receptors are still being stimulated and signals are still traveling toward the brain. Somewhere in the central nervous system, no one is exactly sure where, steady incoming signals seem to be interpreted as the norm, and the original perception of a smell diminishes.

A similar kind of adaptation happens if a person is exposed to an odor day after day. The musty smell of an antique shop is nearly undetectable to its owner, just as the barnyard odor that seems so sharp to a city dweller is hardly noticed by the farmer. Your home probably also has its own unique aroma, but you notice it only at times when you haven't been home regularly—for instance, when you return from a vacation. Originally, too, our ancestors' sense of smell may have functioned as an alarm. A strong odor of the enemy could have been the vital warning to take cover.

Is it true that odors influence our behavior?

There are some obvious ways that odors affect what we do and how we feel. The stink of rotten eggs makes us flinch, while the aroma of a pine forest is pleasing. And the smell of baking bread can make our mouths water in anticipation.

Yet odors may have more subtle influences on human behavior. Because smells play a role in sexual attraction in animals, some scientists speculate that the same may be true of humans. Moreover in 1970, psychologist Martha McClintock noted that young women who lived together in college dorms tended to have the same menstrual cycles.

A similar effect has been observed in women working together in offices. The cause may be the odor of a chemical in the sweat of women. This odor, researchers suggest, acts as a signal that brings the monthly cycles of a group of women into line with the rhythms of a dominant few.

Does sickness have a smell?

There are doctors who rely on their sense of smell as a diagnostic tool, literally finding out what is wrong with a patient by using their noses. Certain diseases apparently have distinctive odors, caused by a change in metabolic processes associated with the patient's condition. A garlic odor is a sign of arsenic poisoning, and a fruity smell on the breath can mean either a diabetic or someone who is starving.

Here are some other illnesses and their distinct smells: German measles smells like plucked feathers; scrofula (a form of tuberculosis) smells like stale beer; typhoid like baking bread; yellow fever like a butcher's shop. Alert surgeons frequently check for bacterial infection by sniffing a patient's bandages. A musty cellar odor can mean an infected wound.

Why do smells create some of our strongest memories?

One of the memory centers of the brain, the hippocampus, is closely connected with the sense of smell. Smell signals make just one stop—in the olfactory bulbs—before making their way straight to the brain.

This nearly direct connection may account for the sometimes surprisingly vivid memories that can be stirred by odors. If you were upset by your first day in school on a long-ago autumn day, the smell of fallen leaves can bring back the experience in excruciating detail. If the smell of blooming honeysuckle accompanied your first kiss, the same smell, even a lifetime later, may take you back in time and place. When the painter Marc Chagall returned to Russia, his original homeland, for the first time in half a century, it was the overpowering scent of wild violets that brought back to him most vividly memories of his youth. Holding two wilted bouquets, he said; "Smell, smell. No other flowers have that smell. I haven't known it in 50 years."

Smell and memory play a more direct role in what foods you like to eat. If a certain food once made you sick, the mere whiff of it can make your stomach queasy. On the happier side, a certain kind of food can be irresistible because of your pleasant associations with it in the past.

***The title of stinkiest** fruit belongs to the durian of east Asia, say most Westerners who sample it. But to Asian gourmets, the spiky, seven-pound, sewer-scented fruit is a delicacy—not just for its sweet raspberry-flavored, custard-like insides, but for its aroma, which they have learned to love.*

Did You Know . . . ?

- **On your tongue are about 10,000 taste receptors.** They are called taste buds, but "taste hairs" would be a more accurate name in that these receptors project like hairs from the walls of the tiny trenches that run between the bumps on your tongue. When you eat, the receptors send signals to the brain, which translates the signals into combinations of sweet, bitter, salty, and sour tastes.
- **Newborn babies have few taste buds.** But soon after birth more buds begin to grow, and by early childhood they cover the top and some of the bottom of the tongue, as well as areas in the cheeks and throat. Since young children have many more taste buds blooming in their mouths than adults, they frequently find foods to be too bitter or spicy. Adults, on the other hand, often seek out bitter or spicy foods because of a declining number of taste buds. In children and adults, each taste bud lives a matter of days before it is replaced.
- **Different parts of your tongue are sensitive to different tastes.** The four primary tastes—sweet, bitter, salty, and sour—are each associated with a specific area on your tongue. The tip of your tongue is most sensitive to sweet and salty tastes, while sour seems to register most strongly on the sides of the tongue. Far to the rear, grouped in a V-shape, are most of the receptors for bitter tastes.
- **The taste buds account for less than 20 percent of the flavor of food.** The sense of smell, with its own separate receptors, mostly determines what we experience as taste. The temperature and texture of food also contribute to its overall flavor. Oddly, though one's sensitivity to saltiness and bitterness seems to increase as food cools, sensitivity to sweetness increases with heat. For instance, a piece of chocolate may have very little taste when cold, taste fine at room temperature, but seem unpleasantly sweet when hot and half-melted.

What does it mean to have acquired tastes?

Most of us have had the experience of hating a certain taste on our first try, then later growing to like it. Known as an acquired taste, this liking generally develops after repeated exposure to a particular taste. When the tongue is stimulated on a regular basis by a bitter food or drink, its sensitivity to that bitterness drops. Your first taste of strong coffee may have been shocking, for example, but it can become a friendly, familiar taste for some people.

However, the food for which you have had to acquire a liking may have tasted just fine from the start to somebody else. A recent study has shown that some people have a genetic inability to taste a bitter chemical that is present in coffee, broccoli, and cabbage; and there may be genetic explanations for food likes and dislikes. Furthermore, some people seem actually to like tastes that others of us find too bitter or sour, for reasons that go back to childhood and to the kinds of meals that were served in the home. The influence of family, both genetic and environmental, is profound in matters of taste, whether they are natural or acquired.

How keen is the sense of taste?

Bitterness can be detected in a solution as weak as one part per 2 million, sourness one part per 130,000, and saltiness one part per 400. It takes much more sweetness to register a sweet sensation—one part per 200.

However, taste buds can be tricked. After you brush your teeth, the usually sweet taste of orange juice seems bitter because of the chemicals left behind by your toothpaste. Conversely, certain chemicals in artichokes make almost anything you put in your mouth for a few minutes afterward seem sweet.

PART IV

The World Within

How curious it is that each of us is born with strong characteristics, which are not at first revealed to anyone— not even to ourselves. Each life is an amazing voyage of personal discovery.

The world is a bewildering place, but nothing is more perplexing than the contradictions within ourselves.

In Search of the Human Personality

Is charisma something you can develop?

For many of us, personality suggests a charismatic quality that tends to attract the attention and admiration of others. We revere it in leaders like Gandhi or Churchill, applaud it in performers with "star quality," and envy it in popular schoolmates.

Charisma (from the Greek for "gift" or "favor") once signified the divine grace bestowed on prophets or saints. Sociologist Max Weber called it a quality "by virtue of which [one] is set apart from ordinary men and treated as endowed with supernatural, superhuman, or [other] exceptional powers or qualities."

Are these attributes within us all, waiting to be tapped? Consultant Doe Lang thinks so. She questioned over 2,000 people in all walks of life. "The majority felt charisma is inborn, but that it could, paradoxically, be developed." Some defined it as sex appeal, energy, or the ability to express one's true self; most of those interviewed cited self-confidence as a key factor.

Where in the brain is your personality?

One way to define personality is to call it the sum of all the feelings, thoughts, and traits that make you unique as a person; but where in the brain those things are organized and

How Pictures of Mystery and Ambiguity Are Used to Test and Interpret Emotions

Developed by psychologist Henry A. Murray in 1936, the Thematic Apperception Test (TAT) involves asking a subject to interpret a series of ambiguous pictures by making up detailed stories about the characters and situations in each one.

While the TAT pictures actually used in tests are available only to professional psychologists, the two pictures on this page share the same kind of ambiguity of meaning as those used in real testing. Like them, they arouse curiosity and lend themselves readily to narrative interpretations and to conjecture. During a TAT the subject usually becomes so absorbed in creating the stories that he or she will express attitudes, feelings, expectations, concerns, and fantasies that might otherwise remain hidden. This can give a skilled therapist insight into the subject's personality strengths and weaknesses.

Although the TAT is said to detect many kinds of personality strengths and weaknesses—anything from feelings of inferiority to achievement potentials—the value of these tests is felt by some to be in doubt. One criticism is that too much depends on the interpretive skills of the person giving the test.

Why is she so intent on the box? What is inside it that calls for such concentration?

Is the man jogging, or running away from an attacker? Such photos are typical of those found in the Thematic Apperception Test.

orchestrated has mystified people since ancient times. Even the word *I* poses riddles. You may imagine your real "I" as a miniature person perched somewhere inside your head, somewhat like a puppeteer pulling strings to make the brain and body perform. But, as artificial intelligence expert Marvin Minsky has written, "This notion of 'homunculus'—a little person inside each self—leads only to a paradox." For the question remains: Who pulls the puppeteer's strings?

In the 19th century, maps of the brain showed specific areas labeled with such personality traits as secretiveness and loyalty. Today, although some functions, like touch and language, can be assigned to places in the brain, the whereabouts of personality remains a mystery.

Do people with different personalities have different brains?

Although science is a long way from connecting every human trait to a telltale wrinkle in brain tissue, researchers have discovered fascinating links between brain structure and the ways different people behave. The British psychologist Hans Eysenck has proposed that a key to the difference between the extroverted and introverted personality—one outgoing, the other reserved—lies in the cerebral cortex, a part of the brain much involved in learning, reasoning, and planning. Activity here can be viewed in brain scans. In the extrovert, the cortex is quiet and seems to welcome noisy, exciting situations that arouse it. The introvert's level of cortical arousal, in contrast, is already high, so the introverted personality does not need much outside stimulation and seems to prefer peace and quiet.

Some support for Eysenck's theory can be found in our daily experience. Extroverts can fall asleep quickly and introverts can't, suggesting that the extrovert's cortex slips easily into a quiet state. Furthermore, the fact that extroverts tend to be less sensitive to pain seems to indicate that their cerebral cortexes are harder to arouse.

PERSPECTIVES

On Personality and Character

Personality is mainly what you are born with; character is the moral dimension—what you do with your gifts and your experiences in life.

Freedom to Act

"We are free when our actions emanate from our total personality, when they express it, when they resemble it in the indefinable way a work of art sometimes does the artist."

—Henri Bergson
Time and Free Will

◆

When Magic Occurs

"The meeting of two personalities is like the contact of two chemical substances: if there is any reaction, both are transformed."

—Carl Jung
Modern Man in Search of a Soul

◆

Shifting Appearances

"Few men are of one plain, decided color; most are mixed, shaded, and blended; and vary as much, from different situations, as changeable silks do from different lights."

—Lord Chesterfield
Letters to His Son

◆

Looking Beyond Mental Deficits

"Rebecca was no child when she was referred to our clinic. She was nineteen, . . . but she could not count change . . . she could never learn to read or write, and she would average 60 or less in IQ tests. . . .

"When I first saw her—clumsy, uncouth, all-of-a-fumble—I saw her merely, or wholly, as a casualty, a broken creature, whose neurological impairments I could pick out and dissect with precision. . . .

"The next time I saw her, it was all very different. I didn't have her in a test situation, 'evaluating' her in a clinic. . . . I saw Rebecca sitting on a [garden] bench. . . . Sitting there, in a light dress, her face calm and slightly smiling . . . She could have been any young woman enjoying a beautiful spring day. This was my human, as opposed to my neurological, vision.

"As I approached, she . . . turned, gave me a broad smile, and wordlessly gestured. 'Look at the world,' she seemed to say. 'How beautiful it is.' And then . . . came . . . odd, sudden poetic ejaculations: 'spring,' 'birth,' 'growing,' 'stirring,' 'coming to life,' 'seasons,' 'everything in its time.' I found myself thinking of Ecclesiastes: 'To everything there is a season, and a time to every purpose under the heaven. . . .' This was what Rebecca, in her disjointed fashion, was ejaculating—a vision of seasons, of times. . . . 'She is an idiot Ecclesiastes,' I said to myself. And in this phrase, my two visions of her . . . met, collided and fused. She had done appallingly in the testing—which, in a sense was designed, like all neurological and psychological testing, not merely to uncover, to bring out deficits, but to decompose her into functions and deficits. She had come apart, horribly, in formal testing, but now she was mysteriously 'together' and composed. . . .

"[Tests] had given me no hint of her positive powers, her ability to perceive the real world . . . as a coherent, intelligible, poetic whole. . . .

"Our tests, our approaches, I thought, as I watched her on the bench—enjoying not just a simple but a sacred view of nature—our approach, our 'evaluations,' are ridiculously inadequate. They only show us deficits, they do not show us powers. . . ."

—Oliver Sacks
The Man Who Mistook His Wife for a Hat

◆

Hanging In There

"Nothing in the world can take the place of persistence. Talent will not; nothing is more common than unsuccessful men of talent. Genius will not . . . the world is full of educated derelicts. Persistence and determination alone are omnipotent. The slogan 'press on' has solved and always will solve the problems of the human race."

—Calvin Coolidge

The Nature-Nurture Question

Is your personality inherited?

The old debate still continues as to whether nature (genetic makeup) or nurture (family and social environment) determines one's personality. The truth is probably that personality results from interaction between the two. One child reared under harsh circumstances may grow up passive and depressed, while another one becomes an ambitious over-achiever. As psychologist Gordon Allport has put it, "The same fire that melts the butter hardens the egg."

Recent research suggests that genes play a significant role in determining certain traits or temperaments, such as aggressiveness, shyness, impulsiveness, and social dominance. There are inherited physiological differences that may at least partly account for different temperaments among children. For example, the nervous systems of some shy children are more easily aroused than those of their more aggressive peers, which might explain the shy child's wariness.

The enormous influence of genes is highlighted dramatically in studies of identical twins who have been reared apart. In some cases these twins have been discovered to have surprisingly similar tastes in everything from politics to clothing and jewelry.

How early in life does a sense of self develop?

After birth, a child gradually becomes aware that he or she has an identity of his or her own, and this awareness grows throughout infancy and childhood. One test that psychologists use to measure the sense of identity is to show toddlers their own reflections in a mirror; if they touch their own face rather than its reflection, they are said to be developing a strong sense of self. This usually happens at about the age of two. Long before they are held up to a mirror, identical twins have grown familiar with their own faces, which means that they show little interest in their reflections.

Finding Demons, Butterflies, and Boats in Inkblots

The famous Rorschach inkblots, a staple of personality assessment for more than half a century, are only ten in number: five in black and white, five in color. When taking the Rorschach test, subjects tell an interpreter what they see in the inkblots, and the interpreter then draws conclusions about the content and manner of the subjects' thinking.

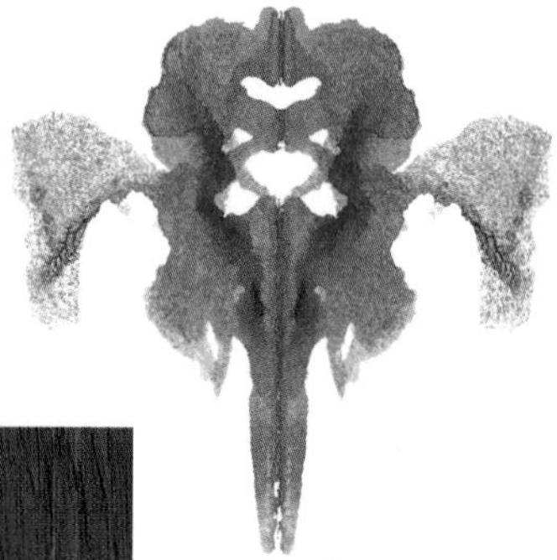

Mock Rorschach inkblot (above) is similar to the real one being examined by the woman at left. What she reads into the blot is the sum total of the test. The technique remains controversial despite its wide use by clinical psychologists.

Do personality tests accurately predict future behavior?

Tests that are supposed to measure mental characteristics have long aroused suspicion. The concern is not just with the reliability and validity of the tests themselves, but with authorities who might use the results to restrict the educational and career opportunities of the people tested.

Probing for significant character traits is especially controversial. Nevertheless, about 600 personality tests have been devised to measure everything from vocational interests to job loyalty and marital compatibility.

Critics cite several shortcomings in personality testing. The same result may be analyzed differently by two or more interpreters. Also, though such tests may give fairly accurate statistical projections of how people will act in the future, they are less accurate in predicting individual behavior, such as if a person will have to be hospitalized for mental illness. Tests of people with normal behavior are less valid than tests of abnormal personalities.

One famous test was invented by Swiss psychiatrist Hermann Rorschach, an artist's son who enjoyed sketching and was nicknamed "Inkblot" as a boy. In a Rorschach test, an interpreter analyzes your reactions to a set of inkblot designs: seeing knives is generally agreed to show hostility; noting movement is said to indicate imagination. The test's value is disputed. One proponent calls its results "not truths but hypotheses."

The MMPI (Minnesota Multiphasic Personality Inventory) consists of labeling as true or false a series of 550 statements, including "I have often thought of suicide" and "I seem to hear things that other people cannot hear." Once widely given, the MMPI is now used mainly in mental-health clinics. After the test was introduced, it became apparent that people might try to "score high" by giving what they thought were normal answers or try to fake mental illness and "flunk" the test with crazy answers. To thwart such tricks, the developers began including statements that almost every honest person would call true, such as "I gossip a little at times."

Theorists and Theories: **What Is Personality?**

Hippocrates, Greek, 5th century B.C.
Personalities are of four types: choleric (hot-tempered), sanguine (confident), melancholic (moody), and phlegmatic (slow to act). These temperaments derive, respectively, from four humors, or internal fluids, that rule our bodies: yellow bile, blood, black bile, and phlegm.

Sigmund Freud, Austrian 1856–1939
The personality has three parts, or forces: the id, representing the instincts you were born with and still harbor in your unconscious mind; the superego, which is the voice of civilization and restraint; and the ego (or "I"), which tries to reconcile the two with each other and with the outside world. There are inevitable conflicts among these forces.

Once the needs of hunger and thirst are met, the id is driven by sexual desire and aggression. In Freudian theory, a young child has sexual feelings toward the parent of the opposite sex and hates and fears the same-sex parent. A boy who does not successfully rechannel such urges may be tormented by an Oedipus complex (after the legendary Greek hero who unknowingly killed his father and married his mother). For girls, similar conflicts can lead to an Electra complex. (When her father, the Greek king Agamemnon, was murdered by his unfaithful wife, Electra took revenge by inducing her brother to kill their mother.)

Alfred Adler, Austrian, 1870–1937
"Striving for superiority" is more critical than the primary urges Freud saw driving the unconscious. People who do not overcome the inferior feelings of childhood have an inferiority complex; mature adults compensate for their limitations by striving for the common good rather than for personal power.

Freud, shown here in 1921, saw the personality as a dynamic interplay of mental forces in conflict.

Carl Gustav Jung, Swiss, 1875–1961
The personality is not set in childhood, as Freud thought, but develops throughout life. The unconscious is not dominated by sexual desire, but has complexes, or clusters of memories and thoughts, which the adult tries to synthesize into a whole self by individuation.

Your unconscious holds not only your own memories but archetypes shared with all: "The collective unconscious contains the whole spiritual heritage of mankind's evolution, born anew in the brain structure of every individual."

Personalities can be divided into two basic types: introverts, who tend to be reserved, and extroverts, who welcome companionship and social excitement.

Karen Horney, American (German-born), 1885–1952
We are shaped primarily by interpersonal relationships, rather than by Freudian biological drives. Personality disorders are misdirected efforts to live with anxiety that originates in "the feeling a child has of being isolated and helpless in a potentially hostile world."

Gordon Allport, American 1897–1967
Your personality structure derives from a unique blend of traits, and Allport compiled a list of almost 18,000 trait-related words in the English language.

Erik H. Erikson, American (German-born), 1902–
Our personality evolves as we face the conflicts inherent in each of eight life stages, from infancy to old age. In adolescence, for example, confronting the question "Who am I?" (an identity crisis) brings a sense of identity.

B. F. Skinner, American, 1904–
Personality is the result of measurable outside forces. Thus, how we think and act can be modified by manipulating our environment. In *Walden Two,* Skinner imagined a utopia in which personalities are shaped by systematic encouragement of desirable behavior.

Abraham H. Maslow, American 1908–1970
We have "an active will toward health, an impulse toward growth, or toward the actualization of human potentialities." We reach our full potential through self-actualization, which includes peak experiences of almost mystical ecstasy.

Can parents deliberately shape a child's personality?

Although some behavioral psychologists have suggested that the personality could be precisely molded by training, research now indicates that a child's temperament is probably predetermined, at least to some extent. That is not to say that parents cannot guide and advise their children and help them to achieve a sense of self-worth. But trying to force a child to fit a particular model would probably be counterproductive. Setting limits for an aggressive child or gently urging a shy one to try new experiences could help youngsters to realize their full potential.

Psychotherapist Alan Loy McGinnis quotes the Hasidic Rabbi Zusya to illustrate the wisdom of trying to develop what is uniquely oneself, rather than radically redesign the personality. Zusya said that when he reached the kingdom of God, he knew he would not be asked, "Why weren't you Moses? Why weren't you David?" but "Why weren't you Zusya? Why weren't you fully you?"

Of Types and Stereotypes

Does your body build influence your personality?

In the 1940's, American psychologist William H. Sheldon developed a system of classifying people's personalities according to body build. Endomorphs, whose bodies are soft and round, were said to be relaxed and sociable; mesomorphs—strong and muscular—were energetic, outgoing, and assertive; and ectomorphs—thin and fragile—were introverted, artistic, and intellectual. Sheldon's scheme was appealing and seemed to fit popular stereotypes. However, most experts now think that his classifications are too simple to account for the wide variety of human physiques and behavior patterns.

Studies of the personnel records of several businesses and professions suggest that taller people are more likely to be hired and promoted than their shorter competitors; but any such height advantage derives from others' subjective expectations rather than from innate leadership traits or abilities of tall people.

In fact, people who have achieved success are generally perceived as taller than they really are. For example, students thought that strangers introduced as professors were taller than those identified as fellow students, and voters overestimated the height of prominent politicians, especially those they admired.

Heat, dust, and drought plague cowboys today just as they did in the Old West.

The Man on Horseback: A Living Legend

We've all met people who were perfect in their jobs. For one, there's the natural-born salesman enjoying his work—and success. We've also met people in the wrong jobs, as, for example, teachers who dislike children. The question arises, what does personality have to do with job choices?

The late 19th century, the heyday of the great cattle drives, produced a legendary hero: the cowboy. Soft-spoken, hard-riding, tough, and resourceful, the cowboy emerged as a modern troubadour, his exploits touted by newspapers and novels, his skills with horse and gun dramatized and exaggerated.

The reality of life on the range was far grittier and more desolate than the romantic image. But the legend endured. Generations of farm boys, city kids, drifters, and people in search of change signed on for this punishing, nomadic life. It has survived the test of experience and still attracts its share of men, young and not so young. Did they start out with personalities that were right for the job, or did the life of a cowboy give them shape?

Musing on this subject in his memoirs, Teddy Roosevelt said, "Cowboys [are from] every land, yet [they] become indistinguishable. . . . All have a certain curious similarity. . . . Sinewy, hardy, self-reliant, their life forces them to be both daring and adventurous, and . . . their faces . . . tell of dangers quietly fronted and hardships uncomplainingly endured."

Are personality traits really consistent?

Ancient Greek poets characterized people by epithets: Homer's heroes were "great-souled" or "many-counseled," while their enemies were evil or cowardly. We still typecast, or stereotype, people as outgoing or shy, honest or dishonest, kind or cruel.

Yet we have all known youngsters who seem lazy at home but are doers at school, or adults who are meek Caspar Milquetoasts in the office but tyrants at home. Because a situation can strongly influence behavior, some psychologists think personality traits are neither stable nor consistent.

In one experiment, groups of eight college students were asked if two straight lines were equal in length. All but one of the group had been told in advance to give the wrong answer; the lone uninformed person almost invariably changed his answer to conform with the others. He ignored the evidence of his senses even when the difference in length was as much as seven inches. Only when one other student agreed with him was he likely to challenge the majority view.

One reason we want to believe people's behavior is consistent is that it makes life easier for us by speeding up decision-making. For example, we avoid lending money to someone who has not paid past debts. Or if we have a personal problem, we turn to someone who seems kind and wise.

We may even find that people want to live up to our expectations, just as

A solitary hang glider, *sailing sunward over the clouds like Icarus reborn, is a symbol of the dreamer and daredevil in us all.*

we try to live up to our expectations of ourselves. In this light, our tendency to expect consistent personality traits is justified and useful. The problem is that we may cling to a negative idea of a person based on mistaken assumptions, and our attitude may cause the undesirable behavior we expect.

When are stereotypes harmful?

Stereotypes are a kind of generalization. As psychologist Gordon Allport has written, "The human mind must think with the aid of categories [generalizations]. We cannot possibly avoid this process. Orderly living depends upon it."

The danger comes when we generalize from observations of a few individuals to create stereotypes for whole groups. Even less rational is holding on to stereotypes that we know are false. Allport tells of an English university student who remarked, "I despise all Americans, but have never met one I didn't like." In this case, the categorization went against even first-hand experience.

Are risk-taking daredevils a special breed?

Just as each of us has optimism or pessimism in varying degrees, sensation seeking is stronger in some people than in others. Certainly, racing drivers or skydivers have a stronger risk-taking trait than most.

It seems obvious that for many thrill-seekers the high of conquering fear is habit-forming. But why some people and not others are drawn to such behavior is unclear. Some psychologists think daredevil pursuits provide a needed outlet from emotionally and physically restrictive jobs, especially for an aggressive personality type who demands pushing the mind and body to their limits.

The tendency of a daredevil in one area to seek other high-risk behavior, including drug and alcohol abuse, hints at a biological cause. One focus of research is the reticular activating system, a neural network at the base of the brain, which in thrill-seekers may need extra stimulation to make the mind feel fully alive. Another theory is that excitement corrects an imbalance of a brain chemical, monoamine oxidase, in daredevils.

Does a certain type of personality guarantee success in life?

There is no single "success" personality, but surveys suggest traits that correlate with professional, business, or political achievement. A Gallup Poll of people listed in *Who's Who in America* pinpointed traits that these high achievers thought important to their success. Frequently cited traits were common sense ("ability to render sound, practical judgments on everyday affairs"); self-reliance; and the ability to get things done efficiently.

Your Handwriting: Variable But Unique

The Appealing but Controversial Art of Graphology

A left-hander's slanting script could be analyzed as "withdrawn" if done by a right-hander.

A great deal about your personality can be read in your handwriting, according to graphologists. Such experts consider handwriting a kind of "brainwriting"—a direct expression of mental impulses in the brain transmitted through the writer's hand to paper. Each person's writing contains characteristic strokes and flourishes that reveal personality traits of the writer, graphologists contend; and they have matched some 300 writing characteristics to specific personality traits. Defended by some, debunked by others, graphology has yet to prove its scientific validity.

If handwriting alone revealed our personalities, judging people would be easy; but graphology is far from being an exact science. Shown below are some writing styles said by graphologist Sheila Kurtz to show positive and negative character traits.

POSITIVE SIGNS		NEGATIVE SIGNS	
Broad-minded	clear, wide e's	Bad-tempered	Temper
Sympathetic	forward slant	Withdrawn	backward slant
Generous	long finals	Impatient	slashed forms: i, t
Enthusiastic	sweeping t bar	Shallow	shallow: t
Communicative	open a's o's	Selfish	compressed strokes + narrow l's + initial hooks
Loyal	round i dot	Narrow-minded	closed letters: a's, o's, e's
Optimistic	optimism	Jealous	small initial loops: m, n, H
Diplomatic	tapering m's, n's	Secretive	looped d
Humorous	initial flourishes, especially m's, n's	Evasive	hook in circle letter: d
		Vain	extra tall t's
Intuitive	spaces between letters	Domineering	arrow t bar

Is handwriting analysis a valid tool for understanding people?

It is important to differentiate between two uses of handwriting analysis. One application is in legal proceedings, where handwriting experts may be asked to give their opinion on whether or not a signature or other writing sample matches that known to be done by a certain person. For this purpose, the testimony of handwriting experts is often admissible in court in cases involving alleged forgeries, disputed wills, false identities, and threatening or extortionate letters. In essence, the courts agree with handwriting analysts that a person's handwriting has unique characteristics, and thus is identifiably different from everybody else's.

Analyzing the *characteristics* of handwriting, however, is quite different from analyzing the *character* of the writer. This latter practice, called graphology, is the second major application of handwriting analysis. Highly controversial, it is claimed by its most enthusiastic proponents to reveal almost everything about personality.

Alfred Binet, co-developer of the intelligence test, called graphology the "science of the future." Graphologists claim that the idiosyncrasies of an individual's handwriting reflect the writer's personality. They refer to handwriting as "brainwriting," meaning that the way a person writes really represents a record of mental impulses, transmitted by the cerebral cortex to the hand. As such, graphologists claim, handwriting becomes an invaluable aid to understanding a person's character.

The belief that handwriting reveals personality dates back centuries. In the 11th century, Chinese painter Kuo Jo Hsu noted, "Handwriting can infallibly show whether it comes from a person who is noble-minded, or from one who is vulgar."

Does graphology reveal more than personality tests do?

One of the few scientific studies of graphology's effectiveness pitted three handwriting experts against standard personality tests. The task was to evaluate the characters of 52 workers. For what it's worth, the graphologists' conclusions proved slightly less accurate than those based on the standard tests. Psychologists caution that neither graphology nor any personality test so far devised should be used as a sole standard to judge the integrity of an individual.

Exactly what is handwriting supposed to tell about you?

Graphologists say that a person's handwriting reveals major and minor personality traits, mood swings, vocational abilities—and such physical problems as heart disease and cancer. These claims are viewed as excessive and in some respects unsupportable by many scientists, but are stoutly defended by proponents of graphology.

In fact, about the only things that cannot be disclosed by handwriting analysis, according to graphologists, are the writer's age, handedness, sex, and race. In Europe and the U.S., thousands of companies use graphologists to help with screening, hiring, and placement of new employees.

Can You Decipher These Famous Names?

They made their mark on history, but their signatures are almost unreadable. To try your hand, write the numbers 1 to 24 on a separate sheet of paper. Then match each number to one of the clues listed below. Answers are on page 321.

- **A.** Polish composer-pianist
- **B.** Novelist (*Oliver Twist*)
- **C.** The little corporal
- **D.** American naval hero
- **E.** Queen of Scots
- **F.** Sailed the ocean blue
- **G.** Called "the Terrible"
- **H.** Italian conductor
- **I.** Romantic poet ("Don Juan")
- **J.** *Der Führer*
- **K.** French painter, lithographer
- **L.** French general, statesman
- **M.** Watergate
- **N.** Florentine artist, engineer
- **O.** *Il Duce*
- **P.** French impressionist
- **Q.** Civil War general
- **R.** Ceiling painter
- **S.** Assassinated U.S. president
- **T.** The Red Baron
- **U.** "Guernica"
- **V.** Austrian psychoanalyst
- **W.** British royal favorite, explorer
- **X.** The Bard of Avon

In Quest of the Ideal Image

Putting Your Mind in Charge of Eating Problems

Modern life makes it easy to take in more calories than we burn, and the result is weight problems. To complicate matters, our bodies work against losing weight. In earlier, harsher times, when food was scarcer and we spent more physical energy to get it, the human body developed a survival technique to avoid starvation. With less food, the body's metabolism slows down, saving energy. Less fat is burned. Since dieting is really a kind of controlled starvation, we must look to our minds for the will and long-term planning to overcome the reluctance of our body to burn its energy reserves of fat. Furthermore, gradual weight loss is healthiest and most lasting, and that requires even more patience and mental discipline.

- **Decide.** If you feel wishy-washy about losing weight, it won't work.
- **Set realistic goals.** After you reach your desired weight, you have the rest of your life to maintain it, so there is no sense in trying to shed pounds at a heroic pace or aiming for a weight that's unnaturally low.
- **Respect calories.** Calorie-counting doesn't work for everyone, but the fact remains that 3,500 calories add up to a pound of fat.
- **Rethink eating.** Snacking between meals erodes willpower and adds calories. Also, food eaten near bedtime is more likely to turn to fat. At meals, remember that feeling full lags about 15 minutes behind what you swallow. Finally, many dieters find a small, tasty meal more satisfying than a large, bland one.
- **Weigh in regularly.** Daily weight fluctuations may have nothing to do with how much you eat, so checking the scales too often can be misleading. But weigh yourself at least once a week, at the same time of day.
- **Avoid fad diets.** Over 90 percent of people who lose weight on fad diets gain it back, one reason being that the pounds lost in the first week or two are mainly water. Also, such diets are often nutritionally unsound.
- **Get some exercise.** Brisk, 10-minute walks reduce tension and elevate mood. Strangely, exercise both burns up calories and makes you less hungry. And it need not be painful: moderate, regular exercise like walking can be as helpful as the more vigorous kind.
- **Learn to love water.** Drinking six to eight glasses a day reduces your appetite and cleanses your system.
- **Reward yourself.** Sticking to a diet for a few days can bring new self-esteem and the fortitude to continue. If you need more tangible rewards, as in the conditioning techniques used to train animals, you can treat yourself every so often to something special (other than food, of course) for persevering.

How much does physical appearance have to do with your self-esteem?

Physical attractiveness evidently can affect the personality. Of course, notions of what makes a person attractive have changed throughout history, and from culture to culture. For instance, the American ideal of beauty today is being tanned, thin, and athletic. It was not always so, nor is it likely to remain the same in the future. However, within the same culture at any given time, most people agree on which individuals are more or less attractive; most people also tend to think that someone with good looks is confident and socially adept.

These perceptions do seem to hold true up to a point. No doubt part of the explanation is that a person who has been treated as attractive tends to develop more self-confidence in dealing with others. In contrast, a less attractive person may have seldom experienced the same kind of ego-building feedback in social situations.

Differential treatment based on appearance seems to begin early in a child's life. In one experiment, women were shown pictures of attractive and unattractive children misbehaving. The women saw the attractive children's bad behavior as temporary, but judged the homely ones to have serious behavioral problems.

Why do some people overeat?

For many people, eating means more than satisfying hunger. They may eat when what they really crave is approval. They may regard food as a reward, especially if it was used as such by their parents or if food was withheld as a punishment for misbehavior. In extreme cases, such feelings can lead to serious eating disorders.

Why do some people starve themselves?

People with anorexia nervosa may diet to the point of starvation, insisting that they are too fat even when they are pitifully emaciated. The ailment is not new, but many doctors blame its current prevalence on society's emphasis on slimness—as expressed in the maxim: "You can't be too rich or too thin." Victims have included such successful people as recording star Karen Carpenter and TV anchorwoman Jessica Savitch.

But why are only certain people susceptible? Although the personality factors that predispose to anorexia are uncertain, many sufferers are perfectionists with low self-esteem. Physiological differences have also been found, including abnormal levels of certain brain chemicals, but these may be results rather than causes of the disorder.

Another eating disorder is binge eating, or bulimia (from a Greek word meaning "ox hunger"). The typical victim is not overweight and seems outgoing and successful. But she pays a price for her appearance: frequent secret binges, in which she may eat several quarts of ice cream at a sitting, are followed by purges using laxatives or vomiting. Usually the victim is depressed and guilt-ridden. A recent study suggests that bulimics may be

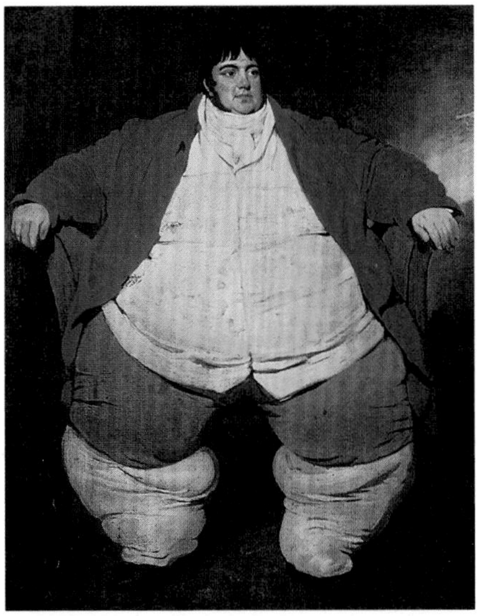

At 740 pounds, *foppish 18th-century English jailer Daniel Lambert probably had a hormonal disorder and fell dead at 39.*

deficient in a hormone that signals a full feeling. Most anorexics and bulimics are female, but men and boys, too, suffer from the disorders. The trap for them is often an exaggerated drive for fitness or athletic achievement.

Though at times extremely hard to treat, eating disorders may be preventable. Among other things, say specialists David B. Herzog and Ingrid L. Ott of Massachusetts General Hospital: "We can help young people feel good about themselves and accept their bodies. A change in our society's attitudes toward food, weight, and body shape may help."

How does our opinion of ourselves relate to how others judge our looks?

Many people think themselves better looking than others rate them. Moreover, any social advantage bestowed by good looks, such as youthful popularity, seems to decline as people age, perhaps because plainer people work harder to develop social skills, while their handsomer peers no longer get the automatic attention they once enjoyed.

Appearance is clearly not the only key to self-respect. Researchers who followed a group of schoolboys from age 10 to early adulthood found that those with consistently high self-esteem were not necessarily the best-looking; the most confident were boys whose parents had set high standards, yet showed respect for their sons' ideas and concern for their welfare. Such findings would certainly apply to girls as well.

Can plastic surgery boost your self-respect?

It was once widely believed that the only good reason to have plastic surgery was to repair disfigurement caused by injury or disease. People who sought surgery for purely cosmetic reasons were judged neurotic or vain. That view is less prevalent today, but the value of cosmetic surgery as a confidence-builder remains an open question and seems to depend on who undergoes the surgery.

"Beauty is not only in the eye of the beholder but in the mind of the beheld," observes one plastic-surgery text. Elective cosmetic surgery is likely to work best for people who have realistic goals: improving a specific feature such as the nose or the eyelids, rather than transforming a perfectly pleasant and ordinary face into the visage of an ideal beauty or a square-jawed football coach.

People with unrealistic expectations may become "scalpel junkies," going from surgeon to surgeon in search of the perfect face. This not only poses risks of infection or scarring, but can cause deep distress as each effort fails to bring the dreamed-of transformation of a shaky ego.

One experiment showed dramatically how a negative self-image can knock perceptions out of kilter with reality. Large scars were applied to people's faces with cosmetics. After showing the subjects their reflections in a mirror, the experimenters pretended to add final touches to their makeup, but actually removed the scars. The subjects were then introduced to strangers. Although none of the strangers knew anything about the "scars," the subjects felt that they were being looked at more often than usual and found unattractive.

Iron Pumpers Can Go Too Far in Others' Eyes

Today's image consciousness has pushed a great many people to try special diets and forms of exercise that promise to remake their bodies into this or that current ideal of physical beauty, male or female. Building bulging muscles by working out with weights, the practice known as pumping iron, has become especially popular among men. Although exercise can boost self-image and give a general feeling of well-being, studies show that big muscles do not give one a better image in the eyes of others.

Instead, diet and exercise that maintain a trim body, neither too muscular nor flabby, seem to be the key to physical attractiveness. When shown silhouettes of various male physiques, women rated a tapered "V" form higher than a very muscular body. Men also found very muscular women unappealing, despite the recent interest of women in muscle-building exercise. While men were found to like a wide range of female body types, the average preference was for a "moderately large bust, moderately small buttocks and moderately large legs."

Body building is no guarantee of appeal.

Understanding the Nature of Deficits

Why are some mental defects called hereditary and others congenital?

If a condition is caused by the set of chromosomes and genes bequeathed by parents to their child, it is said to be hereditary, or genetic. On the other hand, a congenital (birth) defect is one caused by some event during birth or the mother's pregnancy. For example, a baby's brain may have been injured in the womb by drugs or a bad accident; it can also be damaged during a difficult delivery by oxygen deprivation or other traumas.

Among the mental defects known to be hereditary are Down syndrome, or mongolism, and a few other rare forms of mental retardation. A growing number of scientists suspect that genetic factors may underlie personality types and particularly disorders such as manic-depression and schizophrenia; but genes are clearly only part of the story. Environmental influences, such as the family in which one grows up, are also important.

Congenital and hereditary defects need not involve the brain to alter personality. Hearing or vision abnormalities, for example, may lead to a misdiagnosis of mental retardation and adversely affect how children feel about themselves and others. Or a bright child may be judged slow or "odd" because of physical traits linked to a hereditary disorder like Marfan syndrome, which results in a gangly, uncoordinated look, as well as eye and heart problems. Abraham Lincoln is thought to have suffered from this disorder; and some physicians today conjecture that Lincoln's episodes of depression may have been a side effect of Marfan syndrome.

Do mentally retarded children have a special personality?

Hereditary and birth defects obviously affect personality; but mentally retarded people are as varied and unique as normal ones. Children with Down syndrome, for example, have a reputation for being sweet and docile. But this is not always true. In classes that push them to do their very best, some of these children are making unexpected gains—but may also show resentment when pressed.

Down's children, it seems, can not only express complex feelings, but are capable of richer personality development than ever imagined. Computers have worked especially well in teaching these children to read and write. At her computer, one child created a line that amazed even her parents: "I like God's finest whispers."

The Vital Importance of Early Stimulation

When Mary Boss was born with Down syndrome (a form of retardation characterized by a distinctive appearance, a smaller-than-normal brain, and some degree of mental impairment), her parents were determined to make the most of her abilities. Every day for several hours, Mary was played with, exercised, and talked to. The theory is that this intensive early stimulation builds neural connections that might otherwise never be made. The tenacity, devotion—and success—of Mary's parents, and others like them, have changed forever the outlook for retarded children.

Mary Boss at 13 is a competent sixth grader and a keen Scrabble player. Coached by her father (at left), she is even up to a fast game of soccer.

Can mentally retarded people be brilliant?

In the infinite variety of human minds, none is more fascinating than that of the idiot savant, or "wise idiot." These people show astonishing skill in a specific area, yet are mentally retarded, with an IQ of less than 70.

Typically, idiot savants are males (outnumbering females with this condition three to one) who can grasp complex number patterns, such as being able to name the day of the week for any date in a thousand-year span. But an idiot savant's talent may also be in art, mechanics, music, or memory of odd facts.

At 19, blind, suffering from cerebral palsy, and mentally retarded, Leslie Lemke sat down at a piano for the first time and played Tchaikovsky's First Piano Concerto, start to finish, after hearing it on the radio. A five-year-old retarded child named Nadia combined a mature artist's grasp of scale and spatial relationships with an unerring visual memory to create exquisite sketches of animals in motion.

Scientists can only speculate on what causes the behavior of an idiot savant. Somehow, he or she develops the capacity to remember certain things, coupled with an unswerving concentration that tunes out all else.

Curiously, the fields favored by idiot savants—math, music, memory feats—also have a large share of prodigies, people with rare talents who have normal or high IQ's. The brilliant German astronomer and mathematician Karl Friedrich Gauss, for example, did complex calculations in his head as a three-year-old. Musical prodigies include Mozart, Brahms, and Haydn. And prodigious memories are the mark of both idiot savants and great leaders, such as Napoleon, who knew the names of thousands of his soldiers.

A Boy Called Noah

An autistic child can fray but need not break the bonds that unite a family, as Noah Greenfeld's parents found in their endless search for a way into their son's mind. An undersized cerebellum may hold the key to the mystery of autism.

JOSH AND FOUMI Greenfeld's son Noah was a lovely baby. His dark eyes and delicate face had the serene beauty of a finely crafted doll, and he seemed unusually gentle and calm.

But Noah was slow to sit up and crawl, and his parents began to worry. A neurologist they consulted thought the development of his intellect and nervous system was delayed, but his parents insisted that Noah wasn't retarded.

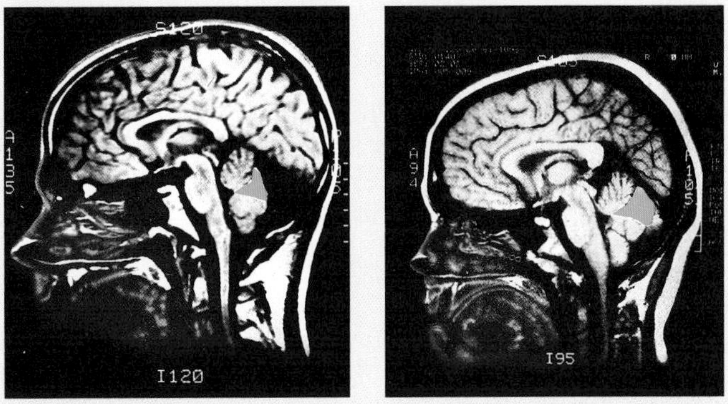

The brain of an autistic person *(left), compared to a normal brain (right), shows reduced size in the cerebellum (colored blue). This area of the brain is not well understood, but such graphic evidence, obtained by a technique called magnetic resonance imaging (MRI), may point the way to the cause of this baffling disorder.*

Noah finally learned to talk in phrases at 18 months and to walk at 27 months—but then he stopped speaking. He barely noticed his surroundings, spent hours alone repeating meaningless gestures and noises, and was prone to temper tantrums.

One doctor after another began to describe Noah as autistic. It is never a very precise diagnosis, and is based almost entirely on a hodgepodge of behaviors exhibited by children like Noah. Since the cause of autism is uncertain, Noah's parents were tormented by unanswered questions: Did they have faulty genes? Had Foumi received the best possible care while pregnant? Had they been meeting Noah's emotional needs? The emotional factor, at least, was at last ruled out, for experts now believe that autism is a physiological disorder of the brain.

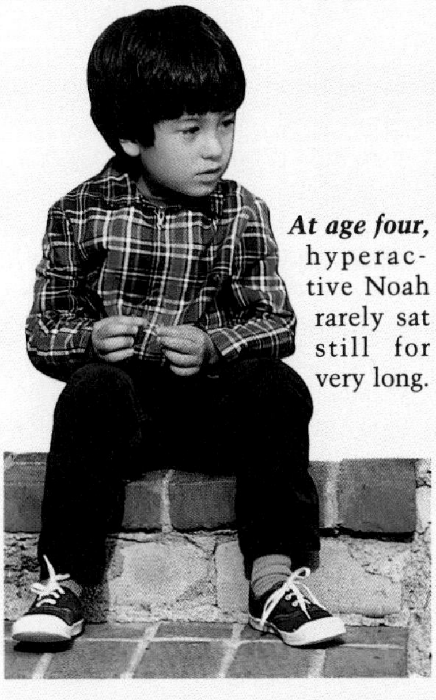

At age four, hyperactive Noah rarely sat still for very long.

Finding treatment for Noah was very difficult. The Greenfelds explored every possible source of help, including instruction in the sign language used by the deaf; they even sought advice from a dog trainer. The most promising treatment was operant conditioning, in which proper responses are rewarded with praise and food. In a program at UCLA, Noah was taught to clap his hands, pick up objects, and imitate simple sounds.

Yet, at four, Noah's chief activities were still "lint-catching, thread-pulling, blanket-sucking, spontaneous giggling, inexplicable crying, . . . wall-hugging, circle-walking, bed-bouncing, jumping, rocking, door-closing, and incoherent babbling addressed to his finger-flexing right hand."

Only 1 out of 50 autistic children becomes a fully normal adult, but almost half become moderately well adjusted. Noah seemed not to be among the more fortunate ones. Even at 16, he was not fully toilet trained. Getting him to dress or brush his teeth was an exhausting daily battle. In their fatigue and frustration, his parents often felt that they could stand no more and would have to put Noah in an institution, but then he would give some encouraging sign—a spoken word, a smile, or a hug—and they would continue.

When Josh developed heart trouble and Foumi's arthritis became severe, however, they had to act. After a brief stay at one center where the overworked staff mistreated him, Noah, nearly 20 at the time, found a haven in a small residential home for developmentally disabled adults.

Few marriages survive the strains of caring for a child like Noah, but the Greenfelds somehow managed. Against all odds, their careers, too, have flourished. Josh is a noted writer who chronicled Noah's early life in three acclaimed books. Foumi also turned to writing, and in 1986 her native Japan awarded her that nation's most prestigious literary prize—for a story about a child like Noah. Her husband attended the award ceremonies in Tokyo and wrote that "as she made her acceptance speech . . . I basked in her happiness—our family at last, somehow, a winner."

When You Take Evasive Action

A Vocabulary of Personality

When we talk about personality, we tend to use certain terms without thinking much about them. Many such terms, though their meanings may seem clear, are given precise definitions by psychologists. These narrower meanings reduce the risk of misunderstandings when psychologists discuss personalities. The following definitions are based in part on a list by psychologist Raymond J. Corsini.

- **Attitude:** A tendency to like or dislike classes of people or things based on one's beliefs and feelings.

  People who seem to believe that all women are emotional can be said to have a prejudiced attitude.

- **Character:** In the broad sense, the same as *personality* if used to refer to a person's total pattern of behavior. However, the word *character* generally implies the added dimension of ethical or moral values.

  Letters of recommendation may refer to a person's trustworthy or emotionally stable character. A person who cheats on an exam is said to have a questionable character.

- **Disposition:** A person's built-in tendency to react to a given situation in a characteristic way; similar to temperament.

  People who smile easily, are kind to others, and are sympathetic listeners are said to have a friendly disposition.

- **Habit:** A learned mode of behavior that is relatively fixed (and hard to change) and occurs again and again in certain situations.

  Taking a vitamin pill every day and fastening one's seat belt before driving are both habits; so are smoking cigarettes and driving too fast.

- **Mood:** An emotional state that may dominate one's outlook and manner of expressing oneself for a period of time.

  Winning a major competition puts one in a euphoric mood; being caught in bumper-to-bumper traffic brings on a depressed or irritable mood.

- **Personality:** The totality of a person's unique psychological qualities, which consistently determines his pattern of behavior in a variety of situations.

  Two boys were assigned to room together in boarding school. Since one was quiet and studious and the other liked to spend all his time partying, they were found to have incompatible personalities.

- **State:** A set of feelings of a certain kind that one is aware of and that cause some reaction in the autonomic nervous system (faster breathing or heart rate, for example). Unlike a trait, a state is only temporary.

  Not being prepared for an exam will cause a state of worrying or stress; but always being upset at exams is a sign of the trait called test anxiety.

- **Temperament:** One's inborn manner of reacting to things. It may show itself at birth or soon after, especially in the way a child expresses emotions and in his or her level of activity.

  Some babies are excitable and active, while others show a calm and passive temperament. Some adults are easy-going and relaxed, while others are high-strung.

- **Trait:** A specific way of behaving that occurs again and again, tends to characterize a person, and is useful in predicting future behavior.

  Someone who gives money to charitable organizations or to friends in need and who gives up leisure time for a worthy cause could be said to possess the trait of generosity.

- **Type:** A category used to classify people who share similar traits.

  People described as Type-A are said to behave in competitive and sometimes hostile ways in reaction to the stresses in their lives.

- **Values:** Qualities that a person has learned to believe are important or worthwhile. They can be principles to live by or goals to be achieved.

  Power and wealth are important to some people; others may find friendship and community service to be of greater significance.

What is a defense mechanism?

Perhaps the most valuable mental asset is self-esteem, a self-image that the individual likes and respects. Without it, we have little chance of possessing what philosophers and scientists have called by many names: a sound ego, an intact psyche, a healthy personality, a fulfilled self, or simply a wise and resourceful mind.

Small wonder, then, that human beings have an array of defenses to protect their self-esteem. Threats come in many guises, such as anxiety, guilt, shame, and conflict between two or more drives or emotions.

At times we consciously face these threats. Often, we automatically repress them, pushing them into our unconscious. Such repression may be the most basic *ego defense mechanism*, a term Sigmund Freud used to describe the ego's effort to resolve conflicts between the primal id, the moralistic superego, and external reality.

Would we be better off without ego defenses?

Defense mechanisms were once considered neurotic, but that view has mellowed. The prevailing opinion is that they are, at times, necessary, if imperfect, solutions to the problem of preserving self-esteem.

The trouble with repressing bad feelings is that they may pop out later. For example, a child may repress anger caused by anxiety over the unpredictable behavior of a parent. As an adult, the child's anger can erupt in rebellion against all authority.

Freud and his successors identified dozens of defense mechanisms, beginning with repression. *Projection* blames somebody else for one's own thoughts or actions. *Rationalization* justifies questionable behavior by defending its propriety. *Reaction formation* is acting exactly opposite to the way you feel, because your real feelings frighten or appall you.

Freud thought that one defense mechanism, *sublimation*, was a powerful constructive force. It involves repressing sexual desires, which later are channeled into good works.

Is a defense mechanism conscious or unconscious?

Psychologists disagree on whether we are aware of using defense mechanisms. Certainly, the end result of a defense mechanism and a conscious decision can look much the same. For example, *undoing* has been called an unconscious defense mechanism in which we think or do something to erase a deed or thought of which we are ashamed—equivalent, in some ways, to conscious atonement.

Are some people stress-free?

As many as one in six people is a "represser" personality who *appears* to feel little stress. Brain scans of some of these stiff-upper-lip types reveal a neurological quirk. Disturbing information is not relayed between their hemispheres as quickly as in a nonrepresser. This lag seems to be a result, not a cause, of the ability to hide emotions, learned in childhood.

Sadly, repressers may pay a price for their composure in hypertension and other ills, as well as in a reduced capacity for intimacy; but various therapies can address these problems.

The Twenty-two Faces of Eve

THE YOUNG WOMAN suffered from agonizing headaches, followed by blackouts. But only when she realized she had tried to strangle her daughter did she seek help. Thus one of the most famous cases of multiple personalities came to light.

In early therapy, her doctor was amazed to witness "Eve White," his bland, self-effacing patient, suddenly become another person: She closed her eyes and pressed her hands against her temples as if in sudden pain. Then her eyes popped open and there was a "reckless smile. In a bright, unfamiliar voice that sparkled, the woman said, 'Hi there, Doc! . . . She's been having a real rough time. . . . Would you give me a cigarette, Doc?'

" 'Who is *she*?'

" 'Why, Eve White, of course. Your long-suffering, saintly little patient.'

" 'Well, who are *you*?' he asked incredulously.

" 'Why, I'm Eve Black.' "

Eve White and Eve Black were just two of the 22 personalities that emerged over time, but only three could coexist in her mind at one time. When one set of three "died," another set would take their place. Some of them, sensing their demise, actually wrote wills.

Toward the end of therapy, a final (22nd) personality emerged, that of Virginia homemaker Chris Sizemore (Eve's real name), who told her story in the book *I'm Eve*. Chris describes her many personalities as "a defense and a unique coping mechanism, which created satellite persons to cope with conflicts that were unbearable."

A tortured Eve White, *unaware of her other personalities.*

Psychiatrists agree, and add that the disorder may stem from sexual or mental cruelty suffered as a child. They call it a dissociative disorder because the self may dissociate, or split apart, into subpersonalities hidden from consciousness.

Although some cases of multiple personality have been exposed as fake, recent research has tended to confirm others as genuine, including Eve's. Most convincing are studies showing a distinctive brainwave pattern for each of a patient's multiple personalities. Normal people cannot simulate different brain waves. The true multiple personality also has selves with unique physical attributes, such as color blindness and allergies.

Joanne Woodward played three *of Sizemore's 22 personalities: she is rational Jane at left and sultry Eve Black at right.*

Personality and Health

Can your personality give you a heart attack?

A highly publicized study conducted in the 1960's reported that Type A people—ambitious, aggressive, and impatient—were more likely to suffer heart attacks than Type B's, who were more relaxed. The quintessential Type A was described in the study as a high-level male business executive, at the peak of his success, in his forties or early fifties.

When further research failed to show any difference between the heart-attack rates of Type A's and Type B's, some researchers decided that the original concept needed refining. They began searching for the "toxic trait" in the Type A personality. Since then, various investigators have proposed that hostility, cynicism, and self-involvement are more critical risk factors for heart disease than ambition; but these conclusions, too, remain hypothetical.

Some studies indicate that Type A's can reduce their heart-attack risk by learning to react more calmly to what they consider unfair criticism and pressure. And whatever your personality type, eating wisely, giving up smoking, exercising, and maintaining blood pressure within normal limits can help keep your heart healthy.

Why are some people more susceptible to disease than others?

Your mental state can make the symptoms of some diseases more distressing and also make you more liable to get sick in the first place, but precisely how biological and personality factors may interact to cause physical illness is uncertain. Of course, our genetic predisposition may underlie both physical and emotional problems, but the relationship between these two factors is still not firmly established. Researchers have, however, investigated the problem, and their conclusion is that susceptibility to disease often has psychological roots. In one study, conducted at West Point, scientists found that Army cadets with intense ambitions for a military career whose scholastic rankings were low were susceptible to mononucleosis.

Have other illnesses been linked to disposition?

It is tempting to attribute diseases whose causes are not understood to personality factors. As Susan Sontag points out in her essay "Illness as Metaphor," before the bacillus that causes tuberculosis was discovered, TB was widely believed to be caused by the patients' passionate natures.

As for other possible links between personality and diseases, recent research has turned up mixed findings. For example, there is now little support for the once popular notion of a single, identifiable "ulcer personality." However, researchers have found evidence that people with certain neurotic traits, such as chronic anxiety, pessimism, and hostility, are particularly likely to become ill by their early forties. One study, begun at Harvard in 1937, followed a group of undergraduates for some 30 years. The men who coped with life immaturely, by running away perhaps, or through fantasy, became ill four times more often than more stable men. The connection is not with any specific disease, but with poor health in general: asthma, headaches, peptic ulcers, and heart conditions show up frequently. Such findings are controversial. Among the criticisms is that neurotics may simply be more likely to complain about physical discomfort than other people.

Narcissus, a mythical youth *in love with his own image, gave his name to a personality disorder marked by self-importance.*

Is narcissism a product of today's "me-first" society?

Narcissism—named for the legendary Greek youth Narcissus, who fell in love with his own reflection in the water—is by no means a new disorder. It seems increasingly common today, but perhaps only because of the "me-first" philosophy that has prevailed of late.

Narcissistic people are often unaware of other people's feelings and needs. They exaggerate their own importance and talent, and if they do not get the attention—even adulation—that they think they deserve, they feel they are victims of personal hostility, like an incompetent actor who blames critics for his poor notices.

The cause of this mind-set is unclear, but psychologists believe the narcissist was probably either overindulged or, paradoxically, deprived as a child. Under a grandiose shell, he or she may feel deeply inadequate.

Why do some people check repeatedly that a door is locked or the oven turned off?

Many of us have had the experience of going back into the house to be sure that we turned off a burner on the stove. But someone continually driven by such anxieties—a chronic worrywart—may have what psychiatrists call an obsessive-compulsive personality. He or she is generally a perfectionist and clings rigidly to familiar ideas and fixed routines.

In extreme cases, this personality quirk may turn into a troublesome disorder, in which a person cannot resist endlessly repeating a gesture that

The Healthy Mind: A Delicate Balance Between Traits That May War With One Another

From Hippocrates' idea that sickness was an imbalance of bodily fluids—blood, phlegm, yellow bile, and black bile—came the medieval notion (below) of four personality types. Today, that system can be used to arrange a continuum of traits on a "personality wheel," which suggests that what makes a trait good or bad is, after all, a matter of balance.

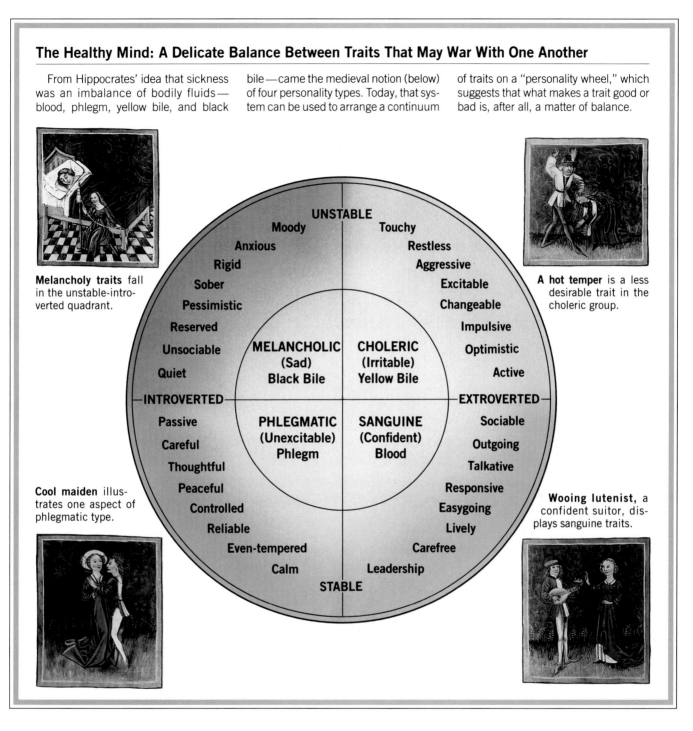

Melancholy traits fall in the unstable-introverted quadrant.

A hot temper is a less desirable trait in the choleric group.

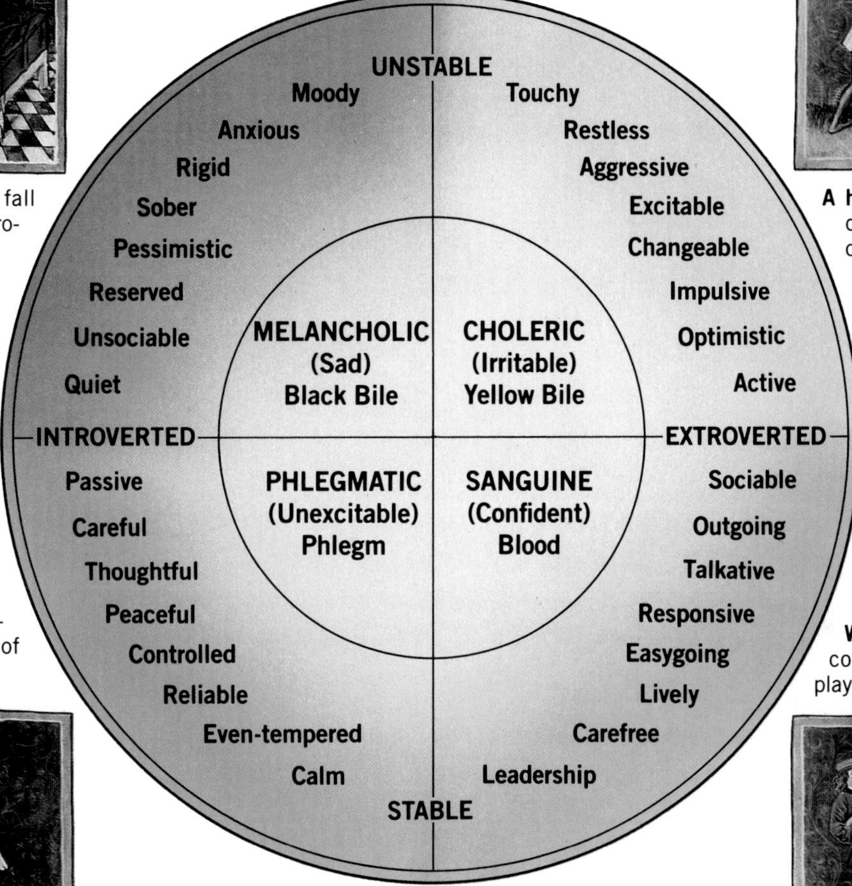

Cool maiden illustrates one aspect of phlegmatic type.

Wooing lutenist, a confident suitor, displays sanguine traits.

he or she knows is irrational or even self-destructive. An example is the man, plagued by an overwhelming fear of infection, who washes his hands hundreds of times a day, until the skin on them is raw and bleeding.

Recent research has uncovered evidence of physiological abnormalities in the brains of some people with obsessive-compulsive disorder. Specific areas in the frontal lobes and in the basal ganglia at the base of the cortex show unusually high metabolic rates. Other studies indicate that the levels of serotonin, a chemical neurotransmitter that is plentiful in these areas, are above normal in obsessive-compulsive patients. Thus, drugs that lower serotonin hold promise in treating obsessive-compulsive behavior.

The new findings in brain research may help to explain a startling report from England about a would-be suicide who shot himself in the head with a .22 rifle because he just couldn't live with his obsessive-compulsive disorder. Remarkably, he recovered from his wound—to find that he had been "cured" of his compulsive hand washing.

Setting the Stage for Change

Is it better to be an optimist or a pessimist?

Although gloomy visions of failure may spur a pessimistic personality to excel, optimists might actually have the power to make their own lives longer, healthier, and more rewarding, recent studies have indicated.

One research method of classifying people as optimistic or pessimistic is to ask them to explain bad events in their lives. Pessimists tend to blame misfortune on permanent, inalterable conditions or on their own ingrained character flaws, and they see any setback as casting a shadow on the rest of their lives. Optimists, on the other hand, feel that their failures are the result of forces they can control and change in the future.

One long-term study, begun in 1946 with about 100 recent Harvard graduates, shows an "impressive . . . relationship between pessimism [at about age 25] and poor health in middle age." Another group, 54 Hall of Fame baseball players, was analyzed from reports on how they explained their slumps. Those who blamed their bad days on their own inner failings died younger than players who felt slumps just happened.

Many well-known people tell of personal victories over pessimism. Perhaps the 20th-century's most famous optimist is Dr. Norman Vincent Peale, author of *The Power of Positive Thinking.* All his life, according to Dr. Peale, he overcame shyness by substituting positive ideas for negative ones before his public appearances.

When the Time Comes to Break a Bad Habit . . .

Generally speaking, habitual nail-biters, foot-tappers, and head-scratchers would love to quit these irksome ways. "I've got to stop doing this," they say to themselves. But, having decided, say, to cut back on coffee drinking, they are often chagrined to find a second cup of coffee in their hands.

Then consider procrastination, a free-floating bad habit that affects every part of one's life. Problems don't go away; they accumulate, gumming up human relations, school assignments, and job performance, and even making people miss their vacation plane flights. Dr. Norman Vincent Peale, an admitted procrastinator who cured himself, described this particular habit as "a villain that can thwart your ambitions, destroy your happiness, even kill you."

The first thing to realize about breaking a habit is that it is going to be tough. It is in the nature of habits that they bypass the conscious mind. This means that you have to retrain yourself from the ground up. Here are some tips on getting started:

- **Focus on the problem.** Many bad habits are so ingrained that you don't notice them. You may want to enlist the help of a friend or relative, who will give you a small signal when you are doing something you want to quit. (The helper in the case should just *signal*, not nag.) Being aware of when you scratch your head or crack your knuckles or whatever is an important first step. Keep notes of the times you find yourself backsliding. This little trick will keep you posted on how you're doing.
- **Choose a time to change.** Don't start on the spur of the moment. Bad habits are often a nervous response to anxiety. So pick a time when you are not likely to be under pressure.
- **Set sensible goals.** And be definite. Get a clear picture of what you want to accomplish and when. But don't take on too much all at once. If there are two habits to quit, tackle them one at a time. Some people find it easier to quit in stages; no coffee after lunch or no finger-drumming at office meetings.
- **Use counter-tactics and substitutes.** To keep away from nail-biting, splurge on a manicure. To avoid coffee, find a fruit juice you like.
- **Relax.** Meditation helps, so take a deep breath and sit back. Imagine yourself in a pleasant place, serenely enjoying your surroundings. Visualize yourself without your bad habit.
- **Persevere.** Backsliding is inevitable for most of us, but don't let it discourage you. Keep on trying.
- **Reward yourself.** When you feel that you are winning the fight against your bad habit, reward yourself. Take a day off, go on a short trip, buy something you've wanted for a long time.

If you want to change your personality, can you do so?

Various forms of therapy and even do-it-yourself exercises may help modify personality traits that you think are denying you happiness or success. If you are uncomfortably shy, like 80 percent of people who have answered surveys on the subject, counselors often suggest starting with simple, attainable goals—a few words of small talk with someone new, for instance—and gradually moving into more difficult situations.

Because of the many forms of psychotherapy—from the Freudian couch to screaming in a group—it is often difficult for a troubled person to know where to look for help. As a rule, proven methods of treatment with a well-trained therapist are the best bet. Just as difficult is the question of whether or not someone will benefit from professional help. Here, the attitude of the client has a great deal to do with the eventual outcome of the treatment. Broadly speaking, if an individual sincerely wants to be helped, it becomes more likely that the therapy will be successful.

No matter what the therapy, much depends on the training, experience, intuition, and sensitivity of the therapist. Naturally, there are differences among therapists, as there are among any group of human beings.

Some people probably go too far in jumping from therapy to therapy in hopes of having their personality revamped into some ideal that does not exist and never did, anywhere, anytime. All this considered, there is no question that many kinds of psychotherapy have helped many thousands of people reach a better understanding and acceptance of who they are, as well as find more effective ways of dealing with life's challenges.

Ivan the Terrible: 16th-Century Sociopath

As a child, he threw dogs off the walls of the Kremlin. As an adult, he murdered thousands, then prayed for their souls. Ivan the Terrible, Russia's most infamous czar, was a notorious example of unbridled power in the hands of a deranged ruler.

Demonic eyes stare from a sculptured head of Ivan IV.

THE FAMOUS STATEMENT that "power tends to corrupt and absolute power corrupts absolutely" seems to fit the violent and sadistic rule of Russia's Ivan IV, known to history as Ivan the Terrible. A close look at Ivan's life, however, shows that "absolute power" was only part of the story. Ivan had a seriously disordered personality that was shaped by violence and terror early in life.

Since he lived over 400 years ago, no sure diagnosis can be applied to Ivan, but his character shows the egocentricity, impulsiveness, and lack of conscience typical of what are today called psychopathic or sociopathic personality disorders. Like many sociopaths, he was intelligent and often charming. But he could slaughter thousands without guilt and then carefully instruct the monasteries to pray for their souls.

Ivan IV was born in 1530. When he was three, his father died and left him the kingdom, but his mother ruled for him—bitterly opposed by the Russian nobility. Intrigue and murder surrounded the child. When he was seven his mother died, probably poisoned. He and his retarded younger brother were left in the center of a furious power struggle among the ruling nobility.

During Ivan's childhood, spent in constant fear of the warring nobles, his emerging personality took a turn toward sadism. He tortured animals by putting out their eyes and slitting their abdomens, and threw puppies from the high towers of the Kremlin. In his teens, while out hunting he amused himself by beating and raping peasants, and then, convinced of his divine dignity, he would go directly to hours of pious prayer.

Surprisingly, Ivan did have a successful first marriage. With his wife, Anastasia, he chose good advisers and began his reign with solid reforms. But after 13 years of marriage, Anastasia died after a long illness, and Ivan, now just 30, became distraught. He was convinced the nobles had poisoned her, and hatred and terror overwhelmed him. He struck back with murderous purges that destroyed even his closest advisers and best military commanders.

Ivan believed he had an absolute divine right to punish any "traitors" as he saw fit. Suspecting that the entire city of Novgorod might be traitorous, Ivan spent five weeks in the city square passing judgment on the hapless citizens. He had them systematically flayed, roasted, and disemboweled until the nearby river was clogged with thousands of bodies. When it was over, as always, he ordered monks to pray for their souls.

Finally, Ivan destroyed all hopes for the future of his dynasty when, in a fit of paranoia toward his son and heir, he beat him to death with a spear. Ivan was overwhelmed with remorse, and for months his howling could be heard outside the palace. Two years later, at the age of 54, the demented czar died suddenly of a mysterious ailment and may have been poisoned. Both he and his people had been victims of a personality that bore within it great potential for good but had been so misshapen by fear, hatred, and uncontrolled power that its horrors eclipsed its accomplishments.

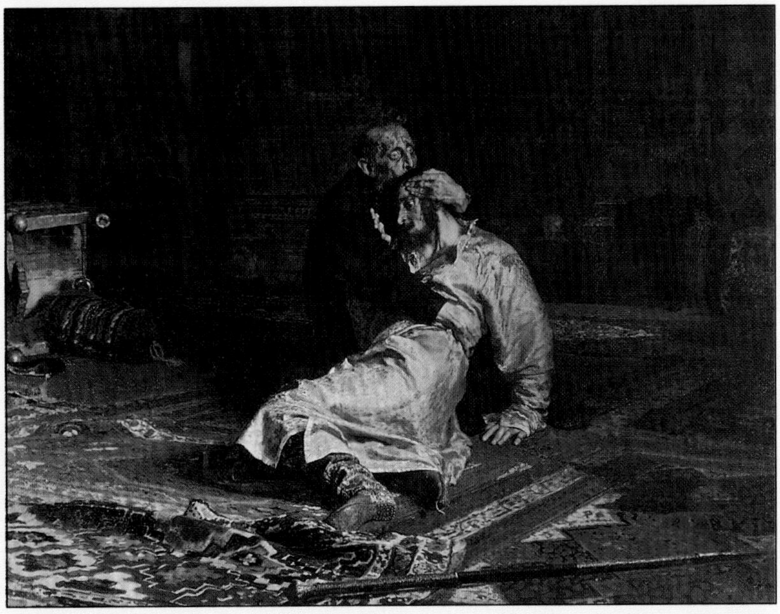

Ivan cradles his son, whom he has just struck a fatal blow with the heavy spear lying in front of them, in this 19th-century oil by Russian artist Ilya Repin.

Unreasoning Fear

What is a phobia?

The difference between a phobia and a sensible fear is the panic that grips a phobic person. A phobia is like a fear gone wild, robbing a person of reason. For example, a respect for the dangers of falling off a cliff reflects a healthy sense of reality; but a panicky preoccupation with heights can prevent a person from working in a tall building or vacationing in the mountains. One of the cruelest aspects of a phobia is that it can dominate a person's thoughts even when the person knows the fear is irrational.

How common are these irrational, consuming fears?

There are hundreds of phobias and over 12 million Americans suffer from them. The American Psychiatric Association separates phobias into three general kinds. The most common kind is agoraphobia, actually a complex group of fears involved with being in public places. Then there are simple phobias and social phobias.

Broadly speaking, simple phobias are connected to one thing or to a specific activity. Among simple phobias are ophidiophobia, fear of snakes; ombrophobia, fear of rain; aerophobia, fear of flying; and ornithophobia, fear of birds. The famous inventor Nikola Tesla suffered from a fear of germs (mysophobia); he never used a handkerchief more than once and went through dozens of napkins at a meal, discarding each after one use.

At the root of a social phobia is a deep fear of suffering humiliation in a social situation. Among the most common is the fear of public speaking. Others are the fear of eating with other people, the inability to urinate in a public lavatory, the dread of socializing with the opposite sex, and the refusal to meet strangers or to appear for job interviews. Clearly, all of these can severely restrict someone's ability to function. To make matters worse, social phobias often cause poor performances, thereby "proving" that the original fear was justified. A person who fears eating in public, for example, may be so nervous that he drops a spoonful of soup on his shirt or knocks over a glass.

Are some people really afraid to go outside their doors?

Of all those who seek help for their phobias, 60 percent suffer from agoraphobia, or panic at being in a place they consider unsafe. Often, agoraphobia is accompanied by a more specific phobia, such as fear of snakes or

The Brothers Who Buried Themselves in Fear

Younger brother Langley appeared briefly at broken window in 1942.

HOMER AND LANGLEY Collyer were respectable and well-to-do young bachelors. Nobody found it strange that they continued to live in the mansion inherited from their parents on New York's Fifth Avenue.

Gradually, however, the brothers withdrew from the world. Today it seems clear that one or both had severe phobias that made ordinary human contact impossible. They barricaded the doors and windows and, foraging by night, accumulated piles of junk that filled the entire house. Unpaid bills left them without water and electricity, so they cooked with kerosene and fetched water from a nearby park.

By the mid-1940's, the junk was so densely packed that Langley crept through narrow tunnels to take food to his now invalid brother. Both were in their sixties. Terrified of burglars, Langley set booby traps designed to send debris down on the heads of intruders.

In March 1947, the police, acting on a tip about a death in the house, worked for hours to get inside. They found Homer's emaciated corpse, but there was no sign of Langley.

Finally, after weeks of searching among 140 tons of junk—ancient toys, tree limbs, a car chassis, 14 grand pianos, and countless other items—they uncovered Langley's crushed body. While taking food to Homer, Langley had sprung one of his own booby traps. And Homer had then starved to death.

Police chop through the roof of the Collyer house in their effort to find Langley in April 1947.

germs. Afraid to venture from their homes, to drive or to use public transportation, or even to walk into a store, many agoraphobes turn into recluses, completely incapacitated.

One agoraphobe, faced with leaving the house, reported that "my hands would go clammy, and my knees would shake, and my muscles would ache, and my eyes would blur, and I'd start to sweat." These panic symptoms are typical of all phobias.

Is there a link between phobias and addiction?

Some phobic people, perhaps as many as 20 percent, resort to alcohol to deaden their panic. A recent study involving a group of alcoholics showed that 25 percent of the men and 17 percent of the women had some type of social phobia. In addition, a common complaint of people trying to stop smoking is that social situations are more frightening without cigarettes; and the use of tranquilizers and other drugs may often be an attempt to conquer the dread of appearing inadequate in public.

Why do people have panic reactions?

Not surprisingly, many researchers think one way a phobia develops is out of a terrifying experience. For example, a child who has been attacked by a dog can develop an intense fear of dogs; or someone who has been in a traffic accident can have a panic attack at the idea of traveling in a car.

Yet not everybody who has had a bad experience develops a phobia. Some phobias seem to run in families, although there is little evidence that they are actually inherited genetically. A fear of snakes or a fear of spiders can simply be learned from a parent.

However, parents need not worry that a phobia lurks in every fear expressed by a child. Most children go through periods of having irrational fears, which they will outgrow. Among the normal, passing childhood anxieties are fears of darkness and of being left alone.

Looking up from the bottom *of the World Trade Center, a phobic person may feel not only the generalized panic of agoraphobia, but claustrophobia (fear of narrow places).*

Can phobias be conquered?

People who seek treatment have an excellent chance of ridding themselves of phobias. Psychologists use a variety of techniques, all of which try to demonstrate that there is nothing intrinsically fearful about the dreaded object or situation.

In one method, called desensitization, therapists begin by teaching the patient how to relax completely and to do so on command. First, the patient is encouraged to face the panic-causing situation in his imagination, then is gradually led to the point of physically confronting his fear. For a victim of claustrophobia (fear of enclosed places), the first encounter might be a picture of the interior of an elevator. Then the patient is asked to imagine himself on an elevator. Next the therapist might accompany the patient on a trip in an elevator. Thus, step by step, the patient is taught that there is nothing to fear.

Another method, known as modeling, involves seeing other people coping with a situation that terrifies the phobic patient. Often the sight of others behaving normally and rationally in a dreaded situation, such as climbing a ladder or mixing in crowds, helps to diminish the phobia.

Wellsprings of Emotion

What is an emotion?

Naming specific emotions—such as love, anger, and fear—is easier than finding an all-purpose definition. In fact there is no scientific consensus on how to define emotion. Most scientists agree that emotions are different from rational thought (cognition), from information known through our senses (perception), and from the storing of information (memory); yet our emotions interact with all these mental functions.

Any explanation of emotions has to consider three factors: (1) what triggers, or arouses, an emotion; (2) how, having been aroused, body and mind respond, or express their reaction; (3) how our physical and mental responses further color the way we experience an emotion. Thus, say most psychologists, the mystery of emotions really involves three mysteries: arousal, expression, and experience.

Not only is the concept of emotion vague and complicated, but also it gets mixed up with other terms, adding to the confusion. Some scientists regard the term *affect* as synonymous with emotion; but to others, affect means only the part of an emotion that we experience consciously, aside from any unconscious or bodily responses. An affect, in this narrower sense, is often used to mean the same

When Your Feelings Are Written on Your Countenance

Researchers believe there are facial expressions that are immediately identifiable, regardless of the age, sex, or nationality of the person. Among these are happiness, sadness, anger, and disgust. Fear and surprise are also widely recognizable, but in some cultures, they are too close to call. Most other facial expressions are strongly influenced by one's upbringing.

Mixed emotions struggle for expression—joy, pride, relief, and exhaustion—as Evelyn Ashford, winner of the 100-meter dash, claims the gold at the 1984 Olympics. A sweet victory indeed, as she was nearly sidelined by injuries.

Pure joy shines from the face of a young Austrian boy, who, in the aftermath of World War II, received a new pair of shoes. The picture is a powerful reminder of the relativity of happiness. Who among us has experienced such rapture over the fulfillment of a modest wish?

as a *feeling* (which, confusingly, also refers to the sense of touch). An emotion that persists becomes a *mood.*

How are our emotions aroused?

Theories abound on what triggers an emotional response. One that makes sense to many of today's scientists starts with the sensing of a "discrepancy." This could be something new, a disturbance, or some other interruption in the normal, expected course of things.

What happens then, at least for a moment or two, is automatic, out of the control of the conscious mind. Several visceral ("gut") reactions occur, amounting to a bodily arousal that, if intense or prolonged, is identical to stress. The heart beats faster, the liver is stimulated by hormones to release more energy-giving sugar into the bloodstream, changes in breathing pump more oxygen to the body, the stomach and intestines tighten (giving "butterflies" to some), the pupils of the eyes dilate, saliva dries up but sweat flows more freely, and skin surface contracts causing a crawly feeling or "goose bumps."

Very quickly, these bodily events register in the conscious mind. The next step—how the mind reacts—depends entirely on the thinking and memory processes of the individual. A situation that causes powerful feelings in one person's mind may produce little feeling in someone else.

Can our minds alone arouse our emotions?

The memory of past experience and how it made us feel can be almost as powerful an emotion-arouser as the event itself. How each of us thinks, and how and what we remember, can heighten—or lessen—the intensity of a feeling. The feelings can then loop back and affect our bodies. The mind alone can cause a visceral reaction if we imagine being aroused. The memory or expectation of a sad event can make us cry; a remembered or imagined argument can make us angry and our hearts beat faster.

PERSPECTIVES

On Emotions

How powerful are our emotions! They override circumstances with ease. Misery can find gloom in rainbows, but a glad heart is resourceful in finding joy.

A Great Charge

"Nothing is so contagious as enthusiasm; it moves stones, it charms brutes. Enthusiasm is the genius of sincerity, and truth accomplishes no victories without it."

—Edward George Earle Bulwer-Lytton

◆

How Hatred Destroys

"When we hate our enemies, we give them power over us—power over our sleep, our appetites and our happiness. They would dance with joy if they knew how much they were worrying us. Our hate is not hurting them at all, but it is turning our own days and nights into hellish turmoil."

—Dale Carnegie
How to Stop Worrying and Start Living

◆

An Abiding Spirit

"Joy seems to me a step beyond happiness—happiness is a sort of atmosphere you can live in sometimes when you're lucky. Joy is a light that fills you with hope and faith and love."

—Adela Rogers St. Johns
Some Are Born Great

◆

A Short Circuit

"Impatience poisons all our joys and prevents us from recognizing happiness. We are made impatient by the impression that happiness is always a little further on. We want to rush through everything to achieve it. But happiness, as a philosopher once wrote, is like a ball chased by a child—when you catch up with it, you give it a kick."

—Luigi Barzini, Sr.
Vita Vagabonda

◆

Perfect Reciprocity

"Cold words freeze people, and hot words scorch them, and bitter words make them bitter, and wrathful words make them wrathful. Kind words also produce their own image on men's souls; and a beautiful image it is. They soothe, quiet and comfort the hearer."

—Blaise Pascal

◆

Luxurious Solitude

"Loneliness is most acutely felt with other people, for with others, even with a lover sometimes, we suffer from our differences—differences of taste, temperament, mood. With other human beings, vision becomes double vision. We are busy wondering, *What does my companion see or think of this?* and *What do I think of it?* The original impact gets lost, or diffused. Alone, we can afford to be wholly whatever we are, and to feel whatever we feel absolutely. That is a great luxury."

—May Sarton
The New York Times

◆

On Being Afraid

"If we take the generally accepted definition of bravery as a quality which knows no fear, I have never seen a brave man. All men are frightened. The more intelligent they are, the more they are frightened."

—George S. Patton, Jr.
American General, World War II

◆

Be Mindful of Your Values

"It is enough if you don't freeze in the cold, and if thirst and hunger don't claw at your insides.
If your back isn't broken, if your feet can walk, if both arms can bend, if both eyes can see, and if both ears can hear, then whom should you envy? And why? Our envy of others devours us most of all.

Rub your eyes and purify your heart and prize above all else in the world those who love you and who wish you well. After all, it might be your last act."

—Aleksandr Solzhenitsyn
The Gulag Archipelago

What Makes Us Truly Human

How necessary are emotions?

Although some philosophers have cast emotions as villains that represent what is most irrational and "animal" in human nature, there is a strong argument for crediting the emotions with all that is worthy and wonderful about human life. If "love makes the world go around," it can also be said that, like love, many other emotions inspire us to improve our own lives and the lives of others.

Moreover, without emotions we could not enjoy great art and literature or root for our favorite team. Fear of punishment is effective in stopping many of us from committing rash or violent acts; if we do lose control, remorse follows. Having emotions may make human life less tidy and predictable, but how drab and spiritless the world would be without them.

Lie Detectors—When Emotions Are Asked to Testify

Most people like to think they can tell when someone is lying—the eyes look shady, the smile lingers too long, the voice cracks. But the truth is that most of us have about a 50-50 chance of figuring out who is lying.

Scientists thought they might have a more accurate way of separating the guilty from the innocent, when, in the 1920's, they tried using electrodes to test the physical response to emotionally charged questions. The polygraph, or lie-detector test, as it is also called, uses electrodes to record changes in the body's heartbeat, breathing, and blood pressure. The test is based on the assumption that the emotional upset of telling a lie will stimulate a significant physical reaction.

Unfortunately, that assumption proved false. As psychologists have since discovered, truthful responses to questions can also trigger physical reactions that can fool a polygraph machine. To those who are innocent, the mere stress of taking a lie-detector test can make them appear guilty. The best way to truly detect a lie, the experts now say, is to know a person's body signals for truthfulness.

Though considered unreliable by most psychologists, lie-detector tests are still used by some banks and government agencies to screen job applicants.

How many emotions are there?

Because emotions shade into one another, researchers cannot agree on what counts as a separate emotion. When does impatience become anger? Or lukewarm acceptance become friendship and then love? Depending on how such questions are answered, the total number of emotions could be dozens or thousands.

Many psychologists have tried to pare down the number of emotions to short lists of the most basic ones. A typical selection is that of psychologist Robert Plutchik, who lists eight: acceptance, anger, anticipation, disgust, fear, joy, sadness, and surprise.

Some researchers suggest that it is senseless to try to count emotions, because the number is virtually limitless. That is, what someone feels depends entirely on the thinking, experience, and memory of the individual—who is unique among all the people who have ever lived.

Is it possible to study feelings scientifically?

A major problem in studying emotions is how to keep the investigators' own emotions and the research environment from affecting the responses of the people being studied. Furthermore, verbal descriptions of emotions—either by the investigator or the subject—can be misleading.

A pounding heart or sweaty palms can signal any number of emotions, from puppy love to fear of flying. Such symptoms can hardly be used as definitive signposts by the scientist.

Nevertheless, the mysterious territory of emotions, straddling the boundary between body and brain, is beginning to yield some secrets. Aristotle's hunch that emotions are partly physical and partly mental is backed by new theories of the function of the brain's limbic system, where thoughts seem to be converted to body reactions, and bodily stresses to feelings.

When do emotions begin?

As the brain develops, emotions grow more complex. Not until about the age of two months is the brain advanced enough to manage the first real smile. Four months later, a baby begins to show a fear of separation.

As we grow older, our expectations increase and we react strongly if these expectations are challenged. For example, if we hope to get a job and then do not, we may feel anger and disappointment and self-doubt. All three feelings occur at once and add up to a complex total response. Similarly, if we fall in love, memories of earlier relationships color our feelings. Our experiences may make us warier, less prone to trust our feelings; or they may, by comparison with the present, make us readier to believe that we have found the real thing.

The Teddy Bear *originated in 1902, named in honor of President Theodore Roosevelt, who refused to shoot a trapped bear. Since that time, legions of Teddies have provided emotional support to children and adults alike. Bear lover James D. Nelson calls them a "prescription for relief of tears and nervous tension."*

Is too much or too little emotion a sign of mental illness?

How people express their emotions—in other words, their behavior—is a significant clue to mental health. However, there is a wide range of behavior that is normal, and a diagnosis of mental illness is rarely made on the basis of one or two seemingly abnormal emotional episodes.

If a person expresses a response to a situation in a way that falls well within the normal range, psychologists say the person is showing *appropriate affect*. On the other hand, people who express less range of emotion are said to have *constricted* affect. The apparent reverse of this affect is seen in people who seem to ride an emotional rollercoaster: laughing one moment and crying the next. This condition is termed *instability of affect*, a sign of an unstable personality or considerable stress. If such emotional responses are severe and long lasting, they are called *affective disorders*.

How does culture influence us?

How emotions are expressed varies from culture to culture, but presumably feelings are much the same anywhere. Psychologists refer to these cultural practices as "display rules." As children grow up, they unconsciously absorb the display rules of their society.

In Japan, for example, a smile is used to mask anger, shame, or any other emotion the smiler wants to hide. Touching someone as a sign of friendship is a common public display in Mediterranean countries but hardly ever seen in the British Isles.

Is it harmful to suppress anger?

"Count to ten! Bite your tongue!" For a while not too many years ago, such advice for avoiding an angry outburst was considered old-fashioned. It was better for mental health, said some psychologists, to "let it all hang out." Now the pendulum has swung back. It isn't always healthy to show anger, say the experts. A public temper tantrum may fuel anger instead of dissipating it. Control, on the other hand, gives calm a chance to prevail and can help avoid a fist fight or a court case.

Are women more comfortable with emotions than men are?

Men and women feel their emotions with equal intensity but they tend to express them differently. In general women are more open about their emotions, admitting to loneliness, embarrassment, and fear. Men tend to cover up such feelings, perhaps because they were brought up to believe that displaying emotion was "unmanly." Men are also quicker to show anger to strangers, especially to other men who challenge them.

Because women have traditionally occupied a subordinate position to their husbands but a dominant role in the care of the family, they have often had to learn to read others' emotions as a form of self-protection and to keep peace.

Historically, as women moved into the workplace, they did so in occupations such as seamstress, elementary school teacher, and nurse, roles that were an extension of their nurturing functions in the home. In particular, nurses were called upon to be compassionate no matter how they felt.

Spontaneous Reactions

Why do we laugh?

Early psychiatric theories connected laughter with a release of aggression and hostility. Jokes and kidding were seen as ways to express forbidden ideas—sometimes unconscious ones—and to play-act antisocial drives. Beyond psychiatric interpretations like these, humor and laughter are obviously valuable social tools, simply because they allow people to relax, let down their guard, and become receptive to new situations.

Most experts feel that incongruity lies at the core of humor. We are prepared for one thing—and something else happens. It startles us, but when we realize we are not in danger, our surprise is released in laughter. An unexpected word, story ending, or gesture can surprise us and make us laugh. Humor takes familiar situations and people, conventional behavior and common attitudes, and looks at them from an unexpected angle, often departing from the accepted standards or attitudes of the day.

Laughter begins early in life. A baby playing peekaboo can be convulsed in giggles, squealing with delight at the disappearance and reappearance of a face or toy. Humor is also universal, as we know from the world-wide popularity of Charlie Chaplin movies.

Just why the incongruous should tickle us has never been fully explained by psychology. W. C. Fields, one of the great masters of comedy, was also at a loss for an explanation, but he gave it a humorous try: "The funniest thing about comedy is that

Tuning In on the Unconscious Messages of Body Language

The gestures, looks, and postures that make up body language can reveal a lot about us, sometimes more than we would like. But the messages are not always as clear as body-language experts contend. Moreover, if you know how the experts interpret body language, you can fool them. A typical interpretation involves

Sending complex nonverbal messages is a skill learned early. The girl above seems to be flirting, playfully using her mother's dress both as a shield and an attractant. Uncertain, the boy keeps back.

Interpreting expressions is risky if you don't know the context. The girls at left appear to be experiencing thrills, ecstasy, fear, even horror—extremes explainable when you know the scene is a rock concert, in this case by David Cassidy.

you never know why people laugh. I know what makes them laugh, but trying to get your hands on the *why* of it is like trying to pick an eel out of a tub of water."

Are fear and anxiety the same emotion?

Many psychologists distinguish between fear, which they see as a reaction to a real threat, and anxiety, which may *feel* a lot like fear but can occur without a specific cause. Generally speaking, if the source is vague, it's called anxiety; if specific, a fear. For example, a child may fear a certain bully, and have anxiety about growing strong and tall.

Except for irrational phobias, fears may function as protective devices. From experience, from parents and other mentors, from watching, listening, and reading, we may learn to fear certain things and events, and we either avoid them or become especially alert and careful if we must face them.

Mild anxieties can also be beneficial, in that they can arouse and motivate us to be fully prepared for an important responsibility, such as a final exam or a public debate. However, too much anxiety can diminish performance. People tend to have their own natural level of anxiety, which may be higher or lower than the next person's. Psychologists call this personality dimension *trait anxiety.* Apprehension about specific circumstances, such as driving in rush-hour traffic, is termed *state anxiety.*

job applicants: if they lean forward during an interview or sit with uncrossed legs, they are pegged as open and friendly. But sitting rigidly, arms and legs crossed, is read as indrawn and hostile. Slouching shows boredom and depression.

Somewhat less debatable are the differences noted between men's and women's body language. For example, men usually point their fingers, while women nod their heads at something they want to indicate. Even these generalizations vary from culture to culture. Job training can also make reading body language tricky. Flight attendants are taught to smile at rude passengers. Credit managers look stern, even when they feel sorry for people unable to pay their bills.

Reading body language correctly takes more than just observing one or two features. All four boys have crossed arms; but there is obviously a great range of feeling in how they face the world—from the cocky boy at left, to the almost fearful one at right.

Why is anxiety hard to control?

Excessive anxiety can make life miserable and is one of the most frequent complaints of people seeking relief from mental turmoil. Often the problem is not just the anxiety but the desperate steps a worried person may take to try to escape it. The threatened feeling seems to arise from within, and since it has no apparent cause, it is very difficult for a person to control.

What is free-floating anxiety?

Freud speculated that the cause of vague yet excessive anxiety lay in childhood, in aggressive impulses and sexual yearnings that a child is taught to repress. If they are not repressed, the child learns that he or she risks disapproval, punishment, and rejection—probably the most frightening of all threats to a child. The forbidden feelings are thus shunted into a child's unconscious. The trouble is that such feelings do not remain completely buried. They lurk at the edge of consciousness, arousing guilt and stirring up old fears of being punished and rejected. The result is anxiety.

Although the Freudian explanation of what he called *free-floating anxiety* is by no means universally accepted today, there is no doubt that generalized anxiety is a widespread psychological condition. Tranquilizers are often prescribed for anxiety, but in recent years, their use has been criticized as promoting addiction. Nonchemical therapies, including self-help strategies, have found greater favor.

The Interplay of Mental Faculties

Does thinking physically alter the human brain?

One of the lessons of childhood is that thinking is hard work, and the more complicated the mental challenge, the more energy it takes. There is ample evidence that learning anything involves a change in the brain, but scientists so far know only the vague outlines of such changes.

It is clear, however, that the changes involved in thinking and learning take relatively huge amounts of energy. Although the human brain accounts for less than two percent of the total body weight, it takes the lion's share of the body's energy. A total of one-fifth of the body's blood and oxygen supply is directed to the brain's maintenance.

With the aid of improved scanning machines and other research tools, scientists are beginning to discover why the brain demands so much energy. Thinking is accompanied by dramatic short-term changes: bursts of electrical energy surge through the brain. Over a longer term, thinking causes alterations that are more or less permanent. New connections are created between brain cells and pressed into action.

Can thinking be observed?

For thousands of years, all anybody knew about thinking had to be *inferred* from its results. For example, from a grade of 100 on a test, researchers might infer that serious thinking had occurred, while a zero suggests the opposite.

In recent years, scientists have been able to observe thinking more directly. One method involves placing electrodes on the scalp of a human volunteer and then noting changes in electrical activity that occur when the person's attention is aroused by a picture, sound, or some other stimulus to the senses. Because the stimulus evokes a response that causes a change in the voltage (potential) between the electrodes on the scalp, this method of observing brain activity is called *evoked potentials*. From it, scientists learned that the first step in thinking—perceiving—triggers electrical changes in the brain, and that the changes correspond to the type and intensity of the stimulus.

Exploring the thinking process by evoked potentials, though still very useful, is crude compared to new methods of revealing brain structures that influence cognition, such as computerized axial tomography (CAT or CT scanning), magnetic resonance imaging (MRI), and positron emission tomography (PET scanning). These techniques do not rely on the placing of electrodes and are not always dependent on outside stimuli. Thus they can detect a broader range of brain activity. Moreover, CAT and MRI afford finer and more selective views since they can be focused from many angles on "slices" of the brain.

We Are All Born With the Capacity for Language

When babies are born, specific areas of the hemispheres of the brain appear to be primed and ready for the development of language. Children have a strong desire to understand their surroundings, and language is crucial to their grasp. This urge for mastery is dramatically illustrated in cases where children of the deaf are born deaf. They learn sign language with little coaching.

Hearing people think in words and images, but deaf people think in sign language. One test established that deaf people confused letters that are similar in sign language—such as Y's, B's or L's—in the same way as hearing people tended to confuse letters that sound alike in speech.

Just as spoken languages differ from country to country, so do sign languages. Though they share the English language, the deaf of the U.S. and England do not generally understand one another's signs.

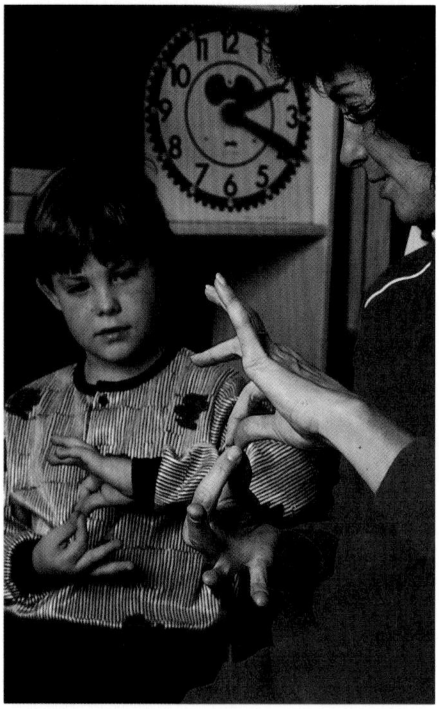

Sign language is not mere words; the gestures convey a complex grammar.

What is meant by knowing?

One perfectly valid definition of knowing something is to have committed it to memory. You know the alphabet, or have a knowledge of the causes of the French Revolution or the basics of algebra or the dates of English monarchies. In this sense, knowing is the end of a chain that begins with perceiving (by the senses), continues through thinking (by which the brain converts external events into images and symbols such as words), and ends in remembering (which stores information in memory, for later retrieval).

Knowing, however, is not only an end result but also the "how to" thought process itself. For this reason, psychologists prefer the term *cognition*, which includes the processes of inquiry and analysis. They use cognition to cover every mental activity that is commonly regarded as thinking or knowing: perceiving, recognizing, learning, conceptualizing, imagining, problem solving, remembering, reasoning, and judging.

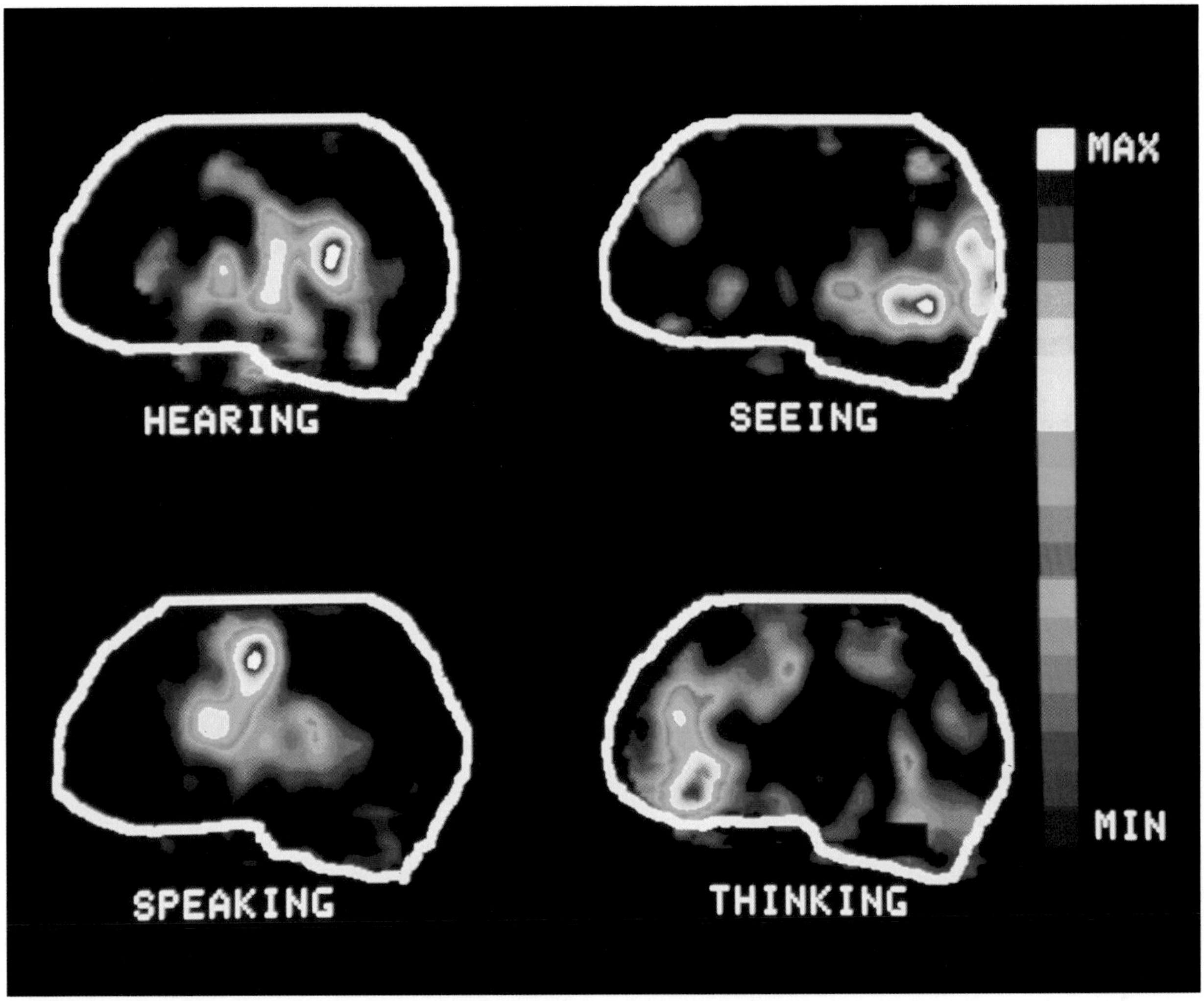

PET scans of the brain, *seen from the side, reveal how a single word activates different parts of the brain, depending on whether it is heard, read, or spoken. White, red, and yellow indicate highest levels of activity; blue, lesser levels. When the subject was asked for a related word, a task involving thinking, the frontal lobe lit up (lower right).*

Where do memories go?

Research suggests that the hippocampus, a structure near the core of the brain, maps and organizes memories, then directs them to other sections of the brain, perhaps to several sections at once. Exactly *what* a memory is made of, however, remains a mystery. There are many theories. One is that a memory is stored as an electrical charge; another is that special "memory molecules" or even entire cells hold memories; a third proposes that remembered information has caused changes in the chemical make-up of some cells. One researcher uses the term *mnemon* to describe a basic unit of memory that guides the formation of other memories.

Although no single site in the brain seems to have a monopoly on memory, the neocortex holds at least some long-term memories. When stimulated electrically, the neocortex, the brain's gray outermost layer, may release a rush of sensations—sounds, sights, smells—from long-ago days.

Can we think without words?

There is little doubt that language—the ability to communicate with words, whether in speech, writing, or signing—is one of the attributes that makes us human, perhaps the most basic one. Says Dr. Philip Lieberman, a linguist at Brown University: "Language facilitates thought. I think it's impossible to conceive of human thought without human language. The two are integral elements tied together."

Yet there are some people who seem to think best not in words but in images. These nonverbal or visual thinkers have included scientists like Albert Einstein and Michael Faraday, who said that their great discoveries came to them first as pictures and spatial relationships, which they then translated into words. Ordinary people, too, seem to do at least some nonverbal thinking. In getting from place to place, for example, most of us form *cognitive maps,* rough guides to the best route, by which we avoid laboriously memorizing each step and turn but reach our destination nevertheless.

Steps in Development

Why don't we remember before the age of three?

Somewhere around the age of one, a baby begins to develop short-term memory. He or she becomes clearly aware of certain objects, such as toys or clothes, and can remember where they have been put away.

Up to about the age of three, remembered scenes seem mostly to be like isolated snapshots—full of color and detail, but lacking a context. The explanation may be that the baby's brain is still growing and has not formed a sufficient network of nerve pathways and connections, the synapses between brain cells, to file new experiences in an organized way.

Normally at about age three, as the child's familiarity with language increases, the brain begins to be capable of recalling long-term memories. Interestingly, the word *infancy* comes from the Latin *infans,* meaning "incapable of speech." Thus the end of infancy literally means the beginning of speech, and there seems to be little doubt that the power of speech has much to do with the capacity for long-term memory, if only as an unmistakable sign that the child's nerve pathways are now ready to handle grown-up challenges.

Are children born with the ability to use language?

The human brain and body have certain structures that are intimately connected with the ability to commu-

Theorists and Theories: **Exploring How People Learn**

Nobel Prize winner Pavlov made his discoveries of conditioned reflexes while investigating the digestive system.

Ivan Pavlov, Russian, 1849–1936

Learning is the response to an external event, or stimulus, to which an organism—human or animal—has become accustomed or, psychologically, *conditioned.* In experiments with dogs, Pavlov gave them food—described today as an *unconditioned stimulus*—and simultaneously rang a bell. The dogs, in an *unconditioned response,* salivated at the scent of food. After many trials the dogs salivated at the sound of the bell. They had learned a *conditioned response* to a *conditioned stimulus.* Thus he defined learning as a behavior change produced by biological conditioning.

Edward Lee Thorndike, American 1874–1949

We learn by trial and error. Thorndike put cats into a closed box with food outside. While scrambling to escape, a cat usually found the right string to pull to open a door. With each experiment, a cat took less time to find the string. Thus, by trial and error, how to find the string was stamped in the animal's brain. Thorndike also developed a *law of effect,* stating that a response followed by satisfaction is more firmly implanted in the mind than one followed by disappointment.

John B. Watson, American 1878–1958

All learning is conditioning. "Give me a dozen healthy infants," Watson wrote "well formed, and my own specified world to bring them up in, and I'll guarantee to take anyone at random to become any type of specialist I might select." Watson insisted that psychology should study only objective, observable behavior. He is called the father of *behaviorism,* and his theories of learning dominated American psychology for the first half of this century.

Edward C. Tolman, American 1886–1959

Learning is the interaction of internal, mental processes with the external events of our environment. Behavior is not learned from trial and error but from thinking and considering alternatives. Thus behavior is not purely mechanistic—a case of reflexes—but involves a mental process. We learn by observation, but we do not always act on what we have learned unless we are motivated.

Burrhus F. Skinner, American, 1904–

Behavior is learned in response to experience. Skinner uses the term *operant conditioning* to describe how humans or animals function, trying to manipulate or control their environment to meet their needs. Central to his view is a concept of reinforcement, by which he means that behavior is likely to occur, or conversely, not to occur as a response to an environmental reaction.

Complicated processes—such as driving a car—are learned by what Skinner calls *chaining or shaping.* Such knowledge is acquired step by step and then applied to a sequence of actions.

Donald O. Hebb, Canadian, 1904–

In *The Organization of Behavior* (1949), Hebb proposed that neural connections of the brain, after repeated stimulation, are strengthened and form what he called cell assemblies—groupings of cells—and these function as memory banks of what we have learned.

Albert Bandura, American (Canadian-born), 1925–

We learn by experience and by observing other people's behavior. We do not use everything we learn; instead we do what brings rewards and what is considered acceptable in our society. We are molded by our thinking, by social rules, and by what we have learned from our models. Learning enables us to change our lives if and when we choose.

nicate in language. These features are not fully formed at birth, but develop over the childhood years to a point where producing and comprehending language are possible.

The vocal tract of a baby, for example, is incapable of anything but mewling, squealing, and babbling. But the vocal tract—lips, tongue, larynx—will *develop* in a year or so in ways that allow the formation of adult speech sounds.

Something similar happens in the brain. There is no doubt that certain areas in a normal baby's brain will develop into the typical language centers of the adult brain, but it will take a few years. In these pre-speech years, according to neuropsychologist Colwyn Trevarthen of the University of Edinburgh in Scotland, babies engage in a nonverbal form of communication, mainly with their mothers. Most psychologists agree that language builds upon such nonverbal roots.

Do thinking and language develop together?

Whether it is truer that the human mind shapes language, or language shapes the mind, is open to debate. We do know a child's ability to use language grows by leaps and bounds. By six months, according to one expert, a baby's skill at distinguishing one voice from another exceeds the comprehension capacity of the most advanced artificial intelligence machine. By 18 months, a child is talking in phrases and has a vocabulary of about 50 words; by three years, a vocabulary of 1,000 words, delivered in sentences of up to five words; and as early as six years, the basic adult vocabulary and grammar are in use.

Yet this astonishing rate of language acquisition lags behind the development of the child's mental faculties, its cognition. At least for the first two years, babies seem to know more than they can say; by age three toddlers are capable of abstract thinking.

With thinking racing ahead of language, some revealing and totally charming ideas come out of the mouths of young children. A 15-month-old girl named Abby, held up to view the ocean for the first time, announces, "Cup!" In psychologists' terms, she has *overextended* the meaning of "cup" to include all liquids. And quite logically, a three-year-old follows a grammatical rule to make plurals by adding *s* and produces "mans," "womans," and "foots."

A Child's Age Is the Key to Handling Concepts

A five-year-old easily grasps that the beakers contain equal amounts of liquid.

Jean Piaget (1896–1980), the Swiss psychologist, developed the theory that a child's thinking matures in stages related to brain development. In his "lemonade" experiment, Piaget showed that children of five and six are not yet ready to grasp more than one dimension at a time. When the lemonade is poured into two equal-sized glasses, they know the amounts are equal, but once the liquid in one glass is transferred to a taller and narrower one, they believe the taller glass holds more. Children of about seven no longer make this mistake. They know that a thing need not change its identity when its appearance changes.

The girl watches the liquid from one beaker poured into a taller, narrower one.

She now indicates that the taller beaker holds more than the shorter one does.

What memories last the longest?

Kinesthetic, or physical motor, memories, are the longest lasting. To a child learning to ride a bicycle, each try is a consuming challenge. But once the knack of bike riding is acquired, 40 years can pass and all it takes to recall the skill is to climb on the seat again.

Psychologists generally agree that memories involving names, faces, dates, images, or situations are less indelible than physical motor memories. Such perceptions first enter the *immediate memory*. There, two things can happen. The perception can be lost after a few seconds. Or, if the perception captures our attention, it is transferred to *short-term memory*, where it can last anywhere from 30 seconds to a few hours. The length of time we hold on to a short-term memory seems to depend on whether we make a special effort to retain it. Finally, in some as yet uncharted sorting process, thoughts and experiences that are deemed worthy enter *long-term memory*, where they may be stored for a lifetime.

Exercising Your Mind

Seeing Is Remembering

Because images are received and stored in pictorial form, they are far easier to recall than words or numbers. See for yourself—try this visual memory test. Study these 21 diagrams for exactly three minutes, then turn to page 321 and check off the diagrams that duplicate the ones on this page.

Are some people born with a good memory?

How much you remember depends to some extent on inborn capacity. Like sharp eyesight or keen hearing, a good memory may be inherited. But in most cases, what counts is your enthusiasm for a subject. An avid sports fan can remember games and players' performance to an extent that is amazing to non-fans. So, too, there are bridge players who can recite the order of bidding and tricks taken in games played years ago. The more you learn of a subject that fascinates you, the easier it is to pick up more. Conversely, if a subject bores you, you will probably have trouble remembering anything about it.

How can you improve your memory?

The first essential seems obvious, but it cannot be stressed enough: to acquire information, you have to pay attention. Then you must relate the information to something you already know, and finally, you have to practice its use. Everyone's mind works differently, so you may want to try a variety of memory devices.

When you need to remember the number of days in a month, chances are you use this rhyme: "Thirty days hath September, April, June, and November. All the rest have 31, except February which stands alone." Or, when struggling with spelling, maybe you say: "*i* before *e* except after *c* or when sounded like *a* as in *neighbor* or *weigh.*" Your memory can be jogged by chunking. That is, grouping information by a common characteristic: you can remember navigational colors and names by the fact that *left, port,* and *red* are short words, *right, green,* and *starboard* are longer.

Isolated bits of information are easily lost; learning in sets of two or three, on the other hand, is often effective. Subjects asked to recall 100 word cards found that the cards were harder to memorize one by one than to memorize by category: it is easier to remember 15 birds or 20 reptiles than it is to recall 100 separate animals.

Then there are useful nonsense statements: "King Philip Came Over For Ginger Snaps," for example, can remind you that plants and animals are classified by their Kingdom, Phylum, Class, Order, Family, Genus, Species. You can make up your own memory tricks, using rhyme, chunks, nonsense sentences, and acronyms such as HOMES for the names of the Great Lakes: Huron, Ontario, Michigan, Erie, and Superior.

For many, visual cues are effective as memory devices. By relating names or other information to, say, ships, pineapples, or lampposts, you can visualize the picture cue and thus call up the original information.

With practice, how much can someone remember?

The distinguished Shakespearean actor and movie star Sir John Gielgud, when in his eighties and at the top of his form, credited memorization with preserving one's mental agility: "If you do only films and television in short takes, the concentration starts to go. It's very important to learn whole plays instead of brief scenes: Sybil Thorndike kept her memory perfect well into her nineties by doing plays. Edith Evans gave up the theater and then couldn't remember a thing."

Such memory feats as reciting whole plays have parallels in the music world. Many musicians, for example, know by heart the scores of entire operas and symphonies, each having hundreds of thousands of notes.

Sharpen Your Wits With Brain Teasers and Puzzles

No one is born knowing how to do crossword puzzles or anagrams; even the most skilled of puzzle-solvers had to learn the ropes. With practice, your ability to solve even the most erudite of games will improve over time. Nearly all puzzles have a trick or set pattern to them. Learning to spot the tricks is part of the fun, and a big part of the solution. Brain teasers and puzzles help enormously to improve the mind's ability to think and reason. Puzzle lovers find the challenge the best mental exercise around.

These questions are adapted from The Triarchic Mind *by Robert J. Sternberg, a professor of psychology at Yale University. His theory is that intelligence is mental self-management. Each of the problems requires selective combination for its solution.* *For answers, see page 322.*

1. **How many flowers** do I have if all of them are roses except two, all of them are tulips except two, and all of them are daisies except two?

2. **You have three boxes** of checkers: one labeled "red checkers," one labeled "black checkers," and one labeled "red and black checkers." Unfortunately, each label is on a wrong box. By taking only one checker from one box, how can you label each box correctly?

3. **On October 1** you go to the first lecture in a weekly series of four lectures. On what date will the final lecture take place?

4. **A camera costs $100,** including the case. The camera costs $80 more than the case. How much does the case cost?

5. **A cookie recipe** calls for three cups of flour. You have only a two-cup container and a seven-cup container, both of which are otherwise unmarked. How can you measure out exactly three cups of flour using only these two containers?

Try Your Hand at Solving the "Toughest Puzzle of All"

The following puzzle, known as the Smith–Jones–Robinson classic, is a masterpiece of its kind. It's an absorbing mental challenge presented in concise and entertaining terms. In one group of 240 people trying it, only six came up with the solution. But there is no "catch" in it, and the answer was worked out by some in five to ten minutes. Every fact is important, and must be considered. *To find the solution, turn to page 322.*

On a train, Smith, Robinson, and Jones are the fireman, brakeman, and engineer, but NOT respectively. Also aboard are three businessmen who have the same names: a Mr. Smith, a Mr. Robinson, and a Mr. Jones.

1. Mr. Robinson lives in Detroit.
2. The brakeman lives exactly halfway between Chicago and Detroit.
3. Mr. Jones earns exactly $20,000 per year.
4. The brakeman's nearest neighbor, one of the passengers, earns exactly three times as much as the brakeman.
5. Smith beats the fireman at billiards.
6. The passenger with the same name as the brakeman lives in Chicago.

WHO IS THE ENGINEER?

Remembering and Forgetting

How does your mind choose what to remember?

Short-term memory has been likened to a scratch pad where you check your arithmetic, or jot down a phone number. You keep the details in your mind only as long as needed to accomplish the project at hand. Then the barely noticed images fade immediately and completely.

For something to enter long-term memory—there to be available days, months, or years later—the image must get past what psychologists term the "gatekeeper of memory"; it must get your full attention. Something novel, noisy, wonderful, horrifying, or of special interest causes you to focus on it. It may then start on the way to becoming established in your memory. Through association with existing memory, through linkages with other remembered events, it builds new traces in the brain.

How durable is long-term memory?

Some psychologists believe that long-term memories are never lost. Unfortunately, this does not mean you can call up a name, face, fact, or figure whenever you want to just because you had a firm memory of the subject in the past. The problem may lie in your retrieval system. The memory may be linked to a special circumstance; if this eludes you, you are left with the "tip of the tongue" phenomenon, where you can almost make the connection. Or the memory may have been suppressed.

Evidence of the stability of long-term memory comes from studying patients who have suffered strokes or mild brain seizures. Sometimes strokes unlock a flood of detailed memories from the distant past.

One elderly woman, described by neurologist Oliver Sacks in *The Man Who Mistook His Wife for a Hat,* awoke one night from a musically based dream, but couldn't stop the music after she woke up. She had suffered a mild stroke that had activated childhood memories. Her recollections were far in excess of anything that could be expected of normal memory. Gradually, both the seizure and the music went away, and the woman was left feeling content. "It was like being given back a forgotten bit of my childhood," she said. Such intense, involuntary reminiscences are occasionally experienced as well by epileptics and migraine sufferers.

When Clive Wearing's hippocampus *was destroyed by a brain inflammation, he lost totally his ability to build new memories. His personality and musical skills are intact, and he remembers and loves his wife. But each meeting is new, he greets her over and over, as though for the first time.*

Does amnesia erase memories?

During the 1940's and 1950's, when severe epileptic disorders were treated by surgically removing part of the brain, doctors found that electrical stimulation of the hippocampus provoked a flood of memories in their patients. Removal of or damage to the hippocampus made it impossible for patients to learn anything new, and at the same time erased memories of events within the past three years. Only older memories were left intact. This kind of amnesia (loss of memory) has proved to be permanent.

Progressive loss of memory is the dire result of Alzheimer's disease, a degeneration of the brain that generally strikes in old age. This, too, is an irreversible loss.

A head injury can also cause amnesia, but often the effect is temporary. For example, the victim of a car crash may lose memories of events just prior to the accident. Scientists call this retrograde amnesia.

Severe emotional stress is another cause of amnesia. Victims of crime and battle-scarred soldiers may protect themselves from the horrors they have experienced by blotting out the memory. Such a mechanism may seem merciful, but can result in deeper emotional trouble, for, it seems, these memories are not lost. Unless the past is retrieved and faced, the stress may fester.

What is a photographic memory?

People with photographic (eidetic) memories say that they can see a page in their mind's eye and can simply read it. The truth of such claims has been demonstrated repeatedly, with eidetikers reciting whole pages from books. In the same way, situations and scenes may be recalled with equally great precision.

Leonardo da Vinci is believed to have had a photographic memory. He was able to draw a detailed portrait of someone after a single meeting. Another famous eidetiker, Napoleon Bonaparte, could glance at a map and thereafter recall every town, hill, and stream on it.

The Man With the Indelible Memory

Solomon Shereshevskii had a memory so perfect that he could recall every minute of his life in graphic detail. This bizarre capacity was further distinguished by the fact that he could "feel" images, "taste" colors, and "smell" sounds.

IMAGINE HAVING A MEMORY so incredibly vivid that late in life you can still clearly recall your mother's face coming into focus as she bent over your crib. Or that words and numbers invoke specific concrete images: the word *blue* always calls up a small blue flag, the number 7 immediately brings to mind a man with a mustache.

A man with such a mind came to the attention of the Russian psychologist Alexander R. Luria in the early 1920's. Luria tells of his experiences with this remarkable man over some three decades in his book *The Mind of a Mnemonist.*

Solomon Shereshevskii, called simply S in the book, worked as a newspaper reporter in Moscow. S first came to see Luria when his editor became so impressed with his ability to remember facts without taking notes that the editor suggested S have his memory tested.

Luria began by reading off lists of numbers and having S repeat them from memory. As the lists got longer (up to 70 numbers) and the tests more complicated, Luria was increasingly astonished. S performed each test without error, and then to Luria's amazement was able to recite everything backward.

S's memory capacity was virtually boundless. Not only was there no limit to what he could remember, but each memory was *indelible.* This means that five, ten, or fifteen years after memorizing a list of numbers, he could recite the list perfectly, forward and backward, and describe in detail the room where the list was first memorized.

Luria also discovered that S's five senses seemed to fuse together whenever his mind recorded something. Recalling any stored impression would result in a state of "synethesia" where memory becomes a medley of sight, sound, touch, taste, and smell. Some scientists now think that the limbic system,

An inability to forget *led to such mental overcrowding that S was not able to function normally.*

which processes sensations, must have been so active in S that it overpowered the brain's ability to discriminate between the senses.

For S this meant that one voice sounded "crumbly and yellow," another like "a flame with fibers protruding from it." He refused to buy ice cream from a woman whose voice made him see "black cinders bursting out of her mouth."

Sounds of some words didn't match their meaning to S. The word for pig (*svinya* in Russian) felt wrong because its sound was "so fine, so elegant." But *khasser* (Yiddish for pig) was just right; it made him think of a pig's "fat, greasy belly caked with dried mud."

Such vivid image-making turned out to be the key to S's ability to memorize a long sequence of numbers. He would first translate the numbers into graphic mental pictures made up of sound, color, taste, smell, and touch, then distribute these snapshots along an imagined road in his mind. To recall them, he would simply walk along the road and "see" everything laid out before his eyes.

In a normal mind, impressions begin to fade almost immediately, making room for new ones. For S, every incoming impression would last for hours, causing memories to back up and crowd each other. To reduce the confusion caused by this pile-up of images, S came up with some novel but ultimately ineffective ways to forget. First he tried covering whole groups of memories with an imaginary canvas. Then he tried writing down all the things he wanted to forget on pieces of paper and burning the paper. But the memories would not go up in smoke. After much practice, though, he was able to will some away.

For all its vivid precision, S's memory had serious drawbacks. Since it was so focused on *concrete particulars,* S had trouble identifying some things we all take for granted. For example, he could not always recognize familiar faces or voices on the telephone. "They change too much," he said. The subtle daily changes in someone's face or voice that the rest of us are able to overlook, challenged S's powers of recognition.

As a person, S seemed a bit awkward, slow, and timid, perhaps due to the phenomenal flood of images in his mind at all times—some of them uncontrollable and very disquieting—which he laboriously tried to sort out. He held dozens of jobs, until he finally settled on being a professional mnemonist—someone who performs memory stunts for paying audiences.

S always thought he was destined for greatness, but his mind was so richly stocked with lifelike images that he spent much of his time daydreaming. Perhaps in one way at least, S's "great thing" did finally arrive. Since its publication in 1968, A. R. Luria's study of S's amazing yet curiously crippled mind has been recognized as a classic work of literature and psychological research.

Magic Carpets—Yours for the Asking

How do we learn to read?

The miraculous capacity to read is tied to the development of a child's brain. Usually children must be at least four years old to have developed the necessary intricate nerve linkages that connect the eyes to both hemispheres of the brain. These pathways must be in place before the young mind can analyze and store the information required to master reading.

The complex brain structures that underlie reading are a clue to why learning to read is so problematic, a surprisingly easy task for some children, painfully hard for others.

There are no foolproof methods of teaching reading. Some beginners respond well to the technique of relating specific sounds to specific symbols, then forming words from these pieces, and finally creating whole sentences. (Sounds are called phonemes, hence this is the phonic method.) Other children's minds have the ability to grasp whole words at once. Whatever the technique, the child always chooses the pace: some learn quickly, others slowly.

***The Flying Dutchman, condemned to sail** till doomsday, glares from the heaving deck of his ship in this painting by Howard Pyle. Manned by a dead crew, the ship is seen by other vessels only in foul weather off the Cape of Good Hope.*

Why is reading important?

No doubt about it: To get anywhere, from holding a job to marketing for the family, you have to be able to read. But reading is more than the deciphering of words and the attainment of literacy.

The cultural historian Jacques Barzun sees reading as the essential stimulus in creating "a well-made Self"—the most fully realized, perfect you that you can be. Reading can accomplish this, says Barzun, because it speaks to our imagination and thus provides an antidote to the daily grind that can "narrow the mind and stifle the spirit." Reading provides "the contrast, the otherness, the novelty and the strangeness; the shock of difference and the recognition of sameness," Barzun believes. "Your imagination must work every minute, reconstructing the lives, events, and emotions depicted in print."

Of course, reading can also benefit us on a very practical level. For example, the size of our vocabulary depends on how much we read, and there is an established correlation between the number of words we know and our ability to do well on all sorts of tests. Although a person can function in today's world after learning about 5,000 words, the vocabulary of a typical five-year-old, much of the potential richness of life and work is denied to such a person.

There is, finally, the pleasure and comfort derived from reading. Richard de Bury, a 14th-century English scholar, wrote of books that "they delight us when prosperity smiles upon us; they comfort us inseparably when stormy fortune frowns on us. . . . If you seek them they do not hide, if you blunder they do not scold, if you are ignorant, they do not laugh."

What can you do if your child can't read?

The efforts of children whose *b*'s looked like *d*'s and whose writing of *was* came out *saw* used to be called mirror writing. By the end of the first grade, these mistakes have usually disappeared—except among some of the 10 to 15 percent of children who have a reading disability known today as dyslexia. These children are not mentally retarded.

The term *dyslexia* covers a wide range of reading disabilities, from mild to severe. What most dyslexics have in common is difficulty in grasping the shapes of letters and relating them to the sounds that the letters symbolize. Many dyslexics also reverse the order of the letters in a word.

Using PET brain scans, researchers are trying to pinpoint the causes of dyslexia. Although the evidence is not conclusive, it appears that dyslexics may have difficulty coordinating the two hemispheres of their brains; and perhaps this explains why many dyslexics are gifted artistically and athletically, talents believed by some psychologists to arise mainly from the right hemisphere.

Any child whose reading skills lag significantly behind those of classmates at the end of the first grade should be tested for dyslexia. Almost all dyslexics can be taught to read, but not always in traditional ways.

How does television influence reading?

Television or no television, in households where books are almost a part of the furniture, children seem to learn to read—and enjoy it, beginning a lifelong habit. On the other hand, reading problems arise in households where parents read little or nothing and the main link with the wider world is through a TV set.

Psychologist Patricia Marks Greenfield has written of "the special power of television for learning," and many of her professional colleagues agree that television need not be a negative force in a child's life. But it does the child no good to be a couch potato and watch passively. Rather, a parent or teacher should discuss the content of TV programs with the child, and encourage him or her to pursue the subject through books or magazines. Teachers and school librarians report that after the airing of a TV version of a story, there is always a great demand for the original book.

PERSPECTIVES

On Books and Reading

Reading is not just for acquiring facts and enjoying fiction. It is the surest avenue to truth. A skillful reader is not easily bamboozled by propaganda.

An Everyday Miracle

"Isn't it amazing how we take them for granted, those little black marks on paper! Twenty-six different shapes known as letters, arranged in endless combinations known as words. Lifeless, until someone's eye falls on them.

"But then a miracle happens. Along the optic nerve, almost at the speed of light, these tiny symbols are flashed to the brain, where they are instantly decoded into ideas, images, concepts, *meanings*.

"The eye's owner is changed too. The little black marks can make him love or hate, laugh or cry, fight or run away. And what do we call this incredible chain of events? Reading.

"The spoken word rushes by and is gone, but the written word remains . . . endures. It can be consulted over and over again . . . forever."

—Arthur Gordon
Guideposts Associates

◆

From the Belle of Amherst

"There is no Frigate like a Book
To take us Lands away,
Nor any Coursers like a Page
Of prancing Poetry."

—Emily Dickinson

◆

A Friend for Life

"A good book is never exhausted. It goes on whispering to you from the wall. Books perfume and give weight to a room. A bookcase is as good as a view, as the sight of a city or a river. There are dawns and sunsets in books—storms, fogs, zephyrs.

"I read about a family whose apartment consists of a series of spaces so strictly planned that they are obliged to give away their books as soon as they've read them. I think they have misunderstood the way books work.

"Reading a book is only the first step in the relationship. After you've finished it, the book enters on its real career. It stands there as a badge, a blackmailer, a monument, a scar. It's both a flaw in the room, like a crack in the plaster, and a decoration. The contents of someone's bookcase are part of his history, like an ancestral portrait."

—Anatole Broyard
The New York Times Book Review

◆

A Golden Time

"When school ends, millions of children will head for the beach or will climb into the family station wagon for a trip to Grandmother's. But none will travel farther than the child with a book who goes only to his own room or to the shade beneath a backyard tree.

"The books of childhood are always with us. Lost in their pages, a child may swim in the bluest sea, rise on the highest swing, engage in the grandest adventure." **—Gene Shalit**
McCall's

◆

To Jog Your Mind

"Reading is to the mind what exercise is to the body."

—Sir Richard Steele

◆

The Pleasure of Rambling

"Digressions, incontestably, are the sunshine;—they are the life, the soul of reading." **—Laurence Sterne**
Tristram Shandy

◆

A Bookowner's Plea

"If thou art borrowed
by a friend,
Right welcome
shall he be
To read, to study,
not to lend
But to return to me.
Not that imparted
knowledge doth
Diminish learning's store,
But books, I find,
if often lent
Return to me no more."

—Inscription in an old book
Owner unknown

Seeing Things in a New Way

What is creativity?

Creativity leaves current knowledge behind and produces something that is new. Or it puts old ideas or familiar things together in a new way. It is free-wheeling, imaginative thinking that leads to fresh insights and revolutionary ideas, and even comes up with useful products.

Creative thought goes outside the usual route, puts aside the accepted formula or pattern or recipe. The results are many and varied: a poem, an opera, a medical diagnosis, a pastry, a better mousetrap, a theory on starlight, a faster way to clean a kitchen.

Do original ideas begin in daydreams?

Whenever you let your thoughts wander and you muse, "What if . . . ?" you nudge your mind to travel beyond the accepted and familiar. Such daydreaming is the source of much of the creativity in our lives. When you come up with a better or easier way to do your job, you are being creative. You are thinking creatively when you can no longer tolerate an explanation like "But that's the way we've always done it."

If our ancestors had not asked "What if . . . ?" they would not have turned stones and bones into tools, cultivated crops from wild plants, drawn pictures, or used written symbols for sounds and ideas. No human progress would have occurred if everybody had done things the way they had been done before. Creative daydreams led us to the industrial revolution, the computer age, and the exploration of space.

Are people with the highest IQ's the most inventive?

A high score on an intelligence test doesn't automatically mean a high level of creativity. Truly original thinking involves nonintellectual factors, such as receptivity to novel ideas and a knack for making connections that hadn't occurred to someone else.

Tests have been developed to identify creative talent. They have shown that top scorers on creativity tests average 23 IQ points lower than top scorers on intelligence tests. The most creative individuals often had trouble with problems that demanded sticking to rigid rules to find the answer.

Is creativity inheritable?

There are famous examples of creativity appearing in generation after generation of a family. Johann Sebastian Bach was born to a line that had produced musicians for the previous 100 years, and three of his children became composers. The Wyeth family has had three generations of artists.

But such examples of a specific creative talent spanning generations are quite rare; and the evidence for some sort of "creative gene" is not strong. It may be that a general kind of creative temperament runs in families, whose members show creativity in diverse fields, such as business, politics, or the arts. In any case, heredity would not be the only factor predisposing an individual to creative thinking. Equally important would be the influence of his or her family environment.

What kind of person is creative?

Creative people tend to be both hard workers and daydreamers. Although they may have a strong nonconformist streak and jealously guard their private moments, they are not necessarily loners. A great many creative people seem to need the stimulation of their colleagues and dive happily into group discussions.

Creativity doesn't blossom overnight; most people spend many years learning their field and *then* make their innovations. They are interested in many areas and have a rich fund of general knowledge. They are skeptical about "right answers" and tend to trust their own instincts. They are persistent, pursuing a problem from different angles until they solve it.

***A little girl reveals** her skill in imaginative play, swiftly positioning the blocks in a pattern that pleases her. Totally absorbed, a child will often talk softly to herself or himself about the moves, which block goes where—and why.*

Can you raise a child to be an innovative thinker?

Childhood is perhaps the most creative period in anybody's life. Preschoolers make dolls talk, play cops and robbers, build with blocks, draw, dance, pilot a spaceship under a table. The let's-pretend games are pure creativity.

At school, a child must learn the correct solutions, the approved method: "Don't color outside the lines. No plaid elephants." Every question has a right or a wrong answer. Albert Einstein thought it was "nothing short of a miracle that the modern methods of instruction have not yet entirely strangled the holy curiosity of inquiry; for this delicate little plant, aside from stimulation, stands mostly in need of freedom; without this it goes to wrack and ruin without fail."

Part of a child's natural creativity is the ability to fantasize, to think beyond the right answer, to wonder why and why not. One way to cultivate this trait, experts suggest, is for parents to strike a balance between challenging a child, exposing him or her to new ideas and activities, and letting the child alone to experiment with toys and games. Reading should be encouraged. The more information that is stored up, the more the child can draw on for creative efforts.

Ironically, many people who are creative as adults have had what no loving parent would choose to give them: an unhappy childhood. Financial crises, divorced parents, and other family difficulties are common in the backgrounds of creative people. The reason may be, according to some authorities on intellectual development, that having to cope with disappointment and hardship makes a child look at things differently than his or her less troubled peers.

Of course, happy children can turn out to be just as creative as miserable ones. Many creative adults thank their parents for providing an environment that valued the free discussion and expression of all kinds of talents and ideas.

René Magritte's entertaining painting, Carte Blanche, *is plausible at first, but on examination becomes more and more complex. Is the horse in front of the trees? Behind them? What of the figure? It is a surprise to discover she is painted on one tree trunk! Magritte wrote, "In my paintings I showed objects situated where we never find them. It was the realization of a real, if not actually conscious desire existing in most people."*

Why is an inventor like a hen?

They both use incubation. According to psychologists, incubation is an essential part of the creative process, which can be divided into the following four basic steps:

Preparation. "Nothing can be created from nothing," said Lucretius, the Roman philosopher. Scientists and artists spend many years exploring their fields, getting to know the great questions that remain and, in effect, choosing the challenges they want to face. Even child prodigies need time to ripen—though they start earlier than less precocious creators. Mozart produced his first symphony at eight, but it was almost a decade before he wrote his first masterpiece.

Incubation. No matter how good the preparation, no matter how clearly the creative problem has been identified, a solution may still be elusive. At this stage, the problem is internalized and the unconscious will work on it.

Illumination. This is the moment when the writer's block evaporates and the shape of the rest of the work becomes clear, when the theory finally takes the twist that fits the facts, when the pieces of the puzzle make a whole. Almost always, preparation and incubation precede this moment.

Verification. To be truly innovative, an idea must meet two requirements. Is it really new? Does it solve the problem? For instance, someone might decide that a creative way to sharpen a pencil is to let the family dog chew on it. That's a novel idea, but it isn't likely to solve the problem.

Courting Creativity

What part of the brain influences a person's creativity?

There is some evidence that, in most people, the right hemisphere of the brain has more to do with creativity than the left, which handles life's day-to-day business: talking, writing, reasoning. The right side has the job of organizing experience, finding patterns in events, and responding emotionally. Imagination and creative ideas are fired up on the right.

The right and left brains communicate through the corpus callosum, a thick bundle of nerve fibers joining the two halves. Indications of the hemispheres' divergent functions have come through the study of accident victims whose corpora callosa have been injured or cut.

Are there barriers to creative thinking?

Researchers in creativity often make the case that education is aimed at developing our ability to learn by rote, to follow the formulas, recipes, and rules. We are urged to home in on *the* right answer. Thus, from an early age, many of us value logic, practicality, and established rules over our creative faculties—imagination, fantasy, insight, and intuition.

Over the centuries, practical persons have scoffed at just about every invention you can name, from the printing press to the automobile. Think how improbable some ideas must have seemed when first presented—such as sweeping floors with air (vacuum cleaners) and pictures traveling through the air (television). Some of the world's most admired artists, Matisse, Braque, Vlaminck, Dufy, and Derain, broke the rules of painting early in the 20th century with their new techniques. Those who knew the rules (people of much lesser reputation today) called the innovators *Les Fauves* (wild men).

Take inspiration and pleasure from play—it will help you look at things freely, as a child does. Games of all kinds, even highly structured ones like chess, loosen up your mind. Perhaps this is because a game is outside the needs of one's life, hence a mental holiday. And when working at play, give it your whole attention—don't be afraid to look foolish at first. As practice makes you more proficient, the benefits of game playing increase.

Why is failure good for creativity?

You learn from your failures, said Charles Kettering, the engineer who invented the automobile self-starter and who, at his death, had developed more major inventions than any other American except Thomas Edison. He used to point out: "From the time a kid starts kindergarten to the time he graduates from college, he will be examined three or four times a year, and if he flunks once, he's out. Now an inventor fails 999 times, and if he succeeds once, he's in. An inventor treats his failures like practice shots."

The founder of IBM, Thomas J. Watson, gave the same kind of advice, "The way to succeed is to double your failure rate." Two-time Nobel Prize winner Linus Pauling said that the trick in coming up with good ideas is to think up a great many ideas and just get rid of the bad ones.

How does one get over writer's block and procrastination?

People put off creative action because they fear that what they produce won't be good enough. The best way to overcome this fear is to begin work on some small aspect of the project, preferably not the beginning. No matter what you want to create, a novel, a concerto, a plastic engine, or a hollyhock variant, there must be some small part—a paragraph, a bar, a linkage, a seam—that you have worked out in your head. Get that on paper or whatever vehicle it demands and work on it until it satisfies you.

By the time you have finished the first element, you will have found another small part to work on and you can link that to the first when you've completed it. Before you know it, you're well on your way.

Making Creativity a Matter of Method

Few human attributes are held in higher esteem than creativity, or are less understood. To be creative requires a form of flexible thinking that most people, although they may not know it, possess to some degree. Contrary to popular myth, creativity can be cultivated. Here are some ways to set the stage.

- **Decide what you want to do,** what your project or your problem is. It could be something as practical as living on your income, or getting a piece of furniture through a doorway that's too narrow. It could be as ambitious as inventing a new system or device, or as personal as expressing yourself in poetry. Bear in mind that without a good idea of what to create, you can't be creative. It often helps to write down what your objectives are or sketch the object you want to build.
- **Be positive** in your attitude. The solution may well be there for you if you work hard enough.
- **Learn all you can** about your subject, more than you think you'll need. The more you know, the better equipped you are to find a solution.
- **Think.** Thinking is hard work, which is why we shy away from it. Don't limit yourself to straight-line, logical thinking. Sneak up on your problem from a new angle. As the biochemist and Nobel Prize winner Albert Szent-Györgyi, says, "Discovery consists of looking at the same thing as everyone else and thinking something different."
- **Incubate.** If the solution doesn't come after your initial efforts, put the problem out of your mind and let your subconscious work on it. Go back to it in a few days and see where you are.
- **Prune.** Review your ideas and set aside the ones that have not worked. Make changes, additions, variations until you come up with your best.
- **Put your ideas to work.** That's the best way of testing them.

The Courage and Genius Of Vincent van Gogh

The brilliant Dutch artist was eccentric, lonely, and the victim of a mysterious, debilitating neurological disorder. But it is his unique vision, compassion, and dazzling creativity—not madness—that are reflected in his powerful paintings.

VINCENT VAN GOGH was a man of astonishing creativity and profound suffering. He was isolated, lonely, and financially dependent on his brother Theo. And during the last 18 months of his life he was plagued by a neurological disorder that led to the famous incident in 1888 when he cut off part of his ear with a razor.

In his last years as an artist Van Gogh worked intensely to develop his use of color and texture into a unique and profound language of emotion. The swirling, turbulent style that he developed has often been linked, wrongly, to his bouts of mental illness. He has been portrayed as a mad genius whose insanity was flung onto the canvas in wild fits of inspiration. But that notion, though widely believed, is a myth. The neurological disease had nothing to do with the fiery intelligence, compassion, and creativity that burst forth in his paintings.

It is true that Van Gogh was a disturbing presence in polite society. He was intense, stubborn, and often disheveled, with a spiritual, ascetic side to his character. During his twenties an interest in the religious life led him to become a lay missionary, working among the poor coal miners of southern Belgium. He lived in a shack, sleeping on the floor. He nursed victims of disease and mine accidents. This chapter of his life ended when his supervisors, who rebuked him for "excessive zeal," dismissed him from his missionary work.

He emerged from the experience shaken, but convinced that his life was to be an intellectual and artistic quest. As he wrote Theo, "If I do not go on seeking any longer, then I am lost." He recalled his passion for art and felt "homesick for the land of pictures."

In the remaining ten years of his life, Van Gogh devoted himself to painting. "What am I in the eyes of most people? A nobody, an eccentric and disagreeable man," he wrote. "I want to show by my work what there is in the heart of such an eccentric man, of such a nobody." He worked incessantly, often producing a painting a day. He also wrote hundreds of letters, to Theo and others, filled with vivid descriptions of the landscapes and people around him, and with analyses of his work in progress.

Sadly, only one of his paintings was sold during his life—*The Red Vineyard,* for a mere $80. When his neurological attacks began, they terrified him. At their most acute, they made work impossible and brought on bizarre, self-destructive behavior that resulted in his being placed in an asylum.

***This self-portrait**, one of a series, was painted shortly after Van Gogh suffered a nervous breakdown.*

Van Gogh's illness was never completely diagnosed during his lifetime, but it has been analyzed posthumously by a number of specialists. One of the theories proposed today is that Van Gogh did not suffer from insanity but was the victim of a type of temporal lobe epilepsy, which is characterized by limbic or psychomotor seizures. Electrical discharges within the centers of emotion in the brain can produce bizarre and violent behavior, followed by amnesia.

The affliction caused Van Gogh's mental instability. Though he painted intensely until the end, he felt a growing despair and, at the age of 37, took his own life.

Some say that one of Van Gogh's last paintings, *Crows Over the Wheatfield,* shows signs of his impending suicide. However, as Vincent wrote to his brother, these "vast fields of wheat under troubled skies . . . express sadness and the extreme of loneliness," but they also are a tribute to "the health and fortifying power I see in the country." It is that combination of suffering and hope expressed in a unique language of color, texture, and intense beauty that Vincent van Gogh bequeathed to the world.

***Crows Over the Wheatfield**, a haunting and vivid portrait of the French countryside, is believed to be Van Gogh's last painting before his death in 1890.*

When You're Caught in a Bind

Monitoring aircraft on a radar screen *is monotonous, but inattention can be fatal. The stress of this job has given many an air-traffic controller a case of peptic ulcers.*

What is stress?

Think back to a moment of crisis in your life—for example, a near car collision on the highway. After the crisis passed, you probably felt weak in the knees, emotionally drained. Your body had risen to the occasion, marshaling all your physical resources. This is a portrait of acute stress.

But a short-term emergency is not what most people mean when they talk about feeling stressed. Generally, what grinds people down are long-term pressures—a too-heavy work load, difficulty in commuting to work, worry about baby-sitting arrangements, poor health, chronic illness, a nagging spouse, money woes.

Characteristically, really stressful pressures are inescapable. And while the particular stresses or combination of problems may not affect everyone negatively, the person complaining of stress finds them intolerable.

Stress spans the whole of human life. Researchers have found that it begins even before birth. When a mother suffers from stress during pregnancy, her baby's birth weight, heart rate, and motor activity are influenced. In old age, fear of isolation and loneliness heighten stress among the elderly and infirm. The consequence of long-term stress: the individual feels anxious, angry, hopeless, or trapped.

How does your body respond to stress?

The body reacts to stressors with certain physiological mechanisms. As with emotional responses, both the nervous system and endocrine glands are involved. The hypothalamus, known as the "stress center," responds to alarming events by alerting the autonomic nervous system and by activating the pituitary gland. In a complex interaction, the pituitary and the thyroid glands move into action and release hormones that ready the body to try to cope with troubling situations.

Your body reacts to stress by increasing the flow of certain hormones, known as a group as steroids. If someone is ineffective at dealing with stress, if the response to stressors is passive, then the body will in time be worn down by constant physiological stimulation for which it can find no constructive outlet.

In an effort to avoid dealing with stress some people turn to alcohol or drugs or seek comfort in bingeing on chocolates. Such self-destructive escape mechanisms usually only make the situation worse and add to the wear and tear on the body.

Researchers have found that stress may even influence the immune system by suppressing the body's killer cells, the defenders against invading infections. Heart disease, arthritis, hypertension, even cancer have been linked to excessive stress.

Is stress bad for you?

A life totally without stress would be boring indeed. In fact, Hans Selye, the Canadian physician who first developed the concept of stress and stressors, believed that stress often furnishes the motivation and the energy to achieve success. Stage fright, which is certainly stressful, may spur an actor to give a better performance; anxiety about academic standing may prod a student to study more.

What are the most stressful of all situations?

Studies indicate the death of a spouse is one of the single most stressful events anyone can experience. Also very stressful are the death of a close relative, a major injury or illness, and divorce. Surprisingly, mere changes in routine can be harmful. People who keep changing shifts from day to night are more prone to stress than those who always work the same schedule. The disturbing of biological body rhythms takes a high toll.

Does everyone react to stress in the same way?

If you are fit, and nothing else is seriously wrong in your life, you can probably manage a fair amount of frustration, delay, unfairness—misfortune in whatever form. But illness or accumulated woes can be disabling. Stresses add up—and subtract from your ability to cope with them.

There are people who claim to thrive on stress, but in all likelihood, they are not experiencing stress as most of us understand the word. Such people generally pride themselves on holding up under pressure; they may even brag about it. But this zest gives away the difference between them and ordinary folk. They are among the fortunate few "stress hardy" people who are charged up by challenges, stirred to curiosity and action by situations that leave the rest of us frustrated, angry, or weary.

Further, there are thrill seekers. Rock climbers defy gravity, surfers skim under great, breaking waves, sky divers throw themselves out onto a thin ocean of air. Stressful? Yes, but the stress is brief, the pleasures of accomplishment are strong; therefore there is no damage to body or spirit.

How can you cope with taxing situations?

Most people know what kinds of things get on their nerves and make an effort to avoid them. People who can't tolerate crowds or standing in long lines can try to get to the supermarket and post office when they are likely to be less crowded.

Setting aside some quiet time just for yourself, even if it is only ten minutes early in the morning, or a solitary walk at lunch time, can help insulate you from the hassles of the day.

Taking time as well for exercise may do more for your resistance to stress than a week's vacation. A chess master was once asked how he survived the pressures of a particularly long and grueling tournament. He credited his stamina to swimming and skiing. Something less ambitious—for example, walking to work—can be just what you need.

Few of us have any control over major stresses—ill health, loss of income or job. But there may be some things you can control. When in the middle of a major dislocation, hold off on optional moves. If you are in the process of divorcing, don't try to change your job. Wait until your life is more settled and you feel better. Remember that stresses are cumulative.

How Stresses in Your Life Can Add Up

This quiz, the Life Change Index Scale, was developed by Dr. Thomas Holmes and a group of researchers at the University of Washington School of Medicine. To rate yourself, look over the events listed here. If a given event happened to you within the last twelve months, write down the index number (1–100) for that event. Add up all the points to get your total, then turn to page 322 to find out what the score means.

		Index Number
1.	Death of spouse	100
2.	Divorce	73
3.	Marital separation from mate	65
4.	Detention in jail or other institution	63
5.	Death of a close family member	63
6.	Major personal injury or illness	53
7.	Marriage	50
8.	Being fired at work	47
9.	Marital reconciliation	45
10.	Retirement from work	45
11.	Major change in the health or behavior of a family member	44
12.	Pregnancy	40
13.	Sexual difficulties	39
14.	Gaining a new family member (through birth, adoption, oldster moving in, etc.)	39
15.	Major business readjustment (merger, reorganization, bankruptcy, etc.)	38
16.	Major change in financial state (either a lot worse off or a lot better off than usual)	37
17.	Death of a close friend	36
18.	Changing to a different line of work	36
19.	Major change in the number of arguments with spouse (either a lot more or a lot less than usual regarding child-rearing, personal habits, etc.)	35
20.	Taking on a mortgage greater than $10,000 (purchasing a home, etc.)	31
21.	Foreclosure on a mortgage or loan	30
22.	Major change in responsibilities at work (promotion, demotion, transfer)	29
23.	Son or daughter leaving home (marriage, attending college, etc.)	29
24.	In-law troubles	29
25.	Outstanding personal achievement	28
26.	Spouse beginning or ceasing work outside the home	26
27.	Beginning or ceasing formal schooling	26
28.	Major change in living conditions (building a new home, remodeling, deterioration of home or neighborhood)	25
29.	Revision of personal habits (dress, manners, associations, etc.)	24
30.	Troubles with the boss	23
31.	Major change in working hours or conditions	20
32.	Change in residence	20
33.	Changing to a new school	20
34.	Major change in usual type and/or amount of recreation	19
35.	Major change in church activities (a lot more or a lot less than usual)	19
36.	Major change in social activities (clubs, dancing, movies, visiting, etc.)	18
37.	Taking on a mortgage or loan less than $10,000 (for a car, TV, etc.)	17
38.	Major change in sleeping habits (a lot more, a lot less, or change in time of day)	16
39.	Major change in number of family get-togethers (a lot more or less than usual)	15
40.	Major change in eating habits (a lot more or a lot less food intake, or very different meal hours or surroundings)	15
41.	Vacation	13
42.	Christmas	12
43.	Minor violations of the law (traffic tickets, jaywalking, etc.)	11

Dealing With Depression

Pensiveness, sadness, feelings of isolation—*emotions common to all—should be regarded as a normal part of life. Not so a severe depression, which can be disabling and may, if prolonged or recurrent, require professional help.*

Doesn't everybody get depressed sometimes?

The word *depression* is used for a wide range of mental states. On one side are passing moods of disappointment, regret, or anxiety that almost everybody has at one time or another. For many of us, Sunday evenings are depressing in this sense, because the weekend is over and the responsibilities, pressures, and uncertainties of the week lie ahead.

On the other side is so-called clinical depression, a harrowing week-after-week emotional despair that is a major health disorder. Although there is a huge gap between an occasional case of Sunday blues and a deep clinical depression, the difference is not in the kinds of moods but in their intensity and duration.

Doctors make a diagnosis of clinical depression when a person suffers most or all of a group of symptoms for longer than two weeks. These include despair, bouts of uncontrollable weeping, lethargy, self-hatred, exhaustion, hypochondria, and, in extreme cases, delusions and hallucinations. A paralysis of will can make the clinically depressed person incapable of functioning at home or at work, at times even unable to get out of bed. Those who suffer from clinical depressions can often see no end to their pain and no prospect of happiness in the future.

Can depression make you physically ill?

In addition to sapping one's energy and playing havoc with sleep and eating patterns, a serious depression may cause aches and pains. It also may make a person more susceptible to infections and diseases.

However, never assume that a depression alone is causing distressing physical symptoms. Any number of other causes may be responsible, including heart disease, thyroid disorder, diabetes, cancer, and nutritional imbalances. Blaming a depression for physical illnesses could delay getting the medical treatment really needed.

Why do we get depressed?

A death in the family, losing a job, even moving to another community can all bring on unhappiness, worry, or grief. Depressions that follow such events are called reactive, meaning that they result from external causes.

Reactive depressions are common and, curiously, in many ways healthy because they help sufferers cope with grief. Most doctors regard this kind of depression as a normal response to upsetting events.

In contrast, endogenous depressions arise from internal factors, either biochemical or genetic. For no apparent reason, a perfectly healthy person will sink into despair. The line between these two sorts of depression is not always clear; and a reactive depression has been known to end in misery and despair.

What's the difference between acute and chronic depression?

Doctors describe a depression as acute when it lasts a few weeks and is reversible, and as chronic when it continues for longer and does not respond to treatment. However, that distinction blurs because acute, severe depressions are often cyclical. That is, they keep occurring, relapsing, and occurring again at intervals varying from weeks to years.

One study reported a relapse rate of 85 percent among people who had received treatment for clinical depression. Another study found that cyclically depressed adults spent as much as one-fifth of their lives in an institution; and 20 percent were chronically handicapped by their depressions.

What are the early symptoms of a deep clinical depression?

An erratic sleep pattern is one early sign that someone is depressed, although all erratic sleepers are certainly not on the verge of a major depression. A pervasive irritability, loss of appetite and sexual desire, constant fatigue for no apparent reason, a lack of perspective about minor reverses: any combination of these may signal the onset of a severe depression.

Because someone who is falling into a deep depression may look and act normal, at least for a while, friends may think that he or she is being overly sensitive. Not realizing that the person is really ill, they say, "Snap out of it" or "Pull yourself together." Giving such advice is like telling a person with heart disease or cancer to get better. Although some severely depressed people do heal on their own, a doctor should always be consulted if the depression persists.

Is there a link between brain chemistry and depression?

Although many severely depressed people feel that their misery is their own fault, the result of a character weakness or a spiritual flaw, this view ignores mounting scientific evidence. One focus of research is the brain's neurotransmitters, chemicals that act as messengers between neurons in the brain. In very depressed people, three such chemicals, dopamine, norepinephrine, and serotonin, appear to stop functioning at full strength.

What is S.A.D.?

Many of us, looking upon the grays and browns of a winter landscape, long for the first green of spring. But there are people whose winter melancholy can turn into a deep depression. Victims of seasonal affective disorder, or S.A.D., they struggle all through the gray months against depression. Their spirits lift only when spring returns with brighter sunshine and longer daylight hours.

In the early 1980's, researchers discovered that the hormone melatonin, secreted by the brain's pineal gland, seems to play a role in S.A.D. The less light available, the more melatonin produced by the pineal gland. It may be that the depression of S.A.D. sufferers is caused by the higher level of melatonin in their blood during the winter months. But why the rise in melatonin causes S.A.D. in some people, and not in others, is unclear.

Some people with S.A.D. have found relief by moving closer to the tropics, where the winters are sunny. For those who can't or don't want to move, doctors suggest sitting under a "grow light"—the kind used to stimulate growth in houseplants—for a few hours each day. This appears to suppress melatonin production and its depressive effects.

Searching for the Manic-Depressive Gene

Tucked away in a corner of Pennsylvania's Lancaster County live the Old Order of Amish, a sect that still clings to a strict and traditional way of living. Because marriage to outsiders is rare, this group offers scientists a concentrated gene pool for research into the links between heredity and disease.

The Amish are remarkable for the completeness of their family records. They themselves have long held the belief that manic depression runs in families. This is expressed by their words "sis im blut"—it's in the blood.

The repository of each individual's genetic inheritance is contained within each cell in the body. The nucleus of the cell usually has 46 chromosomes, and within the chromosomes—which are small, roughly X- or Y-shaped structures—are the genes. The genes are the challenging focus of research in heredity. Is a particular gene responsible for manic depression? And if so, how does it operate?

One theory holds that depression is caused by a gene that fails in the normal synthesizing of the neurotransmitter dopamine, one of the chemicals that allow communication among brain cells. In looking for the faulty gene among the Amish, researchers found two genetic markers. This describes a gene shared by a group of people, as revealed by certain traits. A marker is a clue that the gene being looked for lies nearby. In the case of the Amish, two markers were found on the tip of chromosome 11, indicating that the gene might be found there.

On the other hand, research in Israel, among a group as homogeneous as the Amish, found a genetic marker and determined that the defective gene is found on the X chromosome. This result indicates that there may be more than one gene at work in the transmission of manic depression. Clearly, the search is not over. Other investigations of small groups from North America and Iceland failed to turn up evidence of genetic markers.

Fortunately, the presence of a faulty gene does not doom someone to the disease, although it indicates a predisposition to it. Once the defective gene is found, there is hope that a cure may follow.

Barn-raising among the Amish is a wonder to behold, a tribute to their cooperative way of life. Scores of men and boys swarm over the structure and with practiced skill provide a sturdy, spacious barn for one of their number.

The Black Dog of Despair

Are manic-depressives different from other depressed people?

Manic depression is also known as bipolar depression because it swings between two extremes, or poles, of mood. The poles are elation (mania) on one side and depression on the other. A unipolar depression has no "up," or manic, phase. A manic-depressive can be in a state of irrepressible euphoria and hyperactivity, then sink almost overnight into dejection, passivity, and hopelessness.

In the 1940's, an Australian psychiatrist, John Cade, took a bold gamble by giving his manic-depressive patients doses of lithium salts, which he knew had a calming effect on animals. His hunch proved right, and today lithium is widely used for bipolar depression. Administered with care and the constant checking of blood pressure, lithium is a safe treatment for many manic-depressives. If it fails, electroconvulsive therapy (ECT) may be used to control mood swings.

Is it possible to cure depression?

Since the 1960's, a major weapon against crippling depressions has been antidepressant drugs. They boost the amount of neurotransmitters available in the brain. The trouble with these drugs some of which are known chemically as tricyclic compounds, is that it is largely a matter of trial and error to determine which ones will work, in what dosages, on individual patients. The most careful medical and pharmacological supervision must be exercised.

Most authorities believe that chemical medications alone are inadequate to treat depression or may bring on dangerous side effects, and that their use is best supplemented by psychotherapy, either one-on-one or in a group. Less severely depressed people often respond well to psychotherapy.

For those who remain dangerously depressed despite drugs and therapy, some doctors recommend electroconvulsive therapy (ECT), a refined version of what used to be called "shock treatments." It is a procedure that sends electric currents through the brain. Today ECT is used selectively and at lower strengths than it was in the past, but it remains a treatment of last resort, with the risk of at least some temporary memory loss. Even so, without ECT many patients would remain forever locked in suicidal, hopeless depressions.

"Cowardly Lion" *Bert Lahr began using humor as a defense against stress early in life. Many comedians share this coping mechanism, joking in the face of panic.*

Because the causes of depression remain elusive, the search for a cure is difficult. In fact, medical science does not know exactly why antidepressants and ECT work, only that they do in many cases.

Does depression strike men, women, and children equally?

Twice as many women as men seek treatment for unipolar depression, according to data gathered in the U.S. Some researchers believe that this difference may be linked to hormones. Another factor may be that some men regard admitting a depression as unmanly. Others surmise that men are more likely to avert a depression by physical and mental activity because they have a greater choice of outlets. In contrast, many women, trained from childhood to emulate a feminine stereotype of passiveness and forbearance, may find it difficult to prevent negative feelings from building up.

Depressed children, who were once dismissed as just moody, self-pitying, or spoiled, have attracted growing concern. Serious childhood depression is often difficult to diagnose. Many deeply unhappy children turn in upon themselves, become irritable, and do badly in school. A significant change in a child's disposition should never be ignored. When a sunny, smiling eight-year-old retreats into sulky silence and the behavior lasts more than a couple of weeks, it is probably time to seek help.

Is there a link between creativity and manic depression?

You don't have to suffer mental illness to be a novelist, poet, playwright, painter, or composer, but it does not bar achievement in these fields. Studies show that about one-third of prominent writers and artists are manic-depressives or have mood disturbances such as cyclothymia, which involves mood swings less extreme than those of bipolar depressions. The rate of such illnesses among writers and artists is more than six times the rate in the general population.

Certainly not all, nor even most, great creative minds suffer such torments. Yet for some reason creativity does seem to be curiously entwined with mental illness, particularly the bipolar sort characterized by agonizing swings between deep, spiritless depression and boundless enthusiasm and energy.

Among the famous creators who would probably be diagnosed today as manic-depressives are Virginia Woolf, Ernest Hemingway, Eugene O'Neill, George Frederick Handel, F. Scott Fitzgerald, Edgar Allan Poe, Honoré de Balzac, and Robert Schumann. Manic depression seems to be a special hazard for renowned poets. Among its known and suspected victims have been Samuel Coleridge, Robert Lowell, Lord Byron, Sylvia Plath, Anne Sexton, Percy Shelley, and Hart Crane. Of course, any diagnosis based solely on historical evidence is open to question.

The Up-and-Down Life of Josh Logan

Despite debilitating bouts of manic depression, Josh Logan's talent and inner sense of direction allowed him to write and direct a number of hit shows. His courageous public acknowledgment of his mental illness helped many to seek treatment.

As the director of such popular stage and screen successes as *Annie Get Your Gun*, *Mister Roberts*, *South Pacific*, *Fanny*, *Picnic*, and *Paint Your Wagon*, Joshua Logan was one of the greatest theatrical personalities of our time. He was also a man plagued by devastating mood swings—from soaring highs to crippling lows.

When Logan saw his first professional play at the age of eight, "it was love at first sight." He decided to go to Princeton because of its famed student theater, the Triangle Club, for which he both wrote and directed. His enthusiasm for theater was endless. He spent his summers working with other young college students, such as Henry Fonda and James Stewart, in summer stock productions. His unlimited talent and energy earned him his first directing job on Broadway. His theatrical career was set, and there were times when he found himself working on two shows simultaneously. This level of activity was exhilarating, but it left him "exhausted and dizzy."

Logan kept up this frantic pace until his early thirties. Then, while directing a Rodgers and Hart play, Logan fell into a "blue funk." As he wrote in his autobiography, *Josh*, "something sneaked up on me . . . I knew I felt bad. I knew I felt low . . . but I didn't imagine I was sick." He had to force himself to work, couldn't sleep, and felt "very, very lost." Friends tried to cheer him up, but his depression was so deep that any attempt to help seemed futile.

As time passed, the depression wore off and was replaced by something that Logan described as a "high, whizzing feeling." He became so talkative and flamboyant that "people thought I was drinking." He couldn't stop his mind from racing: "I put out a thousand ideas a minute." He worked at a furious pace and then went out to nightclubs until closing. Sleep was fitful and often impossible.

Alarmed by his frantic behavior, friends called in a team of psychiatrists, who informed him that he was having a severe nervous breakdown and needed immediate hospitalization. The doctors determined that Logan was suffering from acute manic depression, where moods go through cycles of elation (which demanded enormous physical stamina), then swing down to the depths of debilitating despair. It is often associated with people of high energy and creativity, a group to which Logan most definitely belonged.

Though Logan recovered after his hospitalization and went on working successfully for years, he continued to suffer from mood disorders. No treatment, whether with drugs, psychotherapy, or electroshock, was able to halt his emotional roller coaster ride.

By the early 1970's, however, a new era had begun for the treatment of manic depression—the era of lithium carbonate. This simple salt had been found to reduce the wild mood swings of 8 out of 10 manic-depressives, and when Logan tried it, it changed his life. Not only were the maddening bouts of highs and lows stopped, but this drug, unlike others he had tried, did not interfere with his creative work.

Today, thanks to Logan's example and the pioneering efforts of many others, thousands of people are able to escape from the ups and downs of manic depression.

Josh Logan *had no idea he was ill until he had to be hospitalized. Treatment with lithium finally brought an end to his suffering.*

Suicide: The Agonizing Mystery

Why do people commit suicide?

Despite much theorizing, there seems to be no single, underlying motive for suicide. Any number of possible reasons for it have been presented by psychiatrists and psychologists.

Freudian theories linked suicide with an unconscious desire to kill someone else; but that wish is instead deflected to the self. More recent theories propose that self-destruction arises from a generalized murderous rage, or that it represents a last-ditch effort to restore lost self-esteem. There are times when the pain and hopelessness of a terminal illness have led to someone's decision to kill himself or herself. Such suicides are sometimes described as rational, but that is a highly controversial opinion.

Suicide remains a puzzling act, repellent and inexcusable to many. In his book *The Savage God*, A. Alvarez—himself a failed suicide—warns against glamorizing "the shabby, confused . . . crisis which is the common reality of suicide."

Can a severe depression lead to suicide?

Studies have shown that the majority of people who commit suicide have experienced a deep depression. Some authorities feel that the most dangerous point for suicide is not at the very bottom of a depression, which is marked by lethargy and an inability to plan, but when the depression begins to lift.

The same pattern is seen in people who have had a very serious disease, operation, or accident. They are most at risk for suicide when they begin to get better. For this reason, people recovering from severe mental or physical illness need just as much watchful care and love as they did when they seemed to be much worse off.

Is taking one's own life approved in some societies?

In Japan, in the ceremony of harakiri, a dishonored warrior could save his reputation and spare his family disgrace and shame by disemboweling himself publicly. In India, a widow might express her inconsolable grief by throwing herself on her husband's funeral pyre and immolating herself with him. Among the aristocracy of old Europe, it was not unusual for a gentleman to shoot himself if caught in socially disapproved behavior. Condoned and even admired for centuries, these mandates for suicide are no longer strong.

In the Christian and Jewish faiths the commandment "Thou shalt not kill" applies as much to suicide as to murder. (At one time, suicides could not be buried in consecrated ground of the Roman Catholic Church.) The Islamic faith also denies adherents the right to kill themselves.

Are certain types of people more inclined to attempt to kill themselves?

Suicide knows no national boundaries and occurs in all walks of life. Across the world, more than two thousand people kill themselves every day. In the United States, the official annual count of deaths by suicide is about 30,000, or almost 100 a day. Experts, however, double or triple that number, pointing out that many suicides are reported as accidents.

Three times as many women as men try to end their lives but fewer women succeed. Thus more men than women actually die by suicide. For reasons that are not entirely clear, men tend to kill themselves with

The Warning Signs of Suicide

Whenever someone you know—relative, friend, coworker, schoolmate, or neighbor—talks about committing suicide, the threat should be taken very seriously. Get in touch with a close family member, the person's doctor or minister, or a local suicide-prevention agency. In other cases, people who plan to kill themselves may not talk about it. Nevertheless, they may give clues to their intentions.

- **At greatest risk** are those who have attempted suicide in the past. An estimated 75 percent of those who actually kill themselves have made at least one prior attempt. Such a person needs watchful care and support, particularly during times of stress.
- **A change of personality** can signal danger. If someone becomes highly irritable or cries for no apparent reason, there are grounds to act. And when someone who is normally resilient becomes apathetic and resigned, it is time to watch them carefully.
- **Emotional blows**—the loss of a loved one, financial reverses, failure in performance at school or on the job—may trigger the wish to end it all.
- **Expressions of guilt** or self-hatred may indicate an inner despair; remarks like "I think I'm a lot of trouble to everybody; they'd be better off without me" should be taken seriously.
- **Fixation on themes of death,** suffering, or suicide, even if spoken of in jest, should be taken up. It is difficult to do, but may be lifesaving, to reply to such remarks by asking if the person is thinking about suicide.
- **Writing a will,** putting one's affairs in order, can, in certain circumstances, be a warning that the person is preparing to commit suicide.
- **Giving away** of possessions, particularly by young people, is a tip-off that something may be seriously wrong.
- **Withdrawal** from normal activities involving school, sports, or hobbies can be a warning of danger.
- **Alcoholics and drug abusers** make up a high risk group. They account for the great majority of suicides.

Measures to Take Include:

- **Do not ignore danger signals.** Don't assume the crisis will pass. Try to discuss suicide openly and calmly.
- **Hide all dangerous drugs**, including aspirin, all firearms, and car keys.
- **Try to make sure** the potential suicide is not left alone too often or too long.
- **Don't be hesitant** about calling for professional help. Remember, you may help to avert a real tragedy.

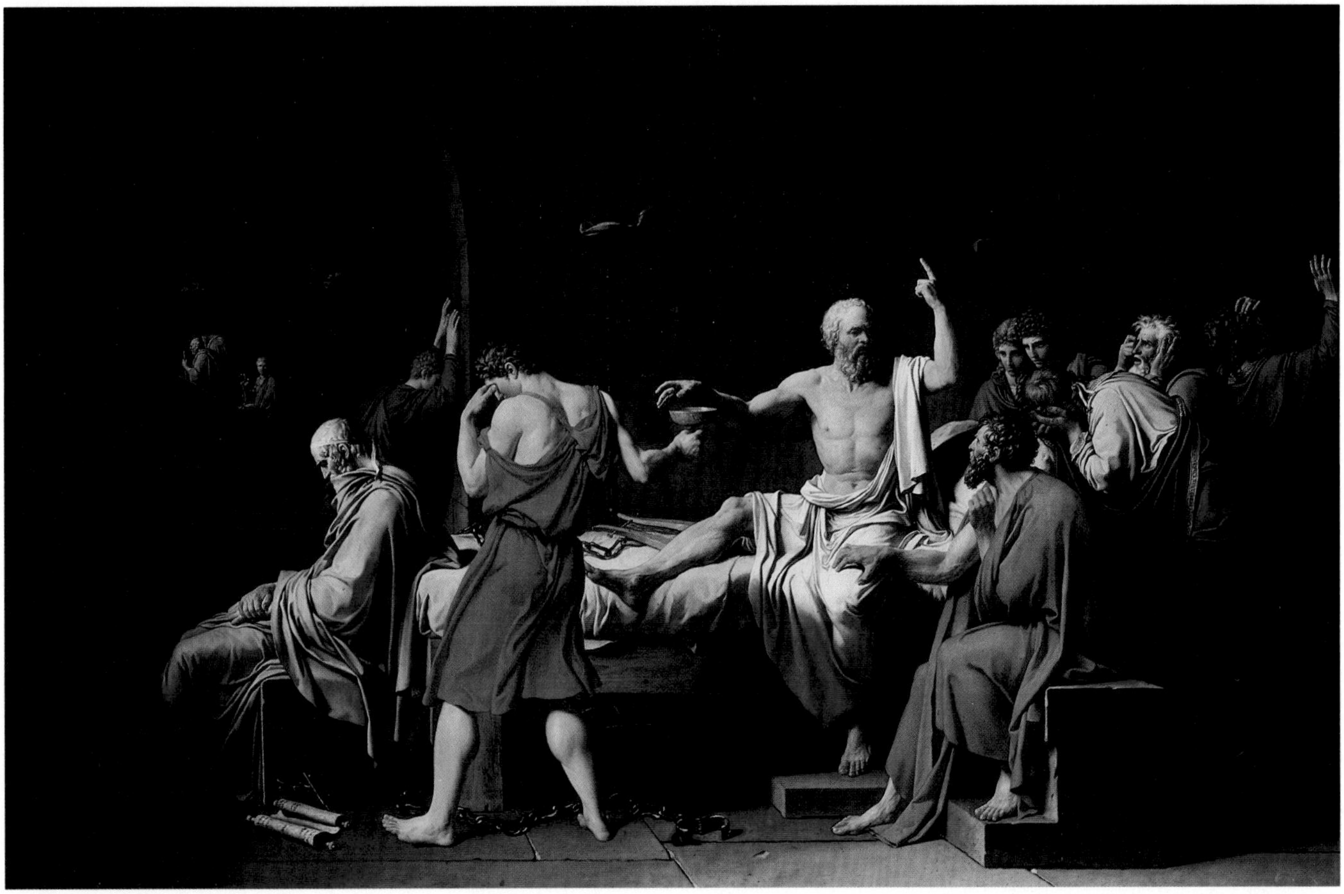

In a romanticized portrayal *of the suicide of Socrates in 4th century B.C. Athens, the French painter Jacques Louis David (1748–1825) shows the philosopher about to accept a cup of poisonous hemlock. Socrates killed himself in defiance of the Athenian court that had sentenced him to death. Some societies have condoned suicide, but Judeo-Christian faiths condemn it.*

guns, by hanging, or by jumping from a height; women by poison. However, guns are increasingly used by young women suicides, ages 15 to 24.

What accounts for the rise in suicide among young people?

Since the 1950's, the rate of suicide in the United States among 15- to 24-year-olds has almost tripled. Some 5,000 deaths a year in this age group are attributed to suicide, and perhaps twice that number are disguised as accidents. Suicide is the third leading cause of death in this age group after homicide and accidents.

One study has shown that 50 percent of all attempted suicides among teenagers are by those who come from broken homes. Some experts believe that the typical suicidal adolescent may not grasp the nature of death and that suicide may thus be a cry for help, or perhaps a way of trying to take revenge on the world.

The disturbing rise in teenage suicide has spurred many communities to take preventive action, using schools and teachers as the first line of defense. A program in New Jersey, for instance, instituted hot lines, teacher awareness of potential problem students, open discussion of suicide in the classroom, and the close cooperation of teachers, psychologists, and social workers. Students surprised school officials by getting closely involved, asking probing questions, and welcoming the idea of the hot lines.

Are feelings of guilt and anger normal after someone commits suicide?

The death of a close relative or friend is never easy; but if the death is by suicide, the unanswerable question "Why?" may cloud the lives of family and friends for years afterward. In one of his rational periods between the attacks of neurological illness that drove him to take his own life, Vincent van Gogh wrote of suicide: "You actually turn your friends into murderers." Moreover, the survivors' feelings of grief, guilt, and even anger may be intensified by a reluctance to talk about how they really feel.

Most survivors say that it helps to talk as soon as possible to someone who understands the complex emotions aroused by the suicide of a loved one. That person may be a minister, doctor, or trusted friend. There are also self-help groups for survivors, which can usually be found through a local hospital, mental health organization, or church group. A great many people have found that it is easier to come to terms with their loss if they are able to meet others who have had a similar experience.

If the grieving friend or relative of a suicide turns to you for help, remember that no matter how awkward or inexperienced you feel, just being there and listening is probably the best help anyone can give.

Gamblers, Misers, Spendthrifts

What's the emotional value of money?

"Nothing else is so rarely about what it is ostensibly about as . . . money," writes columnist Martha Weinman Lear. How people think about money, she observes, often relates to repressed disappointments, or represents a nonviolent, socially acceptable way of venting "the lusts of power and vengeance, the lifelong grievances of childhood."

Of course, money can mean the difference between eating and hunger, or between homelessness and a roof over one's head. But beyond its role in paying for life's necessities, money carries a huge amount of emotional freight for many people who have little to worry about financially. For them, money is tied up with self-esteem, a feeling of power or the lack of it, and a sense of safety and control of one's life, as opposed to feeling constantly at the mercy of circumstances.

When the magazine *Psychology Today* asked its educated, middle-class readers which emotions they linked with money, 20,000 replied. Seventy-one percent said anxiety; 52 percent mentioned depression and anger; and 51 percent "remembered being happy about money at some point."

Interestingly, while 74 percent felt that "money is how we keep score in America," those with the fewest money worries were not necessarily those with the highest incomes. Rather, they were people who felt good about their jobs, personal growth, and relationships with family and friends.

Why are some people cheap?

Who we call cheap depends on our point of view. In families that value frugality, the children tend to grow up thinking that saving money is wise and admirable and spending it is often foolish and self-indulgent.

A desperately poor upbringing can cause a permanent dread of poverty. And cheapness can be a weapon used only against certain people, such as an ex-spouse, or in certain situations, such as giving to charities. This "situational cheapness" may be a substitute for expressing feelings that seem too hostile to admit openly.

Perhaps most serious of all is the kind of cheapness that makes some people hoard everything—money, love, sympathy, praise—because they have always felt emotionally deprived or shortchanged. "Why should I give," they ask, "when I never got?"

As all experienced gamblers know, *"the odds favor the house" (whether casino, racetrack, or bookie). One theory of compulsive gambling is that the thrill of the game provides an escape from internal pressures. In this view, losses are part of the attraction.*

What do misers have in common with big spenders?

Consciously or unconsciously, a feeling of being emotionally deprived can motivate the spendthrift and cheapskate alike. Instead of hoarding, big spenders make up for feeling shortchanged by buying themselves material things. Lavish generosity can result from guilt about having once deprived somebody; or it can be a way of denying a desire to hoard. Of course, generosity may also come from old-fashioned goodness of heart.

Can shopping be addictive?

Shopping as a means of stress reduction can create the compulsive shoppers' syndrome, which some psychologists liken to the problems of binge eaters and alcoholics. Compulsive shoppers splurge in order to feel good and to forget troubling thoughts and emotions. But the relief is always only temporary, and it may take ever bigger splurges to feel good.

Occasionally buying a present to lift your spirits doesn't make you a compulsive shopper. It's a question of degree. If the pattern repeats itself, and the bills get bigger and bigger, it may be time for professional counseling.

When does gambling become a disease?

A willingness to accept risk is a healthy expression of our need to grow, change, solve problems, help ourselves and others. Even people who bet regularly, but not excessively—so-called social gamblers—are as well adjusted as nongamblers, studies show. Social gamblers are people who can "take it or leave it."

Getting high on risk, much like getting high on drugs or alcohol, is at the heart of compulsive gambling. Win or lose, the compulsive gambler craves

The Insatiable Greed of Hetty Green

BACK IN THE LATE 1800'S, the world's richest woman was also the world's stingiest. Though she had millions in the bank, she dressed like a street hag and lived like a pauper.

As a child, Hetty Robinson learned to read from the financial pages, which she would recite to her wealthy father. At age 30 she inherited one million dollars and, over the course of the next 50 years, she shrewdly manipulated stocks and bonds until her fortune grew to nearly $100 million.

Her financial wizardry and infamous stock manipulations confounded such formidable tycoons as Jay Gould and J. P. Morgan and earned her the ignominious title "The Witch of Wall Street." But though she was a genius at making money, she developed an unparalleled hatred of spending it.

When she turned 33, she married Edward Green, another millionaire, but made him sign a prenuptial agreement not to claim any of her money. When he went broke speculating on stocks, they separated, and Hetty, though she had vast wealth, raised her two children under dingy conditions, moving from one cheap hotel to another to avoid paying personal property taxes.

To save money on clothes and laundry soap, she wore the same black dress every day and washed only the bottom portion that touched the ground. Hetty's reluctance to spend money reached horrifying proportions when her son, Ned, injured his knee. She took him to a charity ward to be treated. Unfortunately for Ned, a doctor recognized his millionaire mother and demanded payment. She refused to pay and treated the boy's injury herself. After two years, his leg had to be amputated.

She was far too cheap to pay rent for an office. Instead she conducted her financial dealings from the bank where she kept her fortune, threatening to withdraw it if the bank officers refused to let her use an available desk. When she was feeling particularly unhappy, she would sometimes sit on the marble floor of the bank's vault and admire her notes and securities, which she filed in the specially made pockets of her petticoat. For her meals she would warm up a bowl of oatmeal on the radiator or take out a ham sandwich, unwrapped, from one of her voluminous pockets.

Hetty's lifelong stinginess even played a role in her death in 1916 at the age of 81. She suffered a stroke while arguing over the price of milk. Her son Ned hired nurses to care for her before she died, but had them dress in street clothes for fear that Hetty's condition would worsen if she realized money was being spent to pay nursing bills.

As a final irony, Ned, who inherited much of his mother's vast fortune, became an extravagant spender. He threw his millions away on lavish parties, expensive jewelry, yachts, even diamond-studded chamber pots.

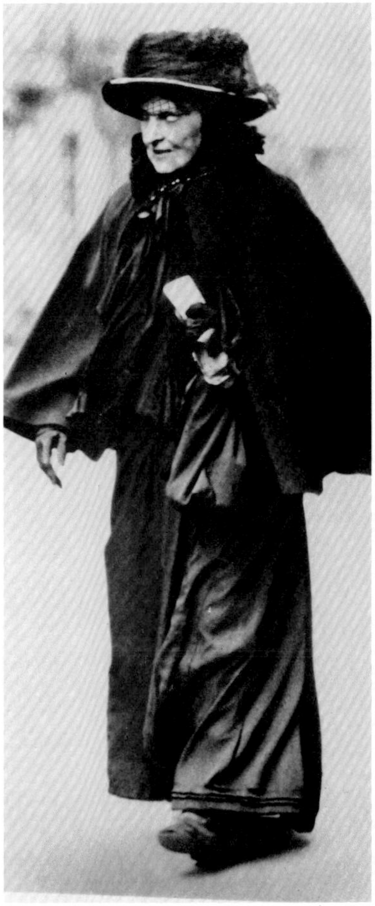

***Hetty Green's** rule was to buy cheap and sell dear. Her dealings earned her millions on Wall Street, but she hated to spend a penny.*

the action. As one put it, "I don't feel alive unless I'm gambling."

In the 1950's, behaviorist B. F. Skinner's experiments with pigeons showed that persistence (addiction) develops when reinforcement (winning) is so variable as to be unpredictable. Almost all compulsive gamblers have had at least one big win and believe they're bound to have another—soon.

How can you spot a compulsive gambler?

Psychologists put compulsive gambling in the category of an "impulse disorder," whose chief symptoms are (1) an inability to resist an impulse, (2) causing harm to oneself and others because of this impulse, (3) increased tension prior to the action, and (4) gratification and a sense of release at the time of the action. A compulsive gambler tends to dislike rules and responsibilities. Guilt or regret may or may not be part of his emotional make-up. He (or she) may appear sociable, but he seldom forms deep attachments. He needs recognition and adulation. He lives for the present. He's often superstitious, prone to believe in signs and omens, and refuses to think about consequences.

New Light on Bad Habits

Are cigarettes addictive?

Up to two-thirds of the adolescents who make it past their second cigarette become habitual smokers, according to a 1988 study reported in the prestigious *New England Journal of Medicine*. Getting hooked on cigarettes, it seems, is quite easy; and the reasons are no longer mysterious.

The nicotine from one puff of a cigarette takes only seconds to reach the brain. Once there, nicotine stimulates the release of brain chemicals, among them acetylcholine. This neurotransmitter and others trigger alertness in mind and body. It is like an excited emotional response, with similar body reactions, such as more rapid heartbeat. As a person continues to smoke, the brain begins to release chemicals called beta-endorphins. Their effect is to calm and relax. Thus smoking has the diabolical ability to give pleasure by both stimulating and calming the nervous system.

Such chemical changes in the brain help explain why some doctors feel that nicotine is as addictive as heroin and why smokers have such a hard time quitting, even when they are well aware of the links with lung cancer and other serious medical problems. The bright side is that the health benefits of quitting are enormous. This is true, a recent study shows, regardless of "how old you are, no matter how long you've smoked."

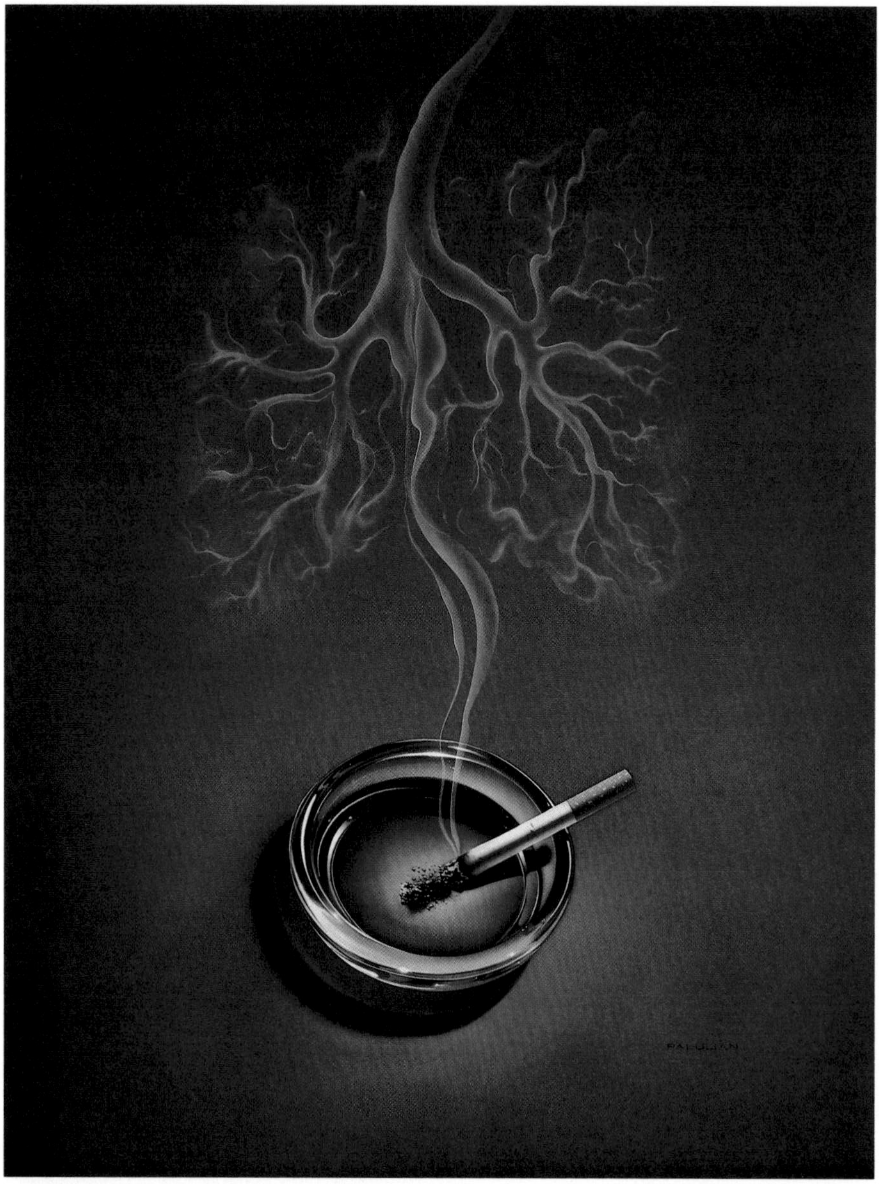

Smoking was once promoted as sophisticated. *Advertisements for cigarettes featured famous people, even opera singers (who claimed to find the smoke soothing). Nowadays, few celebrities are willing to be associated with smoking, and anti-smoking advertisements effectively make the point that smoking is a serious health hazard.*

How can you stop smoking?

Giving up smoking means coping with both physical and mental withdrawal, because smokers are truly addicted. As psychologist Stanton Peele notes, any drug that is successful at relieving tension, pain, and anxiety will be used addictively. Some ex-smokers report such symptoms as nausea and irritability during the several weeks their bodies were adjusting to life without nicotine.

Quitting involves coming to grips with what started you smoking and what keeps you smoking now. Old behavior patterns must be looked at. There are countless books, kits, plans, and clinics that promise to help you stop. Some are expensive. Ask for recommendations from friends who have managed to kick the habit or ask your doctor for advice. The more serious you are about quitting, the better your chances of eventual success.

When chewing gum containing nicotine was introduced a few years ago, it was hailed by some doctors as a good way to treat heavy smokers. After all, the smoke in cigarettes does much of the damage, and eliminating it seems to represent a net health gain.

Many doctors, however, feel that a prescription for nicotine gum, without any accompanying behavioral modification to curb the nicotine habit, runs the risk of trading one addiction for another. Some people who use the nicotine gum to ease their withdrawal symptoms do develop a craving for it. This is hardly surprising, since chewing tobacco, another smokeless nicotine product, can be addictive. Critics of nicotine gum see a parallel with methadone-substitution

programs for heroin addicts, which cure heroin addiction but can produce methadone addicts.

Does cutting down help?

It is tempting for smokers to think they don't have to quit completely but can just cut back on the number of cigarettes they smoke or change to a lower-tar brand. The trouble is that most smokers unwittingly start to inhale more deeply and more often in order to maintain the level of nicotine to which they are habituated.

How does alcohol affect the mind?

It takes only minutes for the alcohol in a sip of beer, wine, or liquor to enter the bloodstream and reach the brain. There alcohol swiftly finds the neocortex, the area of the brain where, among much other activity, many of the signals that affect our social behavior are processed. Some of these signals apparently work to increase our caution and inhibit our gregariousness, raising our anxiety about interacting with people.

Somehow, alcohol counteracts the inhibiting signals in the neocortex, and one result is that people who feel self-conscious at a cocktail party find themselves loosening up after a drink. This may happen, according to one theory, because alcohol blocks the action of a neurotransmitter known as GABA, which is essential for creating anxiety messages in the neocortex.

After a typical drink's worth of alcohol, it takes the liver about an hour to break down the alcohol circulating in the bloodstream. Amounts in excess of roughly an ounce per hour build up in the bloodstream, resulting in more alcohol reaching the brain. The deeper interior parts of the brain are affected, causing sleepiness in some people and belligerence in others. One reason why alcohol produces belligerent behavior, a British study found, is that intoxicated people misread facial expressions. They get into fights because they perceive anger or contempt when none existed.

***In the 1945 movie* The Lost Weekend,** *Ray Milland portrayed a man made sick and desperate by drink. This film, with its vivid scenes of delirium tremens (the D.T.'s), changed the way many people looked at drinking.*

If the alcohol in the bloodstream exceeds a certain critical point, the brain stem, which governs such autonomic functions as breathing, can't function. Death by suffocation follows. This is called acute alcohol poisoning and there is no antidote for it.

Is there a cure for alcoholism?

In terms of numbers of people helped at no charge, Alcoholics Anonymous (AA) is the most successful approach to alcoholism. Not everybody who enters AA is able to stop drinking, but almost everybody who attempts to needs some support system, whether it is AA, family, religion, therapist, or friend.

AA was founded in 1935 by two alcoholics trying to help each other stay sober. Membership is voluntary and anonymous in the sense that only first names are used. One of AA's basic tenets is that alcoholics can—must—stop drinking permanently; that is, no alcoholic is ever really "cured" of the inability to control drinking.

Over the years AA has developed a step-by-step program that has become a model for other self-help groups. The journalist Nan Robertson, a recovering alcoholic herself, summarizes the steps: "We admit we are licked and cannot get well on our own. We get honest with ourselves. We talk it out with somebody else. We try to make amends to people we have harmed. We pray to whatever greater Power we think there is. We try to give of ourselves for our own sake and without stint to other alcoholics, with no thought of reward."

What if there's a relapse?

Conquering an addiction does not mean that a former user will never be tempted again. Facing up to the possibility of a relapse is a key concern of many recovery programs. "Advising people just to say no is not enough," according to Harvard psychologist Howard J. Shaffer. "You need to rehearse exactly how to handle situations when temptation is greatest."

If a recovering addict does have a relapse, or slip, the experience can be intensely upsetting and demoralizing. But, say many psychologists, it's important to remember that a slip can be an opportunity for learning.

Alcoholism and the Family

What makes someone an alcoholic?

There is wide (though not unanimous) agreement among medical scientists that alcoholism should be treated as a disease and that a tendency, or predisposition, to contract it may be inherited. Studies show that children of alcoholics do not have as much of a reaction to one drink as children of nonalcoholics. Consequently, children of alcoholics may find themselves drinking more than their less alcohol-tolerant peers.

Almost all alcoholics have a history of seemingly harmless social drinking. No one is an instant alcoholic, but for some heavy drinkers, alcohol sooner or later gains control.

When Alcoholism Passes From Parent to Child

Apparently, some children inherit a predisposition to alcoholism. This seems to be especially true of one group: men who have alcoholic fathers, have been drinking since their teens, and have a history of violence. Today a technique known as evoked potential offers hope of identifying children who may have inherited this predisposition.

(Of course, a predisposition to alcoholism does not mean someone is destined to succumb to this disease. Evoked-potential tests can warn of this special hazard, and so can give an advantage to young people at risk.)

Evoked potential measures the brain's electrical activity in response to such stimuli as flashing lights. Electrodes are placed on the scalp to pick up the subject's responses, which are initially recorded as brain waves. These waves are then converted into computer graphic brain maps.

Recently, a study compared the evoked potential of two groups of youngsters aged 6 to 18 years. The first group was made up of sons of alcoholic fathers; in the second group were sons of nonalcoholic fathers. The results showed that each group had distinctive brain waves.

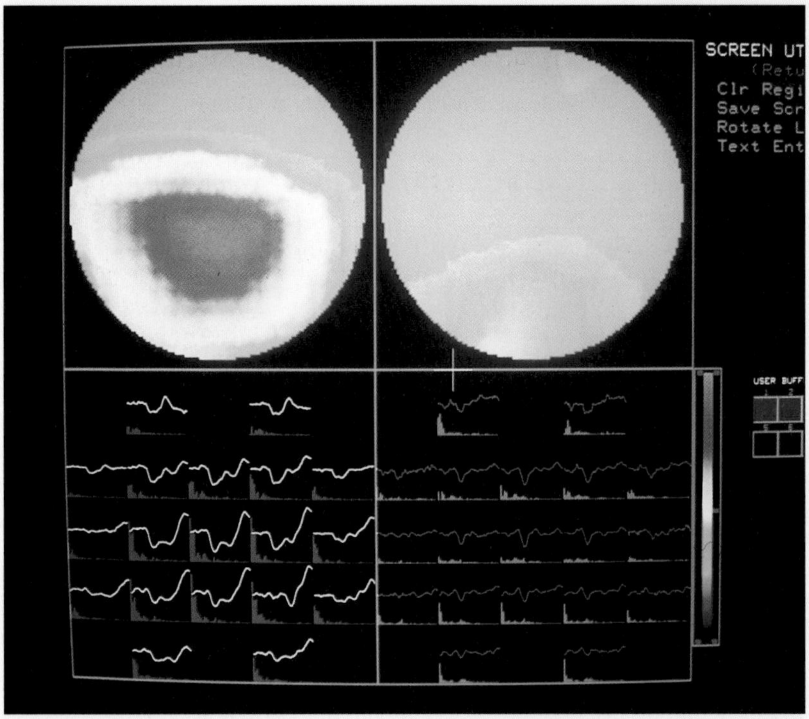

Two contrasting computer maps (the circular areas shown above) illustrate that there is a marked difference between the brain of a child who has not inherited a predisposition to alcoholism (left) and the brain of a potential alcoholic (right).

Why do some experts say an alcoholic's family needs as much help as the alcoholic?

Covering up for an alcoholic spouse or parent, intentionally or unintentionally, can force family members to play a part in maintaining the alcoholic's world of denial and delusion. Typical statements include: "My husband may drink too much sometimes and get belligerent, but it's okay because it gives him relief from his high-pressure job." This makes it easier for an alcoholic to duck the problem.

Psychologists have observed that children of alcoholics learn to deny the neglect they often suffer at the hands of an alcoholic parent. "Every child of an alcoholic receives the knowledge that the bottle is more important to the parent than he or she is," says the poet Robert Bly. Learning to deny such unhappy truths can have lasting effects on a child's emotional development. For this reason, there are self-help groups for grown children of alcoholics.

Is there such a thing as an addictive personality?

Psychiatrists once thought that there was a personality type that was prone to addiction. But since so many personality types are susceptible to addiction, the term *addictive personality* is now little used.

To understand more about the nature of addiction, researchers are now looking into why some people can abuse alcohol or drugs but stop at will, while others become addicts. Dr. G. Douglas Talbott, a leading drug expert, looks upon addiction as a disease that "requires abuse plus genes." Therefore, some are more susceptible to addiction than others.

Talbott's theory might explain why most servicemen who seemed to be addicted to heroin in Vietnam could stop easily when they returned home. The GI's lacked both the biological and psychological components of addiction. His theory might also help explain why nearly all hospital patients who are given narcotics for pain have no trouble stopping once they're well.

"Most Alcoholics are Bankrupt Idealists"

More than 50 years ago, two men, both of them alcoholics, met and talked about their inability to stop drinking. Together, they set out to help others like themselves. There are now A.A. chapters worldwide with a membership of nearly two million.

***The co-founders** of Alcoholics Anonymous, Dr. Bob Smith (left) and Bill Wilson, true to their principles, avoided all personal publicity. Their full names became generally known only after they had died.*

One Saturday afternoon in May 1935, Bill Wilson, a securities analyst from New York, found himself at loose ends in the lobby of the Mayflower Hotel in Akron, Ohio. From one end of the lobby came the sound of voices and of clinking glasses, the sort of convivial sounds that can entice any lonely person into a bar. But Bill Wilson was an alcoholic. For the past few months he had managed to stay sober but only with the support of the Oxford Group, a religious movement, and by trying to help other alcoholics. Now he could feel himself weakening. As he described it later, he was "seized with a thought: I am going to get drunk. Then I panicked. That was really a gift! I had never panicked before at the threat of alcohol."

Realizing his danger, Wilson began a frantic search for help. Through a clergyman whose name he had plucked from a church directory, he tracked down a fellow alcoholic. He recognized that what he needed in his moment of crisis was to talk openly to someone who understood his craving.

The man Wilson found was not only an alcoholic but, unlike Wilson, still an obsessive drinker. A surgeon, Dr. Robert Smith was rapidly losing his patients. Dr. Bob, as he came to be called, was a reserved, conservative man. Wilson, in contrast, was a man of immense drive, who naturally took center stage. It was Wilson's vision and determination that brought Alcoholics Anonymous into being but, without the support of Dr. Bob, he might never have succeeded.

Very gradually, the two men developed a philosophy about the treatment for alcoholism that ultimately became the basic approach of Alcoholics Anonymous. For a brief time at the beginning, Wilson was tempted to create a large, structured organization, one with research facilities. He envisioned affiliation with hospitals and, of course, substantial funding. As he himself said, "Yes, we did dream those dreams. How natural that was, since most alcoholics are bankrupt idealists." But A.A. soon took another turn entirely. It became a loose federation of chapters, funded by the membership. A.A. has never allied itself with any institution or with any political cause. It has never lent its name to any school of therapy for alcoholics. It has remained strictly nonprofessional. Above all, it has offered its members complete anonymity. Wilson, for instance, always greeted new members with a handshake and the words: "I'm Bill. I'm a drunk."

From the first, one of the underlying principles within A.A. has been the recognition of the need among alcoholics for a spiritual rebirth. This realization came to Wilson from a most unexpected source. In the early 1930's, while Wilson was still drinking, he heard about an alcoholic friend who was a patient of the famous Swiss psychiatrist, Carl Jung. Jung believed that the only hope for an end to alcoholism was a spiritual or religious experience—in short, a genuine conversion. Wilson heard about Jung's message when he himself was still at the mercy of his addiction, yet ultimately Jung's words led him to a spiritual awakening. "This concept," Wilson wrote in a letter to Jung, "proved to be the foundation of such success as Alcoholics Anonymous has since achieved . . . this astonishing chain of events actually started long ago in your consulting room."

Wilson lived and worked in New York, while Dr. Bob stayed in Akron, operating at the local hospital and guiding an A.A. group. In November 1950, Wilson visited Bob Smith to discuss A.A. business. He was dismayed to find an exhausted and dying man. Dr. Bob's farewell words to him were, "Remember, Bill, let's not louse this thing up. Let's keep it simple."

Bill Wilson lived for another 21 years, working actively for A.A. Aged 75, he died of pneumonia in Miami Beach, Florida.

The Scourge of Drugs

Is marijuana addicting?

Marijuana is a psychoactive drug, which means it can affect the mind and behavior and alter moods. Any substance with this power (including caffeine) is potentially addictive.

Tetrahydrocannabinol, or THC—the psychoactive substance in marijuana—is a sedative-hypnotic. Even low doses of THC can impair one's motor coordination and confuse one's sense of how much time is passing. Driving a car or operating machinery under the influence of the drug has proven deadly.

Long-term use of marijuana (or pot) can blunt emotions and dull mental faculties and may bring on what psychologists term *amotivational syndrome*—a loss of drive and ambition. This passivity of pot smokers may partly explain why marijuana has the reputation of being harmless.

Much remains to be learned about the long-term effects of marijuana on the mind and behavior, but what is known supports the idea that avoidance is the wisest course. As for the effects on the body, recent evidence shows that smoking marijuana is even harder on the lungs than smoking cigarettes, since habitual pot users inhale deeply and hold the smoke in their lungs before exhaling.

How does cocaine unbalance the mind?

By stimulating the pleasure centers of the brain, cocaine can produce an extraordinary sense of euphoria and mastery. Cocaine intensifies feelings of alertness and pleasure and seems at first to boost performance. The addictive power of cocaine, which is taken as a powder through the nose or burned and inhaled as smoke, was not fully recognized until the 1980's, when incidences of abuse broke out in many areas of the world.

A cocaine high wears off quickly, to be followed by depression and an intense craving for another high. Users may have panic attacks or develop acute paranoia. Because cocaine is a stimulant, it makes the heart beat faster and increases blood pressure; a single dose has been known to cause a massive heart attack or stroke.

Cocaine upsets the brain's delicate chemical balance. One result is that the production of dopamine, a neurotransmitter that helps stimulate pleasure within the brain, is reduced. Coke users seem to wash out all the dopamine in their brains and suffer from chronic anhedonia, or pleasurelessness, without cocaine.

Because cocaine addicts don't usually suffer physical withdrawal symptoms like the delirium tremens of the alcoholic or the shakes and nausea of the heroin addict, cocaine was long considered relatively harmless and nonaddicting. However, if denied the drug, an addict may experience such acute depression and panic that experts revised the definition of withdrawal to include psychological

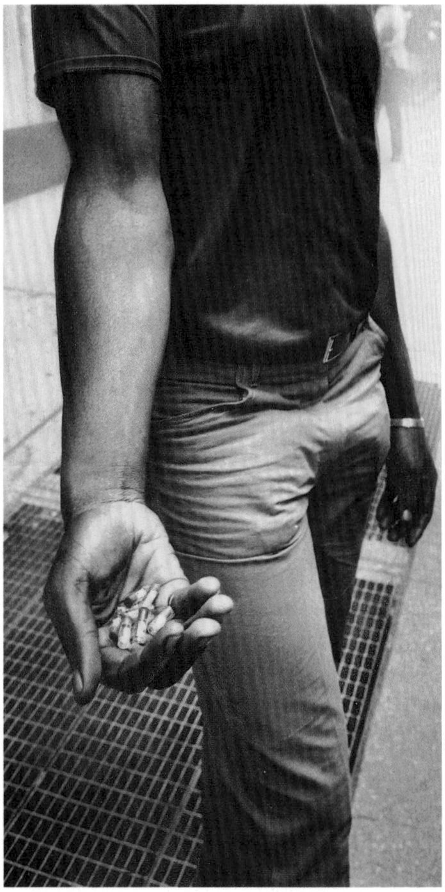

The craving for a fix was so overwhelming *that this heroin addict (above) lost all inhibitions and injected herself in public, right through her clothes.*

His killer wares in the palm of his hand *a dealer (left) brazenly offers vials of crack to passers-by on the crowded streets of New York City.*

symptoms. "Never in my life have I felt such constant anxiety and despair," one ex-addict says of the periods between highs. "I knew that if I didn't get myself into a treatment program in a hurry, I would kill myself."

Can a cocaine addict be cured?

The addictive potential of cocaine is immense. Part of the reason is chemical, part is cultural and social: it is a power drug, used by people who want to be considered "in."

First-time users are almost always supremely confident that they will never get caught in the vicious cycle of anxiety and denial that dominates an addict's life. They cannot imagine themselves desperately craving cocaine, doing anything to get the drug. But it happens again and again. "To keep using coke, I could deal [drugs], I could steal, or I could sell myself," one woman confides, "before I was through, I did all three."

In the temporary euphoria of a cocaine high, an addict can deny the desperate costs of addiction. While high an addict does not have to face losing his or her job, family, friends, and savings. A user can spend more than $1,000 a day to buy cocaine and so prevent being engulfed by despair. Those who have stopped say it takes about one week before the depression and anxiety start to lessen. However, the intense craving for cocaine can last for weeks.

In the mid-1980's researchers found that administering antidepressant drugs to cocaine addicts was sometimes an effective way to break the cycle of craving by helping to restore the brain's chemical balance. But drug counselors warn that use of antidepressants is not a miracle cure for cocaine addiction.

Ex-addicts must avoid situations and people that may tempt them to try cocaine again. In some cases, just talking with one's former drug-using companions is enough to trigger a relapse. Thus recovering addicts must be on guard against anything that will weaken their resolve.

What is crack?

Usually sold in small vials, crack is a form of cocaine that is smoked in a pipe. Unlike cocaine, a single dose of crack is cheap. One vial of crack can cost less than $20. Users of crack report a sense of euphoria that blots out all worries. This peaks within five minutes, only to be followed by feelings of anxiety and depression and an overwhelming craving for more crack. An addict calls this "crashing."

To ward off crashing, crack users can end up smoking cocaine on a continual basis until their money or their lungs give out. To date, there has been no illicit drug that has proven to be so accessible and so addicting. A survey done in the late 1980's indicates that 1 out of 18 American high school seniors may have tried crack.

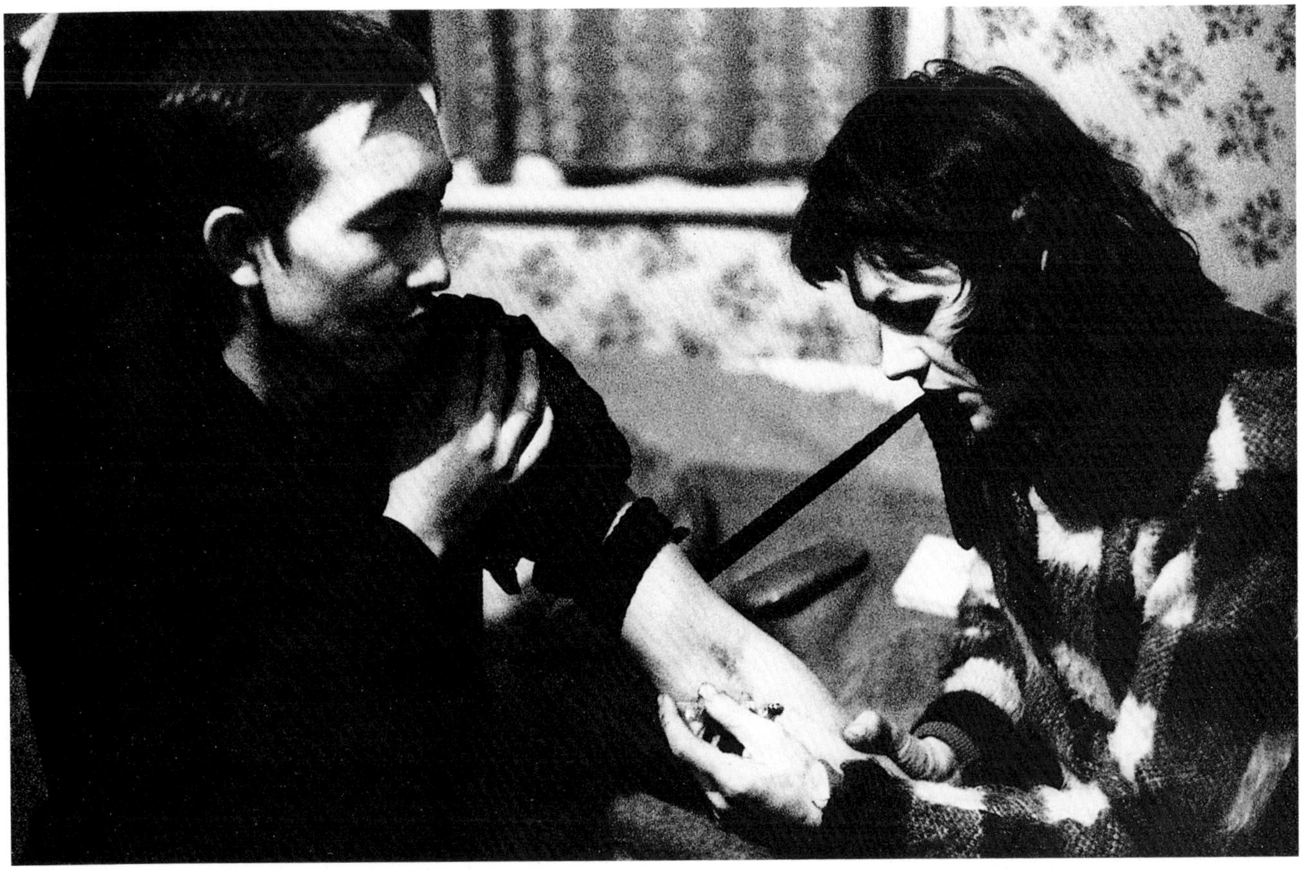

The ravages of drug addiction etched on her face, *a young woman injects another addict with a dose of heroin.*

False Promises, Deadly Risks

***Winner of a silver medal** in the 1972 Olympics, East Germany's swimming star Renate Vogel-Heinrich developed a husky voice and heavy shoulders. When she discovered that her trainers were, secretly, feeding her steroids, she defected to the West in 1979.*

Why do athletes take steroids?

In big-time, mass-audience sports, it is the winners who get most of the glory and money, and for that reason athletes look for any edge they can get against the competition. Some athletes thought they had discovered the answer in the class of chemical compounds called anabolic steroids, a number of which are naturally produced in the body and play important roles in growth and metabolism.

By taking extra doses of certain steroids—sometimes under the supervision of a doctor or trainer, sometimes not—athletes have achieved phenomenal gains in muscle mass and body weight. However, these increases in size and strength appear to come at a high cost to an athlete's long-term health.

Some athletes have been known to take, each day, 10 different types of animal and human steroids, amounting to more than 1,000 milligrams, many times the amount produced naturally in the body. To be sure, some muscles will begin to bulge.

Yet taking excessive amounts of certain steroids has been found to alter permanently the sexual characteristics in women and seriously affect the male sex drive.

The heart and liver also suffer. Doctors are seeing cases of athletes in their twenties who, after prolonged use of steroids, developed such heart-attack warning signs as angina and high blood pressure. Also reported are unusually high rates of liver tumors and liver cancer.

Do steroids affect the emotions?

Often, steroid users find themselves undergoing a personality change. "I felt an aggression I'd never felt before," says one football player. "I got into a fight with . . . a linebacker. I threw him down, pulled his helmet up far enough so I could . . . smash him in the eye." Other athletes find themselves addicted to steroids and complain of terrible fatigue and depression if they try to quit. Though much scientific research remains to be done on the addictive potential of steroids, as well as on their physical and emotional side effects, enough is known to have made the sports world extremely cautious about their use. There is also the question of whether it is fair to pit athletes taking steroids against those who are not.

Can prescription drugs be addicting?

Doctors have learned that some prescription sleeping pills and sedatives can turn their patients into accidental addicts. In the early 1900's, when barbiturates were first prescribed to help insomniacs, doctors were unaware that these powerful sleep inducers, if used for more than a few weeks, produced dependence

Did You Know . . . ?

- **You should avoid drinking alcohol when you're cold.** Though alcohol may taste fiery, it actually cools the body. This is because alcohol dilates the blood vessels, which allows for a rush of more blood to the skin's surface. In the process, body heat is given off.
- **In a test of the addictiveness of cocaine,** laboratory rats were given the choice between food and cocaine. They chose cocaine over food and starved to death.
- **Withdrawal from heroin addiction** may be accompanied by an involuntary twitching of the legs. This is believed to be the origin of the expression "kicking the habit."
- **Crack consists of pea-sized pellets of cocaine.** It is one of the most addictive drugs known. When smoked in a pipe, it makes a crackling sound, hence the name.
- **The hypodermic syringe was invented in 1853.** Soldiers in the American Civil War were among the first to use the needles to inject themselves with morphine.
- **Hashish is made from the resin** of marijuana plants but is much stronger than marijuana. Hashish is usually smoked in a pipe.

and withdrawal symptoms. Later, long-term users of tranquilizers (with such brand names as Librium, Valium, and Xanax) reported similar experiences of addiction.

Amphetamines, the powerful stimulants that some doctors once routinely prescribed for mild depression and weight problems, proved so conducive to abuse that prescriptions for them are rarely written anymore. Today they are prescribed mainly for certain acute conditions, such as extreme obesity, since amphetamines suppress the appetite, and some cases of narcolepsy, in which a person has irresistible attacks of sleepiness.

Many doctors and patients fear the addiction potential of painkillers containing such narcotics as morphine and codeine. For this reason, some doctors refuse to prescribe these opium-related drugs, and some patients who receive such prescriptions decline to take them.

For people who have no history of drug abuse, the temporary use of such narcotics to ease serious pain seldom poses a problem. The best approach is for the doctor and the patient to decide together the right type of medication and dosage for a particular pain, since people's tolerance of pain is highly subjective.

Does the brain have its own painkillers?

Scientists now know that the brain can produce its own natural opium-like chemicals, called endorphins. But the brain releases small amounts of these natural narcotics only in response to the stress of some sort of trauma. Their effect is evident in accident victims, who feel no initial pain after a traumatic injury, for example, or in marathon runners, who are insensible to soreness until after they finish their race. Endorphins can provide only temporary relief.

Do some illicit drugs act like the body's own painkillers?

Opium-based drugs, such as heroin, affect the brain very much like endorphins, the body's natural painkillers. The major difference is that endorphins are released as a temporary reaction to stress, while heroin's effect can be produced for any length of time with a hypodermic needle and enough cash to buy the drug. One theory of heroin and opium addiction is that it, too, is linked to stress: addicts are seeking relief from the psychological stress of coping with life.

However, these illicit drugs prove to be so overwhelmingly powerful that an addict stops needing the drug for psychological relief and develops a physical craving for it. Thus, heroin and opium addicts are caught in a potentially deadly balancing act between satisfying their escalating need for the drug and avoiding a lethal overdose.

***When All-American basketball** star Len Bias was chosen in June 1986 to play for the Boston Celtics, everyone felt he had earned it. Elated by this achievement and perhaps feeling invincible as only a youngster can, Bias tried cocaine—evidently for the first time. Within hours, he was dead of cardiac arrest, aged 22.*

PART V

The All-Important Family

Like a passing parade, families are in full swing when we join them. As we in turn march forward, we carry our family's particular culture into the future.

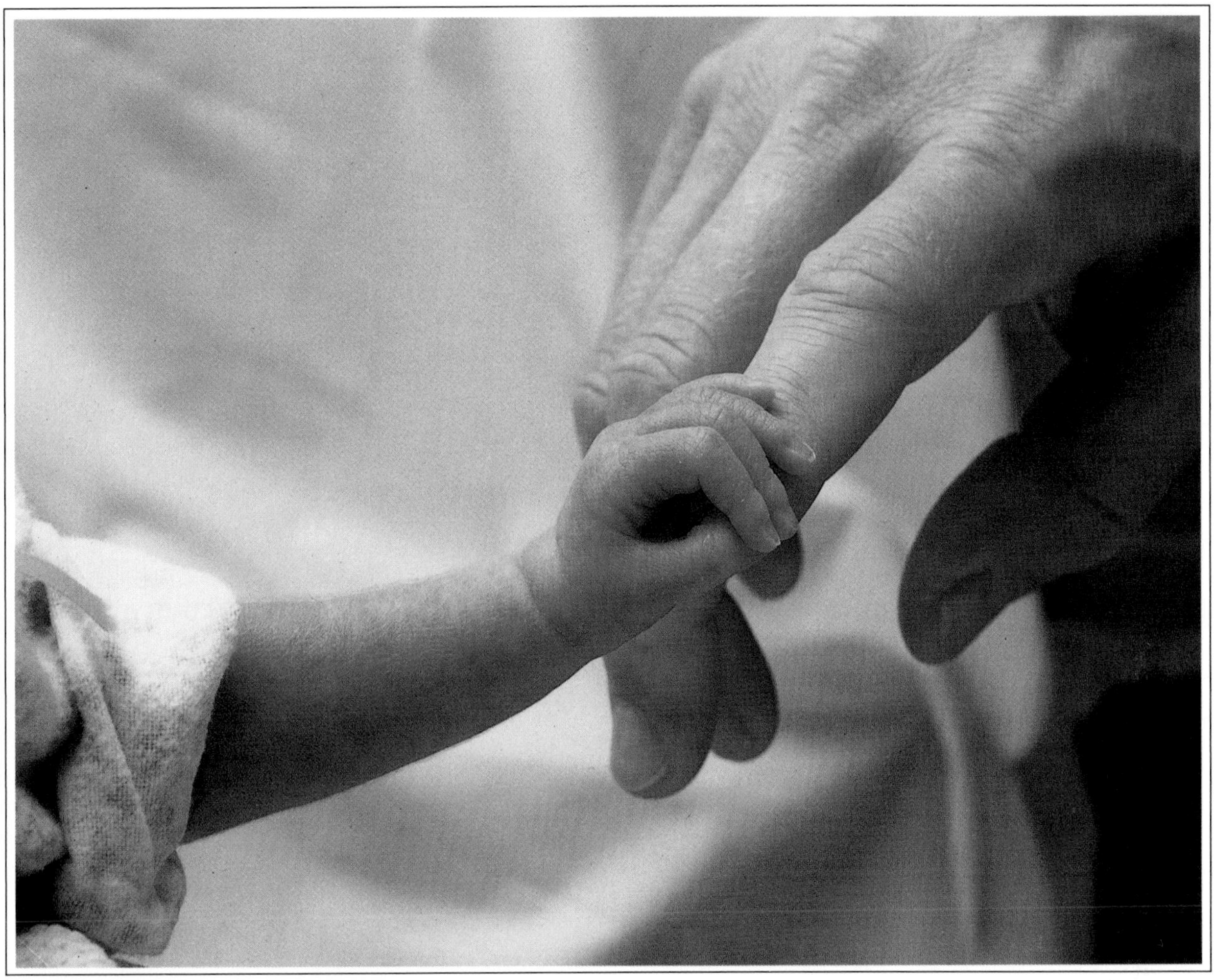

It takes no more than the touch of a tiny hand to seal forever a parent's pledge of love.

Our Personal Beginnings

To what extent does the family shape a child's mind?

Long before they enter school, children absorb basic concepts of morality, faith, fair play, and even fun from observing, listening, and participating in family life. Youngsters learn decision-making from seeing how parents make decisions; they imitate their elders in everything from table manners to patterns of fighting, bickering, and making peace. Social scientists refer to this process of imitation and absorption as *socialization*, or *enculturation*. Socialization within our own families sets the emotional tone that guides us the rest of our lives.

So powerful are these socializing forces that even people who are determined to reject their own family patterns may still be influenced by them. In raising our own children, for example, many of us seem to harbor a strong urge, whether it is mainly conscious or unconscious, to treat them as our parents treated us. Thus systems of reward and punishment, of what is acceptable behavior and what is not, are perpetuated in a family.

***If stories are attached** to dry names and dates, a family tree comes alive, as in this Norman Rockwell painting.*

What exactly is a family?

Most families are, of course, made up of members related by blood or marriage, but the term *family* can describe any group of people drawn together by intimate ties and shared goals. And this sense of family seems sometimes to make people stronger individually and collectively.

Often families will informally "adopt" a friend to share holidays and special occasions with them, describing the friend as "one of the family." Or a youngster may form a close relationship with a relative outside the immediate family, making that person a role model and mentor. Great Britain's Prince Charles had such a relationship with his father's uncle Lord Mountbatten, whose almost legendary achievements in war and peace the young prince profoundly respected. Charles referred to Mountbatten as his "honorary grandfather."

What is more important in shaping our lives, our family environment or our genes?

Specialists continue to argue over whether nature (genes) or nurture (environment in which we grow up) is more important in forming our personalities. Many studies indicate that neither factor is consistently dominant; instead, they modify each other. A 1984 study found that adopted children in Denmark whose natural parents had been criminals got into more trouble with the law than adopted children whose natural parents had no criminal backgrounds. Even so, the number of lawbreakers was significantly less than what might have been expected if the children had been left with their natural parents.

Family tradition and natural ability reinforce each other. The Khan family of Pakistan, whose members have been squash racquets champions over three generations, illustrates this blend of natural talent and family conditioning. Not only have squash championships passed from father to son, but also to brothers-in-law, related not by blood but only by marriage to the Khan family.

PERSPECTIVES

On Home and Family

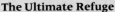

Few words strike deeper than "home" and "family," calling up as they do powerful, private feelings about the most important places and people in our lives.

The Ultimate Refuge

"Home is the place where, when
you have to go there,
They have to take you in."

—Robert Frost
The Death of the Hired Man

◆

Voices From the Past

"We go back to find the security of home, but also *to find in the past the answer to the present.* It would be to misread our early days if we thought of them only as a place of sweetness and light. The past is not completely happy for any of us, and that is as it should be, for it is the birthplace of the self. Here our lives take shape. Here the real self begins its struggle to be known and here, for the first time, we encounter the mystery and otherness of people.

"We must cherish our yesterdays but never carry them as a burden into the future. Each generation must take nourishment from the other and give knowledge to the one that comes after.

"Even if the past was not kind to you, turn it to account, to understanding. Take time to remember. Make an enduring home for your children's memories; then leave them to build, on that foundation, their own house of the future." **—Ardis Whitman**
You Must Go Home Again

◆

An Unfortunate Distinction

"All happy families resemble one another; every unhappy family is unhappy in its own fashion."

—Leo Tolstoy
Anna Karenina

◆

Uniquely Human

"A man's family sets him apart from all other living creatures. Who else has children he can call his own for longer than it takes to set them on their feet or on their way? The most loving animals—the vixen, the bear, the lioness—teach their cubs to make their own world, and to forget them; after the eagle has taught her eaglet to fly, she will see him no more. Calf, colt, grasshopper, dragonfly—go their separate ways as soon as they can. Only man stands with his children from first to last, from birth to death, and to the grave."

—Robert Nathan
So Love Return

◆

Homegrown Chaos

"There is scarcely any less bother in the running of a family than in that of an entire state. And domestic business is no less importunate for being less important." **—Montaigne**
Essays

◆

Stepping Right Along

"On a recent visit, my only child's only child put her arm around my neck and asked me if I knew how many grandparents she had. I, of course, said she had four. Her proud correction was that she had fifteen.

"Fifteen?

"Her mother and father are not married to each other now but are to other people, so that the basic parent count at the moment is four, which, since each of the four has two living parents, means an active grandparent population of eight. Active? Of those eight grandparents, two couples have divorced and each has remarried, adding four grandparents, making twelve—eight steppies and the primary quartet. Everybody's doin' it, so to speak. Then we have the child's then one surviving great-grandparent—a great-grandfather (my ex-father-in-law)—and his second wife: the thirteenth and the fourteenth. My grandchild's stepmother's mother has a sister she regards 'as a twin,' and my granddaughter seriously includes that step-great-aunt and will not put her in a lesser category. Fifteen."

—Harold Brodkey
Reflections

Family Roots and Awareness

How to Capture Your Family History

Family stories are like messages from the past; they tell us where we come from and, often, what to expect of ourselves. They can be simple descriptive anecdotes, such as your grandfather saying, "Your grandmother always forgot to bring the salt along on picnics," or they can be tales of mythic prowess when the same grandfather boasts of his father that "winter or summer, he swam in the river every day of his life." But such stories depend for their existence on someone's memories and recollections, and they can be lost forever unless a real effort is made to record them.

- **How to start collecting**
  Write down any family anecdote you may remember. Don't worry about writing style or the sequence of events. Family history is often fragmentary and contradictory. In fact, it's part of the pleasure to have various versions of one event.

- **Building the record**
  Show your notes to other family members and ask them to add from their storehouse of memories. Be sure to look in family Bibles to see what births, marriages, and deaths were recorded there. Photo albums are a wonderful way to jog memories. If there are unidentified pictures, ask around to see if someone can match names to faces. Old family letters, too, can be mined for information or simply preserved for the quality of the writing.

Be sure to label photos, noting place, date, and names, including last names if there is a possibility of confusion.

- **Reunions and holiday get-togethers**
  Bring along a notebook, a tape recorder, or a video recorder if you have one. These occasions also offer an ideal time to quiz older family members about what they recall. Let them ramble on but also have a list of questions ready to jog their memories.

- **Questions you might ask**
  Where did the family come from? What are its ethnic roots?
  What trades or professions did they follow?
  What were the family's politics?
  How did they survive the depression of the 1930's?
  Were there any black sheep in the family?
  How did various family members meet and marry?
  How many children were there in each branch?
  What wars have the men of the family fought in?
  What was the most exciting thing that ever happened in the family? the best? the worst?
  How did they amuse themselves?
  What kind of books did they read?

- **Learn your family medical history**
  An anecdotal family history can provide valuable information to your doctor in certain situations. So, as part of your record, find out how long family members lived and what caused their deaths. You may discover a predisposition to certain illnesses, such as asthma, heart disease, or diabetes.
  Nowadays, many doctors are also interested in annotated family trees, which are called *genograms.* This kind of background information may be helpful when treating someone for emotional disturbances.

Who's responsible for making family traditions?

Most families do, indeed, have long-standing traditions. But young children are known for converting any memorable experience into instant tradition just by adding the word *always.* After an afternoon of fishing with his father, a young boy will proudly say, "My dad always takes me fishing," or a single summer trip is transformed by "We always go to Canada in the summer."

Even the simple patterns we use to organize activities can be the stuff of family legend: "Don't we always put the lights on the Christmas tree before we do anything else, Mom?"

Part of what keeps families together is creating new memories and passing them along as traditions. Parents are often teased for squirreling away cartons of their children's schoolwork, crafts projects, and the like. But the parents' hope is to keep cherished moments alive and give their children and *their* children, on through succeeding generations, a chance to relive family history.

Is the family crucial to the development of our minds?

A medieval monarch designed an experiment that, unwittingly, demonstrated how vital the family is to mental and emotional development. Convinced that German was the natural language of children, Emperor Frederick II removed a group of newborns from their families and had them cared for by nurses who, on his orders, never spoke to the children or played with them. But instead of spontaneously speaking German, as the emperor had expected, all the children, deprived of meaningful human contact, sickened and died.

Modern investigation confirms what the emperor Frederick sadly learned. When a group of orphaned infants were placed in foster homes for their first year of life, all did significantly better on mental and physical tests at the age of one year than a similar group of babies who had been left in an orphanage.

The Wild Boy of Aveyron

No family ever came forth to claim the strange child captured in the French countryside, and that may explain why the boy could never be taught to speak. Deprived of human contact at a crucial age, his mind may have been too crippled to use words.

Portrait of Victor *shows him a year after capture.*

EARLY ONE JANUARY MORNING in 1800, villagers in Aveyron, southern France, captured a remarkable creature, an 11- or 12-year-old boy who appeared to be wild—he was naked in the winter weather and pocked with scars. Villagers thronged to see this skittish wild boy, who continually tried to escape. How long he had been lost or abandoned or why, no one knew. He took no notice of anyone who talked to him, so that observers guessed that he was deaf and mute. Because of his completely asocial behavior, they assumed he had lived most of his young life without human contact, subsisting on roots, acorns, and raw potatoes.

The "savage boy" quickly became a celebrity and was taken to Paris to be observed by those who thought that life in the wild might be superior to civilization. But as a "noble savage," the boy proved to be a sore disappointment to Parisians, who found him to be "a disgusting, slovenly boy, affected with spasmodic . . . convulsive motions . . . biting and scratching those who contradicted him, expressing no kind of affection for those who attended upon him." The boy was soon diagnosed as an "idiot" and placed in an institute for deaf-mutes.

There, however, he had the good fortune to come under the care of a young doctor named Jean-Marc Itard, who welcomed the challenge of educating the wild child. By close observation Itard discovered that the boy, whom he named Victor, was neither deaf nor mute nor an idiot. But Victor was profoundly unaware of lessons usually taught a child by the family and community. Apparently, the crucial socialization that a family provides had been denied him. Though human, he had learned little about how to live with other people.

With great optimism Itard set out to teach Victor the skills needed to live in society. He had to be toilet trained. He had to be taught how to sit in a chair, how to express emotions without violent outbursts, and ultimately how to speak. After a few months of intensive training Victor was transformed from a wild creature to a clean and controlled boy. He showed affection for Mme. Guérin, Itard's housekeeper, and even learned to say the word "milk" and the phrase "Oh God," which Mme. Guérin often used.

But after such a hopeful start, Victor made little progress. He never learned any more words. Unlike an infant learning to mimic parents and siblings, Victor had almost completely lost the ability to imitate. Somewhere, his bonds with family and community had been severed, and he could never recover from the devastating loss. After his training ceased, Victor lived on in Paris, cared for by Mme. Guérin, until he died at the age of 40, still unable to master words.

Stories of children reared by animals, *such as Mowgli in Rudyard Kipling's* Jungle Books, *reflected a belief, widespread in the 19th century, that there was such a thing as a "noble savage," superior to civilized man. In fact, isolation from a human family is catastrophic for a child.*

Siblings: Homegrown Rivals

Primogeniture: Firstborn Favoritism

Under the system of primogeniture, which prevailed in Europe for hundreds of years, the firstborn son had sole right to inherit his father's land. In countries that retain royal traditions, this practice persists today for succession to the throne: the monarch's oldest son (or daughter, if there is no son) becomes ruler of the realm when the royal parent dies.

History and literature abound with bloody strife centering on succession. The stakes were high. To the king went not just the title and power, but all the royal property as well.

In recent times, regality seems to have lost much of its appeal, perhaps because modern monarchs have little power and a great many headaches, such as being a center of media attention. King George V, who became the British ruler in 1910 because his older brother had died, never wanted the job. His son King George VI, father of Queen Elizabeth II, came reluctantly to the throne after his brother King Edward VIII abdicated in 1936 to marry a twice-divorced American woman. George VI was an unassertive man, uncomfortable with the trappings of office. Nevertheless, in spite of having to conquer a severe stammer, he inspired his people with eloquent speeches in the dark days of World War II.

King George VI of Britain was not a firstborn. He came to the throne only because his older brother gave it up.

Does birth order affect a child's development?

Studies have repeatedly shown that first children, perhaps because they have their parents' undivided attention, at least for a while, tend to be more aggressive and to do better in school than their younger siblings. Surveying the members of the U.S. Congress in 1972, Dr. Richard L. Zweigenhaft found that a majority of the politicians were firstborns.

University of Michigan psychologist Robert B. Zajonc believes that, on average, firstborn children do better on IQ tests because they are born into a home that contains only adults. As infants they are exposed primarily to adult ideas, behavior, and speech.

Researchers observing individual families have found behavior that might explain the IQ differential. New Jersey psychologist Michael Lewis, who studied videotapes of family dinners, found that fathers paid more attention to the oldest child, particularly if that child was a son. And, Lewis reports, in families with three children or more, middle children were virtually ignored at the dinner table.

Some firstborns, however, pay a price for their special status. Parents may be more critical and negative when their eldest child does not live up to expectations. Not surprisingly, first children can become perfectionists who feel great tension resulting from the pressure to do well.

Does birth order create lifelong stereotypes?

Hypotheses about the significance of birth order are drawn from studies of large groups. These studies cannot predict how any given individual will develop or respond in different situations. Psychologists caution against casting children in specific roles: the quiet one, the athletic one, the smart one, the clumsy one. Even positive roles may box children into a confining identity, and it goes without saying that negative typing can provide a harmful self-image that a child may carry throughout his or her life.

What does sibling rivalry mean?

The Austrian psychiatrist Alfred Adler used the term *sibling rivalry* to describe the competition between children in the same family for the affection and attention of their parents. Of course, sibling rivalry existed long before Adler coined the phrase.

Two of the best-known Bible stories deal with bitter feuds between brothers: the hostility between Cain and Abel and the rivalry of Joseph and his brothers. Believing that their father loved Joseph, a younger son, more than all the rest, his older brothers left him in a pit to die.

Is sibling rivalry inevitable?

Competition is natural and normal between children in the same family who must share their parents' love. But that does not mean that it should be allowed to develop into savage fighting. Child psychologist Selma Fraiberg warns parents against using the notion of sibling rivalry to excuse truly unacceptable behavior by their children. "Sibling rivalry is regarded as another prerogative of today's child, and the licensed hostility in this area sometimes reaches the point of barbarity," she maintains.

Although no two families are alike, psychologists have observed certain general patterns of sibling rivalry. It appears to be more intense the closer children are in age. Compared to a brother and sister, children of the same sex are more likely to be either each other's rivals or close companions at various stages in their growing years. A respected older sibling of the same sex may serve as a role model when the younger sibling is shaping his or her own identity.

When the relationship between older and younger siblings is hostile, the older one can become a model not for emulation, but for rebellion. As a result, a younger sibling may be provoked into contrary behavior merely for the sake of being different.

Whatever the spacing of births and the sex of offspring, it is the parents' reactions to sibling rivalry that strongly influence whether the children will develop feelings of intense hostility or will be content with being no more than good-natured competitors.

Should parents treat all children alike?

Parents sometimes assume they can reduce sibling rivalry and avoid playing favorites by treating all their children alike—the same rules, the same expectations, the same opportunities—regardless of differences in age, sex, and temperament. Paradoxically, this behavior often fosters the very rivalry parents are trying to avoid. Psychologists Adele Farber and Elaine Mazlish, authors of *Siblings Without Rivalry,* suggest that instead of thinking of equality in everything from parental attention to music lessons, parents should be sensitive to each child's individual needs.

"To be loved equally," say Farber and Mazlish, "is somehow to be loved less. To be loved uniquely—for one's own special self—is to be loved as much as we need to be loved."

Does sibling rivalry last into adulthood?

In 1959, shortly after British novelist Rebecca West learned that she was to be honored with the title Dame by Queen Elizabeth II, she received an irate telephone call from her older sister, then 75. Since childhood the two had nursed a rivalry that they would not give up even as mature women. "She rang me up and, crying with utterly shameless rage, demanded by what accident this preposterous thing could have happened," wrote West.

Actress Joan Fontaine's autobiography, *No Bed of Roses,* makes clear that she and her older sister, Olivia de Haviland, never resolved their own sibling rivalry. Fontaine says of her sister, "I regret that I remember no one act of kindness from her all through my childhood."

Even where the bitterness of sibling rivalry has long since faded, sometimes a taste of the competition lingers. When Dwight Eisenhower was president of the United States, reporters knew they could provoke him by mentioning his brother Edgar. A year and a half older, Edgar had been Ike's constant rival as a child, and in fact had regularly come out ahead whenever they competed. To reminders that Edgar didn't agree with his latest policy, Ike would reply, "We haven't agreed on anything since we were five years old."

In a study of older siblings, psychologists Joel I. Milgram and Helgola Ross of the University of Cincinnati found that nearly half still had feelings of sibling rivalry and jealousy. Most frequently these adult siblings believed the source of the rivalrous feelings was parental favoritism.

Jacob favored his son Joseph *above all his other sons and that bred bitter sibling rivalry. Here, in a plot to prove the favorite son is dead, Joseph's envious brothers show a stricken Jacob (at left) the bloodstained coat worn by their hated brother.*

Early Influences, Lasting Roles

Is there a best family size?

Books like *Cheaper by the Dozen* and movies like *The Sound of Music* paint a glowing picture of the benefits of a big family: warmth, sharing, and fun, with a ready supply of playmates. They reflect the belief that large families encourage resourcefulness, independence, and responsibility, while discouraging selfishness and feeling sorry for oneself.

Some think that a large family can be a buffer against what they see as the rootlessness and isolation of modern life. "In this era, the idea that there is a large group to depend on gives large families a sense of security and comfort," notes University of Hartford psychologist Michael Kahn.

In contrast, at least one study suggests that as a group children from large families don't do as well in school as those from smaller families and have a higher delinquency rate.

The brunt of raising a family still falls mainly on the woman, despite efforts at equalizing the burden. And the larger the family, the greater a woman's load. The strain can be killing, as one 18th-century husband noted in a letter about his late wife: "Indeed she would sometimes say to me that bearing, tending and burying children was hard work and that she has done a great deal of it for one of her age (she had six children, where of she buried four, and died in the 24 year of her age)."

Are there advantages to being a later-born child?

In some instances, later-born children's rank in the family hierarchy gives them a receptivity to new ideas that the oldest child, busy living up to traditional parental expectations, does not develop.

In a project at Princeton University's Institute for Advanced Study, Frank Sulloway researched the lives of a number of eminent scientists over the last four centuries. He found that a majority of his subjects who initially supported scientific breakthroughs, such as Copernicus's theory of planetary movement and Freud's theory of personality, were later-born siblings; 80 percent of those who opposed these new notions were firstborns.

Lila was six years old *when sister Julie was born. This age difference brought out not sibling rivalry but protectiveness.*

What is the role of the baby of the family?

Even in fairy tales, the youngest child gets more than a fair share of triumphs. When psychologists Brian Sutton-Smith and B. G. Rosenberg analyzed 112 of the Grimms' fairy tales, they found the youngest child came out a winner in battles with everything from evil gnomes to jealous siblings 92 percent of the time.

Sometimes parents deliberately encourage the youngest child to be overly dependent on them. The youngest may seize the opportunity to preserve his or her status. Such children can become manipulative and demanding, lacking a sense of responsibility.

If, on the other hand, parents can bring the wisdom of their accumulated experience to raising their youngest, the last child in line may have some real advantages in realizing his or her own potential. A big brother or sister who provides a positive role model can also contribute to the emotional and social growth of the baby of the family.

Does a one-child family face special challenges?

G. Stanley Hall, a leading American psychologist at the turn of the century glumly concluded that "being an only child is a disease in itself." But today experts have come to an entirely different view of the situation.

An advantage for parents with one child is that they can focus their resources of time and money on a single individual. This is an important consideration for parents who feel no expense is too great in educating their offspring—even through years of graduate school if asked.

In many parts of the world, the trend of couples to want just one child has led to reexamination of an old stereotype involving the only child. Instead of warning parents that such children may need special discipline to avoid becoming self-centered and demanding, psychologists simply advise parents to provide as many opportunities as possible for their only child to mix with other children.

Is it rare for siblings to be close friends all their lives?

One of the consequences of having just one or two children, the choice of more and more couples today, is that parents find that a child seems to grow up and leave the family nest much too soon. To soften the blow, many middle-aged and elderly couples are turning again to their brothers and sisters for companionship and the sense of security that a family can provide.

Behavioral scientists have found that relationships between adult siblings often repeat the long-ago patterns of childhood. For example, if an older sister once acted as a "surrogate mother" when children were young, she often resumes that role years later, maintaining contact among scattered family members.

Studies have shown that brothers as a rule are less likely to keep in contact with one another than are sisters. In fact, rather than calling or writing one another, brothers often keep informed of one another's lives by calling an older sister.

Can the birth order of a wife and husband affect their marriage?

Birth-order roles may play a part in how adults relate to each other in marriage. Two firstborns who marry will have to remember that both cannot simultaneously insist on being the boss. They will have to temper their aggressive instincts with consideration and tolerance for each other, perhaps setting up in advance a system for problem-solving or agreeing on areas of responsibility.

When two youngest children marry, both will have to remember that they cannot revert to the role of dependent baby, demanding everything be done for them. In fact, youngest children may have to remember, whatever the birth order of their spouses, that they cannot expect to be fussed over and pampered the way they were by older siblings.

Middle children have often learned the art of compromise to preserve family harmony. They must remember to speak up for their own desires and not to compromise themselves into unhappiness and dissatisfaction.

A Family's Talents Flourish in Tragedy and Isolation

NOTHING COULD OFFER A MORE startling contrast to the drab life of the Brontë family than the romantic, melodramatic stories they wrote. *Jane Eyre,* by Charlotte Brontë, and *Wuthering Heights,* by her younger sister Emily, novels of passionate love affairs, were both published in 1847.

In the 1939 movie version of Wuthering Heights, *Laurence Olivier played Heathcliff; Merle Oberon, his beloved Cathy.*

From their earliest years, the six children of the Reverend Patrick Brontë lived in isolation in a gray stone parsonage in Haworth on the bleakly beautiful English moors. When the children were very young, their mother died of cancer, and four years later the two oldest children died of tuberculosis.

Charlotte, Emily, Anne, and Branwell, the only son, were left in the care of a kind but undemonstrative aunt and a self-absorbed father. Thrown on their own, the children began to create a world of fantasy. What would have been confining to most people inspired the Brontës. Night after night, in the parsonage's damp sitting room, they recorded their stories in handmade notebooks that measured only two or three inches square (100 have survived and can be deciphered with a magnifying glass). Urging one another on, they created realms peopled with royalty, revolutionaries, and murderers.

Anne, Emily, and Charlotte *(left to right) are shown in a serious mood in an 1834 portrait by Branwell.*

At various times all three sisters left Haworth for teaching positions, but they were always drawn back to their beloved moors and, above all, to their world of writing.

When their work was finally published, the Brontës tried to preserve their anonymity by using the names Currer, Ellis, and Acton Bell. Then the rumor began that these names represented one person, so they revealed the truth.

But the Brontës' success as writers was overshadowed by the alcoholism and drug addiction of their brother. Life at home became a nightmare of paying Branwell's debts and nursing him through delirium tremens. In the autumn of 1848 Branwell died. Three months later Emily succumbed to tuberculosis, and in the spring of the following year Anne perished of the same disease.

In 1854 Charlotte married her father's curate. But her happiness was brief. Less than one year after the wedding, the pregnant Charlotte died on March 31, 1855.

The Private World of Twins

Why are twins so fascinating?

Almost every culture has considered twins to be special. Exactly how special depends on where you are. In Africa, for example, the Yoruba people believed that twins were godlike spirits who had come back to the living world; Yoruba parents were given twin wooden statues to commemorate their babies' births. A group in Tanzania, the Kaguru, thought that twins had dangerous powers, and they were killed at birth. The Tsimshian Indians of British Columbia believed twins to be salmon, magically transformed into children.

Scientists, too, are fascinated by twins. The heredity (gene makeup) of identical twins is so similar that they represent a marvelous opportunity to study the differences caused in human beings by environmental factors, such as interactions with parents, friends, and teachers. In this study of the relationship between heredity and environment—nature versus nurture—identical twins who have been reared apart are particularly appealing to scientists, since the environmental influences on each twin have been separate and distinct, but the twins' genes are the same.

The study of twins is so universal that there is even an official name for it—gemellology, which, like Gemini, the zodiacal sign for twins, derives from *geminus*, the Latin word for "twin." In the United States, there is an annual summer festival held in (where else?) Twinsburg, Ohio, at which pairs from all over the world celebrate their twinhood with look-alike contests and other festivities.

***Twins Marian and Vivian Brown have always delighted** in being indistinguishable. For them, looking identical is fun, and they laugh at the idea that their individuality suffers.*

Is there more than one type of twins?

Most of us know at least one set of twins. That's hardly surprising, since about 1 in 80 human deliveries produces twins. There are two main kinds: *fraternal*, or dizygotic (DZ), and *identical*, or monozygotic (MZ). Fraternal twins occur when two eggs are fertilized by two sperm. They are like ordinary brothers and sisters, except for the fact that they are born together. Although no one knows why, the tendency to have fraternal twins seems to run in families; if they occur in one generation, they have a better-than-average chance of showing up in the next.

Unlike fraternals, identical twins occur randomly, at the rate of about four sets for every 1,000 births. They are created when one egg is fertilized by one sperm and then splits in half. The result: two fetuses with the same genetic makeup. How identical are identical twins? Well, if one set married another set, their children would all be brothers and sisters—genetically speaking.

If they look the same, are they identical twins?

You can't always tell if twins are identical or fraternal by looking at them. Though identicals are always of the same sex, they can sometimes be quite different in personality and appearance, while fraternal twins of the same sex can so closely resemble each other that many people—including the twins themselves—think they are identical. The differences between identicals develop as a result of environmental factors such as the twins' different positions in the womb, their birth order, and their respective eating and playing patterns.

Twins sometimes *need* to know how they are related. For example, if one twin has a bad kidney, he or she can be virtually 100 percent sure that his or her body will accept a kidney from an identical twin but only 85 percent sure of a match from a fraternal twin. Various kinds of tests can be authorized by doctors to determine if twins are fraternal or identical. One clue can be found in handprints and footprints: identical twins should have almost identical patterns.

Should parents encourage twins to be different?

Experience has taught many a parent of twins to avoid two extremes: neither to treat the pair as if they were exactly alike nor to create artificial differences between them. If twins are treated just alike, the identity of one can get lost in the other's.

One pair of five-year-old fraternal twins, believed by their parents to be retarded, could speak only a few words and spent most of their time in a playpen. When the twins' IQ's were tested for school placement, the parents were shocked to learn that while one twin was mildly retarded, the other had intelligence that was at least average. But because the parents had treated both as though they could not learn, neither had made any progress.

However, looking for differences between twins can go too far. Some parents fall into a kind of stereotyping, seeing one as quick, the other as slow; one as smart in school, the other as athletic. Twins, like other children, often develop in spurts, and the twin who fails math this year might get A's next year—unless the child is told he or she is "no good at math." Comparisons can be especially demoralizing to opposite-sex fraternal pairs, because girls and boys have such different rates of development.

More often than not, in raising twins the rule seems to be that there are no rules. One aspect of their special closeness, for example, may be a specially intense period of competition. But whether the issue is dressing alike or choosing the same college, the best idea is to encourage twins to make their own choices. After all, the twins themselves are the ones who will have to live with those choices.

Raising Identicals as Separate Individuals

One of the mysteries posed by twins is how two babies with the same genes, raised in the same family, can turn out very differently. It is a reminder that predicting what kind of person a child will grow up to be is not an exact science.

Hannah and Carrie, the identical twins shown growing up here, were raised by parents who wanted them to be strong, self-confident individuals. That meant acknowledging their differences, adjusting—and making mistakes. Told as a toddler that she was born two minutes before her sister, Hannah adopted the role of older sister for a few months, much to Carrie's consternation.

As two-year-olds, the twins (above) mirrored each other's feelings. As Hannah prepared to slide, Carrie's face knotted in anticipation of the risk. Eight years later (left), when they were asked to sit in look-alike outfits for a portrait, they struck a pose that betrayed, most visibly on Carrie's part (right), impatience with the photographer, each other, and the whole situation.

By age 16, Carrie (left) and Hannah wear different clothes and hairstyles. Excellent students, they chose different schools, have different friends.

Science Looks at Identical Pairs

Do twins share ESP or other special bonds?

It is not unusual for a young twin to say,"We want," rather than "I want." This sense of oneness can sustain twins through rough times. One pair of identicals, Holocaust survivors who had lost their mother, said it was their shared strength that enabled them to endure years of emotional and physical abuse.

For other pairs, though, the relationship can be destructive. June and Jennifer Gibbons are identical twins who spoke mostly to each other, in a private language no one else understood. After committing a number of crimes, including arson, the girls were sentenced to life in a prison for the criminally insane. Adults who know them believe that Jennifer controls her twin; June herself wrote in one of many journals, "This sister of mine, a dark shadow, robbing me of sunlight, is my one and only torment."

Although there is no proof that twins have ESP, there is evidence that many pairs communicate more closely—and more mysteriously—than nontwin siblings. This unusual sensitivity for each other's thoughts and feelings, a kind of heightened empathy, may account for some strange experiences twins have reported. One twin who occasionally feels the urge to call his brother usually finds that his twin has been wanting him to call.

Some twins also say that they have felt each other's pain. One woman whose identical twin was killed in a plane crash reported feeling scorching heat, pain, and then a black void at the time of the crash—before she could possibly have heard the news.

Such closeness makes the death of a twin uniquely difficult for the surviving one, whose sense of loss may be so overwhelming that he or she loses the will to live. One way to prevent this kind of despair is for twins to develop a strong sense of themselves as individuals *while* they are growing up—a process that parents can encourage.

Identicals who do not fully separate *in the womb are called Siamese twins, after Chang and Eng (1811-1874), who were born in Siam. Depending on where they are joined, Siamese twins can sometimes be separated surgically.*

Do twins make better friends?

The ability of twins to tune in to each other can carry over to other people as well, making twins caring and insightful friends. There may be another side to this, however: twins may expect the same level of sensitivity from others, and they may become frustrated if it is not forthcoming. The need for closeness and intimacy that feels natural to twins can seem demanding and unrealistic to nontwins.

What have twin studies revealed about human behavior?

A long-term project at the University of Minnesota has focused on the behavior of identical twins who were separated at an early age and raised apart. By studying this special group, the researchers hope to pinpoint more precisely which kinds of behavior are controlled by the genes we inherit and which by external factors such as the family environment. Their assumption is that different behavior by the twins would indicate an environmental cause, while similar behavior is genetically based.

The Minnesota research suggests that traits such as vulnerability to stress are inherited, but that other traits, such as achievement, aggression, and orderliness, are the result of environmental factors. A tendency to develop certain phobias seems to be inherited: of 15 pairs in the study, 3 shared one or more phobias. One pair had even arrived at the same solution for dealing with fear of water: wading in backward.

The twin studies support the idea of a genetic factor in schizophrenia. If one identical twin has it, the probability is as high as 80 percent that the other does. By contrast, the likelihood that both fraternal twins will have schizophrenia is about 15 percent.

Twins Who Found Each Other

Tony and Roger, identical twins, were separated at birth and reunited two decades later. One had a harsh childhood, the other a secure one. Alike in some ways, different in others, their personalities reveal the tug-of-war between genes and environment.

IT WAS A MOMENT FILLED with drama and fascination when Tony Milasi of Binghamton, New York, and Roger Brooks of Miami, Florida, met for the first time in 1963. They were 24-year-old identical twins who had been separated at birth and reared far apart.

No two people can be more alike than identical twins. A single fertilized egg, which ordinarily produces one individual, divides to become two, and they share every possible inherited characteristic. They also normally grow up together and share a special intimacy throughout their lives. But in those rare, unfortunate cases when they are separated early in life, they may grow up under quite different conditions. When the separated twins are reunited, they become a living experiment for comparing the effects of heredity and environment.

When Tony and Roger were born in 1938, their unmarried and destitute parents could not support them, and they were offered to an immigrant Italian couple named Milasi. Unfortunately, the couple could care for only one child.

Thus the twins were separated. The lucky one, Tony Milasi, grew up in a secure environment.

By contrast, Roger had a traumatic early life, full of insecurity. He was shunted among foster home, hospital, and orphanage. He did not walk until 18 months (versus 12 months for Tony), and at age two he was judged to be five months retarded in his development; he had difficulty combining words and was unable to fit pegs into holes on a board. When he was four, his natural father's wife heard of his plight, took him in, and continued to raise him even after her marriage failed and she decided to move to Florida. Disruption and instability plagued Roger's youth, however—brawling in camp, periods away in boarding school, and two difficult years back with his father. In 11 years, before dropping out to join the air force, he attended eight different schools.

Identical twins *Tony Milasi (sitting) and Roger Brooks discovered each other in their twenties.*

When he was 13 and away at school, Roger dreamed vividly of having a twin. When he learned that his dream was true, Roger was thrilled and longed to find his brother. The twins were not destined to meet, however, until, by an amazing coincidence, a young man who had worked with Tony in New York happened to spot Roger in a restaurant in Florida.

As soon as the twins were reunited, comparisons began. They certainly were physically alike, right down to the same aching wisdom tooth, but there were other unexpected and puzzling similarities. Not only did they use the same after-shave, smoke the same cigarettes, and hold a pen in the same awkward way, they both also used the same obscure brand of toothpaste, imported from Sweden. They had entered military service within eight days of each other, liked the same sports, and enjoyed performing before an audience.

After their reunion Tony and Roger volunteered to undergo extensive testing by a psychologist. In spite of radically different childhood experiences, their overall intelligence scores were practically identical, but both the twins and the psychologist noted substantial differences in personality and emotional development.

Tony, whose security as a child had made him more venturesome, was notably the more extroverted, aggressive, and impatient of the two, with an optimistic, happy-go-lucky approach to life. Roger, perhaps as a result of his own difficult childhood, more readily sympathized with the problems of others, especially children. Experience with his undependable father had created in Roger an intense desire to live responsibly, and as a young man he was willing to endure long hours and boring work in a factory and save for the future. Tony, on the other hand, was slow to settle into a long-term job and had free-spending habits. But he was a natural salesman with great confidence in his ability. Tony, who had never known their father, was more like him than Roger, who had known him and reacted against him.

Roger married a niece of the Milasis, and thus became a member of the family that raised Tony. The twins saw each other daily, but their personality differences did not change. Tony remained talkative and outgoing and was a successful salesman. He became the dominant "big brother" of the two. The quieter Roger worked with the mentally handicapped and as a city councilman. So alike and yet different, these separated twins reveal some of the complex influences of heredity and environment that shape us into who we are.

Forging New Family Ties

The Brady Bunch, ***a television comedy*** *of bliss in a "blended" family (all problems solved in half an hour), left many real-life stepfamilies wondering what they were doing wrong.*

Why are stepparents so often portrayed as cruel and heartless?

Ask people what word they associate with *stepmother* and almost invariably they shoot back, "Wicked," clearly with Cinderella's notorious parent in mind. But while stepmothers get the harshest and most frequent mention in folklore, there are also tales of ruthless stepfathers and conniving stepchildren who cheat the rightful heir out of the family fortune.

The truth of the matter is that, regardless of how real-life stepparents treat their stepchildren, the youngsters are likely to harbor resentments that can turn even the kindest stepparent into a fairy-tale monster.

A stepparent walks into a very difficult situation. Most children of divorce fantasize that their birth parents will someday reunite, a dream that a new marriage shatters. And it is the stepparent whom the child most often blames, however unfairly, for destroying the fantasy.

In a one-adult family, moreover, a child may have a special status as a parent's friend and confidant. The child sees remarriage ruining this relationship and feels anger and jealousy, usually directed at the stepparent.

Along with these powerful feelings, a child may experience what behavioral specialists refer to as *splitting.* Children, psychologists point out, naturally feel contradictory emotions of love and hate for their mothers and fathers, but to solidify the all-important relationships with their parents, they suppress the negative feelings and express the positive ones. With stepparents, there are no such restraints. A child may turn all the hate and anger on the stepparent.

What myths do stepparents have about their stepchildren?

No less an authority than child-care expert Dr. Benjamin Spock admitted that, before his remarriage, he had not anticipated the difficulties that an 11-year-old stepdaughter would present. Frustrated at his unsuccessful attempts to get along with his wife's daughter, he finally sought advice from a counselor who specialized in family problems. "I had been living in a fool's paradise, she told me, naively thinking that any child would accept a stepparent in just a year or two."

Stepparents who rush headlong into a family with dreams of becoming a "superparent" are almost always disappointed. Family therapists advise stepparents that when it comes to dealing with stepchildren, less is often best. In particular, stepparents should not fantasize that they can replace the birth parents in the child's affection. Whatever the shortcomings of birth parents, they will always have a special place in their children's hearts that no one else can fill.

What are children's main fears about their new stepfamily?

Children fear everything from abandonment to losing their own name when they become part of a stepfamily. The latter is a particular concern of teenagers, who worry about how friends will reach them.

In divorce all children feel some sense of abandonment, which can be intensified if they blame themselves somehow for their parents' breakup. To a child, remarriage poses the threat of abandonment once again, of being forsaken for someone new. Youngsters may also feel that the decision to remarry is a sign they are inadequate, the proof being that the parent has chosen another partner.

Does age play a part in a child's ability to adjust to a stepfamily?

Adolescents, in the best of circumstances, challenge family authority in the struggle to establish their own identity. A stepfamily adds a dimension to this struggle, since the teenager now has a target for feelings of rebellion—the new stepparent.

Sex can also compound the adolescent's problem. Despite their own growing sexuality, teenagers are uncomfortable with the idea that parents also have sex lives. And the affection new spouses show for each other may anger an adolescent.

A further complication is the fact that taboos against incest, which develop naturally in a birth-family situation, may be absent in the stepfamily. Experts say that even if no one intends to behave in a seductive fashion, there is a possibility of sexual attraction between teenagers and their stepparents or stepsiblings. Such feelings can be very threatening, especially to youngsters, and parents should be aware of this hazard. Such attractions may call for counseling.

Do girls or boys adjust better to their new positions in stepfamilies?

The divorce of parents, according to Texas psychologist James H. Bray, is harder on boys of elementary-school age than on girls of the same age, but remarriage is apparently harder on the girls. University of Virginia psychologist Mavis Hetherington found girls had more difficulty with social relationships both inside and outside the stepfamily than did boys.

In a study of stepfamilies with children aged 9 to 12, psychologist Glenn Clingempeel found an interesting paradox: relationships between stepmother and stepdaughter were worst when relations between the new couple were best. The stepdaughters felt intense jealousy that another woman had supplanted them in their father's affections. However, the longer the family lived together, the less tense the situation became between stepmothers and stepdaughters.

Stepsons seem to have an easier time than stepdaughters fitting into a new family. However, a stepson is quick to resent a stepfather who tries too hard, especially if he assumes the role of rigid disciplinarian.

How can stepfamilies get off to a good start?

Experts suggest that, if possible, a new stepfamily launch itself in a new home. That way no one will feel like a trespasser on other people's territory. If a move is out of the question, the new stepfamily might try redoing part of the home or reallocating bedrooms to give the feeling of a fresh start—always, of course, discussing any proposed changes with the children.

The parents in the new stepfamily, even before their marriage, should discuss discipline and lines of authority to make sure both agree on the ground rules. Behavioral specialists suggest that for the first year or so, the birth parent should take primary responsibility for disciplining the child. Still, children should understand from the outset that the stepparent has authority to make family rules in the birth parent's absence.

The need for clear rules is just as important when a stepchild comes to visit. The child should never be allowed to "get away with murder," no matter how eager a stepparent is for the child's affection.

If a child lives with a birth parent and a stepparent, the youngster may get anxious about arrangements, or the lack of them, for seeing the absent parent. For this reason the birth parents should try to stay in contact, though it may be difficult. Such communication will prevent a child from playing one parent off the other.

As the handsome prince is about *to fit the glass slipper on Cinderella's dainty foot, her envious stepsisters glare in disbelief. When competition in real stepfamilies becomes heated, this story comes readily to mind, with each side identifying with Cinderella.*

The Adopted Child

"Every son that is born ye shall cast into the river" was Pharaoh's command. To save Moses' life, his mother and sister placed him in a basket in the Nile. The courage and heartbreak of this story have echoed down the centuries.

When should you tell a child that he or she is adopted?

Adoption used to be treated as a family secret to be withheld as long as possible from an adopted child. Parents were often advised against discussing the situation until a child was well into the teenage years. People believed that once the young person's personality was formed, he or she could deal better with the emotion-laden questions adoption raises.

In practice this seldom worked out well. Almost invariably some friend or relative would spill the beans, often causing a child to learn of the adoption secondhand through gossip.

Today there is virtual unanimity that explaining the basic facts of adoption to children should begin early. Of course, giving detailed explanations to very young children will probably have little meaning.

A study under the direction of Rutgers University psychologist David Brodzinsky, a leading authority on adopted children, found that a child had to be at least six years old in order to be able to understand the difference between nonadoptive and adoptive parents. Additional research suggests that for younger children, the notion of another mother, living somewhere else, may be more frightening than informative.

How should children be told of their adoption?

Today's adoptive parents are cautioned about relying on the once-recommended explanation "we chose you because you were so special." Psychologists think that too much talk about being special will only emphasize to the adopted child that he or she is different. This is not necessarily comforting news to adopted children, who may yearn for a family history just like that of all their friends.

A child's adjustment to being adopted only begins with being told. Even more important is to assure the child that the subject will always be open and that questions about it are always welcome. It is, as adoption counselor Bernice Hauser says, "a lifelong process." As children grow, they may want a fuller account of their background. They should know they can talk about their concerns with their adoptive parents at any time, instead of feeling that after the initial explanation, the question of adoption has been buried forever.

What questions do children ask about their adoption?

Of course, children want to know about their birth mother, but for most of them the burning question is not "Who is she?" It is "Why did she give me up?" Since most adoptive parents know little, if anything, about the birth parent, they often rely on a standard explanation: your mother was very young and she had not finished school; she loved you very much and wanted you to have all the things you needed to make you happy; since she could not provide them, she gave you up for adoption.

Sadly, even when this scenario is true, it seldom explains things well enough for an adopted child. In a child's world, events are often seen as either good or bad, with no shades of distinction in between. If the child had been good, the mother would have loved and kept her baby; since she did not, the child must be bad. Burdened with such thoughts, adopted children may find it hard to work out a positive image of who they are and where they belong. And often, creating a healthy self-image involves a trying period for the adoptive parents. The child continually tests the limits of their tolerance with bad behavior just to see if this mother and father, too, will send him or her away.

To help an adopted child deal with the past, some counselors suggest that adoptive parents keep a baby scrapbook, with pictures and mementos starting from the day the parents received the child. In that way the child and the adopted family can emphasize the past that they do share, rather than the past they don't.

Do adopted children face special health risks?

Infants who spend their first few months in institutions, however technically good the care, have more fevers and respiratory infections than normal. These institutionalized children may also lag in growth and weight gain. Fortunately, most of the babies show a dramatic improvement once adopted into a loving home.

If the birth mother of an adoptive baby has received little or no prenatal care, the result can be a low-birth-weight child susceptible not only to physical complications but to certain intellectual ones as well. Some physicians believe that a stressful pregnancy can cause attention-deficit disorder, a condition that impairs the child's ability to concentrate and therefore to learn.

A long-term health problem for adoptees can result from their lack of medical history. When a doctor asks people who have been adopted whether their parents had diabetes or heart disease, in most cases the adoptee can't answer. What could be vital in diagnosis or treatment is unknown.

It is often the need for medical information that prompts adoptees to undertake a search for their birth parents. Not all these searches have happy endings, but in 1986 one mother happily donated a kidney to the daughter she had despaired of ever seeing again after giving her up for adoption 20 years earlier.

Riding an Orphan Train to a New Life

When Charles Loring Brace, a Connecticut philanthropist, went to New York City in the 1850's, he was appalled at the plight of the children of the poor. What he saw fully confirmed the claim of the city's police chief that the children's lives led to "degradation and disgusting habits in the school of vice, prostitution and rowdyism." By one estimate, there were 30,000 orphans or abandoned children living on the streets in the city's unsanitary, crowded slums at this time.

Brace, a man of high principle and humane instincts, was inspired to organize a sweeping and imaginative program. In 1853 he founded the Children's Aid Society. One of the aims of the society was to send the children out of the city, instead of putting them in impersonal institutions. Initially, small groups went to nearby states. Ultimately, large groups were sent to the West, where they were placed in foster homes among America's farming families.

By the time the program ended in 1929, orphan trains had carried nearly 100,000 children to their new homes. It is an extraordinary success story. Many grew up to be farmers, others went on to practice law or medicine, and two became governors, one of North Dakota and the other of Alaska. Thousands of Americans in all walks of life can claim to be descended from these children.

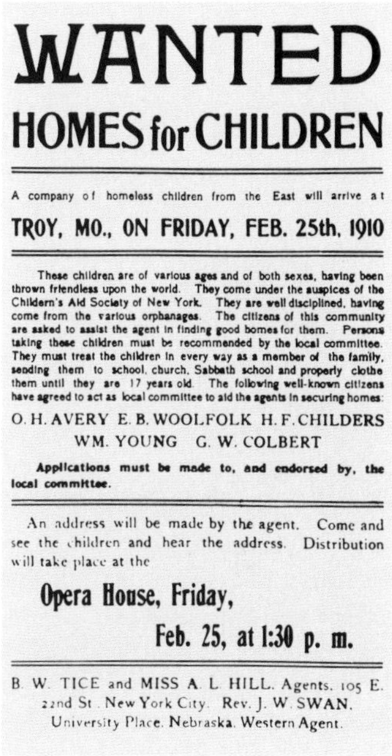
WANTED

HOMES for CHILDREN

A company of homeless children from the East will arrive at

TROY, MO., ON FRIDAY, FEB. 25th, 1910

These children are of various ages and of both sexes, having been thrown friendless upon the world. They come under the auspices of the Childern's Aid Society of New York. They are well disciplined, having come from the various orphanages. The citizens of this community are asked to assist the agent in finding good homes for them. Persons taking these children must be recommended by the local committee. They must treat the children in every way as a member of the family, sending them to school, church, Sabbath school and properly clothe them until they are 17 years old. The following well-known citizens have agreed to act as local committee to aid the agents in securing homes:

O. H. AVERY E. B. WOOLFOLK H. F. CHILDERS
WM. YOUNG G. W. COLBERT

Applications must be made to, and endorsed by, the local committee.

An address will be made by the agent. Come and see the children and hear the address. Distribution will take place at the

Opera House, Friday,
Feb. 25, at 1:30 p. m.

B. W. TICE and MISS A. L. HILL, Agents, 105 E. 22nd St., New York City. Rev. J. W. SWAN, University Place, Nebraska, Western Agent.

Under the benign care of agents of the Children's Aid Society, 12 orphans wait expectantly for their new families in Lebanon, Missouri, in 1909.

Choosing Partners

A World of Difference in Courting Rules

In many cultures the announcement that a young person is ready to take a mate is loud and clear. The occasion may be a girl's first menstrual period or, for a young man, a feat of skill. Whereas some cultures shield a young woman when she reaches marrying age—while her family cements plans for her marriage—others waste no time in pairing off young people. But Western societies often lack clear mandates about when or whom to wed, and young people face making these momentous decisions alone.

Uncertainty is the rule: both may be thinking marriage, but accepting responsibility for its success can be intimidating.

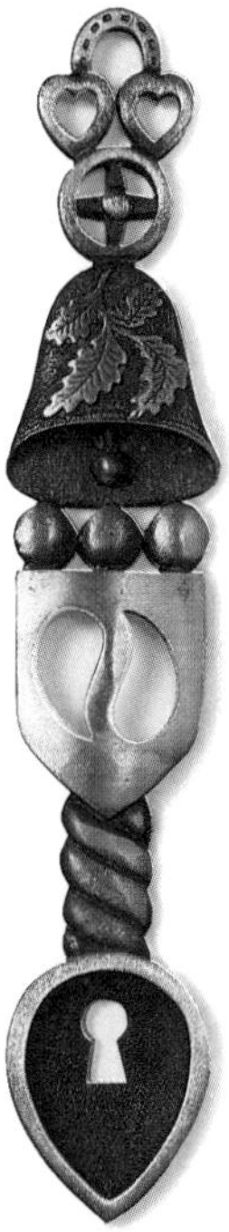

Welsh love spoon signals betrothal.

Young Wodaabe men, members of a West African nomadic tribe in Niger, roll their eyes and show their teeth in an all-male dance competition. Around them, marriageable young women and other members of the tribe appraise their talents. This is one of several Wodaabe rituals that set the rules for courtship and marriage.

When did dating begin?

The practice of an unmarried young woman going out somewhere with an unmarried young man is relatively new. In the early years of this century, "calling" was the socially approved way of getting to know each other. Typically, a young woman might invite a suitor to call on her at home. After arranging a suitable time, she would plan on receiving him in her family's parlor. There he would meet her family, exchange pleasantries, and perhaps listen to the young woman play the piano.

Such meetings were closely supervised, and young women were advised to follow strict rules of etiquette, such as this one: "On no account should the woman accompany her caller to the door nor stand talking while he struggles into his coat."

Such customs might still be with us if there had not been a rapid growth in urban populations. Most city homes simply did not have rooms to spare for entertaining male friends. Getting out of the house became almost a necessity, and by the 1930's the automobile had become the preferred way out. Cars were more than transportation to exciting places, they were like private rooms on wheels.

As courting moved out of the family parlor, a shift occurred in the roles of men and women. When she was a hostess in her own home, a woman could decide how long she wanted her caller to stay and how she would entertain him. With dating no longer homebound, men took more control of where the two went and what they did, since custom made men responsible for the expenses.

How do you know when someone is flirting?

One behaviorist spent years studying the flirting behavior of different cultures, only to conclude that the language of flirting is much the same the world over. Be it Chicago or Tokyo, Moscow or Melbourne, the gestures that show availability, interest, and coyness are similar.

In this universal language the eyes

do a lot of the talking. A common indicator of interest is holding your gaze for just a fraction of a second longer than usual when you look into his or her eyes. Also widely understood is smiling slightly, glancing once, and then lowering the eyes bashfully. Other gestures include making small touching movements, moistening one's lips, and nodding in agreement no matter what the person is saying.

Did You Know . . . ?

- **The hope chest had an unexpected drawback.** It was believed that if a girl used or even tried on anything from her hope chest, she was destined never to marry.
- **How bachelor's buttons came by their name.** A young man thinking he was in love would pick this flower early in the morning and put it in his pocket. If the flower was still fresh at the end of the day, he was assured of wedded bliss. If, however, the flower was wilted, it told him that he could expect nothing but strife in his marriage.
- **Diamond engagement rings have sparkled for 500 years.** A diamond is an enduring stone and when polished has special brilliance. An early use as a token of betrothal can be traced to 15th-century Venice. Within 200 years the custom of presenting a diamond ring to a future bride had spread across Europe.
- **Advertising for a mate is not new.** Wherever men emigrated or colonized and found themselves without wives, mail-order brides became the custom. This was true in the American West and in Australia. Among the Japanese who settled in the United States, picture brides were also an accepted path to matrimony.
- **Courtship by capture, modern-style.** Reenacting this primitive form of courtship, some Eskimo tribes today stage a ritual struggle between a man and his chosen bride. He pretends to drag her away and she resists until her self-esteem is satisfied.

Are there underlying rules for small talk on dates?

The kind of chitchat that occurs after a man and woman first meet—about the weather, clothes, TV and movies, hobbies, and so on—may seem superficial, but it has an important purpose, say some psychologists. Just a few exchanges of small talk may convince a person that he or she should stop the relationship right then and there—or get ready for a full-fledged romance.

Psychologists have tried for years to impose some kind of scientific framework on the perplexing and diverse elements of romance. By analyzing the elements of courting behavior, for example, and giving them names, some researchers hope to explain love in quantifiable terms, just as chemistry explains matter and physics explains forces. One recent effort of this kind focused on small talk.

The study says that we decide whether or not we like somebody's small talk by more or less unconsciously applying four criteria. Although these criteria deal with age-old social skills, such as how to pay and receive compliments gracefully, the researchers give the criteria special names: valence, magnitude, congruence, and authenticity. Here is how the criteria work:

Valence is the tone of the conversation, positive or negative, upbeat or downbeat. Most people prefer a positive valence.

Magnitude is the strength of the other person's signals. "You're not bad-looking" has lower magnitude than "You're gorgeous!"

Congruence rates how the other person's comments about us match our view of ourselves. Finally, small talk is judged for its authenticity—that is, whether the person seems to be sincere or merely trying to impress us with a line of smooth talk.

What's the difference between sexual attraction and love?

Almost everybody, scientist and nonscientist alike, agrees that sexual attraction is different from true love; but it is also apparent that love, even after decades with the same partner, need not exclude sexual attraction. Love itself, if it is considered a desire for more than sexual intimacy, seems to be not one state but several. For example, the feeling of a young couple that they can do nothing alone can mature into a relationship in which each is relatively independent.

Yale psychologist Robert Sternberg suggests that love has three basic elements: intimacy, passion, and commitment. Typically, says Sternberg, passion is the key ingredient in the early stages of courting, but as the relationship matures, intimacy and commitment grow in importance.

The French writer Madame de Staël's definition of love is far more poetic. "Love is a symbol of eternity," she wrote almost two centuries ago. "It wipes out all sense of time, destroying all memory of a beginning and all fear of an end."

What's the surest sign that two people have fallen in love?

If a couple passes the tests of flirtation and small talk, the next step may be love—even though neither may admit or even realize they have fallen in love at the time. One telltale sign is that couples begin to mimic each other's body movements. And when couples begin smiling and sighing in unison, love has arrived.

Why is physical attraction sometimes overwhelming?

According to one theory, there is a "sex nucleus" in the brain's hypothalamus, the lower region of the thalamus at the base of the cerebrum. When someone strikes us as very appealing, this nucleus sends a chemical message to the pituitary gland, which in turn triggers the release of certain sex hormones, such as estrogen and progesterone. Within seconds the heart races and the palms are sweating; and the particularly smitten may feel faint, giddy, or about to swoon.

A Sometimes-Rocky Road

Are women more romantic than men?

It's a subject that will probably be debated until the end of time, but on the evidence to date psychologists tend to feel that women do not fall in love as readily as men. Moreover, women seem to fall out of love more quickly and suffer less long-term distress than men do when a relationship breaks up.

Why this should be so is also a controversial question. One view contends that in cultures where a woman is allowed to choose a mate, as opposed to the family arranging a marriage, the woman must look out for her own interests. She seeks a man who is best able to provide for her and their future children. Some psychologists think that this may explain why it is not uncommon for women to be attracted to men with power—physical, financial, or social.

Men, in contrast, are prone to fall in love quickly and be less critical than women of their beloveds' qualities. According to one study, men are far more likely than women to believe in "love at first sight" and that "true love comes along just once in life."

Do opposites really attract?

Most of us fall in love with those whom we find most similar to ourselves, both in looks and in emotional temperament. There is thus a good deal of relevance in the words of the old song "I want a girl just like the girl that married dear old Dad." This is not to say that men are always searching for a woman who is exactly like their mother; but it is a fact that the mother is the first woman a boy knows, and it would not be surprising if he felt comfortable with a woman who shared some of his mother's characteristics. Furthermore, studies have tended to support the idea that relationships are strongest between two people who are similar to each other in age, intelligence, attitudes, goals, and physical attractiveness.

However, it is perfectly possible to fall in love with one's emotional opposite, though such a couple may be in for some rocky moments. One family therapist suggests that we are often attracted to a person who we feel represents some underdeveloped aspect of our own personality. Each of the pair may feel more complete in the company of the one who seems to supply what's lacking, and for a time both may modify their behavior to please the loved one. After a while, however, the old selves are likely to re-emerge. This may explain why some people, after going out together for a few months, are surprised to find they have almost nothing in common. There has been a gradual reversion to the personalities that existed before the two started dating.

Romeo and Juliet epitomize *a kind of intensity that sometimes attends young love. Thwarted by their parents' implacable loathing, the youngsters entered into a clandestine marriage. Their subsequent effort to meet led to their tragic deaths.*

What happens when you fall out of love?

Recent research indicates that sexual attraction alone, unsupported by other sources of mutual interest and compatibility, cannot sustain a relationship much beyond the two-year mark. In this case, falling out of love is simply a matter of time.

Of course, no relationship ends quite the same way, for quite the same reasons. One generalization that seems to hold up, however, is that two people hardly ever fall out of love with each other at the same time, and the breakup can be devastating to the one who isn't ready for it.

There may be a biochemical basis for the emotional pain that can occur when a love affair ends. When a person is in love, the brain apparently releases a chemical substance called phenylethylamine, which acts like the prescription drug amphetamine to increase mental alertness and physical energy. If the feelings of love are dashed, the brain and body are faced with a sudden loss of phenylethylamine. Consequently "the crash that follows a breakup is much like withdrawal," says Dr. Michael Liebowitz of the New York State Psychiatric Institute. He notes that people who break up often crave chocolate, which is high in phenylethylamine.

A Courtship That Triumphed Against All Odds

A semi-invalid at the age of 39, the poet Elizabeth Barrett seemed doomed to remain locked away from normal life, prisoner of an autocratic father. Attracted by her poetry, Robert Browning began a passionate courtship that swept her fears aside.

No medieval romance of a gallant knight rescuing a fair maiden from a castle can match the love story of Elizabeth Barrett and Robert Browning. But in this romance, the fair maiden was a reclusive 39-year-old semi-invalid. Her castle was an unremarkable house on a quiet street in Victorian London and her rescuer was a poet six years her junior.

It was poetry that brought them together. Early in January 1845, Browning happened upon two volumes of Elizabeth's recently published work. "I . . . love these books with all my heart," he wrote her, "and I love you too." Yet at this time they had never met. "I had a letter from Browning the poet last night," Elizabeth wrote to her oldest friend, "which threw me into ecstasies." She answered him immediately and so began one of the most touching and dramatic courtships of all time.

In **The Barretts of Wimpole Street,** *Charles Laughton (center) played Edward Barrett. His possessiveness caused his daughter Elizabeth (Norma Shearer) to keep Browning's (Fredric March) visits a secret.*

For all practical purposes Elizabeth was a prisoner in her father's house. A man embittered by the loss of his wife, his fortune, and his oldest son, Edward Barrett tyrannized his three daughters and six sons. He forbade any of them to marry. A childhood accident to her spine and symptoms of tuberculosis further restricted Elizabeth's life.

By 1845 she had already been confined for five years to a viewless back room. There she lay all day on a sofa, seeing only her family and a few selected friends. For constant companionship she depended on her maid, Wilson, and her adored spaniel, Flush. Exceptionally well-educated, she devoted her days to reading Greek, Latin, French, and German literature, writing to her friends, and, most important, composing poems.

Then Browning's vibrant personality broke her solitude. At first she wrote to him but refused to see him. She may have been afraid that the intimacy that had gradually developed in their correspondence would end once he saw her. Although endowed with striking black eyes, Elizabeth was not otherwise a beauty. But eventually, and in response to Browning's persistence, she relented. On May 20, five months later, they saw each other for the first time.

No one has ever known what happened at that meeting but Elizabeth's fears proved groundless. Browning's love strengthened. And very gradually Elizabeth, too, allowed herself to respond to him. But the courtship had to be kept secret. Elizabeth was never free of her terror of her father. "We are standing on hot scythes," she wrote, "and because we do not burn our feet by a miracle we have no right to count on the miracle's prolongation." She was careful not to confide in her family, and Browning's visits were limited to three a week and sometimes even canceled.

As Elizabeth's love burgeoned, so did her health. First she ventured downstairs, then outside. Finally, she felt well enough to go walking in the park.

It was a year and four months before Elizabeth dared to take the irrevocable step. She and Browning were married, hastily and secretly, in a neighborhood church. Afterward, she returned home. One week later, while her family was at dinner, cradling Flush in her arms so that he wouldn't bark, she and Wilson slipped out of the house. Meeting Browning, they crossed the English Channel for Paris.

Edward Barrett never forgave his daughter. He returned her letters unopened and refused to hear her name. The Brownings settled in Florence, where Elizabeth, at the age of 43, gave birth to a healthy baby boy. Their marriage was idyllically happy. Both wrote poetry and both became celebrities. But, inevitably, Elizabeth's frail health caught up with her. She died in Florence in 1861, aged 55, with Browning holding her in his arms. Her last word was "beautiful."

Marriage: The Great Commitment

What are the signs indicating a happy, long-lasting marriage?

After studying 200 couples who had been happily married for many years, James R. Hine, a University of Arizona researcher, found some general qualities that characterize a successful marriage and probably predict a union that will endure.

To begin with, both spouses like each other and are happy to be together. In addition, they have interests in common, which leads them to value each other as friends and companions. Both also basically agree on the definition of the roles of males and females in a marriage, and they share similar values, goals, and beliefs. Finally, they have personalities that get along well, even though their temperaments may be different.

Although no test can guarantee that a marriage will be successful, Hine believes that any partnership with these characteristics has a good chance of surmounting the stresses and strains of a long life together.

Can getting married affect your health?

No matter how much two people love each other or how compatible they are, the first year of marriage can

The Traditional Wedding—Still the Favorite

The marriage ceremony is rich in tradition and diversity. Brides and grooms marry on mountaintops and in midair while parachuting. Most couples, however, still prefer the established religious ceremony, complete with bridal attendants and wedding reception.

Through the years, special rituals have sprung up to add to the splendor of the event. Bridal gowns, for example, were for centuries ceremonial and richly colored—usually red. The elegant white wedding dress is relatively new. It dates back to Victorian times when brides showed off their family's wealth by appearing in a white dress, which was intended to be worn only on the wedding day.

The wedding veil, symbolizing youth and virginity, is one of the most ancient traditions. In Moslem countries, the bride's veil is not removed until the wedding feast after the marriage.

Rituals contribute to the wedding reception as well. Toasting the bride and groom by clinking glasses is an ancient trick meant to ward off evil spirits. The wedding cake goes back to Roman times. A wheat cake was first tasted by the bride and groom, then crumbled and sprinkled over the bride's head to ensure fertility. Though wedding customs may change over time, the glory and magic of the marriage ceremony never alters. Today photographs and even videotapes of those moments provide precious keepsakes to be enjoyed in years to come.

Bridesmaids are picked by the bride when she begins to plan her wedding. They arrange for the bride's "shower" of gifts and help her organize her wedding. The duties of the maid of honor include helping the bride dress and carrying the groom's ring.

Sharing wedding cake as husband and wife.

be a difficult period of adjustment for both partners. According to a rating of life's most stressful events, marriage produces more stress than getting fired from a job or going bankrupt.

Most people enter marriage with highly romantic expectations. The everyday reality of living together can often be a letdown when one's partner is not always as attentive, sexy, or entertaining as he or she seemed before the wedding. There may also be a shocking realization that marriage is a social and legal commitment that is quite different from the emotional ties developed during courtship.

In addition, the couple must adjust to new daily routines and changes in eating and sleeping habits. Ties with family and friends also change as the newlyweds relate to them as a couple rather than as individuals. Money, an almost taboo subject during courtship, becomes a major topic of discussion and often argument. Sharing possessions—especially a prized one, such as a car—can also be stressful.

All of these problems can be aggravated if the couple moves to a new area or if one or both start a new job. The results, say psychologists, can be an increase in colds, headaches, high blood pressure, and sleeping disorders. Fortunately, most people do adjust comfortably and soon.

This bride wears her mother-in-law's lace wedding veil and carries a bouquet with sprays of lilies of the valley, which are a traditional symbol of purity.

Does a marriage go through predictable stages?

A marriage grows and changes with time and shifting circumstances. Psychiatrists say that a typical relationship has five major stages. The first is a stage of idealization, the honeymoon phase. Even though the early days of marriage are stressful, each partner usually has positive, happy feelings about the other and a bright outlook on their future. Eventually, a second phase sets in as each begins to recognize his or her mate's shortcomings and realizes that all of life's dreams are not going to come true.

The third phase is a busy and productive time. Raising a family and getting ahead at work absorbs all the couple's time and energy. Often, they become efficient teammates, and the marriage runs along smoothly with problems ignored or set aside.

The fourth phase is a period of redefining roles. The time-consuming responsibilities of being a parent lighten as the children, now adolescents or older, become more independent. Surprisingly these changes can reawaken the parents' own adolescent yearnings, especially if they married young. This period has great potential for growth and change.

The final phase is the postparenting stage. With children no longer the unifying force in the couple's life, they are faced with the need to renew their commitment to each other. For some this can be a time of cantankerous score-settling as each blames the other for life's disappointments. But for couples who have met earlier challenges head-on and evolved with them, this can be the marriage's best and most rewarding stage.

Customs, Expectations, and Human Nature

How do arranged marriages differ from ones based on love?

While most couples in Western societies marry for love, people in many other parts of the world follow the tradition of having marriages arranged. Even in the West, unions arranged by the couple's families occur among some ethnic groups.

Arranged marriages appear to be more durable than ones based on love. In part, this is because the society usually frowns on the breakup of an arranged union and makes getting a divorce difficult. And in such cultures, women often cannot work and support themselves. But some scholars also believe that the partners themselves tend to be more satisfied in the long run, because each goes into the marriage without expecting personal happiness. Since the wife and husband commit themselves to marriage and family rather than romance, they tend to stay together even when they are incompatible.

Furthermore, spouses whose marriage has been arranged usually have strong ties to large families on both sides. This provides a ready source of close family friends, who make up for any lack of companionship in the marriage and provide support and advice when the couple has difficulties.

Weddings Call Forth Splendors

A headdress crowns a Japanese bride.

There are occasions in life when the past holds sway and we revert to the legacies of our ancestors. With many people and in many countries, this is truer of the marriage ceremony than of any other.

In Japan, the Shinto religion, which has roots in the country's ancient mythology, offers the bride a chance to clothe herself in a costume like one worn for generations in her family. In the United States and Canada, many immigrants from all over the world have brought their beloved traditional rituals and objects with them, to be used in their new home.

A wedding is the best occasion to call forth a touch of old customs.

Ukrainian costumes and a special cake add color to a wedding procession.

Is fighting in a marriage always a bad sign?

Arguments that revolve around broad discontents are the ones to avoid. An argument of this type has no clear-cut subject and the complaints are usually hopelessly general, such as "You don't treat me right" or "I can't depend on you."

Arguments that solve nothing are filled with declarations in absolute terms, such as "you never" and "you always," and may degenerate into name-calling and even physical fighting. Afterward, each usually feels resentment toward the other. Clearly such arguments have little hope of being settled except, perhaps, by time.

Quarrels that involve fairly specific disagreements have a better chance of being resolved. An argument might begin "I don't think I should have to cook dinner and clean up afterward. I want you to do one of those chores." This clearly defines the problem and suggests a solution, giving the couple a starting point for negotiating a settlement. The result can be a net gain in understanding each other.

But even this kind of argument can go awry if either person or both do not listen to the other and instead use the time when the other is talking to prepare his or her next argument, often on a side issue. Whenever possible, if argue they must, a couple should aim for a calm, rational discussion of a clearly identified problem. It is also helpful to remember that every disagreement does not put the entire marriage in jeopardy.

Do couples argue about the same things as their grandparents?

Experts say that couples usually quarrel about the time-honored subjects of money, child-raising, and sex. But the way these issues are seen has shifted as the result of changes in roles within the family, particularly when both husband and wife work.

According to a University of Minnesota study, new areas of dispute often center on which partner is to do what chores and how much of the husband's and wife's incomes will be spent together and how much by the individual. How to use leisure time may also be a problem.

Most experts add, however, that whatever the issues in an argument, the real battle may be over who is to be the marriage's dominant partner.

How does a marriage counselor approach a failing marriage?

Marriage counselors today view a marriage and family as a whole working unit, involving the husband and wife, their children, and even their parents. If the marriage is troubled, a major problem is likely to be in the way that these individuals interact. The counselors usually treat the couple together or the family as a group.

In treatment a counselor often tries to help a couple to see how both are unwittingly involved in causing their difficulties. For example, the problem may appear to be a wife who is overly dependent, but she may be unknowingly encouraged by a husband who finds that her reliance on him makes him feel more important. Or an intense disagreement over the best way to raise their children may be rooted in the different ways that each partner was raised. Giving the couple such insights is often the first step in helping them to resolve their difficulties.

But treating the marriage as a whole is rarely the complete answer to a couple's problems. The individuals usually need to make changes too. Often they need to learn more about their own emotions and motives and how to communicate their needs and feelings to each other.

PERSPECTIVES

On Love and Marriage

At the heart of a successful marriage is the commitment—firmly held by two people—that come what may, they will be on each other's side.

A Litmus Test

"If we discovered that we had only five minutes left to say all we wanted to say, every telephone booth would be occupied by people calling other people to stammer that they loved them."

—**Christopher Morley**

◆

Courtly Love

"So through the eyes love attains
the heart:
For the eyes are the scouts of the
heart,
And the eyes go reconnoitering
For what it would please the heart
to possess.
And when they are in full accord
And firm, all three, in the one
resolve,
At that time, perfect love is born
From what the eyes have made
welcome to the heart."

—**Guiraut De Borneilh**

◆

A Beloved Bible Verse

"Love is patient and kind; love is not jealous or boastful; it is not arrogant or rude. Love does not insist on its own way; it is not irritable or resentful; it does not rejoice at wrong, but rejoices in the right. Love bears all things, believes all things, hopes all things, endures all things.

"Love never ends; as for prophecies, they will pass away; as for tongues, they will cease; as for knowledge, it will pass away. For our knowledge is imperfect and our prophecy is imperfect; but when the perfect comes, the imperfect will pass away. When I was a child, I spoke like a child, I thought like a child, I reasoned like a child; when I became a man, I gave up childish ways. For now we see in a mirror dimly, but then face to face. Now I know in part; then I shall understand fully, even as I have been fully understood. So faith, hope, love abide, these three; but the greatest of these is love."

—I Corinthians 13:4–13
Revised Standard Edition

Pierre Loves Natasha

"A joyful, unexpected frenzy, of which Pierre had believed himself incapable, seized upon him. The whole meaning of life, not for him only, but for all the world, seemed to him centered in his love and the possibility of her loving him. Sometimes all men seemed to him to be absorbed in nothing else than his future happiness. It seemed to him sometimes that they were all rejoicing as he was himself, and were only trying to conceal that joy, by pretending to be occupied with other interests. In every word and gesture he saw an allusion to his happiness. He often surprised people by his significant and blissful look and smiles, that seemed to express some secret understanding with them. But when he realized that people could not know of his happiness, he pitied them from the bottom of his heart, and felt an impulse to try to make them somehow understand that all that they were interested in was utter nonsense and trifles not deserving of attention."

—**Leo Tolstoy**
War and Peace

◆

Into the Unknown

"Marriage is a journey toward an unknown destination—the discovery that people must share not only what they don't know about each other, but what they don't know about themselves."

—**Michael Ventura**

◆

The Power of Recall

"When a marriage gets into trouble many people obsessively focus all their energy and attention on the "problem" causing their difficulties. Yet it can often be far more saving at such times to concentrate on the positive feelings that brought the marriage partners together in the first place."

—**Norman Lobsenz**

The Role of Sex in Marriage

The Sweetest Gifts of All

The most appreciated gifts are the ones we don't expect, the gestures that spring from a sudden impulse. For instance, a husband walking down the street sees a pretty blouse. He buys it, brings it home, and presents it with the words, "I happened to see this and thought you would look wonderful in it." The wife might buy a book or magazine on a subject of special interest to her husband. Or she might offer to serve dinner for his friends who are attending their high school reunion.

Costly presents are not the measure of love—neither jewelry nor golf clubs necessarily make the heart light. But thoughtful, knowledgeable gifts—whether writing a difficult letter that is by rights the job of one's spouse, or the offer to take over the vacuuming, or run the Saturday errands—these are pure gold. Here is how you can show concretely that you appreciate what your spouse is doing for you, that you don't take it for granted. Such gifts of love can infuse sweetness and surprise into married life, whether you are newly wed or long married.

A charming bouquet of flowers, offered for no particular reason, can literally bring a breath of spring to an evening's homecoming. It can make life seem civilized, after all.

Do husbands and wives perceive sex differently?

Because of differences in anatomy, body chemistry, and upbringing, men and women tend to have different ideas about the nature of sex and usually enjoy different aspects of it.

Most men, psychologists say, are easily aroused and are concerned primarily with the physical act. A man's feelings of fondness and affection for his wife come into play, of course, but are usually not as important as the physical aspects.

Women, by contrast, tend to need more time to get ready for sex both physically and mentally. They usually need to be more emotionally involved and feel a strong rapport with their mate. A woman's desire can be affected by how well she feels her spouse is performing his roles as a husband and as a father to their children.

Are sexual difficulties signs of deeper marital problems?

Although sexual troubles can be caused by some underlying conflict in the marriage, sexual problems are common even in happy unions. In a study of 100 couples who viewed their marriage as happy—in some cases, very happy—nearly half of the women reported difficulty in becoming aroused or reaching an orgasm; 15 percent never reached orgasm.

Among the men, 10 percent said they experienced difficulties having an erection and more than one-third had premature ejaculation frequently. The researchers who did the survey concluded that "very few people have trouble-free sex lives, even when their marriages are satisfying."

What causes impotence and similar conditions?

More often than not a sexual problem has a psychological cause. A woman may not become sexually aroused because she was raised to feel that sex is dirty or is something that is not done by someone with high moral principles. (Such thinking may affect a man too.) Or she may have been brought up to believe that sex is a duty that a woman must endure to please her husband and to have children.

In other women an inability to respond sexually may be rooted in a fear of becoming pregnant or of not being able to conceive a child. Anxiety about not being able to have an orgasm can also affect a woman's sexual response and actually prevent her from having an orgasm.

In men, an estimated two-thirds of the cases of impotence can be traced to a psychological cause. Often a man may not be able to have an erection because of stress or anxiety, sometimes as a result of family strife, job problems, or financial difficulties. Depression can cause impotence, as can fear of impotence.

Of course, both men and women may find it difficult to become sexually aroused simply because they are unhappy with their spouse or some aspect of their married life. In these cases, treatment or counseling directed toward the basic problem is no doubt needed. Treatment can usually help other sexual problems too. But often all that is needed is a more relaxed approach to sex and better communication between the partners about each one's sexual concerns.

Does lack of sexual desire indicate a physical problem?

Certain illnesses can impair sexual desire—even though the individual can function sexually. An overactive or underactive thyroid, for example, can upset a person's emotional balance. And diabetes can have an effect on both desire and the ability to become aroused.

A drop in sexual desire is often one of the first signs of depression, appearing before such indications as sadness and loss of appetite. In young adults depression is probably the most common cause of a lack of interest in sex.

Drugs can also lower a person's sex drive and, in men, may cause impotence. Among the drugs that can affect sexual performance are some prescription antihistamines, MAO inhibitors used to treat depression, and certain medications prescribed for high blood pressure, most notably reserpine and beta blockers. Alcohol, barbiturates, marijuana, heroin, and cocaine all adversely affect a user's interest in sex.

What happens in a marriage encounter group?

Marriage encounters are seminars for couples. They are usually sponsored by a church or temple and are held over a weekend in a place away from the pressures of home and children. The gatherings are led by a member of the clergy and a specially trained lay couple.

Using techniques that force the husband and wife to react to each other, the leaders try to show couples ways to improve communication. Other topics include how to clarify marital roles, express anger in less harmful ways, and generally become more sensitive to each other's needs.

Attending a marriage encounter will probably not save a badly troubled marriage. The experience is like a refresher course for couples who want to renew the happiness and energy they once felt in their marriage. Gatherings known as marriage-enrichment seminars use the same approach without the religious content.

Keeping Sexual Interest: It's Not All Physical

The key to keeping sex a strong and vital part of marriage, the experts say, is found in being emotionally close to one another and working to strengthen all aspects of your relationship, not just sex. Here are some tips on attaining lifelong intimacy.

- **Make each other a priority.** Schedule the demands of work and children so that you both have some time to spend together every day, not just for sex but simply to be with each other.
- **Accept each other.** Avoid criticizing and trying to reshape each other to fit an ideal. Each should try to ignore the other's irritating habits if they are not serious, and think of the other's good traits, the ones that attracted you to each other in the first place.
- **Talk frequently.** Discuss more than household matters. Increase your closeness by sharing your interests and concerns about work, hobbies, friends, relatives, and other outside involvements. And be sure to listen to one another.
- **Be affectionate.** Make hugging, kissing, back rubbing, and touching a part of your everyday life. Do not limit displays of intimacy to the bedroom.
- **Keep romance alive.** Be attentive to each other and give each other compliments. Remember anniversaries, birthdays, and other special events. Give unexpected gifts. Treat yourselves to a night out.
- **Maintain your appearance.** Try to keep yourselves physically appealing by staying in shape and being neat and clean. Come to bed looking attractive, not with your hair in rollers or your face in need of a shave.
- **Make time for sex.** Set aside some time for sex other than late at night, when you are both exhausted and sleepy. Put the children to bed early; try early mornings, or midday on the weekends.
- **Make sure you have privacy.** Lock the door. Take the phone off the hook or turn on an answering machine.
- **Set the mood.** Dim the lights, put on music you both like, and make sure the room is at a comfortable temperature. If you find a scent arousing, use it very discreetly.
- **Be responsive.** If one of you is not in the mood when the other suggests sex, try to go along anyway; there's a good chance you'll get in the mood. On the other hand, if you start making love and discover you are really not in the mood, feel free to stop.
- **Allow time for foreplay and afterplay.** Try arousing one another slowly, maybe start by just talking. Lie holding one another afterward, relaxing and enjoying your escape from outside cares.
- **Be spontaneous.** Occasionally have unplanned sex or have sex in an unexpected place or a different position to add excitement to your love life.
- **Communicate sexual wants.** Be clear about what you each want without being demanding or critical. Communicate nonverbally too; for example, gently guide your spouse's hand to show how you want to be touched.
- **Experiment with sex.** Continue to learn about and try new techniques, positions, and ways to please each other. Share your fantasies and let each other know what excites you.
- **Learn to give.** Be generous to each other when making love. Never make receiving something in return a condition for giving your partner pleasure.
- **Change your routine.** If you always make love on the same days, try changing them or try making love more than once.
- **Laugh at sex.** Take a playful attitude toward sex and laugh if something you try does not work or is awkward or funny. Be silly together.
- **Expect change.** Be aware that major events, such as becoming parents or changing jobs, as well as lesser stresses can temporarily sidetrack sex. One or both of you may have to put an extra effort into rekindling interest.
- **Grow as a couple.** Realize that even though arousal may take longer as you get older, you can still enjoy sex.

When Things Are Askew

Is jealousy dangerous to a marriage?

Jealousy is normal when a partner is unfaithful, openly flirts with someone else, or engages in other provocative actions. Clearly, such behavior is a sign that a marriage is already in danger and needs help to be saved.

However, irrational jealousy, for which there is no real cause, can tear apart a marriage that otherwise has every chance of surviving. Irrational jealousy is rooted in a fear of losing the loved one to a rival. In some people it can become an all-consuming obsession, almost a form of sickness.

A jealous partner is usually the less powerful, more dependent spouse and often feels insecure. He or she fears being abandoned. In an excessively jealous person, a bout of obsessive concern can be set off if the other partner is late arriving home from work or has an innocent chat with someone at a party. Besides reacting with anxiety to his or her suspicions, the jealous person often becomes angry and depressed as well.

Whether the cause is real or imagined, jealousy can be corrosive to a marriage. Not only is the jealous partner filled with doubts and suspicions but the other spouse is likely to be hurt or irritated by the jealous one's distrust. Help from a marriage counselor, and individual therapy as well, may be needed to address the causes and resolve the conflicts.

The Bigamist: Coward or Swindler?

Women seldom commit bigamy. Even among men it is rare, so its psychological implications have been little studied. Leaving aside the criminal intent of a man who marries in order to fleece an array of wives, there are certain common characteristics shared by the majority of bigamists. Psychologists believe that the bigamist is often self-centered, unable to make an emotional commitment and a gambler to boot. A bigamist may find himself in this questionable state because he lacks the courage to ask one woman for a divorce and cannot stave off another's wedding plans.

In the 1953 movie *The Captain's Paradise,* Alec Guinness plays a bigamist, the captain of a boat sailing between two ports, who keeps a wife in each. The fantasy world of movies can make fun of bigamy, but in the real world wives are emotionally shattered and children often so severely hurt that later in life they are unable to trust men.

The exotic wife, Yvonne De Carlo, in Morocco satisfies Alec Guinness's wish for glamour.

The prim and proper wife, Celia Johnson, in Gibraltar fulfills the captain's desire for domestic tranquillity and respectability.

What effect is having an affair likely to have on a marriage?

Experts estimate that one-half to two-thirds of husbands and one-half of wives have an affair at some time during their marriage. Perhaps two-thirds of all marriages are affected.

Even if the participants in an affair keep it secret, it can have a serious effect on both partners in a marriage. An affair, one researcher noted, produces "internal conflict and guilt feelings on the part of one engaging in such acts, and is anywhere from infuriating to shattering to the other if he or she discovers the truth."

In a study directed by Dr. Bernard L. Greene based on the voluntary responses of 750 unfaithful mates, the reasons for infidelity given most frequently by straying spouses were sexual frustration, curiosity, revenge, and boredom. Many also felt a need to be accepted and recognized as a person—a need that they said was not being met in the marriage. As one researcher noted, an affair may not be the problem but rather a symptom of other, less obvious problems. It may mean that the marriage is already in trouble and must change to survive.

On the other hand, an affair may simply be an excuse to avoid facing marital problems in a mature way, and countless couples happily endorse moral and religious injunctions against adultery.

Men Who Don't Marry

Casanova loved women and they in turn loved him throughout the length and breadth of 18th-century Europe. He wrote his memoirs, recounting his amatory adventures. Since then his name has become synonymous with philandering.

"I HAVE LOVED WOMEN even to madness," Giacomo Casanova once wrote, "but I have always loved liberty more." For nearly two centuries Casanova's name has conjured up visions of a life dedicated to a shameless seduction of women and avoidance of all family ties and responsibilities.

Casanova is often confused with his fictional counterpart, the rake and libertine Don Juan, who was created by the 17th-century Spanish playwright Tirso de Molina. Later Don Juan was the subject of the opera *Don Giovanni* by Mozart and George Bernard Shaw's play *Man and Superman.*

Casanova was born in Venice in 1725 into a theatrical family. Venice at that time was a city devoted to pleasure and amusement, and the boy grew up in a carnival atmosphere. Having no name of consequence or wealth, Casanova knew early in life that he would have to make his own way. He had a first-class mind and taught himself to read Homer in the original Greek and to recite the poetry of Horace in Latin. He studied the chemistry of his time. "His every word is a revelation," a learned Austrian wrote of him, "and every thought a book."

By the time he was 17 years old, Casanova had already embarked on his profligate, adventurous life. For the next 39 years he crisscrossed Europe from Naples to London and Madrid to Moscow. He made and lost fortunes at gaming tables and in dubious financial schemes. He fought duels, advised kings, lived in splendor, and was sometimes forced to take refuge in brothels. Wherever he went, he found women eager to give him their love and devotion. In later life he claimed that he had seduced 122 women, among them highborn ladies, chambermaids, nuns, and actresses. Any number of times along the way he squirmed out of marriage, sometimes by simply leaving town in a hurry.

Casanova's charm *is not readily apparent to modern eyes in this contemporary portrait. Yet he dazzled women far and wide.*

Casanova's name might well have died with him (18th-century Europe swarmed with adventurers and confidence men like him) had he not written his *Memoirs,* a 12-volume documentation of his successes and misfortunes. In these pages, we meet the king of Prussia, Catherine the Great of Russia, Voltaire, and unnumbered scoundrels and rogues.

Casanova has given his name to what is known today as the Casanova complex. This describes men who cannot form enduring relationships with women, whose romances or marriages don't last long, or who must constantly prove themselves by sexual conquest. When someone is called a "regular Casanova," we understand him to be a "love 'em and leave 'em" type.

The question, then and now, is: Why did Casanova behave the way he did? We know that he feared boredom and it was certainly easier to travel, to gamble, and to climb the social ladder successfully unencumbered with wife and family.

Present-day psychologists, however, would look beneath Casanova's exploits to underlying traits and motives. Today's Casanovas are generally judged to be men incapable of developing adult feelings. They are often selfish and self-seeking, and some may just be cynical, indulging in passing pleasures with no thought of anyone else's feelings or well-being. They may have a compulsive desire to justify themselves, or demonstrate a masculinity of which they are not really sure.

Women may be attracted to Casanovas because their intense sexual drive is intriguing. Furthermore, sometimes Casanovas have real skills in the art of persuasion. Whatever the reason, Casanovas seldom have difficulty finding someone to romance. Casanova wrote of himself that he was "neither tender nor gallant nor pathetic. I am passionate." And it may just be that passion is the magnet that attracts women.

Casanova, who lived until the age of 73, spent the last 24 years of life in straitened circumstances. He worked briefly for the Inquisition in Venice, assigned, ironically, to report on the morals of his fellow citizens. In 1776 he wrote: "It is this craze for luxury, and the wantonness of women, and the horrible new freedom in the commerce of love, which, despite the undeniable necessity of stable family life, is the cause that the rotten conditions here grow steadily worse."

Casanova's last 13 years were spent as a librarian at a country estate, dependent on the generosity of an Austrian duke. He was bored and, hoping to make money, he sat down and wrote his memoirs. Although he never found a publisher in his lifetime, his work later became a popular success. It first appeared in 1822, 24 years after his death.

A New Life Begins

In the later months of pregnancy, *a woman is often urged to rest by family and friends. But the early months are the most fatiguing.*

How are a woman's emotions affected during pregnancy?

Frequent mood swings from crying to euphoria are common during pregnancy. It is also natural to have more fantastic or frightening dreams. Such emotional turbulence is due to hormonal and emotional adjustments inherent in pregnancy. Rising levels of progesterone, for example, can have a depressing effect on the mood centers of the brain.

Similarly, when a pregnant woman is profoundly upset or frightened, her brain's hypothalamus causes the release of catecholamine hormones (one of which is adrenaline), which raise blood pressure and heart rate. In rare cases the release of these stress hormones can induce uterine contractions in pregnant women and trigger premature labor.

Do men go through their own form of pregnancy?

Some men go through a range of sympathetic physical changes during their wives' pregnancies known as *couvade,* from the French word for *hatching.* Such symptoms as nausea, heartburn, fatigue, backache, weight gain, and persistent toothaches apparently stem from the emotional conflicts of impending fatherhood.

Some cultures, recognizing this phenomenon, developed elaborate rituals to help men through the difficult times. Only recently have Western cultures given men a formal role in pregnancy. Fathers-to-be are now encouraged to participate in prenatal care and delivery.

How can parents prepare for childbirth?

Many expectant mothers and fathers find they are much more relaxed and confident when they are familiar with the details of pregnancy. "Prepared childbirth" classes, offered by many hospitals, teach prospective parents about the physiological changes that occur during pregnancy and labor.

Certain childbirth classes offer excercises to ease or avoid tension and offset any fears a woman may have about childbirth. Best known is the Lamaze method, named for a French obstetrician, which is designed to teach breathing, relaxing, and massage routines to the mother and her coaching partner.

Is morning sickness real or imagined?

The nausea that frequently accompanies the first months of pregnancy has recently been traced to very low levels of vitamin B_6. However, another cause is the natural slowing down of a pregnant woman's digestive process. Thus food remains undigested in the stomach for longer periods than normal, bringing on nausea and the urge to vomit. Doctors advise keeping meals small and eating easily digestible food. Morning sickness usually abates by the time a pregnancy enters the fourth month.

Some mothers-to-be who feel extremely anxious or negative about pregnancy may experience chronic nausea. But such reactions are rare among women who are well informed about pregnancy.

Can mothers communicate with their unborn child?

By its sixth month, a fetus has fully developed hearing. There has been a lot of talk in recent years about the value of parents' stimulating their unborn children with reading, music, and conversations. Such prenatal schooling is supposed to improve a baby's mental abilities.

To date, there is no evidence that any of these efforts produce changes in a baby's IQ. However, any sustained effort by parents to communicate with their babies can have only a positive effect on their future relationship, and this in turn has proven to be critical to the development of a child's later mental abilities.

Why does a baby cry at birth?

Most babies cry briefly in order to take their first breath. No one can say for sure whether the cry is purely reflexive or whether it reflects distress or pain, but the crying serves a vital purpose. During delivery a baby's oxygen supply is temporarily interrupted, and babies are almost always born in a state of oxygen starvation. Crying clears fluids from the respiratory tract and allows the baby to take in great gulps of air that inflate the lungs.

Does the stress of birth affect a baby's initial view of the world?

A newborn's journey from the womb through the birth canal is arduous at best. To help weather the trip, babies produce high levels of the stress hormones called catecholamines. The rush of these hormones puts the baby in a state of alertness and provides protection against oxygen deprivation until the last moments of delivery.

Some scientists have theorized that this aroused state encourages and strengthens the initial attachment felt by the mother when she first sees her baby. If her baby looks perky and alert, rather than exhausted and passive, the mother responds to her newborn more quickly and more readily accepts her new responsibilities.

What is parent-infant bonding?

The moment a child is born it naturally seeks its mother. Likewise, when mothers and fathers are first presented with their newborns, they follow an instinctive pattern of touching their newborn's face, massaging its trunk, and gazing into its eyes.

Such interaction is crucial to establishing bonding—the growth of attachment between parent and child. Without bonding few parents could happily sustain all the sacrifices that caring for an infant requires, nor could an infant respond to all the new conditions in its environment.

Studies indicate that an ideal time for baby and mother to bond is immediately after birth. The newborn can be placed in its mother's arms for at least 30 minutes before being removed to be examined and washed.

In the past most hospitals would whisk the newborn away to be examined and cleaned before letting the mother hold her child. After delivery, mothers saw their babies only for feeding every three to four hours.

Nowadays if the mother is well and able, hospitals will immediately place the newborn in its mother's arms. Often the newborn will start to nurse immediately. Instead of staying in a nursery, a new baby can stay with its mother in her hospital room.

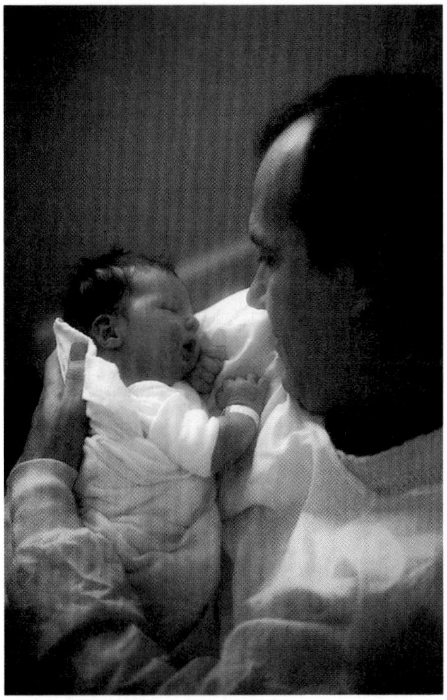

***Holding his infant** shortly after its birth, a young father shares in the miracle of life. Many doctors today allow fathers to be present throughout the delivery.*

Why is parent-infant bonding so important?

Early bonding helps ensure that a baby will get plenty of care. Mothers who are allowed extensive contact with their newborns in the hospital soothed and fondled their one-month-old babies more than mothers who are permitted only minimal contact with their newborns.

For some parents, forming a bond takes time. New mothers may be upset to discover they feel as if their newborn is an odd stranger. Feelings of love will come, however. Recalls one woman after the birth of her first child: "I just assumed that I would feel this overwhelming motherly love for my son . . . as soon as I gave birth to him. Instead, when the doctor handed him to me to hold, I felt as if I were holding a stranger. . . . I didn't feel any closeness or great love for him. . . . It wasn't until several weeks of caring for him at home had passed that I began to develop positive feelings for him and love him."

What causes the postpartum "baby blues"?

The stress of giving birth and the subsequent hormonal changes—plus fatigue from round-the-clock feedings—can give a new mother the "baby blues," known medically as postpartum depression (from the Latin *post,* meaning "after," and *partum,* "birth"). Some postpartum mothers are so prone to weeping that even a story about a faraway tragedy can cause a flood of tears. Often women who have had a miscarriage undergo the same kind of hormonal changes and have similar depressed feelings.

In the great majority of cases, postpartum blues do not last much longer than two weeks. But sometimes they won't go away and can deepen into a serious depression. If this happens, a woman may suffer from despair, irrational fears, and sometimes violent anger toward others, including her baby. This severe form of postpartum depression occurs in perhaps 10 percent of new mothers and requires immediate professional treatment.

What We Know, When We Know It

What reflex actions is a baby born with?

The most important of several involuntary responses found in healthy newborns is the rooting reflex, by which infants instinctively turn toward the stimulus of touch and open their mouths. This reflex enables the newborn child to find nourishment when in contact with the mother's breast and to feed long before being able to see or smell the nipple and know its purpose.

The Moro reflex, named in honor of a German pediatrician who practiced early in this century, occurs when a newborn is startled by loud noises or by a sudden change in position. (In adults the equivalent is called the startle reflex.) Infants will fling out their arms and legs, then clench the fists and pull the arms back in a movement that resembles embracing. Scientists have speculated that the Moro reflex is a primitive gesture that helps the infant cling securely to the mother.

A third kind of involuntary response observed in newborns is the Babinski reflex, named for the French neurologist who described it in detail in 1896. Stroking the bottom of an infant's foot causes the toes to spread and turn upward.

An obstetrician may check a baby immediately after delivery for one or more of these reflexes. Their presence indicates normal development.

What can newborns see?

A newborn baby's visual equipment has not yet matured. The infant can see, but only with blurred vision, and objects beyond about 18 inches are apparently not detectable. This limited eyesight may be a protection against too much visual stimulation at this tumultuous stage of life, when so much else is happening to the baby.

However, as fuzzy and nearsighted as their vision seems to be, babies show a distinct preference for human faces, patterns, sharp outlines, and moving objects. A baby seems to find these more visually arresting than stationary objects, plain surfaces, and solid forms.

The Language of Mother and Baby Makes a Special Bond Between Them

A mother's gentle babble of short syllables, often called baby talk (or motherese), is not only an expression of her love but also baby's best teacher of language. A mother's high-pitched cooing, with its exaggerated stress on vowels, communicates best with babies because a baby's ear is attuned to high frequencies. In a newborn's presence, baby talk seems to come naturally to almost everyone.

Language development appears to be shaped by hearing, cognitive development, motor control of the tongue and lips, and, above all, a parent's verbal stimulation. By the age of four to five weeks, a baby will smile when it hears its mother's voice. Two months later it will answer with responsive gurgles. The baby has actually begun to carry on a conversation, rehearsing for the future, when intelligible words will appear. Although all normal babies eventually learn to talk, the importance of baby talk is that it stimulates babies to get started, say child psychologists.

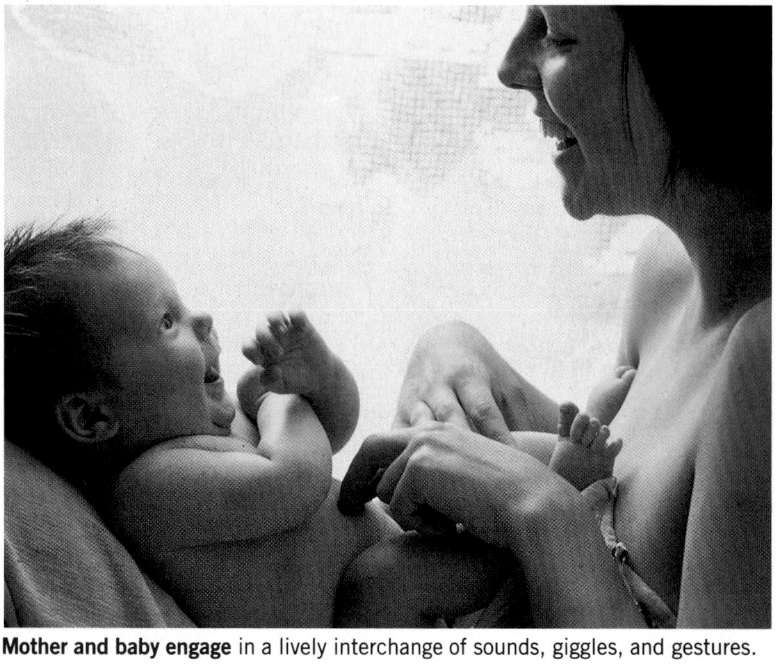

Mother and baby engage in a lively interchange of sounds, giggles, and gestures.

The baby's response seems like conversation.

What can a baby hear?

A baby who has just emerged from the womb has acute hearing and can pick up virtually all the sounds made by the human voice. Within 10 minutes of birth, babies may be able to associate a sound with its source and to turn their heads accordingly.

To determine babies' ability to pick up variations in voice pitch, researchers designed a special artificial nipple that registered the rate of sucking and was connected to a voice recording. Depending upon how rapidly a newborn sucked the nipple, the pitch of a voice recording would go up or down. The researchers found that the babies tended to adjust their sucking rhythms to produce voices that were in the higher, more typically female range. Also, the closer in pitch the voice was to their mother's, the more interest was stimulated in the babies, as expressed by their sucking rates.

Many infants appear to be born with the ability to select the voice of their own mother from among several similar voices. Some psychologists believe that such discrimination is explained by the fact that babies become familiar with their mothers' voices while still in the womb. Another theory is that babies do not actually recognize their mothers' voices, which would have been muffled and distorted if heard in the womb, but rather their distinctive rhythms.

How developed are taste, smell, and touch in a newborn?

Babies come into the world able to detect the difference between sweet and bitter tastes. The ability to discriminate salt and sour follows soon after. Within days of birth, development of the sense of smell, which is critical in further distinguishing among tastes, has begun.

Newborns also have a highly developed sense of touch and will often change their behavior in response to different kinds of touching. For example, being touched or held in one way will calm a newborn, while a slightly different kind of touch will stimulate the baby.

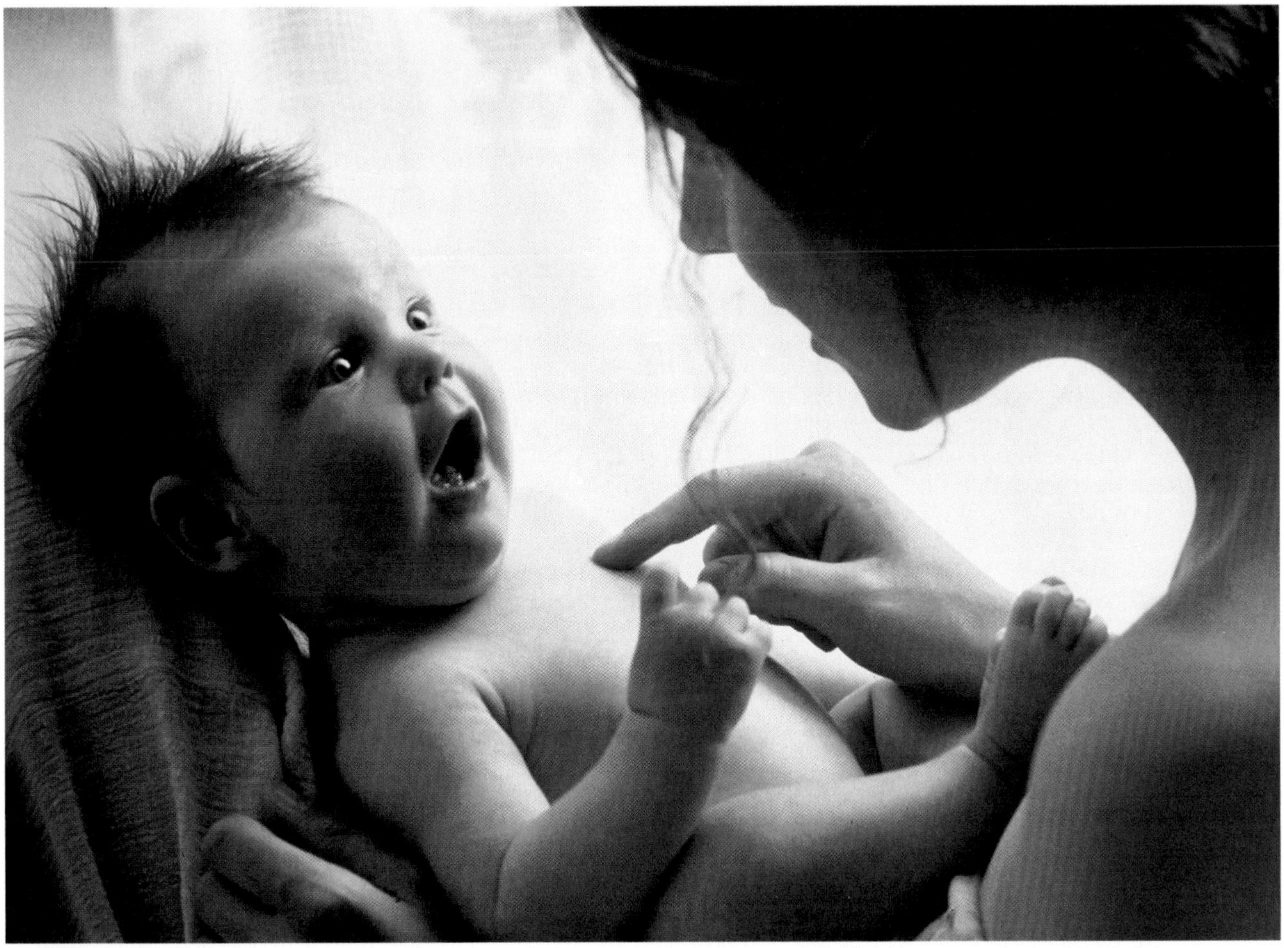

In these intimate moments of cooing and touching, powerful bonds of affection are forged between a mother and her infant.

Little People on the Move

How do motor skills relate to a child's development?

Our motor skills progress from lifting our heads and turning over in the crib, through walking and running, to driving a car, typing, playing the piano, or mastering a sport. Because such skills require close teamwork between brain and body, learning them must await development of portions of the young brain, as well as of the hundreds of muscles, joints, and tendons that perform the physical work involved. Equally important is the formation of nerve fibers, through which brain and body communicate.

From studies of large numbers of infants and toddlers, scientists have constructed a timetable that indicates when most normal children should acquire a certain motor skill, give or take a few weeks or months. If a child varies greatly from these norms, he or she may have a neurological or brain deficit that needs special attention.

The first motor skills mastered by a child employ the gross (large) voluntary muscles in the areas closest to the brain. Most children can hold their heads up before they can control their arms and they crawl before walking.

Fine motor skills requiring the skilled manipulation of hands and feet, fingers and toes, usually develop last. These skills demand coordination with the eye as well as certain advanced cognitive abilities that do not mature until later childhood or even adolescence, such as knowledge of shape, space, and timing.

When do babies start to develop feelings?

Days or even hours after birth, babies evidently have basic sorts of feelings, in that they seem to derive pleasure from sweet tastes and odors, from certain kinds of tactile stimulation, and from the repetition of actions such as rocking and sucking. They also appear to experience discomfort from intense light and sound, from bitter flavors and smells, and from various kinds of physical sensations. And even very young babies sometimes have an increase in pulse rate—a standard physiological reaction of adults to stress—when they are overstimulated.

Cindy steps out, *delicately balanced, and delighted with her new mobility.*

But genuine emotional feelings, which involve the interplay of bodily sensations and experience (and the memory to connect them), do not enter the infant's repertoire until after the eighth month or so. At that time babies begin to appreciate cause and effect, and this makes it possible for them to feel anger and frustration, as, for example, when their desires are thwarted. Children of this age also begin to recognize certain simple incongruities, such as when a parent makes a funny face, and feel amusement.

Sometime around the 18th month, the connections in a child's brain and nervous system are sufficiently developed to begin to register the more complex emotions typical of adults. With the capacity for feelings such as pride, shame, embarrassment, and guilt, the child is launched on a course of emotional development that leads ultimately to self-discipline and control of his or her own life.

When does learning begin?

Before children start school, they have already learned a tremendous amount. Preschool learning was studied in depth by many researchers. The most influential findings were those of Jean Piaget, a Swiss psychologist. Key terms in Piaget's theories are *assimilation*, the process of a child's ingesting new experiences and information, and *accommodation*, the way a child revises his or her responses to adapt to a widening universe.

In Piaget's view, learning in the first 24 months of a child's life is achieved by what he calls "sensorimotor thought." It is an ongoing process of interaction with the environment, in which every solution is acted out by the baby to see if it works. Sensorimotor learning develops in six phases.

In the first month a baby's actions are almost entirely based on reflexes over which the infant has no conscious control. In the second sensorimotor phase (one to four months), the baby becomes able to repeat certain reflexive actions—grasping and sucking, for example—intentionally.

The third phase (four to eight months) finds the baby able to call up and repeat learned responses: shaking a toy, banging a block to produce noise. In phase four (8 to 12 months), the infant can, with prompting, imitate simple actions of other people—for example, engage a parent in a game of making faces. Phase five (12 to 18 months) brings a toddler to the threshold of problem-solving, in that he or she will physically try several solutions to a problem, though unable to imagine which solutions are practical and which are not.

Piaget defines the last sensorimotor phase (18 to 24 months) as the beginning of symbolic thought. In this sixth phase a baby begins to use mental trial and error in place of strictly physical explorations of reality, and is thus more selective in the number of physical solutions attempted. Once this phase arrives, the child is ready for a new burst of cognitive growth. Soon the child will be learning to talk, to solve problems mentally, to play pretend games, to sense the difference between before and after and yesterday and tomorrow, and to grasp that objects continue to exist even when they are out of sight.

How do children learn speech?

Children tend to master speech, just as they acquire motor skills, in predictable stages. For example, most children can produce the sounds formed at the front of the mouth, P, B, M, G, and D, between 24 and 36 months. But they cannot say J or V until they are five or older, presumably because they lack the muscle control and an oral cavity large enough to accommodate the tongue in the configurations needed to produce those sounds.

Children also learn parts of speech in a predictable order, beginning with a variety of nouns. Next come verbs, then a diversity of other parts of speech. The first two-word phrases, such as "Mommy help," appear around two years of age. By age six the average child speaks in sentences, using perhaps 2,600 words and understanding as many as 12,000.

Making Believe

At one moment your four-year-old is on the floor, a roaring lion, shaking its mane; the next, she is a hostess, presiding at a dolls' tea party. Such flexibility and imagination is the special province of childhood, a magical talent, envied by adults whose minds have had to become rooted in practical realities.

Parents are wise to encourage their child's fantasies, which stimulate thinking skills and the ability to get along with other children. Make-believe, say psychologists, leads to smiles, laughter, and a sense of inner peace.

Erika answers the telephone.

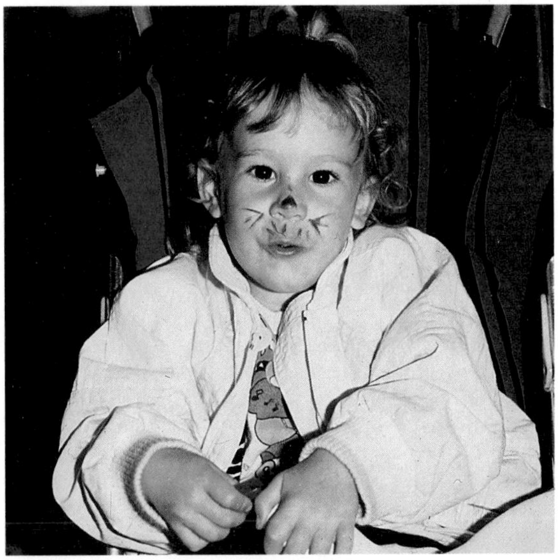

Melissa enjoys being a make-believe cat.

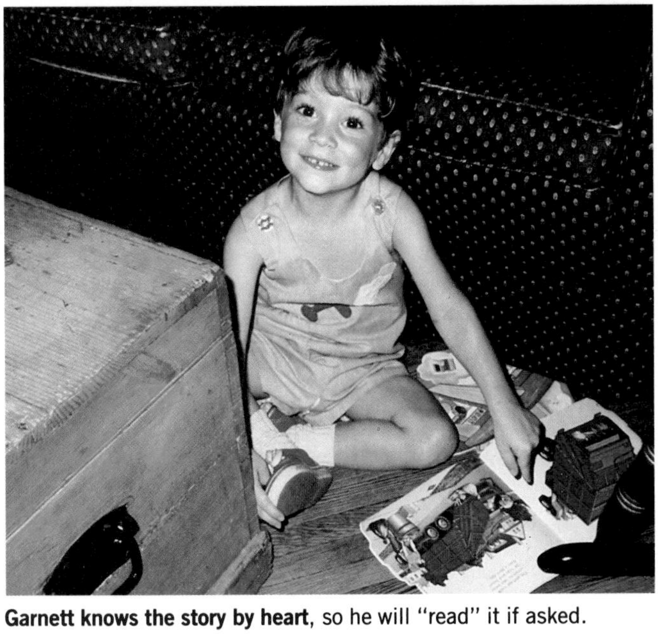

Garnett knows the story by heart, so he will "read" it if asked.

Conrad fits one toy into another, building important things.

Wonderful Discoveries Every Day

Standing within the hushed ramparts of a barn, *Charles watches with fascination as the swallows fly to and fro in the rafters high over his head. At three years of age, Charles is no longer a baby, nor yet as grown up as he imagines. Agile, sturdy, and intelligent, he is endlessly curious, avid for adventure.*

Are children naturally curious?

Many psychologists believe that we are born with some sort of survival instinct for competence, a drive to master our environment and thereby thrive within it. This so-called competence motivation impels even the very young child to be constantly curious, constantly experimenting.

Curiosity and competence motivation, however, are tender instincts. They can be suppressed or nurtured in a child by the negative or positive feedback received from adults.

Negative feedback occurs when children see their efforts to master a skill or concept met with disapproval, disinterest, or even scorn. This gives a child a sense of failure and, if repeated, he or she comes to avoid challenges and to remain dependent on parents and teachers for information and decision-making.

In contrast, repeated success at tasks, together with praise from parents and other adults, produces more curiosity, more independent effort, and increased self-esteem, all of which fuel the child's competence motivation. The result is an optimistic, confident, inquiring youngster.

How can young children develop such different personalities?

The sensitivity and responsiveness of a baby's nervous system are major factors in shaping personality. Child psychologists recognize three basic categories of nervous temperament: difficult; quiet, or slow-to-warm-up; and easy. They are quick to add that there is overlap among these categories and much variation within them.

The so-called difficult child is very active and intense. He or she has a low threshold of tolerance for all kinds of stimulation and cries frequently and lustily. Sleeping, eating, and waking patterns tend to be irregular. These children frustrate easily, and resist even gentle handling, an indication that even touching may sometimes overload their nervous systems.

The quiet, or slow-to-warm-up, child tends to be withdrawn. Because this type of child makes so few demands and is so unresponsive, he or she is in some ways more of a challenge than the difficult child.

The third category—the easy child—is the most common temperament among babies. Parents find these children to be generally in a good mood, usually adjustable, and pleasantly responsive to people and situations most of the time.

Behavior specialists say that the nervous temperaments displayed in the first months of life are likely to prevail throughout the growing years. However, sensitive and informed parents can work wonders with children who have difficult or quiet temperaments, helping them to get along more comfortably with themselves and their world.

Are children born with fears or do they learn them?

Psychologists differ on the question of whether or not certain apparently unconscious and involuntary responses of infants should be called fears. At or soon after birth, a baby has startle reflexes and avoidance reactions, such as recoiling from pain, jerking at a loud noise, or gasping at the sensation of falling. These actions may be unconscious to begin with, but they connect to conscious fears as the infant matures.

The first so-called social fears usually appear by about the 9th or 10th month, when babies are beginning to be aware of themselves as individuals separate from their mothers. Most children experience a predictable progression of fears, with each arising and fading roughly in step with an age-related timetable.

Before their first birthday, children typically develop a fear of strangers. This is followed by separation anxiety (fear of losing the mother or even of letting her out of sight) and often by fear of the bath.

During the second and third years, a toddler's fears may focus on doctors, sudden noises, such as thunder or fireworks, strange animals, and unfamiliar children. Along with these may come dread of the darkness and fear of a flushing toilet.

Can children scare themselves?

As the child's imagination expands, so does the capacity to anticipate or fantasize fearful objects and events. Between ages three and four, children may frighten themselves with imaginary creatures. And they may become unreasonably afraid of the risk of bodily harm, an exaggerated, anticipatory fear that is a by-product of their real experiences with painful falls, bee stings, bruises, or the like.

Most youngsters grow out of their childhood fears, or at least soon put them in some kind of reasonable perspective that makes them less disturbing. If any fears seem to be unusually severe or long lasting, professional help may prove useful.

Bringing Up Baby: A Doctor's Prescription for Busy Parents

Juggling work and family can often seem overwhelming. Here Dr. T. Berry Brazelton, himself the father of three girls and a boy, offers some practical advice for easing the strain on working parents, those two-job couples who are so much a part of our world today. A practicing pediatrician for more than 40 years, Dr. Brazelton has never lost his enthusiasm for helping children (and their parents) over life's rough spots.

- Learn to compartmentalize—when you work, be there, and when you are at home, be at home.
- Prepare yourself for separating each day. Then prepare the child. Accompany him or her to the care giver.
- Allow yourself to grieve about leaving your baby—it will help you find the best substitute care, and you'll leave the child with a passionate parting.
- Let yourself feel guilty. Guilt is a powerful force for finding solutions.
- Find others to share your stress—peer or family resource groups.
- Include your spouse in the work of the family.
- Face the reality of working and caring. No supermom or superbaby fantasies.
- Learn to save up energy in the workplace to be ready for homecoming.
- Investigate all the options available at your workplace—on-site or nearby day care, shared-job options, flexible-time arrangements, sick leave if your child is ill.
- Plan for children to fall apart when you arrive home after work. They've saved up their strongest feelings all day.
- Gather the entire family when you walk in. Sit in a big rocking chair until everyone is close again. When the children squirm to get down, you can turn to chores and housework.
- Take children along as you do chores. Teach them to help with the housework, and give them approval when they do.
- Each parent should have a special time alone with each child every week. Even an hour will do.
- Don't let yourself be overwhelmed by stress. Instead, enjoy the pleasures of solving problems together. You can establish a pattern of working as a team.

Jason's parents share with him *their pleasure in swimming. Whether fearful of water or loving it, small children should never be left alone near water. At shore or pool, full-time adult attention is a must. No amount of training can "waterproof" a tot.*

Playing Is a Child's Job

What is the function of play?

Play is children's work. It has obvious importance in physical development, as the child tries out various kinds of movements that help develop motor skills. But over the long run, play contributes even more significantly to mental development.

Through play youngsters test their creativity, learn to solve problems, explore the physical world, and gain competence. Play helps create a child's social persona, the way he or she behaves in the presence of other people. As children play, they may experiment with a range of different make-believe roles and choose parts of one role or another to build their personalities. Children delight in trying on hats and making faces that turn them into cartoon characters or space travelers or fire fighters. They are happy to become lions and bears, too.

Finally, play teaches about the ways people deal with one another—the rules, rewards, and punishments that go along with performing in the real world—and a child learns these complicated lessons under conditions that are basically benign and pleasurable, at least to adults.

As every parent and baby-sitter knows, however, what may seem like a trivial frustration to an adult can be a monumental insult or setback to a child, calling forth a dramatic expression of anger or grief. Children, in this case, have adult-sized emotions.

Beaming with pride, *Penny and brother Steven display their finger paintings.*

Should parents help select their children's friends?

In their early years children really have no choice in deciding who their playmates are going to be. They play with the children of their parents' friends or acquaintances or at a playground selected by parents. Only as a child grows older and his or her social horizons widen will the child pick out certain playmates from a group to be special friends.

When this begins to happen, usually around the time of nursery school or its equivalent, both child and parents may be in for some trying times. In recent years psychologists have discovered to their surprise that friendships even at the toddler stage are quite complex.

Friendships can be a testing ground for how to express and confront anger and aggression, says Dr. Eugene S. Urbain, a clinical psychologist at the Wilder Child Guidance Center in St. Paul, Minnesota. Moreover, he says, the experience of getting along with friends can teach children important lessons about balancing assertiveness with compromise.

Sometimes, Dr. Urbain has found, a child chooses a friend who represents behavior that the child admires but is too timid to act out. Such a child, for example, might choose a bully or a daredevil for a friend. Although such an association rarely changes a child in any lasting way, worried parents may want to protect their child from what they regard as a bad influence.

Parents have every right not to like or trust a certain friend of their child's, in the opinion of Dr. Caroline Howes, a developmental psychologist at the University of California at Los Angeles. However, the parents' chances of

Caught unawares playing cards, *a little girl takes the practical approach to bidding and sneaks a look at the others' hands. The joys of*

changing their child's mind about a friend depend almost entirely on the parents' tact and sensitivity. If a child is young, a parent can often help a child understand how an overly aggressive friend makes things unpleasant for everybody.

But the older the child, the more he or she is likely to resent a parent's disapproval, especially if the parent shows little interest in hearing the child's point of view. In fact, a parent's unbending disapproval may make a child more determined than ever to keep a friend.

***Going up in a swing** undoubtedly is "the pleasantest thing ever a child can do!"*

How early can a child's IQ be reliably assessed?

It is difficult to test a child's intelligence before he or she attains some degree of verbal proficiency, usually at about age three or four. Until then, the only way to assess intelligence is by observing what the child does naturally and then matching his or her performance against developmental norms for a large number of other children the same age.

Among the factors that have been studied as possible predictors of later intelligence are attentiveness, vocal excitability, frequency and level of activity, irritability, playfulness, and inclination to smile when stimulated. However, though analyzing such behavior patterns may tell where a child's development stands at a specific moment in time in relation to other children, it is not generally a very reliable way to predict the future capabilities and talents of a child. Perfectly healthy, normally intelligent three- and four-year-olds exhibit widely varying development curves, which tend to even out later.

One kind of observable behavior, known as habituation, does seem to have some correlation with later IQ scores. Habituation has to do with the rate at which a child becomes familiar with some new piece of visual information, such as a bright pattern, and loses interest in it. The sooner the baby gets bored and shows an interest in moving on to something else, the better a learner he or she is likely to prove to be.

Early walking and talking are not particularly significant indexes of brightness, in the opinion of most psychologists; but uncommon curiosity, perceptiveness, and determination are good clues. Some researchers think the rate (as distinct from the age) at which a child learns to master language can also be an important predictor of intelligence.

winning are not dampened by the suspicions of her companions. Her "rules of the game" do not yet include the concept of playing fair.

The Basics of Child Development

At what age does socialization begin?

Babies are not born sociable. A child begins life in a state of egocentricity, in which he or she is the center of the universe and everyone around is apparently perceived by the child as an extension of its being.

In experiencing the give-and-take of relationships with its parents, and in becoming aware of feelings of mutual love and trust, a child moves beyond self-involvement to interest in other people. Thus begins the acquisition of the social skills that enable the child to function in the wider world.

Its own cries teach the young infant the first lesson in purposeful social behavior: crying brings comfort and security in the form of parents. By two months a baby has usually discovered that smiling and vocalizing also pay off in keeping people's attention.

As the weeks go by, babies acquire other social signals, such as a variety of noises, hand gestures, and facial expressions. Between three and six months of age, they also start to show a preference for particular individuals in addition to their parents.

Beginning sometime in the second year the toddler usually shows interest in other children of the same age. First, for a period of weeks or months, the child may play separately but side by side with another youngster. Then one day the two of them actually start to play with each other.

Notions of sharing, taking turns, and cooperation do not come easily. Even a three-year-old is still much involved in "me" and "mine," so the first experiences with peer play can be fraught with conflict and tears.

At first glance, these toddlers *seems to be playing together. Actually, though they are keenly aware of each other, they are too young for cooperative play.*

By the time children go to school, *it's clear that half the fun of playing is having friends there with whom they can share their toys, games, and opinions.*

When and how is a child's sexual identity formed?

In their second year children apparently begin to notice physical differences between males and females. A boy becomes aware of the way in which he resembles his father, and a girl, her mother. Almost all boys and girls at some time form an intense attachment to the parent of the opposite sex. However, by age five or six, boys increasingly identify with their fathers and girls with their mothers.

Many psychologists believe that conforming to society's views on what is acceptable sex-role behavior, and what is not, begins in the nursery. There the behavior of boy and girl babies—who are tomorrow's parents—is shaped by the ways their parents handle and play with them. Girls are generally cuddled more than boys, spoken to more gently, and roughhoused with less than boys, with the result that girls come to sense that they are expected to respond in quieter, less assertive ways than boys.

As children grow into preschoolers, information about sex roles is absorbed from many sources: the behavior of their mother and father, the

Noise and derring-do escalate *whenever little boys get together, a fact of life that many a parent finds hard to face.*

kinds of toys and play experiences they are offered, and the attitudes and conduct of their friends.

One recent study looked at how boys and girls, aged two to five, related to young babies. The researchers found no appreciable difference in how either sex played with the babies, except that the boys showed somewhat more interest in baby boys, and girls had a preference for baby girls.

How important is discipline?

Discipline can be thought of as the daily training that parents provide by action, word, and example to shape their children's behavior. Its basic purpose is to steer a child away from dangerous and unacceptable behavior and toward self-control. Almost all research indicates that behavior is most effectively shaped by rewarding acceptable conduct and withholding rewards if conduct is unacceptable. Eventually, by developing (internalizing) self-rewards, children learn self-discipline. As opposed to this kind of active involvement by a child in creating its own behavior, punishment simply suppresses behavior.

By the time a child starts to crawl, parents are already shaping its behavior in many ways—for example, teaching compliance to safety rules. At the toddler stage, lessons in coping and social skills have to be learned. Discipline in middle childhood usually involves the child's work habits and moral standards. By adolescence, a child has normally acquired some measure of self-discipline.

How effective is punishment?

Psychologists have noted three types of punishment. One is power-assertion, an example of which is described in the old saw "Spare the rod and spoil the child." Here, a parent relies on some kind of superior power, whether physical or financial, to force a child to behave in a certain way. Over the long run, power-assertion almost invariably fails in producing a self-disciplined child, since the child has little motivation to develop his or her own standards of behavior.

Some parents try to control their children by threatening to withhold love. Psychologists call this love-withdrawal. It may occasionally be beneficial if the parent is normally affectionate and loving and explains why the child's behavior was wrong.

The method that seems to have the best long-term results is known as induction. In terms their child can understand, parents explain why a certain type of behavior might harm the child or others. Because no threats are involved, the child usually begins to internalize the parents' values, the first step in developing self-discipline.

Fairness and consistency are all-important in administering discipline. A child needs to know the logical connection between actions and consequences. Nothing confuses a child more than having the same behavior punished one week, ignored the next, and rewarded the week after that.

When It's Parent Versus Child

Responding to Fears in the Night

Children are often plagued by troubling nightmares. Parents are well advised to take them seriously, particularly since nightmares can signal a fever or illness. Usually, the nightmares of little children can be traced to anxiety-provoking events, such as going to a new school or a scary movie. It's important that parents respond quickly when a child cries out from a nightmare. If children are left to scream themselves awake, the sound of their own crying will add to their terror. Talking about the fears will help to relieve a child's anxiety. For children who are afraid of the dark, having a night-light or a nearby flashlight can provide added reassurance.

Maxfield Parrish's illustration of a vivid nightmare, complete with menacing monsters.

As for detecting physical abuse, doctors and nurses know that occasional bruises and scrapes, and even more serious accidents, are part of growing up. What arouses suspicion, however, is when neither the parents nor the child seems willing or able to explain how a bruise, burn, or broken bone happened. Often a child will try to hide marks of abuse and offer feeble stories to explain them.

Sexual abuse is one of the most devastating forms of child abuse. Studies show that the majority of the offenders are trusted family members. Incest often goes unreported because its victims are warned not to tell, or if they tell they are not believed. Experts define sexual abuse as not just forced sexual intercourse but "any sexual activity or touching that the perpetrators try to keep secret."

Whether the child molester is a stranger or a family member, it's important that a concerned adult listen closely to what a child may be trying to say about his or her abuser. Parents should focus on their child's need and concerns, and they should remember that reacting hysterically can often be more upsetting to a child than the incident itself; but react they must, for the abuse has to be stopped.

When does punishment become abusive?

Abusive parents are those who have a pattern of punishing their children by hurting or humiliating them, either mentally or physically. Abusive parents are venting their own frustrations with life and take it personally when an infant cries or a toddler misbehaves. They feel they must administer severe punishment to help their child "straighten up." Many such parents have impossibly high expectations for their children and interpret a child's "cannot" as "will not." (A child can also suffer, however, if parents set no standards of performance.)

Typically, child abuse occurs when parents cannot handle the daily stress of child rearing and have nobody to turn to for help. Researchers have found that roughly one-third of the adults known to be child abusers were abused themselves as children. In a crisis, these people apparently cannot help reverting to the way their parents treated them.

What are the signs of child abuse?

Psychologists recognize four types of abuse—neglect, physical abuse, emotional abuse, and sexual abuse. Of these, emotional abuse is the hardest to spot. In its most obvious form, it can involve a parent who constantly shouts and curses at a child, but it can also stem from a parent who is simply cold and unloving or who calmly says cruel and deeply scarring things, such as "I wish you had never been born."

Neglect and physical abuse are easier to determine. A neglected child is usually not cared for properly. In infants, neglect can cause "failure to thrive" syndrome. A baby suffering from this syndrome is emaciated, restless, and resistant to cuddling. If admitted to a hospital, such neglected children eat voraciously.

Is there treatment for children abused by their family members?

Once child abuse has been determined, the next step is to prevent its happening again. This normally means removing the child from the abusive home and placing him or her in a foster home. Abused children are full of fear and anger. They have a hard time trusting adults, and most of them would profit from some kind of therapy aimed at restoring their confidence in themselves and others. Children who have been abused for a long time may need tutoring because the abuse may have affected their cognitive and speech development.

Treating the abusers is difficult, particularly if they were abused themselves as children. However, many abusive parents have turned to self-help groups like Parents Anonymous to learn how to control their anger.

A Mother's Plea

Like many victims of child abuse, Patricia Bissell survived the violence of her childhood, only to find herself abusing her own children, particularly her son Patrick. Here, Mrs. Bissell bravely reveals the tragedy of child abuse that scarred her life.

I WAS BORN IN 1928 TO AN affluent family plagued by demons that must have lurked in dark crooks of the family tree for generations. By any measure, my childhood was a relentless horror. Before I was two years old, my mother died at the hands of an abortionist to whom she had been forced to go by my father.

We went to live with my father's mother, a stern and self-righteous woman who was viewed as a community and church leader. Every memory I have of my early childhood is gripped by overwhelming fear of my father. He beat me practically every day with his leather razor strop—a practice my grandmother endorsed. Other times he locked me in a closet.

Fragments of horror from that time litter my mind. One of the most terrifying was a "parlor trick" my father enjoyed. He would pick me up, hold me firmly atop his shoulders, and, with great laughter, dance about the room. Then he would saunter through a doorway and smash my head into the wall above the door.

I was around six when my father took me to his bed. In addition to rape, the sexual acts that were a part of my childhood are truly unspeakable. I do not know how I physically survived. Even today, my father's stench stains my mind.

When she was seven, her father died. For the next six years Patricia Bissell lived with her grandmother, who continued the brutal beatings. Patricia was certain that her grandmother had also violently beaten her father.

Soon after high school I fell in love with a handsome navy veteran I had met at our church. He was a very shy and gentle man. These qualities were so rare to me that, when he asked me to marry him, I was swept away with joy.

When we were wed in 1947, I was completely confident that our love could overcome the shame of my childhood. I was eager to have children, for I assumed they would love me and I would be able to love them. I did not know that I was infected with a monstrous violence as destructive as any genetic disease.

Almost from the beginning, I battered my children—screaming at the younger ones and beating the older ones with a leather belt. (I never beat them when my husband was around; but he was usually away on business.) I battered the children's self-esteem as much as I battered their bodies—and in some ways those wounds probably were worse.

My son Patrick [whom we nicknamed Wally] became my chief target. As I would furiously flail Wally's legs and back, I'd hold one of his arms to keep him from running. He would stare directly into my eyes with a steady, composed look that instantly catapulted me to the dark scenes of my childhood. So I would swing the belt harder. It would all end in a crescendo of humiliation when I finally conquered that look, and his eyes clouded with pain and fear.

A spark of hope for Wally came from his older sister. For years we knew he had extraordinary stamina and coordination, and she got Wally to join her ballet class, when he was 10. I have wondered whether she was trying to keep him safe from me.

As Wally was making his way through dance schools with brilliant performances, he was also cementing lethal habits: he was drinking heavily and experimenting widely with drugs. He once told an interviewer: "I do good performances, and then I punish myself with drugs. I try to destroy myself. It's a weird kind of cycle." This sense of failure was the terrible legacy I gave my son.

As Patrick Bissell's career as a dancer skyrocketed, he made heavy use of cocaine and alcohol. Just months after his release from a treatment program, his fiancée found him dead from a drug overdose. He was 30 years old.

When the terrible news [of his death] reached us, I was sick with remorse. It was agonizingly clear to me that I had led my child to this tragic end. By this time extensive therapy had helped me understand what I had done to my children–and why. But it was too late to reverse what I'd done. I had taken away everything Wally had needed to be able to handle life.

For a normal person it's nearly impossible to understand how a mother can beat her child. I do not believe that any mortal alone has the strength to break this powerful cycle of horror. My hope is that never again will anyone have to face the kind of searing anguish of my life and the life I gave to my son.

Patrick Bissell *was a brilliant, widely acclaimed ballet dancer, shown here in the role of the Prince in Peter Ilich Tchaikovsky's* Nutcracker.

The Searching Years of Middle Childhood

Who is the middle-aged child?

Psychologists and societies agree that there is a point when a child loses most of its babyishness and, some years later, another point when a child becomes adolescent. Between these two milestones fall the middle years of childhood. Sometime around ages five to seven, a major new thrust begins in a child's social and intellectual life. It is the time when children typically begin their formal education and assume their first social responsibilities, such as watching over younger siblings, doing chores around the house, or taking an active part in religious observances.

How does the mind develop in the middle years of childhood?

Around age six or seven, children normally begin to be able to think with increasing logic about objects and experiences in their everyday lives. For example, they become capable of what psychologists call a reversible mental action: figuring out for themselves that if 2 plus 4 equals 6, then 4 plus 2 also equals 6. The Swiss psychologist Jean Piaget saw this as the start of what he called concrete operational intelligence, meaning the ability to think logically about concrete things.

From concrete operational intelligence it is a relatively short journey to more abstract thought, holding two or more conflicting ideas in the mind at the same time, as well as to thinking morally. In the middle years of childhood, the mind develops the capacity to distinguish right from wrong, hear another person's point of view, play games according to rules, and master the sequential mental tasks upon which reading, arithmetic, and other school tasks are based.

However, there is no cognitive skill that children master uniformly. A child may remain preoperational in some mental tasks for months and even years, but become competent in others before entering first grade. Most children who lag in one or more cognitive skills catch up eventually.

As children attain cognitive skills, they come increasingly to see their minds and their knowledge as sources of strength that they can rely on. This becomes very important as children move on to the next developmental level, adolescence, which typically begins around the age of 12.

What makes a fishing trip so special *is not so much the act of catching fish, but the feelings of pursuing a shared goal, an all too rare occurrence between parent and child. At such times, the generations often see each other with new understanding and respect.*

How can I raise my youngster to share my values?

Parents typically pass on their values not so much by talking about them as by applying them to real situations in family life. Children learn quickly what kinds of behavior their parents approve or disapprove. In being strict about some things and permissive about others, parents are making implicit statements about their own values and the ones they want their children to adopt.

For example, the parent who is very strict about a child being tidy or dressing in some socially approved way, while showing little concern about how the child spends free time or when the child goes to bed, may be inadvertently declaring that superficial appearances and social conformity are of primary importance to the family. And parents who are relaxed about the neatness of a child's room, but firm on the seriousness of getting homework done, are likely to be expressing the high value they place on education and matters of the mind.

Almost always a child will adapt to parental values, but the child will not necessarily internalize them—take them for his or her own—for life. For internalization to occur, a bond of trust must develop between parent and child. Almost unconsciously, a child may observe with what degree of sincerity and consistency the parents live by their declared values. As children grow older, they become quite adept at recognizing uncertainty and confusion in their parents' value system and can become disenchanted with following the rules when deeds do not match words.

Is there a right time for discussing sexuality?

Most children are naturally curious about some aspects of sex and likely to ask questions almost from the time they can talk. The challenge for parents is to give answers that match the child's intellectual and emotional level and do not tell the child more than he or she is ready to hear.

There is no single age or situation that is the right (or wrong) time for introducing the subject of human sexuality to your child. However, children who are approaching the age of puberty and have not yet asked basic questions may need some parental help in getting questions out. Often, the problem is that the child has sensed excessive discomfort or embarrassment on the part of parents and for that reason has chosen to avoid bringing up the subject of sex.

Psychologists say that parents can help themselves and their child by admitting that they, too, are uncomfortable about discussing sex but feel it is too important an issue to neglect. This kind of parental forthrightness and honesty will often put children at ease and allow them to voice their concerns and questions.

PERSPECTIVES

On Children and Parents

Soft, gurgling babies in their parents' arms seem so very unformed. But the truth is, those babies come fully equipped with the blueprint for their adult selves.

Miracles All

"Each second we live is a new and unique moment of the universe, a moment that never was before and never will be again. And what do we teach our children in school? We teach them that two and two make four and that Paris is the capital of France. When will we also teach them what they are? We should say to each of them: Do you know what you are? You're a marvel. You are unique. In all of the world there is no other child exactly like you. In the millions of years that have passed, there has never been a child like you. And look at your body—what a wonder it is! Your legs, your arms, your cunning fingers, the way you move! You may become a Shakespeare, a Michelangelo, a Beethoven. You have the capacity for anything. Yes, you are a marvel."

—Pablo Casals
The Children of Jonestown

◆

Through a Child's Eyes

"In my childhood the days were extremely long. I was high all the time without realizing it; extremely high on elementary things, like the luminosity of the day and the smell of everything—mud, earth, humidity; the delicious smells of cellars and molds; grocery shops."

—Saul Steinberg

◆

A Question of Guidance

"Isidor I. Rabi, the Nobel laureate in physics was once asked: 'Why did you become a scientist rather than a doctor or lawyer or businessman, like the other immigrant kids in your neighborhood?' Dr. Rabi's answer was: 'My mother made me a scientist without ever intending it. Every other Jewish mother in Brooklyn would ask her child after school: "So? Did you learn anything today?" But not my mother. She always asked me a different question. "Izzy," she would say, "did you ask a good question today?" That difference—asking good questions—made me become a scientist!' "

—Donald Sheff
To the Editor,
The New York Times

◆

Parental Balancing Act

"The hardest part of raising children is teaching them to ride bicycles. A father can either run beside the bicycle or stand yelling directions while the child falls. A shaky child on a bicycle for the first time needs both support and freedom. The realization that this is what the child will always need can hit hard."

—Sloan Wilson

◆

A Dose of Realism

"Four magic words, *we can't afford it,* should be a part of every child's education. A child who has never heard those words—or also has never been forced to abide by their meaning—has surely been cheated by his parents. As exercise strengthens the body, frugality strengthens the spirit. Without its occasional discipline, character suffers."

—Morris Mandel
The Jewish Press

◆

The Present Counts

"The child is constantly confronted with the nagging question: 'What are you going to be?' Courageous would be the youngster who could look the adult squarely in the face and say, 'I'm not going to be anything, I already am. . . .' Childhood isn't a time when a child is molded into a human who will then live life; he is a human who is living life. No child will miss the zest and joy of living unless these are denied him by adults who have convinced themselves that childhood is a period of preparation."

—David Elkind
The Hurried Child

The Changed Mind of an Adolescent

In high school, joining the band and many other such extracurricular options reflect the teenager's maturing mental and motor capabilities. Playing music, for example, calls on a youngster's emerging ability to handle abstract concepts; practicing alone sharpens coordination, while group practice brings a sense of belonging and teaches teamwork.

When does adolescence begin and how long does it last?

Adolescence is a period between childhood and adulthood when there is rapid development physically and mentally. It is usually said to start at puberty, when a child begins to mature sexually. But not all youngsters enter puberty at the same age. For some the changes occur at 11 or 12 or earlier; for others, the change comes later. However, regardless of sexual development, the mental changes that mark adolescence are generally well under way by the mid-teens.

Most physical development is complete by the age of 18, and societies often grant youths at this age adult legal privileges, such as the right to vote and marry without parental consent. But by age 18, few people have reached their full mental maturity.

Does maturing early or late have a lifelong effect?

Most adolescents are keenly aware of their physical development and constantly compare themselves with others. But in addition to this heightened self-consciousness, adolescents can experience long-term psychological effects from maturing earlier or later than most of their peers. Such difficulties seem to hit boys harder. Girls tend to escape lasting effects, although they can feel absolutely miserable when they are obviously ahead of or behind their peers physically.

Boys who mature at an early age and become taller and stronger than other adolescents have a great advantage. Their classmates usually admire them, think of them as more attractive, and often select them as leaders. They tend to excel on school sports teams and date the most desirable girls. Both their parents and teachers are likely to treat them more as adults.

Studies show that the preferential treatment accorded early-developing adolescents tends to build self-confidence that lasts into adulthood. Many men who matured early think of themselves as having leadership ability. Personality tests also indicate that, compared to late maturers, they have more self-control and are more responsible. They are usually more successful in their jobs.

Men who mature late, the studies indicate, tend to have a more flexible approach to life than early maturers. Although they are generally more assertive, rebellious, and impulsive, they are more perceptive. The advantages of maturing early seem to disappear once men move into their forties.

How does the way children think change around puberty?

Around 11 or 12 years of age, most children start to understand the links that make it possible to put people, things, or events into certain categories. Understanding these links is the first step in learning to work with abstract concepts.

For example, instead of thinking about school just in terms of particular teachers and activities, a typical 12-year-old is beginning to comprehend the broader abstract idea of education that connects them. This marks the start of what Jean Piaget calls formal operational intelligence, using the word *formal* to mean being able to think about the *form* of things and ideas. With this new ability to put things in abstract categories, express them as concepts, and manipulate concepts logically, adolescents are able to deal with future events and hypothetical "what if" situations.

Given a problem that can be solved only by testing the various alternatives—for example, mixing liquids to find the combination that produces a certain color—most young adolescents can form a general plan of what they must do to solve the problem and set about finding the answer by systematically eliminating all the other possibilities. Children just a couple of years younger usually take a random, unorganized approach when trying to solve problems of this type.

Does a person's thinking change during the teenage years?

The changes that are occurring in the adolescent brain can be tracked fairly precisely by testing the youngster's ability to handle abstract concepts. Young adolescents become able to deal with one abstract concept at a time but are confused if they try to manage two abstract ideas together.

Starting between the ages of 14 and 16, however, most adolescents develop an aptitude for relating abstract concepts to one another and to themselves and the wider world. For example, a teenage girl might perceive how the idea of conformity relates to the idea of individualism and become able to identify the areas of her own life where she is a conformist and where she is an individualist.

How do teenagers' mental changes affect their attitudes about rules and authority?

As adolescents become capable of more sophisticated thinking in their middle teens, they may also grow less rigid about their ideas. This is especially true of ideas related to rules and society, according to psychologist Lawrence Kohlberg, who studied the development of moral judgment. Young adolescents, Kohlberg said, tend to think in absolute terms, believing, for example, that everyone should always obey rules and respect authority. They have what psychologists call an authoritarian bias.

By the middle to late teens, however, many youngsters have the capacity to develop flexible views, whether they actually do so or not. They can understand how laws vary in different cultures and at different times, depending on the needs of the society. Older teenagers, for instance, are capable of appreciating the need to change a law that is not effective.

Is there a biological basis for the changes in the way an adolescent's mind works?

A growing body of evidence suggests that the brain begins to undergo a dramatic physical change in late childhood and early adolescence. The brain apparently sheds about a third of the nerve connections in the cerebral cortex, which controls thinking and most sensory perception and movement. Researchers are not certain about what causes the change, but some speculate that it is triggered by hormones released during the process of maturing.

Psychologists are also not sure if or how the change affects thinking. Some researchers believe that the large number of connections in the brains of children overwhelms thought processes, and this prevents them from being able to concentrate for very long. If this is true, then the loss of some of the connections might be what allows a teenager to concentrate and think logically.

The change may also be a way of streamlining the brain and making it more efficient by getting rid of excess or little-used connections. One observable result is that the brain needs less energy to function. It also requires less rest. As a result, adolescents need about two hours less sleep than they did when younger.

By spending the summer abroad, *these teenagers prove (to themselves as well as to adults) that they are getting old enough to plan their own schedules and keep commitments. As teenagers begin to manage on their own, parents must walk a narrow line between encouraging their children's independence and giving them too little guidance.*

Teenage Tug-of-War

Is adolescence always emotionally stormy?

Teenagers are renowned for their need to test their independence and rights. Surveys show, however, that the majority of parents and teenagers get along "fairly well." This may be because most parents, at least in Western cultures, expect their teenagers to challenge traditional customs and values.

Though teenagers do indeed rebel against parental standards, psychologists have discovered that tension arises most often from two specific sources: first, when adolescents simultaneously want and fear independence; second, when parents waver between treating them as adults and children. Thus it is the timing of new rights and responsibilities, not disagreements over values, that underlies much of the friction between teenagers and their parents.

What is a teenage identity crisis?

During adolescence it's normal for a youngster to ask: Who am I? What do I want out of life? These questions express the teenager's concern about fitting in with the adult world.

Psychologist Erik Erikson likens a child's passage through adolescence to the action of a trapeze artist who swings from one trapeze to another—the youngster must leave the safe haven of childhood and reach out for the independence of adulthood. But in between, there is the unsupported flight known as adolescence.

Erikson sees most teenagers sooner or later facing an identity crisis—not so much a "crisis" in the sense of an emergency, but a point when the adult personality can develop in one direction or another. It occurs when teenagers are not yet sure what kind of person they want to be or how they wish to be perceived. Sometimes, teenagers feel that personality traits they don't have or don't wish to have are being imposed upon them by their friends or parents. For example, a teenage boy may see himself as lacking in athletic abilities and will be confused and angry if his parents insist on telling him he is a fine athlete.

Both praise and criticism may be felt as ploys to control and are tough for a teenager to accept with equanimity. The poet T. S. Eliot, for example, is said never to have forgiven his mother for overpraising (in his opinion) a poem he wrote as a teenager.

Why are teenagers so susceptible to peer pressure?

"But everyone's doing it" seems to be a universal rallying cry of teenagers when confronted by parental disapproval. Conforming to the customs of a group can make a teen feel like he or she fits in. This sense of belonging is an important need as teens traverse the difficult years of being no longer children but not yet adults.

Some teenagers are more susceptible to peer pressure than others. Dr. Lynn Ponton, the director of the Adolescent Psychiatric Unit at the University of California, San Francisco, finds that teens whose parents set few rules or guidelines turn to their peers to help them form their values.

How important is friendship during the teenage years?

Friendships can be devastating or elating as they teach adolescents about themselves and their place in the world. Forming friendships is one of the best ways that teens can learn who they are on their own, away from their families.

According to University of Michigan psychologists Elizabeth Douvan

Why some teenagers adopt outrageous behavior, *while others seem to move smoothly into the adult world, is a mystery that has baffled the older generation for centuries. On the surface, at least, the peacock-coiffed pair at left seems to be more troubled by the idea of independence than does the smiling graduate with his proud father, above.*

and Joseph Adelson, teens go through three different types of friendship as they mature. From ages 12 to 15, youngsters are interested in friends who can share common activities and are easy to get along with.

The emphasis changes during the years 15 to 17. Teenagers at this stage seek friends who hold common opinions on such subjects as clothes and dating partners. Most cliques or groups are based on these shared viewpoints. Teenagers tend to band together and model themselves after the leaders of their clique, be it the star quarterback, the class brain, or the most conspicuous daredevil.

At times, teens can identify so strongly with their clique that they become very intolerant of outsiders. Psychologists note that intolerance of this kind may help teens protect themselves against identity diffusion, a state in which teenagers feel overwhelmed by too many choices about who they would like to be.

Finally, as adolescents enter their late teens (ages 17 to 19), they begin to feel more confident about themselves and are able to look for individuality in their friends.

*"**Teenage telephonitis**" can drive parents wild but offers teenagers privacy and independence in exchanging feelings, opinions, and gossip with peers.*

How do parents influence their teenagers' self-esteem and motivation to succeed?

Studies show that teenagers with low self-esteem typically have parents who are indifferent to either the successes or failures (or both) of the children. Lacking clear directions and goals, such children find it difficult to develop initiative. When this happens, children tend to form a negative self-image and give up trying anything new or challenging, including making new friends.

On the other hand, some parents can be so overprotective that they undermine their children's effort to grow up, and the children develop a fear of school. Psychologists have found that teenagers who suffer from school phobia are deeply afraid of leaving their family home and being separated from their parents.

Whether teenagers develop a high or low degree of motivation depends greatly on what their parents expect of them. If parents set high but achievable standards and express love and support for their teenagers' abilities, then adolescents will probably be reasonably confident of attaining success. Motivation will naturally follow. Parents who are overly critical and whose standards are impossibly high, however, may raise teenagers who avoid challenges for fear they will fail.

Is girls' motivation to succeed different from boys'?

Up until adolescence, girls tend to do better in school than boys. But during high school, boys start getting the higher grades. One reason may be that certain boys begin to realize that their academic success could be the road to prestigious jobs. As a result, pressure to succeed increases for boys.

In the past, girls have typically received mixed signals about what constitutes success and achievement. While being told that academic excellence was vital, girls were encouraged to seek only those goals that rewarded them for their social skills, not their intellectual or athletic ability.

Such mixed messages caused a number of girls to suffer from a syndrome that psychologist Matina Horner called "fear of success." As they grow older, this anxiety can prevent young women from achieving good grades in college or choosing a rewarding profession simply because these achievements might be considered unfeminine.

Trials and Individual Choices

A sense of being indestructible *is common among teenage boys the world over. Here, young daredevils risk goring as they taunt bulls, a July ritual in Pamplona, Spain.*

Why do teenagers take risks?

Teenagers tend to see the dangers in daredevil stunts as real for everyone but themselves. According to child psychologist David Elkind, they believe in their own "personal fable," which holds that "bad things will happen to other people but not to us." Lack of experience, wishful thinking, and a need to prove himself or herself can make a teenager oblivious to the perils inherent in most risks.

Risk-taking is often associated with rites of passage, which initiate a teenager into the privileges of adulthood, such as taking one's first drink of alcohol. Not all rites of passage are dangerous. Obtaining a driver's license or graduating from high school helps prove that a teenager is ready for the responsibilities of adulthood.

How much do teenagers need to know about sex?

One of the myths of adolescence is that teenagers know more than enough about sex. Despite explicit sexuality in movies, TV, and rock videos, a great many teenagers are woefully ignorant about sex.

Much of teenagers' naïveté about sex may be due to the fact that they are still learning to reason abstractly and don't fully understand the laws of probability. For example, a survey of sexually active teenage girls who did not use birth control revealed that half relied on wishful thinking to prevent pregnancies. They were convinced they wouldn't get pregnant because they didn't want to.

Teenagers need to learn that they can control their sexuality. This is particularly important, since teenagers often think that being sexually aroused inevitably becomes so overwhelming that they cannot be blamed for "losing their heads" and forgetting that intercourse causes pregnancy.

In most Western cultures, it falls to the parents to instruct their children about sex and, more important, about acceptable sexual behavior. Health experts advise parents to avoid lecturing about sex. Instead, parents should be sensitive to their child's level of interest and be ready with information when the child asks. As children mature, so do their questions. Parents then should provide frank and explicit answers.

Parents should make their views and standards very clear to their teenage children. "In shaping the values of young people," says Michael Carrera, a health-science professor at Hunter College, "parents are more powerful than any clinic, any [sex-education] teacher, any peer."

Why is teenage pregnancy on the rise?

Much of the blame for the alarming increase in teenage pregnancies has been placed on the media and on society's general permissiveness over the past 20 years. Sexually explicit movies and songs extol promiscuity with no reference to its consequences.

The inability of teenagers (and some adults) to grasp the seriousness of having children is also to blame. Many teenagers who feel neglected or isolated see having a child as a quick way of getting attention from friends and family. Many teenage girls think that having a baby means having someone to love. They are unprepared for the long-term sacrifices involved in caring for their babies.

Teenagers who are doing poorly in school are especially at risk of getting pregnant and dropping out. Typically, these teenagers are from lower-income families; they have no goals for the future and feel that motherhood is their only option. Thus, having illegitimate children is no longer widely seen as a stigma. For many girls, having a baby has almost become an accepted rite of passage. Reports one teacher at an inner-city high school: "Back in the 1960's, babies were mistakes. Now, if you haven't had a kid by the age of 18, [they think] there's something wrong with you."

Because many teenage girls are not fully developed physically, they have higher percentages of high-risk pregnancies. Health professionals note that most teenage mothers receive little or no prenatal care and thus have more birth complications and babies with lower than normal birth weights.

What can be done to prevent these pregnancies?

Abstinence from sexual intercourse is believed by most parents and religious groups to be the only acceptable method of birth control for teenagers. However, the statistics suggest that the parental message isn't getting across. In fact, the United States has the highest rate of teenage pregnancy in the Western world.

American educators and health workers are looking at ways other countries try to control the number of teenage pregnancies. The teenage pregnancy rate in Sweden is lower than in the United States by two-thirds. By age 12, Swedish children are given a firm education in reproduction, including contraception. "The idea is to dedramatize and demystify sex so that familiarity will make the child less likely to fall prey to unwanted pregnancy and venereal disease," says Annika Strandell of Sweden's National Board of Education. Stress on both the threat of sexually transmitted diseases and the risk of pregnancy seems effective.

Theorists and Theories: **What Causes a Different Sexual Orientation?**

Views on what determines sexual orientation have changed through the ages. Ancient writings testify that homosexuality has been present since earliest times. In Athens, Greece, in the fourth century B.C. it was an accepted form of love for many. Although some religions have tolerated homosexuality, it has been vigorously condemned since biblical days by both the Jewish and the Christian faiths.

Aristotle, Greek, fourth century B.C.

This philosopher believed that homosexuality derives from an inborn tendency, which is strengthened by habit.

Voltaire, French, 1694–1778

Homosexuality is a passing experience, which comes at a time when a growing boy's appearance is least distinguishable from a girl's. "When age has made the resemblance vanish," Voltaire wrote, "the errors cease."

Carl Heinrich Ulrichs, German, 1825–1895

Attempting to analyze homosexuality scientifically, Ulrichs theorized that the body had one sex and the soul another. Homosexuals belong to a third sex, for which he coined the word *Urnings*.

Richard von Krafft-Ebing, German, 1840–1902

Homosexuality is a hereditary trait. He believed that it is a sign of physical and mental degeneration.

Henry Havelock Ellis, English, 1859–1939

Advocating free sexual expression for homosexuals as well as heterosexuals, Ellis saw homosexuality as an inborn trait and a natural form of sexual activity.

Sigmund Freud, Austrian, 1856–1939

Young people may have erotic feelings toward both sexes, but by adulthood one's sexual drive is more commonly directed toward the opposite sex. Homosexuals do not follow this pattern, Freud says, because in some cases their excessive attachment to the parent of the opposite sex makes them fearful of violating incest taboos. Freud also suggested that homosexuality could result from a child's excessive attachment to the same-sex parent, a narcissistic attachment that the child would later try to duplicate in a homosexual relationship.

Although Freud's views are somewhat ambiguous, his theories have been interpreted as implying that homosexuality is often a treatable condition.

Alfred C. Kinsey, American, 1894–1956

His pioneering surveys of large groups found that homosexual behavior was more common than believed. While 4 percent of men were completely homosexual, 37 percent had had some homosexual experience and 13 percent had had more homosexual than heterosexual experience. Among women, Kinsey found that 3 percent were exclusively homosexual but 28 percent had had some lesbian experience.

Current Theories

Today, treatment is directed toward helping people adjust to their orientation if they feel maladjusted because of it. For those who wish to change, there are behavioral therapies that may be effective. Homosexuality is no longer considered a mental disorder by the American Psychiatric Association.

Among the first sex researchers, Havelock Ellis wrote *Studies in the Psychology of Sex* between the years 1897 and 1928.

Scientists are exploring a variety of possible reasons for homosexuality. One research project has investigated the possible role of prenatal hormones in the development of sexual orientation and how a child's subsequent upbringing can affect any such orientation.

Another project discovered that some lifelong homosexual men react differently to the hormone estrogen than do heterosexual men, but no definite conclusions were drawn about a possible link with sexual orientation.

Yet another study apparently found evidence that neither psychological nor biological influences can be singled out as the sole causes of homosexuality and that the home environment has little to do with sexual orientation.

Edging Into Adulthood

When do we become emotionally mature?

Reaching age 20, give or take a year, is generally viewed as the end of growing up; and one's twenties are considered the first decade of adulthood. Although young adults are physically and mentally mature, most are still developing emotionally.

In their early adult years, most grown children are still emotionally dependent on their parents and often turn to them for help in making important decisions. At this age, too, many young adults have not yet accepted their parents as individuals and still see them mainly as authority figures. Some grown children may harbor resentment about being dependent on their parents.

By their late twenties, most people have acquired a greater perspective on their parents. They are more confident about their own judgment and less concerned about parental approval or disapproval. They finally begin to see their parents as individuals.

Is early adulthood one stage of life or several?

The years between about 20 and 40—after adolescence but before mid-life—are often termed early adulthood. However, there is some evidence that adults, like children and adolescents, may go through developmental stages that are linked to age brackets. This is a controversial view.

Many psychologists question whether a timetable of age-related changes can be widely applied. They argue that the major shaping forces of adult life are the external events that affect it. Starting a job, getting married, having children, being fired or divorced may be as influential as reaching a certain age.

Singles Living Together

Many young people today think they are being innovative when they elect to live together without a marriage contract. But living-together arrangements have been around since the beginning of time. For centuries many societies made marriage impossible for people who were too poor, were unable to divorce, or were of different faiths.

In some cultures, however, young people were allowed to live together in trial marriages. In northern Europe in the late 1700's, many poorer parents could not allow their older children time off from farming for courtship. To solve the problem, young men and women practiced "hand-fasting." Here a young couple would meet at the annual fair and mutually agree to a trial marriage. If the relationship lasted a year, then the couple was permitted to wed. On the other side of the world, Japanese farmers took hand-fasting one step further. Because offspring were needed to help in running a farm, couples could defer marriage until a baby was conceived.

Today's couples, however, seem not to be trying out marriage, so much as living together as a part of a strong dating relationship. Sociologist Rodney Stark has theorized that adolescence is so prolonged by education that living together has become another rite of passage before reaching adulthood.

In socially approved trial marriages of the past, parental consent was always required. That is not the case today. A study done by psychologist Eleanor Macklin of unmarried college students who were living together revealed that nearly half were afraid their parents would find out about the arrangement. And most, she says expressed "sorrow at not being able to discuss or share the relationship with their parents."

What puzzles researchers now is why more and more couples are choosing not to marry. Dr. Joyce Brothers suggests that perhaps these younger couples had lived with unhappily married parents and saw marriage as a joyless institution. However, living together does not allow people to avoid moral or legal duties. Recent court rulings state that couples who live together have an implied contract with their partners.

How strong is the evidence for stages in adult life?

From studies of 40 men in all walks of life, Yale psychologist Daniel Levinson concluded that men have four developmental stages between ages 17 and 40. Together with other periods later in life, he called these stages "the seasons in a man's life."

The first period, lasting roughly from age 17 to 22, covers the time when a man gains independence from his parents and develops what Levinson calls the Dream, or what the young man feels he should achieve in order to view himself as successful. Following this is a period during which he establishes himself as an adult, pursuing his Dream by starting a career, finding a mate, and often starting a family.

Around age 28, a man begins a period of reassessment. He may decide that he is not going to achieve his Dream and feel the urge to change parts of his life. This transitional phase usually ends by age 33. For many men it is extremely stressful.

The last phase of young adulthood is settling down, which usually occupies the rest of the man's thirties. Whether in family, work, or other concerns, the goals of this period, says Levinson, are "to speak more strongly with one's own voice, and to have a greater measure of authority."

Why is it so hard to pin down stages in adult life?

Researchers who challenge Levinson's work point out that the men he studied were born during the Depression years. Would the same stages be seen in men born in the optimistic years following World War II or in members of the post–baby boom generation? Answers to such questions await further studies.

Efforts have been made to find stages in the lives of adult women. But whether married or unmarried, with or without children, women today seem to lead less predictable lives than men, and it is difficult to detect any pattern in how their attitudes and expectations change with age.

The Dark Passage of Herman Melville

Desperate for freedom of spirit, the young Melville went to sea. His greatest book,* Moby Dick, *so powerfully portrayed his inner conflicts that it offended the delicate tastes of the public and critics. His creative gifts did not survive this rejection.

***This portrait** of Melville shows him at age 28.*

As a boy, Herman Melville believed that travel was his passport to a larger world. "I frequently fell into long reveries about distant voyages and travels," he once recalled.

Melville's quest for a place in the world was the more difficult because of his father's bankruptcy in 1830 and subsequent death two years later. From the age of 13, Melville's life was overshadowed by hardship and want.

Brought up by an impoverished, widowed mother, who clung to pretensions of gentility, Melville felt suffocated by his circumstances. In 1839, at 19 years of age, he signed up for a voyage to Liverpool. Melville was thrust abruptly into the coarse, brutal reality of life at sea. It was a swift, painful transition from youth to adulthood.

When Melville returned, he tried a variety of jobs but nothing suited him. In 1841, he shipped out again, this time from Fairhaven, Massachusetts, on the whaler *Acushnet.* He learned to harpoon whales, and he sailed through the treacherous waters of Cape Horn into the Pacific. But when the *Acushnet* reached the Marquesas Islands in the South Pacific, he jumped ship.

There, in a secluded valley, he found refuge among a tribe called the Typees, who were reputedly cannibals. Undaunted, Melville was determined to try life in a simple society, which he believed offered more than existence in his own complex civilization.

Later he wrote admiringly of the happiness of the Typees and, quoting the French philosopher Jean-Jacques Rousseau, he attributed it to a "buoyant sense of a healthful physical existence." Still, while Melville lived among them, he kept a wary eye on their diet. Finally, fearing for his life, he escaped on an Australian whaler. Later he transferred to the U.S. naval frigate *United States* and sailed home. His travels had lasted from the age of 21 to 25 and provided him with the substance of his novels.

In later years, he told his friend and fellow writer Nathaniel Hawthorne that his growth had not begun until his 25th year. It was at that age, with no settled profession, that Melville decided to profit from his travels by writing about them. Then, as now, accounts of exotic and faraway places like the South Seas were avidly read. Melville's books *Typee* (1846) and *Omoo* (1847) were popular successes.

Melville married in 1847 and his first child was born two years later. Other novels followed, then, faced with the responsibilities of a family, he began a new novel in 1851, drawing from his experiences on the *Acushnet.* In 18 months, Melville wrote the 900 pages of *Moby Dick,* a book which is now esteemed as a masterpiece but at the time was ignored and even reviled by some. The somber undertones of *Moby Dick* and the use of symbolism and allegory were not to the taste of Melville's reading public.

Melville was in many ways a tormented man, never at peace with himself or his God. Yet these very torments gave his writing its power and richness. It is amazing to think that he wrote eight novels in as many years and that, except for one novel published posthumously, a few short stories, and some verse, his creative life effectively came to an end at the age of 36. Battered by criticism and neglect of his works, Melville retreated into himself. He supported his family with a small legacy and with wages from working as a customs inspector on the New York City docks. He died in September 1891 at the age of 72.

***The excitements and dangers** of hunting the sperm whale inspired Melville to write his classic novel,* Moby Dick.

The Family Under Pressure

Raising Children Alone

Whatever the difficulties may be of bringing up children in a two-parent family, they are compounded in a family headed by one person. The majority of single parents are women—divorced, separated, widowed, or never married. These parents are almost always forced to go to work. In some cases, there is outside help, but money is usually in very short supply.

Apart from the financial stresses and anxieties of maintaining a household, a single parent faces the problem of obtaining reliable child care. She or he may put the children in a day-care center or find someone to stay with them at home, but it will be an added expense. When the children get sick, job priorities must be weighed against family responsibilities.

Despite the pressures on a single parent, psychologists have found some positive consequences for both parent and child. Women discover that they are able to make major decisions and carry them through alone—and gain confidence and pride in their self-sufficiency. The children show more responsibility at an earlier age. Finally, psychologists believe that a single-parent family offers a healthier environment for raising children than one that is constantly torn by family strife.

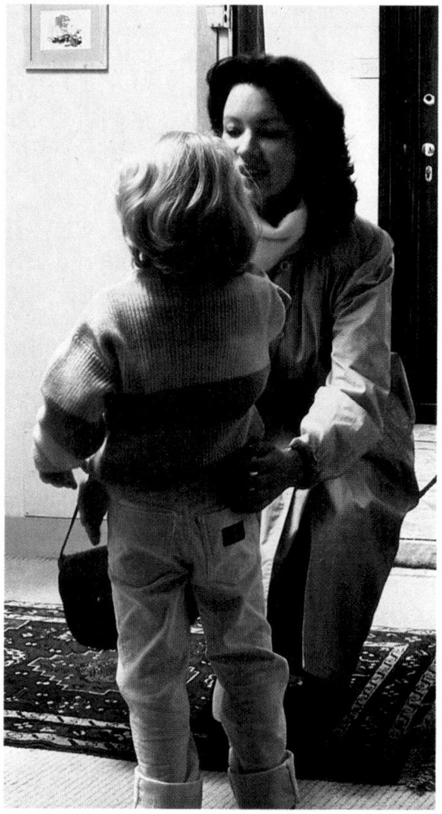

Arriving home after work and exchanging hugs are the high points of a single mother's day and a great moment for the child too.

How common is domestic violence?

Researchers believe that more violence occurs within the family than anywhere else in society. After studying 6,000 households, one sociologist concluded that 1.8 million American women each year were subjected to serious physical abuse, such as being kicked, hit, or struck with an object. This means a woman is mistreated in about 1 home in 20. Children are thought to be mishandled about as frequently as spouses. The elderly also compose an identifiable group of abuse victims. Often they are targets of the frustrations of family members who care for them.

In addition, many spouses, children, and old people, though not beaten, suffer severe emotional abuse in the form of being constantly ridiculed, belittled, and criticized. This may be almost as harmful as being physically brutalized.

What factors contribute to violence in the home?

Spouse and child abuse seems to be most common in families where the parents are very young or poor or where one or both of them have drug or alcohol problems. Family violence also tends to perpetuate itself. Abused children are four times more likely to grow up to become abusive mates and parents than people raised in homes where they were not mistreated.

The notion that domestic violence is limited to poor families is mistaken. The truth, researchers say, is that abuse in middle- and upper-income homes is less likely to be reported.

Abusers apparently feel little personal risk when venting frustrations on other family members, who are usually economically dependent on them. At the same time, these abusive individuals gain a feeling of power and control that they often lack in their work and social life.

Why has the number of divorces risen so much in recent decades?

Throughout the Western world the divorce rate generally climbed in the 1960's and 1970's, then leveled off in the 1980's. This reflects the passage of the post–World War II baby boom generation through its twenties, the decade of life when people are most likely to get divorced.

One key cause is a change in values. More people today evidently feel that commitment to staying married and raising children together is less important than personal fulfillment and happiness. Other factors contributing to the high divorce rate include the increased economic independence of women as more of them work, and the declining influence of family, ethnic, and religious ties that reinforce the commitment to marriage.

Along with these social changes, the divorce laws have been greatly modified. They make it much easier to dissolve a marriage; often mutual consent is all that is legally required.

Does a child's age affect how he or she responds to the parents' divorce?

A family breakup is stressful for a child of any age. In the case of young children, who some psychologists feel are most vulnerable to the stresses of divorce, the effects may not be immediately apparent. Years or even many decades later, the child may have to contend with feelings that originated in his or her parents' breakup.

Until recently, it was widely believed that the older the child, the less risk of psychological damage from divorce. But new studies challenge this view. The teenage years are a time of testing roles and establishing a self-identity. The disappearance of the family structure at this crucial period has been compared to the removal of a safety net when it is most needed. During a divorce and its aftermath, parents are rarely able to provide the kind of patience, understanding, and stability that an adolescent needs.

Divorce can also thrust financial and child-care responsibilities on a teenager. The youngster may be asked to get a part-time job to help out. And an adolescent may have to provide emotional support to the parent he or she lives with at the very time most other teenagers are trying to separate psychologically from their parents.

These stresses compound other teenage problems: peer pressure involving drugs and alcohol, sexual experimentation, daredevil behavior. By contrast, children who were younger when the divorce occurred have time to recover their equilibrium before reaching their teens.

Is joint custody best for young children after divorce?

Under joint custody, the youngster lives with each parent for an equal amount of time, typically spending half of a week with each. Advocates maintain that it is better for the child than the more traditional arrangement in which the mother has custody and the child spends time with the father on weekends and during the summer. With shared custody, they say, the child does not experience the emotional loss of a parent and is not so estranged from the father.

However, studies directed by California psychologist Judith Wallerstein raise some questions about the benefits of joint custody. Since a girl is "no longer part of her mother's protective orbit," she observes, joint custody may weaken mother-daughter ties, which help the youngster develop her identity. If there was bitterness and anger between parents who share custody of a child, Wallerstein found, those feelings tended to be aggravated by the frequent contact the antagonists had to have with each other. If the parents were on friendly terms, however, there were few problems of any kind.

Children on the Streets: The Terrible Plight of Runaways and Throwaways

Children have always fantasized about running away from home to solve their problems and to seek their fortunes. They usually get as far as the end of the block and turn back. But hundreds of thousands of children run away not to follow a dream but to escape from families that abuse them physically and emotionally. If life is grim for these young people at home, it is just as grim or grimmer out on the streets. Their tragedy is that there are few safe havens for them. When the streets are their only refuge, they are doomed to an existence that offers only sex for money and drugs for forgetfulness.

Runaways live in abandoned buildings, in bus depots, and under bridges. They survive by stealing, foraging in garbage, and selling their bodies.

To keep loneliness at bay, street children often band together in "families" or form close-knit partnerships.

Reappraisal at Mid-life

Do men undergo a predictable mid-life crisis?

Most people think of middle age as beginning around their 40th birthday. Some psychologists say that the transition into middle age is nearly always a period of readjustment, with men affected more than women.

Along with emotional upheaval and self-review may come such problems as marital distress, extramarital affairs, sudden career changes, impotence, and depression. Men may also develop heightened concern about their health and mortality.

Other experts question the idea that all men experience this so-called mid-life crisis. "Some men do appear to reach a state of crisis," one study found, "but others seem to thrive. More typical than either of these responses is the tendency for men to bury their heads and deny and avoid all the pressures closing in on them."

Does menopause cause psychological problems?

Menopause is the natural end of a woman's menstrual periods. It results from a gradual decline in the function

One Way to Test Your Happiness

Most of us know when we're unhappy, and we're often aware of fleeting joyous moments. But the question "How happy are you?" can be difficult to answer. Based on traits found to be common among happy, well-adjusted people, this quiz by Robert Harrington can help you assess your happiness.

Choose the response to each question closest to your own feeling or situation. (And don't attempt to pick those that seem "happiest"—they aren't necessarily what they appear.) If none of the listed choices is quite right, you may check two, but no more.

1. Given your pick of the following jobs, which would you choose?
a. A difficult, challenging assignment. If you can bring this off, you'll be promoted to an executive job. **b.** A job you can excel in because it's ideally suited to your energies and talents. **c.** A fairly modest job that involves working closely with a very powerful, important person.

2. Do you enjoy doing favors?
a. Yes. I seldom refuse when asked. **b.** Yes, when it's convenient and will really help someone. **c.** Not really. But I oblige when I feel I owe it to the person or if there's some compelling reason.

3. Which description best fits your usual sleeping pattern?
a. Sound sleeper, little trouble falling asleep. **b.** Light sleeper, easily awakened. **c.** Sound sleeper, difficulty falling asleep.

4. Are there occasions when you need to be alone?
a. Absolutely. My most peaceful, creative moments are when I am by myself. **b.** No. I love having people around. **c.** No. I don't mind being alone, but wouldn't say I have a need for it.

5. How important do you feel it is to keep your surroundings neat and orderly?
a. Very important. I can put up with sloppiness in others, but never in myself. **b.** Important. In fact, I wish I were more orderly. **c.** Fairly important. I'm rather neat and don't care much for mess or squalor. **d.** Unimportant. I'd rather be in a messy house where people are relaxed than in a tidy one where everybody's fussy and uptight.

6. Which of the following would you be *least* likely to want for a friend? The person who is . . .
a. Snobbish and pretentious. **b.** A bully, cruel to those who can not fight back. **c.** Crude, pushy, ill-mannered.

7. In the past six months, how many times did illness keep you home?
a. None. **b.** One. **c.** Two or more.

8. Something distressing has happened to a loved one—the death of someone close, perhaps. Your reaction?
a. I'd try to console him and cheer him up. **b.** I'd be as upset as he was—when he hurts, I hurt too. **c.** I'd let him know I am sorry but would continue to treat him the way I normally do.

9. How punctual are you?
a. Extremely punctual. I have an exact time sense. **b.** Quite *un*punctual. Even with an early start, I never get anywhere on time. **c.** It varies. I'm punctual for some things, late for others. **d.** Quite punctual. I usually arrive when I'm supposed to.

10. How long do you remain angry with someone who has been unfair to you?
a. For a long time. I don't easily forgive bad treatment. **b.** I wouldn't get angry. Anger is the product of a troubled mind. **c.** Not long. I get angry, but seldom hold a grudge. **d.** I don't stay angry but will usually avoid the person from then on.

11. You inherit several million dollars. How would you react?
a. I'd be delighted! **b.** I'd anticipate problems but accept the money anyway. **c.** I'd be very worried about handling such a huge sum—it would mean starting a whole new life.

12. What would you find most appealing in a marriage partner?
a. Good-looking. **b.** Rich. **c.** Intelligent. **d.** Compatible. **e.** A terrific lover. **f.** Understanding.

13. Which statement best describes your social style?
a. I tend to keep to a small circle of close friends. **b.** I'm active socially and know hundreds of people. **c.** I have a lot of friends but don't stay in touch with them. I usually associate with whoever comes to see me.

14. With which of the following would you agree?
a. Time flies, almost in a blur. **b.** Time moves slowly. **c.** Days are long, but weeks and months speed by. **d.** Days seem fast, weeks and months slow.

15. How do you feel about your present situation—personal qualities, friends, family, career, prospects for the future?
a. Wonderful! **b.** Pretty good. My situation may not be marvelous, but it's okay, and improving steadily. **c.** Fair. But I'm striving for a much better future. **d.** My feelings vary. Sometimes I feel good about myself, sometimes not.

Turn to page 322 to check and analyze your score.

of her ovaries and usually occurs during her late forties or early fifties. The most uncomfortable symptom for many women is hot flashes. These feelings of extreme warmth result from chemical shifts in the brain that cause blood vessels to dilate and constrict irregularly.

Other physical and psychological effects commonly attributed to "raging hormones" include headaches, backaches, irritability, nervousness, and depression. But only some women report having such reactions.

In popular belief, menopause is a crucial stage of development, "the change of life." But there is no evidence for this. Most women have made the transition to middle age well before the onset of menopause.

Is it difficult for parents to face an "empty nest"?

Surveys have found that the younger generation's exit is a problem for only a very small number of parents, usually ones for whom having children fills a sense of being needed. Instead of regretting that their children have left, most parents express relief, often feeling a sense of having accomplished a major task in life. Empty nesters are generally happier and more satisfied with their lives than before their children left.

Does having a grown child at home put a strain on parents?

Since the mid-1980's, census figures show that more and more children in their twenties are living with parents. Many are so-called boomerang kids, who returned home after going to college or living on their own. The reasons for the change probably include the high cost of housing, relatively lower starting salaries, and an older age for marriage.

In a society that expects a youngster to leave home as early as possible, a child may have a sense of failure for not leaving or having to return. Parents may believe that they are at fault for not having given the youngster a desire to be independent.

Paul Gauguin's Famous Mid-life Crisis

The crisis in the life of Paul Gauguin, by profession a stockbroker in Paris, came in 1883, when he was a married man of 35.

Though Gauguin was successful in his work, he had long felt the lure of painting. For some 10 years, he had attended art classes in the evenings and painted on Sundays. He was strongly attracted to the rising school of Impressionists and could afford to buy the works of painters like Degas, Cézanne, Renoir, and Pissarro.

Very gradually over the decade of the 1870's, painting grew into an obsession for Gauguin. No matter what the cost, he was determined to quit his job and devote himself to his art alone.

Totally self-centered and by nature an optimist, Gauguin was certain that he could rely on his commercial training to sell his work. Mette, his wife, thought differently. The life of an impoverished artist held no appeal. She packed up her five children, her husband's collection of paintings, and returned to her homeland, Denmark.

Despite his efforts, recognition eluded Gauguin. Undeterred, he turned his back irrevocably on his family in 1888. "In order to preserve my moral strength," he wrote to Mette, "I have gradually suppressed the tender feelings of my heart."

Gauguin, aged 43, was still cocky and self-confident.

In 1891, miserably poor, unable to sell his pictures, Gauguin sought a simpler—and cheaper—life in Tahiti. Except for one brief trip back to Paris, he lived among the Polynesians and produced his most famous paintings. Despite failing eyesight, sickness, and poverty, Paul Gauguin painted furiously to the last. He died in 1903, one month short of 55 years old.

Early on in his stay in Tahiti, Gauguin painted these two Polynesian women sitting on the beach. In 1895 he wrote, "The world I am discovering . . . is a Paradise."

Facts and Fallacies About Old Age

How fast is the over-65 population growing?

Many more people are reaching the age of 65 than ever before, thanks in part to medical advances and better nutrition. The technological improvements in central heating and air-conditioning have also helped to increase the longevity of older people, whose health is often seriously affected by extremes of temperature.

The over-65 population now accounts for more than one-tenth of the population in many Western countries, including the United States, Canada, and the United Kingdom.

Demographers used to liken the overall population to the shape of a pyramid. The bottom of it was supported by a broad base of newborns, followed by a middle-sized tier of adults. At the top, there was a thin layer of the elderly. But the number of Americans over 65 has more than doubled in the past 25 years, which has resulted in "squaring the pyramid."

What are some of the myths and realities of old age?

The aging process begins the moment we are born. As we grow older, wear and tear take their toll. With age, there is a gradual loss of lean muscle tissue and bone mass. If there is too much bone loss, the bones become brittle and are more likely to break. The hunched back that sometimes afflicts the elderly is not due to poor posture, but is the result of tiny fractures in the brittle vertebrae of the spine.

However, not all health problems of the elderly are caused by old age. Upon visiting her doctor for a pain in her shoulder, one great-grandmother was told: "Well, you know, that shoulder is 83." She snapped back: "So is the other one, but it doesn't hurt a bit." Further examination revealed a severe sprain.

Much of the aging process can be slowed by proper nutrition and physical activity. Men and women over 65 who took up a regime of exercise and weight lifting actually increased their muscle and bone mass.

Many older people are more sensitive to the effects of medication than when they were younger. With age, the liver, which is responsible for breaking down the compounds in food and drugs, works more slowly. So do the kidneys, whose job it is to clear waste out of the body. Thus symptoms such as dizziness and memory loss, which are often associated with old age, may be the result of an adverse reaction to certain foods or even to prescription drugs. Some drugs, such as the tranquilizer Valium and the arthritis painkiller Feldene, have caused a number of harmful side effects among the elderly.

Age has a way of sneaking up on us, *but for people fully engaged in life, like this mountain fiddler, it holds no terrors. In fact, winners in fiddling contests are seldom the young performers, however agile. The prizes generally go to seasoned oldsters, who have more than a few bewitching tricks in their bows.*

Do older people feel isolated and unneeded?

"In the past," says historian Ronald Blythe, "the reason why old age was venerated was that it was extraordinary. . . . [Today] to be old is to be part of a huge and commonplace problem." As the body begins to wear and slow down, old age requires the virtues of patience and contemplation. However, these virtues can seem unimportant in a society that places great value on work, speed, and instant communication.

According to David Gutmann, a professor of psychiatry at Northwestern University medical school, the long period of old age provides a natural balance to the long years of childhood. The years of childhood give a child time for needed education, while a long old age provides for experienced teachers and grandparents who can act as "emeritus parents."

Old age is a time when one can begin to take the long view and see the shape and meaning of one's life as a whole. Thus, the elderly are natural instructors. Sadly, it is a fact of life in many Western societies that the elderly often live alone or with others of their own age group, and are separated from children and grandchildren.

How can adult children best help their elderly parents?

Many adult children who find themselves with an infirm elderly parent express feelings of confusion over the new roles they must play. Whereas parents once seemed all-powerful, they are now vulnerable and need help and protection.

The adult child may have to take over the role the parents once occupied. In the process, adult children may realize how much psychological security their parents provided.

The practical problems of taking care of an ailing parent or relative can be physically, emotionally, and financially draining. These demands often seem to leave no choice but to give up one's normal social life, but psychologists advise against doing this.

Most adult children are in the prime of their careers and have children of their own when their parents and relatives begin to need care. Often adult children feel caught between the needs of their own children and the needs of their parents.

Finding room for elderly parents in an already full house is also a major problem. Moreover, support services, such as home nursing, are expensive. Thus, adult children face the prospect of placing an infirm family member in a nursing home.

As the over-65 population grows, alternatives to nursing homes are being created. Retirement villages are one answer, although they are generally affordable only by the well-to-do. They offer private apartments, dining halls for those who can't or don't wish to cook, as well as a complete health-care center. Such a specialized community provides both independence and security to an older person.

For the aging or infirm parent, leaving home is sure to be difficult. Except where a sudden illness forces the issue, elderly parents should be involved in choosing where, when, and if a move should be made.

PERSPECTIVES

On Aging

It's hard for the young to be satisfied with what they are. But in old age, when one's hand has been played, many of us find we didn't do so badly after all.

Sage Advice

"If I'd known I was going to live this long, I'd have taken better care of myself." **—Eubie Blake**

◆

How Precious Is Time

"Days were plentiful and cheap when I was young. Like penny candy. I always had a pocketful—and spent them casually. Now my supply is diminished, and their value has soared. Each one becomes worth its weight in the gold of dawn. Suddenly I live in unaccustomed thrift, cherishing hours the way lovers prize moments. Even at that, when the week is ended, it seems I've gone through another fortune. A day doesn't go as far as it used to."

—Dewey Gill

◆

Personal Landmarks

"When I was five, my mother woke me up and took me to the window on the landing. She showed me Halley's Comet streaking across the sky. She told me to remember it always, because, my mother said, it comes around only once every 76 years. And 76 years is a long time.

"Well, that's almost how old I am now—76. The years seem to have gone by as fast as Halley's Comet. But I don't think of myself as old.

"I still think of myself as the boy on the landing looking out of the window." **—Henry Fonda**

◆

Compensations

"Age loves to give good precepts to console itself for being no longer able to give bad examples."

—La Rochefoucauld

◆

A Clear, Crisp View

"I have no romantic feelings about age. Either you are interesting at any age or you are not. There is nothing particularly interesting about being old—or being young, for that matter." **—Katharine Hepburn**

Recipe for Staying Young

"1) Avoid fried meats, which angry up the blood. 2) If your stomach disputes you, lie down and pacify it with cool thoughts. 3) Keep the juices flowing by jangling around gently as you move. 4) Go very light on the vices such as carrying on in society. The social ramble ain't restful. 5) Avoid running at all times. 6) Don't look back; something may be gaining on you."

—Satchel Paige

◆

Richly Seasoned

"Alonso of Aragon was wont to say in commendation of age, that age appears to be best in four things—old wood best to burn, old wine to drink, old friends to trust, and old authors to read." **—Francis Bacon**

◆

Savoring Experience

"The compensation of growing old was simply this: that the passions remain as strong as ever, but one has gained—at last!—the power which adds the supreme flavor to existence, the power of taking hold of experience, of turning it round, slowly, in the light." **—Virginia Woolf**

◆

In the Front Lines

"A man over 90 is a great comfort to all his elderly neighbors: he is a picket-guard at the extreme outpost; and the young folks of 60 and 70 feel the enemy must get by him before he can come near their camp."

—Oliver Wendell Holmes

◆

A Birthday Toast

"Like rare French Brandy
Like a Georgian house
Like a first edition
Like a catnip mouse
Like a Chippendale chair
Like a Bach motet
The older you grow
The dearer you get."

—Anonymous

Time Travelers Among Us

From the Vantage of Old Age, A View Like No Other

One of the last human faculties to develop is an appreciation of time, for it comes only with having traveled the long road to old age. (At age 10, we speak of having once been a child and wonder what strange world 15-year-olds inhabit.) Then, somewhere late in life, we gain a broader scope. Older people can see patterns to life that younger people only theorize about. Increasingly, as their numbers grow, the elderly are better understood as repositories of family history—and indeed, as sources of information about history generally, whether war, politics, or the vast social changes of the 20th century.

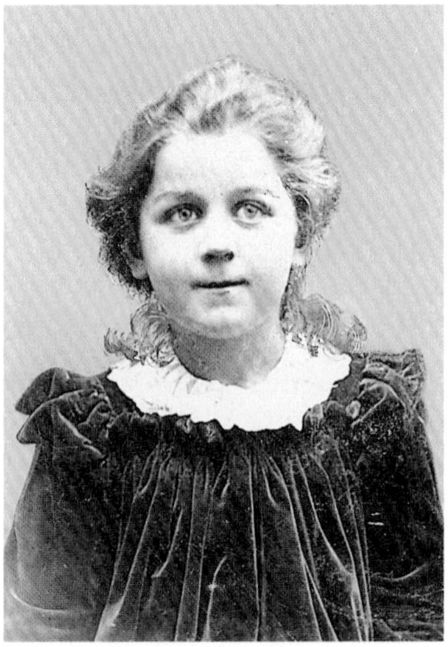

An 1899 portrait of an 8-year-old girl.

Age 20 in 1911, before the Great War.

Looking back from her high 90's (pictured here in 1988), she muses on her childhood in rural Denmark, where her veterinarian father was the first person in town to own an automobile. She compares that excitement with the first moon landing. She considers civility to be the great gift of the past, communication (telephone and TV) the special joy of today. "I always want to know: And then what."

Who are the "old old"?

With so many people living past age 65, scientists started to call those in their late seventies and eighties the "old old." Today more than 25 percent of all Americans over age 65 can expect to live on into their eighties.

In the words of one geriatrician (a doctor who studies old age), being old no longer necessarily means feeling "sick, senile, sexless, spent, or sessile [immobile]." The majority of those over 85 today are in good health and live on their own. Because modern medicine can cure many diseases that once caused early death or disability, medical experts now talk of increasing the "health span," not the life span. The goal is to "add life to your years, not years to your life."

For most of us, the life expectancy is not much beyond the biblical "three score and ten." But the prospect of all our years being healthy and fulfilling is increasing dramatically.

Do men and women react differently to old age?

Noted psychiatrist Carl Jung said that in the later years, men tend to discover their "tender feelings," and women their "sharpness of mind." Researchers have noted an interesting paradox: the greater the gender differences in youth, the more likely there will be a gender reversal in old age.

In modern society, sex roles also tend to blend with age. Older men are sometimes surprised to discover sensitive feelings in themselves, and women may be startled by their newfound sense of assertiveness. But as one indomitable 80-year-old put it: "The biggest advantage of living this long is that I don't have to give a damn what anyone thinks. I can do just what pleases me."

Are the "golden years" really golden?

Retirement usually brings reentry of a working spouse into the home. Contrary to the popular opinion that such a change increases marital strife, studies show most couples manage it well, especially when financially secure. The most communicative couples fare the best. In planning for their retired years, couples need to talk and listen to each other's goals and wishes for their future years together.

Being Old Old

After Malcolm Cowley published his essay on aging, "The View From 80," many fans wrote urging a sequel by the author when he reached 90. "I can't do that yet," replied Cowley, but he offered these insights "from the intervening vantage point of 86."

MEN OF MY AGE GROUP—or "cohort," as social observers call it—are by now more numerous than one would think. We seem to be the subject of more and more studies and reports which call us the "old old." Most of them, I note, are written by younger scholars looking from the outside. It is time for more testimony—and advice—direct from the old old horse's mouth. How does a man *feel* when he enters the second half of his ninth decade?

Sometimes he feels terrible, as had better be admitted. "After 70," a friend told me, "if you wake without any pains at all, you're dead." Infirmities accumulate, as they have a habit of doing in spite of gerontologists. Daily routines are harder to carry out and take more time. The old old man can no longer depend on his instinctive reflexes. He has to learn new methods of doing everything, as if he were starting over in early childhood. How to get into bed and out again, how to stand up, how to sit in what sort of chair, how to walk and even how to crawl, if he has to.

***Alert in mind** though tentative in movement, an old man finds his best bet is a straight-backed chair.*

Women seem able to live for years without companions, but an old man is more fragile. If he has a wife of his own age, he is lucky; having a daughter is the next best thing, but any woman in the house is better than none if she can cook and make beds.

As a matter of fact, the offer of help from any quarter should be gratefully accepted—an arm across the street, a place on a crowded bus, a served plate at a dinner eaten in the living room. No matter if it conflicts with a man's desire to be independent. Accept, accept is the rule. Let younger persons exult in their strong arms and their confident stride or in their eagerness to be helpful. An old old man has other reasons for self-esteem, including simple pride in survival.

I always make a mental survey of any room, noting the location of chairs, tables, and light switches. I keep a light burning all night in the bathroom. That is the room where most falls occur, and falls are the greatest hazards of the old old. I have found that shower stalls and bathtubs never have enough handgrips within easy reach, especially if the bather is bending over (another hazard) to wash his feet.

A friend says, "The best part of your day is over when the alarm clock rings." Getting up becomes chiefly a moral problem, but my advice is to place both feet firmly on the floor, bend forward from the hips, rise to an erect posture, and take one sideward step to keep your balance. That sideward step is useful in many situations; practice it.

For a man of uncertain balance, the big problem is pulling on his pants. It is something that can't be done in the middle of a room without danger of falling. No, the safe procedure is to stand next to a wall, or better still in the angle formed by a wall and a bureau so you can steady yourself with an elbow while standing on one foot. Be content if you don't put both of your own legs into one leg of the pants.

I avoid basement stairs, which are always perilous. For other stairs, I grasp the railing firmly, take one step up or down, then pause to survey what is ahead. I take the other steps more quickly, but I count them as I go. Remembering the number of steps is an interesting game and it can prevent stumbling in the darkness.

Deep, comfortable overstuffed chairs or sofas may become prison cells for the old old man, but he can escape from incarceration if they have at least one firm arm. Grasping the arm, he inches forward then pushes himself to his feet, always adding that sideward step to keep his balance. Solidly made hard-bottom chairs are safest.

Walking is the crowning achievement, besides being the best form of exercise. Have your feet wide apart, raise each of them in turn to avoid stumbling (don't shuffle), and move forward in a sort of duck waddle; it isn't elegant, but it is relatively secure. Avoid sudden stops and be deliberate in changing direction, always leaning on your cane. Have the cane in your hand even when you aren't using it. Pause often.

There is truly a reward for following such self-imposed rules, tedious as they may seem to be. The old old man can wake without apprehension, prepared for whatever the day might bring. He has earned for himself the privilege of surviving in this miraculous world as a free agent, not as a patient subject to regulations imposed by others. He can say to himself on going to bed, "Some of my sills have rotted, but there are no leaks in the attic."

Why Some Are Senile, Some Are Brilliant

How does the brain change with age?

By age 80, the brain will have lost, on average, 7 percent of its peak weight. As the brain ages, it loses neurons, and the speed of some types of thinking can slow down. Uncorrected hearing loss and failing vision also impair mental alertness.

However, the older brain compensates by increasing its "crystalline intelligence," or the ability to solve problems by using previously acquired knowledge and solutions. Experience proves to be the best teacher and something the aged clearly have more of than the young.

What is senility?

Senility (also known as senile dementia) is the general name for a wide variety of conditions with a variety of causes, known and unknown. In most cases, it is a slow, debilitating condition that eventually results in permanent mental impairment. Irreversible senility occurs in about 15 percent of the over-65 population. The first sign is forgetfulness, followed by a loss of judgment. One man with such symptoms went into the men's room of a restaurant to dab out a spot on his pants and emerged wearing soaking-wet trousers—which he had washed in the sink.

Typically, a senile person has problems coping with his or her environment. As the condition progresses, apathy can sometimes set in. Senility eventually may reduce the desire or the ability to wash, dress, or feed oneself. At this stage, the senile person requires constant care and monitoring. "That affects every aspect of the caregiver's life," says Elaine Brody of the Philadelphia Geriatric Center, "and there is no feedback—no cooperation, no affection."

Hardening of the arteries, or arteriosclerosis, was once blamed for almost all types of senility among the aged. Researchers have found that other diseases, such as Huntington's and Alzheimer's, which are incurable, also result in senility. Multiple small strokes are another cause of progressive mental disability. Unfortunately, researchers don't yet understand how to arrest the senility that strokes and diseases cause.

Alzheimer's disease is the leading cause of irreversible senility. It alone is responsible for more than half of the cases of senility in the over-65 population. Though its cause is not yet known, some experts suspect a genetic defect, especially when the disease strikes prematurely. In fact, the German physician Alois Alzheimer, who first discovered the disease in 1907, was looking for clues to explain dementia in people under the age of 65. During an autopsy, he found that their brain tissue was tangled and mired in the debris of atrophied cells.

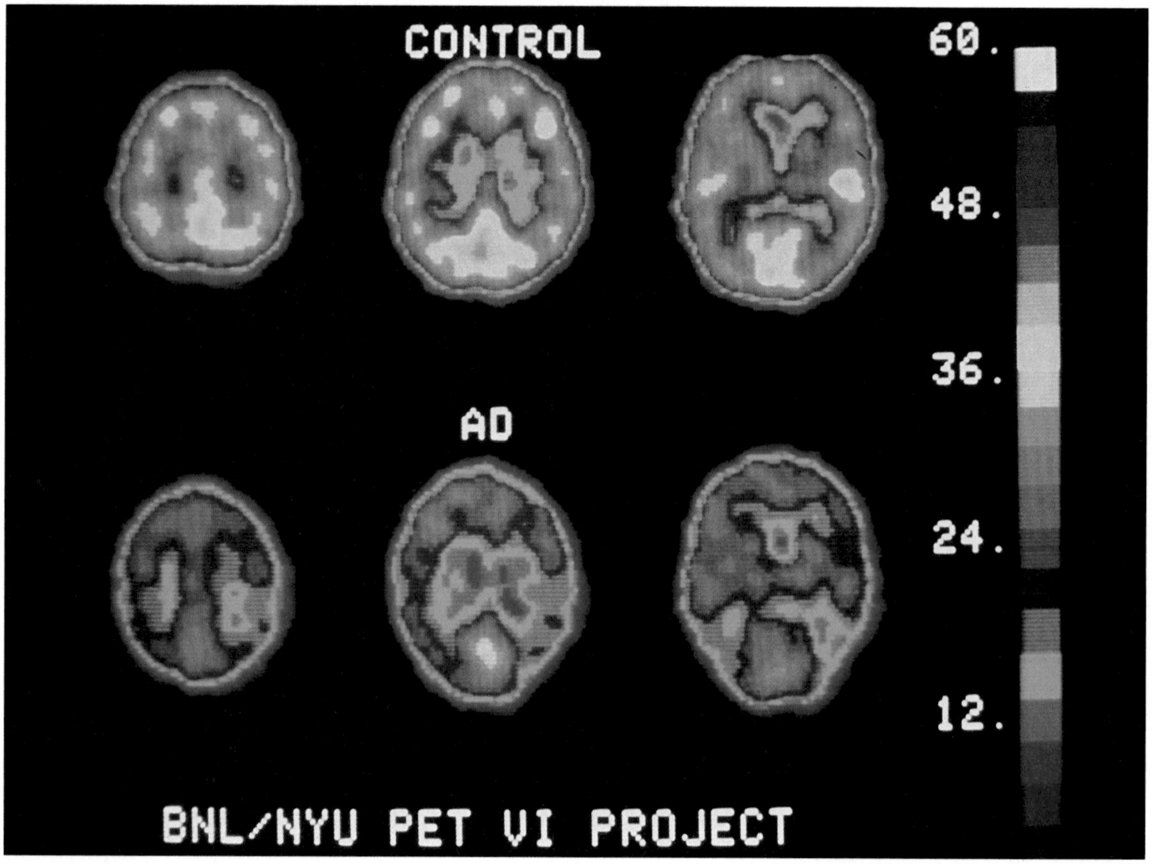

The brain needs glucose to function. *The healthy brain (top) is absorbing the normal amount of glucose, as indicated by the red and yellow; the brain of a presumed Alzheimer's patient (bottom) is unable to take in as much.*

Is senility ever reversible?

As with any other disease, diagnosis is the key to effective treatment. Occasional forgetfulness is common through all stages of life. However, many people mistakenly think that memory lapses among the old are an incontestable sign of senility.

The myth of senility has been part of Western culture for ages. Samuel Johnson wrote about it back in the 18th century: "There is a wicked inclination in most people to suppose an old man decayed in his intellects. If a young or middle-aged man . . . does not recollect where he laid his hat, it is nothing; but if the same inattention is discovered in an old man, people will . . . say, 'His memory is going.' "

Illnesses such as the flu, anemia, even appendicitis can cause forgetfulness and confusion in the elderly. If the older person is depressed over the death of a loved one, forgetfulness is even more common. Adjusting to new living quarters can also create mental disruption in old people who were used to the familiarity and comfort of their old surroundings.

The expectation of senility is harmful to an aging person's self-esteem and can cause serious medical problems to be overlooked. Before a diagnosis of irreversible senility can be made, a thorough medical examination should rule out drug toxicity, illness, and other physical problems. For every 100 older persons who have symptoms of senility, 30 have senile behavior that will largely disappear with proper medical treatment.

George Bernard Shaw described retirement *as "a working definition of hell." He himself never retired. When he died in 1950 at age 94, he was still writing cantankerous letters, pruning his trees, and working on a play, "Why She Would Not," left unfinished.*

Can intelligence improve with age?

Researchers have discovered that the mind, like the rest of the body, needs activity to stay fit. The more active the aging mind, the sharper its memory and problem-solving ability. It's never too late to learn new things.

Older people can sometimes suffer from "information overload," since the loss of neurons may affect their short-term memories. However, once new material has been learned, older people can do as well as their younger colleagues at remembering it. The best way for the aged to acquire new information is for them to activate their long-term memories. To do that, they must be allowed to discover the new material at their own pace. The less outside interference, the better. Says one retiree who started his own company at the age of 65: "God has given us certain talents. And he gave them to us to use."

Old age can be a time of great intellectual growth and achievement. A number of well-known artists and business professionals have done their best work after the age of 60. When Vladimir Horowitz's performances began to displease him, the brilliant pianist retired at the age of 78 to work on his technique. At the age of 81, he made a triumphant return to the concert stage. Famed artist Georgia O'Keeffe took up pottery in her late eighties when her eyesight became too weak for painting. At age 80, the Spanish painter Goya drew a picture of a very old man with the inscription: "I am still learning."

Talking With Your Doctor

How can you get the best possible care from your doctor?

Whenever you consult a doctor, don't be afraid to ask questions. One study found that patients who came to a doctor's office with three prepared questions were more satisfied after their visits than people who came unprepared. Studies also show that patients who ask questions tend to respond better to treatment.

You should definitely ask for an explanation of any scientific terms that you don't understand. If the doctor recommends tests, be sure that you understand their nature and purpose. Some diagnostic procedures are potentially damaging; even X-rays carry a risk. Ask what the doctor hopes to learn from such exams and whether they are really necessary to determine the kind of care you should get.

If a doctor proposes hospitalization for surgery, ask if alternatives are available. Some operations can be done safely on an outpatient basis, and some can be avoided entirely by changes in diet, exercise, medication, or other home measures.

A Patient's Guide to Intelligent Pill-Taking

When illness strikes, if you are an active participant in your own care or that of a relative, the therapy is likely to be much more effective. You can monitor the course of the treatment—in this case the taking of pills—and also dispel to some extent the feelings of helplessness that often accompany illness.

- **Report any allergic reactions** to medicine that you have had in the past. Tell your physician about this before he or she prescribes a drug.
- **If taking other medicine,** tell your physician about it, so that interactions between the different medicines can be considered.
- **Learn the name** of the drug prescribed and why you are supposed to take it.
- **Exactly how and when** should you take the medicine? Its effect can depend on what you eat and drink with it and whether it is taken before, during, or after meals.
- **Follow the instructions** on your medicine exactly. If the prescription says four times a day, ask the doctor what hours would be best, or at least what the *intervals* should be.
- **Ask about adverse reactions** that are possible with the prescribed medicine, and what you should do if you experience any of them.
- **Should you abstain from alcohol** while you are taking the medicine?
- **Will the medicine make you drowsy?** Is it safe for you to drive while using it?
- **Try to use the same pharmacist** for all your prescription medication needs. That way he or she will be able to call to your and your physician's attention any harmful drug interaction.
- **If you have trouble** opening those child-resistant caps, ask your pharmacist to place your medicine in an easy-to-open container.
- **How should you store your medicine?** Ask your pharmacist. See if it requires refrigeration or needs to be kept out of the sunlight.
- **Store all medicine** out of your children's reach.
- **Never pretend to a child** that medicines are candy.
- **Dispose of medications** that are past their expiration date. They will no longer be fully effective and could be dangerous to use.
- **Get rid of old medicines** by flushing them down the toilet. Do not place them in the garbage can.
- **If you might be pregnant,** don't take any medicine without first checking with your physician.
- **Don't treat yourself** with anyone else's medicine.
- **Do not stop taking medicine** prematurely. If you feel there is a reason to stop taking the medication before you're supposed to, consult with your physician first.
- **When traveling,** keep prescriptions in their original containers and in your carry-on luggage. Also, take medications on "home" time until you adjust.

Once you understand and agree to follow your doctor's advice, be sure to remember it all. Take notes or ask for written instructions. If you are in a state of considerable anxiety or discomfort, consider bringing someone close to you to the doctor's office. Your companion can act as your advocate and present the questions that should be asked.

How involved should you be in your medical care?

You can and should take part in decisions about your treatment. The first step is to be well informed about your condition: this not only lets you feel in control, it may help you to get well.

You can say no to what your doctor recommends or seek the opinion of another doctor. (Insurance policies now require second opinions in some cases.) If a physician's attitude, availability, fees, or reputation turns out to be unsatisfactory, it is probably best to pay any bill you agreed upon (provided it is not unreasonable) and look for another doctor who will suit your needs better. Sometimes, a person must make a choice between staying near home, where acceptable care is offered, and traveling to another place where better care is available. For example, a highly recommended surgeon for the type of operation you need may practice in a distant city.

You also have responsibilities. Give the doctor full and accurate information: when symptoms began; whether you had a rash or fever; what pills and medications (both prescribed and over-the-counter) you take; diets and allergies. Don't hide facts about yourself or your family that might affect how you respond to treatment: alcohol and drug use, mental illnesses, serious emotional disorders.

Once your treatment has started, report any side effects. Don't decide to stop the treatment without consulting your doctor.

Surveys show that most patients want more information than their doctors volunteer. They don't wish to take over decision-making from their doctor but do want to understand what's going on.

The Changing Role of the Doctor in Family Health Care

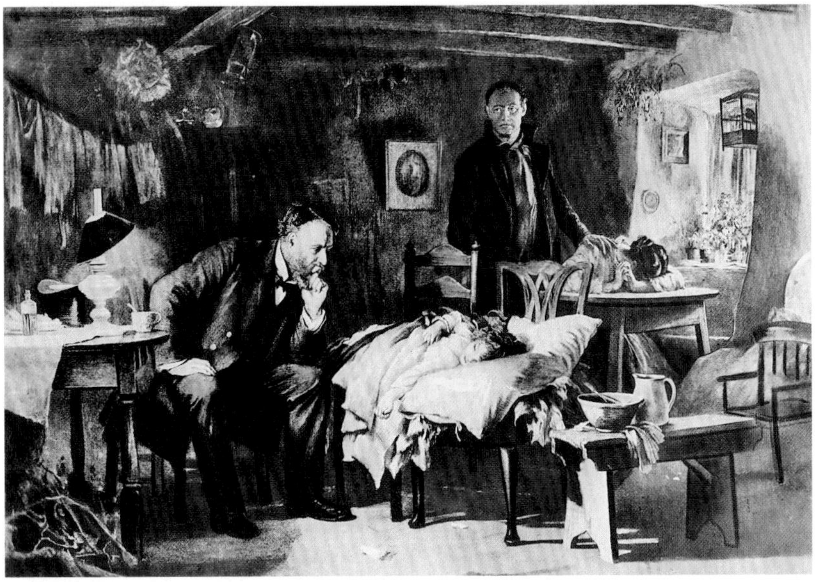

"The Doctor" accurately portrayed the concern of the physician at the desperate condition of a little girl. Whatever happened, he was there in this dark hour.

Nostalgia for the good old family doctor will not bring back this cherished paragon. Today, no single doctor could possibly keep up with all the technological advances in all fields of medicine. Hence, specialists are here to stay.

Whereas the old family doctor could carry in his bag most of the medicines available at the time, today's doctors have literally thousands of pharmacological options, to say nothing of such highly advanced diagnostic equipment as CAT scans and angiograms, which the old family doctor wouldn't recognize.

Moreover, the diseases that old family doctors treated have also changed. Diphtheria, smallpox, scarlet fever, whooping cough, and the like, which once accounted for about 90 percent of a doctor's practice, have been all but wiped out. Doctors today generally deal with the chronic diseases of arthritis, diabetes, and high blood pressure.

Why is it sometimes so difficult to communicate with doctors?

Communication is always a two-way street. The patient and physician share the blame if they fail to understand each other. Effective communication requires listening attentively as well as speaking clearly.

Doctors, for their part, are not necessarily good communicators. Although some medical schools have introduced courses in doctor-patient relationships, medical training does not automatically impart the ability to explain technical subjects clearly or to understand patients' emotions.

Nor are doctors free of irrational feelings. Surveys have found that certain patients arouse particular dislike. They include hypochondriacs, patients who question the doctor's authority, and those who seem to have caused their own problems.

Perhaps most troubling to doctors are the people who need the most sensitive understanding: incurable patients. Cancer survivor Alice Stewart Trillin comments, "Patients often say that their doctors seem angry with them when they don't respond to treatment. I think this is more than the result of overdeveloped medical egos. It is necessary for doctors to become a bit angry with patients who are dying, if only as a way of separating themselves from someone in whom they have invested a good bit of time and caring." However, as one doctor points out, "Patients ought not to have to treat their doctors—at least that should not be among the patient's primary concerns."

How can patients be better communicators?

It is difficult for most people to accept that being sick makes them different from their normal selves. Their perceptions and emotions may be temporarily out of kilter. When you are ill, you tend to be frightened, in pain, angry at having to be at the mercy of other people, and uncomfortable with the invasion of your privacy by medical technology. Like the narrator of a story by surgeon Richard Selzer, you may resent "miscreant doctors who warm their arrogant fingers in the orifices of their unwary patients."

Furthermore, you may have had almost no experience with being sick until you are struck by a major illness. As Dr. Lewis Thomas writes, "Most of us can ride almost all the way through life with no experience of real peril, and when it does come, it seems an outrage, a piece of unfairness."

With all these emotions at work, it may take a Herculean effort for a patient to discuss his or her condition rationally and objectively. That is why it makes sense for a seriously ill person to ask a trusted relative or friend to deal with doctors and nurses.

What about the search for new cures?

Too frequently tales of medical miracles lead people on expensive and ultimately disappointing quests for a cure that sounds too good to be true—and is. Beware of remedies that promise instant health, that cost huge sums, or that cannot be used without giving up standard medical treatment. For instance, leaving a major cancer center in desperate pursuit of a "cure" outlawed in the United States is a prescription for tragedy. At the end of your travels you will more likely find a quack than a cure.

The Role of Emotions

What makes a person a hypochondriac?

The unflattering stereotype of a hypochondriac—a faker or crybaby who pretends to be ill or in pain to get sympathy—arouses a mixture of amusement and scorn in many people. Hypochondria is viewed seriously, however, by medical organizations like the American Psychiatric Association, which lists it as a somatoform disorder, meaning a mental condition that has bodily (somato-) symptoms. Doctors realize, moreover, that it is entirely possible for a chronic complainer to have a serious disease.

There is some evidence that hypochondriacs are abnormally sensitive to bodily sensations such as hunger, cold, and minor aches and pains. Hypochondria is also the subject of several psychological theories, one of which proposes that people whose childhood illnesses brought them gratifying attention later become morbidly preoccupied with illness. And simply reading about disease can cause mild hypochondria, as medical students soon learn.

Hypochondriacs frustrate doctors, who expect their patients to want to get well. Yet hypochondriacs resent a doctor's telling them they are not sick. The ideal doctor for a hypochondriac is probably one who neither dismisses the patient's complaints nor gives in to irrational demands to do unnecessary tests.

One Harvard psychiatrist has had some success in teaching groups of hypochondriacs to live with discomfort. Breathing and meditation exercises help these patients to focus on bodily processes without thinking of them as alarming symptoms.

Does being ill change your personality?

Some sick people, finding themselves in a state of helpless dependency, become childishly self-involved. For others, the loneliness of being ill is the worst problem; such patients may welcome the sustaining fellowship in a hospital ward. A few crave solitude like Charles Lamb, who wrote: "How sickness enlarges the dimensions of a man's self to himself! He is his own sympathizer, and instinctively feels that none can so well perform that office for him. He cares for few spectators to his tragedy."

If you are sick, it is a good idea to try to delay important decisions until you are better. Studies show that illness impairs reasoning ability.

Writer Morton Hunt comments: "If I become ill again, I mean to postpone any major decisions. If for some reason I'm moved to change my will, for example, I shall not do it during my next bout with the flu."

How do doctors react to being patients?

The doctor most likely to treat patients with understanding is one who has been ill himself. Dr. Lewis Thomas writes: "I wish there were some easier way to come by this level of comprehension for medical students and interns, maybe electronic models like the simulated crash landings used for pilot training. Every young doctor should know what it is like to have things go catastrophically wrong, and to be personally mortal. It makes for a better practice."

An Effort to Make Hospitals More User-Friendly

The American Hospital Association (AHA) endorses a "patient's bill of rights," summarized below, intended to assure patients that they will be treated with care and respect. The AHA asks hospitals to post the list prominently and to give a copy to every patient. However, a hospital can decide what is proper treatment, and is not legally bound to observe these rights. Moreover, a private hospital may send nonemergency patients who cannot afford treatment to a public institution.

The hospital shall give patients the right to:

1. Receive emergency medical care when needed.

2. Be treated in a considerate and respectful manner.

3. Obtain the name of the physician overseeing their care and be able to consult with any private physician or specialist affiliated with the hospital.

4. Know the name and duties of any person providing them with care.

5. Have any diagnosis, treatment, and likely outcome explained in easy-to-understand terms.

6. Receive a full explanation of a recommended nonemergency treatment—including its risks and alternatives—before consenting to it.

7. Refuse treatment and be told what to expect as a result.

8. Have privacy and expect physicians and hospital staff to be discreet when discussing their case.

9. Have all records kept confidential except when a law or an insurance payment requires disclosing them.

10. Request and receive any normal hospital service.

11. Be told, on leaving the hospital, about any continuing care needed—or be told why moving to another hospital or care facility would be better and what the alternatives to it are.

12. Request the names of other institutions that are involved in their treatment, such as clinics, laboratories, and medical schools.

13. Refuse to take part in research and not be given experimental treatment without having it fully explained and consenting to it.

14. Examine the charges and receive an explanation of them, even if the bill is being paid by an insurance company or a social services agency.

15. Know what hospital rules and regulations apply to them.

16. Not be discriminated against because of race, color, religion, sex, national origin, or source of payment.

17. Have surroundings free of tobacco smoke both in their rooms and in halls and other common areas.

18. Criticize hospital policies and services and suggest changes in them to hospital administrators or the department of health without fear of being mistreated as a result.

The Road From Sickness to Health

Dr. Oliver Sacks is a clinical neurologist and the author of the book* A Leg to Stand On. *In it he recounts his experiences after a serious injury to his left leg and takes the reader step-by-step through the process of his recovery, both physical and spiritual.

"One moment I was running like a madman," wrote Oliver Sacks, "the next, I was lying at the bottom of a short, sharp cliff, with my left leg twisted grotesquely beneath me." As a result of this accident, which took place on a Norwegian mountain, he tore his thigh muscles. In great pain, Sacks was flown to London and operated on within 48 hours.

For 18 days, he lay on his back in a small, windowless room, his leg encased, as he described it, in a "cylinder of chalk." He endured intense pain and terrifying fantasies, in which he knew for sure that "the leg had vanished. I could no longer remember having a leg. I could no longer remember how I had ever walked or climbed."

When the time came to take his first steps, Sacks faced the moment with great uncertainty. "How could I stand, without a leg to stand on? How could I walk, when I lacked legs to walk with? How could I act, when the instrument of action had been reduced to an inert, immobile, lifeless, white thing? So I stood, or was stood, supported not by my legs, but by crutches and physiotherapists, in a strange, and rather terrifying, stillness—[which] occurs when something momentous is about to happen. And suddenly—into the silence, the silent twittering of motionless frozen images—came music, Mendelssohn, *fortissimo*. And, as suddenly, without thinking, without intending whatever, I found myself walking, easily—joyfully, *with* the music. And, as suddenly, in the moment that this inner music started—in this self-same moment the *leg came back*.

"Now, suddenly, I was whole, I was well. At least I could feel what wholeness, wellness, felt like, where they had been unimaginable—beyond thought, beyond hope—before. I found I felt completely different: no longer prostrate, passive-dependent, like a patient, but active, erect, able to face a new world—a real world, *a world now made possible*, instead of the shifting half-world of patienthood and confinement.

"The return of health and strength—convalescence—was intoxicating and I continually misjudged what I could or should do. When I stole a look at my chart and saw 'Uneventful Recovery,' I thought: 'They're mad. Recovery *is* events, or rather advents—the advent of new and unimaginable powers—events, advents, which are births or rebirths.'

"Now I was free—morally free, as well as physically free—to make the long trek, the return, which still lay before me. Now the moral obscurity and darkness was lifted, as well as the physical darkness, the shadow. I was flying with joy—joy which was to last, and deepen, for six weeks, which transformed, and transfigured the world, and made of everything a new wonder and festivity."

Within a week, Sacks was moved from the hospital to a convalescent home. "The gap, the abyss, between sickness and health—this was what the Convalescent Home was for—we had become invalids, in-valid. We had resided in sickness too long. And we had not only harbored it, but become sick ourselves—developed the attitudes of inmates and invalids. Now we needed a double recovery—a physical recovery, and a spiritual movement *to* health."

***Sacks is a best-selling** author and a specialist in neurological disorders.*

At the Home, Sacks met a fellow patient, "a little grizzled man, a diabetic, who had just had an amputation and was much plagued, he confessed, by vivid phantoms. 'What about you? What happened?' he asked, with a glance at the cast. I told him. 'Isn't that the darnedest thing!' He turned to the others. 'Doc here's got a leg, but no feeling in the leg—and I've got the feeling, but no leg to go with it. You know—we could make one good leg between us. I'll donate the feeling and you give the leg.'

"Communication in the Home was instant and profound. There was a transparency, a dissolution of the usual barriers between us. This sharing of normally hidden and private feelings—feelings, indeed, often hidden from oneself—and the depths of concern and companionship evoked, the giving and sharing of priceless humor and courage—this seemed to be remarkable in the extreme, unlike anything I had ever known and beyond anything I had imagined."

Six weeks later, Sacks was discharged from the Home. "My adventure," he wrote, "was ending. But I knew that something momentous had happened, which would leave its mark, and alter me, decisively, from now on. A whole life, a whole universe, had been compressed into these weeks: a density of experience neither given to, nor desired by, most men; but one which, having happened, would refashion and direct me."

A Patient's View of Hospitals

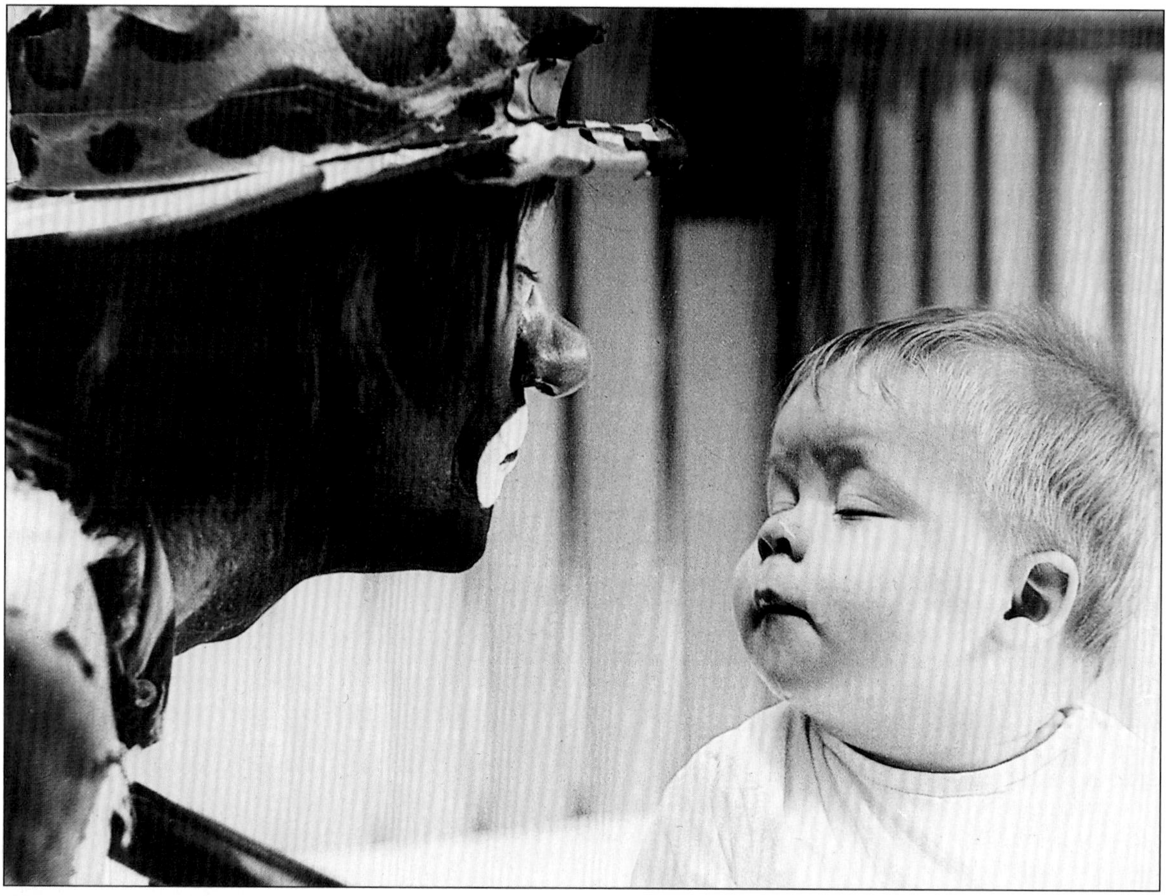

If humor really is the best medicine, *no one was better qualified to dispense it than famous circus clown Emmett Kelly, Jr., shown here visiting the crib of a little patient in Woonsocket Hospital, Rhode Island.*

How can you keep control of your life in a hospital?

As one writer has observed, when you enter a hospital, you feel like the guest of a giant in a fairy tale. You are not sure whether you are invited to dinner, or whether you *are* the dinner. Studying the patient's bill of rights, provided to hospital patients in the United States, can help relieve some of your anxieties.

When possible, bring a spokesperson to the hospital—a family member or close friend who can run interference with the hospital staff. If you have no spokesperson, see if your hospital has an ombudsman to look out for patients' needs, or find an understanding nurse or social worker. Your doctor, too, may be permitted to mediate among the specialists who sometimes make you feel more like a laboratory specimen than a person.

Questions can and should be asked of anyone charged with your care, especially when drugs or tests are involved. Overworked staff members can make mistakes, and overmedication can be a problem. But don't hesitate to ask for pain relief when you need it. Hospitals may be reluctant to dispense painkilling drugs for fear that patients will suffer ill effects or become addicted.

What small things can make a hospital stay more comfortable?

Even when the care is excellent, being in a hospital is no vacation. One medical administrator kept a diary of the people who came into her room during a brief hospital stay. Counting nurses, technicians, and orderlies, she logged as many as 75 visitors a day. Hospital noise, rigid schedules, and unappetizing food also make for a less than pleasant experience.

Music can be helpful. A radio with headphones lets the patient listen to music without bothering other patients. In one study, soothing music actually enabled people to use less medication for postoperative pain.

Is a positive, happy attitude really good medicine?

Many people believe that a happy mental outlook can directly defeat physical disease. In *Anatomy of an Illness as Perceived by the Patient,* writer Norman Cousins described his battle with a severe joint ailment called ankylosing spondylitis. Told that his doctors could do no more for him, he checked out of the hospital and spent weeks watching Marx brothers movies and other comedies. Cousins believes that laughter and the positive feelings it aroused in him were vital factors in his recovery.

Centuries earlier, wise observers of the human condition noted a connection between laughter and health. The Book of Proverbs tells us that "a merry heart doeth good like a medicine."

One researcher reports that the sense of well-being and alertness imparted by laughing 100 times a day is equivalent to that derived from 10 minutes of rowing.

Some doctors remain skeptical. But others agree that laughter eases pain and may help the respiratory system by exercising the lungs. There is also evidence that laughter and other positive emotions can influence the immune system, perhaps by stimulating production of certain hormones. Recognizing the value of humor, some hospitals encourage visits from clowns or provide "laughter rooms," where comic films are shown.

There is a danger, however, in putting so much faith in positive thinking that you blame yourself—or some other person—for not trying hard enough to get well. Marcia Angell, M.D., has written in the *New England Journal of Medicine:* "In our desire to pay tribute to gallantry and grace in the face of hardship, we sometimes credit these qualities with cures, not realizing that we may also be implying blame when there are reverses. At a time when patients are already burdened by disease, they should not be further burdened by having to accept responsibility for the outcome."

What's the best way to help a child who must be hospitalized?

Young children are naturally frightened of being separated from their families, as well as by hospital procedures. Parents are often allowed to stay in the hospital and, of course, can bring their child's favorite toys.

Lying to children about their illness is almost never a good idea. Learning the truth will make them feel betrayed. Children can usually understand what is happening to them if it is sensitively explained. They may even be less fearful if they have a chance to rehearse their experiences by playing doctor—bandaging a doll, for example, or giving it "medicine."

Parents, too, need reassurance. They may be plagued by guilt when a child becomes ill, fearing that the child's sickness must somehow be their fault. Such guilt is almost always baseless and can divert attention from the person who needs their full support: the child.

Who should decide when it is time to leave the hospital?

As a patient, you have a right to decide when to go home, but be sure to discuss the medical consequences with your doctor. Hospital stays are generally becoming shorter, partly to cut costs and partly to minimize the effects of bed rest, which can be physically and mentally debilitating.

Shorter hospital stays, however, may mean that you will need help after being discharged. You or your spokesperson should start to plan for your convalescence early in your hospital stay. A social worker or, in some hospitals, a discharge specialist can help arrange for nursing or rehabilitation aid. Especially if you live alone, a temporary stay in a convalescent or nursing home may be advised.

Do people who push themselves get better faster?

Mental attitude obviously plays a part in how different people progress when convalescing from a serious illness, but trying to rush one's recovery can be deadly. One man recovering from a heart attack may start doing push-ups in the hospital, while another hesitates (and rightly so) to get out of bed. Ask your doctor for specific recommendations on when to resume your usual activities.

Remember that after a long illness, you are likely to feel disoriented as well as weak. It is no time for Spartan heroics. A convalescent could do worse than to heed the old-fashioned advice given to a character in Samuel Butler's novel *The Way of All Flesh.* Return to ordinary living gradually, Butler's doctor advised, starting with a visit to the zoo: "I prescribe a course of the larger mammals."

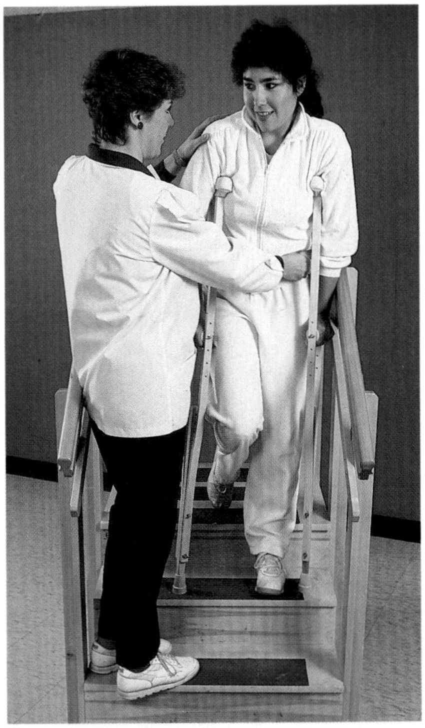

A therapist helps *a patient regain the muscle control needed to climb stairs.*

Physical therapy for children *can be presented as play. This child, diving into a sea of colored balls, is gaining valuable practice in coordination.*

Decisions at the End

How has modern medical technology affected our understanding of death?

Death was once a relatively simple event. It occurred when the heartbeat and breathing ceased. Now some people whose hearts and lungs no longer work can be revived and then maintained for days or even years on mechanical respirators. Failed hearts can be replaced by transplanted ones.

Many people who have been brought back from "death" by methods such as cardiopulmonary resuscitation tell of dramatic and inspiring out-of-body experiences. Religious believers regard such reports as proof of an afterlife, but skeptics say they are simply hallucinations.

The new medical technology forces a reexamination of traditional definitions of life and death. Scientists now know that the brain, not the heart or some other organ, is the essential regulator of body functions. The heart is simply a wonderful pump. Thus there is growing support for defining death as brain death, that is, the cessation of function of the whole brain. A brain-dead person is unconscious, has no reflexes, and cannot breathe or maintain a heartbeat spontaneously. The electroencephalogram (EEG) of such a person would be generally flat, without the regular oscillations that indicate brain function.

Brain death would occur naturally within a few minutes after the heart stopped, since none of the oxygen essential to life would be carried to the brain tissues by circulating blood. But because resuscitation techniques can mimic circulation, some nations and many U.S. states have passed laws recognizing either brain death or heart and lung failure as a criterion for declaring a person dead.

Some scientists and philosophers go further. They believe that death occurs when the neocortex—the part of the brain responsible for consciousness, which they regard as the essential feature of an individual human life—no longer functions. By this definition, a patient like Karen Ann Quinlan, whose breathing and heartbeat continued for years while she was in what is usually called a "persistent vegetative state," would be considered dead.

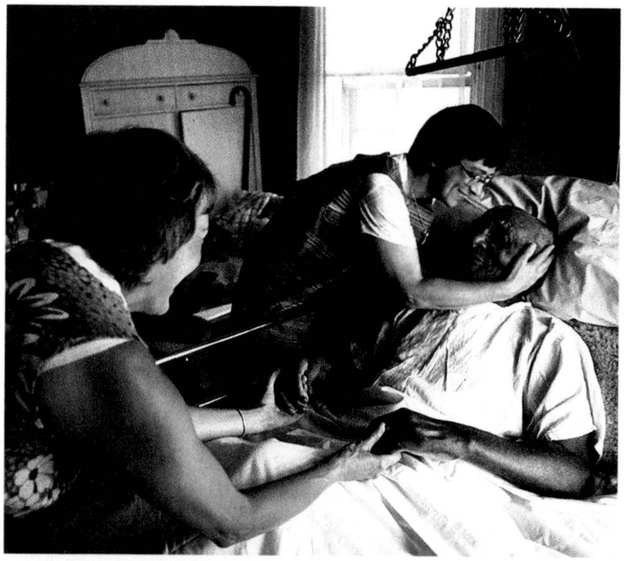

***A nurse comforts** a patient (left) in the homelike surroundings of a hospice, while another visitor holds the man's hands in a tight grip. Expressions of emotional support are encouraged by the hospice movement in caring for the terminally ill. Medication is given at regular intervals rather than at the onset of pain. An emphasis on personal attention (below) effectively shores up patients' morale.*

Why is it important to have a definition of death?

It has almost always been important to be able to pinpoint the time of death in criminal cases, and the time of death can also be significant in matters of inheritance. But in recent years, many new ethical issues have arisen centering on exactly when death occurs. Now that successful transplants of hearts and livers (as well as of kidneys, corneas, and other body parts) are becoming common, there is a new urgency to determining when a potential organ donor is dead. Then, too, it has become medically possible to keep many moribund patients alive indefinitely. The financial and emotional costs of so doing can be astronomically high.

The needs and wishes of the dying patient remain paramount, however. A consensus is growing that critically ill or injured people have the right to demand or reject the use of so-called heroic measures involving machines that keep vital body organs function-

The Iron-Willed Compassion of Dame Cecily Saunders

ONE OF THE MOST SENSITIVE and emotional of all ethical issues today concerns the ability of modern medicine to prolong the life of a terminally ill patient. The modern hospice movement was designed to offer such patients an alternative. Hospices stress humane care and, above all, the dignity of the dying.

St. Christopher's, which opened in London in 1967, was the first institution of the movement. It owes its founding to the vision and determination of Dame Cecily Saunders, a social worker who became a doctor. "What I did," she says, "was to allow patients to speak for themselves, to suggest what we ought to do to give them safe conduct."

The philosophy of the hospice movement holds that someone has the right to die when the time comes without the intervention of

Dame Cecily Saunders

high-technology medicine. The movement does not believe in prolonging life but neither does it believe in hastening death. It does not favor euthanasia. Dame Cecily Saunders has said, "I believe that to make voluntary euthanasia . . . lawful would be an irresponsible act . . . abrogating our true respect and responsibility to the frail, the old and the dying."

Since 1967 hospices have spread around the world. In the United States they now number almost 1,700. They must be certified just like hospitals and are always under the direction of doctors. Many patients stay at home, where they can be cared for by the family in comfortable, less intrusive surroundings under the supervision of doctors and nurses. The emphasis is on medical teamwork. Each patient's case is reviewed at least once a week by everyone concerned.

People sometimes ask Dame Cecily, "How can you work at St. Christopher's? It must be so depressing." She answers by saying that, of course, there are moments of distress and tension, but "amongst all this there is also joy and fulfillment."

ing. By the same token, it is increasingly seen as a right of patients to say whether or not their organs should be made available for transplantation after their deaths.

How can you be sure that your wishes about terminal care will be followed?

Hospitals often fear that family members will hold them liable for letting patients die who might possibly have survived if all available life-saving techniques had been used. Thus, unless they have specific written instructions to the contrary, hospital staffs usually must maintain life by every means at their disposal, including the use of machines that do the work of the heart and lungs.

If you do not wish heroic measures to be used to revive you when you are dying if it would be a matter of prolonging the dying process, you can sign what is termed a *living will.* This is easy enough to arrange, but it means making an advance decision on the question of how you want (or don't want) to die.

Many states recognize living wills. Even where there is no specific law endorsing such documents, doctors will generally respect the patient's advance directives when making decisions about terminal care.

There are standard forms for making a living will; or specific wishes can be drawn up in consultation with a doctor and legal adviser. Copies should be given to one's doctor, lawyer, and next of kin, and the will should be periodically reviewed, resigned, and redated to make clear that there has been no change of mind. If you do change your mind, you can revoke the living will at any time.

Your living will can be used, too, to express your wishes about donating your organs after you die. In some states, you can provide for the donation of any or all organs by signing a statement on your driver's license.

Do hospitals have unlimited authority in treating mentally incompetent people?

One way to make sure that somebody speaks for your best interests in the hospital when you cannot is to execute a durable power of attorney for health care. In it you designate and authorize a person to make medical decisions on your behalf if you should become mentally incompetent; an ordinary power of attorney becomes invalid in these circumstances.

It is up to you to make sure that the person you designate as your "attorney" fully understands what you want done—or not done—in the event that you are unconscious, slip into a coma, or in some other way lose possession of your mental powers. Taking the person entirely into your confidence before a crisis arises can give you control over your own care and may provide guidance for your loved ones at a time when they are under great emotional stress.

New Information About Death

***A medieval painting by Hieronymus Bosch** depicts a common element in near-death experiences: the perception of a tunnel with brilliant light at its end.*

Should people be told when they have a terminal illness?

Surveys show that the vast majority of people would want to be told if they were terminally ill. The people surveyed included both those who were ill and those in good health.

There are practical reasons for honesty. Patients need to put their affairs in order, provide for their families, and make informed decisions about their treatment. Psychologically, too, when patients feel desperately ill and suspect that they will not recover, they, their families, and hospital staff members all suffer from the strain of pretending that nothing is wrong.

This does not mean removing all hope. Many once incurable diseases are now curable, and even when a disease has no known cure, no one can predict when a medical breakthrough will come. Nor can anyone unerringly predict how a particular patient will respond to treatment.

How do most people react emotionally to terminal illness?

It takes time to adjust to losing a loved one; but a dying person must adjust not only to a single loss but to the idea of losing everybody and everything that has brought happiness, comfort, and pleasure in life. In her book *On Death and Dying,* Elisabeth Kübler-Ross originally divided this adjustment to one's own imminent death into five stages: denial of approaching death; anger at fate, God ("Why me?"), and doctors, or other bearers of bad tidings; bargaining ("If I can just live until my son graduates . . . "); depression as the inevitability of loss sinks in; and finally acceptance. Recognition of these stages, based on interviews with many dying patients, has deeply affected our understanding and care of the terminally ill.

But individual reactions vary. Not everyone experiences each stage or goes through them all in a prescribed order. For example, some people seem to give up almost immediately; others never reach acceptance; still others shift back and forth between denial and depression. And many severely ill people lack the strength for a whole repertoire of emotions.

Can you predict how a person will handle approaching death?

Individuals tend to react to terminal illness much as they did to earlier life crises. Just as everyone's life has both highs and lows, a terminally ill person will have up days and down days. One doctor compares dying to swimming "in the hollows of the waves."

Some people face death with particular grace. Senator Hubert Humphrey showed characteristic candor, speaking openly about his fatal cancer, cheering up fellow patients, and even joking with the press. One day, as his death neared, he was asked what he had talked about in a meeting with President Jimmy Carter. Humphrey quipped that he had promised not to run against him in 1980.

Not everyone can be so buoyant. But many people are sustained by a strong religious faith. Others become acutely aware of small pleasures and welcome every minute of life, every human encounter, as a gift. Literary agent Betty Marks, stricken by diabetes and cancer, told health writer Jane Brody: "There's been a reward to my illness—discovering how much people care for me. What has moved me to tears has not been my disease, but each time I talked to a friend and one of us said, 'I love you.' "

How do you talk to a terminally ill person?

It is never easy to be around someone who is close to death. Experience with severe illness may be helpful, but experts say there is no formula for giving comfort.

Be guided by the person's wishes and let the conversation flow in the direction of least resistance. The terminally ill person may or may not want to talk about dying. You might approach the issue with a gentle inquiry about the nature of the disease—but let the matter drop if you sense the least discomfort or anxiety.

Remember that denial can be a refuge for a dying person. In a book about his battle with fatal leukemia, journalist Stewart Alsop wrote: "A kind of protective mechanism took over, after the first shock of being told of the imminence of death. I remember seeing much the same process at work in combat. There is the first sudden shock of realizing that the people on the other side are really trying to kill you. But soon a kind of unhappy inner stolidity takes over, coupled with a strong protective instinct that the shell or the bullet or the mine will kill somebody else, not me. In this way the unbearable becomes bearable, and one learns to live with death by not thinking about it too much."

Above all, don't isolate a friend or relative with a terminal illness. Remember that the person is still the individual you know and love. Isolation may be the most distressing problem faced by people with AIDS, who are often treated like modern-day lepers. Indeed, like leprosy, this dread disease is actually not transmitted by casual contact. There is no reason for a friend to avoid such simple human gestures as visiting an AIDS patient and offering a hand to hold.

Can you prepare for your death before it becomes imminent?

Many psychologists believe that fear of death is a universal human emotion. Yet many of us find a meaning in death that makes it acceptable. We may be consoled by the religious belief that physical death is the beginning of a higher spiritual existence, or by the thought that after death, as one scientist said, "my molecules will return to the universe."

Whatever their beliefs about an afterlife happen to be, many people see a form of immortality in creative achievements—books, musical compositions, scientific discoveries—or simply in the memories friends and relatives will preserve. Others find solace in leaving their bodies to science, donating their organs to save another life, or endowing worthy causes.

The Testimony of Survivors' Near-Death Experiences

In recent years the medical techniques of resuscitation have advanced greatly and cases of near-death experiences have become much more common. People who would have died of cardiac arrest, for instance, can now be brought back to life.

There are nine traits that define the near-death experience, though it is seldom that anyone experiences all nine of them. The presence of at least one of these symptoms is enough to constitute a near-death experience, according to psychiatrist Raymond Moody. Moody believes that psychologist Kenneth Ring's research into 102 experiences of this kind has validated some of his own findings.

- **A sense of being dead.** At first many people don't realize that they are experiencing near death. They find themselves floating above their bodies. Feeling confused, they wonder, "How can I be up here, looking at myself down there?"
- **Peace and painlessness.** An illness or accident frequently brings on intense pain, which suddenly vanishes during a near-death experience. Research by Ring shows that 60 percent of people who have had such an experience describe peace and painlessness.
- **Out-of-body experience.** People often feel that they are rising up. Most say they are not simply a point of consciousness but seem to be in some kind of body. Ring says 37 percent have out-of-body experiences.
- **The tunnel experience.** This generally occurs after an out-of-body experience. For many, a portal or tunnel opens and they are propelled into darkness. Some hear a "whoosh" or they hear a humming sound or feel an electric vibration.The sense of heading toward an intense light is common to almost all tunnel experiences.
- **People of light.** Once people pass through the tunnel, they usually meet beings of intense light, who permeate everything and fill them with love. As one person said, "I could describe this as 'light' or 'love' and it would mean the same thing." They frequently meet dead friends and relatives, though the glowing beings can't always be identified. In Ring's research, 16 percent saw the light.
- **The Being of Light.** After meeting several beings of light, there is usually a meeting with a Supreme Being of Light. Whatever the name given to this holy presence, most want to stay with him forever.
- **The life review.** The Being of Light often takes the person on a review of life, presenting it from a third-person perspective, almost like watching a movie. The person not only sees every action but also sees its effect on people in his or her life. The Being of Light helps put the events of life in perspective.
- **Rising into the heavens.** Some people report a rise into the heavens, which enables them to see the universe from the perspective of astronauts.
- **Reluctance to return.** Many people find these surroundings so pleasing that they want to stay. Some are angry at doctors for bringing them back.

The Shock of Loss

Is there a normal way of reacting to the death of a loved one?

Most experts agree that people tend to pass through stages of bereavement. There is no rigid pattern, however, and the following outline suggests only the more typical reactions. The stages vary according to age, sex, personality, and circumstances.

Adjusting to the death of a loved one is in many ways like accepting the idea of one's own approaching death. Almost always, the first stage is shock and numbness. You may feel that the tragedy is unreal or is happening to someone else. Although you appear dazed, even unfeeling, this period gives you merciful time to adjust, and you are able to cope effectively with necessary details and arrangements. Many practical matters, including the funeral, may be handled while you are in an almost trancelike state.

Later will come acute pangs of grief, like the waves of pain that follow the initial numbness of a physical injury. The pangs can be so severe that you cry uncontrollably, or scream, tear your hair, and beat your chest—all dramatic but normal reactions.

Often you go through a period of searching, as if looking for a lost object. Although you know that the person is dead, you refer to him or her in the present tense and listen anxiously for the loved one's footsteps. After his wife's death, essayist C. S. Lewis wrote: "I am beginning to understand why grief feels like suspense. It comes from the frustration of so many impulses that had become habitual. Thought after thought, feeling after feeling, had H for their object. Now their target is gone. I keep on, through habit, fitting an arrow to the string; then I remember that I have to lay the bow down."

You may dream about the dead person or even see him or her near you. Such hallucinations are so common that they are considered normal. Perhaps, as novelist Gabriel García Márquez writes of an elderly widow's feelings, they are like the pains "that amputees suffer in the leg that is no longer there." Losing someone close to you is like losing part of yourself.

In giving comfort, remember that it is natural for a bereaved person to idealize or exaggerate the qualities of a lost loved one. Be understanding, too, when a mourner alternates between desperately seeking your help and seeming to reject it. That is normal.

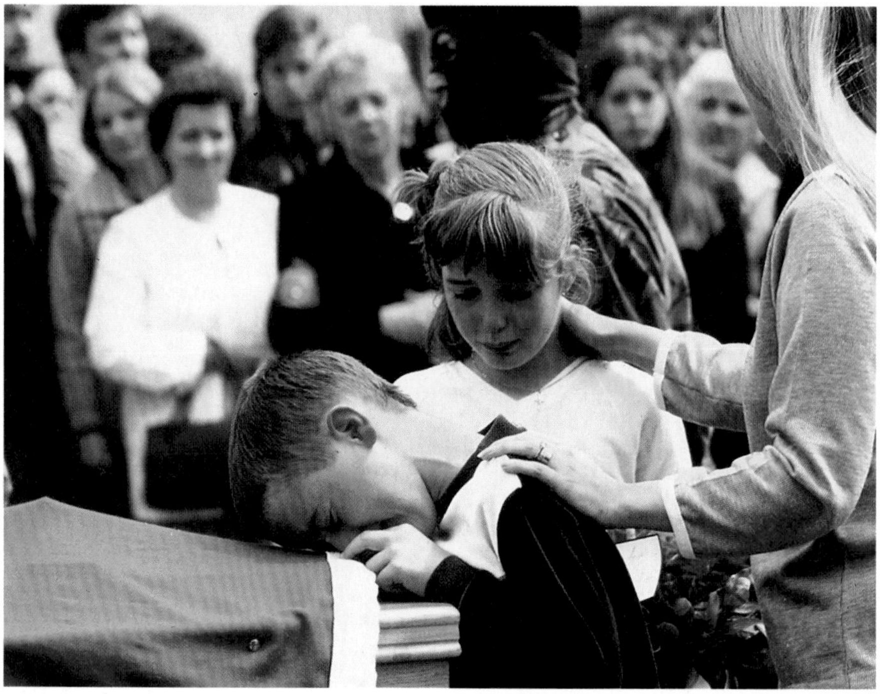

A family is wrenched by grief *at the burial of a victim of civil strife in Northern Ireland. The feelings of desolation that follow death are intensified in such circumstances. The deep bitterness on both sides reverberates as one such blow is followed by others.*

How do you finally recover from grief?

You may never fully overcome your sense of loss. In time, however, although you do not forget the dead person, your memories tend to become more realistic. You recognize that the person was human, that your relationship had ups and downs, that your life was not entirely dependent on him or her. As you come to accept the death, you are able to resume social activities and reorder your life.

Months after her husband died, novelist Rhoda Tagliacozzo wrote: "What I know now is that even if we love them inordinately, people are not ours to possess. In fact, we barely own ourselves, and we need to keep re-inventing our lives in order to move along."

Are anger, guilt, and depression normal in bereavement?

Anger is a common reaction to death. It may be directed at doctors who you feel didn't try hard enough. Or the target could be yourself: "If only I hadn't let her borrow the car!" or "If only I'd urged him to go to the doctor earlier." You may also be angry at God or at the dead person for abandoning you, however unintentionally. These are natural attempts to find a meaning in the death and scapegoats to blame for a disaster that you find unacceptable.

Of course, sometimes the blame for a death is inescapable. In such a situation, you will probably be unable to accept your loss until you forgive the person responsible—whether it is yourself or someone else.

Fortunately, grieving rarely reaches the depths of apathy and hopelessness that doctors call clinical depression. Occasionally, grief takes on an extreme form that leads to suicidal thoughts. A mourner who becomes suicidally depressed needs immediate professional help.

Can grief make you physically ill?

Insomnia and loss of appetite are common during bereavement and may make you unusually susceptible to fatigue, weakness, and infection. There is evidence, too, that the immune system may be suppressed by grief, as by other forms of emotional stress. Some medical studies have also indicated that heart rhythm irregularities become more common in the first weeks or months after the death of a spouse. But experts disagree as to whether these actually cause illness.

Is it possible to "die of a broken heart"?

One study found unusually large numbers of widowers died within six months of their wives' deaths; over half these men died from coronary disease. Other studies have also found high mortality rates among bereaved spouses, especially widowers. After the first year, heart disease declines as a cause of death, but spouses then seem to face a greater risk from infectious disease, accidents, and cirrhosis.

More recent research suggests that the "broken-heart effect" may be less potent than generally believed. A 10-year study of Israelis who had lost sons in war or accidents—a tragedy certainly comparable to a spouse's death—found no overall difference in mortality between bereaved parents and other men and women of the same ages. There was, however, an exception to this general finding: widowed or divorced mothers whose sons had died did have a higher than normal mortality rate.

An editorial in the *New England Journal of Medicine,* which published the study of bereaved Israelis, suggests that instead of trying to measure the ill effects of grief, scientists "may do better to emphasize human resilience and the power of life" on the part of the survivors. In any case, good general health and the support provided by other close relationships are vital assets in overcoming the sometimes almost unbearable sense of loss at the death of a loved one.

PERSPECTIVES

On Death and Bereavement

Poet John Donne said of death in his* Holy Sonnets, *"One short sleep past, we wake eternally And death shall be no more; death thou shalt die."

Living to the Last

"By all means begin your folio; even if the doctor does not give you a year—even if he hesitates about a month, make one brave push and see what can be accomplished in a week.

"And even if death catch people, like an open pitfall, and in mid-career, laying out vast projects, . . . flushed with hope, and their mouths full of boastful language . . . is there not something brave and spirited in such a termination? . . .

"Death has not been suffered to take so much as an illusion from his heart. In the hot-fit of life, a-tiptoe on the highest point of being, he passes at a bound on to the other side. The noise of the mallet and chisel is scarcely quenched, the trumpets are hardly done blowing, when, trailing with him clouds of glory, this happy-starred, full-blooded spirit shoots into the spiritual land."

—**Robert Louis Stevenson**
Virginibus Puerisque

◆

Caught Off Guard

"I opened the drawer of my little desk and a single letter fell out, a letter from my mother, written in pencil, one of her last, with unfinished words and an implicit sense of her departure. It's so curious: one can resist tears and 'behave' very well in the hardest hours of grief. But then someone makes you a friendly sign behind a window . . . or one notices that a flower that was in bud only yesterday has suddenly blossomed . . . or a letter slips from a drawer . . . and everything collapses."

—**Colette**
Letters From Colette

◆

In Quiet Sympathy

"There's a Hebrew proverb about 'wearing out' grief—if you bottle it up, you'll never soften it. So, when meeting a friend for the first time after there has been a death close to him, offer condolences. Keep it brief and simple; then ask a question that will allow him to keep his composure. It can be related to the death, but not to his feeling of loss. Ask if most of the family were able to attend the funeral, or if he plans to go away for a while. If you are alone and the death was recent, the person may want to talk of nothing else, may *need* to talk of nothing else."

—**Barbara Walters**
How to Talk With Practically Anybody About Practically Anything

◆

A Sweet Return

"There is no fence or hedge round time that has gone. You can go back and have what you like if you remember it well enough."

—**Richard Llewellyn**
How Green Was My Valley

◆

From the Holy Bible

"For everything there is a season,
and a time for every matter under heaven:
a time to be born, and a time to die;
a time to plant, and a time to pluck up what is planted;
a time to kill, and a time to heal;
a time to break down, and a time to build up;
a time to weep, and a time to laugh;
a time to mourn, and a time to dance;
a time to cast away stones, and a time to gather stones together;
a time to embrace, and a time to refrain from embracing;
a time to seek, and a time to lose;
a time to keep, and a time to cast away;
a time to rend, and a time to sew;
a time to keep silence, and a time to speak;
a time to love, and a time to hate;
a time for war, and a time for peace.
What gain has the worker from his toil?"

—**Ecclesiastes 3:1–9**
Revised Standard Edition

A Long, Lonely Time

When Queen Victoria died in 1901, aged 81, *she was still in mourning for her husband, Prince Albert, who had died 40 years earlier. She avoided public functions, wore widow's weeds, kept his bedroom as it had been, and used black-edged paper for her correspondence.*

Is it healthier to express grief or hold it in?

Many experts believe that letting your feelings out is essential to working through your grief. They think a show of bravery, keeping your emotions under tight control, may invite later psychological problems.

In Shakespeare's tragic play *Macbeth,* when Macduff hears that his wife and children have been murdered, a character urges him: "Give sorrow words. The grief that does not speak whispers the o'er-fraught heart and bids it break."

But not everyone is comfortable with the vocal expressions of grief encouraged at some funerals. Psychiatrist Colin Murray Parkes writes: "There is an optimal 'level of grieving,' which varies from one person to another. Some will cry and sob, others will betray their feelings in other ways. The important thing is for feelings to emerge into consciousness. How they appear on the surface may be of secondary importance."

How can you best console a bereaved person?

It is not easy to know what to say or do in the presence of grief. Some of us hesitate to talk about the dead person for fear of causing pain. Even doctors have trouble dealing with the survivors' emotions when a patient dies. They may prescribe sedatives, delaying the grieving process. One widow was enraged when given a sleeping pill to calm her after her husband's death in the emergency room: "I should not sleep," she said. "Now is the time to grieve for my Joe."

Some phrases intended to comfort have the opposite effect. "You'll get over it in time" or even "I know how you feel" may mean little to a person struggling with the shock of bereavement. A sympathetic touch is often more consoling than words.

Probably the most helpful response is simply to be there. Offer help with practical tasks. Above all, be prepared to listen, to let the person express anger, sorrow, or other strong feelings—even anger at you for not being the missing loved one.

Showing your own sadness can be supportive. A young widower was shocked when his father cried at the funeral; the son had always thought of his father—and all grown men—as "tough." But realizing that tears were apt, he felt free to cry himself.

A sympathy note can give valuable support. The best ones are often brief and share positive memories. When the wife of Justice Oliver Wendell Holmes died, Harold Laski, a lifelong friend, wrote to Holmes: "I learned almost the first time I saw her that she had, with all her reserve and reticence, a genius for affection. And to see you together was a lesson in the beauty of love. I know that things can never be the same for you again. But I want you to remember that your house was made by her for me as for others a place of loving pilgrimage and that while we live she will be remembered with deep affection."

Are bereaved families helped by seeing the body after death?

Many psychologists think viewing the dead body is a critical step in coming to terms with the death, although some people have found that it leaves them only with grim memories. Individual preferences and customs vary and should be respected.

An especially heartrending decision is whether parents should see the body of their stillborn baby. In the *Journal of the American Medical Association,* a physician described the time as a third-year medical student he delivered a stillborn baby. After this agonizing experience, the senior doctor insisted on showing the parents the baby. His motive was not to confront the parents with death but to reassure them about life. "I want you to look closely," the resident said to the crying mother. "He has five perfect fingers on each hand. His arms and legs are perfectly developed and normal. Although the bones in the skull have shifted in the birth process, the head is normally developed in every way. You can have a normal baby."

As they left the parents alone with their infant, the student looked back. "The mother was still sobbing," he wrote. "But she was touching the tiny hand. I had had my first lesson in the art of medicine."

How long does it usually take to recover from the death of a loved one?

After a death, there is often an immediate rallying round of relatives. When that is over, the days can be particularly lonely for the closest survivors. This is a time when friends can help by visiting and, not too long after, beginning to extend invitations.

While acute mourning may last for a year or more, the loss of a loved one leaves one changed, forever. The nature of this change varies, and certain events and anniversaries can revive old sorrow.

Some people find it difficult to get beyond the stage of denying the death of a loved person. They may "enshrine" the dead by keeping his or her room just as it was. One widower even had his wife's body reburied close to his house, so that he could watch her grave from his window.

Self-help groups such as Widow-to-Widow programs or Compassionate Friends (for bereaved parents) can often prevent these extreme reactions or lessen the pain by counseling. Sometimes professional help is needed. Certain psychiatrists claim success with "re-grieving" therapy, in which a person who is numbed by denial is confronted with the reality of his or her loss.

Deaths have other long-term effects, even for less intimate friends. Former *New York Times* columnist Anna Quindlen admits that when two people she had not seen for years suddenly died, she was "selfishly troubled by the fact that parts of a mosaic had worn away. That mosaic was the picture of my life, with all the little moments intact. I was not willing to see it erode, to recognize that of two people who had shared a particular moment, an exchange, a vignette, only one of us was left to remember it." She observes, "You realize that like everyone else you are standing upon sand; that someday, if you live long enough, your past will exist only in your own mind."

How should you tell a child about a death in the family?

For Rhoda Tagliacozzo, "the two hardest words in the language" were: "Daddy died." Yet too much delay in telling a child such news does not help either the parent or the child.

Experts say that by age three, and perhaps even earlier, children can understand death on some level. Just as children's intellectual ability develops in stages, along the lines proposed by Jean Piaget, so does their view of death. Younger children, for example, generally cannot conceive of death being irreversible.

Some counselors urge that parents talk to preschoolers about death before they have to face it. The occasion may come with the death of a distant relative or of a pet. As in telling children about sex, the subject should be introduced gently, with no more detail than the child can handle.

Parents may not wish to let a child see their own grief when a spouse or another child dies, but crying together can be comforting. Children need to talk about the dead person, just as adults do; this can clear up possible misunderstandings about death. If a child had argued with the dead parent—or brother or sister—the child may feel responsible for the death.

Using euphemisms, such as referring to death as sleep, is not recommended. Children may then be afraid of going to sleep themselves. If they do not understand that dead people no longer feel, they may worry that the person will be hurt by cremation or by earth piled on the coffin. One mother reassured her son by showing him that it did not hurt to cut the dead ends of his hair; it only hurt when she tugged at the living roots.

Experts urge that children be allowed, though not forced, to attend the funeral; otherwise they may feel isolated from the support of family and friends. By all means discuss with your child your religious interpretation of death, so that he or she can share the consolation of your faith.

Mourning Rituals Are Beneficial to Survivors

In all cultures, ceremonies that follow a death are tributes to the dead and rites of passage for the survivors. Mourners often draw support from the religious rites that give meaning to the death, as well as from the presence of relatives, friends, and associates. The ritual of burial can help people face the ending of a life and gives the opportunity to say good-bye in the company of others who will miss the dead person.

- In nearly all cultures, mourners put aside new, flashy, or highly individualistic clothing and fashions. In the West it is customary for mourners to wear black, while in much of the Far East it is proper to wear white.
- Jews observe the custom of shiva, a seven-day mourning period in which friends call on the bereaved family and reminisce about the deceased. On the seventh day, the mourners take a symbolic walk outside to show their return to normal living.
- The word *quarantine* derives from the Italian word for *40*, which was the traditional number of days an Italian widow was expected to stay sequestered in the house after her husband's death.
- Mourning can take many forms. The Taj Mahal in Agra, India, is one of the most magnificent buildings in the world. It was finished in 1648 by the Mogul Emperor Shah Jahan as a monument commemorating his beloved wife.

PART VI

The Outside World

As in the storybooks of childhood, we "set out to seek our fortunes" in the larger world. How we fare depends in large measure on our own attitudes.

Here the world is in perfect scale with the human spirit—
a tree-shaded marketplace where one can stock up on the necessities of life.

School: A Room Full of Strangers

Why is the first day of school so hard?

Most children going to a school for the first time experience some degree of what experts call separation anxiety. Suddenly, the idea of being cut off from one's mother (or father, or both) and left among strange people in alien surroundings, if only for a few hours, can fill a child with emotions that are close to panic.

Children sometimes respond by reverting to infantile behavior. A five-year-old may act like a toddler, crying for Mom or Dad to stay. Fortunately, most children are rather quick to adapt and such desperate behavior does not usually last long.

Some psychologists suggest that parents take a child to visit the teacher and classroom in advance as a way of reducing a child's anxieties. As a rule, the calmer the parents are, the calmer their children will be. However, remoteness will not reassure a child. Rather, the parent should matter-of-factly try to convey the idea that child, teacher, and parent will be able to work out any problems together.

When the time comes for a parent to leave a child at school, a clear good-bye is important. If the parent tries to sneak out, the child may feel his or her trust has been betrayed and become even more upset at the parent's sudden disappearance.

If a child seems apprehensive about school, it may be helpful to bring a favorite toy from home. One teacher had her kindergarteners create a family photo album during their first week of school. For many of them, it was comforting to turn to their albums when they felt anxious about being away from home. Treasured reminders can often comfort children whose longing for home may interfere with their enjoyment of the new experience of school.

When should a child be taught to read?

What is called "reading readiness" is a hotly debated topic in educational and psychological circles. In the past, nursery schools and kindergartens focused on teaching four- and five-year-olds basic social and motor skills: how to follow instructions, participate in group activities, and hold a crayon or pencil for best results. Not until the first grade, when they were six or so, were most children considered emotionally and mentally ready to be taught reading and arithmetic.

Today, however, many parents are persuaded that their children need a head start in life, and that early reading is the key to future success. Thus many parents pressure nursery schools to offer reading programs at the four-year-old level.

Such early training is wonderful for some children, but it may cause others to hate reading. Psychologist David Elkind worries about preschoolers who are pushed to read but don't pick it up as fast as some of their classmates. Such children may feel like failures and give up on school and themselves. Reports one preschool teacher: "Young children don't know how to distinguish between effort and ability. If they try hard to do something and fail, they may conclude that they will never be able to accomplish a particular task."

Wriggling, fidgeting, or just staring off into space, *these children at a Newfoundland kindergarten graduation*

Though some parents continue to request early reading programs (and some children continue to benefit from them), most educators are happy with first graders who simply know how to get along in the classroom. Interestingly, kindergarten teachers in Scandinavia adhere to the custom of not teaching reading, writing, or math skills to their pupils.

What is the most important influence upon a child's education?

Good students have parents who care about education. A supportive parent can be the difference between a child's academic success and failure. When Thomas Alva Edison went to school at age eight, his teacher thought the boy was mentally retarded. His mother, a former teacher, knew her son was more than capable of learning. She took him out of school and proceeded to teach him not only the three R's, but, recalled Edison, "the love and purpose of learning." Her confidence in his abilities laid the groundwork for one of America's most remarkable inventors. "My mother was the making of me," he said years later.

A study sponsored by the National Science Foundation confirmed that the greatest impact on a student's performance is parental encouragement. Without parental backing, children seem to have great difficulty in understanding what school is good for. Of course, parental support is no guarantee of academic success, but lack of it makes school a lot tougher for most children. Parents who show no interest in their children's education tend to produce students who do poorly and may drop out.

The best kind of support is active and specific. Parents should insist that homework be done, they should encourage children to discuss what they like and dislike about their subjects, and they should praise a well-done assignment. Some parents may be shy or insecure about their own academic abilities, but this should not prevent them from speaking up if they believe a teacher is misguided about their child's performance or capabilities.

How important is a teacher's expectation of a student?

High expectations by a teacher can encourage a student to do better, whereas low expectations may result in a mediocre performance. A series of tests that proved this was devised by psychologist Robert Rosenthal.

In his first experiment in 1968, Rosenthal told teachers that certain students were expected to "bloom" academically in the coming year. He said that his predictions were based on the results of tests he gave the children at the beginning of the school year. Testing, however, had nothing to do with Rosenthal's predictions, which were entirely random. The students that the teachers thought were "bloomers" outperformed the rest of the class. When retested at the end of the year, they had gained an average of 15 IQ points over the "nonbloomers."

Evidently a teacher's high expectations alone can create a positive self-fulfilling prophecy in a student. Unfortunately, low expectations seem to be just as potent and can be a source of academic failures.

ceremony demonstrate that, so far, school has done little to dampen their spontaneous reactions to the world.

New Parental Concerns

Nothing beats a demonstration when it comes to learning about light.

How to Make the Most of Your Study Time

- Set aside a regular time and place for study. If your home tends to be noisy in the afternoon and at night, try studying in the morning before school.
- Study time should be divided into short chunks. Avoid all-night cramming. Sometimes studying with others can help you understand and retain information.
- For an overview of a new subject, try reading a popular account first. Pictures and illustrations can help flesh out abstract ideas and unfamiliar times.
- Make study interesting by focusing on people behind historical dates and scientific discoveries. Often, a historical movie or novel makes a period come alive.
- When faced with a great deal of reading, scan the material first, looking at the first and last sentence of each paragraph.
- To keep track of a book's main ideas, make a brief, informal outline listing the author's important points as you read.
- When taking notes, write down ideas on one side of a file card. Paraphrase or summarize the information in your own words and mark down the source. Give each card a short heading; this will help you to organize your notes more easily.

What effect are computers having in the classroom?

Many teachers find that computers are excellent for learning that requires rote and repetition, such as multiplication tables or spelling. A computer can be programmed to ask questions, give the student time to respond, and then tell the student if the answer is correct. Some children like the fact that the computer is impersonal, allowing them to work at their own pace. As one seven-year-old put it: "The computer doesn't yell."

Computers have limitations as teaching tools. They can help students practice reading, for instance, but they cannot actually teach them how to read. However, they can improve on the process of learning by providing games that develop logical thinking. As more and more jobs require knowledge of computers, educators seem to have little choice but to instruct children in how to use and master the machines.

Should parents intervene when a child is having trouble?

Although parents want to be supportive of their children, they cannot shield them from all that is disagreeable. When a child complains that a certain teacher is mean or unfair, parents' first step should be to determine the facts as best they can. By encouraging the child to talk about specifics, parents can usually get a clearer idea of whether they need to talk to the teacher. Sometimes, either the child or the teacher has simply had a bad day. However, if the child keeps coming home unhappy, it is time to arrange a talk with the teacher.

Usually a teacher is just as anxious as a parent to discuss ways of improving the situation. If the teacher does not seem willing to improve things, the parents may have to go to the principal or even to the school board. In some cases, transferring their child to another teacher's class may be an option to consider.

What are learning disorders?

Some types of physical or neurological disorders can make learning nearly impossible. Such disorders are tricky to diagnose, and children who have persistent problems in learning should be observed by a specialist. Once diagnosed, children with learning disorders can be helped by proper treatment or various types of training.

Some disorders have been linked to a scrambling of the brain's neural connections. One result is that numbers and letters appear inverted. For reasons not yet clear, boys are more likely to have reading problems than girls. Other disorders may stem from mild hearing or vision impairment.

Children with learning disorders are often teased by their classmates, which can make them feel inferior. Thus, an early diagnosis can help a child get the extra help he or she needs. Teachers familiar with learning disorders say that building a child's self-esteem is essential. Confident children seem better able to take their disorder in stride and achieve despite it.

Is hyperactivity a learning disorder?

All children are active, but a few are extraordinarily so and are considered hyperactive. They may sleep only a few hours at a time. When awake, they are constantly in motion, darting from one activity to another. Because their attention span is extremely short, learning is blocked.

Doctors sometimes prescribe a stimulant called Ritalin for such children. This drug has the paradoxical effect of making hyperactive children more manageable. Some scientists say the drug works by wiping out the brain's overabundance of natural stimulants and replacing them with milder synthetic ones. Ritalin can be addictive; experts recommend that it be used with caution. In some cases, more conservative treatments, such as exercise and diet, may be enough.

Is there a profile of the dropout?

Until the middle of the 19th century, schooling was often considered a luxury, available to sons and daughters of the wealthy. One idea behind compulsory education was to offer all children the means to improve their chances in life.

Today, not all students see schooling as the ticket to a better future. Some see it as a dead end and drop out, not believing that dropouts face a lifetime of low-paying jobs. One study reveals that most dropouts have these four characteristics: a distrust of authority figures, unrealistic aspirations, a facade of toughness, and an acute sensitivity to rejection.

Dropouts leave school for many reasons. A few leave to help earn money for their families. Most, however, have a long history of problems with teachers and schoolwork. They choose to quit in order to avoid further failure.

PERSPECTIVES

On Teaching and Learning

From the day we are born until the end of life, we are teachers, every one of us. We teach by example, and we learn by the example of others.

A Solid Foundation

"All I really need to know about how to live and what to do and how to be I learned in kindergarten. Wisdom was not at the top of the graduate-school mountain, but there in the sandpile at Sunday School. These are the things I learned:

Share everything.

Play fair.

Don't hit people.

Put things back where you found them.

Clean up your own mess.

Don't take things that aren't yours.

Say you're sorry when you hurt somebody.

Wash your hands before you eat.

Flush.

Warm cookies and cold milk are good for you.

Live a balanced life—learn some and think some and draw and paint and sing and dance and play and work every day some.

Take a nap every afternoon.

When you go out into the world, watch out for traffic, hold hands, and stick together.

Be aware of wonder."

—**Robert Fulghum**
All I Really Need to Know I Learned in Kindergarten

◆

The Power of Praise

"As I was giving a master class for young pianists in Saarbrücken, West Germany, in September 1985, I felt that one student would do even better if given a pat on the back. I praised him before the whole class for what distinguished his playing. He immediately outdid himself, to his amazement and that of the group. A few words brought out the best in him.

"How happy and proud the first praise I remember receiving made *me* feel! I was seven, and my father asked for help in the garden. I worked as hard as I could and was richly rewarded when he kissed me and said, 'Thanks, son, you did very well.' His words still ring in my ears more than six decades later.

"At 16, I was in the midst of a personal crisis arising from differences with my music teacher. Then the renowned pianist Emil von Sauer, Liszt's last surviving pupil, came to Budapest and asked me to play for him. He listened intently to Bach's Toccata in C major and requested more. I put all my heart into playing Beethoven's 'Pathétique' sonata and continued with Schumann's 'Papillons.' Finally, Von Sauer rose and kissed me on the forehead. 'My son,' he said, 'when I was your age I became a student of Liszt. He kissed me on the forehead after my first lesson, saying, "Take good care of this kiss—it comes from Beethoven, who gave it to me after hearing me play." I have waited for years to pass on this sacred heritage, but now I feel you deserve it.'

"Nothing in my life has meant as much to me as Von Sauer's praise. Beethoven's kiss miraculously lifted me out of my crisis and helped me become the pianist I am today. Soon I in turn will pass it on to the one who most deserves it.

"Praise is a potent force, a candle in a dark room. It is magic, and I marvel that it always works."

—**Andor Foldes**
Beethoven's Kiss

◆

Pluses and Minuses

"One needs two things before one is 30. One needs achievement, the thrill of achievement, which, once one has it, the taste never leaves. All the talk about excellence makes me rather sick because it's preaching. But the person who has, as a young person, had the thrill of achieving something he knows damn well is really beyond his reach, he never loses that yearning. . . . and the second thing is, one needs to learn what one cannot do—the limitations. . . . And one needs to learn this before one is 30 or one is defenseless before life."

—**Peter Drucker**
"An Interview With Peter Drucker"

Of Boredom and Bullies

What if a child is bored in school?

A young lawyer, using his Ph.D. in physics to launch himself into the brand-new field of computer-program patent law, credits his father with giving him the motivation to earn two advanced degrees and apply them swiftly and directly. As a child, he would occasionally complain about being bored with his schoolwork. When he did, his father would say, "Take another look. It's my opinion that only boring people are bored." What the father knew, and the son had to learn, was that usually when we say we are bored, what we mean is something else.

Sometimes children say they are bored in school because they don't understand what's expected of them. Others may find the work too easy and need more challenging assignments. Some children, rather than say they are tired of sitting still and studying, think it's more impressive to say they are bored. Little children who frequently complain of boredom usually have not been taught how to listen and follow instructions.

Pleading boredom can also hide a child's lack of understanding of certain subjects. The work may, in fact, be too hard, and the child could need special attention.

Of course, there is no denying that learning such things as spelling and multiplication tables can be tedious. But most children accept such tedium as the price of going on to more grown-up studies.

Why are some children bullies?

Bullies are at the top of the list of things that many schoolchildren worry most about. The classic bully is someone who needs to feel in control by dominating others. Psychologists have found that bullies are often raised by parents who do not teach them how to negotiate or share.

These parents typically resort to harsh and arbitrary physical punishment that reflects their own moods more than anything else. After many early lessons in erratic parental attacks, a bully misreads the actions of others. When a youngster accidentally bumps into a bully in the lunch line, for instance, the bully will mistake it for an attack and start a fight.

Because a bully has never learned the value of sharing or cooperation, getting along with others is not a priority. Often bullies become more unhappy and aggressive with age. They are more likely to drop out of school and have trouble with the law.

What's the best way to deal with a bully?

When children are attacked by a bully, they often feel ashamed and don't want to talk about it. Like adult victims, they blame themselves for being attacked. Studies show that children who are fragile or appear unusual in any way are the ones most likely to be picked on by a bully.

In such cases, the parents should tell the school authorities of the bully's assault. Should a child under attack hit back? Some psychologists say yes, if the bully isn't too much larger and walking away has not worked.

Do social pressures to conform affect learning?

As children enter adolescence, they feel social pressures beginning to war with the priority of learning. Recognition for athletic abilities or for leadership skills can be far more important to some youngsters than good grades.

Teenagers want to be treated as individuals, yet fear doing things that may set them apart from their peers. Being with one's peer group protects teenagers from feeling isolated or inadequate. For example, the very bright student may try to hide his or her academic abilities so as not to stand out from the crowd.

Caught napping in a 19th-century classroom, *a student risked bringing the wrath of his schoolmaster down upon himself—quite literally. Schools have come a long way since those dire days, when children's needs and capabilities were little recognized.*

An Expert Describes the Teacher's Task

For 40 years Gilbert Highet taught the classics, first at Oxford and then at Columbia University. In his book* The Art of Teaching*, published in 1950, he described the personal qualities and professional requirements that make a good teacher.

GILBERT HIGHET had no doubt that teaching was the best and most satisfying calling. His conviction is clear at the very beginning of *The Art of Teaching*. "Leisure is one of the three greatest rewards of being a teacher," he wrote. "The teacher's second reward is that he is using his mind on valuable subjects [and] the third reward is very closely linked. That is the happiness of making something. You take the living mind, and mold it."

What, Highet asked, makes a good teacher? "Most necessary of all, he must know the subject. Teaching is inseparable from learning. Every good teacher will learn more about his subject every year—every month, every week if possible. A teacher must believe in the value and interest of his subject as a doctor believes in health."

It is also essential, Highet emphasized, that a teacher like his subject. "Of course, nearly every teacher dislikes some part of his subject. But to dislike the entire subject, to be a history teacher and be bored by history, that must be either a constant pain or a numbing narcosis.

"The third essential of good teaching is to like the pupils. It is easy to like the young because they are young. They have no faults, except the very ones which they are asking you to eradicate: ignorance, shallowness, and inexperience."

Highet was sure that a teacher must know the names and faces of his pupils. "It is a *must*. The young are trying desperately hard to become real people, to be individuals. If you wish to influence them in any way, you must convince them that you know them as individuals. Never assume that you are addressing a group of types. That calm, fair-haired girl with the cheerful smile may turn out to be a cruel satirist. The earnest hobbledehoy who writes down everything rather slowly may be three or four years ahead of the rest of the class."

Highet saw teaching as a test of willpower and determination. "Consider how many different kinds of resistance the teacher has to overcome. To begin with, the young do not like work. They would rather be playing football, or sitting in the movies eating popcorn. Nor do the young like authority. They are natural anarchists. They would prefer a world of unpredictable disorder, without duties or responsibilities. The young must be taught to respect the principle of authority.

"Also, the young hate concentration. It is an effort, an unfamiliar and painful effort. Watch a boy doing his homework when he thinks he is not observed. He will read ten lines, then draw a funny face, then try to read ten lines more, then rearrange all the books on his table and sharpen all his pencils, make a dash at the book and read 25 lines, and then sit panting and vacant-eyed for at least 3 minutes before beginning the struggle once more.

"Concentration must be learned. It should be learned in school. Take the same boy who reads his book grudgingly, five lines at a time, and increase the urgency of his study—somehow, anyhow—make the choice clearer to him, and the importance of his study paramount—put him to work on the prize essay—and then watch. 'Turn that radio off!' he shouts. He clears the table. He sits fixed in one position. Sometimes, when he is really intent, he will miss meals and forget about sleep. All this because he has chosen one aim and discarded others.

"Many youngsters also resent the domination of one mind. They reject suggestions just in order to assert their own independence, as a horse will jerk its head when it is ridden on a tight rein. It is one of the aims of teaching to provoke their resistance, and then to direct it into the right channels.

For many years, *Gilbert Highet's radio talks on literary subjects delighted millions of listeners.*

"It is very difficult to teach anything without kindness. Pupils should feel that the teacher wants to help them, wants them to improve, is interested in their growth, is sorry for their mistakes and pleased by their successes and sympathetic with their inadequacies. Learning anything worthwhile is difficult. Some people find it painful. Everyone finds it tiring. Few things will diminish the difficulty, the pain, and the fatigue like the kindness of a good teacher. Every teacher dislikes *some* pupils. But if any teacher finds himself disliking *all* his pupils, he should change his character, and if that fails, change his job."

Gilbert Highet was 26 years old when he began teaching classical literature at Oxford. Beginning in 1937, he taught at Columbia, where, until he retired in the 1970's, he was a favorite among the students. "Teaching," he wrote, "is not a science. It is more like painting a picture or making a piece of music. You must throw your heart into it."

What Intelligence Tests Are All About

Tests for the College Bound

Most colleges consider a strong vocabulary the key to intellectual development because it allows for greater precision in the expression of ideas. They use vocabulary tests to help screen applicants. Students also need to show their mastery of math and the ability to solve problems using mathematical concepts. Another part of the test measures the ability to analyze problems using logic. The multiple-choice format allows tests to be scored quickly by computers.

A Sample of a College-Placement Vocabulary Test

Choose the word out of the four that is the best definition of the first word, and mark your response on a separate sheet of paper. For example:

A. **author** *(a) name (b) originator (c) reporter (d) scholar*
B. **uncouth** *(a) cruel (b) bold (c) uncultured (d) robust*

In the first example you should have marked (b), originator, as the best definition. In the next example the correct answer is (c), uncultured.
Turn to page 322 for the answers.

1. **surplus** (a) an excess (b) coins (c) salaries (d) a surplice
2. **sagacious** (a) thoughtless (b) wise (c) old (d) sarcastic
3. **ingenuity** (a) cleverness (b) artifice (c) haste (d) novelty
4. **hypothesis** (a) a supposition (b) a relation (c) a provision (d) proof
5. **cudgel** (a) a club (b) to hide (c) to sneak (d) an injury
6. **odious** (a) detestable (b) ill-smelling (c) pleasant (d) peculiar
7. **derisive** (a) silly (b) scornful (c) troublesome (d) miserable
8. **harbinger** (a) forerunner (b) a message (c) a port (d) a bird
9. **finesse** (a) the end (b) a veneer (c) delicate skill (d) fine
10. **unmitigated** (a) unabated (b) undisturbed (c) relieved (d) unfinished
11. **enigma** (a) a riddle (b) a contrivance (c) a taint (d) contempt
12. **salience** (a) saline (b) projection (c) old-fashioned (d) metaphorical
13. **obsequious** (a) obscure (b) yielding (c) secluded (d) aloof
14. **germane** (a) German (b) contagious (c) relevant (d) different
15. **specious** (a) kind (b) roomy (c) plausible (d) special

Measure Your Understanding of Elementary Mathematics

Select the correct answer to each question. *The answers are on page 322.*

1. Which of the following fractions is less than $\frac{1}{3}$?
(a) $\frac{22}{63}$ (b) $\frac{4}{11}$ (c) $\frac{15}{46}$ (d) $\frac{33}{98}$ (e) $\frac{102}{303}$
2. What is the perimeter of the square if the length of each side of the square is $\frac{2x}{3} + 1$?
(a) $\frac{8x + 4}{3}$ (b) $\frac{8x + 12}{3}$
(c) $\frac{2x}{3} + 4$ (d) $\frac{2x}{3} + 16$ (e) $\frac{4x}{3} + 2$
3. The approximate distance, s, in feet that an object falls in t seconds when dropped from a height is obtained by the use of the formula $s = 16t^2$. In 8 seconds the object will fall
(a) 15,384 feet
(b) 1,024 feet
(c) 256 feet
(d) 2,048 feet
(e) none of these

Who created the first useful intelligence test?

In the early 1900's, the French government asked psychologist Alfred Binet to create an intelligence test that would identify retarded children in need of special schooling. Designing such a test proved extremely difficult.

First, Binet had to define intelligence and then find a way to capture intelligence in small parts—the test questions. To Binet, intelligence meant "judgment, otherwise called good sense." His tests attempted to measure how well children managed their everyday life by asking them to identify pictures of common objects, tell time, and work with numbers.

How are intelligence tests scored?

Binet's intelligence tests were based on the assumption that there is an average level of mental competence measurable at each age. Thus, he tried out different questions and kept in the final tests the ones that the majority of children at each age level that he sampled answered correctly.

These assumptions of average ability established the *mental age* standard of the test, while the actual age of the child was called the *chronological age.* To find a child's *intelligence quotient,* or IQ, the child's mental age was divided by his actual age. For example, a 10-year-old who had the mental age of an 11-year-old had an IQ score of 1.1.

Later, psychologists eliminated decimals by multiplying the score by 100. Thus, a 1.1 score on a Binet test becomes an IQ of 110. This type of scoring considers an IQ of 100 as average for a child at any given age.

How are adult intelligence test scores measured?

Once a person reaches adulthood, chronological years begin to outstrip mental years as measured by Binet. Therefore, his test and its scoring had to be revised to take this into account. Using graphs and statistics of adult scores, psychologists designed a way

Test Your Ability to Grasp Spatial Relationships

How well can you visualize a house from its floor plans? Can you read maps easily? Such questions relate to what psychologists call spatial skills, an often overlooked aspect of intelligence. Spatial skills can be measured in a number of different ways. For example, one test asks you to visualize three-dimensional objects from a two-dimensional illustration. Most of us take this ability for granted, but it is an important component of over-all intelligence.

In this block-counting and analysis test, the task is to count the number of blocks in each pile. For example, count the blocks at the right. The correct number is four blocks. Only three blocks would be shown in the test, but here we have revealed the hidden block that supports the structure. The answers are on page 322.

A

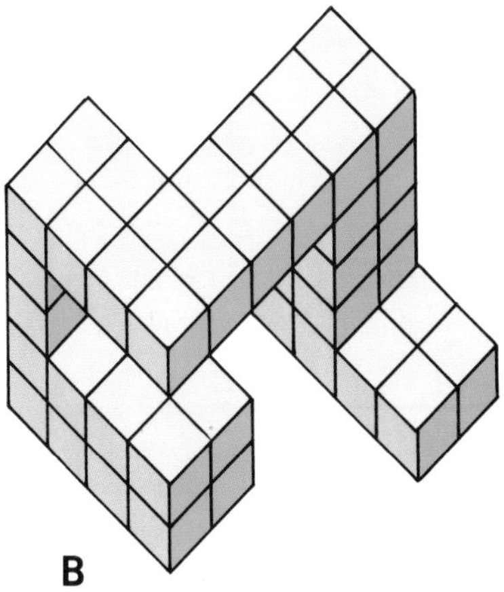

B

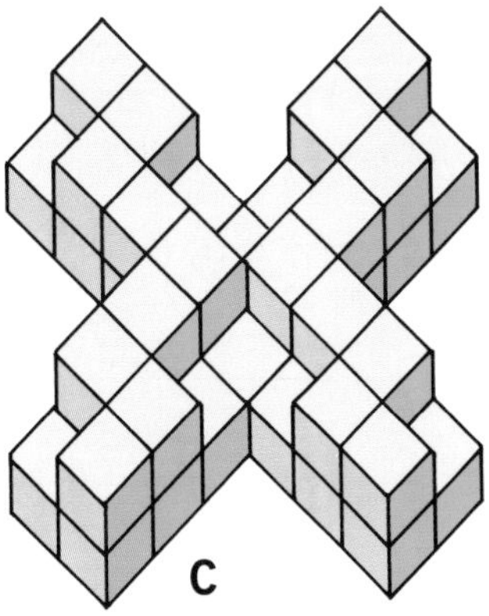

C

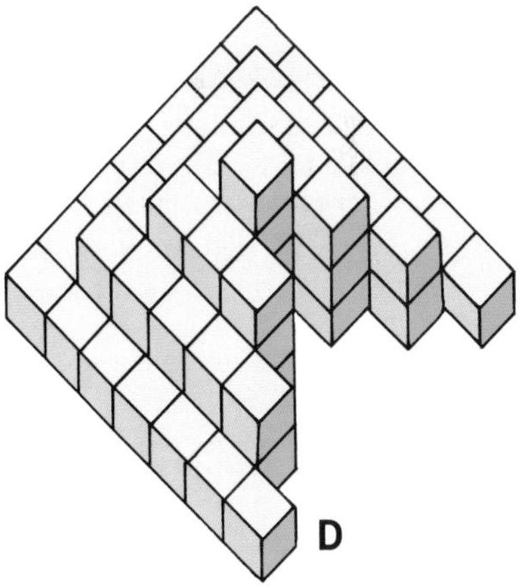

D

to assign a numerical value of 100 to an average adult IQ score.

While intelligence tests have been useful in providing an objective standard with which to measure certain abilities, they cannot predict with certainty an individual's future performances. An IQ score can change. If adults are intellectually challenged, their IQ scores will increase.

Why is it hard to design a test that is fair to everyone?

Standardized tests are intended to be as fair as possible, so people from all backgrounds can be evaluated by the same impartial standards. The only way test designers can evaluate a new test is to try it on a sample group of people. The sample should closely resemble those for whom the test is intended. However, no one group can fully represent an entire population. For example, one person may be able to answer a question on snow, while another may have never seen snow.

Can test anxiety be cured?

Many students who do poorly on tests become so anxious over tests that they fall into a pattern of underachieving. To combat anxiety, experts advise test-taking practice. Above all, a child should be encouraged to keep tests in perspective. Tests can be taken again. It's vital that children know that no test can completely measure their ability or willingness to learn.

What different types of tests are available today?

The Wechsler Adult Intelligence Scale is one of the most widely used intelligence tests today. It attempts to measure an individual's over-all mental strengths and weaknesses, not just the knowledge of vocabulary and math. For instance, the Wechsler asks subjects to arrange a group of pictures in a sequence that creates a meaningful story.

Achievement tests measure *mastery* of a specific subject. An example is the Metropolitan Achievement Tests. Aptitude tests, on the other hand, are designed to show a student's *potential* for acquiring skills and knowledge.

The best-known aptitude tests are the Scholastic Aptitude Tests, or SAT's. Typically, these examinations measure mathematical ability, vocabulary, and reading comprehension. The SAT's help appraise the ability of a student to succeed in college.

Vocational interest tests are yet another category, designed to measure one's inclination toward different jobs. The Strong-Campbell Interest Inventory test asks students to check off those activities they like and dislike. A vocational counselor can tell the student which jobs are held by people with similar interests.

Choosing Work That's Right for You

There Are Jobs Out There for Animal Lovers

Like many an infant, the soapy cub is upset by her bath.

Dripping wet from the tub, Marissa continues her reproaches.

Wherever there are animals—in the wild or in zoos, parks, wildlife refuges, farms, racetracks, or, for that matter, towns and cities—there are jobs caring for or working in the interests of animals. For example, there are people who track the migration of various species of birds, those who are concerned with populations of marine animals, and those who monitor the living conditions of domesticated animals.

Here, Fred Sterling, a manager of mammals at the New York Zoological Society, sets about giving a bath to a snow leopard cub. One of three cubs, this infant, Marissa, was not doing well, and needed hand rearing. (She was reintroduced to her siblings later, when she was older and able to hold her own.)

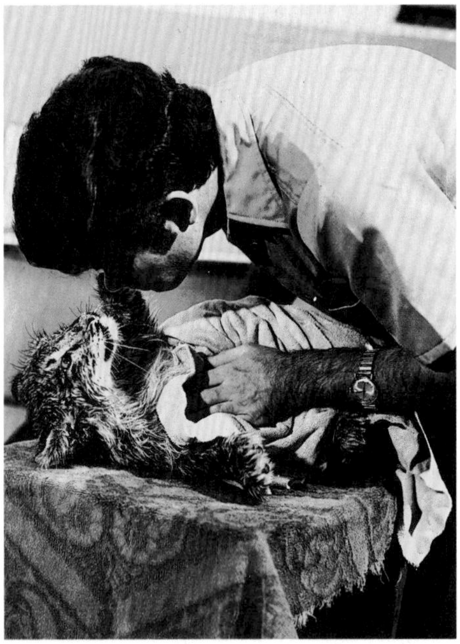

Toweled dry, the tired baby begins to relax.

A thorough drying is provided by a blower.

Are teenagers who work better prepared for adult jobs?

Having part-time and summer jobs does not automatically make teenagers more responsible, better employees, or happier in their adult work. Much depends on the job, the individual, and the individual's attitude. Circumstances and the values instilled by the family, rather than simply working as a teenager, seem to be the key factors in how young people do in their adult jobs.

A California study supports the old idea that working makes youngsters feel better about themselves and helps them focus their sights. Teenage students with jobs showed greater self-reliance than peers who were not working. This was especially true of the girls studied. The girls, too, showed a greater interest in getting more education than did either nonworking teenagers or working boys.

Working did not seem to affect the California teenagers' grades in school. But when adolescents put in long hours on a job or start working at a young age, they tend to miss out on sports and other extracurricular activities, experiences that many psychologists think are important for developing an ability to work with others.

What factors influence a person's choice of a first job?

A few people decide early in life what they want to do and then follow a prescribed path of schooling or training to reach their goal. More often, a young person takes the best job available, and that leads to a lifetime of working in a particular field.

A first job depends on where a young person happens to live, what businesses are hiring there, and what jobs are open. Sex can also be a factor, since women and men tend to be drawn disproportionately to certain jobs: women, for example, into elementary school teaching and men into construction trades. The economy also plays a role: in a slump, jobs are scarce and a young person may have to lower his or her sights.

Finally, both *who* you know and *what* you know are important. Frequently an individual finds a job through a friend, relative, or other helpful person, such as a teacher. However, with a college degree the minimum requirement for jobs in many areas—and advanced training and degrees a must in most professional and technical fields—what you know can be the ticket to a good job.

How do you choose the right job?

There is probably no single "right" job for anybody. Out of the estimated 20,000 types of occupations available in modern society, there are likely hundreds that an individual could perform well and find rewarding. Although circumstances narrow one's choices, there are still many more possibilities than most people realize.

Chance always plays a part in finding a job you like, but vocational counselors believe that a person can improve the odds by analyzing his or her ambitions, interests, and aptitudes. One person may want to earn a lot of money. Others may give priority to being active, helping people, or having a low risk of ever being laid off. Personal interests, such as a love of the outdoors or a fascination with computers, may point the way to a job a person enjoys and respects. Job counselors also urge reading about various careers and talking to people in the fields that are of most interest.

When do most people usually settle down in a job?

What some psychologists call "reality shock" is the discovery by some first-time jobholders that the work is more demanding than school led them to believe, allowing little time for fun and relaxation. Dissatisfaction may also occur because young workers are rarely given much decision-making power until months or even years after being hired. In occupations that help others, such as nursing and social work, disillusionment can set in when the work does not seem to be as morally rewarding as expected or when one's efforts do not seem to be adequately appreciated.

Faced with such disappointments, some young workers look for more compatible work. But most eventually settle down in a field by their late twenties and pursue advancement. Sadly, the price of adjustment may be a loss of idealism and commitment.

People Whose Pictures Shape Our Lives

We live in pictorial times. Every day, television, movies, books, magazines, signs, posters, and advertisements fill our eyes and minds with a wealth of images. We all know the saying, "One picture is worth a thousand words." How true this is can be judged by the fact that in October 1984, when NBC-TV rebroadcast a 5-minute BBC report on famine in Ethiopia, the network switchboard lit up. This was the beginning of a massive worldwide relief effort.

Every form of graphic expression creates an industry in its own right, providing jobs. Photography is particularly rewarding; we all like to know about our fellow human beings, seeing them at work or play. When photographer Roger Ressmeyer was working in a town south of Ottawa, he was enchanted by a little girl in a beautiful white dress "almost like a wedding gown," getting ready for her first communion. Her brother was about to go play baseball when he met them (at right).

The children agreed to pose for a picture. Reports the photographer: "Trevor handed his sister Angela his baseball bat so that he could get the family cat, Dot, into the picture."

Pluses and Minuses on the Job

Can your job affect your personality?

Most people's self-esteem is closely tied to their work. When people meet for the first time, the first questions almost always involve jobs, and the answers tend to spark interest or deaden it. Many of us tend to stereotype people by the kind of work they do. Considering that a job takes about half of a working adult's waking life, it is not surprising that psychologists see work as a significant influence on a person's outlook and behavior.

One 10-year study found that people who have to think and use their judgment to perform complicated tasks at work tend to develop an intellectual flexibility that they carry over into the other parts of their lives. They seem to be generally more independent-minded and open to new experiences than those who perform more routine jobs. They also tend to select intellectually engaging activities for their leisure pursuits, such as learning a language or investigating the history of their area.

Working Conditions in the Not-So-Good "Good Old Days"

In the popular TV program *Upstairs, Downstairs,* the aristocratic Bellamy family (upstairs) is always considerate toward the household staff (downstairs). The staff, in turn, is unfailingly deferential to the Bellamys.

However, belowstairs reality in those bygone days was quite different. The work was arduous, including such duties as hauling jugs of hot water upstairs (and later emptying basins) for every family member and any guests four times a day. Houses were stuffed with furniture and bric-a-brac—a nightmare to keep clean. Servants commonly worked seven days a week, 16 hours a day, with few holidays. Servants' food and sleeping conditions ranged from meager to atrocious, and the pay was paltry. A rigid caste system existed among servants, with those above frequently tyrannizing those below.

Job security was nonexistent. Far from being valued members of the household, servants were often dismissed at a whim, and their places were easily filled from the ranks of great numbers of unemployed.

So, before you wish yourself back in those spacious times, with all the great houses and graceful living, be careful to wish yourself into the select upstairs segment of the population.

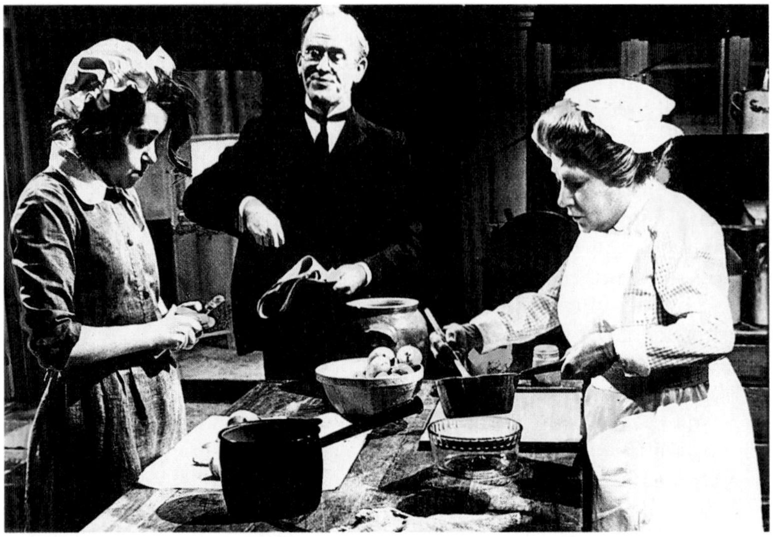

The exemplary butler Hudson (Gordon Jackson) reproves the clumsy scullery maid Ruby (Jenny Tomasin), while Mrs. Bridges (Angela Baddeley) prepares dinner.

Does job satisfaction result in better performance?

Common sense says that a happy worker will be more productive than someone who is dissatisfied. However, many experts believe that the connection between satisfaction and good performance is just the opposite of what most people assume. Instead of happiness contributing to greater job accomplishments, it is the sense of accomplishment from doing well on the job that makes the worker feel competent and happy. But cause and effect are not clear-cut: being satisfied and performing well may be reciprocal, with each affecting the other.

Most studies confirm that unhappy workers are absent more often and are more likely to change jobs than are contented workers. Of course, many dissatisfied employees stay on and continue to do just passable work because they fear not getting paid for excessive absences and being unable to find another job.

What factors besides money motivate people to work?

For most people the need to earn an income is the primary incentive for having a job. But other factors can play powerful roles. Among them are our need to feel productive, to master challenges, to be creative, and to be involved with activities that we enjoy and admire.

Equally important, a job can build feelings of competence and self-esteem, especially in a society that expects people to have regular paid work, and in which individuals attain social status through their jobs. Many people also cite the companionship of their coworkers as a reason to work. Which of these factors are most important depends on the individual and his or her background, expectations, and goals.

In most surveys of job attitudes, a clear majority of professionals, in con-

Skyscrapers have come to symbolize *the world of business; to some extent, the image limits our understanding of jobs in general. Desk work is only part of the story. The ever-present regiments of suppliers, salespeople, and maintenance personnel are essential too.*

trast to other groups, report enjoying their work. This is probably partly explained by the high income levels in such professions as medicine and law. But significantly, university professors were the most happily employed group. More than 90 percent said they would choose the same job, despite the relatively low pay. Also, in the moderately paid field of journalism, more than 70 percent reported being content. These high percentages suggest that intellectual challenge and some degree of autonomy are strong elements in determining how much a person likes work.

At least one experiment suggests that the promise of money may reduce productivity. When test subjects were asked to solve a set of puzzles, the people who were promised payment for correct solutions lost interest when the time was up. But many of those who were offered no reward continued to try to solve the puzzles after the experiment had ended.

What makes somebody a good boss?

Most experts now discredit the belief that a good manager is a born leader with certain definable traits, such as intelligence, confidence, assertiveness, empathy, and organizational skill. They also tend to dismiss the notion that leaders are born of circumstances. This once-popular idea holds that instead of being the right kind of person, a successful manager is simply someone who happens to be in the right place at the right time; and events then mold the lucky individual into an effective leader.

Today, most researchers believe that the capability of a manager depends on how his or her leadership style fits the work situation involved. According to one expert, the most revealing trait of leaders is whether they tend to give priority to getting a job done or to having good relations with their workers. In general, job-oriented managers fare better in situations where workers already get along well with one another and the task to be done is clearly defined. But when establishing good relations among workers is a major concern and the group's goals are less obvious, managers who excel at personal relations are more likely to be successful.

It is easier in some respects to define ineffective management practices than to describe what makes a good leader. A manager is not likely to get the best out of employees, for example, if he or she is constantly giving mixed signals, delegating responsibilities but not power, and failing to define the job to be done.

The effectiveness of an individual manager may change with circumstances. For example, an entrepreneur can be outstanding in spurring a small group to start a successful enterprise but may not be good at handling the complex organizational problems of the expanding corporation.

Facing Up to Success or Failure

What are the characteristics of successful people?

Psychologists believe that some people have a need for achievement that drives them to accomplish tasks in much the same way that hunger stimulates a person to eat. The exact motivation behind this drive varies from person to person. Some people no doubt are impelled by a desire for money, fame, or prestige. Others may be driven to attain certain cherished goals or to gain power. Still others may be motivated by a dread of failing or of not living up to their own or others' expectations.

Whatever the motives, studies suggest that people who feel a need to achieve are usually oriented toward the future and set long-term goals. Surprisingly, they tend not to set extremely tough objectives for themselves. Instead, they aim at moderately difficult goals that they have a realistic chance of reaching. They also show a persistence in solving problems and generally prefer to work with people who are capable rather than just amiable.

Successful people also tend to be independent thinkers. Rather than relying on the judgment of others, they usually establish their own standards and judge their own success in meeting them. Many start their own businesses. They tend to have a strong sense of being competent and believe that their success is the result of their own abilities and hard work.

An Aptitude Test to Reveal Your Mechanical Abilities

Taking an aptitude test may reveal skills you never knew you had. Some schools and businesses use tests of this kind to aid in the selection of trainees for technical jobs. Occupational aptitude tests can help identify various kinds of abilities. Aspiring draftsmen, for instance, are tested for their ability to trace lines, while would-be bookkeepers need to show they can read numbers quickly and accurately.

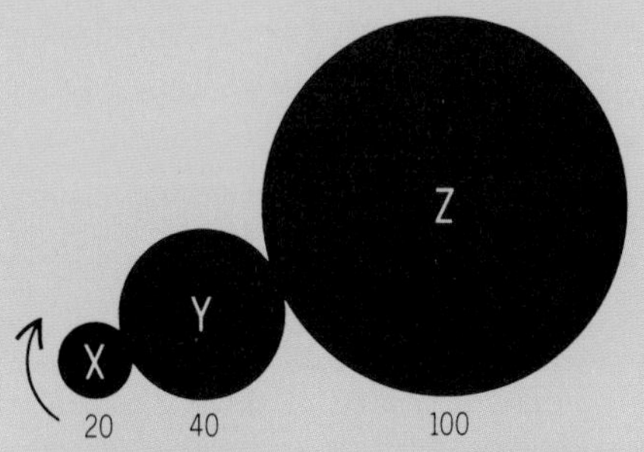

Assume that X, Y, and Z in the diagram above are gears. Gear X has 20 teeth, and drives Gear Y. Gear Y has 40 teeth, and drives Gear Z. Gear Z has 100 teeth.

1. If X turns in the direction shown by the arrow, Y will move:
   (a) In the same direction as the arrow.
   (b) In the opposite direction to the arrow.
   (c) Partly in the same direction as the arrow, and partly counterclockwise.
2. If X turns in the direction shown by the arrow, Z will move:
   (a) In the same direction as the arrow.
   (b) In the opposite direction to the arrow.
   (c) Partly in the same direction as the arrow, and partly counterclockwise.
3. If Z makes a complete turn, X will make:
   (a) 1/5 of a turn.
   (b) 5 turns.
   (c) 1 1/4 turns.
4. If X makes a complete turn, Z will make:
   (a) 1/5 of a turn.
   (b) 5 turns.
   (c) 1 1/4 turns.
5. If X makes a complete turn, Y will make:
   (a) 2 turns.
   (b) 1/2 turn.
   (c) 20 turns.

Answers are on page 322.

A Simple Way to Test Your Attention to Detail

Give yourself about 20 seconds to decide if the numbers in the following pairs are exactly the same. On a separate sheet of paper, write down which of the numbered pairs match. The answers are on page 322.

1.	347612. . .347612	6.	2981. . .2791
2.	960521498. . .960521478	7.	29560418347. . .29560418347
3.	3726. . .3726	8.	520. . .530
4.	851079225. . .851079225	9.	3151684. . .3151684
5.	1438926. . .1438928	10.	65972. . .65972

Do most people like their jobs?

When American workers were asked in a national survey if they would choose the same job again, only half said yes. Finer analysis of the results indicated that about two-thirds of professionals were satisfied with their work while less than a quarter of blue-collar workers were happy. White-collar workers fell in between with about half saying they would select the same job again.

Why do some people have a fear of success?

According to many researchers, people are often afraid of being too successful and may actually sabotage their own chances of getting ahead. Of course, there are many good reasons why a person might not want advancement, such as concerns about being overworked, facing greater stress, and shouldering additional responsibilities. Some of us may also see a job as simply a way to earn money while reserving a deeper commitment for family or other involvements outside the job.

When they use the term *fear of success,* psychologists are usually referring to people who profess ambition but unconsciously undermine their own chances of success. Such people may not work to capacity or may downplay their abilities. "One possible reason," says psychologist Don E. Hamachek, "is that success establishes a precedent, a standard to be lived up to, a performance level to be maintained, and this may be frightening to individuals who have basic doubts about their ability to sustain a high level of personal performance." In effect, by not trying to achieve to their full potential, these workers cushion themselves against the possibility that they might fail.

Work is not the only place where fear of success occurs. It may also hamstring achievement in school grades, sports, and personal goals, such as losing weight. Indeed, some psychologists think that most people have some area in which they are afraid of succeeding.

What are the psychological effects of being fired?

Whether it's called a layoff, involuntary early retirement, or being fired, losing a job hurts. The feeling of loss is deep because a person's sense of identity is usually closely linked with work. "In our society, you are what you do," says a psychiatrist who specializes in occupational counseling. "That gets stripped from you when you get fired. You become, in a sense, vocationally naked."

Emotionally, a person who has lost a job is likely to go through several stages of reaction, according to reseacher Carole Hyatt. The first is usually shock and disbelief. This may be followed by concern about making ends meet and by anger and frustration. Then self-doubt and a feeling of shame may set in before the individual finally comes to accept the situation. People who are unhappy with their jobs may be an exception. After the initial shock, they may actually feel relief more than anything else.

Like other stressful events, job loss can take a physical toll. A person who has been let go has a greater chance of having headaches, colds, gastrointestinal upsets, and high blood pressure. Loss of a job can also place a great strain on relations within a family.

PERSPECTIVES

On Work

In all our striving for advancement, it's well to keep this in mind: Success is getting what you want; happiness is wanting what you get.

A Healthy Workout

"Work is a basic biological need of man. The question is not whether we should or should not work, but what kind of work best suits each individual. In order to function normally, man needs work as he needs air, food, sleep, social contacts, or sex." **—Hans Selye**

◆

Three Keys to Success

"What do young managers need? . . . They need to know the contents of the toolbox, the elementary tools—whether you are talking of accounting or marketing. They are not that hard to learn, and I think one ought to learn them.

"Secondly, I think they need to know quite a bit about themselves. How do you work? What kind of person are you? What are you good at? What have you done uncommonly well, and why? And what can you learn from it? Learn to use what you are good at. I don't believe very much in overcoming weaknesses because I don't know how one does it.

"The third thing I'd say young managers need—the phrase is probably communication skill—but I don't mean that. It is very largely a realization that unless they take responsibility for making themselves understood, they won't be. . . . It is also saying it is my job to make sure I make myself understood. It is not other people's job to pick it up. . . . The smart way to tell them is not to tell them but to go and ask for advice."

—Peter Drucker
An Interview With Peter Drucker

◆

Crossing T's, Dotting I's

"In the end, it is attention to detail that makes all the difference. It's the center fielder's extra two steps to the left, the salesman's memory for names, the lover's phone call, the soldier's clean weapon. It is the thing that separates the winners from the losers, the men from the boys and very often, the living from the dead. Professional success depends on it, regardless of the field."

—David Noonan
Esquire

◆

Beware Myopia

"It is said that sheep may get lost simply by nibbling away at the grass and never looking up. That can be true for any of us. We can focus so much on what is immediately before us that we fail to see life in larger perspective." **—Donald Bitsberger**
Forward Day by Day

◆

Two Sides of One Coin

"Success and failure. We think of them as opposites, but they're really not. They're *companions*—the hero and the sidekick."

—Laurence Shames
Esquire

◆

Front and Center

"If you wish in this world to
advance
Your virtues you're bound to
enhance
You must stir it and stump it
And blow your own trumpet
Or, trust me, you haven't a
chance." **—W. S. Gilbert**
Iolanthe

◆

The Real Test

"To laugh often and much; to win the respect of intelligent people and the affection of children; to earn the appreciation of honest critics and endure the betrayal of false friends; to appreciate beauty, to find the best in others; to leave the world a bit better, whether by a healthy child, a garden patch or a redeemed social condition; to know even one life has breathed easier because you have lived. This is to have succeeded."

—Ralph Waldo Emerson
Unlimited Power

The Special World of Working Women

Coping with the demands *of impending motherhood is all part of the job these days. In fact, studies show that being moderately active improves a pregnant woman's well-being. Women employed in strenuous jobs are advised to stop work at six months.*

Are women conditioned not to succeed?

Differences in the ways that boys and girls are treated at school may affect their later performance at work. Specifically, many psychologists believe that much of what is learned in the classroom about interacting with others and being rewarded has a lifelong influence on a person's self-esteem, morale, and ability to get ahead.

At least until recently, more boys than girls participated in competitive team sports during the school years. Some successful women say that this meant they had to learn the lessons of team play on the job, rather than in school athletics. One such lesson is the ability to take losses in stride, without being devastated by them.

Although most schools today go to great lengths to offer equal opportunity to both sexes, teachers unwittingly seem to give boys more attention than girls. In fact, one study showed that boys are the objects of their teachers' attention up to five times more frequently than girls are.

Boys may receive so much more notice in part because they are more likely to misbehave and require discipline, especially in the earlier grades. But studies also suggest that boys speak out and seek help more frequently than girls and that teachers call on them more often. All this may help to develop an assertiveness and an ability to deal with authority that the youngsters carry over into their adult jobs.

Perhaps even more important to later self-confidence on the job, boys are more often praised for the quality of their work, according to the studies. When girls receive praise, it is usually for good behavior. Even being criticized seems to work in boys' favor. Because they are more frequently berated for their conduct, boys tend to become less sensitive to criticism and tend not to see it as an indication of a lack of ability on their part. When girls are faulted, on the other hand, it is likely to be for the quality of their schoolwork, making them less sure of their skills.

Of course, many women succeed in their jobs despite these and other obstacles. And a much greater number of girls are now growing up with the goal of becoming successful in a job.

What psychological barriers do women face in the workplace?

Many people make unconscious assumptions about what jobs men and women can and cannot do well. In one experiment, a group of people was told a story that involved a surgeon. Most of the group automatically assumed the surgeon was a man even when there were clues that the person in question was a woman. People may similarly suppose that a nurse is a woman.

Other studies suggest that people tend to undervalue some types of work produced by women. When one group was given an essay with a man's name listed as the author, they rated it higher than a comparable group rated the same essay with a woman's name cited as the writer.

Although such biases may be unintentional, they can limit the positions to which women are promoted. And since women themselves often share such assumptions, unconscious discrimination of this sort may restrict a woman's aspirations at work.

How is a woman's success viewed compared with a man's?

Studies indicate that we tend to evaluate the achievements of men and women very differently. When a man performs a job successfully, people are most likely to credit his ability. But when a woman does well, they tend to attribute her success to good fortune. As researcher Kay Deaux of Purdue University says, "What is skill for the male is luck for the female."

Deaux and others who have studied the role of a person's sex in the workplace say that this bias also affects the perception of failure, but with a reverse twist. When a man does not perform as well as expected, people usually blame it on bad luck or on the man's not trying hard enough. If a woman fails, however, they tend to attribute it to her lack of ability. Even successful women seem to share these assumptions.

The inequitable view of women's work performance, Deaux suggests, is rooted in people's expectations about each sex. Most of us are raised to believe that men have the ability to do their jobs, but we usually have lower expectations for women. As a result, a woman's success is ascribed to luck.

How are children affected by working mothers?

In some respects, having a mother who works may actually be an advantage for children, according to several studies. Daughters especially seem to benefit from having a working mother as a role model. These girls tend to be high achievers and develop a sense of independence. They look up to their mothers and feel confident about their own abilities.

Sons whose mothers hold down a job seem to develop a more positive attitude about the capability of working women in general. But in one study, sons of mothers who stayed home got higher school grades than boys whose mothers had to be out of the house on jobs.

Both boys and girls usually have more household chores to do when their mothers work. Researchers believe that this helps build a sense of responsibility and bolster children's feelings about their competence. Children with employed mothers also seem generally to have more contact with their fathers.

What are the psychological effects of combining a job with motherhood?

Surveys indicate that women still bear the major responsibility for housekeeping and child rearing in most homes. As a result, a working mother may find herself physically and emotionally drained by trying to meet what are assumed to be her responsibilities. Invariably, too, frustrating and stressful conflicts arise among her roles as mother, worker, spouse, and homemaker. For example, the problem of what to do when a child is sick and must stay home or go to the doctor can pose tremendous interpersonal and emotional ramifications. Such difficulties are compounded when a woman is a single parent or hates her job.

On the other hand, some studies suggest that working wives and mothers generally have happier marriages and better physical and mental health. Working can be a positive experience for a woman if she has a pleasant, rewarding job and the support and help of her husband and children, who make a habit of pitching in and gently but firmly reminding her that she does not have to do and be everything for everybody all the time. Then, psychologists say, a mother who works can develop an increased sense of self-worth from the wider contact with the outside world provided by a job she likes.

Day-care centers can be places *of fun and learning, where children absorb lessons in getting along with others their age.*

Recharging Your Batteries

Trekking through the Himalayas in Nepal *may not be everyone's idea of a vacation; but for this intrepid New York graphic designer it proved the perfect way to get away from it all. Said she, "It was the most exhilarating experience of my life."*

How important is leisure?

Many psychologists see leisure as an essential counterbalance to work. Overwork can contribute to harmful stress and can diminish the ability to concentrate and to perform a job effectively. Leisure activities refresh and revitalize the body and the mind.

The brain, according to experts, needs stimulation of various kinds in order to stay in top form. Some of us do not mind repetitive daily routines, but others are bored by them, especially if they continue over weeks and months. When this occurs, the brain adapts by reducing its level of activity, but then the brain has mechanisms that kick in and arouse a need for stimulation. A craving for a change of pace, even a desire for excitement, can occur. Leisure, by offering a change of routine, can be one way of getting the brain working at the top of its form again.

Too much change, however, can be as bad as no change at all. If your schedule is never the same from day to day, you may begin to long for peace and quiet and for time to relax and restore yourself. Cravings like these may be linked to the levels of neurotransmitters in your brain.

What is the healthiest way to approach a vacation?

Anyone setting out on a vacation should firmly resolve to put day-to-day responsibilities not only out of sight but out of mind. The most beneficial vacations are real breaks from everyday life. It is also important to approach a vacation with an open mind. This means being willing to accept what the vacation has to offer, come what may, and being ready to savor the new and the different. It means being able to relax despite the minor inconveniences of travel that invariably arise.

Some people want constant stimulation during their vacations. They must see everything on their itinerary and end their evenings in a disco. Others prefer to sightsee for a couple of hours a day and then take advantage of free time to unwind. "Real relaxation lies in the enjoyment of experience," says one specialist in the use of leisure. If family or friends are along, this expert urges, it is important to spend some time alone every day. This need be no more than 20 minutes, but too much togetherness can bring its own irritations.

No one has written more felicitously about getting away from it all than the American author John Steinbeck in his book *Travels With Charley*. "A trip, a safari, an exploration, is an entity, different from all other journeys. It has personality, temperament, individuality, uniqueness. A journey is a person in itself; no two are alike. And all plans, safeguards, policing and coercion are fruitless. We find after years of struggle that we do not take a trip; a trip takes us. Tour masters, schedules, reservations, brass-bound and inevitable, dash themselves to wreckage on the personality of the trip. In this a journey is like marriage. The certain way to be wrong is to think you control it."

Why do some people find it so difficult to relax?

Workaholics tend to see time off as time wasted. They typically feel that every minute has to be devoted to attaining the goals they have set for themselves. They may be corporate presidents or college students, but they share an inability to relax.

An excessive and compulsive drive for achievement may be based on a distortion of a deeply ingrained work ethic. Counselors have found that one way to persuade workaholics to relax is to convince them that time off will improve their productivity, that giving themselves time to refuel will enable them to perform twice as well.

For many, taking it easy is something they must actually learn to do. They have to consult "leisure counselors," who may advise them to try to discover the hidden benefits of leisure by seeking out activities as far removed as possible from the daily routines of the job. A counselor might also recommend that dedicated workaholics join a leisure-oriented club or make a list of things they have always secretly wanted to do.

What is the best way to spend leisure time?

People's ideas of how to use their leisure vary greatly, of course. For some the perfect way is to settle down with a good book. For others it may be working in the garden, or dancing till dawn on a Caribbean cruise, or backpacking through the Himalayas. Upbringing and personal tastes, researchers believe, determine which leisure activity is most fulfilling.

Sometimes, social pressure has a lot to do with the choice of a leisure pursuit. People seeking to conform to a fashionable ideal, such as going to a popular resort or an exotic locale, or owning a boat or vacation home, often do so at the risk of increasing their stress rather than reducing it. A simpler, more restful—not to mention less expensive—vacation might have been a better way to recharge mentally and physically.

Does your mind always return from vacation when you do?

Even after a marvelous vacation, many people are glad to be home again in familiar surroundings. Others may feel out of synch and disoriented. They are victims of post-vacation dysphoria, or "vacation lag."

This condition results from the mind's reaction to the contrast between an easygoing holiday existence and the pressures of everyday life. It may be especially acute for people in very stressful occupations or for those stuck in jobs they dislike intensely.

One tip for beating post-vacation anxieties: plan to come home a few days before you have to report back to work. A few quiet days of reorientation may make returning to the job easier to handle.

Sometimes vacation lag can push people to make positive changes in their lives. They may simply add extra leisure activities to their week. Or they may decide to change jobs or seek career or psychiatric counseling.

What if you just can't get away?

The value of vacations can hardly be overstated. However, if job pressures prevent you from taking the time off that you have earned, a few stolen moments in the middle of the day can be effective in reducing stress and bringing the change of pace you need. Many companies today encourage longer and more frequent break times, because experts have shown that periodic rest breaks increase worker productivity. Taking a break can also inspire creative solutions to intractable problems.

A few days of slumping *and forgetting appearances can help dispel the tension of work and recharge inner batteries.*

Charting a New Course

Should older people keep working as long as possible?

Movie producer David Brown advises: "Work yourself to death. It's the only way to live." Comedian George Burns insists that he can't stop working: he's booked to play at London's Palladium when he is 100.

Others think older workers should retire to make way for the young. This was one reason why the German chancellor Otto von Bismarck in 1881 introduced pensions for people over 65. For many years retirement at 65 was the rule, but nowadays it is not generally mandated. Nevertheless, more and more people are retiring early. And while some discover that "the golf course is only good for about three months," others agree with the 73-year-old author of a letter to *Modern Maturity* who wrote, "If I'd known it was this good, I'd have retired 70 years ago."

The choice seems to depend on the individual and the work he or she does. Monotonous work is rarely rewarding enough to keep people on the job when they can afford to quit, but managers often thrive by staying in harness. And creative people can produce at any age. However, in mathematics and physics major discoveries have been made almost exclusively by scientists in their early years.

A Look at Low-Key Retirement

There's nothing to say that retired people must make big changes in their lives—such as selling their homes and moving to retirement communities. There's no law that says retired people have to structure every moment of their newfound freedom either (unless they really want to). Many people are content to live just the way they always have, but with more time for coffee in the morning and the newspaper in the evening. There is, after all no need to rush anymore.

Family, friends, and associates may urge starting a new business, or investing in a new enterprise. But it's *your* retirement, so suit yourself.

Pets often benefit from retirement, as owners give them more time. This dog's whiskers are perfectly groomed. (Oft-observed, the resemblance of pet and owner has no scientific explanation.)

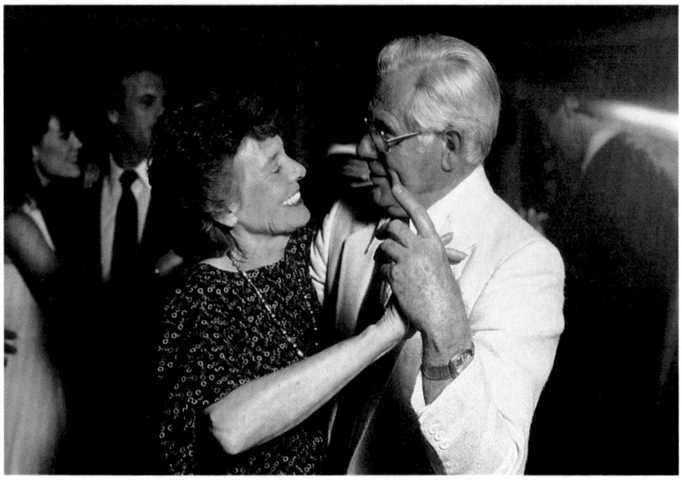

Dancing to those old favorite tunes is one of the sweetest, easiest ways to recapture your youth. Dancing is first-class exercise, too.

Do some personality types adjust better to retirement than others?

Psychologists have drawn up a scale of personalities according to their adjustment to aging, giving the highest rating to the "reorganizers," who find new activities readily. Business managers and professionals who are used to planning their own schedules generally fall into this category. Unless executives have made firm retirement plans, however, they may still be dismayed by the sudden loss of power and prestige that comes with quitting work.

Falling into another well-adjusted category are "disengaged" people, those who enjoy cutting down on activities. Instead of moping, they turn inward to a less demanding, more contemplative life.

People who are used to strenuous physical work may be frustrated when failing strength ends their working life and limits their activities. And, oddly, people who have had to punch a time clock for 40 years may find themselves at loose ends.

What do people fear most about retirement?

Illness and death top the list of fears. We've all heard of someone who died within six months of retiring. But the idea that retirement causes early death is a myth. Serious illness more often precedes than follows retirement. Sheila Miller, Ph.D., of the Scripps Gerontology Center at Miami University of Ohio, adds, "It's not uncommon for people who retire early because of poor health to experience a slight improvement in health."

Many people are afraid they will

not have enough money to live on when they retire, and thus give careful thought to pre-retirement financial planning. While sufficient income does not guarantee happiness in retirement, it removes a major worry.

People who have been wrapped up in their work may also fear an emptiness in their lives. Depression can follow retirement, but even if someone does suffer from it, studies show that it is almost always temporary.

Boredom is another common fear. "What do you do with your time?" is probably the question retirees hear most often. But in one survey conducted for the National Council on Aging, only 6 percent of them actually had trouble keeping busy.

The joking lament of the retiree's wife—"I married you for better or for worse, but not for lunch"—hides a real concern. Conflicts can arise if a bored husband wanders restlessly around the house or tries to take over tasks that his wife is used to doing. Married women whose careers started late in life may be even more frustrated than retired men when they are forced to return home full-time.

School can be wonderful the second time around! *Unlike the youngsters in the class, older people have a wealth of experience to draw upon.*

When should you begin to plan activities or hobbies for your retirement?

Some fortunate people find rewarding part-time activities related to their former work—like the retired executive chef who designs ice sculptures for banquets. Others devote more time to favorite hobbies, from carpentry to bird-watching.

Yet you can take up a new interest at any age. You may feel more freedom to experiment when neither your livelihood nor your sense of identity depends on your becoming an instant expert. Judith Viorst writes of her friend Irene, who at 68 "tells me it isn't too late to take up tennis. But then nothing is ever too late for Irene, who recently began to write a novel. And a few years ago embarked on singing lessons. And prior to that took science courses at Harvard. And still dreams of learning to paint, play a musical instrument, pay a visit to Iceland and tap-dance."

What are the greatest rewards of retirement?

Among the pleasures frequently cited by retired people are the following: more time for family and friends, a deeper relationship with a spouse, the pursuit of cherished dreams such as achieving a long-sought perfection in the garden, the freedom to study a language, to write a novel, or to take off on a trip around the world.

Retired people also find that they relish being their own boss and that time spent working for a favorite cause or charity is one of the compensations for leaving the workplace.

Perhaps the most valuable reward was described in a tongue-in-cheek article by former executive George Nelson in *The New York Times*. He had read about the need to plan carefully for an active retirement. On his first day at home, he set up a busy schedule consisting of a two-mile walk, two art and literature classes, and service for two volunteer organizations. "Everything seemed exactly right. A misfortune occurred, however. My wife, thinking I was to begin a new life, turned off the alarm. I overslept by three hours. I was frantic.

" 'Don't panic,' said my wife. 'Just have a good breakfast.'

"Which I did.

" 'Then go get the papers.'

"Which I did.

"On the way back, I noticed that the sun was shining and that the park benches were empty. My wife came along and said, 'Why don't we sit down?'

"Which we did.

"I was getting ready to leave for my 2 p.m. class, but some kids turned up with bats, gloves and a ball, and said they needed an umpire. I couldn't resist. The game didn't end until 5:30 p.m. Then we went home and had dinner. . . .

"If things keep up this way, my whole retirement will be ruined."

Honing Athletic Skills

Truly a soccer genius, *the Brazilian called Pelé tells of entering a strange, calm zone of invincibility when playing at his peak. Other great athletes report similar feelings.*

Is the mind as important as the body in athletics?

Well-conditioned muscles, a strong heart, and healthy lungs are standard equipment for good athletes. But scientists are increasingly aware of the fundamental role of the mind in orchestrating athletic performance.

The mind underlies athletic skill in two general ways. First, the brain acts upon a flood of information reaching the senses. Some brains seem to do this faster and more efficiently than others, and athletic ability depends in part upon how quickly or surely the brain responds to signals and then directs the body to move.

Athletic performance is also controlled by the mind in a more subtle way, not yet fully understood. Many top athletes (and weekend competitors as well) talk about "mental toughness" and "mental preparation" being the difference between winning and losing, playing well or poorly. No two athletes define this attitude the same way, but what seems to be involved is learning how to tune out distractions and pressures and concentrating utterly on the moves of the game. There is apparently a fine line, furthermore, between concentrating too hard, which causes an athlete to tense up and commit errors, and a kind of automatic and relaxed concentration, which allows peak performance. Sports psychologist Jim E. Loehr describes the desired attitude as "managing mental energy."

Thus, athletics brings into play not one specific function of the mind but a whole catalogue of mental activities: cognition, emotions, and both conscious and unconscious responses to signals received by the senses. At least up to the limit of their physical prowess, individuals can improve their athletic performances by training their minds as well as their bodies.

What are an athlete's most important senses?

Sensors in the muscles, tendons, and joints provide the brain, through the nervous system, with constant updates on the positions of the arms and legs. Your eyes supply a wealth of data ranging from spatial orientation to strategic information on the actions and whereabouts of opponents.

Not only does the inner ear give us our sense of balance, but hearing often serves as the "eyes in the back of the head," to help us sense our overall situation. Learning to interpret sounds can also give you a valuable edge in a sport. For example, the thwack of your opponent's tennis racquet can help you anticipate the speed, direction, and spin of the ball you are about to return.

Why are the right body moves more mental than physical?

Whether you're a batter who has solved the mystery of how to hit a dipping, darting ball or a marathon runner struggling toward the finish line, much of the training that has brought you to your level of achievement has conditioned your mind, not your body. Your performance is really a reflection of how your training has fine-tuned the way your brain regulates the movements of your body.

Data from receptors surges along your nerves into the brain in a continuous stream. Only a fraction of this data is selected for retention (by some as yet unknown process, whose selectivity may differ from person to person); the rest fades within a second. Then, according to one theory, the retained bits of information are sent to short-term memory, where they are compared to experiences drawn from long-term memory. Your brain then decides upon a reaction, consults long-term memory again to call up the patterns of learned motor skills that are stored there, and finally issues the commands that get your body moving in the required way.

From the initial sensing to the movement by the body, the entire process usually takes no more than half a second. In the world of sports, where seconds are divided into a hundred parts, a reaction time increased or decreased by a few hundedths of a second can mean the difference between defeat and victory.

How are athletic skills learned?

Most sports require well-tuned motor skills and a highly developed sense of spatial orientation, or of exactly where your body is in space from moment to moment. Both of these functions are primarily the concern of the right brain, and they are learned by imitation and repetition. Thus three words sum up what is necessary to reach your potential in a sport: practice, practice, practice. A powerful golf swing, a deft soccer dribble, or an accurate cue stroke in billiards—each is the result of the brain summoning up, and then issuing orders to duplicate, patterns that have been imprinted on long-term memory by repeating the correct movements over and over.

In their first efforts to learn a sport, beginners often bemoan getting bogged down "thinking about the mechanics" of what they are doing. This is necessary because the left brain is active at this point in the learning process. But as the movements are repeated and corrected and repeated again, they become indelibly etched on long-term memory until conscious effort is no longer required to perform them. When a skill is so well learned as to be almost instinctive, it will seldom be lost. Riding a bike is perhaps the classic example of this type of learned skill.

Is a tough sports competitor basically aggressive?

A fierce competitor on the playing field can be a pussycat off the field. Ex-pro footballer Roosevelt Grier, for example, was known as an unforgiving competitor on the field, but was happy off the field absorbed in an unlikely hobby: needlepoint.

Though many top athletes do seem to share some aggressive personality traits, these attributes are apparently just as common in other successful people. Psychologists have found it difficult to devise a test that will reveal what combination of personality traits, if any, marks a talented athlete for superstar status.

Is there such a thing as a born athlete?

The genes you are born with set certain limits on athletic ability. Such qualities as the shape and size of bones and muscles are genetically determined and strongly influence what sports you are best suited for and how good you can get at any of them. For example, someone with genes that project a height of over 6 feet and big bones is not likely to become a top jockey, nor is a person endowed with a short, slight body build likely to become a successful heavyweight boxer.

Tuning out distractions, *internal and external, is a skill shared by top athletes, but few acquire it so young as this Olympics hopeful, the archery prodigy Denise Parker, competing here at age 13.*

Beyond this, of two people who seem equally matched in physical attributes and who have undergone the same conditioning, one may be clearly more "athletic" than the other. One explanation seems to be that the brain and nervous system of the better athlete have somehow been genetically programmed for faster reaction times, smoother coordination, and other traits that are important for athletic achievement, such as agility, running speed, manual dexterity, and various kinds of strength.

How important is an athlete's will to win?

"Winning isn't everything," said football coach Vince Lombardi, "it's the only thing." Lombardi was talking about glory and riches going to the winners of a contest, not to the also-rans, and in that sense he was at least partly right. But thinking obsessively about the abstract, relatively distant goal of winning may distract the athlete's mind from the task at hand, say some sports psychologists. They feel that the critical factor in success is the athlete's ability to focus his or her concentration on the game, move after move, play after play.

In the heat of competition an athlete's short-term memory is constantly monitoring choices as to which pieces of information are significant. A totally focused competitor makes those choices faster and better, freeing part of the mind to plan strategy and anticipate the actions of an opponent.

Some athletes more than others seem to have the power to tap the sources of psychic energy that allow them to concentrate and anticipate. Many athletes and coaches talk of motivation—or desire, as it is frequently called—as a key variable. The desire to perform at a level approaching absolute perfection is a trait shared by all super athletes.

Mind Over Muscle

Can anybody be a great athlete?

While there seem to be natural athletes, this does not mean that there are natural world-class athletes, people for whom it is easy to become the best in their sport. Whatever their game, the world's top athletes have spent years pushing their bodies and minds to achieve just one or at most a small collection of skills. This is probably the reason why few world-class athletes excel at more than one sport or even more than one aspect of a sport. Skiers, for instance, tend to be excellent at either downhill racing or negotiating slalom courses, seldom both.

Of course, once every decade or so, a "sports genius" appears. This may be someone who plays the game better than anyone had thought possible. In the 1980's the hockey player Wayne Gretzky fit this description. Over half a century before him, there was Babe Ruth, whose combined talent as a pitcher and a batter has never been equaled before or since.

Or someone may appear like Jim Thorpe, who excelled in a dozen sports. Such people are blessed with many natural motor skills, which perfectly match the sports they choose, and an uncanny knack for learning quickly. They are extremely rare.

Visualizing the flight of his shots *and where they would land helped Jack Nicklaus rank among the best in golf for over two decades.*

How do athletes practice in their minds?

To a greater or lesser extent, ever since tests of physical skill began, individual athletes have probably used some form of what today's sports psychologists call visualization. This is the technique of mentally rehearsing the moves and timing necessary to achieve a superior level of performance. For example, Jack Nicklaus and other golfers have described making every shot in their imagination before they hit it, and in his Olympic gold-medal performances diver Greg Louganis used visualization as part of his preparation for every dive.

In recent years the elements of the technique have been analyzed and applied systematically to train both individuals and teams. The training stresses three steps: setting a goal, learning to relax, and visualizing a successful outcome. This approach has seemed to produce better performances in Olympic athletes, although separating the benefits of one type of training from another is difficult when, of course, both mental and physical preparation are involved.

What makes visualizing work?

Some athletes liken visualization to learning a skill by watching an instructional film or video. Others report they experience more of a feeling than an image, as if they were playing the game rather than observing it. Dr. Kay Porter and Judy Foster, authors of the book *The Mental Athlete,* have suggested that "visualizing specific movements, performance techniques, or personal endeavors creates neural patterns in the brain. The more one visualizes, the more ingrained these neural patterns become. Since it is the brain that tells the muscles what to do—when and how to move—the stronger the patterns, the more perfect the movement."

Visualization, say its proponents, is not just for top athletes. Even those with modest personal goals can use their minds to improve their performance and heighten their enjoyment of many kinds of activities.

"Sir, You Are the Greatest Athlete in the World"

Jim Thorpe was a member of the Sac and Fox tribe and the great-grandson of the warrior Black Hawk. He was brought up on the open plains of Oklahoma, where his pride in his heritage spurred him on to make the most of his inborn physical skills.

Thorpe starred *on both offense and defense and kicked field goals with precision. He was 6 feet 2 inches tall and weighed 185 pounds.*

IN 1950, WHEN JIM THORPE was 61 years old, a national poll was taken among sports broadcasters and writers. They were asked to name the greatest all-around athlete of the first half of the 20th century. Of the 393 people polled, 252, two out of three, picked Jim Thorpe for first place.

Thorpe, who was born on May 28, 1888, liked to credit his phenomenal athletic skills to his childhood training in the Indian Territory of today's Oklahoma. "I was never content," he said, "unless I was trying my skill in some game against my playmates or testing my endurance and wits against a member of the animal kingdom."

When he was 15 years old, he was asked to enter the Carlisle Indian School (now closed) in Pennsylvania. Word of his great natural athletic potential had reached Glenn "Pop" Warner, Carlisle's famous football coach. Warner was perfect for Thorpe. Demanding but never dictatorial, he could coax the best out of Thorpe. Warner once recalled: "No college player I ever saw had the natural aptitude for football possessed by Jim Thorpe." Beyond his unique physical talents, Thorpe was also endowed with the ability to concentrate and with an irrepressible enthusiasm for sports. "Football," Warner said, "was just a good time for Jim. I never saw him snarl. Most of the time he just laughed, talked to the boys on the other team; he enjoyed himself."

Not long after Thorpe joined Carlisle's football squad, headline writers were calling the team, with reason, Thorpe's Indians. In four years of playing for Carlisle, Thorpe led the school to victory in 43 games out of a total of 50 games played. In 1911 he was picked for the All-American team.

The following year, Thorpe also won 10 gold medals in intercollegiate track and field events. He was the obvious choice for the U.S. Olympic team, which was to compete in the 1912 Stockholm games.

Thorpe, along with the rest of the team, spent the Atlantic crossing in intense training. But he had his own very personal approach to the coming challenges. In Stockholm he was observed by a teammate taking a piece of chalk, drawing a line on the sidewalk, carefully pacing out 23 feet, and then simply standing and gazing thoughtfully at the measured distance, as though visualizing it in his mind. When the time came to make the broad jump, he cleared 23 feet, 2⁷⁄₁₀ inches.

Competing in two categories of track and field events, he won the 200-meter race and the 1500-meter race, the broad jump, the discus throwing, 110-meter high hurdles, and the shot put. With no previous training, he came in third in javelin throwing and pole vaulting. To this day, his feats remain an unparalleled accomplishment. Jim Thorpe was presented with his two gold medals by the Swedish king, Gustav V, with the words, "Sir, you are the greatest athlete in the world."

Back home, Thorpe, now a beloved national hero, a major star, was greeted with adulation and parades wherever he went. Then in January 1913 a newspaper reported and Thorpe readily admitted that he had once earned money playing baseball. The Amateur Athletic Union immediately disallowed Thorpe's amateur standing and rescinded his eligibility as an Olympic contender. He was forced to return his medals, his wins were stricken from the record. There was an outcry across the country and abroad, but the AAU remained self-righteously adamant.

In 1913 Thorpe became a professional. He signed on to play baseball for the New York Giants, under the tough, unforgiving John J. McGraw. It was an unhappy relationship for both men, which ended when McGraw called Thorpe a "dumb Indian" and Thorpe chased him around the field.

Thorpe played professional football up to the end of the 1920's. But, inevitably, his days as an athlete were numbered. When the Depression came, he was hard hit. For a while he worked as a painter for a Los Angeles oil company. "No one knew me," he said, "and I was lost in the oblivion of paint buckets and brushes while I painted filling stations and trucks." He was given some bit parts in Hollywood movies. Traveling in his broken-down car, he went on lecture tours, an unlikely profession for someone as laconic and plainspoken as he.

But Thorpe was never forgotten. Beginning in the 1950's, agitation grew to persuade the AAU to return his awards and reinstate his records. Jim Thorpe died of a heart attack on March 28, 1953. In 1973 the AAU restored his amateur status. Ten years later, in 1983, the International Olympic Committee gave his medals to his family.

Hitting Your Stride

What causes an athlete to have a hot streak?

Most people who play a sport regularly have experienced periods when it seems they can do everything right, almost without effort: an average baseball player bats over .500 for a series, a hockey goalie has a run of miraculous saves, a tennis player pulls off a string of fabulous returns. Among athletes, who refer to it as being in "the zone" or "the groove," such a streak is often revered as almost magical. Their awe is not new. In ancient times when games were dedicated to the gods, extraordinary feats were considered divinely inspired, a nod of favor from a deity.

Many statisticians, on the other hand, see nothing mysterious in a hot streak. They compare it to those times when tossing a coin turns up a string of consecutive heads or tails. And some coaches and sports psychologists contend that finding "the zone" is simply the payoff for endless hours of practice and training.

Still, any athlete would choose to have peak performances, day in and day out, for as long as he or she plays the game. But no athlete can do that. Why? One theory is that the conscious mind is the villain. "Your conscious mind always wants to help you," says professional archer and coach Tim Strickland, "but usually it messes you up." In this view, the answer probably lies somewhere in the more primitive areas of the brain, below the level of consciousness, where training has imprinted the perfect execution of the required skills on motor memory. During a hot streak, instructions from these areas may directly control visual and motor coordination, without having to pass through the conscious mind. And perhaps a streak ends (and a slump begins) when the conscious mind reasserts itself in the process.

What causes an athlete to "choke"?

When a professional golfer misses a one-foot putt to lose a tournament, or an Olympic champion makes a mistake and fails badly, they often say

Joggers like their sport's casualness—all it requires is less than an hour, running shoes, and maybe an open road. With a friend, it's also fun.

The joy of winning, as seen in the movie *Chariots of Fire.*

How Fitness Became a Way of Life

The award-winning British movie *Chariots of Fire* was released in 1981 at the peak of a fitness craze in America. The film depicted the exhilaration of running in the 1924 Olympics and undoubtedly inspired many a would-be runner to try a jog, at least around the block. But running has proved to be no ordinary fad. Runners could not stop talking about the euphoric feelings they often experienced during and after a vigorous workout. Moreover, medical evidence shows that exercising, which improves your circulation and strengthens your heart, can help prevent certain diseases. With some exceptions, the prescription for well-being is simple: exercise. It not only makes you feel good, it can also improve your health.

they "choked" or "clutched." One reason athletes perform below their abilities, whether for an instant or over longer periods, is difficulty in coping with stress. Athletic competitions are stressful in themselves. The ability to control that stress through concentration is part of the challenge of sports. But when stress gives way to panic or even mild anxiety, the athlete can lose his or her concentration and perform poorly.

To help athletes cope with stress, many psychologists advocate relaxation training. Meditation and breathing techniques of the sort once practiced only by mystics are today helping many athletes prevent stress from affecting their performances. These techniques seem to stimulate a natural relaxation response by diverting the conscious mind from the situation that is causing the stress.

Certain exercises, such as closing the eyes and breathing deeply, affect the hypothalamus and decrease the activity of the sympathetic nervous system, one of the body's main activators. This brings relaxation and enables a person to regain control of his or her emotions. Through training, some athletes can learn to trigger this response in themselves.

What is runner's high?

Runner's high, a feeling of physical and mental well-being, can occur during or after a period of exercise that makes the cardiovascular system work harder for longer than it does in most activities. For example, about 30 to 45 minutes of jogging may produce the feeling in many people. A common misconception is that runner's high is caused exclusively by the release of endorphins, brain chemicals that cause pleasure and reduce pain in a manner similar to opiate drugs. But researchers say that endorphin release does not tell the whole story.

Exercise puts the body into stress and causes the release of a battery of neurochemicals that, in turn, triggers a host of physiological reactions. Stimulation of the sympathetic nervous system, along with activation of the endocrine system's adrenal medulla, causes (among other effects) your heart rate to increase, more oxygen to be delivered to your brain, and even your pupils to dilate, which improves eyesight. All of this contributes to the feelings of runner's high.

What happens if you become addicted to exercise?

Many psychologists once believed that exercise addiction was a healthy substitute for substance abuse, and that the only side effect was physical fitness. This may not be so, new research indicates. Just like other addicts, those hooked on exercise can get so wrapped up in their sport that they exercise at all costs. Nothing—even personal injury or emergencies at home or at work—can keep them from their daily dose of exercise. When deprived of exercise, such "addicts" may experience withdrawal symptoms, ranging from crankiness to severe anxiety and depression.

In some cases exercise-dependent people have psychological needs similar to those with anorexia. Runners who regularly log more than 45 miles per week have also been shown to have high blood levels of certain stress hormones. Both men and women who train intensively for long periods have experienced abnormalities of the reproductive system.

Contrary to popular belief, exercise addiction cannot be fully explained as an acquired chemical dependence on the brain's natural opiates, the endorphins, which are released during physical exertion. Rather, say some experts, there may be an increased dependence on the over-all feelings of well-being associated with exercise. Some people may find, for example, that it takes them longer and longer to feel the pleasant effects of runner's high. Thus they run more and more to attain the feeling they crave.

Can your mind tell you when you've exercised enough?

A popular adage says, "No pain, no gain." But scientific wisdom says that you have gone too far, too fast, when a little stiffness or mild soreness turns to real pain. Experts advise fitness buffs to use their heads: begin a new exercise program gradually and be moderate in workouts.

Dedication *made Australian aborigine Evonne Goolagong a star in the 1970's.*

Studies have shown that even light exercise, such as a brisk walk, for as little as 20 to 30 minutes three times a week can improve cardiovascular fitness. For those who wish to make weight loss a goal of their workouts, research has shown that 30 minutes of vigorous walking or cycling every day can help you lose weight, even without dieting. Interestingly, the same time spent swimming, while equally beneficial to your muscle tone and cardiovascular system, may have no effect on weight. Scientists think that your body eventually retains or increases fat to offset a loss of body heat caused by immersion in water.

All in all, experts say, the benefits of exercise far outweigh the drawbacks. As long as moderation and good judgment are a part of every workout, an exercise program can help you lead a healthier, happier life.

When Emotions Run High

Does anger help athletic performance?

Anger, frustration, self-pity, all of the so-called negative emotions generally have a bad effect on athletic performance. They create tension, drain energy, and divert one's attention from the task at hand.

The ability to recover quickly from setbacks and to shield the mind from distractions of all kinds is a trait common to top athletes. Many incorporate mental strategies into their training that are designed to help them keep a positive attitude, whether the problem is an irritating action by an opponent, their own lapses in concentration, or the general hubbub and tension of a sports event.

Occasionally an athlete comes along who seems able to use anger to elevate his or her level of play. Anger (or at least what looks like it to observers) becomes a positive force, not a negative emotion. An example was the tennis player John McEnroe in his late teens and early twenties.

Are competitive sports good for children?

Athletic competition has long been touted as "character-building," fostering, among other qualities, good sportsmanship. Children naturally tend to use sports as a gauge by which to measure their own and others' abilities. More and more experts, however, are warning that in contests for children organized by adults, the teaching of traditional values and even basic motor skills is ignored, in favor of an emphasis on victory at any price. Some psychologists even contend that contact sports lead to antisocial behavior by instilling the idea that hurting others is acceptable.

On the physical side, no child should be pushed to develop a specific skill, such as throwing or kicking, that will put one part of the body continually under great strain. The result could be severe and lasting injury.

Despite the hazards of overemphasis on winning, most researchers feel that organized sports can be beneficial in teaching children motor and social skills, provided that coaches always

The Daunting Presence of Masked Men

A catcher's mask in baseball has an old-fashioned use: protection.

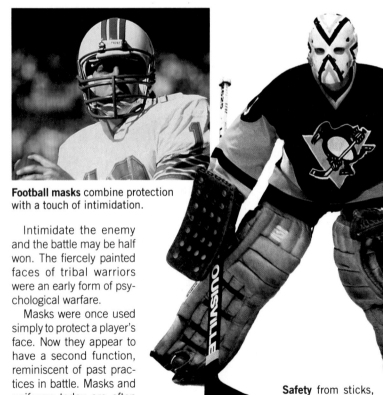

Football masks combine protection with a touch of intimidation.

A fencer is anonymous—and mysterious—behind the mask.

Intimidate the enemy and the battle may be half won. The fiercely painted faces of tribal warriors were an early form of psychological warfare.

Masks were once used simply to protect a player's face. Now they appear to have a second function, reminiscent of past practices in battle. Masks and uniforms today are often designed with intimidation in mind, used as much to throw foes off their game as to prevent injury.

Safety from sticks, pucks, and fists is the primary benefit of an ice hockey goalie's mask; but goalies choose masks that intimidate too.

keep in mind that children mature at different rates, both emotionally and physically. Children should also be urged to try several sports until they find one suited to their natural abilities. Striving for personal bests, rather than winning, should be stressed.

What happens when a boxer gets punch drunk?

First written about medically in 1928, the punch-drunk syndrome—describing a veteran boxer who slurs his speech, shuffles and stumbles, and can't keep his thoughts straight—is not the result of a spectacular knockout, but the cumulative effect of countless blows. A professional boxer can deliver a punch packing 100 times the force of gravity. Such a blow can send an opponent's brain crashing against his skull, causing bleeding and even death. But the lighter jabs can also damage brain tissue. Over the years these minor injuries can build up and, evidence suggests, eventually lead to damage in such vital brain areas as the cerebral cortex.

The repeated hammerings are also thought to be time bombs. Many boxers exhibit no obvious symptoms until years after they have left the ring. The threat is seen as so great by some doctors that they have called for a total ban on boxing. Others cry foul, saying that more research must be done before taking so drastic a step.

Amid this controversy, boxing—once widely pursued just for its exercise value—is enjoying a resurgence among some fitness groups. Proponents say that protective gear, such as newly designed helmets, makes it safe. Critics say that the headgear offers no protection and may cause greater damage by increasing the brain's rotation inside the skull.

At a French rugby game, a fan experiences despair and frustration.

Why Sports Events Are So Compelling

Sports fans brave traffic jams, zero-degree weather, and hours sitting on hard wooden seats (or standing) just to watch games being played. This dedication, if not fanaticism, can often be traced back to the fans' early years. As children many dreamed that one day they, too, might star in a sport they loved. Even after such hopes have died, their fascination with sports remains.

Psychologists see the identification with a team as an expression of masculinity, an age-old bonding of man to man. But women, too, are loyal fans. Certainly allegiance to a team gives fans a sense of belonging to a community. In Washington, D.C., for instance, where almost everyone comes from somewhere else, the involvement with their professional football team, the Redskins, is so intense that one year the government came to a near standstill during a crucial game.

In a world of uncertainties and ambiguities, sports offers clear-cut answers. There are definite and well-understood rules. A game is won, lost, or tied. Afterward, fans may argue endlessly about what might have been, but words will not alter the outcome.

While most fans show elation at victory and sadness or disgust at defeat, in recent years sports events seem increasingly to provide the spark for violent mob behavior. The 1989 soccer game in England at which nearly 100 fans died may serve as the ultimate example of uncontrollable crowd emotions. Yet most fans seek only the thrill and excitement of the game and the pleasure they get from watching their favorite players.

Is exercise good for your mind?

There is no doubt about it, exercise can make you feel better—and not just physically. Research has shown that people who exercise regularly tend to have a better self-image than those who do not. They also seem less likely to be anxious or depressed, and generally better able to cope with stress. Involvement in some sort of vigorous exercise program has even helped reduce the symptoms of patients diagnosed as clinically depressed. And exercise may help older people forestall memory loss, as well as keep reflexes and reasoning sharp.

Whether the benefits of exercise just make common sense (you feel better mentally because you are in better shape) or reflect some specific change in the brain is not completely clear. Some researchers feel that both brain chemistry and physical fitness play a part. Scientists now know, for instance, that exercise causes the brain to release certain kinds of pleasure-producing chemicals.

How We Choose Our Friends

Three buddies hang around together *at their New Orleans elementary school in the years following court-ordered desegregation. The same age, the same size, and, more than likely, having the same interests, the boys are oblivious of race.*

What is friendship?

The words "friend" and "free" come from the same root word, suggesting that one aspect of friendship is the freedom to be ourselves in the company of another person. "A friend," said Ralph Waldo Emerson, "is a person with whom I may be sincere." Most friendships begin with shared interests or activities, which gradually develop into mutual trust, openness, affection, and loyalty.

We like people who are similar to ourselves, who share our attitudes and values. When someone agrees with us, or makes the same choices we do, we gain confidence in our own views. Proximity can also influence our choice of friends, be they coworkers or neighbors. Most of us tend to enjoy the companionship of people of the same economic status and level of education. As we become older and our experience grows, our expectations of friendship change.

Sometimes we find ourselves attracted to people who are different and who can provide us with a fresh perspective. A very reserved person and an uninhibited person can often complement each other; one friend gains a sense of stability while the other achieves spontaneity. Yet, for the relationship to endure, the "opposite" friends may still need a common bond, and perhaps find it in a shared activity or sense of humor.

Friends can help fill other needs—for self-esteem or for reaching one's potential. When friends share an altruistic goal, such as a concern for justice or the cultivation of the arts, they are fulfilling Aristotle's description of "friendships of virtue."

Are first impressions right or wrong?

Most of us, based on past experience, unconsciously create categories of people we like and don't like. If outgoing people have disappointed us, but quiet ones helped us, we'll rate quietness as a positive quality when we evaluate a person. If you meet someone who powerfully reminds you of your demanding algebra teacher, you are likely to be wary. Similarly, you're apt to be attracted to a person whose face or manner resembles that of a good friend.

Relying on first impressions can be risky. We may misjudge another person. A negative first impression can prevent us from getting to know someone who might have become a good friend.

Do we actually need friends?

There are some cultures in which friendships are not valued. The Seri Indians of northern Mexico, for example, have no word for friend, and friendly relationships don't appear to exist among them. Yet, the historical record suggests that most human beings form alliances of one kind or another beyond their immediate families. As part of a wider circle, the individual finds practical support. Today this still holds true. A friendly neighbor may drive you to the doctor if you're sick; a close friend may calm you down during an emergency.

In fact, according to psychologists, contact with friends and family, and affiliation with a club or religious group, can help you live longer. Studies have shown that socially isolated people are more likely to experience a variety of health problems, including heart disease and asthma, than people with many social contacts.

Do some people need more friends than others?

Some people are happy with a few close friends; others have a tremendous number of friends and are eager to have more. The musician Liberace is said to have once held a party for 5,000 of his "closest" friends.

Adolescents, in particular, may feel they need many friends to show that they are "popular," or socially approved and desirable. Friends are very influential in adolescence, furnishing emotional support. Some groups of friends set trends that others all too willingly follow.

What qualities are most valued in friendship?

Most highly prized among all the attributes of friendship are loyalty and trust. This includes the ability to keep a personal confidence.

People like to be sure that they can rely on their friends in an emergency, and they want to feel that their friends will stick by them when the going is rough. And most people also expect that real friends will be open and honest about their feelings and opinions. Everyone hopes that a friendship will offer warmth and affection. Many people believe it is important to be able to share their jokes and sense of fun with their friends.

Are friendships between women different from those between men?

It's difficult to generalize about male and female friendships. Among the many studies on the subject, one showed that when with friends, women tend to talk about family, health, weight, food, and clothing. The majority of men reported discussing current events and sports.

Generally speaking, men are reserved about personal problems, and do not air their insecurities even with friends of long standing. Women, on the other hand, are less inhibited about seeking personal advice from their close friends.

PERSPECTIVES

On Friendship

Making friends is something like building an auxiliary family for oneself. We are at liberty to seek as many friends as we may want or need—or as few.

The Unexpected Gift

"Is there any miracle on earth to compare with that of discovering a new friend, or having that friend discover you? So much is at stake, but I will gladly risk everything to give a promising relationship a chance."

—Alex Noble
Moments of Stillness

◆

Elusive Intimacy

"As close as marbles in a bag we touch each other: the close touch of dearest love, of treasured friendship of brother and sister, husband and wife, parent, child and grandchild. We touch one another like marbles. In the touching, as with marbles, our point of contact is so small that geometry knows no formula to compute the minuteness of the touching points. It is a challenge to know thyself. But it is an even greater challenge to know another." **—Paul R. Beall**

◆

There Are Limits

"The paradox of friendship is that it is both the strongest thing in the world *and* the most fragile. Wild horses cannot separate friends, but whining words can. A man will lay down his life for his friend but will not sacrifice his eardrums."

—Sydney J. Harris
Field Newspaper Syndicate

◆

Balancing Act

"Very often conversations are better among three than between two, for the reason that then one of the trio is always, unconsciously, acting as umpire, interposing fair play, seeing that the aggressiveness of one does no foul to the reticence of another." **—Christopher Morley**

◆

The Quiet Question

"The real test of friendship is: Can you literally do nothing with the other person? Can you enjoy together those moments of life that are utterly simple? They are the moments that people look back on at the end of life and number as their most sacred experiences."

—Eugene Kennedy
U.S. News & World Report

◆

Tried, True, and Comfortable

"It does seem so pleasant to talk with an old acquaintance who knows what you know. I see so many new folks nowadays who seem to have neither past nor future. Conversation has got to have some root in the past, or else you have got to explain every remark you make, and it wears a person out." **—Sarah Orne Jewett**

◆

Worth Working For

"Relationships seldom die because they suddenly have no life left in them. They die slowly, either because people do not understand how much upkeep, time, work, love, and caring they require, or because people are too lazy or afraid to try."

—David Viscott

◆

On Keeping Your Friends

"Though a seeker since my birth,
Here is all I've learned on earth,
This the gist of what I know:
Give advice and buy a foe.
Random truths are all I find
Stuck like burs about my mind.
Salve a blister. Burn a letter.
Do not wash a cashmere sweater.
Tell a tale but seldom twice.
Give a stone before advice.

"Pressed for rules and verities,
All I recollect are these:
Feed a cold to starve a fever.
Argue with no true believer.
Think-too-long is never-act.
Scratch a myth and find a fact.
Stitch in time saves twenty stitches.
Give the rich, to please them, riches.
Give to love your hearth and hall.
But do not give advice at all."

—Phyllis McGinley
A Garland of Precepts

The Importance of Keeping in Touch

How do you maintain a lifelong friendship?

Many things work against a continuing friendship—moving away and the demands of business and family, to name a few. While shallow friendships fade quickly, an increase in affluence can also ruin a friendship. Through generosity that cannot be reciprocated, wealthier friends may make their old friends who have less money feel uncomfortable.

Many of us know people who resumed a friendship after years without contact. But for most friendships to survive, friends must set aside time for one another. The activities that fostered the relationship in the first place, such as fishing or other sports, are most likely to keep it strong.

Maintaining a friendship requires time, energy, and thought. Many people who live far apart have found that writing letters and telephoning are effective in preserving a feeling of closeness. The historian Henry Brooks Adams once wrote, "One friend in a lifetime is much; two are many; three are hardly possible."

How to Write a Friendly Letter

SUCH A SWEET GIFT—a piece of handmade writing, in an envelope that is not a bill, sitting in our friend's path when she trudges home from a long day spent among wahoos and savages, a day our words will help repair. They don't need to be immortal, just sincere. She can read them twice and again tomorrow: *You're someone I care about, Corinne, and think of often, and every time I do, you make me smile.*

The first step in writing letters is to get over the guilt of *not* writing. You don't "owe" anybody a letter. Letters are a gift. The burning shame you feel when you see unanswered mail makes it harder to pick up a pen and makes for a cheerless letter when you finally do. *I feel bad about not writing, but I've been so busy,* etc. Skip this. Few letters are obligatory, and they are *Thanks for the wonderful gift* and *I am terribly sorry to hear about George's death.* Write these promptly if you want to keep your friends. Don't worry about the others, except love letters, of course. When your true love writes *Dear Light of My Life, Joy of My Heart,* a response is called for.

Some of the best letters are tossed off in a burst of inspiration, so keep your writing stuff in one place where you can sit down for a few minutes and dash off a note. Envelopes, stamps, address book, everything in a drawer so you can write fast when the pen is hot.

A blank white 8½" × 11" sheet can look as big as Montana if the pen's not so hot—try a smaller page and write boldly. Get a pen that makes a sensuous line, get a comfortable typewriter, or a friendly word processor.

Sit for a few minutes with the blank sheet of paper in front of you, and let your friend come to mind. Remember the last time you saw each other and how your friend looked and what you said and what perhaps was unsaid between you; when your friend becomes real to you, start to write.

Write the salutation—*Dear You*—and take a deep breath and plunge in. A simple declarative sentence will do, followed by another and another. As if you were talking to us. Don't think about grammar, don't think about style, just give us your news. Where did you go, who did you see, what did they say?

If you don't know where to begin, start with the present: *I'm sitting at the kitchen table on a rainy Saturday morning.* Let the letter drift along. The toughest letter to crank out is one that is meant to impress, as we all know from writing job applications; if it's hard work to slip off a letter to a friend, maybe you're trying too hard to be terrific. . . .

Don't worry about form, it's not a term paper. When you come to the end of one episode, just start a new paragraph. The more you write, the easier it gets. . . .

Don't tear up the page and start over when you write a bad line—try to write your way out of it. Make mistakes and plunge on. Let the letter cook along and let yourself be bold.

Probably your friend will put your letter away, and it'll be read again a few years from now—and it will improve with age.

And 40 years from now, your friend's grandkids will dig it out of the attic and read it, a sweet and precious relic of the ancient 80's that gives them a sudden clear glimpse of the world we old-timers knew. You will have then created an object of art. Your simple lines about where you went, who you saw, what they said, will speak to those children and they will feel in their hearts the humanity of our times.

You can't pick up a phone and call the future and tell them about our times. You have to pick up a piece of paper.

***Garrison Keillor,** who offers this advice on letter-writing, wrote the best-selling book,* Lake Wobegon Days.

Can friendships be unequal?

Some "unequal" friendships, such as one between a teacher and a student, may not be as unequal as they appear to be. According to Freud, people of higher status are often amply rewarded by seeing in a younger friend the person they used to be.

People may also look for unequal relationships. Some like to play the role of a child who always needs support. Others like to behave as though they were parents, and look for friends with, apparently, more problems than they have or with plenty of obvious faults they can "correct."

Over the long run, friends usually need to feel that they are getting as much as they are giving.

Are there degrees of friendship?

In her book *Among Friends,* Letty Cottin Pogrebin identifies seven degrees of friendship. "Acquaintances are the people you know by name or face, 'familiar strangers.' Neighbors are a special breed of acquaintance." They can become friends but, even when no intimacy develops, we often rely on neighbors. We look out for their house as they watch ours.

In a third category are confederates: people who serve a specific purpose. They are, very often, unequal in status. A patron of the arts and a painter might fit this description. Pals, in Pogrebin's system of classification, are generally equals who enjoy some shared activity without intimacy. Close kin are often overlooked in a discussion of friends, but they are frequently among one's oldest, most intimate friends.

Coworkers fall into the sixth category. They may be friends or not, but it should be noted that coworkers deserve a separate category because, "in terms of time, the people you work with every day probably see more of you than anyone else does."

Last and best are true friends. "Friendship is a heart-flooding feeling," Pogrebin writes, "that can happen to any two people who are caught up in the act of being themselves, together, and who like what they see."

Two Friendships That Changed a Country

Friendships are usually such a personal matter that it is surprising to discover that certain ones have transcended the purely personal and have left a lasting imprint on history. Take, for instance, the friendship between Thomas Jefferson and John Adams. They were introduced in June 1775, and despite the differences between Jefferson, the Virginia patrician, and Adams, the blunt New Englander, they were soon linked in friendship by a shared loyalty to the ideals and aims of the American Revolution. Throughout the first years of the Republic, they labored together to lay down the principles that would serve to guide the country. Although deep political differences kept them apart for 12 years, they were reconciled in 1812. Dr. Benjamin Rush, speaking of the American Revolution, told Adams, "Some talked, some wrote . . . but you and Mr. Jefferson *thought* for us all."

Shared convictions and beliefs were the cornerstone of the 51-year friendship between Elizabeth Cady Stanton and Susan B. Anthony. From 1851 on, they fought side by side to establish a woman's right to vote, to hold property in her own name, and to retain her children after a divorce. Their skills complemented each other perfectly. Susan Anthony was the spokeswoman of the movement while Elizabeth Stanton refined their ideas and wrote speeches. "United," she said of their friendship, "no ordinary obstacles, differences or dangers ever appear to us insurmountable."

Fittingly, Thomas Jefferson (left) and John Adams (far left) died within five hours of each other. On the day of their death, the young nation was celebrating the 50th anniversary of the founding of the United States.

Elizabeth Stanton (left), mother of seven, ran a model household. Her abolitionist husband never encouraged her in her fight for women's rights. Susan Anthony did not marry but her Quaker parents backed her crusade.

Reaching Out to Strangers

The Good Samaritan rescued a stranger *and provided care without thought of recompense. This great kindness lives on, as others follow his example.*

What is the "altruistic paradox"?

With no thought of reward, the Good Samaritan in the Bible stops to help a man who has been beaten and robbed. That is the essence of the altruistic act: unselfishly giving help when it is needed, no strings attached.

This presents a paradox to many experts on human behavior. These scientists assume that we do something—that is, we behave in a certain way—because we get or expect a reward for doing so, and we do not do something because the cost of doing it would be great. This is called the rewards/costs model of human behavior. An example of reward-motivated behavior is putting in extra hours on the job to win a promotion. An example of cost-motivated behavior is refraining from punching your boss in the nose when you don't get the promotion, since that would probably cost you your present job and make it hard to get future jobs.

Altruistic acts don't seem to fit the rewards/costs model. There is no apparent reward, and there are almost always costs: from being a few minutes late for an appointment to sacrificing one's life.

Is selfishness really at the root of altruism?

Some psychologists argue that a person gets a hidden reward for altruism. The benefit is feeling good, or at least avoiding guilt for not helping. This reasoning attempts to preserve the rewards/costs model and explain away the altruistic paradox, but it sidesteps some large issues, such as where the good or guilty feelings come from in the first place and why some people are more altruistic than others. Perhaps most tellingly, it cannot explain why we feel good just knowing somebody is being helped, even when we have nothing to do with helping and receive no credit.

What is empathy?

Although it is often used as a synonym for compassion or helping, the word *empathy* does not really describe moral behavior that is good (or bad) but simply the ability to feel what someone else is feeling. For example, a boy in kindergarten may be aroused when a classmate gets a bump on the head and starts to cry, because the boy knows what a bump feels like. However, just because the boy has felt empathy, his next emotion is not necessarily compassion: he could give the crying classmate either a comforting pat or a shove or he could quickly lose interest altogether.

Is caring about others inborn or learned?

Recent research suggests that the age at which we start to care about others' feelings is younger than previously thought. At birth, the brain may be equipped with certain neurons and circuits that allow it to feel what others are feeling: that is, to have empathy. Indirect support for this theory comes from studies of people who lack empathy, such as sociopaths and patients suffering from chronic schizophrenia, autism, and other less severe conditions that affect emotional behavior. Increasingly these conditions are being linked to underlying biological causes.

Injuries to the right hemisphere of the brain, for example, can affect a person's ability to express feelings by gestures and voice inflections. People with damaged parietal lobes may fail to respond to the emotional nuances conveyed by changes in someone's voice tone. These and similar consequences of brain damage suggest that "normal" may include being born with a brain that has the capacity to develop empathy.

Dr. Leslie Brothers, a California Institute of Technology psychiatrist, has made a specialty of investigating the links between the brain's circuits and the emotion of empathy. She feels that a child's capacity for empathy grows as the brain and central nervous system mature. Thus, to some extent, the neural equipment we are born with determines how empathic we will turn out to be.

However, developmental psychologists stress that the role of the parent and society should not be underrated. It is from them that children learn how to channel empathy into the kind of caring, helping behavior that is called altruism.

What makes an altruist?

The consensus of psychologists is that three ingredients are essential for the making of a caring, helping person. First, the brain must be normal to begin with and develop normally. There is mounting evidence that damage to certain areas of the brain affects a person's ability to be responsive to the feelings of others.

Second, a child must grow up in a society where compassion is valued. Every society has unwritten laws of conduct, called social norms, that influence an individual's behavior. One such norm is that people should help somebody in trouble. This unwritten rule seems to have greater force in close-knit segments of society, such as a group held together by religious and ethnic bonds. Its influence is weaker where there is social upheaval, such as in a neighborhood that is having an influx of strangers.

Another widespread social norm is the Golden Rule—do unto others as you would have them do unto you—which social psychologists call the norm of reciprocity. As children grow to adulthood, they absorb these norms and make them part of their personal moral codes, a process psychologists call internalizing values. Sometimes, the lessons are formal, taught by teachers; other times, they are acquired as part of living.

Finally, parents have a key role in the making of an altruist. Studies of people who have faced great personal risk to help others reveal that most such individuals have at least one parent with extremely high moral values, and questions of right and wrong were discussed openly and often as they grew up. However, simply talking about altruism is not enough. A parent must practice what he or she preaches. Otherwise, the child will learn hypocrisy, not altruism.

How Young Children Learn About the Feelings of Others

Infants and toddlers act and react in ways that certainly look like empathy, caring, and helping, whether or not the behavior is conscious or very developed. Babies a few days old often start to cry if other babies nearby are fussing noisily. One psychologist calls this a kind of "emotional contagion," which may be the behavioral precursor of empathy. That is, the joint crying may lay down circuits in the babies' brains that will later allow them consciously to feel empathy.

But for many years, the sense of what someone else is feeling—followed by the urge to help if the person is in distress of some sort—was thought to be a skill children learned, like talking or reading. The influential Swiss psychologist Jean Piaget believed that children could not experience how someone else felt until they could understand it cognitively, and that did not occur until about age 7. Later, Lawrence Kohlberg, who studied the development of moral reasoning in children, also concluded that age 7 marked the beginning of the kind of thinking that developed into altruism.

Now, however, it is believed that by the age of 2, children may be able to comprehend the pain of someone to whom they are emotionally close, like their mother, and actually to experience the other's discomfort as their own. In one typical experiment, a mother pretends to hurt her finger and her 2-year-old girl promptly begins to rub her own hand in sympathetic distress. Within six months or so, these feelings have been vastly refined. By age 2½, "toddlers clearly realize that someone else's pain is different from their own, and know how to comfort them," according to Dr. Marian Radke-Yarrow of the National Institute of Mental Health. "From around 2 or 3," she adds, "you begin to see children develop their own style of empathy, with some showing increasing awareness of other people's plights, while others seem to turn away." Upbringing may influence that difference in the children's concern for others. Studies suggest that children are more empathic when their mothers reprimand them for upsetting another child and point out the other youngster's distress.

When Mom pretends to hurt her finger, her two-year-old seems to feel pain.

As they grow older, children seem to gain a perspective that bolsters their ability to empathize with others. Instead of reacting only to someone's immediate condition, they can understand a person's general life situation. They can feel concern for a seriously ill person's plight, for example, even though at that moment the person does not seem to be ill.

Making a Difference in the Lives of Others

Can altruism go too far?

In Charles Dickens's novel *Bleak House,* a character named Mrs. Jellyby neglects her own children but is constantly engaged in noble causes, such as aid for the poor girls of a faraway land called Borrioboola-Gha. Mrs. Jellyby illustrates the wisdom of the old saw "Charity begins at home."

Even when altruism is practiced close to home, it must not risk smothering the independence of a loved one, and the would-be altruist must be sensitive to the needs and likes of the person being helped. For instance, a dutiful son tells sheepishly of sending weekly bouquets to his convalescing mother, completely forgetting that she was allergic to many kinds of flowers. And a widowed father in his seventies may not have the heart to tell his daughter-in-law that the casseroles she brings on Saturday violate almost all his dietary rules.

Why do people resent their benefactors?

Even if a benefactor has no thought of being superior or manipulative, the recipient must contend with feelings of inferiority. These feelings are often heightened when a condition of receiving aid is being judged weak or helpless. Rather than accept this judgment, some people refuse to take help.

At work in this complicated equation is what psychologists call the principle of equity. People who are helped usually feel best when they can return the favor. Their self-esteem depends on showing that they don't need charity and can be generous, too. However, the urge to reciprocate can be weakened by mistrust of the original helper's motives. The recipient may feel that there were strings attached or that the helper could and should have done more.

Is helping others good for you?

The warm feeling you get from making someone feel better may prolong your own life. A 14-year study of 2,700 people in Tecumseh, Michigan, found a decline in the mortality rate of men who did volunteer work, compared with that of men who didn't. Another study, at Harvard, showed a rise in disease-fighting antibodies in the saliva of students seeing a film about the work among Calcutta's poor of Mother Teresa, one of the most admired altruists of this or any other era.

From surveys of people regularly involved in helping others, the picture emerges of altruism lightening depression and bringing increased energy. Many volunteers speak of a "helper's calm" much like the runner's high that comes with exercise. Helping people, like exercise, seems to have a calming effect on the brain and body and may reduce heart stress by curbing anger and irritability.

A Heartwarming Movie of Old-Fashioned Morality

James Stewart played Bailey, Donna Reed his wife. *Wonderful Life* was his favorite film.

In 1945 film director Frank Capra decided to make *It's a Wonderful Life.* For six years, people had suffered through the horrors of World War II. Now Capra wanted to show that decency and kindness endured.

The film's hero is altruistic bank owner George Bailey, who has always sacrificed his own dreams for the well-being of his hometown. His nemesis is a greedy, unscrupulous businessman, Henry F. Potter, who craves to control and dominate the town of Bedford Falls. Bailey has somehow managed to keep his family's small bank afloat, and only the bank stands between the townspeople and their exploitation by Potter. In a dramatic ending the townspeople reward Bailey's years of selflessness with a last-minute gesture that saves the bank—and the town.

In an outpouring of goodwill and hard cash, Bailey's fellow citizens express their recognition of all that he has done over the years to make their town a better place to live.

The Indomitable Spirit of Mother Hale

When mothers take drugs during pregnancy, their babies are born addicted. These infants then face the torture of withdrawal. For over 20 years, Clara McBride Hale has made it her personal mission to help these babies through their agony.

ON FEBRUARY 7, 1985, Clara McBride Hale sat in the gallery of the U.S. Congress listening to President Ronald Reagan describe her in his State of the Union message as a "true American hero." Since 1969 Clara Hale has devoted herself to caring for the babies of drug addicts. In a sense, these babies have been "on drugs" for nine months and, from the moment of birth, suffer through the torments of withdrawal.

Clara McBride was born in 1905 in Philadelphia, where she graduated from high school. She moved to New York in 1931, after she married Thomas Hale, who ran a floor-waxing business. In 1938 he died of cancer, leaving her with two children, Nathan, 7, and Lorraine, 5 (later she adopted a son, Kenneth). To support the children, Clara Hale worked as a cleaning woman. But she so disliked leaving her children with others that she decided to stay at home and care for the children of other working women, charging two dollars a week per child.

She established an informal day-care center in her Harlem apartment. The 6 or 7 children she took in returned home on weekends, but her touch with them was so sure and so loving that, Clara Hale said, "everyone called me Mommy." Ever since then she has been known as Mother Hale.

By 1969 her own children had gone through college and were working. It seemed time to take it easy. But that didn't happen. One day her daughter, Lorraine, was walking through a Harlem park and spotted a young woman addict so deeply drugged that she could barely hold her baby in her arms. "Here's a place where you can get help for your baby," Lorraine told her, giving the young woman her mother's address.

The next day the woman arrived on the doorstep of the Hale apartment. Clara Hale recalls that her first reaction was bewilderment. Then it occurred to her that Lorraine could explain the mystery. She told the young woman to wait and went to call her daughter. "When I came back, only the baby was waiting." Word spread rapidly among drug addicts, and soon Mother Hale was looking after 22 babies.

***A deep faith** has sustained Mother Hale. "I never had a problem that I couldn't go to God with for help."*

Addicted babies can be seriously handicapped at birth both physically and mentally. There is damage to the brain and central nervous system, which usually results in slowed mental and physical development. At one month an addicted baby may be at the same stage of development as a 2-day-old normal baby. As addicted babies grow older, they have trouble crawling and walking. They have learning difficulties. Without early treatment, these children are likely to become drug addicts themselves.

During their first weeks, as the babies go through withdrawal, they scratch, vomit, suffer from diarrhea, and cry continuously. Helping them demands a commitment that few people have the power to sustain. Though Mother Hale may look slight, standing only 5 feet 2 inches tall, her indomitable determination has kept many babies alive. Hospitals treat these infants with blood transfusions and put them into incubators, but modern medicine cannot supply what Mother Hale gives in such abundance: love and devotion. "You pet them a lot," she says, "and give them a lot of milk because they are always hungry." She paces back and forth with them through the night, and she croons over them as she moves gently back and forth in her bentwood rocker.

In 1975 Mother Hale moved to a house on 122nd Street that was renovated for her by the City of New York. When a baby arrives at Hale House, she cares for it in her own bedroom until, a month or so later, the baby is over the worst of its addiction. Then, it is moved downstairs to join the other children. Most babies stay about a year and a half.

At one time, Clara Hale, before she accepted a baby, made it a condition that the mother go for drug rehabilitation. She wanted her babies to be reunited with their families rather than be put up for adoption or placed in foster homes. She was almost always successful. As of 1989, out of some 800 children, only 16 had to be adopted. The rest went back to drug-free mothers. Crack, however, presents a new and terrible challenge. "For the first time since we've been in the business, we don't know where the mothers are," says Lorraine Hale, now executive director at Hale House. "She walks in the front door. She walks out the back door, and we don't see her again."

Although in her mid-eighties, Clara McBride Hale refuses to give up her work with the innocent victims of drug abuse. "How can I give them up?" she asks. "How can I tell myself I have given my share? How do I know what my share is?"

Answers

Page 38, Horses and Riders

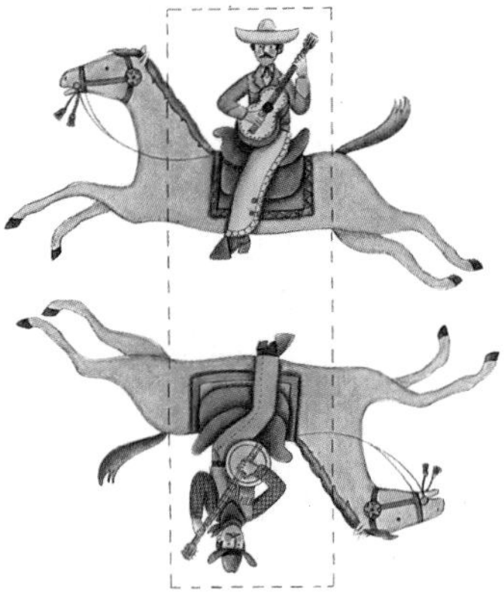

Take the copy you have made of panel A (the riders that you have traced or machine copied) and turn it 90 degrees from its original position in the book. Then slide the panel-A cutout between the backs of the two horses in panel B, until the riders mount their horses—actually newly created horses galloping in different directions from the original, rather droopy nags in the untouched panel B.

Page 38, Six Matchsticks and Nine Dots

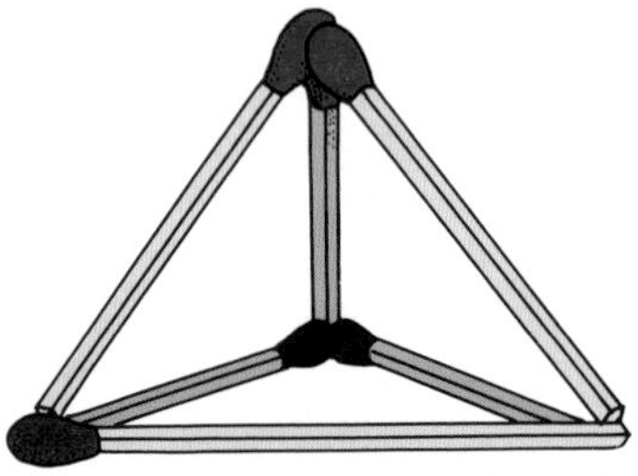

The trick is to arrange the six matches into a three-dimensional pyramid whose sides and bottom form four equilateral triangles. Most people assume the matches must lie flat.

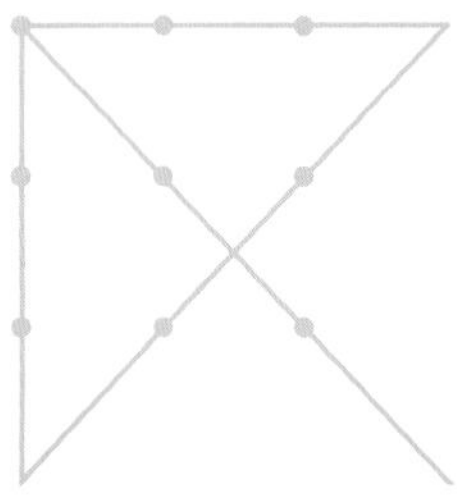

To solve this problem, all four of the lines must extend beyond the square of dots. Most people fail to see beyond the square.

Page 69, Who Is This?

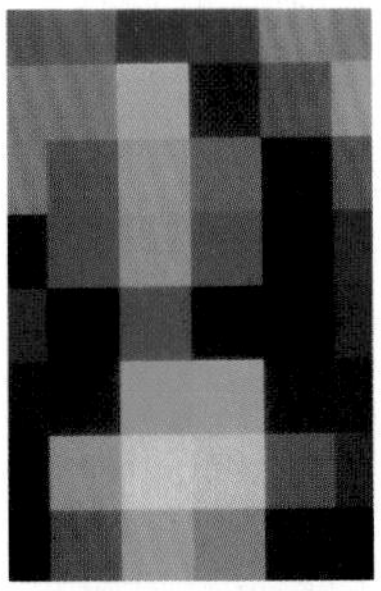

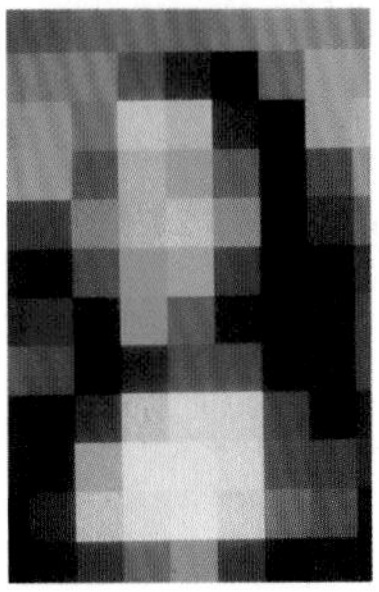

As more color blocks are added, the famous face of Mona Lisa, drawn by Leonardo da Vinci, comes into view.

Page 112, How Observant Are You?

To test your powers of recall, try to answer the following questions. The answers are given in the upside-down lines at the end of the questions.

1. How many people are in the painting?
2. Is there one parasol, or more than one?
3. How many chairs are there?
4. Is there a table?
5. Does each man have a hat? A cane?
6. Are the two flags the same or different?
7. Is the wind blowing from the right or from the left?
8. Is the sun shining from the right or from the left?
9. Are there more than ten boats, or fewer than ten?
10. Are they all sailboats?

The answers: 1) 4; 2) more than one; 3) 4; 4) no; 5) yes, yes; 6) different; 7) from the left; 8) from the left; 9) more; 10) no.

Page 114, Black-and-White Muddle

The hidden object in the photo is a dalmatian (a breed of dog with white coat and dark spots), sniffing the fallen leaves on the ground. Stored memories help us identify objects by their patterns, even when the objects merge confusingly with the background.

Page 123, Mirror Maze

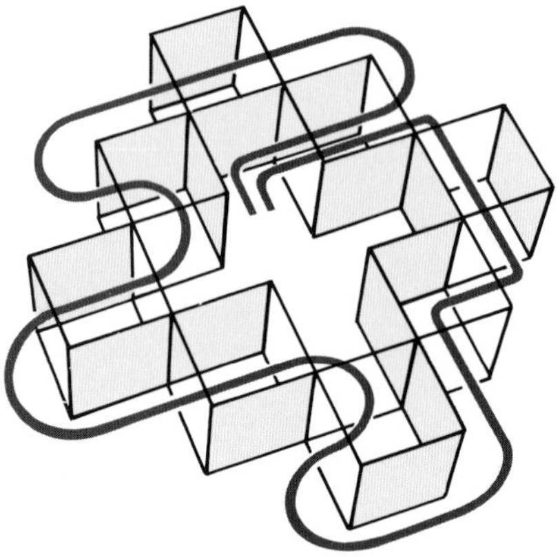

The correct path, which can be taken in either direction, is drawn at left. The doll's mirrored images give visual clues as to which sides of the rooms are mirrored (shown shaded) and which are open.

Page 153, Famous Names

1. R Michelangelo
2. N Leonardo da Vinci (signed backward)
3. S John F. Kennedy
4. H Arturo Toscanini
5. W Sir Walter Raleigh
6. K Toulouse-Lautrec
7. D John Paul Jones
8. O Mussolini
9. M Richard Nixon
10. X William Shakespeare
11. E Mary, Queen of Scots
12. L Charles de Gaulle
13. V Freud
14. P Degas
15. J Hitler
16. A Chopin
17. B Charles Dickens
18. G Ivan the Terrible
19. U Picasso
20. F Christopher Columbus
21. I Lord Byron
22. T Baron Manfred von Richthofen (The Red Baron)
23. Q Robert E. Lee
24. C Napoleon

To handwriting experts or cryptographers, signatures are nothing more than a uniquely individual way of signing one's name. Quite a few of these famous signatures are difficult to decipher. A score of 18 to 21 is good; 22 to 24 makes you an expert cryptographer.

Graphologists, on the other hand, believe that a person's signature reveals a great deal about the writer's personality. When analyzing the signature of Mussolini (8), for example, one graphologist concluded that Il Duce's highly vertical, pinched writing showed a man consumed with self-interest.

Page 176, How Sharp Is Your Memory?

Many of the designs shown below are identical to the ones you saw on page 176. On a separate piece of paper jot down the number underneath each design you recall seeing.

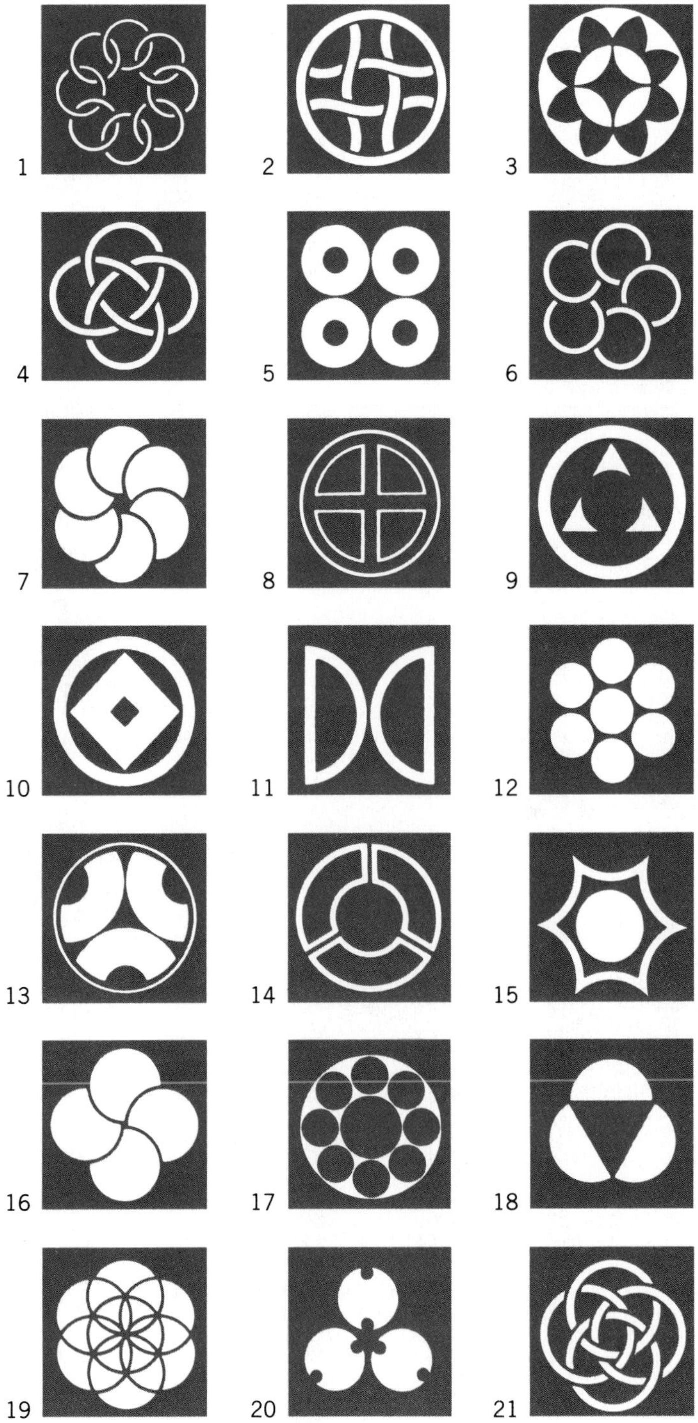

These are the 11 numbers to have written down: 1, 3, 4, 5, 7, 12, 13, 14, 15, 17, and 19. Give yourself two points for each design correctly noted. Subtract one point for each design incorrectly noted. Perfect: 22; Superior: Over 15; Good: 12–15; Fair: 9–12; Poor: Below 9.

Page 177, Brain Teasers

1. Three. Aside from the roses, there must be one tulip and one daisy; aside from the tulips, one rose and one daisy; aside from the daisies, one rose and one tulip. The trick is to realize that the word "all" can also stand for one type of flower.

2. Because all the boxes are mislabeled, take a checker from the box labeled "red and black" checkers and put the correct label on it (if the checker you take out is red, label the box "red"; if black, then label it "black"). With one box correctly labeled, you can now switch the labels on the two remaining mislabeled boxes. The point is that taking a checker from a box labeled either "red" or "black" tells you nothing, since you might reach into the one that is mixed and, like all of them, mislabeled. Since you know that all the boxes are mislabeled, choose one from the box marked "red and black" checkers and label the box with the color of the checker you pull out; then each of the remaining boxes must contain what the other one says it does.

3. October 22.

4. $10. The camera costs $90, which is $80 more than the case. Many people assume the camera costs $80, forgetting the "more." To find out the cost of the case, first subtract the $80 from $100 and then split the difference.

5. Fill the seven-cup container with flour. Use the two-cup container to remove two cups of flour from the seven-cup container. Empty those two cups back into the flour bag. Again, fill the two-cup container from the seven-cup one. You've now removed four cups of flour from the seven-cup container. Thus, there are now three cups of flour remaining in the larger container.

Adapted from *The Triarchic Mind.*

Page 177, "The Toughest Puzzle of All"

The brakeman, who lives halfway between Chicago and Detroit, also lives near Mr. ______, who earns three times as much as he does. Mr. ______ can't be Mr. Robinson, as Mr. Robinson lives in Detroit. He can't be Mr. Jones, as Mr. Jones's $20,000 a year isn't divisible by three. Therefore the brakeman's neighbor must be Mr. Smith.

The passenger whose name is the same as the brakeman's lives in Chicago. He can't be Mr. Robinson, as Mr. Robinson lives in Detroit. He can't be Mr. Smith, as Mr. Smith is a neighbor of the brakeman, who lives halfway between Chicago and Detroit. Therefore he must be Mr. Jones.

Therefore the brakeman's name is also Jones.

Smith beats the fireman at billiards, therefore the fireman must be Robinson.

Therefore the engineer is Smith.

Page 187, Life Change Index Scale, Interpreting Your Score

Dr. Thomas Holmes and his colleagues have shown a relationship between recent life changes and the onset of illness. Listed below are the score categories and the associated probability of illness during the next two years for a person with a score in a certain range. Of course, individuals vary a great deal.

0–149	No significant problem.
150–199	Mild Life Crisis level with a 37% chance of illness.
200–299	Moderate Life Crisis level with a 51% chance of illness.
300 or over	Major Life Crisis level with a 79% chance of illness.

Page 260, "One Way to Test Your Happiness" Quiz

Check your answers against the list below. Give yourself one point for each of your answers that matches these.

1. b	4. c	7. a or b	10. c	13. c
2. b	5. c	8. c	11. a	14. d
3. a	6. b	9. d	12. d	15. b

According to this quiz, if you got two points or fewer, there is not much joy in your life. A score of four to six suggests that you experience many happy moments. Seven points or more indicates a happy person, at least by this criteria. Following is a brief explanation of Robert Harrington's reasoning in rating answers for happiness. The numbers refer to the questions involved.

A happy person likes to do useful, productive work, to use his or her abilities fully (1) and enjoys helping people, but is not self-sacrificing (2). At night, sleep researchers have found, a happy individual has little trouble falling asleep (3). He or she tends to be self-sufficient and can enjoy both solitude and company but is dependent on neither (4, 13). Generally, happy people are orderly and punctual (5, 9).

Though tolerant of people's minor flaws, the happy person dislikes cruelty and destructiveness (6). He or she is healthy (7), has no hangups about prosperity (11), and refuses to participate in other people's negative emotions (8)—or cling to his or her own (10). When choosing a mate, a happy person will pick a congenial, compatible figure rather than someone romantic and glamourous (12). Being busy and absorbed, a happy person tends to feel days pass quickly, though in larger units—weeks, months, years—time may seem to move slowly (14). Finally, the happy person has a sense of progress, improvement, of getting somewhere (15).

Page 290, College Placement Vocabulary Answers

1. a	4. a	7. b	10. a	13. b
2. b	5. a	8. a	11. a	14. c
3. a	6. a	9. c	12. b	15. c

Page 290, Elementary Mathematics Answers

1. (c). $^{15}/_{45}$ would be $^{1}/_{3}$. With a larger denominator, the fraction $^{15}/_{46}$ is less than $^{1}/_{3}$.
2. (b). Since the perimeter of a square is 4 times the length of a side, it is:
   $$4\left(\frac{2x}{3}+1\right), \text{ or } \frac{8x+12}{3}$$
3. (b). By simple substitutions, $s = 16 \times 8 \times 8$, or 1,024.

Page 291, Spatial Relationships Test

A. 63 or 64 blocks
B. 56 blocks
C. 46 blocks
D. 70 blocks

Page 296, Mechanical Ability Test

1. b	2. a	3. b	4. a	5. b

Page 296, Attention to Detail

There are six pairs of numbers that match.
They are pairs numbered 1, 3, 4, 7, 9, and 10.

Index

A

B

Page numbers in **bold** type refer to illustrations and captions.

D

Page numbers in **bold** type refer to illustrations and captions.

E

F

Page numbers in **bold** type refer to illustrations and captions.

Page numbers in **bold** type refer to illustrations and captions.

Q

R

Page numbers in **bold** type refer to illustrations and captions.

T

Page numbers in **bold** type refer to illustrations and captions.

Credits and Acknowledgments

Hundreds of publications were consulted in the course of preparation of ABC's OF THE HUMAN MIND, notably *Brain, Mind and Behavior* by Floyd E. Bloom and Arlyne Lazerson, published by W.H. Freeman and Company; *The Mind* by Richard M. Restak, M.D., published by Bantam Books; *Psychology and Life* by Philip G. Zimbardo, published by Scott, Foresman and Company; and *Psychology Today: An Introduction* by Richard R. Bootzin, Gordon H. Bower, Robert B. Zajonc and Elizabeth Hall, published by Random House.

Text

Grateful acknowledgment is made for permission to excerpt or adapt featured material from the following works:

American Association for the Advancement of Science. "Machinations of Thought" by M. Mitchell Waldrop. **Science**, Vol.6,No.2. Copyright © 3/85 by American Association for the Advancement of Science. **A New Slant, Inc.** Sheila Kurtz, "Handwriting Traits to Watch For." *Botom Line/Personal*, 5/30/88. Used by permission of Sheila Kurtz, President, A New Slant, Inc. **Atheneum Publishers.** *Breaking Tradition: The Story of Louise Nevelson* by Natalie S. Bober. Copyright © 1984 by Natalie S. Bober. Reprinted by permission of Atheneum Publishers, an imprint of Macmillan Publishing Company. *The Senses of Animals and Men* by Lorus and Margery Milne. Copyright © 1962 by Lorus Milne and Margery Milne. Reprinted by permission of Atheneum Publishers and Andre Deutsch Ltd. **Georges Borchardt, Inc.** "Sick Thinking" by Morton Hunt. *The New York Times Magazine*, 1/3/88. Copyright © 1988 by Morton Hunt. **The Christian Science Monitor**, 4/27/88. "Acquiring Taste" by Louise Miller Mann. **Cosmopolitan**. "How Happy Are You" by Robert Harrington. Copyright © 1978 by The Hearst Group. **Dodd Mead & Co., Inc.** "The Open World" by Edwin Way Teal, from *Heirlooms*, Margaret T. Applegarth, editor. Copyright © 1967 by Margaret T. Applegarth. **Doubleday and Company, Inc.** *How to Talk With Practically Anybody About Practically Anything* by Barbara Walters. Copyright © 1970 by Barbara Walters. Excerpts by Mary C. Bateson and Michael Josephson from *Bill Moyers: A World Of Ideas* by Betty Sue Flowers. Copyright © 1989 by Public Affairs Television, Inc. **W. H. Freeman and Company.** *Wide Awake at 3:00 A.M. by Choice or by Chance?* by Richard M. Coleman. Copyright © 1986 by Richard M. Coleman. **Guideposts Associates, Inc.** *Those Little Black Marks* by Arthur Gordon. Copyright © 1980 by Guideposts Associates, Inc. **Harper & Row Publishers, Inc.** *The Gulag Archipelago* by Aleksandr I. Solzhenitsyn. Copyright © 1973 by Aleksandr I. Solzhenitsyn. English language translation Copyright © 1973, 1974 by Harper & Row Publishers, Inc. *He: Understanding Masculine Psychology* by Robert A. Johnson. Copyright © 1974 by Religious Publishing Co. **Harvard University Press.** *The Man With a Shattered World* by A. R. Luria. Copyright © 1972 by Michael Cole. Foreword Copyright © 1987 by Oliver Sacks. **Houghton Mifflin Company.** *The Origin of Consciousness in the Breakdown of the Bicameral Mind* by Julian Jaynes. Copyright © 1976 by Julian Jaynes. **International Paper Co.** *How to Write a Personal Letter* by Garrison Keillor. Copyright © 1967 by International Paper Co. **Janklow & Nesbit Associates.** "Reflections—Family" by Harold Brodkey, *The New Yorker*, 11/23/87. **Alfred A. Knopf, Inc.** *Peter the Great: His Life and World* by Robert K. Massie. Copyright © 1980 by Robert K. Massie. *So Love Return* by Robert Nathan. Copyright © 1958 by Alfred A. Knopf, Inc. Reprinted by permission of H. N. Swanson, Inc. *The Art of Teaching* by Gilbert Highet. Copyright © 1950 by Gilbert Highet, renewed 1978 by Helen MacInnes Highet. Reprinted by permission of Alfred A. Knopf, Inc., and Curtis Brown Ltd. **LDAP, Inc.** *Mammoth (TM) Book of Fun and Games* by Richard B. Manchester. Copyright © 1979 by Hart Associates. Reprinted by permission of LDAP, Inc. "Mammoth" is a registered trademark of LDAP, Inc. **The Lighthouse, The New York Association for the Blind.** *What Do You Do When You Meet a Blind Person?* **McCall's.** "Children's Books" by Gene Shalit. Copyright © 5/64 by *McCall's*. Reprinted by permission of the author. **McGraw Hill, Inc.** *The Children of Jonestown* by Kenneth Wooden. Copyright © 1981 by Kenneth Wooden. Comment by Pablo Casals. **William Morrow & Co., Inc.** *The Twins Who Found Each Other* by Bard Lindeman. Copyright © 1969 by Bard Lindeman. **New American Library**. *Fonda: My Life* as told to Howard Teichmann. Copyright © 1981 by Howard Teichmann and Orion Productions, Inc. **New Leaf Publications Ltd.** "Is Raoul Wallenberg Still Alive?" by Gerald Clark. Copyright © 1980 by Gerald Clark, *Saturday Night* 7/80, reprinted by permission of the author. **The New York Times Company.** "Life in the 30's" by Anna Quindlen. Copyright © 3/31/88 and 11/10/88. "Show and Tell: My First Day of Retirement." by George Nelson. Copyright © 5/10/86. "On Parenting" by Donald Sheff. Letters to the Editor: *The New York Times* 1/12/88. Reprinted by permission of Donald Sheff. "The Rewards of Living a Solitary Life" by May Sarton. Copyright © 4/8/74. "About Men: Being Old Old," by Malcolm Cowley. Copyright © 1985. "A Test of Will" by A. Alvarez. Copyright © 11/13/83. "A Friend for Life" by Anatole Broyard. *The New York Times Book Review.* Copyright © 2/22/87. **Newsweek, Inc.** "Bringing Up Baby: A Doctor's Prescription for Busy Parents" by Dr. T. Berry Brazelton. Copyright © 1989. "The ABC's of Prescription Drugs" by Norman B. Geller, M.D. Copyright © 1988. **North American Syndicate.** "There Are Limits" by Sydney J. Harris, North American Syndicate, release date 9/24/76. Reprinted by permission of North American Syndicate, Inc. **New York University Press.** *Contributions to Business Enterprise* by Peter Drucker. Copyright © 1970 by New York University. **F. E. Peacock Publishers, Inc.** *Current Personality Theories* by Raymond J. Corsini. Copyright © 1977 by Raymond J. Corsini. **Pergamon Press, Inc.** *Journal of Psychosomatic Research*. Vol.ll, pp.213-218. The Holmes and Rahe Social Readjustment Rating Scale. Copyright © 1967, Pergamon Press, Inc. **Psychology Today**. "Knowing Near Death" by Paul Perry. Copyright © 9/88 by *Psychology Today.* **The Reader's Digest Association, Inc.** "Moments of Stillness" by Alex Nobel. Copyright © 3/88. "Into the Unknown" by Michael Ventura. Copyright © 5/88. Reprinted by permission of Michael Ventura. "A Mother's Plea" by Patricia Bissel. Copyright © 10/88. "Paul R. Beall's Christmas Message" by Paul R. Beall. Copyright © 4/83. "Beethoven's Kiss" by Andor Foldes. Copyright © 11/86. "You Must Go Home Again" by Ardis Whitman. Copyright © 4/86. "The Power of Recall" by Norman Lobsenz. "What Men Live By" by Christopher Morley. Copyright © 3/88. "A Litmus Test" by Christopher Morley. Copyright © 1/83. Reprinted by permission of Blyth Morley Brennan. **Selezione.** "Vita Vagabonda" by Luigi Barzini, Sr. Copyright © 1/88. **Simon & Schuster, Inc.** *The Man Who Mistook His Wife for a Hat* by Oliver Sacks. Copyright © 1985 by Oliver Sacks. Reprinted by permission of Summit Books, a Division of Simon & Schuster, Inc., and John Farquharson Ltd. *Winston Churchill's Afternoon Nap* by Jeremy Campbell. Copyright © 1986 by Jeremy Campbell. Reprinted by permission of Simon & Schuster, Inc. **Time Inc.** "The World of Steinberg" by Robert Hughes, *Time*, 4/17/78. **U.S. News & World Report.** "Why a Good Friend Is Hard to Find," interview with Eugene Kennedy, 9/26/83. **Viking Penguin, Inc.** *The Triarchic Mind* by Robert J. Sternberg. Copyright © 1986 by Robert J. Sternberg. Reprinted by permission of Viking Penguin, Inc., and John Brockman Associates, Inc. *The Love Letters of Phyllis McGinley* by Phyllis McGinley. Copyright 1954 by Phyllis McGinley. Copyright renewed © 1982 by Phyllis Hayden Blake. **Villard Books.** *All I Really Need to Know I Learned in Kindergarten* by Robert Fulghum. Copyright © 1986 by Robert L. Fulghum. **John Wiley & Sons, Inc.** *The Body in Time* by Kenneth Jon Rose. Copyright © 1988 by Kenneth Jon Rose.

Illustrations

1 American Red Cross. **2** *upper left* Carol Donner/Renard Represents Inc.; *upper right* John Barr/Gamma-Liaison; *lower left* Jean-Loup Charmet; *lower right* National Gallery of Art, Washington, Collection of Mr. and Mrs. Paul Mellon. **3** *upper* Culver Pictures; *lower* Marina Raith/Eltern Syndication/Gruner + Jahr AG & Co. **5** *top* Courtesy of Jane Polley; *lower* James Fraser/Impact Photos. **6** The Freud Museum, London. **9** Kaiser Porcelain Limited. **11** Michael Melford/The Image Bank. **13** John Neitzel. **15** David Madison/Duomo Photography Inc. **17** Collection Israel Museum, Jerusalem/ Photography by Moshe Caine. **18** *left* Sally Garnett; *right* Melissa Wanamaker. **20** Scala/Art Resource, N.Y. **21** © Karsh, Ottawa/Woodfin Camp & Associates. **22** The Hildebrand Brothers. **23** Movie Star News. **24** The Bettmann Archive. **25** *left* The Bettmann Archive; *right* Ray Manley/Shostal-SuperStock International. **26** Memory Shop. **28** John Launois/Black Star. **29** *top* Abby Aldrich Rockefeller Folk Art Center, Williamsburg, Virginia; *bottom* John Loengard. **30** *upper* Giraudon/Art Resource, N.Y.; *bottom* National Archives. **31** *top* AP/Wide World Photos; *lower left* Seny Norasingh/Light Sensitive; *lower right* J.B. Diederich/Contact Stock Images. **32** © Lawrence Schiller/Alskog from the book *Marilyn*/Photo Researchers. **33** Collection, The Museum of Modern Art, New York. **34** By courtesy of the Trustees of Sir John Soane's Museum, London. **36** Images Colour Library Ltd., Leeds & London. **37** Courtesy of the Leo Baeck Institute, New York. **38** *top* Ray Skibinski; *bottom* Carolyn Croll. **39** Nancy Durrell McKenna. **41** The Freud Museum, London. **42** Sue Coe/© 1986 Discover Publications. **44** National Institutes of Health, Bethesda, Maryland. **45** *top* Reproduced by courtesy of the Board of Trustees of the Victoria & Albert Museum from *Louis Wain—King of the Cat Artists 1860-1939* by Heather Latimer; *below* © Guttmann-Maclay Collection, The Bethlem Royal Hospital and The Maudsley Hospital. **46** Courtesy of Dr. Benjamin Harris, University of Wisconsin-Parkside. **48** Brown Brothers. **49** Collection of the Whitney Museum of American Art. **50** AP/ Wide World Photos. **51** Greg Robinson courtesy of the San Francisco Examiner. **52** *upper* Frederick Ayer III/Photo Researchers; *bottom* C.S. Perkins/Magnum. **53** Werner Forman Archive/National Museum of Man, Ottawa. **54** Giraudon/Art Resource, N.Y. **55** Courtesy of Richard Comerford. **56** Jean-Loup Charmet. **57** *left* Giraudon/Art Resource, N.Y.; *right* From the collections of Henry Ford Museum & Greenfield Village. **59** *top* National Archives; *bottom* Dick Ruhl. **61** Robert B. Livingston, M.D., University of California, San Diego. **62** Carol Donner/Renard Represents Inc. **64** *upper left* Phoebe Dunn; *upper right* Courtesy of Inez Deaton; *lower* Illustration by Orietta Agostoni. **65** Neil O. Hardy. 66 *left* Howard Sochurek; *right* Laszo Kubinyi. **67** Children's Hospital and Medical Center. **68** Howard Sochurek. **69** Ed Manning/Blocpix ® Images, Stratford, Connecticut. **70** From *Psychology and Life* by Philip G. Zimbardo, © 1988 by Scott, Foresman and Company, Reprinted by permission. **71** *left* Courtesy U.C.L.A. School of Medicine/Photography by Howard Sochurek; *right* Howard Sochurek. **72** Judy Skorpil. **73** Jane Hurd Studio. **74** James A. McInnis. **75** From *The Making of Mind* by A.R. Luria, Harvard University Press, Reprinted by permission, © 1979 by The President and Fellows of Harvard College. **76** Jane Hurd Studio. **79** *top*

Tom Ives/Sygma; *lower* Murrae Haynes/The Picture Group, Inc. **80** Charleston Evening Post/Photography by Brad Nettles. **81** *left* The Historical Society of Pennsylvania; *right* Reproduced by courtesy of the Trustees of the British Museum. **82** Faculté de Médecine, Besançon. **83** Brain Imaging Center, University of California, Irvine. **85** From *Psychology and Life* by Philip G. Zimbardo, © 1988 by Scott, Foresman and Company, Reprinted by permission. **86** Jane Hurd Studio. **87** Robert Skelton. **88** Howard Sochurek. **89** Homer Sykes/Woodfin Camp & Associates. **90** Neil O. Hardy. **91** *left* Sagamore Hill National Historic Site; *right* Theodore Roosevelt Collection, Harvard College Library. **92** *left* New York Public Library, Picture Collection; *right* Henry Wolf Productions Inc. **95** *top* The Bettmann Archive; *bottom* Nationalmuseet, Copenhagen. **96** *left* Reproduced from *Some Must Watch While Some Must Sleep* by William C. Dement, with the permission of W. W. Norton & Company, Inc. © 1972, 1974, 1976 by William Dement; *right* Greg Couch. **97** Reproduced from *Basic Psychology* by Henry Gleitman, with the permission of W. W. Norton & Company, Inc. © 1987. **98** Brown Brothers. **99** Walter Chandoha. **100** Courtesy of Viacom Enterprises. **102** Simon Marsden. **104** The Bettmann Archive. **105** Hans Hinz/Artothek. **106** Memory Shop. **107** *top* Windsor Castle, Royal Library, © 1989 Her Majesty The Queen; *middle* New York Public Library, Picture Collection; *bottom* Clayton Price. **108** © Bill Redic. **111** Phoebe Dunn. **112** The Metropolitan Museum of Art, Purchased with special contributions and purchase funds given or bequeathed by friends of the Museum, 1967. **114** Ron James. **115** *top* Jane Hurd Studio based on a photo by J. Taposchaner/FPG International; *remainder* Jane Hurd Studio. **116** *left* Ray Skibinski; *right* From *Psychology and Life*, by Philip G. Zimbardo, © 1988 by Scott, Foresman and Company, Reprinted by permission. **117** *bottom* Morris Karol; *remainder* Ray Skibinski. **118** Art Staff. **119** Reproduced from *Ishihara's Tests for Color Blindness*, published by Kanehara & Co. Ltd., Tokyo. **120** From *Psychology and Life*, by Philip G. Zimbardo, © 1988 by Scott, Foresman and Company, Reprinted by permission. 121 *left* © 1988 M.C. Escher Heirs/Cordon Art, Baarn, Holland; *right* Art Resource, N.Y. **122** *upper left* Kaiser Porcelain Limited; *upper right* Reproduced with permission from Boring, E.G. (1930) "A New Ambiguous Figure," *American Journal of Psychology*, Vol. 42, pp. 444-5; *bottom left* Reproduced from *Geometrical Designs and Optical Art: 70 Original Drawings* by Jean Larcher, published by Dover Publications, Inc., in 1974; *bottom right* Nancy Mace. **123** Reprinted from *Games* Magazine, New York, © 1981, PSC Games Limited Partnership. **124** *left* Herman W. Kitchen; *upper right* James A. McInnis; *lower right* Reprinted by permission of The Putnam Publishing Group from *The Video Primer* by Richard Robinson, © 1983 by Richard Robinson. **125** From *Seeing: Illusion, Brain and Mind* by John P. Frisby, Oxford University Press © John P. Frisby 1979. **126** *left* Movie Still Archives; *right* © Karsh, Ottawa/ Woodfin Camp & Associates. **128** *top* Jane Hurd Studio; *bottom* Courtesy of Drs. Michael E. Phelps & John C. Mazziotta, U.C.L.A. School of Medicine. **129** © 1988 Michael Beasley:TSW-Click/ Chicago. **130** AP/Wide World Photos. **131** Courtesy Dogs for the Deaf. **132** AP/Wide World Photos. **133** Kevin Horan. **134** Ulli Seer/The Image Bank. **135** *left* Culver Pictures; *right* Diana Walker/Gamma-Liaison. **136** *upper left* John Stubblefield/Four By Five; *upper right* John Neitzel; *bottom* Melchior Digiacomo/The Image Bank. **137** Cambridge University Library. **138** Jane Hurd Studio. **139** *top* Blair Seitz/Photo Researchers; *lower* The Delta Society. **140** *left* Jane Hurd Studio; *right* From *Behold Man* by Lennart Nilsson, published by Little, Brown and Company, Boston. **141** Louie Psihoyos/Contact Stock Images. **142** Ted Spiegel/Black Star. **143** Library, New York Botanical Garden, Bronx, New York. **145** Linda Benedict-Jones. **146** *upper* Peter M. Fiore; *bottom* Larry Dale Gordon/The Image Bank. **148** *left* Will & Deni McIntyre/ Photo Researchers; *right* Morris Karol. **149** Culver Pictures. **150** Burk Uzzle/Archive Pictures Inc. **151** H. Sund/The Image Bank. **152** *top* Robert Douglas DeLisle; *bottom* Sheila Kurtz, President, A New Slant, Inc., New York & London. **153** From *What's the Big Idea and 35 Other Unusual Puzzles* by Don Rubin, © 1979 by Don Rubin, Reprinted by permission of Harper & Row, Publishers, Inc. **155** *left* Reproduced by kind permission of the President and Council of the Royal College of Surgeons of England; *right* Jerry Wachter/Focus on Sports. **156** Mario Ruiz. **157** *top* Children's Hospital and Health Center, San Diego; *bottom* Allan Grant. **159** Memory Shop. **160** The Bettmann Archive. **161** *center* Based on a diagram from *Know Your Own Personality* by Hans Eysenck & Glenn Wilson, © 1975 by H.J. Eysenck & Glenn Wilson, all rights reserved, reprinted by permission of Viking Penguin, a division of Penguin Books USA, Inc.; *remainder* The Bettmann Archive. **163** *top* Soviet Life from Sovfoto; *bottom* Sovfoto. **164** UPI/Bettmann Newsphotos. **165** Richard Berenholtz. **166** *left* American Red Cross; *right* David Madison/Duomo Photography Inc. **168** Richard Flynn. **169** Courtesy of the National Museum of American History, Smithsonian Institution- /Photography by Michael Freeman & Robert Golden. **170** *left* Keystone; *right* Sally & Richard Greenhill. **171** Harvey Lloyd. **172** Blair Seitz/Photo Researchers. **173** Drs. M. Posner, M. Raichle, & S. Petersen, Washington University of Medicine, St. Louis. **174** Sovfoto. **175** © Marcia Weinstein. **176** From *Mammoth ™ Book of Fun & Games* by Richard B. Manchester, © 1979 by Hart Associates, reprinted by permission of LDAP, Inc. **177** Joe Krush. **178** Courtesy of Mrs. Deborah Wearing, The Amnesia Association, St. Charles' Hospital, London. **179** Ray Skibinski. 180 Delaware Art Museum, Wilmington. **182** Michael Melford/The Image Bank. **183** National Gallery of Art, Washington, Collection of Mr. and Mrs. Paul Mellon. **185** *top* Giraudon/Art Resource, N.Y.; *bottom* Stedelijk Museum, Amsterdam. **186** Tom Sobolik/Black Star. **188** Linda Benedict-Jones. **189** Jerry Irwin. **190** The Kobal Collection. **191** From *Josh: My Up and Down, In and Out Life* by Joshua Logan, © 1976 Delacorte Press. **193** The Metropolitan Museum of Art, Wolfe Fund, 1931, Catharine Lorillard Wolfe Collection. **194** Bob Krist/Black Star. **195** Brown Brothers. **196** © 1980 Dickran Palulian. **197** Movie Still Archives. **198** Leonard Lessin. **199** Courtesy of Alcoholics Anonymous. **200** *left* Angel Franco/Woodfin Camp & Associates; *right* Ian Berry/ Magnum. **201** Ian Berry/Magnum. **202** AP/Wide World Photos. **203** Focus on Sports. **205** William Huber. **206** Printed by permission of the Estate of Norman Rockwell, © 1959 Estate of Norman Rockwell. **208** Courtesy of Alma Guinness. **209** *top* Bibliothèque Nationale; *bottom* Library of Congress. **210** © Karsh, Ottawa/Woodfin Camp & Associates. **211** National Museums and Galleries on Merseyside, Walker Art Gallery, Liverpool. **212** Courtesy of Lisa Keen and Robert Keen. **213** *top* Memory Shop; *bottom* National Portrait Gallery, London. **214** © 1981 Kathryn McLaughlin Abbe & Frances McLaughlin Gill. **215** *top* Courtesy of Edmund H. Harvey, Jr.; *middle* James Salzano; *bottom* Anne K. Price. **216** National Portrait Gallery, Smithsonian Institution. **217** Courtesy of Shirley Milasi. **218** Memory Shop. **219** By special permission of the Sutton Place Foundation/Photography by John Neitzel. **220** Private Collection. **221** *top* State Historical Society of Missouri; *bottom* The Kirk Pearce Collection, Lebanon, Missouri. **222** *upper left* D. Cody/FPG International; *upper right* John Neitzel; *bottom* © Carol Beckwith, from *Nomads of Niger*, published by Harry N. Abrams, Inc. **224 & 225** Memory Shop. **226 & 227** Courtesy of Cordelia Menges. **228** *upper* © E.A. Heiniger/Rapho/Photo Researchers; *bottom* © Katrina Thomas. **230** Roy Morsch/The Stock Market. **232** Memory Shop. **233** Courtesy of Armando Preziosi, Bologna. **234** Elliott Erwitt/Magnum. **235** Beermann/Four By Five. **236 & 237** Marina Raith/Eltern Syndication/Gruner + Jahr AG & Co. 238 Nadine R. Willis. **239** *upper left* Courtesy of Carol Seabrooks; *upper right* Courtesy of Sharon Fass; *bottom left* Sally Garnett; *bottom right* Cecilia Conrad Miller. **240** © 1967 John Loengard. **241** Courtesy of Lisa Drescher. **242** *top* Courtesy of Penny Howard; *bottom* © 1955, 1983 Ruth Orkin. **243** *top* A Kinsa photo courtesy of Eastman Kodak Company; *bottom* © 1955, 1983 Ruth Orkin. **244** Jack Reznicki. 245 Photograph by Steve Wall © 1983. **246** Illustration by Maxfield Parrish, used by permission of Charles Scribner's Sons, an imprint of Macmillan Publishing Company, from *Poems of Childhood* by Eugene Field (New York: Scribner's, 1904). © 1904 Charles Scribner's Sons. **247** AP/Wide World Photos. **248** Four By Five. 250 Jonathan Wallen. **251** Theodora Hausman. **252** *left* James Fraser/Impact Photos; *right* Courtesy of Jane Polley. **253** Michael Philip Manheim/The Stock Market. **254** SuperStock International. **255** The Bettmann Archive. **257** *left* Courtesy of the Berkshire Athenaeum, Pittsfield, Massachusetts; *right* Shelburne Museum, Shelburne, Vermont. **258** Giuseppe Molteni. **259** Mary Ellen Mark/Library. **261** *top* Dan McCoy/Black Star; *bottom* Scala/Art Resource, N.Y. **262** Dan McCoy/Black Star. **264** Courtesy of Alma Guinness. **265** Bob Ziering. **266** © Dr. Mony de Leon/Peter Arnold, Inc. **267** © Karsh, Ottawa/ Woodfin Camp & Associates. **269** The Bettmann Archive. **271** Henry Grossman. **272** George Beaubien/The Woonsocket Call. **273** Blair Seitz/Photo Researchers. **274** Linda Bartlett. **275** © Radio Times/Courtesy of St. Christopher's Hospice. **276** Scala/Art Resource, N.Y. **278** Homer Sykes/Woodfin Camp & Associates. **280** The Bettmann Archive/BBC Hulton. **283** John Lewis Stage/The Image Bank. **284 & 285** Ottmar Bierwagen. **286** John Barr/Gamma-Liaison. **288** The Bettmann Archive. **289** Elliott Erwitt/Magnum. **291** © 1960 Science Research Association, Inc., Reprinted by permission, © 1974 Arco Publishing, Inc. From *The Dental Admissions Test* by David R. Turner. **292** New York Zoological Society. **293** © 1989 Roger Ressmeyer/Starlight. **294** Photofest. **295** Alan Berner. **296** From *Mammoth ™ Book of Fun & Games* by Richard B. Manchester, © 1979 by Hart Associates, reprinted by permission of LDAP, Inc. **298** James A. McInnis. **299** Robert Knowles/Black Star. **300** Thomas Asbridge. **301** Tom Grill/ Comstock. **302** *upper* Jack Reznicki; *bottom* Tom Grill/ Comstock. **303** Yvonne Hemsey/ Gamma-Liaison. **304, 305 & 306** Focus on Sports. **307** UPI/Bettmann Newsphotos. **308** *left* David Madison/Duomo Photography Inc.; *right* Photofest. **309** Focus on Sports. **310** *upper left* Focus on Sports; *middle* Dan Helms/Duomo Photography Inc.; *right* Focus on Sports; *bottom left* David Madison/Duomo Photography Inc. **311** M. Passmore/All-Sport, London. **312** Bill Eppridge, *Life* Magazine © Time Inc. **314** Jim Brandenburg. **315** *upper left* Boston Athenaeum; *upper right* Courtesy of The New-York Historical Society, New York City; *bottom* Culver Pictures. **316** Reproduced by courtesy of the Trustees, The National Gallery, London. **317** David Hathcox. **318** *upper* Memory Shop; *bottom* Photofest. **319** John Chiasson/Gamma-Liaison. **320** *top* Carolyn Croll; *middle left to right:* Ray Skibinski; Nancy Mace; Ron James; *bottom left to right*: Ed Manning/Blocpix ® Images, Stratford, Connecticut; Scala/Art Resource, N.Y.; Reprinted from *Games* Magazine, New York, © 1981, PSC Games Limited Partnership. **321** From *Mammoth ™ Book of Fun & Games* by Richard B. Manchester, © 1979 by Hart Associates, reprinted by permission of LDAP, Inc.

Efforts have been made to contact the holder of the copyright for each picture. In several cases these have been untraceable, for which we offer our apologies.